LIVING PHILOSOPHY

LIVING PHILOSOPHY

A HISTORICAL INTRODUCTION TO PHILOSOPHICAL IDEAS

THIRD EDITION

LEWIS VAUGHN

New York | Oxford University Press

Oxford University Press is a department of the University of Oxford.
It furthers the University's objective of excellence in research, scholarship,
and education by publishing worldwide. Oxford is a registered trade mark
of Oxford University Press in the UK and certain other countries.

Published in the United States of America by Oxford University Press
198 Madison Avenue, New York, NY 10016, United States of America.

© 2021, 2018, 2015 by Oxford University Press

Cataloging-in-Publication Data is on file with the Library of Congress.

ISBN: 978-0-19-008151-5

Printing number: 9 8 7 6 5 4 3 2 1
Printed by Quad/Graphics, Inc., Mexico

Brief Contents

Contents

CHAPTER 9 DESCARTES: DOUBT AND CERTAINTY 216

CHAPTER 10 FROM HOBBES TO HUME 235

LIST OF READINGS

Preface

This third edition of *Living Philosophy*—like the first—is designed to guide students in a survey of the historical march of philosophical ideas, encouraging an appreciation of the significance of these ideas in Western and Eastern thought. *Living Philosophy* provides this guidance in five fundamental ways: it tells a coherent story of philosophical thought from the pre-Socratics to the present; it provides the cultural and intellectual background for this story; it explains why the major issues and arguments are important and relevant today; it includes substantial, well-chosen excerpts from the philosophers' works; and it presents all these elements in a way that engages and stimulates student interest and understanding.

To foster a serious understanding of philosophy, *Living Philosophy* includes solid coverage of critical-thinking skills and argument basics as well as practice in reading philosophical works. Students learn how to *do* philosophy—to think and write philosophically—when they get encouragement and practice in analyzing and critiquing their own views as well as those philosophers they study. To this end, *Living Philosophy* emphasizes philosophical writing, reinforced with step-by-step coaching in how to write argumentative essays on philosophical topics and supported by multiple opportunities to hone basic skills.

In addition to these core elements, *Living Philosophy* further engages today's learners with abundant illustrations and graphics; marginal glosses, questions, and quotations; profiles of a diverse array of philosophers; and ample representation of non-Western and nontraditional sources and voices.

CHAPTERS AND READINGS

Eighteen chapters span the breadth of the historical development of philosophy, both Western and Eastern, from ancient times to the present day. Attuned to recent discussions in the field regarding issues of diversity and representation, *Living Philosophy* includes important voices not often found in introductory textbooks:

Women philosophers are represented not only in Chapter 16, "Feminist Philosophers," but also throughout the text; students will meet Themistoclea, Arignote, Theano, Diotima, Hypatia, Hildegard of Bingen, Mary Wollstonecraft, Simone de Beauvoir, Harriet Taylor, Hélène Cixous, Martha Nussbaum, Alison Jaggar, Jan Crosthwaite, Judith Thurman, Annette Baier, Virginia Held, Elizabeth Anderson, Louise Antony, Alison Ainley, and Eve Browning Cole.

Non-Western philosophers represented include Avicenna, Averroës, Maimonides, Buddha, Lao-Tzu, and Confucius. Chapter 6, "Eastern Thought," is unique among introductory textbooks in its coverage of Hindu philosophy as well as Buddhism, Daoism, and Confucianism.

MAIN FEATURES

- **A comprehensive introductory chapter that lays the groundwork for philosophical thinking.** Through examples drawn from philosophical literature and everyday life, this chapter explains clearly the nature and scope of philosophy and how it relates to students' lives. This first chapter also covers how to devise and evaluate arguments and guides students in thinking and reading critically about philosophical issues—and supplements this coverage with an appendix on deductive and inductive arguments. The chapter includes a questionnaire to survey students' philosophical attitudes, prompting immediate engagement with the relevance of philosophy to their lives and concerns and affording an opportunity to evaluate how the course changes their understanding of these issues.
- **Critical-thinking questions that correspond to relevant passages in the main text.** These questions, located in the margins of the text, invite students to draw out the implications of the material and to think critically about the assumptions and arguments found there. The questions are numbered and highlighted and easily lend themselves to both writing assignments and class discussion. The point of their marginal placement is to prompt students to think carefully and analytically as they read.
- Four types of text boxes demonstrate the value and relevance of philosophy:
  - **"Then and Now"** These boxes address how particular philosophical ideas and issues of the past have affected contemporary thinking, demonstrating that many of the same questions that have concerned noted philosophers also arise continually in contemporary science, society, ethics, religion, politics, medicine, and more. Each box ends with discussion questions that prompt critical thinking and philosophical reflection.
  - **"Portrait"** Each of these profiles the lives and work of compelling figures in philosophy, past and present, Western and non-Western or nontraditional, and men and women. Some feature a philosopher from the past whose story adds a human and historical dimension to the ideas discussed in the chapter, while others profile a contemporary thinker who is grappling with similar important issues today. The point of these features is, of course, to show that philosophy is very much a living, relevant enterprise.
  - **"Details"** These boxes supplement selected issues or concepts mentioned in the main text with more detailed information and discussions. They too end with discussion questions.
  - **"Writing and Reasoning"** These essay prompts ask students to critically examine the strengths and weaknesses of the views discussed throughout the chapter. Students can get help in answering essay questions in the appendix: "How to Write a Philosophy Paper."

Living Philosophy supplements these features with other elements to make the material even more engaging and accessible:

- **Marginal quotes** These pithy, compelling quotes from an array of philosophers appear throughout the text, inviting students to join the ongoing conversation of philosophy.
- **Key terms, marginal definitions, and end-of-book glossary** Key terms in each chapter appear in boldface at their first appearance in a chapter, and a marginal definition helps students learn the term within its immediate context. A list of the chapter's key terms appears at the end of each chapter. Finally, a glossary of those key terms and definitions provides an essential reference for students as they review and prepare for tests as well as draft their own philosophical essays and arguments.
- **Chapter Objectives** This list at the beginning of each chapter scaffolds student learning by providing both structure and support for previewing, note taking, and retention of content.
- **Review Notes** Concluding each chapter, this feature revisits the chapter objectives and encourages students to reflect and review.
- **An index of marginal quotes** This supplemental index helps students locate the words of philosophers that seem especially insightful or inspiring.
- **Timelines** Featuring philosophers' lives and important events, this visual learning tool on the inside front and back covers helps students appreciate the historic significance of philosophical ideas by placing them within a larger context.
- **Engaging, relevant visuals** Appearing throughout the book, these have been selected or created to deepen student engagement with and understanding of complex ideas and abstract concepts. In addition, captions for these images include brief and open-ended questions to help students "read" visuals with the same critical attention they learn to bring to written texts.
- **For Further Reading** Located at the end of each chapter, these useful references point students to sources that will enhance their understanding of chapter issues and arguments.

NEW TO THIS EDITION

- **A completely revised chapter on the contemporary period (Chapter 17)**—This chapter takes on some of the most pressing, complex issues of twenty-first-century life, addressed by many of the clearest and freshest voices: Kwame Anthony Appiah, cosmopolitanism; Martha Nussbaum, religious tolerance; Lawrence Blum, racism; Martin Luther King, Jr., civil rights; David Chalmers, consciousness and zombies; Stephen Gardiner, climate change; and Jacques Derrida and Helene Cixous, deconstruction.
- **A revised chapter on the meaning of life (Chapter 18)**—This chapter discusses how philosophers have clarified and explored the topic of life's meaning. It covers the main philosophical perspectives on the subject and explains the views of thinkers past and present, including Arthur Schopenhauer, Paul Edwards, Leo Tolstoy, Lucretius, Julian Baggini, Susan Wolf, E. D. Klemke, Iddo Landau, and Christopher Belshaw. It discusses in more depth the views of both subjectivists and objectivists and critiques reasons often given for

thinking that life is meaningless: because life is brief and death is sure, because we and our world are so miniscule compared to the inconceivably vast universe, because life is filled with misery and loss, and because there is no god or creator to give us a plan for living.

- **Many online resources added at the end of each chapter**—These supplement the books and papers already listed in "For Further Reading."
- **An added appendix on deductive and inductive arguments**—It covers basic deductive argument patterns and explains how to evaluate enumerative inductions, analogical induction, and inference to the best explanation.
- **More readings**—Excerpts from Plato's *Euthyphro* have been added as well as selections from Donald Robertson, Lawrence Blum, David Chalmers, Stephen Gardiner, and Iddo Landau.
- **Numerous updates**—In several chapters, concepts have been clarified, and minor errors have been corrected.

ANCILLARIES

- Ancillary materials are available on the Oxford University Press **Ancillary Resource Center (ARC)** and include the following:
  - An **Instructor's Manual** containing brief summaries of each reading, summaries and goals for each chapter, sample syllabi, and useful Web links and other media resources for each chapter
  - A **Test Bank** containing about 30 multiple-choice, 20 true/false, 10 fill-in-the-blank, and 10 essay/discussion questions and answers per chapter
- The **Companion Website** for both students and instructors is available at www.oup.com/he/vaughn_livingphil3e. It includes the following:
  - Introduction to Book/Author:
    - Table of Contents
    - About the Author
  - Instructor's Resources:
    - A downloadable version of the Instructor's Manual
    - PowerPoint lecture outlines
  - Student Resources:
    - Summaries and goals for each chapter
    - Key terms and definitions for each chapter
    - Web links and other media resources for each chapter
    - Self-quizzes for practice, containing about 15 multiple-choice, 10 true/false, 5 fill-in-the-blank, and 5 essay/discussion questions and answers per chapter, some of which are from the Test Bank in the ARC

ACKNOWLEDGMENTS

A text like this is not possible without the help of a lot of talented and conscientious people. At the top of the list are my fine editors at Oxford University Press—most notably Andrew Blitzer and Robert Miller, as well as Anna Deen. Throughout the formative stages of this text, many astute reviewers provided invaluable suggestions and criticisms, and the book is much better for it. Many thanks to:

Luisa Benton
Richland College

Ralph J. Brabban II
Chowan University

Ronald James Butzu
Wayne State University

Chung Yu Chang
Montclair State University

Mary Angelec Cooksey
Indiana University East

Anthony T. Flood
North Dakota State University

Luisa Forrest
Richland College

Edward J. Grippe
Norwalk Community College

Charles R. Hogg
Grand Valley State University

Mark A. Horton
Nagatuck Valley Community College

Alexander Izrailevsky
Salt Lake Community College

Matthew Johnson
Milwaukee State University

Stewart Kelly
Minot State University

Jacob Kidd
Blinn College

Erik Kostiuk
*Mt. San Antonio College,
Chaffey College*

A. J. Kreider
Miami Dade College

Klaus Ladstaetter
Washburn University

David Lopez
American River College

John B. Min
College of Southern Nevada

Dane Muckler
Jefferson College

Christian Perring
Dowling College

Michael Reed
Eastern Michigan University

Octavio Roca
Miami Dade College

Stephanie Semler
*Northern Virginia
Community College*

Nancy Shaffer
*California University of
Pennsylvania*

Srujesh Shah
College of Lake County

Michael Sturm
Kishwaukee College

Anthony Thomas
Kishwaukee College

Ruth Zollars
*Neosho County Community
College*

CHAPTER 1

Why Philosophy

CHAPTER OBJECTIVES

1.1 PHILOSOPHY: THE QUEST FOR UNDERSTANDING

- Know the practical and theoretical benefits of studying philosophy.
- Take an inventory of your philosophical beliefs.
- Know the four main divisions of philosophy and the kinds of questions they examine.

1.2 SOCRATES AND THE EXAMINED LIFE

- Understand why Socrates declared, "The unexamined life is not worth living."
- Explain the Socratic method and how Socrates used it in search of understanding.

1.3 THINKING PHILOSOPHICALLY

- Define *argument*, *statement*, *conclusion*, and *premise*.
- Know the two conditions that must be met for an argument to be *good*.
- Define *deductive argument*, *inductive argument*, *valid*, *sound*, *cogent*, *strong*, and *weak*. Understand inferences to the best explanation and how their strength is evaluated.
- Be able to identify arguments in the form of *modus ponens*, *modus tollens*, affirming the consequent, and denying the antecedent.
- Be able to identify arguments in various contexts and tell whether they are valid or invalid, sound or not sound, strong or weak, and cogent or not cogent.
- Understand the guidelines for reading and appreciating philosophy.
- Be aware of common fallacies and know how to identify them in various contexts.

1.1 PHILOSOPHY: THE QUEST FOR UNDERSTANDING

The title of this text, *Living Philosophy*, is meant to suggest two themes: first, that philosophy, after two-and-one-half millennia, is still alive and relevant and influential; and second, that philosophy is not only for studying but also for living—that is, for guiding our lives toward what's true and real. Philosophy, even with its ancient lineage and seemingly remote concerns, applies to your life and your times and your world. Philosophy achieves this immediacy by being many good things at once: it is enlightening, thought provoking, life changing, liberating, theoretical, and practical. The world is full of students and teachers who can attest to these claims. More importantly, you will find proof of them in the remainder of this text—and in the writings of the great philosophers, in your effort to understand what they say and the reasons they give for saying it, and in your honest attempts to apply philosophy to your life.

Philosophy is the name that philosophers have given to both a discipline and a process. As a discipline, philosophy is one of the humanities. It is a field of study out of which several other fields have evolved—physics, biology, political science, and many others. As a process, philosophy is a penetrating mode of reflection for understanding life's most important truths. This mode is called the **philosophical method**—the systematic use of critical reasoning to try to find answers to fundamental questions about reality, morality, and knowledge. The method, however, is not a master key used exclusively by professional philosophers to unlock mysteries hidden from common folk. The philosophical method is the birthright of every person, for we are all born with the capacity to reason, to question, to discover. For thousands of years, great minds like Aristotle, Plato, Confucius, Descartes, Aquinas, and Sartre have used it in their search for wisdom, and what they found has changed countless lives. But amateur philosophers like you have also used it—and continue to use it—to achieve life-altering understanding that would have eluded them otherwise.

The Good of Philosophy

Philosophy is not just about ideas; it's about *fundamental* ideas, those upon which other ideas depend. A fundamental belief logically supports other beliefs, and the more beliefs it supports the more fundamental it is. Your belief or disbelief in God, for example, might support a host of other beliefs about morality, life after death, heaven, hell, free will, science, evolution, prayer, abortion, miracles, homosexuality, and more. Thanks to your upbringing, your culture, your peers, and other influences, you already have a head full of fundamental beliefs, some of them true, some false. Whether true or false, they constitute the framework of your whole belief system, and, as such, they help you make sense of a wide range of important issues in life—issues concerning what exists and what doesn't, what actions are right or wrong (or neither), and what kinds of things we can know and not know. Fundamental beliefs, therefore, make up your "philosophy of life," which informs your thinking and guides your actions.

"Science gives us knowledge, but only philosophy can give us wisdom."

—Will Durant

---

philosophical method
The systematic use of critical reasoning to try to find answers to fundamental questions about reality, morality, and knowledge.

---

1. Suppose you had a fundamental belief that the mind, or soul, does not survive the death of the body. What other beliefs would this fundamental belief be likely to support?

"Philosophy should be responsive to human experience and yet critical of the defective thinking it sometimes encounters."

—Martha Nussbaum

Perhaps now you can better appreciate philosophy's greatest *practical* benefit: it gives us the intellectual wherewithal to improve our lives by improving our philosophy of life. A faulty philosophy of life—that is, one that comprises a great many false fundamental beliefs—can lead to a misspent or misdirected life, a life less meaningful than it could be. Philosophy is the most powerful instrument we have for evaluating the worth of our fundamental beliefs and for changing them for the better. Through philosophy we exert control over the trajectory of our lives, making major course corrections by reason and reflection.

The Greek philosopher Socrates (469–399 BCE), one of Western civilization's great intellectual heroes, says, "The unexamined life is not worth living." To examine your life is to scrutinize the core ideas that shape it, and the deepest form of scrutiny is exercised through philosophy. This search for answers goes to the heart of the traditional conception of philosophy as a search for wisdom (the term *philosophy* is derived from Greek words meaning "love of wisdom"). With the attainment of wisdom, we come to understand the true nature of reality and how to apply that understanding to living a good life.

Philosophy's chief *theoretical* benefit is the same one that most other fields of inquiry pursue: understanding for its own sake. Even if philosophy had no practical applications at all, it would still hold great value for us. We want to know how the world works, what truths it hides, just for the sake of knowing. And philosophy obliges. Astronomers search the sky, physicists study subatomic particles, and archeologists hunt for ancient ruins, all the while knowing that what they find may have no practical implications at all. We humans wonder, and that's often all the reason we need to search for answers. As the great philosopher Aristotle says, "For it is owing to their wonder that people both now begin and at first began to philosophize."

For many people, the quest for understanding through philosophy is a spiritual, transformative endeavor, an ennobling pursuit of truths at the core of life. Thus several philosophers speak of philosophy as something that enriches or nurtures the soul or mind. Socrates, speaking to the jurors who condemned him for practicing philosophy on the streets of Athens, asks, "Are you not ashamed that, while you take care to acquire as much wealth as possible, with honor and glory as well, yet you take no care or thought for understanding or truth, or for the best possible state of your soul?" In a similar vein, the Greek philosopher Epicurus (341–270 BCE) says, "Let no young man delay the study of philosophy, and let no old man become weary of it; for it is never too early nor too late to care for the well-being of the soul." And in our own era, the

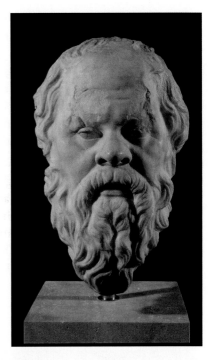

Figure 1.1 Socrates (469–399 BCE).

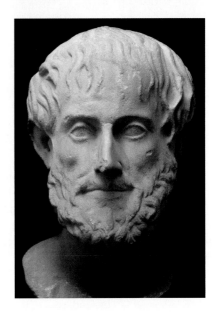

Figure 1.2 Aristotle (384–322 BCE).

2. Is it possible to lead a meaningful life without self-examination?

philosopher Walter Kaufmann (1921–1980) declares, "Philosophy means liberation from the two dimensions of routine, soaring above the well-known, seeing it in new perspectives, arousing wonder and the wish to fly."

Along with philosophical inquiry comes freedom. We begin our lives at a particular place and time, steeped in the ideas and values of a particular culture, fed ready-made beliefs that may or may not be true and that we may never think to question. If you passively accept such beliefs, then those beliefs are *not really yours*. If they are not really yours, and you let them guide your choices and actions, then they—not you—are in charge of your life. You thus forfeit your personal freedom. But philosophy helps us rise above this predicament, to transcend the narrow and obstructed standpoint from which we may view everything. It helps us sift our hand-me-down beliefs in the light of reason, look beyond the prejudices that blind us, and see what's real and true. By using the philosophical method, we may learn that some of our beliefs are on solid ground and some are not. In either case, through philosophy our beliefs become truly and authentically our own.

DETAILS

Your Philosophical Beliefs

Where do you stand on the fundamental issues in philosophy? Here is your chance to take inventory of your views. After you finish this course, take the survey again. You may be surprised at how your perspective has changed or become more nuanced. Answer with these numbers: 5 = true; 4 = probably true; 3 = neither probable nor improbable; 2 = probably false; 1 = false.

1. The God of traditional Western religions (an all-knowing, all-powerful, all-good deity) exists. _____

2. This God does not exist. _____

3. The apparent design of the universe shows that it had an intelligent designer. _____

4. The theory of evolution is a better explanation of the apparent design of biological life than the theory of "intelligent design." _____

5. Right actions are those commanded by God; wrong actions are those forbidden by God. _____

6. God does not make actions right or wrong by commanding them to be so. _____

7. At least some moral norms or principles are objectively true or valid for everyone. _____

8. Moral standards are relative to what individuals or cultures believe. _____

Philosophical Terrain

Philosophy's sphere of interest is vast, encompassing fundamental beliefs drawn from many places. Philosophical questions can arise anywhere. Part of the reason for this is that ordinary beliefs that seem to have no connection with philosophy can become philosophical in short order. A physiologist may want to know how our brains work, but she ventures into the philosophical arena when she wonders whether the brain is the same thing as the mind—a question that science alone cannot answer. A lawyer studies how the death penalty is administered in Texas, but he does philosophy when he considers whether capital punishment is ever morally permissible. A medical scientist wants to know how a human fetus develops, but she finds it difficult to avoid the philosophical query of what the moral status of the fetus is. An astrophysicist studies the Big Bang, the cataclysmic explosion thought to have brought the universe into being—but then asks whether the Big Bang shows that God caused the universe to exist. On CNN you see the horrors of war and famine, but then you find yourself grappling with whether they can be squared with the existence of an all-powerful, all-knowing,

3. Has your thinking recently led you to reflect on philosophical questions? If so, how did the thought process begin, and what fundamental belief did you end up contemplating?

9. Mind and body consist of two fundamentally different kinds of stuff—nonphysical stuff and physical stuff. ____

10. The mind, or soul, can exist without the body. ____

11. Our mental states are nothing but brain states (mind states are identical to brain states). ____

12. No one has free will. ____

13. Persons have free will (some of our actions are free). ____

14. Although our actions are determined, they can still be free (free will and determinism are not in conflict). ____

15. We can know some things about the external world. ____

16. We cannot know anything about the external world. ____

17. Truth about something depends on what a person or culture believes. ____

18. Libertarianism is the correct political theory. ____

19. Welfare liberalism is the correct political theory. ____

20. Meaning in life comes from outside ourselves, from God or some other transcendent reality. ____

21. Meaning in life comes from within ourselves. ____

and all-good God. Or you wonder what your moral obligations are to the poor and hungry of the world. Or you ponder whether government should help people in need or leave them to fend for themselves.

We can divide philosophy's subject matter into four main divisions, each of which is a branch of inquiry in its own right with many subcategories. Here's a brief rundown of these divisions and a sampling of the kinds of questions that each asks.

metaphysics The study of reality.

Metaphysics is the study of reality in the broadest sense, an inquiry into the elemental nature of the universe and the things in it. Though it must take into account the findings of science, metaphysics generally focuses on basic questions that science alone cannot address. Questions of interest: Does the world consist only of matter, or is it made up of other basic things, such as ideas or mind? Is there a spiritual, ideal realm that exists beyond the material world? Is the mind the same thing as the body? Are the theories of science true, or are they just convenient fictions? How are mind and body related? Do people have immortal souls? Do humans have free will, or are they determined by forces beyond their control? Can they be both free and determined? Does God exist? How can both a good God and evil exist simultaneously? What is the nature of causality? Can an effect ever precede its cause? What is the nature of time? Is time travel possible?

"And what, Socrates, is the food of the soul? Surely, I said, knowledge is the food of the soul."

epistemology The philosophical study of knowledge.

Epistemology is the philosophical study of knowledge. Questions of interest: What is knowledge? What is truth? Is knowledge possible—can we ever know anything? Does knowledge require certainty? What are the sources of knowledge? Is experience a source of knowledge? Is mysticism or faith a source? Can we gain knowledge of the empirical world through reason alone? If we have knowledge, how much do we have? When are we justified in saying that we know something? Do we have good reasons to believe that the world exists independently of our minds? Or do our minds constitute reality?

axiology The study of value, including both aesthetic value and moral value.

ethics The study of morality using the methods of philosophy.

Axiology is the study of value. The study of moral value is known as **ethics**. Ethics involves inquiries into the nature of moral judgments, virtues, values, obligations, and theories. Questions of interest: What makes an action right (or wrong)? What things are intrinsically good? What is the good life? What gives life meaning? What makes someone good (or bad)? What moral principles should guide our actions and choices? Which is the best moral theory? Is killing ever morally permissible? If so, why? Are moral standards objective or subjective? Is an action right merely because a culture endorses it? Does morality depend on God? What makes a society or state just?

Aesthetic values are examined in the field of philosophy known as **aesthetics**, the study of the feelings, judgments, and views involved in our appreciation and experience of the arts or other objects deemed beautiful. Aesthetics addresses questions that interest not only philosophers but also plenty of nonphilosophers who are affected by what they call beauty in the arts as well as in the natural world. What, if anything, gives an object aesthetic value? Is there such a thing as an aesthetic experience, and if so, how does it differ from other kinds of experiences? Can art be a source of truth or knowledge? Does the perception of beauty have anything to do with moral concerns? Can an art object be beautiful and yet express a moral perspective that is despicable? Can some art objects be reasonably judged to be better than others—or are there no standards at all for judging one object superior to another? That is, can anything be *objectively* beautiful?

Logic is the study of correct reasoning. Questions of interest: What are the rules for drawing correct inferences? What is the nature and structure of deductive arguments? How can propositional or predicate logic be used to evaluate arguments? Upon what logical principles does reasoning depend? Does logic describe how the world is—or just how our minds work? Can conclusions reached through inductive logic be rationally justified?

logic The study of correct reasoning.

In addition to these divisions, there are subdivisions of philosophy whose job is to examine critically the assumptions and principles that underlie other fields. Thus we have the philosophy of science, the philosophy of law, the philosophy of mathematics, the philosophy of history, the philosophy of language, and many others. When those laboring in a discipline begin questioning its most basic ideas—ideas that define its subject matter and principles of inquiry—philosophy, the most elemental mode of investigation, steps in.

Philosophical questions arise everywhere, most conspicuously from news about technology, science, social injustice, and moral conflict. On any given day, news stories can provoke philosophical questions like these:

If we humans are causing climate change that is leading to global catastrophe and suffering, what are we morally obligated to do about it? Do we have a duty to save or protect future generations? If addressing the problem will require sacrifice now, who should do the sacrificing?

Are nations morally obligated to accept all immigrants (to have more or less open borders)? If a nation admits immigrants, what are the permissible selection criteria it can use to decide which immigrants to accept? Is it morally right, for example, to accept all white Christians but turn away all dark-skinned Pakistanis? Do rich nations have a moral obligation to accept refugees—the poor, oppressed, or persecuted? What rights, if any, do undocumented ("illegal" or "unauthorized") immigrants have?

What is *racism*? Are all whites racist? Can people of color be racist? What is *white privilege*? What are the moral obligations of those who have benefited from white privilege?

Are there limits to the right of free speech? Should speech be censored or punished if it is deemed harmful or offensive? In a pluralistic world, tolerance of human difference is an important value, but do we have a duty to be tolerant of the intolerant?

Who should get health care, who should supply it, and who should pay for it? Do people have the right to a decent minimum of health care?

Will the AI (artificial intelligence) machines of the future have moral rights? Must we consider them persons—or just tools?

Is it morally permissible to use autonomous killer robots in warfare? If such a machine kills an innocent person, who is morally responsible?

Some believe we may be part of a virtual-reality world created by an advanced civilization. If this is true, how would we know it? How could we argue against such a possibility?

Do nonhuman animals have moral status? That is, are they worthy of moral concern for their own sake, not just because of their relationship with humans?

Although this text covers mostly Western philosophy, it's important to keep in mind that non-Western civilizations have also produced distinctive traditions of philosophical inquiry, some of which arose thousands of years ago. (See Chapter 6: "Eastern Thought.") China, Japan, and India have been especially fruitful ground for provocative ideas and unique perspectives on philosophical issues that concern both East and West. In the past, Western philosophers took little notice of non-Western thought, but that has changed. Studying the philosophical traditions of non-Western cultures—a field called "world philosophy"— seems more worthwhile than ever in our age of globalization and increasing cultural diversity.

1.2 SOCRATES AND THE EXAMINED LIFE

There is no better way to understand and appreciate the philosophical quest for knowledge than to study the life and work of Socrates, one of philosophy's greatest practitioners and the most revered figure in its history. Socrates wrote no philosophy, but we know about his thinking and character through his famous pupil Plato, who portrayed him in several dialogues, or conversations (notably in *Euthyphro, Crito,* and *Apology*).

For millennia Socrates has been inspiring generations by his devotion to philosophical inquiry, his relentless search for wisdom, and his determination to live according to his own high standards. As mentioned earlier, he famously said that "the unexamined life is not worth living," and he became the best example of someone living his life by that maxim.

For Socrates, an unexamined life is a tragedy because it results in grievous harm to the soul, the immaterial, divine part of a human. The soul is harmed by lack of knowledge—ignorance of one's own self and of the most important

"There's a difference between a philosophy and a bumper sticker."
—Charles Schulz

"The point of philosophy is to start with something so simple as not to seem worth stating, and to end with something so paradoxical that no one will believe it."
—Bertrand Russell

4. Socrates says that a good man can never be harmed. What do you think he means by this?

PORTRAIT

Plato

No philosopher—with the possible exception of Aristotle—has had a deeper and more lasting effect on Western thought than Plato (c. 427–347 BCE). He was born in Athens into an influential aristocratic family and grew up during the perilous years of the Peloponnesian War, a struggle between Athens and the Peloponnesian states. He was a student and admirer of Socrates, who turned Plato's mind toward philosophy and the pursuit of wisdom. He was horrified by Socrates' execution in 399 BCE for impiety and corruption of Athenian youth, so he left Athens, traveling widely, possibly to Sicily and Egypt. When he returned to Athens, he founded the Academy, a teaching college regarded

Figure 1.3 Plato (c. 427–347 BCE).

as the first university, and devoted the rest of his life to teaching and writing philosophy. (The Academy endured for hundreds of years until it was abolished by the Eastern Roman emperor Justinian I.) The Academy's most renowned student was Aristotle, who entered the school at age seventeen and remained for twenty years.

Plato's thinking is embodied in his dialogues, twenty-five of which exist complete. They were written during a span of fifty years and have been divided into three periods: early, middle, and late. The early dialogues include *Euthyphro, Apology, Crito, Meno,* and *Gorgias.* These early works portray Socrates as a brilliant and principled deflater of his contemporaries' bogus claims to knowledge. The middle dialogues include *Phaedo, Republic,* and *Theaetetus;* the late ones consist of *Critias, Parmenides, Sophist, Laws,* and others.

values in life (the good). But knowledge of these things is a mark of the soul's excellence. A clear sign that a person has an unhealthy soul is her exclusive pursuit of social status, wealth, power, and pleasure instead of the good of the soul. The good of the soul is attained only through an uncompromising search for what's true and real, through the wisdom to see what is most vital in life. Such insight comes from rational self-examination and critical questioning of facile assumptions and unsupported beliefs. To get to the truth, Socrates thinks, we must go around the false certitudes of custom, tradition, and superstition and let reason be our guide. Thus he played the role of philosophical gadfly, an annoying pest to the people of Athens, prodding them to wake up and seek the wisdom within their grasp.

We know very little about Socrates' life. He spent all his days in Athens except for a term of military service when he soldiered in the Peloponnesian War.

THEN AND NOW

Socrates Café

The Socratic method is alive and well in the twenty-first century; Christopher Phillips, author and educator, has seen to that. He has traveled from one end of the country to another to facilitate philosophical discussions based on the Socratic method. These informal gatherings attract people of all ages from all sorts of backgrounds and life experiences. He calls the dialogues *Socrates Cafés*. They are held in coffeehouses, day care centers, senior centers, high schools, churches, and other places, and they have had a profound effect on him and on many people who have participated in such discussions. As Phillips says:

> For a long time, I'd had a notion that the demise of a certain type of philosophy has been to the detriment of our society. It is a type of philosophy that Socrates and other philosophers practiced in Athens in the sixth and fifth centuries B.C. A type that utilized a method of philosophical inquiry that "everyman" and "everywoman" could embrace and take for his or her own, and in the process rekindle the childlike—but by no means childish—sense of wonder. . . .
>
> The Socratic method of questioning aims to help people gain a better understanding of themselves and their nature and their potential for excellence. At times, it can help people make more well-informed life choices, because they now are in a better position to know themselves, to comprehend who they are and what they want. It can also enable a thoughtful person to articulate and then apply his or her unique philosophy of life. This in turn will better equip a questioning soul to engage in the endless and noble pursuit of wisdom.
>
> —*Socrates Café* (2001)

Phillips is the author of several books, including *Socrates Café* and *Six Questions of Socrates: A Modern-Day Journey of Discovery through World Philosophy*. He is also co-founder of the Society for Philosophical Inquiry (www.philosopher.org), which supports the creation and development of Socrates Cafés around the globe. He says there are now over six hundred Socrates Cafés worldwide.

Socrates Cafés usually begin with a question such as "What is sanity?" "When is life not worth living?" or "Is there such a thing as human nature?" The list of possible questions is long and varied. If you were to participate in a Socrates Café, what question would you most like to address?

Socratic method Question-and-answer dialogue in which propositions are methodically scrutinized to uncover the truth.

He was married and had three sons. He spent much of his time roaming the streets of Athens, speaking with anyone who would listen. His habit was to ask people seemingly simple questions about their views on virtue, religion, justice, or the good, challenging them to think critically about their basic assumptions. This sort of question-and-answer dialogue in which propositions are methodically scrutinized to uncover the truth has become known as the **Socratic method**.

Usually when Socrates used it in conversations, or dialogues, with his fellow Athenians, their views would be exposed as false or confused. The main point of the exercise for Socrates, however, was not to win arguments, but to get closer to the truth. He thought people who pursued this noble aim as he did should not be embarrassed by being shown to be wrong; they should be delighted to be weaned from a false opinion. Nevertheless, the Socratic conversations often ended in the humiliation of eminent Athenians. They were enraged by Socrates, while many youths gravitated to him. He was soon indicted, tried before a jury, and convicted of disrespecting the gods and corrupting the youth of the city.

1.3 THINKING PHILOSOPHICALLY

As we have seen, to think philosophically is to bring your powers of critical reasoning to bear on fundamental questions. When you do this, you are usually clarifying the meaning of concepts, constructing and evaluating philosophical theories, or devising and evaluating logical arguments. This latter task constitutes the principal labor of philosophy. Socrates, Plato, Aristotle, Descartes, and other great thinkers do not deliver their philosophical insights to us without argument, as if we are to automatically accept their views with no questions asked. Philosophers provide *reasons* for thinking their ideas are plausible—that is, they give us arguments. And if we believe what they say, it should be because there are good reasons for doing so. Likewise, if we expect intelligent people to accept *our* philosophical views, we must argue our case. Since the philosophy we read will most likely contain arguments, our understanding of the text will hang on our ability to identify and understand those arguments.

Reasons and Arguments

As you might have guessed, the term *argument* does not refer to heated disagreements or emotional squabbles. An **argument** is a group of statements in which one of them is supported by the others. A **statement** (or claim) is an assertion that something is or is not the case and is therefore the kind of utterance that is either true or false. In an argument, the statement being supported is the **conclusion**, and the statements supporting the conclusion are the **premises**. The premises are meant to provide reasons for believing that the conclusion is true. A good argument gives us good reasons for accepting a conclusion; a bad argument fails to provide good reasons. In philosophy—and in any other kind of rational inquiry—accepting a conclusion (statement) without good reasons is an elementary mistake in reasoning. Believing a statement without good reasons is a recipe for error; believing a statement for good reasons increases your chances of uncovering the truth.

When we do philosophy, then, we are likely at some point to be grappling with arguments—we are trying to either (1) devise an argument to support a statement

"The chief benefit, which results from philosophy, arises in an indirect manner, and proceeds more from its secret, insensible influence, than from its immediate application."
—David Hume

"Astonishment is the root of philosophy."
—Paul Tillich

5. Socrates never seems adversarial or combative in his dialogues. What effect do you think this approach has on those who enter into dialogue with him?

"Science gives us knowledge, but only philosophy can give us wisdom."
—Will Durant

argument A group of statements in which one of them (the conclusion) is supported by the others (the premises).

statement (or claim) An assertion that something is or is not the case and is therefore the kind of utterance that is either true or false.

conclusion In an argument, the statement being supported by premises.

premise A statement that supports the conclusion of an argument.

Figure 1.4 Hitler was a master persuader, relying not on good arguments but on emotional rhetoric. How many people today would be persuaded by a contemporary politician with Hitler's rhetorical talents?

or (2) evaluate an argument to see if there really are good reasons for accepting its conclusion.

Note that *argument* in the sense used here is not synonymous with *persuasion*. An argument provides us with reasons for accepting a claim; it is an attempted "proof" for an assertion. But persuasion does not necessarily involve giving any reasons at all for accepting a claim. To persuade is to influence people's opinions, which can be accomplished by offering a good argument but also by misleading with logical fallacies, exploiting emotions and prejudices, dazzling with rhetorical gimmicks, hiding or distorting the facts, threatening or coercing people—the list is long. Good arguments prove something whether or not they persuade. Persuasive ploys can change minds but do not necessarily prove anything.

Now consider these two simple arguments:

Argument 1

> It's wrong to take the life of an innocent person. Abortion takes the life of an innocent person. Therefore, abortion is wrong.

Argument 2

> God does not exist. After all, most college students believe that that is the case.

In Argument 1, the conclusion is "abortion is wrong," and it is backed by two premises: "It's wrong to take the life of an innocent person" and "Abortion takes the life of an innocent person." In Argument 2, the conclusion is "God does not exist," which is supported by the premise "After all, most college students believe that that is the case." Despite the differences between these two passages (differences in content, the number of premises, and the order of their parts), they are both arguments because they exemplify basic argument structure: a conclusion supported by at least one premise.

Though the components of an argument seem clear enough, people often fail to distinguish between arguments and strong statements that contain no arguments at all. Suppose we change Argument 1 to this:

> Abortion is wrong. I can't believe how many people think it's morally okay. The world is insane.

"Philosophy asks the simple question, what is it all about?"
—Alfred North Whitehead

Now there is no argument, just an expression of exasperation or anger. There are no statements giving us reasons to believe a conclusion. What we have are some unsupported assertions that may merely *appear* to make a case. If we ignore the distinction between genuine arguments and nonargumentative material, critical reasoning is undone.

The simplest way to locate an argument is to *find its conclusion first, then its premises.* Zeroing in on conclusions and premises can be a lot easier if you keep an eye out for *indicator words.* Indicator words often tag along with arguments and indicate that a conclusion or premise may be nearby.

Here are a few conclusion indicator words:

consequently	*as a result*
thus	*hence*
therefore	*so*
it follows that	*which means that*

Here are some premise indicator words:

in view of the fact	*assuming that*
because	*since*
due to the fact that	*for*
because	*given that*

Just remember that indicator words do not *guarantee* the presence of conclusions and premises. They are simply telltale signs.

Assuming we can recognize an argument when we see it, how can we tell if it is a good one? Fortunately, the general criteria for judging the merits of an argument are simple and clear. A good argument—one that gives us good reasons for believing a claim—must have (1) solid logic and (2) true premises. Requirement (1) means that the conclusion should follow logically from the premises, that there must be a proper logical connection between the supporting statements and the statement supported. Requirement (2) says that what the premises assert must in fact be the case. An argument that fails in either respect is a bad argument.

There are two basic kinds of arguments—deductive and inductive—and our two requirements hold for both of them, even though the logical connections in each type are distinct. **Deductive arguments** are intended to give *logically conclusive* support to their conclusions so that if the premises are true, the conclusion absolutely must be true. Argument 1 is a deductive argument and is therefore supposed to be constructed so that if the two premises are true, its conclusion cannot possibly be false. Here it is with its structure laid bare:

Argument 1

1. It's wrong to take the life of an innocent person.
2. Abortion takes the life of an innocent person.
3. Therefore, abortion is wrong.

> "One's philosophy is not best expressed in words; it is expressed in the choices one makes . . . and the choices we make are ultimately our responsibility."
> —Eleanor Roosevelt

6. Recall some statements that you have heard or read in which strong assertions were made but no argument was presented. Did the assertions prove anything? What was your reaction at the time? Were you persuaded or impressed by them?

deductive argument An argument intended to give logically conclusive support to its conclusion.

Do you see that, given the form or structure of this argument, if the premises are true, then the conclusion *has to be true?* It would be very strange—illogical, in fact—to agree that the two premises are true but that the conclusion is false.

Now look at this one:

Argument 3

1. All dogs are mammals.
2. Rex is a dog.
3. Therefore, Rex is a mammal.

DETAILS

How to Win Every Argument

The eminent philosopher Walter Sinnott-Armstrong says that too many people think arguments are fights or competitions. But such verbal wrestling matches, he says, will not help you win in any way that really matters. As he sees it,

> If you see a conversation as a fight or competition, you can win by cheating as long as you don't get caught. You will be happy to convince people with bad arguments. You don't mind interrupting them. You can call their views crazy, stupid, silly or ridiculous, or you can joke about how ignorant they are, how short they are or how small their hands are. None of these tricks will help you understand them, their positions or the issues that divide you, but they can help you win—in one way. . . .

But things will turn out better, he says, if you engage in argument in the philosophical sense:

> [S]uppose you give a reasonable argument: that full-time workers should not have to live in poverty. Then I counter with another reasonable argument: that a higher minimum wage will force businesses to employ less people for less time. Now we can understand each other's positions and recognize our shared values, since we both care about needy workers.
>
> What if, in the end, you convince me that we should increase the minimum wage because there are ways to do so without creating unemployment or underemployment? Who won? You ended up in exactly the position where you started, so you did not "win" anything, except perhaps some minor fleeting joy at beating me. On the other side, I gained a lot: more accurate beliefs, stronger evidence and deeper understanding of the issues, of you and of myself. If what I wanted was truth, reason and understanding, then I got what I wanted. In that way, I won. Instead of resenting you for beating me, I should thank you for helping me. That positive reaction undermines the common view of arguments as fights or competitions, while enhancing our personal relationships.[1]

Again, there is no way for the premises to be true while the conclusion is false. The deductive form of the argument guarantees this.

So a deductive argument is intended to have this sort of airtight structure. If it actually does have this structure, it is said to be *valid*. Argument 1 is deductive because it is intended to provide logically conclusive support to its conclusion. It is valid because, as a matter of fact, it does offer this kind of support. A deductive argument that fails to provide conclusive support to its conclusion is said to be *invalid*. In such an argument, it is possible for the premises to be true and the conclusion false. Argument 3 is intended to have a deductive form, and because it actually does have this form, the argument is also valid.

An elementary fact about deductive arguments is that their validity (or lack thereof) is a *separate issue* from the truth of the premises. Validity is a structural matter, depending on how an argument is put together. Truth concerns the nature of the claims made in the premises and conclusion. A deductive argument is supposed to be built so that *if* the premises are true, the conclusion must be true—but in a particular case, the premises might *not* be true. A valid argument can have true or false premises and a true or false conclusion. (By definition, of course, it cannot have true premises and a false conclusion.) In any case, being invalid or having false premises dooms a deductive argument.

Inductive arguments are supposed to give *probable* support to their conclusions. Unlike deductive arguments, they are not designed to support their conclusions decisively. They can establish only that, if their premises are true, their conclusions are probably true (more likely to be true than not). Argument 2 is an inductive argument meant to demonstrate the probable truth that "God does not exist." Like all inductive arguments (and unlike deductive ones), it can have true premises and a false conclusion. So it's possible for the sole premise—"After all, most college students believe that that is the case"—to be true while the conclusion is false.

If inductive arguments succeed in lending very probable support to their conclusions, they are said to be *strong*. Strong arguments are such that if their premises are true, their conclusions are very probably true. If they fail to provide this very probable support, they are termed *weak*. Argument 2 is a weak argument because its premise, even if true, does not show that more likely than not God does not exist. What college students (or any other group) believe about God does not constitute good evidence for or against God's existence.

But consider this inductive argument:

Argument 4

1. Eighty-five percent of the students at this university are Republicans.
2. Sonia is a student at this university.
3. Therefore, Sonia is probably a Republican.

This argument is strong. If its premises are true, its conclusion is very likely to be true. If 85 percent of the university's students are Republicans, and Sonia is a university student, she is more likely than not to be a Republican too.

"Philosophy, when superficially studied, excites doubt; when thoroughly explored, it dispels it."
—Francis Bacon

inductive argument An argument intended to give probable support to its conclusion.

When a valid (deductive) argument has true premises, it is a good argument. A good deductive argument is said to be *sound*. Argument 1 is valid, but we cannot say whether it is sound until we determine the truth of the premises. Argument 3 is valid, and if its premises are true, it is sound. When a strong (inductive) argument has true premises, it is also a good argument. A good inductive argument is said to be *cogent*. Argument 2 is weak, so there is no way it can be cogent. Argument 4 is strong, and if its premises are true, it is cogent.

For a more detailed discussion of arguments, see Appendix B: Deductive and Inductive Arguments.

Reading Philosophy

Unfortunately, arguments in philosophical essays rarely come neatly labeled so you can find and evaluate them. You have to do that work yourself, a task that requires careful reading and thinking. The process can be challenging because,

---

DETAILS

Valid and Invalid Argument Forms

Valid Argument Forms

Affirming the Antecedent
(*Modus Ponens*)
If *p*, then *q*.
p.
Therefore, *q*.

Example:
If Spot barks, a burglar is in the house.
Spot is barking.
Therefore, a burglar is in the house.

Denying the Consequent
(*Modus Tollens*)
If *p*, then *q*.
Not *q*.
Therefore, not *p*.

Example:
If it's raining, the park is closed.
The park is not closed.
Therefore, it's not raining.

Invalid Argument Forms

Affirming the Consequent
If *p*, then *q*.
q.
Therefore, *p*.

Example:
If the cat is on the mat, she is asleep.
She is asleep.
Therefore, she is on the mat.

Denying the Antecedent
If *p*, then *q*.
Not *p*.
Therefore, not *q*.

Example:
If the cat is on the mat, she is asleep.
She is not on the mat.
Therefore, she is not asleep.

in the real world, arguments can be simple or complex, clearly stated or perplexing, and apparent or hidden. This is true for philosophical essays as well as for any other kind of writing that contains arguments. In some philosophical prose, the relationship between the conclusion (or conclusions) and the premises can be complicated, and even good arguments can be surrounded by material irrelevant to the arguments at hand. The remedy for these difficulties is instructive examples and plenty of practice, some of which you can get in this chapter.

Let's begin by identifying and analyzing the argument in the following passage. The issue is whether humans have free will or are compelled by forces beyond their control to act as they do. The statements are numbered for ease of reference.

Figure 1.5 How much is a watch like the universe? Everything depends on the relevant similarities and differences.

> (1) The famous trial lawyer Clarence Darrow (1857–1938) made a name for himself by using the "determinism defense" to get his clients acquitted of serious crimes. (2) The crux of this approach is the idea that humans are not really responsible for anything they do because they cannot choose freely—they are "determined," predestined, if you will, by nature (or God) to be the way they are. (3) So in a sense, Darrow says, humans are like windup toys with no control over any action or decision. (4) They have no free will. (5) Remember that Darrow was a renowned agnostic who was skeptical of all religious claims. (6) But Darrow is wrong about human free will for two reasons. (7) First, in our everyday moral life, our own commonsense experience suggests that sometimes people are free to make moral decisions. (8) We should not abandon what our commonsense experience tells us without good reason— and (9) Darrow has given us no good reason. (10) Second, Darrow's determinism is not confirmed by science, as he claims—but actually conflicts with science. (11) Modern science says that there are many things (at the subatomic level of matter) that are not determined at all: (12) They just happen.

Figure 1.6 Clarence Darrow (1857–1938).

Indicator words are scarce in this argument, unless you count the words "first" and "second" as signifying premises. But the conclusion is not hard to find; it's sentence 6: "Darrow is wrong about human free will for two reasons." Locating the conclusion enables us to see that some statements (statements 1 through 4) are neither conclusion nor premises; they are just background information on Darrow's views. Most argumentative essays contain some supplemental information like this. Statement 5 is irrelevant to the argument; Darrow's agnosticism has no logical connection to the premises or conclusion.

Statement 12 is just a rewording of statement 11. After this elimination process, only the following premises and conclusion (statement 6) remain:

(6) But Darrow is wrong about human free will for two reasons.

(7) First, in our moral life, our commonsense experience suggests that sometimes people are free to make moral decisions.

(8) We should not abandon what our commonsense experience tells us without good reason.

(9) Darrow has given us no good reason.

(10) Darrow's determinism is not confirmed by science, as he claims—but actually conflicts with science.

(11) Modern science says that there are many things (mostly at the subatomic level) that are not determined at all.

Statements 7 through 11 are the premises. They are all meant to provide support to statement 6, but their support is of unequal weight. Statement 10 gives independent

PORTRAIT

Hypatia

Hypatia (c. 370–415) was the greatest philosopher of her day. She lived in the Greek city of Alexandria, which in the fourth century was the intellectual epicenter of the world, excelling in scientific and philosophical learning. It also was the home of the famed Library, which contained thousands of scholarly manuscripts drawn from the best thinkers of ancient times, including the works of Plato and Aristotle. In this rich environment, Hypatia achieved fame as a Neoplatonist philosophy teacher, an astronomer, and a mathematician. At around age twenty-five or thirty, she became the director of the school of the renowned philosopher Plotinus—a very high honor since women were tradition-

Figure 1.7 Hypatia (c. 370–415).

ally not appointed to such offices. Another indication of her sterling reputation was that she was appointed by a Christian government even though she was known to be a pagan.

She taught the works of the "pagan" philosophers such as Plato and Aristotle, and students came from far-flung places for the privilege of being her students. She also is thought to have written three commentaries on noted mathematical treatises.

In 415, Cyril, the bishop of Alexandria, arranged for Hypatia's murder at the hands of a Christian mob: she was pulled from her chariot, hauled to a church, stripped naked, and skinned alive with oyster shells. Cyril, on the other hand, was later canonized.

support to the conclusion without the help of any other premises, so it is an *independent* premise. We can say the same thing about statement 11; it too is an independent premise. But notice that statements 7, 8, and 9 are *dependent* premises supporting the conclusion. That is, taken separately, they are weak, but together they constitute a plausible reason for accepting statement 6. Statement 10 directly supports the conclusion, and in turn is supported by premise 11.

Now take a look at this passage:

> (1) As the Islamic clerics cling to power in Iran, students there are agitating for greater freedom and less suppression of views that the clerics dislike. (2) Even though ultimate power in Iran rests with the mullahs, it is not at all certain where the nation is headed. Here's a radical suggestion: (3) The Islamic republic in Iran will fall within the next five years. Why do I say this? (4) <u>Because</u> the majority of Iranians are in favor of democratic reforms, (5) and no regime can stand for very long when citizens are demanding access to the political process. (6) Also, Iran today is a mirror image of the Soviet Union before it broke apart—there's widespread dissatisfaction and dissent at a time when the regime seems to be trying to hold the people's loyalty. (7) Every nation that has taken such a path has imploded within five years. (8) Finally, the old Iranian trick of gaining support for the government by fomenting hatred of America will not work anymore (9) <u>because</u> Iran is now trying to be friends with the United States.

The conclusion is statement 3, and the premises are statements 4 through 9. The first two statements are extraneous. Statements 4 and 5 are dependent premises and so are statements 6 and 7. Statements 8 and 9 constitute an argument that gives support to the passage's main conclusion (statement 3). Statement 8 is the conclusion; statement 9, the premise. Notice also that the sentence "Why do I say this?" is not a statement.

So remember: When you read a philosophical essay, you are not simply trying to glean some facts from it as you might if you were reading a science text or technical report. Neither are you following a storyline as if you were reading a mystery novel (though philosophy papers sometimes contain their share of mysteries). In most cases, you are tracing the steps in an argument, trying to see what conclusion the writer wants to prove and whether she succeeds in proving it. Along the way, you may encounter several premises with their accompanying analyses, clarifications, explanations, and examples. You may even run into a whole chain of arguments. In the end, if you have read well and the writer has written well, you are left not with a new set of data or a story ending, but a realization—maybe even a revelation—that a conclusion is, or is not, worthy of belief.

The best way to learn how to read philosophy well is to read philosophy often. You will probably get plenty of chances to do that in your current philosophy course. Having a few rules to guide you in your reading, however, may help shorten the learning curve. As you read, keep the following in mind.

> "Philosophy is a kind of journey, ever learning yet never arriving at the ideal perfection of truth."
> —Albert Pike

7. Suppose you are presented with written material containing statements and arguments that strike you as irreverent or unorthodox. Would you be able to read such a text with an open mind? Can you recall a case when you did just that?

"Small amounts of philosophy lead to atheism, but larger amounts bring us back to God."

—Francis Bacon

1. Approach the text with an open mind. If you are studying philosophy for the first time, you are likely—at least at first—to find a good bit of the material difficult, strange, or exasperating, sometimes all three at once. That's normal. Philosophy is an exploration of the rugged frontiers of our knowledge of fundamental things, so much of this new territory is likely to seem daunting or unfamiliar. There's also an excellent chance that your first visits to this terrain will be vexing, perhaps even infuriating, because you may sometimes disagree with what you read.

There is no shame in experiencing any of these reactions. They come with the territory. But if you are to make any headway in philosophy, you need to try your best to counteract these attitudes and feelings. Remember, philosophy at its best is a fair-minded, fearless search for truth. Anything that interferes with this noble quest must be overcome and cast aside.

Avoid making a judgment about an essay's ideas or arguments until you fully understand them and have fairly considered them. Make sure you are not reading with the intent to prove the conclusions false (or true). Be open to the possibility that the essay could give you good reasons to change your mind about something.

Try to maintain a neutral attitude toward the writer, presuming that she is neither right nor wrong, neither sinner nor saint. Don't assume that everything a renowned philosopher says must be true, and don't presuppose that everything a philosopher you dislike says must be false. Give the writer the same attention and respect that you would give a friend who is discussing a serious issue with you.

If you are reading the work of a famous philosopher and you find yourself thinking that his or her ideas are obviously silly or ridiculous, think again. The odds are good that you are misunderstanding what you read. It is wiser to assume that the text offers something of value (even if you disagree with it) and that you need to read more carefully.

2. Read actively and critically. Philosophical reading is intense. It cannot be rushed. It cannot be crammed. It cannot be done while your mind is on automatic pilot.

Philosophical reading is *active* reading. Instead of reading just to get through a piece of writing, you must take your time and ask yourself what key terms and passages mean, how the argument is structured, what the central thesis is, where the premises are, how certain key ideas are related, whether the main conclusion conflicts with propositions you know are true, even how the material compares with other philosophical writing on the same subject.

Philosophical reading is also *critical* reading. In critical reading, you ask not just what something means but also whether a statement is true and if the reasoning is solid. You ask if the conclusion really follows from the premises, whether the premises are true, if the analysis of a term really makes sense, if an argument has been overlooked, if an analogy is weak, whether there are counterexamples to key claims, and whether the claims agree with other things you have good reason to believe.

3. Identify the conclusion first, then the premises. When you first begin reading philosophical texts, they may seem to you like dark thickets of propositions into which you may not enter without losing your way. But your situation is really not that bad. In argumentative writing (the kind you are most likely to encounter in philosophy), you can depend on there being, well, an argument, a conclusion backed by premises. There could, of course, be several arguments that support the main argument, and the arguments could be complex, but these sets of conclusion-plus-premises will all serve as recognizable guideposts. If you want to penetrate the thicket, then, you must first identify the argument (or arguments). And the key to doing that is to find the conclusion first, then look for the premises.

When you find the main conclusion, you thereby identify the main point of the essay, and you then have the number-one clue to the function of all the rest of the text. Once you uncover the point that the writer is trying to prove, finding the supporting premises becomes much easier. And when you isolate the premises, locating the text that explains and amplifies the premises gets easier too. Therefore, the first—and most important—question you can ask about a philosophical essay is, *"What claim is the writer trying to prove?"*

4. Outline, paraphrase, or summarize the argument. Understanding an essay's argument is so important that testing whether you really "get it" is crucial. You can test your grasp of the argument by outlining, paraphrasing, or summarizing it. If you can lay out an argument's premises and conclusion in an outline, or if you can accurately paraphrase or summarize the argument, you probably have a pretty good understanding of it. Very often students who think they comprehend an argument are surprised to find that they cannot devise an adequate outline or summary of it. Such failures suggest that, although outlining, paraphrasing, or summarizing may seem to some to be unnecessary, it is not—at least not to those new to philosophy.

5. Evaluate the argument and formulate a tentative judgment. When you read philosophy, understanding it is just the first step. You also must do something that many beginners find both difficult and alien: you must make an informed judgment about what you read. Simply reiterating what the writer has said will not do. Your judgment is what matters here. Mainly, this judgment is your evaluation of the argument presented by the writer—an assessment of (1) whether the conclusion follows from the premises and (2) whether the premises are true. Only when the answer is yes to both these questions can you say that the conclusion of the argument is worthy of acceptance. This kind of evaluation is precisely what your instructor expects when she asks you to critique an argumentative essay in philosophy.

Fallacious Reasoning

You can become more proficient in reading and writing philosophy if you know how to identify fallacies when you see them. **Fallacies** are common but bad arguments. They are defective arguments that appear so often in writing and speech that philosophers have given them names and offered instructions on how to recognize and avoid them.

Many fallacies are not just failed arguments—they are also deceptively plausible appeals. They can easily appear sound or cogent, misleading the reader. Their potential for slipperiness is another good reason to study fallacies. The best way to avoid being taken in by them is to study them until you can consistently pick them out of any random selection of prose. Here are some of the more prevalent ones:

Straw Man. The *straw man* fallacy is the misrepresentation of a person's views so they can be more easily attacked or dismissed. Let's say you argue that the war in Afghanistan is too costly in lives and money, and your opponent replies this way:

> *My adversary argues that the war in Afghanistan is much too difficult for the United States and that we ought to, in effect, cut and run while we can. But why must we take the coward's way out?*

Thus, your point has been distorted, made to look more extreme or radical than it really is; it is now an easy target. The notion that we ought to "cut and run" or "take the coward's way out" *does not follow* from the statement that the war in Iraq is too costly.

The straw man kind of distortion, of course, proves nothing, though many people fall for it every day. This fallacy is probably the most common type of fallacious reasoning used in politics. It is also popular in many other kinds of argumentation—including student philosophy papers.

Appeal to the Person. Closely related to the straw man fallacy is *appeal to the person* (also known as the ad hominem fallacy). Appeal to the person is the rejecting of a statement on the grounds that it comes from a particular person, not because the statement, or claim, itself is false or dubious. For example:

> *You can safely discard anything that Susan has to say about government. She's a dyed-in-the-wool socialist.*

> *Johnson argues that our current welfare system is defective. But don't listen to him—he's a conservative.*

Ad hominem arguments often creep into student philosophy papers. Part of the reason is that some appeals to the person are not so obvious. For example:

> *Swinburne's cosmological argument is a serious attempt to show that God is the best explanation for the existence of the universe. However,*

---

fallacy A common but bad argument.

straw man The fallacy of misrepresenting a person's views so they can be more easily attacked or dismissed.

appeal to the person (ad hominem fallacy) The fallacy of rejecting a statement on the grounds that it comes from a particular person, not because the statement itself is false or dubious.

"This is patently absurd; but whoever wishes to become a philosopher must learn not to be frightened by absurdities."
—Bertrand Russell

Figure 1.8 Politics is rife with fallacies—especially straw man, appeal to the person, and slippery slope. What fallacies in politics have you heard or read lately?

> *he is a well-known theist, and this fact raises some doubts about the strength of his case.*
>
> *Dennett argues from the materialist standpoint, so he begins with a bias that we need to take into account.*
>
> *Some of the strongest arguments against the death penalty come from a few people who are actually on death row. They obviously have a vested interest in showing that capital punishment is morally wrong. We therefore are forced to take their arguments—however convincing—with a grain of salt.*

Each of these arguments is defective because it asks us to reject or resist a claim solely because of a person's character, background, or circumstances—things that are generally irrelevant to the truth of claims. A statement must stand or fall *on its own merits.* The personal characteristics of the person espousing the view do not necessarily have a bearing on its truth. Only if we can show that someone's dubious traits somehow make the claim dubious are we justified in rejecting the claim because of a person's personal characteristics. Such a circumstance is rare.

Appeal to Popularity. The *appeal to popularity* (or appeal to the masses) is another extremely common fallacy. It is arguing that a claim must be true not because it is

appeal to popularity
The fallacy of arguing that a claim must be true not because it is backed by good reasons but simply because many people believe it.

backed by good reasons but simply because many people believe it. The idea is that, somehow, there is truth in numbers. For example:

> *Of course there's a God. Everyone believes that.*

> *Seventy percent of Americans believe that the president's tax cuts are good for the economy. So don't try to tell me the tax cuts aren't good for the economy.*

> *Most people believe that Jones is guilty, so he's guilty.*

In each of these arguments, the conclusion is thought to be true merely because it is believed by an impressive number of people. The number of people who believe a claim, however, is irrelevant to the claim's truth. What really matters is how much support the claim has from good reasons. Large groups of people have been—and are—wrong about many things. Many people once believed that Earth is flat, mermaids are real, and human sacrifices help crops grow. They were wrong.

Remember, however, that the number of people who accept a claim *can* be relevant to its truth if the people happen to be experts. Twenty professional astronomers who predict an eclipse are more reliable than one hundred nonexperts who swear that no eclipse will occur.

genetic fallacy Arguing that a statement can be judged true or false based on its source.

Genetic Fallacy. A ploy like the appeal to the person is the *genetic fallacy*—arguing that a statement can be judged true or false based on its source. In an appeal to the person, someone's character or circumstances is thought to tell the tale. In the genetic fallacy, the truth of a statement is supposed to depend on origins other than an individual—organizations, political platforms, groups, schools of thought, even exceptional states of mind (like dreams and intuitions). Look:

> *That new military reform idea has gotta be bunk. It comes from a liberal think tank.*

> *At the city council meeting Hernando said that he had a plan to curb the number of car crashes on Highway 19. But you can bet that whatever it is, it's half-baked—he said the plan came to him when he was stoned on marijuana.*

> *The U.S. Senate is considering a proposal to reform affirmative action, but you know their ideas must be ridiculous. What do they know about the rights of the disadvantaged? They're a bunch of rich white guys.*

equivocation The fallacy of assigning two different meanings to the same significant word in an argument.

Equivocation. The fallacy of *equivocation* is assigning two different meanings to the same significant word in an argument. The word is used in one sense in a premise and in a different sense in another place in the argument. The switch in meaning can deceive the reader and disrupt the argument, rendering it invalid or weaker than it would be otherwise. Here's a classic example:

> *Only man is rational.*

> *No woman is a man.*

Therefore, no woman is rational.

And one other:

You are a bad writer.

If you are a bad writer, then you are a bad boy.

Therefore, you are a bad boy.

The first argument equivocates on the word *man*. In the first premise, *man* means humankind; in the second, male. Thus, the argument seems to prove that women are not rational. You can see the trick better if you assign the same meaning to both instances of *man*. Like this:

Only humans are rational.

No woman is a human.

Therefore, no woman is rational.

In the second argument, the equivocal term is *bad*. In the first premise, *bad* means incompetent; in the second, immoral.

Appeal to Ignorance. As its name implies, this fallacy tries to prove something by appealing to what we *don't* know. The *appeal to ignorance* is arguing either that (1) a claim is true because it hasn't been proven false or (2) a claim is false because it hasn't been proven true. For example:

> *Try as they may, scientists have never been able to disprove the existence of an afterlife. The conclusion to be drawn from this is that there is in fact an afterlife.*

> *Super Green Algae can cure cancer. No scientific study has ever shown that it does not work.*

> *No one has ever shown that ESP (extrasensory perception) is real. Therefore, it does not exist.*

> *There is no evidence that people on welfare are hardworking and responsible. Therefore, they are not hardworking and responsible.*

The first two arguments try to prove a claim by pointing out that it hasn't been proven false. The second two try to prove that a claim is false because it hasn't been proven true. Both kinds of arguments are bogus because they assume that a lack of evidence proves something. A lack of evidence, however, can prove nothing. Being ignorant of the facts does not enlighten us.

Notice that if a lack of evidence could prove something, then you could prove just about anything you wanted. You could reason, for instance, that since no one can prove that horses *can't* fly, horses must be able to fly. Since no one can disprove that you possess supernatural powers, you must possess supernatural powers.

"There are more things in heaven and earth, Horatio, than are dreamt of in your philosophy."
—William Shakespeare

appeal to ignorance The fallacy of trying to prove something by appealing to what we don't know. It is arguing that either (1) a claim is true because it hasn't been proven false or (2) a claim is false because it hasn't been proven true.

False Dilemma. In a dilemma, you are forced to choose between two unattractive possibilities. The fallacy of *false dilemma* is arguing erroneously that since there are only two alternatives to choose from, and one of them is unacceptable, the other one must be true. Consider these:

> *You have to listen to reason. Either you must sell your car to pay your rent, or your landlord will throw you out on the street. You obviously aren't going to sell your car, so you will be evicted.*

> *You have to face the hard facts about the war on drugs. Either we must spend billions of dollars to increase military and law enforcement operations against drug cartels, or we must legalize all drugs. We obviously are not going to legalize all drugs, so we have to spend billions on anticartel operations.*

The first argument says that there are only two choices to consider: either sell your car or get evicted, and since you will not sell your car, you will get evicted. This argument is fallacious because (presumably) the first premise is false—there seem to be more than just two alternatives here. You could get a job, borrow money from a friend, or sell your DVD player and TV. If the argument seems convincing, it is because other possibilities are excluded.

The second argument asserts that there are only two ways to go: spend billions to attack drug cartels or legalize all drugs. Since we won't legalize all drugs, we must therefore spend billions to assault the cartels. The first (either/or) premise, however, is false; there are at least three other options. The billions could be spent to reduce and prevent drug use; drug producers could be given monetary incentives to switch to nondrug businesses; or only some drugs could be legalized.

Begging the Question. The fallacy of *begging the question* is trying to prove a conclusion by using that very same conclusion as support. It is arguing in a circle. This way of trying to prove something says, in effect, "X is true because X is true." Few people would fall for this fallacy in such a simple form, but more subtle kinds can be beguiling. For example, here's the classic instance of begging the question:

> *The Bible says that God exists.*

> *The Bible is true because God wrote it.*

> *Therefore, God exists.*

The conclusion here (God exists) is supported by premises that assume that very conclusion.

Here's another one:

> *All citizens have the right to a fair trial because those whom the state is obliged to protect and give consideration are automatically due*

judicial criminal proceedings that are equitable by any reasonable standard.

This passage may at first seem like a good argument, but it isn't. It reduces to this unimpressive assertion: "All citizens have the right to a fair trial because all citizens have the right to a fair trial." The conclusion is "all citizens have the right to a fair trial," but that's more or less what the premise says. The premise—"those whom the state is obliged to protect and give consideration are automatically due judicial criminal proceedings that are equitable by any reasonable standard"—is equivalent to "all citizens have the right to a fair trial."

When circular reasoning is subtle, it can ensnare even its creators. The fallacy can easily sneak into an argument if the premise and conclusion say the same thing but say it in different, complicated ways.

Slippery Slope. The metaphor behind this fallacy suggests the danger of stepping on a dicey incline, losing your footing, and sliding to disaster. The fallacy of *slippery slope,* then, is arguing erroneously that a particular action should not be taken because it will lead inevitably to other actions resulting in some dire outcome. The key word here is *erroneously.* A slippery slope scenario becomes fallacious when there is no reason to believe that the chain of events predicted will ever happen. For example:

> *This trend toward gay marriage must be stopped. If gay marriage is permitted, then traditional marriage between a man and a woman will be debased and devalued, which will lead to an increase in divorces. And higher divorce rates can only harm our children.*

This argument is fallacious because there are no reasons for believing that gay marriage will ultimately result in the chain of events described. If good reasons could be given, the argument might be salvaged.

Composition. Sometimes what is true about the parts of a thing is also true of the whole—and sometimes not. The fallacy of *composition* is arguing erroneously that what can be said of the parts can also be said of the whole. Consider:

> *Each piece of wood that makes up this house is lightweight. Therefore, the whole house is lightweight.*

> *Each soldier in the platoon is proficient. Therefore the platoon as a whole is proficient.*

> *The monthly payments on this car are low. Hence, the cost of the car is low.*

Just remember, sometimes the whole *does* have the same properties as the parts. If each part of the rocket is made of steel, the whole rocket is made of steel.

slippery slope The fallacy of arguing erroneously that a particular action should not be taken because it will lead inevitably to other actions resulting in some dire outcome.

composition The fallacy of arguing erroneously that what can be said of the parts can also be said of the whole.

"Philosophy should quicken life, not deaden it."

—Susan Glaspell

division The fallacy of arguing erroneously that what can be said of the whole can be said of the parts.

Division. If you turn the fallacy of composition upside down, you get the fallacy of *division*—arguing erroneously that what can be said of the whole can be said of the parts:

> *The house is heavy. Therefore, every part of the house is heavy.*

> *The platoon is very effective. Therefore, every member of the platoon is effective.*

> *That herd of elephants eats an enormous amount of food each day. Therefore, each elephant in the herd eats an enormous amount of food each day.*

WRITING AND REASONING   CHAPTER 1

1. What is the difference between an argument and a set of accusations? or expressions of outrage?

2. How is reading philosophy different from, say, reading a physics text? or reading a novel?

3. What is philosophy's greatest practical benefit? Do you think studying philosophy could change your life goals or your fundamental beliefs? Why or why not?

4. What is the philosophical method? Who can make use of this approach to important questions? Can only philosophers use it? Have you used it? How?

5. Devise an argument in favor of the proposition that people should (or should not) be punished as Socrates was for speaking their minds.

6. Write a Socratic dialogue between yourself and a friend. Imagine that your friend declares: "Everyone lies. No one ever tells the truth." Show that those statements are false.

7. Choose one of your fundamental beliefs that you have not thought much about and write an argument defending it or rejecting it.

8. The straw man fallacy is rampant in political debates. Give an example of this tactic being used by commentators or politicians, or make up an example of your own.

9. Think about the political commentators you've read or listened to. What fallacies have they been guilty of using?

10. Socrates died for his principles. What ideas in your life would you be willing to die for?

REVIEW NOTES

1.1 PHILOSOPHY: THE QUEST FOR UNDERSTANDING

- Studying philosophy has both practical and theoretical benefits. To some, the pursuit of knowledge through philosophy is a spiritual quest.

- Taking an inventory of your philosophical beliefs at the beginning of this course will help you gauge your progress as you study.

- The four main divisions of philosophy are metaphysics, epistemology, axiology, and logic. There are also subdivisions of philosophy that examine basic issues found in other fields.

1.2 SOCRATES AND THE EXAMINED LIFE

- For Socrates, an unexamined life is a tragedy because it results in grievous harm to the soul, a person's true self or essence. The soul is harmed by lack of knowledge—ignorance of one's self and of the most important values in life (the good).

- The Socratic method is a question-and-answer dialogue in which propositions are methodically scrutinized to uncover the truth. Usually when Socrates used it in conversations with his fellow Athenians, their views would be exposed as false or confused. The main point of the exercise for Socrates, however, was not to win arguments but to get closer to the truth.

1.3 THINKING PHILOSOPHICALLY

- An argument is a group of statements in which one of them is meant to be supported by the others. A statement (or claim) is an assertion that something is or is not the case and is therefore the kind of utterance that is either true or false. In an argument, the statement being supported is the conclusion, and the statements supporting the conclusion are the premises.

- A good argument must have (1) solid logic and (2) true premises. Requirement (1) means that the conclusion should follow logically from the premises. Requirement (2) says that what the premises assert must in fact be the case.

- A deductive argument is intended to give logically conclusive support to its conclusion. An inductive argument is intended to give probable support to its conclusion. A deductive argument with the proper structure is said to be valid; a deductive argument that fails to have this structure is said to be invalid. If inductive arguments succeed in lending probable support to their conclusions, they are said to be strong. If they fail to provide this probable support, they are termed weak. When a valid (deductive) argument has true premises, it is said to be sound. When a strong (inductive) argument has true premises, it is said to be cogent. In inference to the best explanation, we begin with premises about a phenomenon or state of affairs to be explained. Then we reason from those premises to an explanation for that state of affairs. We try to produce not just any explanation but the best explanation among several possibilities. The best explanation is the one most likely to be true.

- The guidelines for reading philosophy are: (1) Approach the text with an open mind; (2) read actively and critically; (3) identify the conclusion first, then the premises; (4) outline, paraphrase, or summarize the argument; and (5) evaluate the argument and formulate a tentative judgment.

KEY TERMS

appeal to ignorance	conclusion	false dilemma	premise
appeal to popularity	deductive	genetic fallacy	slippery slope
appeal to the person	argument	inductive	Socratic method
argument	division	argument	statement
axiology	epistemology	logic	straw man
begging the	equivocation	metaphysics	
question	ethics	philosophical	
composition	fallacy	method	

Note

1. Walter Sinnott-Armstrong, "How to Win Every Argument," *Time*, July 2, 2018, Ideas and Society section.

For Further Reading

Simon Blackburn, *Oxford Dictionary of Philosophy* (Oxford: Oxford University Press, 1994, 2005). A concise guide to hundreds of philosophy topics; many entries are of substantial length.

Ted Honderich, ed., *The Oxford Companion to Philosophy* (Oxford: Oxford University Press, 1995). A good one-volume philosophy reference featuring many excellent articles on philosophical issues.

Norman Melchert, *The Great Conversation: A Historical Introduction to Philosophy* (New York: Oxford University Press, 2010). An excellent introduction to the major philosophers and their works with in-depth annotations of readings.

Louis P. Pojman and Lewis Vaughn, ed., *Classics of Philosophy*, 3rd edition (New York: Oxford University Press, 2010). The most comprehensive anthology of Western philosophy available.

Bertrand Russell, *The Problems of Philosophy* (New York: Oxford University Press, 1959). A very readable classic work by an eminent philosopher. Focuses mostly on issues in epistemology.

Lewis Vaughn, *Great Philosophical Arguments: An Introduction to Philosophy* (New York: Oxford University Press, 2012). A text with readings organized by topic and by the standard arguments that have occupied thinkers throughout the centuries.

Lewis Vaughn, *The Power of Critical Thinking,* 5th edition (New York: Oxford University Press, 2015). A student-friendly introduction to logic, critical thinking, and philosophical writing.

Online Resources

Stanford Encyclopedia of Philosophy, https://plato.stanford.edu/index.html

Guide to Philosophy on the Internet, http://legacy.earlham.edu/~peters/philinks.htm

Routledge Encyclopedia of Philosophy, https://www.rep.routledge.com

Internet Encyclopedia of Philosophy, https ://www.iep.utm.edu

PhilPapers.org

Philosophy Pages, http://www.philosophypages.com/dy/index.htm

Ethics Updates, http://ethicsupdates.net

American Philosophical Association, https://www.apaonline.org

Philosophy Now, https://philosophynow.org

CHAPTER 2

The Pre-Socratics and the Sophists

CHAPTER OBJECTIVES

2.1 THALES AND ANAXIMANDER

- Understand how Thales contributed to the direction and method of philosophical inquiry and how his approach differed from traditional ways of answering questions about the world.
- Know the reasons why Thales chose water as the fundamental stuff of the world.
- Understand how Anaximander's theory about the cosmos differed from Thales'.
- Be able to recount Anaximander's explanation of why the Earth is suspended in space.

2.2 HERACLITUS

- Be able to explain Heraclitus' concept of the *logos*.
- Understand Heraclitus' view of the *logos* as a "harmony of opposites."
- Explain Heraclitus' maxim "all are in flux, like a river."
- Be able to describe Empedocles' theory of evolution and how it differs from Darwin's.
- Articulate the main beliefs of the Pythagoreans.

2.3 PARMENIDES

- Discuss the important conceptual distinctions that Parmenides introduced to philosophy, and define *rationalism* and *empiricism*.
- Explain Parmenides' theory of the One, and recount his reasoning behind it.
- State Parmenides' main contribution to philosophical inquiry.
- Understand Zeno's paradox of motion and his use of the dialectic form of argument.

2.4 DEMOCRITUS

- Recount the ways in which Democritus' theory of the cosmos differs from Parmenides'.
- Define *ancient atomism*, and explain Democritus' concepts of atoms and the void.
- List the differences between Democritus' atoms and those of modern science.

2.5 PROTAGORAS AND THE SOPHISTS

- Explain who the Sophists were and what role they played in Greek culture.
- Define *rhetoric, sophistry, subjective relativism,* and *cultural relativism.*
- Summarize Protagoras' views and Plato's refutation of them.
- Evaluate the criticisms that have been aimed at subjective and cultural relativism.
- Articulate and justify your views on relativism.

Philosophy began in ancient Greece in the sixth century BCE among thinkers who broke with age-old tradition to ponder important matters in an entirely novel way. Humans had for centuries been devising answers to fundamental questions: What is the nature of the world? What is it made of—one kind of stuff or many kinds? Does the world have an origin or has it always existed? Why is the world the way it is? What makes things happen—gods, magic, or something else? What is the reality behind the appearances of reality? Their answers were generally drawn from mythology and tradition, from old stories about the gods, or from hand-me-down lore and law. But the first philosophers—called **pre-Socratics** because most of them came before Socrates (fifth century BCE)—refused to take this path. It is mostly their *way* of seeking answers about the world, rather than the answers themselves, that distinguished them and made them the first philosophers. Once this philosophical fire was lit, it spread to later thinkers in the ancient world, a period of about a thousand years, from approximately 600 BCE to around 500 CE. It was in this era that Western philosophy first established itself, defined almost all its main areas of study, and gave us philosophical heroes (most notably, Socrates, Plato, and Aristotle) who continue to influence our thinking on important ideas and issues.

Other civilizations—Egypt, Babylon, Persia, China, and Assyria—wondered about the world and its mysteries. But only the ancient Greeks, beginning with the pre-Socratics, sidestepped the old ways of thinking and tried to let reason and experience guide them to the truth. They sought to justify their theories rather than swallow them whole. From our modern perspective, some of their answers may, at first glance, seem incredible. But thinkers were working from a knowledge base that was two and a half millennia behind ours and at the dawn of philosophical investigations. They nevertheless managed some impressive reasoning and even some conclusions that foreshadowed ideas in modern times, and the fundamental questions they asked are still being asked today.

pre-Socratics The first philosophers, most of whom flourished before Socrates (fifth century BCE).

"Science gives us knowledge, but only philosophy can give us wisdom."
—Will Durant

2.1 THALES AND ANAXIMANDER

Figure 2.1 Thales of Miletus (c. 625–547 BCE).

"The most difficult thing
in life is to know yourself."
—Thales

According to tradition, Thales (c. 625–547 BCE) was the first philosopher. He hailed from the city-state of Miletus, a seaport on the coast of Ionia (now Turkey). He is therefore sometimes referred to as a Milesian, as are two other like-minded philosophers (Anaximander and Anaximenes) who came from the same place. In ancient Greece he and his new way of thinking garnered a great deal of respect for an odd reason: he was said to have predicted the solar eclipse of 585 BCE and to have derived his prediction without appeals to divine or other-worldly forces. On this account he has also been called the first scientist, for in those times there was no clear distinction between philosophy and science.

Only tiny fragments of Thales' writings survive, so scholars have had to rely on reports of his views written by ancient authorities (by Aristotle, for instance). Thales' greatest contribution to both philosophy and science is his method. He set out to look for natural—not mythic—explanations for natural phenomena, and he insisted that such accounts be as simple as possible, preferably accounting for everything by positing a single substance or element. This, as it turns out, is also the preferred approach of modern science.

Thales thought the best candidate for the ultimate stuff of the world was water. (The traditional Greek view was that the universe is composed of earth, air, fire, and water.) He has been interpreted as holding that water is the source of all that exists and in some way is what everything consists of. Aristotle gives this summary of Thales' view:

Aristotle: *Metaphysics*

[Water is] the element and first principle of the things that exist . . . that from which they all are and from which they first come into being and into which they are finally destroyed.[1]

1. Consider the phenomenon of fire. How might Thales explain its existence? How might a traditional religious thinker explain it?

Why would Thales think water is so elemental? He might have been convinced by water's capacity to convert into different forms—into a liquid, solid (ice), or gas (steam or vapor). Perhaps he reasoned that since water can change into these forms, it might change into other states of matter as well. Maybe behind material objects that seem to have nothing to do with water (like stones, for example), there is an essential substance that arises from water. Or he might have noticed, as Aristotle suggested, that water is essential to nourishment, to growth, to life itself (after all, the human body is more than two-thirds water). If water is important to so many natural processes, perhaps somehow it is the basis of *all* material processes.

The Milesian philosopher Anaximander (c. 610–546 BCE) was said to be the pupil and successor of Thales. He is credited with drawing a map of the world, providing naturalistic accounts of the weather, and devising a model of the universe consistent with geometric principles. Like Thales, he sought natural explanations for the origin and composition of the universe, and his views on the subject were an improvement over Thales' water theory.

As Anaximander saw it, Thales erred when he asserted that everything came from water. Anaximander assumed, as many Greeks did, that things exist in opposition to one another. Darkness and light, wet and dry, hot and cold—these are in conflict, and each member of an opposing pair alternates between overpowering the other member and being overpowered. Thus we see day turn into night, then night yield to day in a never-ending cycle. As Anaximander puts it, the opposing factors "make reparation to one another for their injustice according to the ordinance of time."[2] But if everything started out as water, how could its opposite (fire) ever arise? To exist, a thing must be pitted against an opposing thing. But if there were no opposites to contend with one another (because there was only water), how could anything appear?

Anaximander's answer is that everything came from a formless, imperishable substance called *apeiron* (the boundless or indefinite). It is the beginning of all that now exists, but it has no beginning itself.

Anaximander's ideas about the Earth constitute another departure from traditional opinion. Thales thought the Earth was floating on water like a raft, but this view raises a question that Aristotle posed: What supports the water? Anaximander's answer is that the Earth is a flat cylinder or flat disk suspended in space at the center of the universe. It doesn't need to be supported by matter of any kind; it is held in place by virtue of its being in the center of everything and equidistant from all points. Anaximander believes that for any action or state, there must be a reason for it, and the Earth has no reason to move in any particular direction—no reason why it should move up, down, or sideways. So it must rest in the middle. Aristotle restates the theory like this:

"Philosophy asks the simple question, what is it all about?"
—Alfred North Whitehead

2. How does Anaximander explain the Earth's suspension in space? What assumption does he make? Is his assumption well founded?

Aristotle: *On the Heavens*

[T]here is no reason why what is situated in the middle and is similarly related to the edges should move upwards rather than downwards or sideways. But it cannot move in opposite directions at the same time. So it necessarily rests where it is.[3]

Figure 2.2 Ancient Greece.

"I went in search of myself."
—Heraclitus

"Whatever comes from sight, hearing, learning from experience: this I prefer."
—Heraclitus

2.2 HERACLITUS

Heraclitus flourished around 500 BCE in Ionia, living and working in the city of Ephesus. He wrote a book, but only about a hundred sentences of it have survived, and those are presented in the form of epigrams, concise statements meant to cleverly express a truth or insight. He thus earned a reputation as a philosopher of obscure assertions and sly riddles. He derived his views from introspection and experience and sorted things out through reason. About this approach he says that his primary aim was to go "in search of myself." Taken as a whole, his writings reveal a coherent and comprehensive worldview encompassing both humanity and the cosmos.

Heraclitus' central idea is the **logos**—the *principle, formula,* or *law* of the world order. To understand the *logos* is to understand reality, to grasp the divine, eternal pattern underlying all of nature and all of humankind.

A fundamental aspect of the *logos* is summed up by Heraclitus' famous maxim: "all are in flux, like a river"[4] or, as others have phrased it, "you cannot step twice into the same river." A river's water is continually changing so that when you step into the river a second time, the water is entirely different from what it was the first time. For Heraclitus, everything flows; every part of the universe is in flux. But behind the changing appearances, there is an unchanging pattern. Underlying the flux of things, there is a sameness, something that unifies the changes, something that enables us to identify a river as a river despite its dynamic, ever-changing composition, something that unifies the many into the one. Heraclitus seems to imply that this *something* is the *logos* itself.

At its core, says Heraclitus, the *logos* is a harmony of opposites. Everything exists and changes through a process of conflict between opposite elements. He declares that "all things come into being through opposition"[5] and that "all things take place in accordance with strife and necessity."[6] Without "strife" and "war" of opposites, the things of this world would not be. Music depends on an opposition between low and high notes. Hot would not exist without cold. Day occurs because night does. And a bow can fling an arrow because the two are held in tension through the string. The *logos* ensures that a balance of opposing powers is preserved and that they are all part of the same divine reality. Thus Heraclitus asserts that "all things are one."

Heraclitus' world order is more nuanced than that of most of the other pre-Socratics. He thinks the cosmos is eternal—it had no beginning but has always existed. Moreover, it is a rational force. The *logos*, he says, "steers all things," for it is a divine "thought" operating according to its own logic. From this picture of reality, Heraclitus derives moral guidance for humankind. We should strive to maintain balance and moderation in our lives, just as the *logos* does:

Figure 2.3 Heraclitus (fl. 500 BCE).

logos Heraclitus' central idea—the *principle, formula,* or *law* of the world order.

3. Is Heraclitus' *logos* a supreme being? That is, is the *logos* an all-powerful person? Does Heraclitus believe that the universe requires such a being to sustain the universe? Do you? Why or why not?

"[T]he lover of wisdom associating with the divine order will himself become orderly and divine."

—Plato

Heraclitus: *Fragment*

Moderation is the greatest virtue, and wisdom is to speak the truth and to act according to nature, giving heed to it.[7]

THEN AND NOW

The (Ancient) Theory of Evolution

In the nineteenth century Charles Darwin propounded the theory of biological evolution, explaining that evolution operates through what he called "natural selection." The basic idea (which is now a matter of scientific consensus) is that offspring of organisms differ physically from their parents in various ways, and these differences can be passed on genetically to their offspring. If an offspring has an inherited trait (such as sharper vision or a larger brain) that increases its chances of surviving long enough to reproduce, the individual is more likely to survive and pass the trait on to the next generation. After several generations, this useful trait, or adaptation, spreads throughout a whole population of individuals, differentiating the population from its ancestors.

Figure 2.4 Empedocles (c. 495–435 BCE).

The basic outlines of natural selection, however, didn't originate with Darwin. It was first articulated in rough form twenty-five centuries ago by a pre-Socratic philosopher named Empedocles.

Using observation and imagination, Empedocles (c. 495–c. 435 BCE) maintained that animals were not created whole by a deity and placed on the Earth. They evolved. In the beginning, he says, there existed a hodgepodge of weird creatures with mismatched parts and deformities. "[There were] many neckless heads," says Empedocles, "Naked arms wandered, devoid of shoulders, and eyes strayed alone, begging for foreheads." The creatures that were ill formed for survival in their environment died out, but those with characteristics that gave them a survival advantage lived and reproduced their kind for generations.

Which theory is simpler (i.e., is based on the fewest assumptions): Darwin's theory or the theory that a deity created biological life at once and whole? Why?

PORTRAIT

Pythagoras and the Pythagoreans

Among all the pre-Socratics, Pythagoras (c. 550–500 BCE) is the most famous yet the most obscure. His name is, of course, attached to the Pythagorean theorem, a geometry-class staple, and the phrase "music of the spheres" can be traced to him. (The phrase refers to the notion that as the heavenly bodies whir about in space, they make a harmonious noise.) We know he came from Samos off the coast of Ionia (Asia Minor) to settle in southern Italy, where he established a religious-philosophical society that practiced asceticism. But we know little else. In most cases it's difficult to tell whether ideas or doctrines came from Pythagoras himself or from his many followers, the Pythagoreans. Part of the problem is that he wrote nothing down, and neither did the early Pythagoreans (conflicting schools of his followers were active for at least eight hundred years). All the schools claimed to trace their philosophical and religious roots back to the man himself, although they differed substantially in their views.

Figure 2.5 For the Pythagoreans, the universe has a mathematical structure, and the mysteries of the world could be uncovered through mathematics.

The Pythagoreans, claiming the authority of the master, taught the doctrines of an immortal soul and reincarnation (metempsychosis) in which the soul travels through cycles of death and rebirth, being born again and again into the form of humans, gods, or animals. Pythagoras is supposed to have remembered his former lives and once scolded someone for beating a dog that Pythagoras claimed was a dear friend in animal form. It is no surprise, then, that Pythagoreans insisted on a vegetarian diet. They didn't want to risk eating someone they knew. Some of them also devised strange dietary restrictions—for example, the absolute prohibition against eating beans.

The heart of the Pythagoreans' worldview was their profound, even mystical, reverence for numbers. They discovered the concepts of the square of numbers and of odd and even numbers. Most importantly, they realized that numerical ratios could exactly describe the steps on a musical scale. This led to the metaphysical view that the universe has a mathematical structure, that the orderliness of the cosmos is based on numbers, that the mysteries of the world could be uncovered through mathematics. (Modern science, of course, also uses numbers to describe and explore natural phenomena.) In a departure from other pre-Socratic doctrines, this view focused the Pythagoreans on the *form* of the universe instead of the matter or stuff it was made of.

The obsession with mathematics led many Pythagoreans to mystical excesses. They assigned numbers to abstract ideas—mind was equivalent to 1; maleness to 2; femaleness to 3; and justice to 4. Ten, being the sum of these four numbers, had special mystical significance.

They also thought the soul can be purified and united with the divine through contemplation of pure ideas—especially numbers. So a course of study for the devout followers of Pythagoras included geometry, astronomy, and music. Faith was not required, but intellect was.

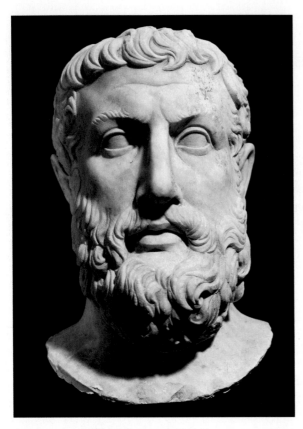

Figure 2.6 Parmenides (c. 515–450 BCE).

> "You must learn all things, both the unwavering heart of well-rounded truth and the opinions of mortals in which there is no true warranty."
>
> —Parmenides

rationalism The view that through unaided reason we can come to know what the world is like.

empiricism The view that our knowledge of the empirical world comes solely from sense experience.

> "[What exists] is now, all at once, one and continuous."
>
> —Parmenides

2.3 PARMENIDES

Parmenides (c. 515–450 BCE) was the most ground-breaking and influential philosopher of the pre-Socratics. We know little about his life—not much more than that he lived in Elea (a Greek colony on the southern coast of Italy) and taught the famous master of paradoxes, Zeno. We also know that through the centuries he won the attention and admiration of several eminent thinkers, from Plato to Plutarch to Hegel. Like the other pre-Socratics, he contributed more to the shape of philosophical inquiry than to its content.

Parmenides' claim to fame rests mostly on his systematic employment of deductive argument. He seems to have been the first thinker outside the field of mathematics to reason deductively and consistently from basic premises to interesting conclusions. In the process, he cemented basic distinctions that have been essential to philosophical inquiry to this day. For one thing, he contrasted reason and the senses. He contended that knowledge of the world could be acquired only through reason, only through a deductive chain of reasoning such as he himself used. The senses, however, were unreliable. In philosophy these two approaches to knowledge are known as rationalism and empiricism. (Both are discussed in later chapters.) **Rationalism** is the view that some or all of our knowledge about the world is gained independently of sense experience. **Empiricism** says that our knowledge of the world comes solely from sense experience. In the coming centuries, many great minds would choose sides in this debate and offer further arguments for and against them. Parmenides takes the path of reason and thus earns the title of the first rationalist philosopher. At stake in this controversy—which continues in our own century—is whether knowledge is possible, how (if at all) knowledge is acquired, and what the extent of our knowledge is (whether we know what we assume we know).

Parmenides also brought out a distinction that philosophers have pondered ever since Thales: the contrast between *reality* and *appearances*—between what is real and what only appears to be real. He holds that almost all of the things we think exist in the world—movement, change, multiplicity, diversity, sensory qualities—are illusions. We may believe that all these are actual, but we would be mistaken. Only reason can reveal the truth.

Parmenides' reasoning on this point goes like this: "What is not" (what is nothing) cannot possibly exist. You cannot sensibly think or talk about "what is not" (what cannot possibly exist). To think or talk of "what is not" is to think or talk of nothing—and that's not possible.

DETAILS

Zeno's Paradoxes

Zeno of Elea (not to be confused with Zeno of Citium, the Stoic) was a fifth-century BCE philosopher and ardent supporter of his distinguished teacher Parmenides. He hoped to defend Parmenides' One—the single, motionless, changeless, eternal world—against critics who thought the idea was nonsensical. Zeno's strategy was to demonstrate the absurdity of the critics' views—specifically to show that com-

Figure 2.7 Zeno's paradox of motion.

monsense propositions such as "more than one thing exists" and "motion is possible" are false. He does this by establishing that each seemingly obvious proposition implies other propositions that contradict each another. The resulting contradiction proves that the original proposition cannot be true. That is, the proposition yields a paradox.

Here, for example, is one of Zeno's arguments against the possibility of motion. (1) Suppose you intend to walk from where you are now to your next class. (2) Before you get to your destination, you must go half the distance. But before you get half the distance, you must go half the distance to that point (one-quarter of the distance). And before you get half the distance to that point, you must go half the distance again (one-eighth of the distance). And so on forever, for an infinite number of halfway points. (3) So you will never get to your next class; you cannot even *begin* the trip. (4) Our commonsense view of motion leads to a paradox—common sense says you can get to class, but logic says you never will. Therefore our commonsense view of motion must be mistaken.

In devising his arguments, Zeno created something else—his distinctive form of argument in which he states the proposition to be examined and draws out its implications, revealing the proposition's weaknesses. Aristotle labeled this kind of argument *dialectic* and called Zeno the "inventor of dialectic." Much later, as you will see, dialectic would be perfected by Socrates.

Most people would dismiss these arguments out of hand because the reasoning is in such obvious conflict with the full range of our perceptions. Nevertheless, for over two millennia, thinkers have pondered Zeno's paradoxes, sometimes offering possible solutions, sometimes gaining important insights into the concepts of infinity, space, and motion. Scientists and philosophers have always taken a special interest in them, and that alone suggests that they are far more than logical curiosities.

Which is the simpler explanation of our perceptions—that our senses somehow give us evidence of an objective world, or that all our perceptions are very elaborate illusions? Explain.

4. What is Zeno's argument against motion? How does it support Parmenides' view of the universe? Why would most people not accept Zeno's argument?

Figure 2.8 Parmenides says that reality is one: "whole and of a single kind and unshaken and perfect."

What follows from this? Parmenides maintains that because we cannot sensibly speak of "what is not," we cannot sensibly speak of things changing. To say that something changes is to suggest that it varies from what it was to what *it is not*—and that's impossible. Likewise we cannot speak of something moving. That would mean that it changed its location from where it was to where it *was not*, and that we cannot say. Further, there can be no coming into existence or passing out of existence:

Parmenides: *On Nature*

How could what is perish? How could it have come to be? For if it came into being, it is not; nor is it if ever it is going to be. Thus coming to being is extinguished, and destruction unknown.[8]

"No one ever touched Zeno without refuting him, and every century thinks it worthwhile to refute him."
—Alfred North Whitehead

Parmenides doesn't stop there. He also reasons that whatever exists now must be as it always was. To contend that a property has been added or subtracted implies that something *is not* the way it used to be. In addition, he says, the universe ("what is") is uniform throughout. There is no emptiness in the cosmos: every part is filled, every part is the same; there is no empty space. The universe does not consist of a multiplicity of objects and forces; it is *one* thing—solid, uniform, and perfect. It is the One. Thus one thing must be uncreated, imperishable, and eternal. As Parmenides says:

Parmenides:
On Nature

[What exists] is now, all at once, one and continuous.... Nor is it divisible, since it is all alike; nor is there any more or less of it in one place which might prevent it from holding together, but all is full of what is.[9]

All these implications conflict with common sense. We are quite sure we can think and talk about what does not exist. We can coherently think about invisible rabbits, hypothetical planets, our long-dead ancestors, zero gravity, and angels dancing on the head of a pin. The idea that virtually everything we believe about the world is an illusion seems preposterous. But Parmenides' conclusions are not the truly valuable part of his views. What is of immeasurable worth is his method—his fearlessly letting reason guide him where it may. Parmenides is credited with being the first to go down this royal road, and philosophers who came after him have had to take it into account.

2.4 DEMOCRITUS

Parmenides confronted ancient philosophers with a disturbing challenge to common sense: the universe is one solid eternal object without empty space and therefore without motion or plurality, a world inaccessible by sensory means but known well through reason. The task was not merely to reject Parmenides' theory but also to come up with a reasonable alternative, one that did justice to the evidence of the senses. The strongest answer came from the ancient Greek *atomists* Leucippus and his student Democritus (c. 460–370 BCE).

Ancient atomism is the theory that reality consists of an infinite number of minute, indivisible bits called *atoms* moving rapidly in an infinite *void*, or empty space. Leucippus first proposed the idea, and Democritus developed it in his writings, which were wide-ranging and voluminous. (Most of Democritus' work has been lost, but many later commentators have provided the missing details.) Of all the early Greek notions about the nature of the universe, Democritus' theory comes closest to that of modern scientists. The views of the atomists were influential (and controversial) for centuries after those thinkers were long gone. The Christian church condemned ancient atomism, and the doctrine seemed to lie dormant for centuries, but since the scientific revolution, it has been held in high esteem as a surprisingly modern (and generally accurate) view of the cosmos.

Parmenides had claimed that motion was impossible because there is no empty space (no "what is not," no nothingness), and without empty space there can be no unfilled area to move into. For the same reason, he says, there can be only *one* thing, the One—the solid, indivisible "what is." Multiple things require empty space, for there must be space between things to render them separate; otherwise, once again, there would be only one solid mass without gaps or holes. Democritus, however, slightly qualified Parmenides's no-space principle and thus showed how both motion and pluralism were possible. He posited the *void*—space that does not contain objects or things but is nevertheless *not the same as nothing* ("what is not"). The void is a kind of "what is."

5. How does Parmenides argue for the existence of the One? Do you accept his arguments? Why or why not?

"No-thing exists just as much as thing."

—Democritus

ancient atomism The theory that reality consists of an infinite number of minute, indivisible bits called atoms moving randomly in an infinite void, or empty space.

6. How does Democritus' theory of the universe differ from that of Parmenides? Which view do you think is closer to the truth? Why?

Figure 2.9 Democritus on a 100-drachma 1967 banknote from Greece.

So the world need not be one solid, uniform thing; it can be broken up by the void so there is room for movement and room to accommodate the many.

Democritus says of atoms what Parmenides says of the One: each one is indivisible (the root of *atom* means "uncuttable"), indestructible, solid through and through (containing no empty space), changeless, and eternal. Yet Democritus' atomic theory can explain change, destruction, creation, and variation better than Parmenides' oneness view. Although atoms have most of the properties of the One, they can also vary in *shape* (some are sharp, some are round, for example), *size*, and their *organization* in the void (some are grouped together, some are far apart, and some are arranged in other configurations). As they whirl around, they collide with one another, allowing atoms with the same shape to clump together. If the clumping is extensive enough, it can form objects that we can detect with our senses. Depending on the size, shape, and arrangement of the clumps, they can coalesce into water, grains of salt, fish, trees, chairs, stars, and human bodies. New objects come into being by grouping together, and existing objects are destroyed when the clumps disperse. Life arises from combinations of atoms; death comes with atomic dispersal.

Through his atomic theory, Democritus tried to account for many other phenomena—for example, sense experience, weather, mind, and the creation of the universe. Even souls are conglomerations of atoms (very fine spherical atoms, Democritus thinks). Like everything else in the cosmos, souls exist for a while and then disintegrate, dispersing their atoms back into the void.

In Democritus' view, the world is mechanistic. Things happen in a particular way because the blind machinery of nature makes them happen that way. There is no need to invoke deities or other agents of purpose or design to explain the state of the universe.

Democritus and modern physics both refer to things called *atoms*, but they understand the term in different ways. Unlike Democritus' atoms, the atoms of twenty-first-century science are known to be destructible, divisible (into other particles such as quarks and electrons), mostly hollow (because of the empty space in them), and impermanent. Yet Democritus' basic insight—that matter is made up of fundamental indivisible units—has yet to be refuted. For all modern physicists know, matter may indeed consist of indivisible, elemental entities—units of matter that are smaller (and stranger) than modern atoms.

2.5 PROTAGORAS AND THE SOPHISTS

In fifth-century BCE, Athens was not merely a city, but a city-state evolving into an empire. It was affluent, influential, and powerful—a burgeoning democracy led by Pericles, the renowned statesman and general who helped usher in Athens' Golden Age. Under his leadership, literature and the arts flourished, democracy blossomed, and the city gleamed with breathtaking monuments and buildings, including the Parthenon, which stands to this day.

Like any prosperous city, Athens bustled with commerce and the usual routines of social life, but it also buzzed with claims, issues, and disputations in the legislature

---

"Nothing occurs at random, but everything occurs for a reason and by necessity."

—Democritus

---

7. According to Democritus (and modern science), is empty space nothing? What role does empty space (or the void) play in Democritus' theory?

"Sweet exists by convention, bitter by convention, color by convention; but in reality atoms and the void alone exist."

—Democritus

(the assembly), the courts, and the marketplace. From these activities arose the need among Athenians to learn the skills that could increase their chances of success. The Athenian education system was too rudimentary to help much, and the first college (Plato's Academy) was yet to be founded and, in any case, was attended by only a lucky few. Into this setting stepped the **Sophists**, itinerant professors who, for a fee, would teach a range of subjects that could be of practical or intellectual benefit: **rhetoric** (the art of verbal persuasion), argument, law, ethics, politics, history, mathematics, literary criticism, grammar, religion, music, and more.

Historically, the Sophists have gotten mixed reviews for their brand of teaching. On one hand, they drew many eager students (generally the "best men," the aristocrats and their children). The demand for the blessings of higher education that the Sophists promised was high, and their emphasis on practical applications and self-improvement made their lectures even more attractive. Some scholars give the Sophists credit for helping shift the focus of philosophy away from the metaphysical speculations of early thinkers like Thales and Parmenides toward more humanistic inquiries such as ethics, rhetoric, and politics. Socrates himself made this shift, and some think the Sophists helped pave the way for him.

Figure 2.10 Protagoras (c. 490–420 BCE).

On the other hand, these popular professors alarmed the moral and religious conservatives of Athens. The Sophists were mostly naturalists like the pre-Socratics, preferring naturalistic explanations for phenomena and downplaying conventional accounts that attributed causes to the gods. They also taught that moral beliefs and legal codes were determined neither by the gods nor nature. Morality and the law were human inventions, varying from society to society depending on local circumstances. Even the Sophists' instruction in argument became suspect because it provided the means to question tradition and inquire into the basis of morality. Argument fostered critical thinking or intellectual cleverness, either of which could subvert the established order.

Plato, Aristotle, and other thinkers had concerns about the Sophists too. Plato contrasted the intellectual honesty of Socrates with the motives and rhetorical slipperiness of the Sophists. Socrates sought understanding for its own sake; the Sophists sought money for their services. Socrates searched for real knowledge; the Sophists wanted only the appearance of knowledge. Socrates engaged in argument to get at the truth; the Sophists were interested only in ways to win arguments. As one Sophist proclaimed, I can "make the weaker argument the stronger." (These

"The art of the sophist is the semblance of wisdom without the reality, and the sophist is one who makes money from an apparent but unreal wisdom."

—Aristotle

Sophists Itinerant professors who, for a fee, would teach a range of subjects that could be of practical or intellectual benefit.

rhetoric The art of verbal persuasion.

8. How did the Sophists threaten the established order of Athens? Were the citizens of the city right to resent the Sophists? What if the Sophists moved into your neighborhood and began teaching? What would be your attitude toward them?

"The recipe for perpetual ignorance is: be satisfied with your opinions and content with your knowledge."
—Elbert Hubbard

relativism The doctrine that the truth about something depends on what persons or cultures believe.

subjective relativism The notion that truth depends on what a person believes.

cultural relativism The idea that truth depends on what a culture believes.

Figure 2.11 Subjective relativism implies that Hitler's slaughter of millions of Jews was morally right. For if he sincerely believed that what he did was right, then he was right.

charges are reflected in terms derived from "Sophist": *sophistry* and *sophistic*, both referring to specious reasoning, such as the use of fallacies like those noted in Chapter 1.)

Probably Plato's most serious allegation against the Sophists is that they espoused **relativism**, the view that the truth about something depends on what persons or cultures believe. That is, a statement is true if some person or society believes it to be true: truth is relative to persons or cultures. Truth depends on what people accept as true, not on the way things are; there is no *objective* truth. When the believer in question is a person, the doctrine is known as **subjective relativism**; when a whole society believes, it's **cultural relativism**. In either case, most philosophers—beginning with Plato—have been skeptical of this notion of truth.

In Plato's time, the leading proponent of subjective relativism was the famed Sophist Protagoras (c. 490–420 BCE). He is renowned for his relativistic adage, "Man is the measure of all things, of existing things that they exist, and of nonexisting things that they do not exist."[10] In other words, reality is what you believe it to be. But Plato rejected subjective relativism, accusing Protagoras of unwittingly refuting himself:

Plato: "Theaetetus"

Protagoras, for his part, admitting as he does that everybody's opinion is true, must acknowledge the truth of his opponents' belief about his own belief, where they think he is wrong.[11]

"Custom is the law of fools."
—Sir John Vanbrugh

Plato's point is that if, according to subjective relativism, all sincerely held beliefs are equally true, then someone's assertion that relativism is true is just as true as someone else's assertion that relativism is false. So if subjective relativism is true, then it's false. The doctrine undermines itself and is therefore unfounded.

In general, modern philosophers are as skeptical of relativism as Plato was. They are aware that relativism has some very odd implications that render it implausible. For example, if we could make a statement true just by believing it to be true, we would be infallible. We could not possibly be in error about anything that we sincerely believed. We could never be mistaken about where we parked the car or what we said about jellybeans or what some general said about carpet bombing. Personal infallibility is, of course, absurd, and this possibility weighs heavily against subjective relativism.

The same criticism can be launched against cultural relativism. According to this view, individuals aren't infallible, but societies are. The beliefs of whole societies cannot be mistaken. But this notion of societal infallibility is no more plausible than the idea of individual infallibility. Is it plausible that no society has ever been wrong about anything? Never been wrong about the causes of disease, the best form of government, the owning of slaves, the burning of witches?

Applying relativism to morality (called *moral relativism*) can yield results that are even more unpalatable. Subjective relativism, for instance, implies an implausible *moral equivalence*. It says that the sincere moral views of any individual are as good or as true as those of any other. If the serial killer and cannibal Jeffrey Dahmer approved of his slaughtering seventeen people, then it is morally right. If you disapprove of the slaughter, then it is morally wrong. By the lights of moral subjectivism, Dahmer's view is no better or worse than yours.

Equally troubling, cultural relativism implies that other cultures are beyond moral criticism; we cannot legitimately criticize them because each culture is the maker of its own moral truth. We cannot accuse another culture of immoral behavior because whatever behavior that culture genuinely endorses is moral. To accept this implication of cultural relativism is to say that if the people of Germany approved of the extermination of millions of Jews in World War II, then the extermination was morally right. But this is implausible. Our moral experience suggests that we can and do condemn other societies for morally heinous acts.

Cultural relativism also has a difficult time explaining the moral status of social reformers. We tend to believe they are at least sometimes right and society is wrong. When we contemplate social reform, we think of such moral exemplars as Martin Luther King, Jr., Mahatma Gandhi, and Susan B. Anthony, all of whom agitated for justice and moral progress. But one of the consequences of cultural relativism is that social reformers could *never* be morally right. By definition, what society judges to be morally right is morally right, and since social reformers disagree with society, they could not be right—ever. But surely on occasion it's the reformers who are right and society is wrong.

Figure 2.12 Cultural relativism implies that social reformers such as Martin Luther King, Jr. were morally wrong.

9. What is subjective relativism? What is cultural relativism? How does Plato argue against subjective relativism? What are some of the implications of relativism? Are you a cultural relativist? Why or why not?

"If Protagoras is right, and the truth is that things are as they appear to anyone, how can some of us be wise and some of us foolish?"

—Socrates

THEN AND NOW

Moral Relativism and Tolerance

Figure 2.13 KKK Klansmen in traditional white robes demonstrating outside a courthouse in New York City.

Protagoras may or may not have thought much about whether his relativism encouraged tolerance toward other cultures, but plenty of people today think moral relativism and tolerance go hand in hand. Their thinking might go something like this: If the values of one culture are no better or worse than those of another, then there is no basis for hatred or hostility toward any culture anywhere.

Tolerance is, of course, both morally praiseworthy and beneficial to our fractured planet of conflicting values. But in promoting tolerance, cultural relativism has no advantage over moral objectivism (the view that some moral norms are valid or true for everyone).

First note that moral objectivism does not entail intolerance. It says only that some moral beliefs are better than others; it does not imply anything about how objectivists should behave toward those they think are in moral error. Some objectivists are intolerant; many are not. But cultural relativism can easily justify intolerance and cannot consistently advocate tolerance. If there are intolerant cultures (and there surely are), then since cultures make rightness, intolerance in those cultures is morally right. For sincerely intolerant societies, the persecution of minorities and the killing of dissidents may be the height of moral rectitude.

In addition, cultural relativists who insist that everyone should embrace tolerance are contradicting themselves. To say that tolerant behavior is right for everyone is to assert an objective moral norm—but cultural relativism says there are no objective moral norms. The moral objectivist, however, can plausibly claim that the moral requirement of tolerance is universal.

Are you a cultural relativist? Why or why not?

Socrates (as portrayed by Plato) seems to have noticed a more mundane objection to Protagoras' relativism. If relativism were true, Socrates says, Protagoras might quickly become unemployed. Relativism says that whatever anyone believes is just as true as what anyone else believes. If so, then no one can claim to be wiser than others—and there is no reason to think Protagoras is any wiser than the dullest man in Athens. So how can he legitimately claim to impart wisdom?

10. Does cultural relativism entail tolerance? Why or why not?

WRITING AND REASONING   **CHAPTER 2**

1. What was the pre-Socratics' greatest contribution to the development of philosophical inquiry? What was Thales' contribution? Parmenides'?

2. In what ways did Parmenides' and Democritus' views conflict? Which view seems most reasonable to you?

3. What prescient theory did Empedocles develop? What modern-day theory does it resemble? What are the differences between them?

4. What is Zeno's paradox of motion? Sometimes the best way to attack a paradox is to dissolve it—that is, to show that one of the premises in the supporting argument is unfounded. Try your hand at detecting such an error.

5. Is subjective relativism true? Why or why not?

REVIEW NOTES

2.1 THALES AND ANAXIMANDER

- In the pre-Socratic era, Western philosophy first established itself, defined almost all its main areas of study, and gave us philosophical heroes.

- The ancient Greeks, beginning with the pre-Socratics, refused to follow the traditional ways of thinking and tried to let reason and experience guide them to the truth.

- Thales' greatest contribution to both philosophy and science is his method. He set out to look for natural—not mythic—explanations for natural phenomena, and he insisted that such accounts be as simple as possible.

- Thales has been interpreted as holding that water is the source of all that exists and in some way is what everything consists of.

- Anaximander contended that everything came from a formless, imperishable substance called *apeiron* (the boundless or indefinite). It is the beginning of all that now exists, but it has no beginning itself.

2.2 HERACLITUS

- Heraclitus' central idea is the *logos*—the principle, formula, or law of the world order. To understand the *logos* is to understand reality, to grasp the divine, eternal pattern underlying all of nature and all of humankind.

- For Heraclitus, everything flows; every part of the universe is in flux. But behind the changing appearances, there is an unchanging pattern—the *logos*.

- Heraclitus thinks of the cosmos as eternal—it had no beginning and has always existed. It is also a rational force. The *logos*, he says, "steers all things," for it is a divine "thought" operating according to its own logic.

2.3 PARMENIDES

- Parmenides' fame rests mostly on his systematic employment of deductive argument. He seems to have been the first thinker outside the field of mathematics to reason deductively and consistently from basic premises to interesting conclusions.

- He also made two distinctions that became of prime importance in philosophy: reason and the senses, and appearance and reality.

- Parmenides says reality consists of the One, which is eternal, uniform, solid, perfect, and uncreated.

2.4 DEMOCRITUS

- Democritus put forth the theory known as *ancient atomism*—the view that reality consists of an infinite number of minute, indivisible bits called atoms moving rapidly in an infinite void, or empty space.

- Contrary to Parmenides, Democritus posited the *void*—space that does not contain objects or things but is nevertheless *not the same as nothing*.

- In Democritus' view, the world is mechanistic. Things happen in a particular way because the blind machinery of nature makes them happen that way. There is no need to invoke deities or other agents of purpose or design to explain the state of the universe.

- Democritus and modern physics both refer to things called *atoms*, yet they understand the term in different ways. But Democritus' basic insight—that matter is made up of fundamental indivisible units—has yet to be refuted.

2.5 PROTAGORAS AND THE SOPHISTS

- Sophists were itinerant professors who, for a fee, would teach a range of subjects that could be of practical or intellectual benefit, including rhetoric, argument, law, ethics, and politics.

- The Sophists were mostly naturalists like the pre-Socratics, preferring naturalistic explanations for phenomena and downplaying conventional accounts that attributed causes to the gods.

- They also taught that moral beliefs and legal codes were determined neither by the gods nor nature. Morality and the law were human inventions, varying from society to society depending on local circumstances.

- The leading proponent of subjective relativism was the famed Sophist Protagoras. He is renowned for his relativistic adage, "Man is the measure of all things, of existing things that they exist, and of nonexisting things that they do not exist."[12] In other words, reality is what you believe it to be.

- Plato rejected subjective relativism. The conclusion of his argument is that if subjective relativism is true, then it's false; the doctrine undermines itself and is therefore unfounded.

- Both subjective and cultural relativism have implausible implications.

KEY TERMS

ancient atomism	logos	relativism	subjective
cultural relativism	pre-Socratics	rhetoric	relativism
empiricism	rationalism	Sophists	

Notes

1. Aristotle, *Metaphysics* (1.3, 983 b18–27), in *The Pre-Socratic Philosophers*, ed. G. S. Kirk, J. E. Raven, and M. Schofield (Cambridge: Cambridge University Press, 1983), 80.
2. Anaximander, in *An Introduction to Early Greek Philosophy*, trans. John Manly Robinson (Boston: Houghton Mifflin, 1968), 34.
3. Aristotle, in *Early Greek Philosophy*, trans. Jonathan Barnes (New York: Penguin Books, 1987), 74.
4. Heraclitus, in Robinson, *An Introduction to Early Greek Philosophy*, 89.
5. Heraclitus, in Robinson, *An Introduction to Early Greek Philosophy*, 89.
6. Heraclitus, in Robinson, *An Introduction to Early Greek Philosophy*, 93.
7. Heraclitus, in Robinson, *An Introduction to Early Greek Philosophy*, 101.
8. Parmenides, in Robinson, *An Introduction to Early Greek Philosophy*, 113.
9. Parmenides, in Robinson, *An Introduction to Early Greek Philosophy*, 113–114.
10. Plato, "Theaetetus," in *The Collected Dialogues*, ed. Edith Hamilton, trans. F. M. Cornford (Princeton, NJ: Princeton University Press, 1961), 856.
11. Plato, "Theaetetus," in Hamilton, *The Collected Dialogues*, 876.
12. Plato, "Theaetetus," in Hamilton, *The Collected Dialogues*, 856.

For Further Reading

Jonathan Barnes, trans., *Early Greek Philosophy* (London: Penguin Books, 1987).

Anthony Gottlieb, *The Dream of Reason: A History of Philosophy from the Greeks to the Renaissance* (New York: W. W. Norton, 2000).

Stephen Greenblat, *The Swerve: How the World Became Modern* (New York: W. W. Norton, 2011).

Ted Honderich, ed., *The Oxford Companion to Philosophy* (Oxford: Oxford University Press, 1995).

Edward Hussey, *The Pre-Socratics* (New York: Hackett, 1995).

Christopher Janaway, "Ancient Greek Philosophy I: The Pre-Socratics and Plato," in *Philosophy 1: A Guide through the Subject*, A. C. Grayling, ed. (Oxford: Oxford University Press, 1995), 336–397.

G. S. Kirk, J. E. Raven, and M. Schofield, *The Pre-Socratic Philosophers*, 2nd edition (Cambridge: Cambridge University Press, 1983).

Mary Ellen Waithe, ed., *A History of Women Philosophers*, vol. 1, 600 BC–500 AD (Dordrecht: Martinus Nijhoff, 1987).

Online Resources

Stanford Encyclopedia of Philosophy, "Presocratic Philosophy," https://plato.stanford.edu/entries/presocratics

Internet Encyclopedia of Philosophy, "Presocratics," https://www.iep.utm.edu/presocra

History of Philosophy (without Any Gaps) Podcast, https://historyofphilosophy.net

The Perseus Digital Library, http://www.perseus.tufts.edu/hopper

CHAPTER 3

Socrates: An Examined Life

CHAPTER OBJECTIVES

3.1 THE PHILOSOPHICAL GADFLY

- Appreciate that in contrast to Socrates' outward appearance, he was charismatic, inspiring, brilliant, and persuasive, profoundly affecting the lives of those around him, gaining both followers and detractors.
- Understand why his words had such a powerful effect on those he encountered.

3.2 THE SOCRATIC METHOD

- Know what the *Socratic method* is and how it can be used to expose errors in ethical thinking.
- Define *reductio ad absurdum* and explain how this kind of argument is used in Socratic dialogues.
- Be able to create a Socratic dialogue that demonstrates the inadequacies of a moral concept.

3.3 KNOWLEDGE AND IGNORANCE

- Explain the differences between Socrates' approach to philosophical discourse and that of the Sophists.
- Understand how Socrates views the connection between knowledge and virtue.
- Know why Socrates says that nothing can harm a good man and that an unexamined life is not worth living.

3.4 SOCRATES' TRIAL AND DEATH

- Summarize the arguments Socrates made to the Athenian jury and be able to evaluate them.
- Relate Socrates' explanation of why he is called wise and has "such an evil fame."

Figure 3.1 Socrates (c. 469–399 BCE).

Socrates devised no grand systems of metaphysics, epistemology, or logic as Plato and Aristotle did, but his influence on these two intellectual giants was profound.

Unlike many great philosophers, he affects people as much by his character as by his ideas. Through the power of his words and the extraordinary force of his personality, he has helped make philosophy relevant to the daily lives of ordinary people. At a time when most philosophy was directed at cosmological speculations (à la Thales, Parmenides, and others), Socrates turned to critically examining people's basic concepts, core beliefs, and moral thinking. After him, philosophy was never the same.

3.1 THE PHILOSOPHICAL GADFLY

Socrates (c. 469–399 BCE) was born and raised in Athens and spent all his days there except for a term of military service in which he soldiered in the Peloponnesian War. In battle he was said to be courageous, levelheaded, and steadfast. In civilian life he was passionate yet self-controlled; down to earth yet propelled by high ideals and concern for the spiritual self; plain-spoken yet intellectually sophisticated. Except for his preoccupation with philosophy, his life was outwardly commonplace—the son of a stonemason or sculptor, a married man, and the father of three sons. By all accounts he was ugly, having a pig nose, bulging eyes, outsized lips, a prominent potbelly, and a peculiar gait. His looks were not helped by his slovenly appearance (barefoot and unkempt), which fit well with his indifference to material concerns and conventional expectations.

Once at a banquet, Socrates showed that he could be a good sport about his looks—and make a serious point to boot. One of Socrates' friends—a handsome young man named Critobulus—challenged Socrates to a beauty contest in which each of them would try to persuade the judges (the audience of partygoers) that he was the more beautiful. Socrates argued in his characteristic style.

Xenophon: *Symposium*

Socrates: Do you hold, then, that beauty is to be found only in man, or is it also in other objects?

Critobulus: In faith, my opinion is that beauty is to be found quite as well in a horse or an ox or in any number of inanimate things. I know, at any rate, that a shield may be beautiful, or a sword, or a spear.

S: How can it be that all these things are beautiful when they are entirely dissimilar?

C: Why, they are beautiful and fine if they are well made for the respective functions for which we obtain them, or if they are naturally well constituted to serve our needs.

S: Do you know the reason why we need eyes?

C: Obviously to see with.

S: In that case, it would appear without further ado that my eyes are finer ones than yours.

C: How so?

S: Because, while yours see only straight ahead, mine, by bulging out as they do, see also to the sides.

C: Do you mean to say that a crab is better equipped visually than any other creature?

S: Absolutely . . .

C: Well, let that pass; but whose nose is finer, yours or mine?

S: Mine, I consider, granting that Providence made us noses to smell with. For your nostrils look down toward the ground, but mine are wide open and turned outward so that I can catch scents from all about.

C: But how do you make a snub nose handsomer than a straight one?

S: For the reason that it does not put a barricade between the eyes but allows them unobstructed vision of whatever they desire to see; whereas a high nose, as if in despite, has walled the eyes off one from the other.

C: As for the mouth, I concede that point. For if it is created for the purpose of biting off food, you could bite off a far bigger mouthful than I could. And don't you think that your kiss is also the more tender because you have thick lips?

S: According to your argument, it would seem that I have a mouth more ugly even than an ass's . . .

C: I cannot argue any longer with you, let them distribute the ballots . . . [1]

The ballots for choosing the most handsome were cast and counted, and every vote went to Critobulus. In mock dismay, Socrates declared that Critobulus must have bribed the judges.

Despite his unpleasant features, in face-to-face encounters Socrates had a powerful impact on those he conversed with. He exuded an inexplicable charisma that was especially attractive to the young. He unsettled his listeners, prompting them to critically inspect their beliefs and to question their pursuit of fame, money, power, and pleasure. This is how Alcibiades, a bright associate of Socrates, describes the effect:

> "Are you not ashamed of heaping up the greatest amount of money and honour and reputation, and caring so little about wisdom and truth and the greatest improvement of the soul, which you never regard or heed at all?"
>
> —Socrates

Plato: *Symposium*

When we hear any other speaker, even a very good one, he produces absolutely no effect upon us, or not much, whereas the mere fragments of you [Socrates] and your words, even at second-hand, and however imperfectly repeated, amaze and possess the souls of every man, woman, and child who comes within hearing of them. And if I were not afraid that you would think me hopelessly drunk, I would have sworn as well as spoken to the influence which they have always had and still have over me. For my heart leaps within me more than

2. What emotional effect does Socrates have on Alcibiades? Why does Alcibiades react this way?

"[Socrates] is the only person who ever made me ashamed, which you might think not to be in my nature, and there is no one else who does the same."

—Alcibiades

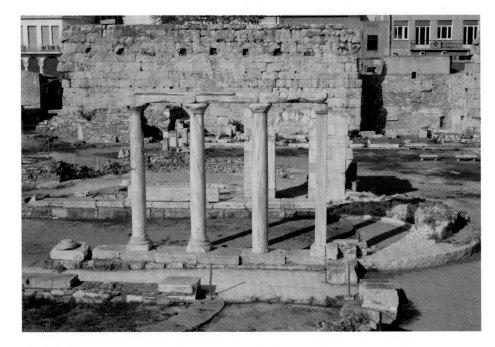

Figure 3.2 Ruins of the ancient Agora in central Athens.

Plato:
Symposium

that of any Corybantian [frenzied] reveler, and my eyes rain tears when I hear them. And I observe that many others are affected in the same manner. I have heard Pericles and other great orators, and I thought that they spoke well, but I never had any similar feeling; my soul was not stirred by them, nor was I angry at the thought of my own slavish state. But [Socrates] has often brought me to such pass, that I have felt as if I could hardly endure the life which I am leading (this, Socrates, you will admit); and I am conscious that if I did not shut my ears against him, and fly as from the voice of the siren, my fate would be like that of others,—he would transfix me, and I should grow old sitting at his feet. For he makes me confess that I ought not to live as I do, neglecting the wants of my own soul, and busying myself with the concerns of the Athenians; therefore I hold my ears and tear myself away from him. And he is the only person who ever made me ashamed, which you might think not to be in my nature, and there is no one else who does the same.[2]

3. Does Socrates believe that his dialectic can lead toward truth—or does he believe as the Sophists do that truth is relative?

To Socrates, this kind of self-examination is essential to living a good life. Nothing, he says, is more important than the care of one's soul (the inner person), and the only way to nurture it is through philosophical reflection.

3.2 THE SOCRATIC METHOD

Socratic method
Question-and-answer dialogue in which propositions are methodically scrutinized to uncover the truth.

In one form or another, the **Socratic method** has been part of Western education for centuries. It is one of the ways that philosophy is done, a powerful procedure for applying critical thinking to many statements that may seem out of reason's reach.

As Socrates uses it, the method typically goes like this: (1) Someone poses a question about the meaning of a concept (for example, What is justice?); (2) Socrates' companion

PORTRAIT

Early Women Philosophers: Themistoclea, Arignote, and Theano

As we've seen (Chapter 2), Pythagoras inspired a long line of followers—Pythagoreans—dating from the sixth century BCE well into the new millennium. What isn't so well known is that many of these followers were women, distinguished philosophers in their own right. Here is part of Mary Ellen Waithe's discussion of three of them:

> The ancient sources indicate that women were active in early Pythagorean societies and may have played a central role in the development of early Pythagorean philosophy. Diogenes Laertius reports that:
>
> > Aristonexus asserts that Pythagoras derived the greater part of his ethical doctrines from *Themistoclea*, the priestess of Delphi.
>
> Early Pythagoreans viewed the cosmos or universe as orderly and harmonious. Everything bears a particular mathematical relationship to everything else. Harmony and order exist when things are in their proper relationship to each other. This relationship can be expressed as a mathematical proportion. One of the "sacred discourses" is attributed to Pythagoras' daughter, *Arignote*. According to Arignote:
>
> > The eternal essence of number is the most providential cause of the whole heaven, earth and region in between. Likewise it is the root of the continued existence of the gods and daimones, as well as that of divine men.
>
> Arignote's comment is consistent with one attributed to her mother, *Theano of Crotona*, in that all that exists, all that is real can be distinguished from other things through enumeration. The eternal essence of number is also directly related to the harmonious coexistence of different things. This harmony can be expressed as a mathematical relationship. In these two ways, number is the cause of all things.

Mary Ellen Waithe, "Early Pythagoreans," in *A History of Women Philosophers* (Dordrecht: Martinus Nijhoff, 1987), 11–12.

gives an answer; (3) Socrates raises questions about the answer, proving that the answer is inadequate; (4) to avoid the problems inherent in this answer, the companion offers a second answer; (5) steps (3) and (4) are repeated a number of times, ultimately revealing that the companion does not know what he thought he knew. This negative result may seem uninformative, but it is actually a kind of progress. False answers are eliminated, opinions are improved, and perhaps the truth is a little closer than before.

Let's watch Socrates in action. Here is his conversation with Thrasymachus, a teacher eager to demonstrate that Socrates is not as wise as people say he is.

4. What proposition does Socrates set out to examine in his dialogue with Thrasymachus?

The question is "What is justice?" and Thrasymachus insists that justice is whatever is in the interests of the strongest—that is, might makes right.

Plato: *The Republic*

5. Is justice merely the interest of the stronger as Thrasymachus says? Does Socrates succeed in showing that Thrasymachus is wrong?

"In appearance Socrates was universally admitted to be extraordinarily ugly, but it was the kind of ugliness which fascinates."
—W. K. C. Guthrie

Listen, then, he [Thrasymachus] said; I proclaim that justice is nothing else than the interest of the stronger. And now why do you not praise me? But of course you won't.

Let me first understand you, I [Socrates] replied. Justice, as you say, is the interest of the stronger. What, Thrasymachus, is the meaning of this? You can not mean to say that because Polydamas, the pancratiast [an athlete], is stronger than we are, and finds the *eating* of beef conducive to his bodily strength, that to eat beef is therefore equally for our good who are weaker than he is, and right and just for us?

That's abominable of you, Socrates; you take the words in the sense which is most damaging to the argument.

Not at all, my good sir, I said; I am trying to understand them; and I wish that you would be a little clearer.

Well, he said, have you never heard that forms of government differ; there are tyrannies, and there are democracies, and there are aristocracies?

Yes, I know.

And the government is the ruling power in each state?

Certainly.

And the different forms of government make laws democratical, aristocratical, tyrannical, with a view to their several interests; and these laws, which are made by them for their own interests, are the justice which they deliver to their subjects, and him who transgresses them they punish as a breaker of the law and unjust. And that is what I mean when I say that in all states there is the same principle of justice, which is the interest of the government; and as the government must be supposed to have power, the only reasonable conclusion is, that everywhere there is one principle of justice, which is the interest of the stronger.

Now I understand you, I said; and whether you are right or not I will try to discover. But let me remark, that in defining justice you have yourself used the word "interest" which you forbade me to use. It is true, however, that in your definition the words "of the stronger" are added.

A small addition, you must allow, he said.

Great or small, never mind about that: we must first inquire whether what you are saying is the truth. Now we are both agreed that justice is interest of some sort, but you go on to say "of the stronger"; about this addition I am not so sure, and must therefore consider further.

Proceed.

I will; and first tell me, Do you admit that it is just for subjects to obey their rulers?

Figure 3.3 A 1998 Greek stamp showing Socrates.

I do.

But are the rulers of states absolutely infallible, or are they sometimes liable to err?

To be sure, he replied, they are liable to err.

Then in making their laws they may sometimes make them rightly, and sometimes not?

True.

When they make them rightly, they make them agreeably to their interest; when they are mistaken, contrary to their interest; you admit that?

Yes.

And the laws which they make must be obeyed by their subjects,—and that is what you call justice?

Doubtless.

Then justice, according to your argument, is not only obedience to the interest of the stronger but the reverse?

What is that you are saying? he asked.

I am only repeating what you are saying, I believe. But let us consider: Have we not admitted that the rulers may be mistaken about their own interest in what they command, and also that to obey them is justice? Has not that been admitted?

Yes.

Then you must also have acknowledged justice not to be for the interest of the stronger, when the rulers unintentionally command things to be done which are to their own injury. For if, as you say, justice is the obedience which the subject renders to their commands, in that case, O wisest of men, is there any escape from the conclusion that the weaker are commanded to do, not what is for the interest, but what is for the injury of the stronger?[3]

As you can see, Socrates uses his question-and-answer approach to show that Thrasymachus' definition of justice is wrong. In particular, he applies a common form of argument called ***reductio ad absurdum***. The basic idea behind it is if you assume a set of statements, and you can derive absurd or false statements from it, then you know that at least one of the original statements must be rejected. So in the preceding dialogue, Socrates says in effect, let's assume that Thrasymachus is right that justice is whatever is in the interest of the powerful, and that people are just if they obey the laws made by the powerful. It is clear, however, that the powerful sometimes make mistakes and demand obedience to laws that are *not* in their best interest. So if Thrasymachus' definition of justice is correct, then it is right for people to do what is in the interest of the powerful, and it is also right to do what is *not* in the interest of the powerful. His idea of justice then leads to a logical contradiction and is therefore false.

Here in the dialogue *Euthyphro* is another example of Socrates at work. He not only shows that his interlocutor (Euthyphro) does not know what he thinks he knows but brings to the surface a crucial question about the relationship between morality (piety) and divinity—a question debated among philosophers (and others) to this day. Socrates asks, in effect, Are actions right because God commands them, or does God command them because they are right? To choose the first option is to say that God *makes* morality. To choose the second is to say that morality exists independently of God's will and even he must obey it. For many modern theists, the second option is far more palatable than the first, for the first one seems to imply that morality is completely arbitrary.

6. What is *reductio ad absurdum?* How does Socrates use it in his discussion with Thrasymachus?

reductio ad absurdum
An argument form in which a set of statements is assumed, and absurd or false statements are derived from the set, showing that at least one of the original statements must be rejected.

Plato: *Euthyphro*

Euth. Piety, then, is that which is dear to the gods, and impiety is that which is not dear to them.

Soc. Very good, Euthyphro; you have now given me the sort of answer which I wanted. But whether what you say is true or not I cannot as yet tell, although I make no doubt that you will prove the truth of your words.

Euth. Of course.

Soc. Come, then, and let us examine what we are saying. That thing or person which is dear to the gods is pious, and that thing or person which is hateful to the gods is impious, these two being the extreme opposites of one another. Was not that said?

Euth. It was.

Soc. And well said?

Euth. Yes, Socrates, I thought so; it was certainly said.

Soc. And further, Euthyphro, the gods were admitted to have enmities and hatreds and differences?

Euth. Yes, that was also said.

Soc. And what sort of difference creates enmity and anger? Suppose for example that you and I, my good friend, differ about a number; do differences of this sort make us enemies and set us at variance with one another? Do we not go at once to arithmetic, and put an end to them by a sum?

Euth. True.

Soc. Or suppose that we differ about magnitudes, do we not quickly end the differences by measuring?

Euth. Very true.

Soc. And we end a controversy about heavy and light by resorting to a weighing machine?

Euth. To be sure.

Soc. But what differences are there which cannot be thus decided, and which therefore make us angry and set us at enmity with one another? I dare say the answer does not occur to you at the moment, and therefore I will suggest that these enmities arise when the matters of difference are the just and unjust, good and evil, honourable and dishonourable. Are not these the points about which men differ, and about which when we are unable satisfactorily to decide our differences, you and I and all of us quarrel, when we do quarrel?

Euth. Yes, Socrates, the nature of the differences about which we quarrel is such as you describe.

Soc. And the quarrels of the gods, noble Euthyphro, when they occur, are of a like nature?

Euth. Certainly they are.

Soc. They have differences of opinion, as you say, about good and evil, just and unjust, honourable and dishonourable: there would have been no quarrels among them, if there had been no such differences—would there now?

Euth. You are quite right.

Soc. Does not every man love that which he deems noble and just and good, and hate the opposite of them?

Euth. Very true.

Soc. But, as you say, people regard the same things, some as just and others as unjust,—about these they dispute; and so there arise wars and fightings among them.

Euth. Very true.

Soc. Then the same things are hated by the gods and loved by the gods, and are both hateful and dear to them?

Euth. True.

Soc. And upon this view the same things, Euthyphro, will be pious and also impious?

Euth. So I should suppose.

Soc. Then, my friend, I remark with surprise that you have not answered the question which I asked. For I certainly did not ask you to tell me what action is both pious and impious: but now it would seem that what is loved by the gods is also hated by them. And therefore, Euthyphro, in thus chastising your father you may very likely be doing what is agreeable to Zeus but disagreeable to Cronos or Uranus, and what is acceptable to Hephaestus but unacceptable to Here, and there may be other gods who have similar differences of opinion.

Euth. But I believe, Socrates, that all the gods would be agreed as to the propriety of punishing a murderer: there would be no difference of opinion about that.

Soc. Well, but speaking of men, Euthyphro, did you ever hear any one arguing that a murderer or any sort of evil-doer ought to be let off?

Euth. I should rather say that these are the questions which they are always arguing, especially in courts of law: they commit all sorts of crimes, and there is nothing which they will not do or say in their own defence.

Soc. But do they admit their guilt, Euthyphro, and yet say that they ought not to be punished?

Euth. No; they do not.

Soc. Then there are some things which they do not venture to say and do: for they do not venture to argue that the guilty are to be unpunished, but they deny their guilt, do they not?

Euth. Yes.

Soc. Then they do not argue that the evil-doer should not be punished, but they argue about the fact of who the evil-doer is, and what he did and when?

Euth. True.

Soc. And the gods are in the same case, if as you assert they quarrel about just and unjust, and some of them say while others deny that injustice is done among them. For surely neither God nor man will ever venture to say that the doer of injustice is not to be punished?

Euth. That is true, Socrates, in the main.

Soc. But they join issue about the particulars—gods and men alike; and, if they dispute at all, they dispute about some act which is called in question, and which by some is affirmed to be just, by others to be unjust. Is not that true?

Euth. Quite true.

Soc. Well then, my dear friend Euthyphro, do tell me, for my better instruction and information, what proof have you that in the opinion of all the gods a servant who is guilty of murder, and is put in chains by the master of the dead man, and dies because he is put in chains before he who bound him can learn from the interpreters of the gods what he ought to do with him, dies unjustly; and that on behalf of such a one a son ought to proceed against his father and accuse him of murder. How would you show that all the gods absolutely agree in approving of his act? Prove to me that they do, and I will applaud your wisdom as long as I live.

Euth. It will be a difficult task; but I could make the matter very clear indeed to you.

Soc. I understand; you mean to say that I am not so quick of apprehension as the judges: for to them you will be sure to prove that the act is unjust, and hateful to the gods.

Euth. Yes indeed, Socrates; at least if they will listen to me.

Soc. But they will be sure to listen if they find that you are a good speaker. There was a notion that came into my mind while you were speaking; I said to myself: "Well, and what if Euthyphro does prove to me that all the gods regarded the death of the serf as unjust, how do I know anything more of the nature of piety and impiety? for granting that this action may be hateful to the gods, still piety and impiety are not adequately defined by these distinctions, for that which is hateful to the gods has been shown to be also pleasing and dear to them." And therefore, Euthyphro, I do not ask you to prove this; I will suppose, if you like, that all the gods condemn and abominate such an action. But I will amend the definition so far as to say that what all the gods hate is impious, and what they love pious or holy; and what some of them love and others hate is both or neither. Shall this be our definition of piety and impiety?

Euth. Why not, Socrates?

Soc. Why not! certainly, as far as I am concerned, Euthyphro, there is no reason why not. But whether this admission will greatly assist you in the task of instructing me as you promised, is a matter for you to consider.

Euth. Yes, I should say that what all the gods love is pious and holy, and the opposite which they all hate, impious.

Soc. Ought we to enquire into the truth of this, Euthyphro, or simply to accept the mere statement on our own authority and that of others? What do you say?

Euth. We should enquire; and I believe that the statement will stand the test of enquiry.

Soc. We shall know better, my good friend, in a little while. The point which I should first wish to understand is whether the pious or holy is beloved by the gods because it is holy, or holy because it is beloved of the gods.

Euth. I do not understand your meaning, Socrates.

Soc. I will endeavour to explain: we, speak of carrying and we speak of being carried, of leading and being led, seeing and being seen. You know that in all such cases there is a difference, and you know also in what the difference lies?

Euth. I think that I understand.

Soc. And is not that which is beloved distinct from that which loves?

Euth. Certainly.

Soc. Well; and now tell me, is that which is carried in this state of carrying because it is carried, or for some other reason?

Euth. No; that is the reason.

Soc. And the same is true of what is led and of what is seen?

Euth. True.

Soc. And a thing is not seen because it is visible, but conversely, visible because it is seen; nor is a thing led because it is in the state of being led, or carried because it is in the state of being carried, but the converse of this. And now I think, Euthyphro, that my meaning will be intelligible; and my meaning is, that any state of action or passion implies previous action or passion. It does not become because it is becoming, but it is in a state of becoming because it becomes; neither does it suffer because it is in a state of suffering, but it is in a state of suffering because it suffers. Do you not agree?

Euth. Yes.

Soc. Is not that which is loved in some state either of becoming or suffering?

Euth. Yes.

Soc. And the same holds as in the previous instances; the state of being loved follows the act of being loved, and not the act the state.

Euth. Certainly.

Soc. And what do you say of piety, Euthyphro: is not piety, according to your definition, loved by all the gods?

Euth. Yes.

Soc. Because it is pious or holy, or for some other reason?

Euth. No, that is the reason.

Soc. It is loved because it is holy, not holy because it is loved?

Euth. Yes.

Soc. And that which is dear to the gods is loved by them, and is in a state to be loved of them because it is loved of them?

Euth. Certainly.

Soc. Then that which is dear to the gods, Euthyphro, is not holy, nor is that which is holy loved of God, as you affirm; but they are two different things.

Euth. How do you mean, Socrates?

Soc. I mean to say that the holy has been acknowledge by us to be loved of God because it is holy, not to be holy because it is loved.

Euth. Yes.

Soc. But that which is dear to the gods is dear to them because it is loved by them, not loved by them because it is dear to them.

Euth. True.

Soc. But, friend Euthyphro, if that which is holy is the same with that which is dear to God, and is loved because it is holy, then that which is dear to God would have been loved as being dear to God; but if that which dear to God is dear to him because loved by him, then that which is holy would have been holy because loved by him. But now you see that the reverse is the case, and that they are quite different from one another. For one (*theophiles*) is of a kind to be loved cause it is loved, and the other (*osion*) is loved because it is of a kind to be loved. Thus you appear to me, Euthyphro, when I ask you what is the essence of holiness, to offer an attribute only, and not the essence—the attribute of being loved by all the gods. But you still refuse to explain to me the nature of holiness. And therefore, if you please, I will ask you not to hide your treasure, but to tell me once more what holiness or piety really is, whether dear to the gods or not (for that is a matter about which we will not quarrel) and what is impiety?

Euth. I really do not know, Socrates, how to express what I mean. For somehow or other our arguments, on whatever ground we rest them, seem to turn round and walk away from us.[4]

3.3 KNOWLEDGE AND IGNORANCE

Why does Socrates persist in asking questions that often annoy or embarrass his interlocutors? Why doesn't he just give lectures or impart his wisdom in some other way? What does he hope to accomplish through his peculiar way of doing philosophy?

First, whatever Socrates hoped to achieve with his approach, he was certainly not trying to be a Sophist (see Chapter 2). Socrates and the Sophists were indeed alike—alike enough to lead many in his day to brand him a Sophist. (The playwright

7. What are the main differences between Socrates and the Sophists? What do they have in common?

"Let him that would move the world first move himself."
—Socrates

8. Why does Socrates say that nothing can harm a good man either in life or after death?

"[T]here's one proposition that I'd defend to the death, if I could, by argument and by action: that as long as we think we should search for what we don't know we'll be better people—less fainthearted and less lazy—than if we were to think that we had no chance of discovering what we don't know and that there's no point in even searching for it."
—Socrates

"Not life, but good life, is to be chiefly valued."
—Socrates

Aristophanes did just that in his play *Clouds*.) But unlike the Sophists, Socrates thought of his method as a way to pursue the truth, not as a means to win rhetorical victories. Unlike them, he was no relativist insisting that truth depends on who you are or where you're from. The Sophists were teachers who charged a fee for their tutelage. Socrates charged nothing and denied that he taught anything, asserting instead that he merely guided people to discover wisdom within themselves.

Socrates' strange method and mission spring from his ideas about the soul and how to live a good life. He insists again and again that nothing in this life is more important than the care of the soul, the true self. Your soul is harmed or helped by your own actions: doing wrong damages your soul, and doing right benefits it. Nothing else and no one else can affect the welfare of your soul as much. Thus Socrates asserts that "nothing can harm a good man either in life or after death" and that doing injustice is far worse than suffering injustice inflicted by others. This view explains why he thought it better to stick to his moral principles and face execution than to give up his principles and live.

Socrates couples this moral perspective with an extraordinary thesis: virtue is knowledge. For him, *knowledge* refers to both knowing *what* virtue is and knowing *how* to apply that understanding to life. This knowledge is self-knowledge and is comparable to the know-how possessed by expert craftsmen. They understand everything about their craft, including how to practice it. Likewise those who know virtue in this sense will grasp it and conduct their lives by it. They will attain a good life and benefit their soul. Socrates believes that people who have this kind of wisdom will automatically behave accordingly. To know the virtues is to have them. He thinks people naturally tend to pursue the good if they know what the good is. If they don't pursue it, it's because of ignorance: they don't know anything about virtuous living. So virtue comes from knowledge, lack of virtue is due to ignorance, and the welfare of the soul hangs in the balance.

Now Socrates' famous dictum takes on richer meaning: "The unexamined life is not worth living." It's not worth living because it harms the soul and makes life unsatisfying. An unexamined life is likely to be a wretched life, an existence bereft of the good that moral knowledge brings.

Socrates considered it his duty to help people attain the necessary moral understanding. That is the purpose behind his dialectic, and the reason he pestered the Athenians so relentlessly. And he was not afraid to rebuke them for their upside-down priorities:

Plato: *Apology*

9. Why does Socrates equate virtue with knowledge? Is this formula plausible?

[W]hile I have life and strength I shall never cease from the practice and teaching of philosophy, exhorting any one whom I meet and saying to him after my manner: You, my friend,—a citizen of the great and mighty and wise city of Athens,—are you not ashamed of heaping up the greatest amount of money and honour and reputation, and caring so little about wisdom and truth and the greatest improvement of the soul, which you never regard or heed at all?[5]

DETAILS

Socrates in the Clouds

In Socrates' day, conservatives and liberals struggled to defend their social positions and worldviews, just as they do in our own time. In fifth-century BCE Athens the contest was traditional ideas and values against the new learning of the naturalistic (nontheistic) philosophers and the relativistic and rhetorically tricky Sophists. Aristophanes, a well-known comedic playwright, championed the conservative view and wrote the play *Clouds* to attack what he considered the causes of social decay. For satirical purposes, he chose a likely character to embody the distressing trends: the well-known Socrates.

Socrates is portrayed as a top Sophist and the buffoonish head of a school called the Thinkery, which teaches nonsense along with sophistic logic and rhetoric. The lead character is a farmer who is tormented by his creditors and wants to learn how to outsmart them by rhetorically transforming right into wrong and the weaker argument into the stronger. At the school he discovers that the students learn such wisdom as which end of a mosquito does the buzzing and how far

Figure 3.4 The celebrated playwright Aristophanes. His play *Clouds* was performed in Athens for the first time in 423 BCE.

a flea can jump. He finds Socrates suspended in air in a basket, declaring that "only by being suspended aloft, by dangling my mind in the heavens and mingling my rare thought with the ethereal air, could I ever achieve strict scientific accuracy . . . The earth, you see, pulls down the delicate essence of thought into its own gross level."

Throughout the play, Socrates and the Thinkery are shown to be ridiculous and depraved. The farmer is finally disillusioned by it all when his son announces that it can be shown with the new logic that a son's beating his father or mother is morally right.

Clouds presents us with distorted pictures of both Socrates and the Sophists. The Sophists were never so inane, and Socrates was not only not a Sophist, he was a critic of theirs, an opponent of relativism, and a believer in the power of reason to search out the truth. But the play gives us a sense of the kinds of issues that divided traditionalists from the new thinkers and raises important questions about truth, rhetoric, education, and critical thinking. On the other hand, some scholars argue that *Clouds*—with its grotesque portrait of Socrates as a loony Sophist—may have contributed to the suspicions among Athenians that led to Socrates' trial and execution.

Is using rhetoric as the Sophists did (making the bad argument sound good) morally permissible? Why or why not?

10. Why does Socrates think that a preoccupation with material goods is bad?

So to Socrates, a clear sign that a person has an unhealthy soul is her exclusive pursuit of social status, wealth, power, and pleasure instead of the soul's well-being. The good of the soul is achieved only through an uncompromising search for what's true and real, through the wisdom to see what is most vital in life.

It seems that if anyone possessed such wisdom or had insight into moral matters, surely Socrates did. But he often claimed to be ignorant and to be as lacking in wisdom as those he questioned. Some of his professions of ignorance are meant to be ironic: he plays the role of eager pupil to get his interlocutors to act the teacher and thereby lay bare their ill-formed arguments. At other times, he seems to be making an honest but qualified admission: he does not have a complete and final theory of ethics or virtue as the gods are thought to have. He must, as everyone else must, continually apply his probing interrogations to expose error and get ever closer to the truth. He and anyone who follows this path must settle for less than perfect knowledge. But for mortals, that is enough.

11. Socrates never seems adversarial or combative in his dialogues. What effect do you think this approach has on those who enter into dialogue with him?

3.4 SOCRATES' TRIAL AND DEATH

12. If you were in Socrates' position, would you choose death over exile? Why or why not?

Eventually Socrates was indicted and charged with disrespecting the gods approved by the state, acknowledging new gods, and corrupting the youth of the city. He was tried before five hundred jurors, a majority of whom voted to convict him. His sentence was death or exile, and he chose death by poison rather than leave his beloved Athens. In his dialogue *Apology*, Plato (who was present at the proceedings) recounts the events of the trial, including Socrates' address to the jurors. Socrates is portrayed as a man of brilliant intellect and unshakeable integrity who would not compromise his principles, even to escape death.

The trial occurred in a volatile atmosphere that worked against Socrates. The people of Athens had only recently restored democracy to the state after a year of tyrannical rule, and two of Socrates' acquaintances had sided with the latter. Another had committed treason. In addition, many Athenians worried that intellectuals were spreading new ideas that could subvert traditional beliefs concerning nature, morality, and religion—and these radical thinkers included Socrates and the Sophists. Of course Socrates had also stirred resentment against him by subjecting many Athenians to his uncomfortable cross-examinations.

"The only good is knowledge and the only evil is ignorance."
—Socrates

Socrates denies the charges and rebuts the accusations that he is "guilty of wrongdoing in that he busies himself studying things in the sky and below the earth; he makes the worse into the stronger argument, and he teaches these same things to others." He declares that not only has he not harmed anyone, he has actually done Athenians a service by arguing with them and turning their attention to the well-being of their souls.

"To fear death, my friends, is only to think ourselves wise, without being wise: for it is to think that we know what we do not know. For anything that men can tell, death may be the greatest good that can happen to them: but they fear it as if they knew quite well that it was the greatest of evils. And what is this but that shameful ignorance of thinking that we know what we do not know?"
—Socrates

He contends that his reputation as a pernicious intellectual is based on a misunderstanding. A follower of his had once asked the oracle of Delphi if there was any man in Athens wiser than Socrates, and the oracle said that there was not. But Socrates knew that he was not wise, so he went about Athens interrogating people who were thought to have great wisdom. In all cases he found that they thought

Figure 3.5 Ruins of the Temple of Apollo at Delphi, the sacred venue of the oracle.

themselves wise but were actually far from it. The oracle, he concluded, must have meant that he was wisest because he did not assume he knew things that he in fact did not know.

Here is Socrates' speech to the jury:

Plato: *Apology*

How you, O Athenians, have been affected by my accusers, I cannot tell; but I know that they almost made me forget who I was—so persuasively did they speak; and yet they have hardly uttered a word of truth. But of the many falsehoods told by them, there was one which quite amazed me—I mean when they said that you should be upon your guard and not allow yourselves to be deceived by the force of my eloquence. To say this, when they were certain to be detected as soon as I opened my lips and proved myself to be anything but a great speaker, did indeed appear to me most shameless—unless by the force of eloquence they mean the force of truth; for if such is their meaning, I admit that I am eloquent. But in how different a way from theirs! Well, as I was saying, they have scarcely spoken the truth at all; but from me you shall hear the whole truth: not, however, delivered after their manner in a set oration duly ornamented with words and phrases. No, by heaven! but I shall use the words and arguments which occur to me at the moment; for I am confident

DETAILS

Socrates' Last Minutes

Figure 3.6 The reputed ruins of Socrates' prison in Athens.

In the last moments of Socrates' life, while he waited in prison for his sentence (death by poison) to be carried out, he discussed with friends the nature of the soul and immortality, speaking in the same calm and clear voice that he always used. Earlier they had tried to persuade him to escape, to safely live out his days far away from Athens. They were ready to engineer his getaway; even the guards would probably look the other way. But he refused their offer, explaining that he could not break the laws of the state even though it had treated him unjustly. In the end he was serene, even content, while his tearful friends in the room with him were overcome with grief. Phaedo, a follower of Socrates, recounts to his friend, Echecrates, the final conversation:

> Socrates said: You, my good friend [the jailer], who are experienced in these matters, shall give me directions how I am to proceed. The man answered: You have only to walk about until your legs are heavy, and then to lie down, and the poison will act. At the same time he handed the cup to Socrates, who in the easiest and gentlest manner, without the least fear or change of color or feature,

Plato:
Apology

in the justice of my cause: at my time of life I ought not to be appearing before you, O men of Athens, in the character of a juvenile orator—let no one expect it of me. And I must beg of you to grant me a favour: If I defend myself in my accustomed manner, and you hear me using the words which I have been in the habit of using in the [market], at the tables of the money-changers, or anywhere else, I would ask you not to be surprised, and not looking at the man with all his eyes, Echecrates, as his manner was, took the cup and said: What do you say about making a libation out of this cup to any god? May I, or not? The man answered: We only prepare, Socrates, just so much as we deem enough . . . Then holding the cup to his lips, quite readily and cheerfully he drank off the poison. And hitherto most of us had been able to control our sorrow; but now when we saw him drinking, and saw too that he had finished the draught, we could no longer forbear, and in spite of myself my own tears were flowing fast; so that I covered my face and wept over myself, for certainly I was not weeping over him, but at the thought of my own calamity in having lost such a companion. Nor was I the first, for Crito, when he found himself unable to restrain his tears, had got up and moved away, and I followed; and at that moment. Apollodorus, who had been weeping all the time, broke out in a loud cry which made cowards of us all. Socrates alone retained his calmness: What is this strange outcry? he said. I sent away the women mainly in order that they might not offend in this way, for I have heard that a man should die in peace. Be quiet, then, and have patience. When we heard that, we were ashamed, and refrained our tears; and he walked about until, as he said, his legs began to fail, and then he lay on his back, according to the directions, and the man who gave him the poison now and then looked at his feet and legs; and after a while he pressed his foot hard and asked him if he could feel; and he said, no; and then his leg, and so upwards and upwards, and showed us that he was cold and stiff. And he felt them himself, and said: When the poison reaches the heart, that will be the end. He was beginning to grow cold about the groin, when he uncovered his face, for he had covered himself up, and said (they were his last words)—he said: Crito, I owe a cock to Asclepius; will you remember to pay the debt? The debt shall be paid, said Crito; is there anything else? There was no answer to this question; but in a minute or two a movement was heard, and the attendants uncovered him; his eyes were set, and Crito closed his eyes and mouth.

Such was the death, Echecrates, of our friend, whom I may truly call the wisest, and justest, and best of all men I have ever known.

Was the guilty verdict in Socrates' trial just? Was his execution just? Why or why not?

Plato, *Phaedo*, *The Dialogues of Plato*, trans. B. Jowett (New York: Hearst's International Library, 1914), 268–271.

to interrupt me on this account. For I am more than seventy years of age, and appearing now for the first time in a court of law, I am quite a stranger to the language of the place; and therefore I would have you regard me as if I were really a stranger, whom you would excuse if he spoke in his native tongue, and after the fashion of his country: Am I making an unfair request of you? Never mind the manner, which may or may not be good; but

Plato:
Apology

---

13. What is the misunderstanding that Socrates says has led to his tarnished reputation?

think only of the truth of my words, and give heed to that: let the speaker speak truly and the judge decide justly. . . .

I will begin at the beginning, and ask what is the accusation which has given rise to the slander of me, and in fact has encouraged Meletus to prefer this charge against me. Well, what do the slanderers say? They shall be my prosecutors, and I will sum up their words in an affidavit: 'Socrates is an evil-doer, and a curious person, who searches into things under the earth and in heaven, and he makes the worse appear the better cause; and he teaches the aforesaid doctrines to others.' Such is the nature of the accusation: it is just what you have yourselves seen in the comedy of Aristophanes, who has introduced a man whom he calls Socrates, going about and saying that he walks in air, and talking a deal of nonsense concerning matters of which I do not pretend to know either much or little—not that I mean to speak disparagingly of any one who is a student of natural philosophy. I should be very sorry if Meletus could bring so grave a charge against me. But the simple truth is, O Athenians, that I have nothing to do with physical speculations. Very many of those here present are witnesses to the truth of this, and to them I appeal. Speak then, you who have heard me, and tell your neighbours whether any of you have ever known me hold forth in few words or in many upon such matters. . . . You hear their answer. And from what they say of this part of the charge you will be able to judge of the truth of the rest.

As little foundation is there for the report that I am a teacher, and take money; this accusation has no more truth in it than the other. Although, if a man were really able to instruct mankind, to receive money for giving instruction would, in my opinion, be an honour to him. There is Gorgias of Leontium, and Prodicus of Ceos, and Hippias of Elis, who go the round of the cities, and are able to persuade the young men to leave their own citizens by whom they might be taught for nothing, and come to them whom they not only pay, but are thankful if they may be allowed to pay them. . . .

---

14. What does Aristophanes have to do with Socrates' reputation?

I dare say, Athenians, that some one among you will reply, 'Yes, Socrates, but what is the origin of these accusations which are brought against you; there must have been something strange which you have been doing? All these rumours and this talk about you would never have arisen if you had been like other men: tell us, then, what is the cause of them, for we should be sorry to judge hastily of you.' Now I regard this as a fair challenge, and I will endeavour to explain to you the reason why I am called wise and have such an evil fame. Please to attend then. And although some of you may think that I am joking, I declare that I will tell you the entire truth. Men of Athens, this reputation of mine has come of a certain sort of wisdom which I possess. If you ask me what kind of wisdom, I reply, wisdom such as may perhaps be attained by man, for to that extent I am inclined to believe that I am wise; whereas the persons of whom I was speaking have a superhuman wisdom, which I may fail to describe, because I have it not myself; and he who says that I have, speaks falsely, and is taking away my character. And here, O men of Athens, I must beg you not to interrupt me, even if I seem to say something extravagant. For the word which I will speak is not mine. I will refer you to a witness who is worthy of credit; that witness shall be the God of Delphi—he will tell you about my wisdom, if I have any, and of what sort it is. You must have known Chaerephon; he was early a friend of mine, and also a friend of yours, for he shared in the recent exile of the people, and returned with you. Well, Chaerephon, as you know, was very impetuous in all his doings, and he went to Delphi and boldly asked the oracle to tell him whether—as I was saying, I must beg you not to interrupt—he asked the oracle to tell him whether any one was wiser than I was, and the Pythian prophetess answered, that there was no man wiser. Chaerephon is dead himself; but his brother, who is in court, will confirm the truth of what I am saying.

"[W]hile I have life and strength I shall never cease from the practice and teaching of philosophy."

—Socrates

Why do I mention this? Because I am going to explain to you why I have such an evil name. When I heard the answer, I said to myself, What can the god mean? and what is the interpretation of his riddle? for I know that I have no wisdom, small or great. What then can he mean when he says that I am the wisest of men? And yet he is a god, and cannot lie; that would be against his nature. After long consideration, I thought of a method of trying the question. I reflected that if I could only find a man wiser than myself, then I might go to the god with a refutation in my hand. I should say to him, 'Here is a man who is wiser than I am; but you said that I was the wisest.' Accordingly I went to one who had the reputation of wisdom, and observed him—his name I need not mention; he was a politician whom I selected for examination—and the result was as follows: When I began to talk with him, I could not help thinking that he was not really wise, although he was thought wise by many, and still wiser by himself; and thereupon I tried to explain to him that he thought himself wise, but was not really wise; and the consequence was that he hated me, and his enmity was shared by several who were present and heard me. So I left him, saying to myself, as I went away: Well, although I do not suppose that either of us knows anything really beautiful and good, I am better off than he is—for he knows nothing, and thinks that he knows; I neither know nor think that I know. In this latter particular, then, I seem to have slightly the advantage of him.

Then I went to another who had still higher pretensions to wisdom, and my conclusion was exactly the same. Whereupon I made another enemy of him, and of many others besides him. Then I went to one man after another, being not unconscious of the enmity which I provoked, and I lamented and feared this: But necessity was laid upon me,—the word of God, I thought, ought to be considered first. And I said to myself, Go I must to all who appear to know, and find out the meaning of the oracle. And I swear to you, Athenians, by the dog I swear!—for I must tell you the truth—the result of my mission was just this: I found that the men most in repute were all but the most foolish; and that others less esteemed were really wiser and better. I will tell you the tale of my wanderings and of the "Herculean" labours, as I may call them, which I endured only to find at last the oracle irrefutable. After the politicians, I went to the poets; tragic, dithyrambic, and all sorts. And there, I said to myself, you will be instantly detected; now you will find out that you are more ignorant than they are. Accordingly, I took them some of the most elaborate passages in their own writings, and asked what was the meaning of them—thinking that they would teach me something. Will you believe me? I am almost ashamed to confess the truth, but I must say that there is hardly a person present who would not have talked better about their poetry than they did themselves. Then I knew that not by wisdom do poets write poetry, but by a sort of genius and inspiration; they are like diviners or soothsayers who also say many fine things, but do not understand the meaning of them. The poets appeared to me to be much in the same case; and I further observed that upon the strength of their poetry they believed themselves to be the wisest of men in other things in which they were not wise. So I departed, conceiving myself to be superior to them for the same reason that I was superior to the politicians. . . .

This inquisition has led to my having many enemies of the worst and most dangerous kind, and has given occasion also to many calumnies. And I am called wise, for my hearers always imagine that I myself possess the wisdom which I find wanting in others: but the truth is, O men of Athens, that God only is wise; and by his answer he intends to show that the wisdom of men is worth little or nothing; he is not speaking of Socrates, he is only using my name by way of illustration, as if he said, He, O men, is the wisest, who, like Socrates, knows that his wisdom is in truth worth nothing. And so I go about the world, obedient to the god, and search and make enquiry into the wisdom of any one, whether citizen or stranger, who appears to be wise; and if he is not wise, then in vindication of the oracle

15. What does Socrates say is the reason for his "evil name"?

16. Why does Socrates think he knows more than the people who claim to have wisdom?

"This man here [Socrates] is so bizarre, his ways so unusual, that, search as you might, you'll never find anyone else, alive or dead, who's even remotely like him."

—Alcibiades

THEN AND NOW

Your Examined/Unexamined Life

If there is anything from Socrates that is applicable to the twenty-first century, it is his admonition to live an examined life. Do you live such a life? The following statements express some fundamental beliefs—beliefs that countless people hold but may never have thought much about. Read each statement and select the ones that you sincerely believe. Then recall if you have ever seriously questioned these beliefs. (Passing thoughts and idle revelry do not count.) Be honest. This little experiment could be very revealing—and helpful as you think about your life and values.

1. God exists and watches over me.
2. God sometimes answers prayers.
3. There is a heaven.
4. I have both a body and an immortal soul.
5. My emotions are not under my control; they just happen.
6. It is wrong to criticize other cultures.
7. It is wrong to judge other people's actions.
8. The moral principles that I was raised to believe are the right ones.
9. Political conservatives are wrong about most issues.
10. Political liberals are wrong about most issues.
11. I make free choices; all my decisions are up to me.
12. I can come to know some things by faith alone.
13. My emotions are my best guide to what is morally right or wrong.
14. People are basically bad.
15. People are basically good.

Plato:
Apology

---

17. What is Socrates' explanation for the oracle's pronouncement about him?

I show him that he is not wise; and my occupation quite absorbs me, and I have no time to give either to any public matter of interest or to any concern of my own, but I am in utter poverty by reason of my devotion to the god.

There is another thing: Young men of the richer classes, who have not much to do, come about me of their own accord; they like to hear the pretenders examined, and they often imitate me, and proceed to examine others; there are plenty of persons, as they quickly discover, who think that they know something, but really know little or nothing; and then those who are examined by them instead of being angry with themselves are angry with me: This confounded Socrates, they say, this villainous misleader of youth!—and then if somebody asks them, Why, what evil does he practise or teach? they do not know, and cannot tell; but in order that they may not appear to be at a loss, they repeat the ready-made charges which are used against all philosophers about teaching things up in the clouds and under the earth, and having no gods, and making the worse appear the better cause; for they do not like to confess that their pretence of knowledge has been detected—which is the truth; and as they are numerous and ambitious and energetic, and are drawn up in battle array and have persuasive tongues, they have filled your ears with their loud and inveterate calumnies. And this is the reason why my three accusers, Meletus and Anytus and Lycon, have set upon me; Meletus, who has a quarrel with me on behalf of the poets; Anytus, on behalf of the craftsmen and politicians; Lycon, on behalf of the rhetoricians: and as I said at the beginning, I cannot expect to get rid of such a mass of calumny all in a moment. And this, O men of Athens, is the truth and the whole truth; I have concealed nothing, I have dissembled nothing. And yet, I know that my plainness of speech makes them hate me, and what is their hatred but a proof that I am speaking the truth?—Hence has arisen the prejudice against me; and this is the reason of it, as you will find out either in this or in any future enquiry.

I have said enough in my defence against the first class of my accusers; I turn to the second class. They are headed by Meletus, that good man and true lover of his country, as he calls himself. . . . He says that I am a doer of evil, and corrupt the youth; but I say, O men of Athens, that Meletus is a doer of evil, in that he pretends to be in earnest when he is only in jest, and is so eager to bring men to trial from a pretended zeal and interest about matters in which he really never had the smallest interest. And the truth of this I will endeavour to prove to you.

Come hither, Meletus, and let me ask a question of you. You think a great deal about the improvement of youth?

Yes, I do.

Tell the judges, then, who is their improver; for you must know, as you have taken the pains to discover their corrupter, and are citing and accusing me before them. Speak, then, and tell the judges who their improver is.—Observe, Meletus, that you are silent, and have nothing to say. But is not this rather disgraceful, and a very considerable proof of what I was saying, that you have no interest in the matter? Speak up, friend, and tell us who their improver is.

The laws.

But that, my good sir, is not my meaning. I want to know who the person is, who, in the first place, knows the laws.

The judges, Socrates, who are present in court.

What, do you mean to say, Meletus, that they are able to instruct and improve youth?

Certainly they are.

What, all of them, or some only and not others?

All of them.

By the goddess Herè, that is good news! There are plenty of improvers, then. And what do you say of the audience—do they improve them?

Yes, they do.

And the senators?

Yes, the senators improve them.

But perhaps the members of the assembly corrupt them?—or do they too improve them?

They improve them.

Then every Athenian improves and elevates them; all with the exception of myself; and I alone am their corrupter? Is that what you affirm?

That is what I stoutly affirm. . . .

And now, Meletus, I will ask you another question—by Zeus I will: Which is better, to live among bad citizens, or among good ones? Answer, friend, I say; the question is one which may be easily answered. Do not the good do their neighbours good, and the bad do them evil?

Certainly.

"People think the world needs a republic, and they think it needs a new social order, and a new religion, but it never occurs to anyone that what the world really needs, confused as it is by much learning, is a new Socrates."

—Søren Kierkegaard

18. Why does Socrates say that Meletus is a doer of evil?

Plato:
Apology

And is there any one who would rather be injured than benefited by those who live with him? Answer, my good friend, the law requires you to answer—does any one like to be injured?

Certainly not.

And when you accuse me of corrupting and deteriorating the youth, do you allege that I corrupt them intentionally or unintentionally?

Intentionally, I say.

But you have just admitted that the good do their neighbours good, and evil do them evil. Now, is that a truth which your superior wisdom has recognized thus early in life, and am I, at my age, in such darkness and ignorance as not to know that if a man with whom I have to live is corrupted by me, I am very likely to be harmed by him; and yet I corrupt him, and intentionally, too—so you say, although neither I nor any other human being is ever likely to be convinced by you. But either I do not corrupt them, or I corrupt them unintentionally; and on either view of the case you lie. If my offence is unintentional, the law has no cognizance of unintentional offences: you ought to have taken me privately, and warned and admonished me; for if I had been better advised, I should have left off doing what I only did unintentionally—no doubt I should; but you would have nothing to say to me and refused to teach me. And now you bring me up in this court, which is a place not of instruction, but of punishment.

It will be very clear to you, Athenians, as I was saying, that Meletus has no care at all, great or small, about the matter. But still I should like to know, Meletus, in what I am affirmed to corrupt the young. I suppose you mean, as I infer from your indictment, that I teach them not to acknowledge the gods which the state acknowledges, but some other new divinities or spiritual agencies in their stead. These are the lessons by which I corrupt the youth, as you say.

Yes, that I say emphatically.

Then, by the gods, Meletus, of whom we are speaking, tell me and the court, in somewhat plainer terms, what you mean! for I do not as yet understand whether you affirm that I teach other men to acknowledge some gods, and therefore that I do believe in gods, and am not an entire atheist—this you do not lay to my charge—but only you say that they are not the same gods which the city recognizes—the charge is that they are different gods. Or, do you mean that I am an atheist simply, and a teacher of atheism?

I mean the latter—that you are a complete atheist.

What an extraordinary statement! Why do you think so, Meletus? Do you mean that I do not believe in the godhead of the sun or moon, like other men?

I assure you, judges, that he does not: for he says that the sun is stone, and the moon earth.

Friend Meletus, you think that you are accusing Anaxagoras: and you have but a bad opinion of the judges, if you fancy them illiterate to such a degree as not to know that these doctrines are found in the books of Anaxagoras the Clazomenian, which are full of them. And so, forsooth, the youth are said to be taught them by Socrates, when there are not infrequently exhibitions of them at the theatre (price of admission one drachma at the most); and they might pay their money, and laugh at Socrates if he pretends to father these extraordinary views. And so, Meletus, you really think that I do not believe in any god?

I swear by Zeus that you believe absolutely in none at all.

Nobody will believe you, Meletus, and I am pretty sure that you do not believe yourself. I cannot help thinking, men of Athens, that Meletus is reckless and impudent, and that he has written this indictment in a spirit of mere wantonness and youthful bravado. Has he

19. What is the contradiction that Socrates sees in Meletus' opinion about corrupting the young?

"Philosophy asks the simple question, what is it all about?"

—Alfred North Whitehead

not compounded a riddle, thinking to try me? He said to himself: I shall see whether the wise Socrates will discover my facetious contradiction, or whether I shall be able to deceive him and the rest of them. For he certainly does appear to me to contradict himself in the indictment as much as if he said that Socrates is guilty of not believing in the gods, and yet of believing them—but this is not like a person who is in earnest. . . .

Some one will say: And are you not ashamed, Socrates, of a course of life which is likely to bring you to an untimely end? To him I may fairly answer: There you are mistaken: a man who is good for anything ought not to calculate the chance of living or dying; he ought only to consider whether in doing anything he is doing right or wrong—acting the part of a good man or of a bad . . .

[I]f you say to me, Socrates, this time we will not mind Anytus, and you shall be let off, but upon one condition, that you are not to enquire and speculate in this way any more, and that if you are caught doing so again you shall die—if this was the condition on which you let me go, I should reply: Men of Athens, I honour and love you; but I shall obey God rather than you, and while I have life and strength I shall never cease from the practice and teaching of philosophy, exhorting any one whom I meet and saying to him after my manner: You, my friend—a citizen of the great and mighty and wise city of Athens—are you not ashamed of heaping up the greatest amount of money and honour and reputation, and caring so little about wisdom and truth and the greatest improvement of the soul, which you never regard or heed at all? And if the person with whom I am arguing, says: Yes, but I do care; then I do not leave him or let him go at once; but I proceed to interrogate and examine and cross-examine him, and if I think that he has no virtue in him, but only says that he has, I reproach him with undervaluing the greater, and overvaluing the less. And I shall repeat the same words to every one whom I meet, young and old, citizen and alien, but especially to the citizens, inasmuch as they are my brethren. For know that this is the command of God; and I believe that no greater good has ever happened in the state than my service to the God. For I do nothing but go about persuading you all, old and young alike, not to take thought for your persons or your properties, but first and chiefly to care about the greatest improvement of the soul. I tell you that virtue is not given by money, but that from virtue comes money and every other good of man, public as well as private. This is my teaching, and if this is the doctrine which corrupts the youth, I am a mischievous person. But if any one says that this is not my teaching, he is speaking an untruth. Wherefore, O men of Athens, I say to you, do as Anytus bids or not as Anytus bids, and either acquit me or not; but whichever you do, understand that I shall never alter my ways, not even if I have to die many times. . . .

[The vote is taken and he is found guilty by 281 votes to 220.]

And so he proposes death as the penalty. And what shall I propose on my part, O men of Athens? Clearly that which is my due. And what is my due? What return shall be made to the man who has never had the wit to be idle during his whole life; but has been careless of what the many care for—wealth, and family interests, and military offices, and speaking in the assembly, and magistracies, and plots, and parties. Reflecting that I was really too honest a man to be a politician and live, I did not go where I could do no good to you or to myself; but where I could do the greatest good privately to every one of you, thither I went, and sought to persuade every man among you that he must look to himself, and seek virtue and wisdom before he looks to his private interests, and look to the state before he looks to the interests of the state; and that this should be the order which he observes in all his actions. What shall be done to such a one? Doubtless some good thing, O men of Athens, if he has his reward; and the good should be of a kind suitable to him.

20. What is the contradiction regarding the gods that Socrates says Meletus has put forth?

21. What error does Socrates accuse the Athenians of committing? How is the jury likely to react to Socrates' claim?

"He who is not contented with what he has, would not be contented with what he would like to have."

—Socrates

22. Why does Socrates say that he is arguing for the Athenians' sake?

Plato:
Apology

Figure 3.7 The death of Socrates.

23. What is Socrates' counterproposal regarding sentencing? How is the jury likely to react to this suggestion?

24. According to Socrates, what is the greatest good of man? Why does he insist that the unexamined life is not worth living?

"And what, Socrates, is the food of the soul? Surely, I said, knowledge is the food of the soul."

—Plato

25. Why does Socrates say that death is probably a good?

What would be a reward suitable to a poor man who is your benefactor, and who desires leisure that he may instruct you? There can be no reward so fitting as maintenance in the Prytaneum [free meals for life at state expense], O men of Athens, a reward which he deserves far more than the citizen who has won the prize at Olympia in the horse or chariot race, whether the chariots were drawn by two horses or by many. For I am in want, and he has enough; and he only gives you the appearance of happiness, and I give you the reality. And if I am to estimate the penalty fairly, I should say that maintenance in the Prytaneum is the just return. . . .

Some one will say: Yes, Socrates, but cannot you hold your tongue, and then you may go into a foreign city, and no one will interfere with you? Now I have great difficulty in making you understand my answer to this. For if I tell you that to do as you say would be a disobedience to the God, and therefore that I cannot hold my tongue, you will not believe that I am serious; and if I say again that daily to discourse about virtue, and of those other things about which you hear me examining myself and others, is the greatest good of man, and that the unexamined life is not worth living, you are still less likely to believe me. Yet I say what is true, although a thing of which it is hard for me to persuade you. Also, I have never been accustomed to think that I deserve to suffer any harm. Had I money I might have estimated the offence at what I was able to pay, and not have been much the worse. But I have none, and therefore I must ask you to proportion the fine to my means. Well, perhaps I could afford a mina, and therefore I propose that penalty: Plato, Crito, Critobulus, and Apollodorus, my friends here, bid me say thirty minae, and they will be the sureties. Let thirty minae be the penalty; for which sum they will be ample security to you.

[2nd vote: The jury decides for the death penalty by a vote of 360 to 141.]

Not much time will be gained, O Athenians, in return for the evil name which you will get from the detractors of the city, who will say that you killed Socrates, a wise man; for they will call me wise, even although I am not wise, when they want to reproach you. If you had waited a little while, your desire would have been fulfilled in the course of nature. For I am far advanced in years, as you may perceive, and not far from death. . . .

The difficulty, my friends, is not to avoid death, but to avoid unrighteousness; for that runs faster than death. I am old and move slowly, and the slower runner has overtaken me, and my accusers are keen and quick, and the faster runner, who is unrighteousness, has overtaken them. And now I depart hence condemned by you to suffer the penalty of death—they too go their ways condemned by the truth to suffer the penalty of villainy and wrong; and I must abide by my award—let them abide by theirs. I suppose that these things may be regarded as fated—and I think that they are well. . . .[6]

"It was the first and most striking characteristic of Socrates never to become heated in discourse, never to utter an injurious or insulting word—on the contrary, he persistently bore insult from others and thus put an end to the fray."

—Epictetus

WRITING AND REASONING   **CHAPTER 3**

1. Could the execution of someone for saying unpopular things happen in the United States? Why or why not? Are there countries in the world where such things happen regularly? Is the execution of someone for his or her offensive speech ever justified? Explain.

2. What do you think Socrates would think about modern consumer societies?

3. Socrates is often regarded as the noblest of the great philosophers. Is this opinion justified? Why or why not?

4. Write a Socratic dialogue between yourself and a friend. Imagine that your friend declares, "Everyone lies. No one ever tells the truth," and you want to show that those statements are false.

5. Write a Socratic dialogue between two fictional characters. Imagine that the opening statement is "Courtesy to others is always a cynical attempt to serve your own interests. Respect for people has nothing to do with courtesy."

REVIEW NOTES

3.1 THE PHILOSOPHICAL GADFLY

- Socrates is one of philosophy's greatest minds and the most revered figure in its history. He changed the course of philosophical inquiry, and his influence on philosophy's two most admired thinkers—Plato and Aristotle—was profound.

- Socrates was passionate yet self-controlled, down-to-earth yet propelled by high ideals and concern for the spiritual self, and plain-spoken yet intellectually brilliant.

- People have been impressed as much by Socrates' character as by his words.

- He insisted that nothing is more important than the care of one's soul and that the only way to nurture it is through philosophical reflection.

3.2 THE SOCRATIC METHOD

- Socrates introduced the Socratic method, or dialectic—one of the ways philosophy is done, a powerful procedure for applying critical thinking to many statements that may seem out of reason's reach.

- Through his brand of question-and-answer dialogue, Socrates often demonstrated that people who thought themselves wise were not wise at all. For example, he showed that Thrasymachus' concept of justice was unfounded.

- The Socratic method often takes the form of *reductio ad absurdum*.

3.3 KNOWLEDGE AND IGNORANCE

- Socrates' method and mission spring from his ideas about the soul and how to live a good life. He asserts that nothing in this life is more important than the care of the soul, the true self. Your soul is harmed or helped by your own actions: doing wrong damages your soul, and doing right benefits it.

- For Socrates, virtue is knowledge. He believes that to know the virtues is to have them, for people naturally tend to pursue the good if they know what the good is. If they don't pursue it, it's because of ignorance: they don't know anything about virtuous living.

- To Socrates, a clear sign that a person has an unhealthy soul is her exclusive pursuit of social status, wealth, power, and pleasure instead of the soul's well-being. The good of the soul is achieved only through an uncompromising search for what's true and real, through the wisdom to see what is most vital in life.

3.4 SOCRATES' TRIAL AND DEATH

- Socrates was arrested and charged with disrespecting the gods approved by the state, acknowledging new gods, and corrupting the youth of the city. He was tried before five hundred jurors, a majority of whom voted to convict him. His sentence was death or exile, and he chose death by poison rather than leave his beloved Athens.

- Socrates denied the charges against him and contended that he did not teach metaphysics and did not try to make bad arguments look good. He declared that he had done Athenians a service by arguing with them and turning their attention to the well-being of their souls.

KEY TERMS

reductio ad absurdum	Socratic method

Notes

1. Xenophon, *Symposium*, "Banquet," IV. 64, v. 4, trans. O. J. Todd (London: William Heinemann, 1922), Internet Archive, http: the_bundle.archive.org.
2. Plato, *Symposium*, trans. B. Jowett (New York: Hearst's International Library, 1914), Classics, http://classics.mit.edu/Plato/symposium.html.

3. Plato, *The Republic*, *The Dialogues of Plato*, vol. 2, trans. B. Jowett (New York: Hearst's International Library, 1914), 18–20.
4. Plato, *Euthyphro*, translated by Benjamin Jowett (from The Internet Classics Archive, classics.mit.edu/Plato/euthyfro.html).
5. Plato, *Apology*, *The Dialogues of Plato*, vol. 3, trans. B. Jowett (New York: Hearst's International Library, 1914), 118.
6. Plato, *Apology*, *The Dialogues of Plato*, trans. B. Jowett (Oxford: Hearst's International Library Co., 1896).

For Further Reading

Jonathan Barnes, trans., *Early Greek Philosophy* (London: Penguin Books, 1987).

David Gallop, trans., *Plato: Defence of Socrates, Euthyphro, Crito* (Oxford: Oxford University Press, 1997).

Anthony Gottlieb, *The Dream of Reason: A History of Philosophy from the Greeks to the Renaissance* (New York: W. W. Norton, 2000).

W. K. C. Guthrie, *Socrates* (Cambridge: Cambridge University Press, 1971).

Ted Honderich, ed., *The Oxford Companion to Philosophy* (Oxford: Oxford University Press, 1995).

Christopher Janaway, "Ancient Greek Philosophy I: The Pre-Socratics and Plato," *Philosophy 21: A Guide through the Subject* (Oxford: Oxford University Press, 1995).

Gregory Vlastos, *Socrates: Ironist and Moral Philosopher* (Ithaca, NY: Cornell University Press, 1991).

Mary Ellen Waithe, ed., *A History of Women Philosophers*, vol. 1 (Dordrecht: Martinus Nijhoff, 1987).

Robin Waterfield, trans., *Plato: Republic* (Oxford: Oxford University Press, 1993).

Online Resources

Stanford Encyclopedia of Philosophy, "Socrates," https://plato.stanford.edu/entries/socrates

Internet Encyclopedia of Philosophy, "Socrates," https://www.iep.utm.edu/socrates

History of Philosophy (without Any Gaps) Podcast, https://historyofphilosophy.net

The Perseus Digital Library, http://www.perseus.tufts.edu/hopper

Philosophy Pages, "Socrates: Philosophical Life," http://www.philosophypages.com/hy/2d.htm

Philosophy News, "Who Is Socrates?" https://www.philosophynews.com/post/2018/02/23/Who-is-Socrates.aspx

CHAPTER 4

Plato: The Really Real

CHAPTER OBJECTIVES

4.1 PLATO'S LIFE AND TIMES

- Appreciate Plato's influence on Western thought and why he has been so highly regarded.
- Know the main events in Plato's life, and explain their significance for philosophy and the history of ideas.
- Understand the role that Socrates plays in Plato's dialogues.

4.2 KNOWLEDGE AND REALITY

- Define *relativism* and *skepticism*, and understand how Plato responded to these doctrines.
- Understand the three necessary and sufficient conditions for knowledge and why true belief alone does not qualify as knowledge.
- Understand Plato's reasoning in arriving at his theory of knowledge.
- Define the *Forms*, and explain how Plato thinks they are related to the material world.
- Know the story of Socrates and his questioning of the slave boy, and be able to explain what conclusion Socrates draws from this experience.
- Define *rationalism* and *empiricism*, and know which doctrine Plato accepted and why.

4.3 ALLEGORY OF THE CAVE

- Recount Plato's Allegory of the Cave, and explain what significance it has for him.
- Explain how the allegory may allude to Socrates.

4.4 IMMORTALITY, MORALITY, AND THE SOUL

- Understand the early Greek concept of the soul and how it changed over time.
- Explain Plato's two arguments for immortality—the arguments from recollection and affinity.

- Explain Plato's concept of the tripartite soul and why he thinks the soul must have more than one aspect.
- Explain why Plato thinks it's more beneficial to be just than unjust.
- Recount the story of the ring of Gyges, and explain what Glaucon thought it proved.

4.5 THE INDIVIDUAL AND THE STATE

- Define *democracy*, *meritocracy*, and *aristocracy*.
- Explain the makeup of Plato's ideal society and what he views as the central tenet of personal and community morality.

Plato's influence on Western thought has been immense. He was the first to labor systematically in the full range of philosophical subjects—from epistemology and metaphysics to ethics, aesthetics, politics, and mathematics. And he was the first to bring these studies together under one banner—*philosophy*—and to maintain that this intellectual enterprise is the only way to attain true wisdom. Along the way he covered terrain that few others, if any, had ever trod, probing the nature of happiness, love, education, beauty, mind, language, the soul, immortality, and the good. He is rightly called the "father of Western philosophy" because most of its branches of inquiry can trace their beginnings to him, and they cannot be deemed complete without taking him into account. Even if he had written nothing, his contribution to the West would still be immense, since he both transmitted to us the wisdom of his beloved teacher Socrates and bequeathed the results of his own genius to his best student, Aristotle.

On the fact of Plato's influence and genius, eminent philosophers from our own era concur:

> The safest general characterization of the European philosophical tradition is that it consists of a series of footnotes to Plato.—**ALFRED NORTH WHITEHEAD**[1]

> Plato and Aristotle were the most influential of all philosophers, ancient, medieval, or modern; and of the two, it was Plato who had the greater effect upon subsequent ages. I say this for two reasons: first, that Aristotle himself is an outcome of Plato; second, that Christian theology and philosophy, at any rate until the thirteenth century, was much more Platonic than Aristotelian.—**BERTRAND RUSSELL**[2]

> It is pointless to ask who is the world's greatest philosopher: for one thing, there are many different ways of doing philosophy. But we can say what the various qualities of great philosophers are: intellectual power

and depth; a grasp of the sciences; a sense of the political, and of human destructiveness as well as creativity; a broad range and a fertile imagination; an unwillingness to settle for the superficially reassuring; and, in an unusually lucky case, the gifts of a great writer. If we ask which philosopher has, more than any other, combined all these qualities—to that question there is certainly an answer, Plato.—**BERNARD WILLIAMS**[3]

4.1 PLATO'S LIFE AND TIMES

"If I were again beginning my studies, I would follow the advice of Plato and start with mathematics."

—Galileo

1. Why does Plato say the best and wisest rulers are those schooled in philosophy as well as politics? In Plato's view, what does philosophy have to do with being a good ruler?

Plato (c. 427–347 BCE) was born in Athens into an influential aristocratic family and grew up during the perilous years of the Peloponnesian War, a struggle between Athens and the Peloponnesian states. His family expected him to have a career in politics, but Socrates involved him in the larger and nobler pursuit of wisdom through philosophy. He became Socrates' greatest student, and Socrates turned out to be the best and wisest man he had ever known. His world was upended, however, when in 399 BCE Athens's democratic government found Socrates guilty of impiety and the corruption of Athenian youth. The sentence was exile or death by poison, and in accordance with his principles, Socrates chose death and was executed. Plato was twenty-eight.

Disgusted by the unjust treatment of his teacher and friend, Plato left Athens. He traveled widely, visiting the Greek cities Megara and Syracuse, southern Italy, Sicily, and possibly Egypt. He met with notable mathematicians and philosophers, including the followers of Pythagoras and Heraclitus; but he also encountered many who seemed, to his dismay, to prize pleasure and luxury above virtue.

In 387 BCE, he returned to Athens and founded the Academy, a college and research center often regarded as the first university. Ostensibly its aim was to train future rulers, for Plato insisted that the best and wisest rulers are those schooled in philosophy as well as politics. It focused on a wide range of studies, from botany to dialectic to political theory, and it gained renown for its investigations in mathematics and astronomy. (The Academy endured for hundreds of years until it was abolished by the Eastern Roman emperor Justinian I.) The Academy's most distinguished student was Aristotle, who entered the school at age seventeen and remained for twenty years.

Figure 4.1 Plato speaking with a student at the Academy.

Plato's thinking is embodied in his dialogues, twenty-five of which exist complete. They were written during a span of fifty years and have been divided into three periods: early, middle, and late. The early dialogues include *Euthyphro, Crito, Meno, Protagoras,* and *Gorgias.* These works portray Socrates as a brilliant and principled deflator of his contemporaries' bogus claims to knowledge. The middle dialogues include *Phaedo, Symposium, Republic,* and *Theaetetus.* These encompass Plato's best-known ideas in epistemology and metaphysics. The late dialogues include *Parmenides, Sophist, Critias,* and *Laws.* They document Plato's evolving views on the *Republic* and on other themes from the earlier periods.

PORTRAIT

Diotima of Mantinea

Diotima of Mantinea is said to have been one of the very few women philosophers of note in the ancient world. She is mentioned in Plato's *Symposium* where Socrates claims to have talked with her years earlier and found that she had some insightful things to say about the nature of beauty and love. Scholars have generally doubted that she ever existed, maintaining that she was a fictitious person invented by Plato—his one and only fabricated character in his dialogues. But some have argued that although her existence cannot be proven beyond all doubt, the weight of evidence actually favors her historical authenticity.

The philosophical views attributed to her differ substantially from Plato's. In addition to her positions on love and beauty, she's credited with thoughtful discussions of personal identity, the transmigration of souls, the good, the doctrine of ideas, the role of reason, and immortality. Diotima's theory of the latter is especially interesting. Mary Ellen Waithe points out that, unlike Plato, Diotima rejected the notion of an immortal soul that transmigrates:

> Rather, her concept of immortality is that one becomes immortal through the process of generating one's own qualities in the beloved. One becomes immortal because one's qualities survive in the person of the beloved, and not because one's soul continues to live.

Mary Ellen Waithe, "Diotima of Mantinea," *A History of Women Philosophers*, ed. Mary Ellen Waithe (Dordrecht: Martinus Nijhoff, 1987), 109.

Scholars tend to regard the early dialogues and *Apology* (which is not in dialogue form) as mostly reflecting the ideas of the historical Socrates. They hold that the dialogues from the middle and late periods generally convey Plato's own thinking, even though he often has his words coming from Socrates. But whether the presumed speaker is Socrates or Plato, observant readers get the sense they are entering into the mind of an extraordinary philosopher and a great writer. There are reasons why Plato is deemed such a towering figure in the world of ideas, and they are to be found in his dialogues.

4.2 KNOWLEDGE AND REALITY

Plato and Socrates believed that we can *know* things, that there are truths to be discerned about reality. They thought there is a way the world is and that we can come to know what that way is: we can attain knowledge. But the Sophists rejected this view. For them, knowledge of objective reality is *not* attainable, because truth is relative. (Recall that relativism is the view that the truth about something depends on

"Desires are only the lack of something: and those who have the greatest desires are in a worse condition than those who have none, or very slight ones."
—Plato

"You are young, my son, and, as the years go by, time will change and even reverse many of your present opinions. Refrain therefore awhile from setting yourself up as a judge of the highest matters."
—Plato

2. Do you think Plato is right to reject relativism? Why or why not?

skepticism The view that we lack knowledge in some fundamental way.

"Death is not the worst that can happen to men."
—Plato

what persons or cultures believe.) There is no objective reality to be discovered; there are only beliefs (or opinions, as Plato says) that people endorse. Plato thought there was urgent need to show that the Sophists were wrong. He knew that if the Sophists were right, philosophy would be an empty exercise, knowledge would be impossible, and wisdom would be merely a philosopher's dream.

If Plato could prove his case, it would also constitute a formidable reply to skeptics. **Skepticism** is the view that we lack knowledge in some fundamental way. Skeptics may deny that we have knowledge of anything or maintain that we lack knowledge of only some things, such as an external world, physical objects, or other minds. In any case, they hold that many or all of our beliefs are unfounded. A standard skeptical argument says we lack knowledge because we have no way of distinguishing between beliefs that we take to be instances of knowledge from beliefs that are clearly *not* instances of knowledge. From either a skeptical or relativist standpoint, then, we have only beliefs; knowledge is a lost cause.

Believing and Knowing

But what if a belief we have for no particular reason just happens to be true—isn't that knowledge, or at least as good as knowledge? Accidental truth of a belief was good enough for the Sophists but not for Plato. He and most other philosophers past and present say knowledge has three necessary and sufficient conditions: to know a proposition (1) you must *believe* it, (2) it must be *true*, and (3) you must have good *reasons* for—be justified in—believing it true. On this traditional account, merely believing something is not enough; what you believe must be true. A belief does not count as knowledge unless it is true. But a mere true belief is not knowledge either, because you can have a true belief and yet not genuinely know. Let's say you believe for no reason that three ducks are now swimming on Walden Pond, and suppose your belief is true—there really are three ducks swimming on Walden Pond. Does your true belief count as knowledge? According to Plato, no—because you have *no reason* to think that three ducks are now swimming on Walden Pond. You have only a true belief by accident, a lucky guess, and that's not knowledge. As Plato says:

Plato: *Meno*

True opinions are a fine thing and do all sorts of good so long as they stay in their place, but they will not stay long. They run away from a man's mind; so they are not worth much until you tether them by working out the reason. . . . Once they are tied down, they become knowledge.[4]

So for Plato, knowledge is justified true belief. (Philosophers disagree about the exact nature of the required justification or reasons, but most accept that knowledge is true belief that is in some sense backed by good reasons.) The Sophist may claim to sometimes have true beliefs (accidentally), but to Plato they are a long way from being knowledge.

Plato takes for granted that we can identify false beliefs and that we can grasp mathematical, conceptual, and logical truths. Therefore, he says, we must be able to acquire knowledge. We know that $2 + 5 = 7$; that a triangle has three sides; and that if A is larger than B, and B is larger than C, then A is larger than C. Moreover, these truths are objective: they are true regardless of what we think. We do not invent them out of our imaginations; we discover them. No matter how hard we try, we cannot make $2 + 5 = 9$.

Plato reasons that if such truths are objective, they must also be about *real things*. But what sort of real things? Certainly not the objects of our sense experience, he says. These are forever changing from moment to moment, and whatever property an object has (red, tall, good, or bad) can be viewed from a perspective in which it seems the opposite of what it was. From one perspective, we may see blue, but from another standpoint, we may see not-blue. Plato concludes that since a sensory property can both be and not be, it is not a reliable indicator of fully real things.

So Plato contends that the truly real things we can come to know are not of the physical world. Consider: No one can draw a perfect line, or square, or triangle; there are always imperfections, even if only at the molecular level. But scientists and mathematicians study perfect lines, squares, and triangles. The objects of their investigations do exist, but they cannot be the objects of sense experience. Plato concludes that they must exist as ideal, changeless things in an immaterial reality beyond sense experience. Ponder this also: Think *dog* or *chair* or *tree*, and ask yourself what the object of your thought is. It is obvious that the mental object remains completely unchanged despite the radical changes that occur in any particular dog, chair, or tree. Thus the objects of knowledge exist, Plato says, but they

3. Why doesn't true belief count as knowledge? What would be the effect on society if no one ever had a good reason to believe a proposition?

"Opinion is the medium between knowledge and ignorance."
—Plato

4. Do you agree that sense experience does not give us knowledge? Why or why not? Scientific research is based ultimately on sense experience. Does science give us knowledge?

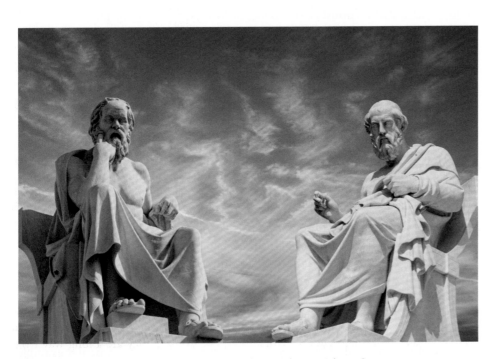

Figure 4.2 Statues of Socrates and Plato at the modern Academy at Athens, Greece.

are not particular, individual sensory things. They are general and abstract objects of the mind.

Plato holds that our sense experience gives us not knowledge but opinion—fallible, transitory belief. Mere opinion is what the Sophists traffic in. Real, immutable, certain knowledge is obtained through the intellect. Only through our powers of reason can we reach beyond the physical world to take hold of real knowledge of lasting truths. As Plato says in *Phaedo*:

Plato: *Phaedo*

Do sight and hearing afford mankind any truth, or aren't even the poets always harping on such themes, telling us that we neither hear nor see anything accurately? And yet if those of all the bodily senses are neither accurate nor clear, the others will hardly be so; because they are, surely, all inferior to those? Don't you think so?

Certainly.

So when does the soul attain the truth? Because plainly, whenever it sets about examining anything in company with the body, it is completely taken in by it.

That's true.

So isn't it in reasoning, if anywhere at all, that any realities become manifest to it?

Yes.[5]

Reason and the Forms

So for Plato, reality comprises two worlds: the fleeting world of the physical accessed through sense experience; and the eternal, nonphysical, changeless world of genuine knowledge accessed only through reason. In spelling out the contents of the latter, Plato articulates the central notion of his philosophy: the **Forms**. He propounds two closely related meanings of *Forms*. In one sense of the term, the Forms (also called Ideas) are perfect conceptual *models* for every existing thing, residing only in the eternal world penetrated by reason alone. They are the ideals, or standards, that we can first come to know and then use to assess the notions and objects we encounter in everyday experience. Through reason, we can access the Form of "table" and thus know the ideal template of "table." With this knowledge we can understand the essence of a table and use this understanding to make judgments about all physical tables. Likewise when we access the Form "courage," we know what the ideal of courage is and can use this knowledge to appraise a particular instance of courage. As Plato sees it, the truly real world is the world of the independently existing Forms—the domain of the perfect and everlasting. In fact, Plato thinks the Forms are *more* real than the objects detected through sense experience. With knowledge of the really real, we can understand the "less real" realm of the imperfect and transitory.

Plato also thought of the Forms as *properties* that can be had by several particular things—in other words, the Forms are universals. Every blue thing is a particular instance of the universal of blueness. Every triangular thing is a particular example

Forms In Plato's philosophy, the objectively real, eternal abstract entities that serve as models or universals of higher knowledge.

of the universal of triangularity. Particulars reside in the temporary, imperfect world of the material; universals are found in the eternal, perfect world of the really real.

In either sense, the Forms bring order to the world. We can comprehend items in the physical realm because they "participate in" (or "partake of") the Forms, and

5. How are the Forms supposed to help us understand the material world?

DETAILS

Critiques of the Forms

Plato's theory of the Forms is probably his most famous and controversial doctrine. Through the centuries it has been subjected to numerous critiques and interpretations—including some from Aristotle and Plato himself. In the dialogue *Parmenides*, Plato imagines the old philosopher Parmenides and his student Zeno discussing the Forms with the young Socrates. Parmenides lodges some tough criticisms against Plato's Forms, criticisms that Socrates is at a loss to answer satisfactorily. In his own works, Aristotle raised many of these same objections. Scholars have been impressed by Plato's willingness to attack his own brainchild, and they have debated whether he is actually criticizing himself or faulting common misunderstandings of the theory.

The most widely discussed criticism in *Parmenides* is also one that Aristotle brings up. It's called the "third man argument." It may be tough to grasp at first, so several readings are recommended. This is how the scholar G. M. A. Grube explains it:

Figure 4.3 Painting depicting Platonic philosophers, by Giorgio de Chirico (1888–1978).

> [I]f you postulate one Idea [Form] to account for the fact that all big things are big, you are still left with two classes of big things— the Idea and the particulars—and you still have to explain why both those classes of big things are big. You will then have to have a further Idea for both classes to participate in, and then in the same way a third Idea to account for the fact that the first and the second Idea have a common predicate, big, and so on *ad infinitum.*

Plato's concept of two realities—an earthly, transitory, imperfect world, and an ideal, perfect, eternal world—had a huge influence on Christian doctrine. In what ways are Plato's two worlds like the Christian realms of heaven and earth?

G. M. A. Grube, *Plato's Thought* (Indianapolis: Hackett, 1980), 33.

6. Try to accurately paraphrase the "third man" objection to the Forms. Do you agree with the criticism? Why or why not?

7. Do you think the doctrine of innate knowledge is plausible? Why or why not?

the physical world achieves order and resists chaos because it also participates in the Forms. A brown horse participates in the Forms of brown and horse. A courageous act participates in the Form of courage. A beautiful child participates in the Forms of beauty and child.

So acquiring knowledge, or wisdom, is a matter of clearly discerning the Forms. But how do we do that? Plato says we must use the same approach that Socrates took when he searched for knowledge: dialectic. Through logical argument and the crucible of questions and answers, Socrates looked for the meaning of concepts such as "justice" and "piety," weeding out the erroneous concepts while trying to edge ever closer to the truth. The implicit aim was to uncover the Form of justice and the Form of piety and thus grasp true wisdom.

For Plato, the greatest of the Forms is the Form of the good. To grasp the Forms is not only to achieve a supreme wisdom, but also to acquire the highest virtues, to receive the blessings of those virtues, and to become a better person. Ultimately, the serious searcher for knowledge will reach the summit of understanding in the Form of the good. To attain this Form is to understand the final and complete explanation for everything—to come to know the best way for anything to exist, to know what is the highest good for everything in the world.

Plato suggests that even before we begin to pursue the Forms, they are already in our minds waiting to be uncovered. How is this possible? His answer is the doctrine of *innate knowledge*. He thinks knowledge of these immaterial ideals is already present at birth, inscribed in our minds (our immortal souls) in a previous existence. We are born with this knowledge, and we somehow acquired it before our present lives. Accessing this knowledge then is a matter of using reason to *recall* what we previously knew in another life.

To many ears, this recall theory may sound preposterous. But in *Meno*, Plato attempts a brilliant demonstration of it. In the dialogue, he depicts the character of Socrates discussing innate knowledge with Meno. To prove his point, Socrates calls over an unschooled slave boy and asks him a series of questions about a geometry problem. Socrates draws a two-foot-by-two-foot square (four square feet), then tells the boy to draw another one that is twice the size of the first. Initially the boy thinks that doubling the length of each side of the square will produce a square twice as large as the first. So he draws a four-foot-by-four-foot square (sixteen square feet) but sees right away that that answer cannot be correct. As Socrates asks further questions, the boy comes to the right answer on his own. Socrates says that he merely helped the boy recollect knowledge that he already possessed, bringing innate knowledge to consciousness.

Plato: *Meno*

Soc: What do you say of him [the slave boy], Meno? Were not all these answers given out of his own head?

Men: Yes, they were all his own.

Soc: And yet, as we were just now saying, he did not know?

Men: True.

Soc: And yet he had those notions in him?

Men: Yes.

Soc: Then he who does not know still has true notions of that which he does not know?

Men: He has.

Soc: And at present these notions are just wakening up in him, as in a dream; but if he were frequently asked the same questions, in different forms, he would know as well as any one at last?

Men: I dare say.

Soc: Without any one teaching him he will recover his knowledge for himself, if he is only asked questions?

Men: Yes.

Soc: And this spontaneous recovery in him is recollection?

Men: True.

Soc: And this knowledge which he now has must he not either have acquired or always possessed?

Men: Yes.

Soc: But if he always possessed this knowledge he would always have known; or if he has acquired the knowledge, he could not have acquired it in this life, unless he has been taught geometry; for he may be made to do the same with all geometry and every other branch of knowledge. Now, has any one ever taught him? You must know that, if, as you say, he was born and bred in your house.

Men: And I am certain that no one ever did teach him.

Soc: And yet has he not the knowledge?

Men: That, Socrates, is most certain.

Soc: But if he did not acquire this knowledge in this life, then clearly he must have had and learned it at some other time?

Men: That is evident.

Soc: And that must have been the time when he was not a man?

Men: Yes.

Soc: And if there have been always true thoughts in him, both at the time when he was and was not a man, which only need to be awakened into knowledge by putting questions to him, his soul must have always possessed this knowledge, for he always either was or was not a man?

Men: That is clear.

Soc: And if the truth of all things always existed in the soul, then the soul is immortal. Wherefore be of good cheer, and try to recollect what you do not know, or rather do not remember.

Men: I feel, somehow, that I like what you are saying.

Soc: And I, Meno, like what I am saying. Some things I have said of which I am not altogether confident. But that we shall be better and braver and less helpless if we think that we ought to inquire, than we should have been if we indulged in the idle fancy that there was no knowing and no use in searching after what we know not;—that is a theme upon which I am ready to fight, in word and deed, to the utmost of my power.[6]

"No civilization, including Plato's, has ever been destroyed because its citizens learned too much."
—Robert McKee

8. Does Socrates' questioning of the slave boy prove that to know something is to recall it from a previous existence? What does Socrates prove?

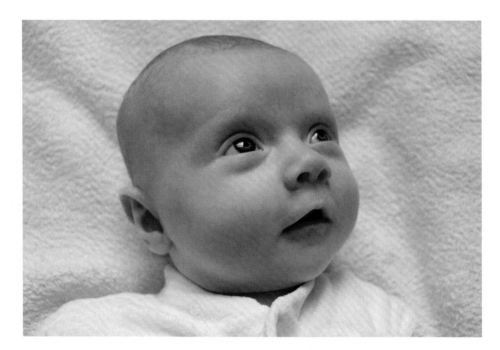

Figure 4.4 Plato accepts the theory of innate knowledge, a common doctrine among rationalists. He thinks our knowledge is already in us at birth. But is it plausible that this baby already knows geometry or physics and that adults just need to help her remember it? Some scientists would say yes, for they have uncovered evidence that neurons establish connections without any prodding from experience.

"If women are expected to do the same work as men, we must teach them the same things."

—Plato

rationalism The view that some or all of our knowledge about the world is gained independently of sense experience.

empiricism The belief that knowledge of the world comes solely from sense experience.

9. Do you consider your views on knowledge closer to rationalism or empiricism? Why?

Many thinkers reject Plato's notion of a preexisting state in which we acquire knowledge, and they are skeptical of the claim that we are born with knowledge. But the idea of innate knowledge in some fashion is still attractive to some philosophers, for it would explain how we could possess knowledge (the truths of mathematics, for example) without relying on sense experience.

Plato's Rationalism

Plato's theory of knowledge is a *rationalist* view. As discussed earlier, **rationalism** is the view that some or all of our knowledge about the world is gained independently of sense experience. Plato was the first great rationalist, but many other eminent philosophers have also taken a rationalist stance: for example, René Descartes (1596–1650), Benedict Spinoza (1632–1677), and Gottfried Leibniz (1646–1716). The opposing view is known as **empiricism**, the doctrine that knowledge of the world comes solely from sense experience. We may come to know logical and mathematical truths through reason, but we can know nothing of the world except through our senses. The great empiricists include John Locke (1632–1704), George Berkeley (1685–1753), and David Hume (1711–1776).

THEN AND NOW

Modern Platonism

Figure 4.5 Do numbers exist independently of human beings somewhere in a timeless ethereal realm?

Platonism refers to views derived from Plato's doctrines, especially his theory of Forms. In the twenty-first century, Platonism is alive and well in the form of mathematical Platonism, a kind that has widespread acceptance among mathematicians. Mathematical Platonism says that mathematical entities—such as the number 3; 2 + 2 = 4; all prime numbers; and *pi*—are abstract objects that exist independently of the thoughts and practices of rational beings.

Suppose you think of the number *pi*—what is it exactly you are thinking about? Platonists might say you are thinking of an object that exists somewhere beyond space and time and that has certain properties regardless of what you or anyone else thinks or does.

A typical objection to mathematical Platonism is that it proposes a great divide between mathematical concepts and the human mind, between the mathematical world and the world we live in. If such a divide exists, it would seem to make human interaction with the mathematical realm inexplicable or maybe even impossible. How can the mind, living as it does in this material world, know anything about the imperceptible, strange mathematical entities that exist in an entirely alien sphere that is neither physical nor mental?

Mathematical Platonists have offered answers to this question, and the debate continues—all because of something Plato said almost twenty-five centuries ago.

Do you think mathematical Platonism is plausible? Why or why not?

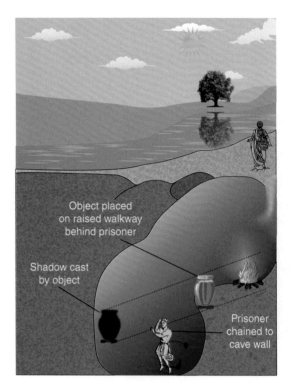

Figure 4.6 Plato's Allegory of the Cave.

The debate between rationalists and empiricists has been raging for hundreds of years, with Plato making the opening move in the fifth century BCE. The discussion continues today in both philosophy and science. Both sides have the burden of explaining how we come to know mathematical and logical truths as well as such facts as the existence of material objects, the shape of the Earth, and the movements of subatomic particles.

4.3 ALLEGORY OF THE CAVE

In the *Republic*, Plato presents what is probably the most famous tale in Western philosophy: the "Allegory of the Cave." Through the persona of Socrates, Plato tells a story that works on many levels. Primarily the allegory illustrates facets of Plato's theories of knowledge and metaphysics, but it can also be seen as a metaphor for the search for ultimate wisdom through philosophy.

Imagine, Plato says, prisoners chained for life against a wall in a cave so that they can see only shadows on the opposite wall. The shadows appear because behind and above the wall to which the prisoners are chained there burns a fire, and between the fire and the prisoners is a raised walkway along which people pass carrying vessels, statues, and replicas of animals. The prisoners see the shadows of these artifacts on the wall and hear the people's voices echoing off of it, and they mistakenly believe that these sights and sounds are the real world. But the real world—the truth—lies above the darkened cave out in the bright sunlight.

Plato: *The Republic*

"Plato described ordinary life as unthinking, lived in a dim cave of shadowy reflections, but said that it is possible to leave the cave and see things in sunlit clarity as they actually are."

—Huston Smith

And now, I said, let me show in a figure how far our nature is enlightened or unenlightened:— Behold! human beings living in an underground den, which has a mouth open towards the light and reaching all along the den; here they have been from their childhood, and have their legs and necks chained so that they cannot move, and can only see before them, being prevented by the chains from turning round their heads. Above and behind them a fire is blazing at a distance, and between the fire and the prisoners there is a raised way; and you will see, if you look, a low wall built along the way, like the screen which marionette players have in front of them, over which they show the puppets.

I see.

And do you see, I said, men passing along the wall carrying all sorts of vessels, and statues and figures of animals made of wood and stone and various materials, which appear over the wall? Some of them are talking, others silent.

You have shown me a strange image, and they are strange prisoners.

Like ourselves, I replied; and they see only their own shadows, or the shadows of one another, which the fire throws on the opposite wall of the cave?

True, he said; how could they see anything but the shadows if they were never allowed to move their heads?

And of the objects which are being carried in like manner they would only see the shadows?

Yes, he said.

And if they were able to converse with one another, would they not suppose that they were naming what was actually before them?

Very true.

And suppose further that the prison had an echo which came from the other side, would they not be sure to fancy when one of the passers-by spoke that the voice which they heard came from the passing shadow?

No question, he replied.

To them, I said, the truth would be literally nothing but the shadows of the images.

That is certain.

And now look again, and see what will naturally follow if the prisoners are released and disabused of their error. At first, when any of them is liberated and compelled suddenly to stand up and turn his neck round and walk and look towards the light, he will suffer sharp pains; the glare will distress him, and he will be unable to see the realities of which in his former state he had seen the shadows; and then conceive some one saying to him, that what he saw before was an illusion, but that now, when he is approaching nearer to being and his eye is turned towards more real existence, he has a clearer vision,—what will be his reply? And you may further imagine that his instructor is pointing to the objects as they pass and requiring him to name them,—will he not be perplexed? Will he not fancy that the shadows which he formerly saw are truer than the objects which are now shown to him?

Far truer.

And if he is compelled to look straight at the light, will he not have a pain in his eyes which will make him turn away to take refuge in the objects of vision which he can see, and which he will conceive to be in reality clearer than the things which are now being shown to him?

True, he said.

And suppose once more, that he is reluctantly dragged up a steep and rugged ascent, and held fast until he is forced into the presence of the sun himself, is he not likely to be pained and irritated? When he approaches the light his eyes will be dazzled, and he will not be able to see anything at all of what are now called realities.

Not all in a moment, he said.

He will require to grow accustomed to the sight of the upper world. And first he will see the shadows best, next the reflections of men and other objects in the water, and then the objects themselves; then he will gaze upon the light of the moon and the stars and the spangled heaven; and he will see the sky and the stars by night better than the sun or the light of the sun by day?

Certainly.

Last of all he will be able to see the sun, and not mere reflections of him in the water, but he will see him in his own proper place, and not in another; and he will contemplate him as he is.

Certainly.

10. If this allegory is taken as a representation of the search for, and the impediments to, wisdom, what does the cave represent? What do the shadows on the wall represent?

"Justice in the life and conduct of the state is possible only as first it resides in the hearts and souls of the citizens."

—Plato

"Wise men speak because they have something to say; fools because they have to say something."

—Plato

11. The prisoners react with disdain and violence to the enlightened one. Are there parallels in history of this sort of treatment for people with unconventional views?

Plato: *The Republic*

He will then proceed to argue that this is he who gives the season and the years, and is the guardian of all that is in the visible world, and in a certain way the cause of all things which he and his fellows have been accustomed to behold?

Clearly, he said, he would first see the sun and then reason about him.

And when he remembered his old habitation, and the wisdom of the den and his fellow-prisoners, do you not suppose that he would felicitate himself on the change, and pity them?

Certainly, he would.

And if they were in the habit of conferring honours among themselves on those who were quickest to observe the passing shadows and to remark which of them went before, and which followed after, and which were together; and who were therefore best able to draw conclusions as to the future, do you think that he would care for such honours and glories, or envy the possessors of them? Would he not say with Homer,

> 'Better to be the poor servant of a poor master,'

and to endure anything, rather than think as they do and live after their manner?

Yes, he said, I think that he would rather suffer anything than entertain these false notions and live in this miserable manner.

Imagine once more, I said, such an one coming suddenly out of the sun to be replaced in his old situation; would he not be certain to have his eyes full of darkness?

To be sure, he said.

And if there were a contest, and he had to compete in measuring the shadows with the prisoners who had never moved out of the den, while his sight was still weak, and before his eyes had become steady (and the time which would be needed to acquire this new habit of sight might be very considerable), would he not be ridiculous? Men would say of him that up he went and down he came without his eyes; and that it was better not even to think of ascending; and if any one tried to loose another and lead him up to the light, let them only catch the offender, and they would put him to death.

No question, he said.

This entire allegory, I said, you may now append, dear Glaucon, to the previous argument; the prison-house is the world of sight, the light of the fire is the sun, and you will not misapprehend me if you interpret the journey upwards to be the ascent of the soul into the intellectual world according to my poor belief, which, at your desire, I have expressed—whether rightly or wrongly God knows. But, whether true or false, my opinion is that in the world of knowledge the idea of good appears last of all, and is seen only with an effort; and, when seen, is also inferred to be the universal author of all things beautiful and right, parent of light and of the lord of light in this visible world, and the immediate source of reason and truth in the intellectual; and that this is the power upon which he who would act rationally either in public or private life must have his eye fixed.

I agree, he said, as far as I am able to understand you.

Moreover, I said, you must not wonder that those who attain to this beatific vision are unwilling to descend to human affairs; for their souls are ever hastening into the upper world where they desire to dwell; which desire of theirs is very natural, if our allegory may be trusted.

Yes, very natural.

And is there anything surprising in one who passes from divine contemplations to the evil state of man, misbehaving himself in a ridiculous manner; if, while his eyes are blinking and before he has become accustomed to the surrounding darkness, he is compelled to fight in courts of law, or in other places, about the images or the shadows of images of justice, and is endeavouring to meet the conceptions of those who have never yet seen absolute justice?[7]

12. What is the moral (or morals) of Plato's allegory?

"Excellence is not a gift, but a skill that takes practice. We do not act rightly because we are excellent; in fact we achieve excellence by acting rightly."

—Plato

Scholars have read this story in different ways, but the most obvious interpretation centers on the individual's struggle to acquire the highest form of knowledge, the Forms. In this reading, the prisoners represent the majority of people who have only transitory beliefs to guide them, who are in the darkness of ignorance, believing that their sensory experience, dim reflections, and shallow thinking reveal all that exists. If a prisoner is released from his chains and is shown the true source of the shadows, he will not believe his eyes, and he will prefer to think as he always has—just as people will often prefer comfortable commonplace assumptions to deeper understanding. If he is dragged into the light, his eyes will hurt, and he will be disoriented, just as the truths of philosophy—the eternal Forms—can at first seem strange and frightening. But if he stays in the light, his eyes will eventually adjust; the persistent seeker of wisdom will gradually grasp the Forms and bask in the light of understanding. When he finally does see things as they really are in the full sunlight, he will pity the prisoners he left behind and will return to the cave to enlighten them—just as Socrates and Plato try to rescue people from their ignorance and turn them toward genuine wisdom. But those who dwell in darkness will revile the enlightened former prisoner, thinking him a ridiculous fool, and might even put him to death for spreading heresy. Athenians treated Socrates in a similar way, executing him for trying to nudge others toward real knowledge—a fate that has often befallen those who have dared speak unconventional truths.

4.4 IMMORTALITY, MORALITY, AND THE SOUL

The early Greeks held diverse ideas about the soul and immortality. In the epic poetry of Homer—the defining literary tradition of Greek civilization—the soul (*psyche*) is a pitiable thing, a far cry from the modern notion of soul as the supremely important essence of the real person. As one scholar describes it:

G. M. A. Grube: *Plato's Thought*

But it is as well to remember that in Homer life after death is but a shadowy counterpart of full-blooded life on earth. The souls fly to Hades shrieking like bats, they cannot speak to Odysseus [the ancient Greek hero] until a draft of living blood has restored a little life to them, and the dead Achilles complains that he would rather be a servant to the poorest man on earth than king among the dead. There is no suggestion that the psyche is in any way man's highest or noblest part. There is nothing spiritual about Homer's souls and his dead would gladly come back to life, however painful.[8]

For many early Greeks, to have a soul is merely to be alive; not having a soul is to be dead. The soul was not laden with much more importance than that. This link between soul and life, however, was eventually expanded: everything living (including animals and plants) was supposed to have a soul. Some thought the soul

"The price good men pay for indifference to public affairs is to be ruled by evil men."

—Plato

Figure 4.7 In Greek mythology, Charon the oarsman ferries the souls of the recently deceased across the river Styx in Hades, carrying them from their former lives to the world of the dead.

13. How does the early Greeks' view of the soul differ from that of Christians'?

hardly different from the body. Both were made of the same stuff but differed only in configuration. The body was material; the soul was too, but its matter was finer. For those who took this bodily view, the relationship between mind and body didn't matter nearly as much as it did to philosophers of later centuries. In any case, the soul did not have the importance that later thinkers would give it. And whatever concept of the soul was prevalent, the idea of immortality was not necessarily part of it.

At the end of the fifth century, however, the soul was generally thought to be more than just a sign of life. It was assumed to be the seat of emotions and desires, the center of practical thinking, or the possessor of moral virtues. Socrates and Plato declared that the intellect is the highest, most divine part of a human, and intelligence is the greatest function of the soul. Through reason the soul guides a person's life and restrains the immoderate actions and reckless passions of the body. It is the soul that grasps eternal truths (the Forms), and it is philosophy that frees the soul from the bewildering and blinding influence of the senses. Little wonder, then, that Socrates urged Athenians to take care, above all, of their souls by continually searching for knowledge.

The Immortal Soul

In the *Apology*, as Socrates waits in prison for his sentence to be carried out, he reflects on life after death and the fate of the soul. He considers two prospects: (1) that death is oblivion, like an eternal sleep without dreams, or (2) that the soul lives on after the body dies and can engage in conversations with the previously departed. He doesn't say which possibility is actual, but he hopes for the latter.

In the *Phaedo* and other dialogues, Plato, through the persona of Socrates, sets forth arguments for the soul's immortality. One is the argument from recollection, which Socrates illustrates with the story of the slave boy and the geometry problem

"Plato wove historical fact into literary myth."
—Michael Shermer

(discussed earlier). We acquire knowledge, says Socrates, by recalling what our souls knew (knowledge of the Forms) before we were born. If he is right, it seems our souls do not perish with our bodies, and this suggests that immortality is at least a plausible theory.

To this line, Plato has Socrates add the so-called affinity argument. There are two types of being or existence, Socrates asserts. There is the type of existence that is "human, mortal, multiform, non-intelligible, dissoluble, and never constant in relation to itself." The body is most similar to what has this type of existence. In contrast, there is the type of existence that is "divine, immortal, intelligible, uniform, indissoluble, unvarying, and constant in relation to itself."[9] The soul is most akin to what has this type of existence and therefore probably shares in all these attributes, including being both divine and immortal.

14. What is Plato's affinity argument for immortality? Does the argument prove what Plato thinks it does?

The Three-Part Soul

As you can see, Plato believes that soul and body are very different entities—that is, he assumes that dualism is true. **Dualism** is the view that the mind (or soul) and matter (or body) are two disparate things. Soul and body consist of different kinds of stuff. (As we will see later, in the seventeenth century Descartes famously arrived at the same conclusion, as have many others who came before and after him.) Plato is a very sophisticated dualist because he thinks the soul has a complex internal structure: he claims that the soul has three distinct parts or aspects.

dualism The view that the mind (or soul) and matter (or body) are two disparate things.

He recognizes that a simple, unitary soul could not account for psychological conflict, the internal struggles that humans are obviously prone to. He reasons that internal conflict in the soul cannot happen unless the soul consists of more than one part:

Plato: *The Republic*

It's clear that the same one thing cannot simultaneously either act or be acted on in opposite ways in the same respect and in the same context. And consequently, if we find this happening in the case of these aspects of ourselves, we'll know that there are more than one of them.[10]

Plato provides an example of the kind of psychological conflict involved:

[T]here's a story I once heard ... about how Leontius the son of Aglaeon was coming up from the Piraeus [Athens' main port], outside the North Wall but close to it, when he saw some corpses with the public executioner standing near by. On the one hand, he experienced the desire to see them, but at the same time he felt disgust and averted his gaze. For a while, he struggled and kept his hands over his eyes, but finally he was overcome by the desire; he opened his eyes wide, ran up to the corpses, and said, "There you are, you wretches! What a lovely sight! I hope you feel satisfied!"[11]

Plato: *The Republic*

15. Why does Plato believe the soul must have more than one part? Do you agree that the soul must be tripartite? Why or why not?

Plato's tripartite soul has these aspects: (1) *appetite* (the "avaricious" part), which desires satisfaction of the bodily cravings for food, drink, sex, sleep, and other useful or pleasurable things; (2) *spirit* (the "competitive" part), which wants to preserve a sense of self and serve ambition (and is thus motivated to maximize honor, self-esteem, recognition, success, and winning); and (3) *reason* (the philosophical or intellectual part), which should pursue truth (both practical and theoretical), regulate the other two parts, and rule the soul as a whole.

Plato believes he is on solid ground when he asserts that the reasoning part should dominate the soul. An eminent Plato scholar explains:

Julia Annas: *An Introduction to Plato's* Republic

There are two main reasons why it is appropriate for reason to rule the soul. . . . One is that it is the only part that cares for the interests of the whole soul and not just itself, whereas the other two parts care only for themselves and not for the whole of which they are parts. . . . Reason, then, is the source of practical judgement about what is best for the person as a whole. The other ground for reason's rule over the whole soul is that a life which is shaped by devotion to the aim of reason, searching for truth, is a better life for the person to lead than a life shaped by devotion to the ends of the other parts.[12]

"The philosopher whose dealings are with divine order himself acquires the characteristics of order and divinity."

—Plato

The Moral Soul

With his notion of a three-part soul, Plato is able to shed light not only on human psychology but also on the foundations of morality. Most of his treatment of the latter is found in the *Republic*, which is ostensibly about the workings of the ideal state (or society) but is largely about the nature of morality (justice) and the necessary conditions for human happiness. The discussion begins in the *Republic*'s first chapter with the Sophist Thrasymachus insisting that justice is nothing more than rules devised by the strong and imposed on the weak. He then argues that the moral man will always be at a disadvantage compared to the immoral. It pays to be immoral, he declares; being moral is for suckers. Here is Thrasymachus making the point:

Plato: *The Republic*

"You fool, Socrates, don't you see? In any and every situation, a moral person is worse off than an immoral one. Suppose, for instance, that they're doing some business together, which involves one of them entering in association with the other: by the time the association is dissolved, you'll never find the moral person up on the immoral one—he'll be worse off. Or again, in civic matters, if there's a tax on property, then a moral person pays more tax than an immoral one even when they're both equally well off; and if there's a hand-out, then the one gets nothing, while the other takes a lot. . . .

"So you see, Socrates, immorality—if practiced on large enough scale—has more power, license, and authority than morality. And as I said at the beginning, morality is really the advantage of the stronger party, while immorality is profitable and advantageous to oneself."13

The challenge to Plato, then, is to show that Thrasymachus is wrong, that the moral person will in the long run fare better than the immoral one. Thrasymachus thinks it's more beneficial to be unjust than just—or to *appear* just while actually being unjust. The fundamental question here is, Which is the best way to live—unjustly or justly? More precisely, which kind of life is *good in itself* (inherently good), not just good because the consequences of living that way are advantageous? The question is about the inherently good life and not the consequences of living a particular way, because it is possible for both just and unjust living to result in positive benefits. (A just man's good reputation, for example, might afford him advantages; an unjust man can always turn circumstances his way.) So this is essentially what Plato is up against: he must demonstrate that the poor, sick, reviled, homeless *moral* man has a better life (is happier) than the rich, healthy, respected, powerful *immoral* man.

Plato answers this challenge by referring to his concept of the tripartite soul. A man is moral and behaves morally, he says, when the three parts of the soul act in harmony and fulfill their purpose—that is, when each part performs its proper function well. A man's soul is in harmony when *appetite* motivates him to act confidently and satisfy basic needs; when *spirit* pushes him to achieve success, honor, and recognition; and when *reason* rules wisely over appetite and spirit and ensures balance among all three. To achieve this state of harmony is to be a just person, and a just person acts justly. As Plato says:

[Morality's] sphere is a person's inner activity: it is really a matter of oneself and the parts of oneself. Once he has stopped his mental constituents doing any job which is not their own or intruding on one another's work; once he has set his own house in order, which is what he really should be concerned with; once he is his own ruler, and is well regulated, and has internal concord; once he has treated the three factors as if they were literally the three defining notes of an octave—low, high, and middle—and has created a harmony out of them and however many notes there may be in between; once he has bound all the factors together and made himself a perfect unity instead of a plurality, self-disciplined and internally attuned: then and only then does he act—if he acts—to acquire property or look after his body or play a role in government or do some private business. In the course of this activity, it is conduct which preserves and promotes this inner condition of his that he regards as moral and describes as fine, and it is knowledge which oversees this conduct that he regards as wisdom; however, it is any conduct which disperses this condition that he regards as immoral, and the thinking which oversees this conduct that he regards as stupidity.14

The result of having this harmonious and just soul, Plato says, is enduring happiness—the priceless byproduct of the good life. The balance, stability, and integration of the inner parts of ourselves dispel internal conflict and make true

"And now—Plato's words mock me in the shadows on the ledge behind the flames: 'the men of the cave would say of him that up he went and down he came without his eyes.'"
—Daniel Keyes

16. What is Thrasymachus' theory of morality? How does it differ from Plato's?

Plato: *The Republic*

"Reading Plato should be easy; understanding Plato can be difficult."
—Robin Waterfield

17. According to Plato, when is a person moral, or just? How does a person achieve true happiness?

"[O]ther thinkers have philosophised since the time of Plato, but that does not destroy the interest and beauty of his philosophy."

—Frederick Charles Copleston

18. Why does Plato believe the moral life is better than the immoral life? Do you agree? Why or why not?

happiness possible. This kind of happiness is more profound than a fleeting surge of pleasure or a period of gladness: this is a deep, durable satisfaction that is not affected by the ups and downs of fortune.

The inner state of the immoral person, however, is disharmony, where the three aspects of the personality pull against one another, each one wanting something that conflicts with the wants of the other two. Desire struggles with spirit for dominance; reason controls neither; the result is unwise, self-defeating action and internal chaos. Such internal strife and external foolishness is the essence of unhappiness.

This is Plato's reply to Thrasymachus and others who assert that the best life is an immoral one. The unjust life is out of balance, he says, with inner conflict among the parts of the soul wreaking psychological pain and external calamity. From an immoral life may come transitory enjoyment but no true happiness. But the just life, despite any outward misfortune and the disdain of the unjust, is the most beneficial and, in the best sense of the word, the happiest.

DETAILS

The Ring of Gyges

In the *Republic*, Glaucon, who is Plato's older brother, asks Socrates whether justice is good in itself or only a necessary evil. Playing the devil's advocate, Glaucon puts forth the hypothesis that egotistic power seeking in which we have complete freedom to indulge ourselves might be the ideal state of existence. However, the hypothesis continues, reason quickly shows us that others might seek to have the same power, which would interfere with our freedom and cause a state of chaos in which no one was likely to have any of one's desires fulfilled. So we compromise and limit our acquisitive instincts. Justice or a system of morality is simply the result of that compromise. It has no intrinsic

Figure 4.8 What would you do with the ring of Gyges? Would having it turn you to evil or good?

value but is better than chaos and worse than undisturbed power. It is better to compromise and limit our acquisitive instincts.

To illustrate his point, Glaucon tells the story of a shepherd named Gyges who comes upon a ring, which at his behest makes him invisible. He uses it to escape the external

4.5 THE INDIVIDUAL AND THE STATE

In the *Republic*, Plato proposes a political theory that has challenged thinkers and stimulated debate ever since. He argues that the only kind of society that can ensure people get their due is a **meritocracy**, a system of rule by an elite distinguished by abilities and achievements. He contrasts meritocracy with a form of government he strongly opposes: **democracy**, rule by the people as a whole. In his view, democratic rule is mob rule, the reign of a rabble too easily swayed by emotional appeals and bad arguments. Plato had plenty of experience with democratic rule, for in his day Athens was a democracy in which governmental decisions were made by direct vote of adult male Athenians. There were no representatives of the citizenry, because the citizens themselves made political or governmental decisions. (Greek democracy was far from rule by all the people, for only free men were full citizens, and women and

meritocracy A system of rule by an elite distinguished by abilities and achievements.

democracy Rule by the people as a whole.

sanctions of society—its laws and censure—and to serve his greed to the fullest. Glaucon then says:

> Suppose there were two such rings, then—one worn by our moral person, the other by the immoral person. There is no one, on this view, who is iron-willed enough to maintain his morality and find the strength of purpose to keep his hands off what doesn't belong to him, when he is able to take whatever he wants from the market-stalls without fear of being discovered, to enter houses and sleep with whomever he chooses, to kill and to release from prison anyone he wants, and generally to act like a god among men. His behavior would be identical to that of the other person: both of them would be heading in the same direction.

Glaucon asks whether it is implausible to suppose that we all would do likewise. Then he offers a thought experiment that compares the life of the seemingly just (but unjust) man who is incredibly successful with the life of the seemingly unjust (but just) man who is incredibly unsuccessful. Which would we choose? Socrates counters that to be just is indeed always better than to be unjust. Immorality corrupts the inner person, making one truly worse off psychologically and spiritually.

This story about the ring always engenders many questions. But the one that hits closest to home is this: What would you do with the ring?

Plato, *Republic*, trans. Robin Waterfield (Oxford: Oxford University Press, 1993), 359d–360c.

slaves were excluded.) He never forgot that it was a democratic vote of his fellow citizens that committed the ultimate injustice by condemning to death his teacher and role model, the venerable Socrates.

Plato's political theory dovetails with his theory of the soul as well as with his epistemology and ethics. He argues that the makeup and functioning of the ideal society is directly analogous to the makeup and functioning of the soul, or mind. As we have seen, Plato maintains that the soul is composed of three fundamental components: appetite; spirit; and reason, or the intellect. The just, or moral, person will be a well-balanced composite of these; each performing its own distinctive function in harmony with the others, with the appetites and spirit ruled and coordinated by reason. In similar fashion, Plato says, a society consists of three types of people, each one identified according to which of the soul's components predominates:

1. Those who are moved by appetites (*producers*—laborers, carpenters, artisans, farmers).
2. Those who are moved by spirit (*auxiliaries*—soldiers, warriors, police).
3. Those who are moved by reason (*guardians*—leaders, rulers, philosopher-kings).

In a just society, these three perform their proper functions, with the producers and auxiliaries being led and controlled by the guardians. The just state is a harmonious community governed by reason, just as a moral or virtuous person is a tripartite being presided over by the rational faculty of the soul.

Plato says citizens are assigned to one of the three functions based on their aptitude and performance, and once appointed, they are expected to remain in that class and not cross over to another. This scheme reflects his theory of ethics. To be virtuous and happy, he says, we must act according to our talents and aptitude, striving for excellence in the endeavors nature has chosen for us.

Plato, then, envisions an **aristocracy** (a society ruled by a privileged class)—not an aristocracy of the rich, landed, or well born, but of the intellect. The guardians are true philosopher-kings. They wield all the political power by virtue of their greater talents and intelligence. In the ideal republic, the guardians—contrary to the usual custom—cannot own property, for owning property might tempt them to govern for personal gain rather than for the good of society. This powerful elite can include women and anyone from the lower classes, because the only qualification for becoming a ruler is simply to be of superior intelligence and character.

To modern minds, some of the elements of Plato's society may sound both wrong and alien. His ideal state rests on massive inequality among citizens who are sorted into three classes marked by unequal shares of power and privilege. Granted, people are assigned to different classes according to merit, but inequality is still the rule. Plato maintains that equals should be treated equally, but to him the classes deserve different treatment because they are *not equal*. They are different. For Plato, all men are not created equal.

Then there is the authoritarianism of Plato's state, in which no one gets to choose their own role in life. In general, once assigned to a social role, citizens cannot jump to a different one. There is no social mobility except *within* a class and in the case of guardians being chosen from lower classes.

---

19. According to Plato, how are the just person and the just society alike?

"Plato was a bore."
—Friedrich Nietzsche

---

20. To determine citizens' aptitudes and talents (and thus their place in society), Plato favored testing them while they are young. Is it possible to discover the best career for someone this way? What about people who discover or develop their true talents late in life—those, for example, who are poor students but turn out to be geniuses in adulthood like Einstein? Is Plato too optimistic about the ease of discovering a person's true calling?

aristocracy A society ruled by a privileged class.

"Democracy is a charming form of government, full of variety and disorder, and dispensing a sort of equality to equals and unequals alike."
—Plato

Criticism has also been leveled at Plato's assumption that the unity of the community trumps personal liberty. For example:

> Plato does not—or does not *quite*—seem to regard the community as an organic entity in its own right, to which the rights of individuals are subordinated. On the contrary, when he talks about the happiness of the whole community . . . he seems to mean the happiness of all the inhabitants. Philosophers have to become rulers because they, with their knowledge of goodness, are the only ones who can produce goodness and happiness in everyone in a community.
>
> Still, from our point of view, we require very strong arguments in support of the view that the unity of the political state is such a good thing that it justifies loss of what we are bound to regard as individual freedom. We never get these kinds of arguments in Plato, however . . . Plato simply takes the value of the unity of the state as self-evident. Perhaps it is more accurate to say that what he takes as obvious is that dissension or disruption of unity is bad, and a cause of misery.[15]

In the following selection from the *Republic*, Plato has Socrates explain to his companions his concept of morality within individuals and communities. The discussion is narrated by Socrates.

21. Don't we reward athletes, doctors, lawyers, and business executives according to their merit and not by democratic vote? Should our leaders be chosen the same way, as Plato suggests? Why or why not?

22. Do you agree with Plato that unity of the community is much more important than personal liberty? Why or why not?

23. How would you defend democracy against Plato's criticisms?

Plato: *The Republic*

"All right," I said. "See if you think there's anything in what I say. From the outset, when we first started to found the community, there's a principle we established as a universal requirement—and this, or some version of it, is in my opinion morality. The principle we established, and then repeated time and again, as you'll remember, is that every individual has to do just one of the jobs relevant to the community, the one for which his nature has best equipped him."

"Yes, that's what we said."

"Furthermore, the idea that morality is doing one's own job and not intruding elsewhere is commonly voiced, and we ourselves have often said it."

"Yes, we have."

"So, Glaucon," I said, "it seems likely that this is in a sense what morality is—doing one's own job. Do you know what makes me think so?"

"No," he answered. "Please tell me."

"We've examined self-discipline, courage, and wisdom," I said, "and it occurs to me that this principle is what is left in the community, because it is the principle which makes it possible for all those other qualities to arise in the community, and its continued presence allows them to flourish in safety once they have arisen. And we did in fact say that if we found the other three, then whatever was left would be morality."

"Yes, that's necessarily so," he said.

"But if we had to decide which of these qualities it was whose presence is chiefly responsible for the goodness of the community," I said, "it would be hard to decide whether it's the unanimity between rulers and subjects, or the militia's retention of the lawful notion

> "Until philosophers are kings, or the kings and princes of this world have the spirit and power of philosophy, and political greatness and wisdom meet in one, and those commoner natures who pursue either to the exclusion of the other are compelled to stand aside, cities will never have rest from their evils—no, nor the human race, as I believe—and then only will this our State have a possibility of life and behold the light of day."
>
> —Plato

Plato: *The Republic*

---

24. Do you think Plato exaggerates the consequences of allowing a person to abandon his own career path and do another person's job? Explain.

---

25. Do you think you could be happy in Plato's ideal community? If you did agree to live in such a society, what benefits or advantages would you gain and lose?

"Democracy passes into despotism."
—Plato

about what is and is not to be feared, or the wise guardianship which is an attribute of the rulers, or the fact that it is an attribute of every child, woman, slave, free person, artisan, ruler, and subject that each individual does his own job without intruding elsewhere, that is chiefly responsible for making it good."

"Yes, of course that would be a difficult decision," he said.

"When it comes to contributing to a community's goodness, then, there's apparently a close contest between the ability of everyone in a community to do their own jobs and its wisdom, self-discipline, and courage."

"There certainly is," he said.

"And wouldn't you say that anything which rivals these qualities in contributing towards a community's goodness must be morality?"

"Absolutely."

"See if you also agree when you look at it from this point of view. Won't you be requiring the rulers to adjudicate when lawsuits occur in the community?"

"Of course."

"And won't their most important aim in doing so be to ensure that people don't get hold of other people's property and aren't deprived of their own?"

"Yes."

"Because this is right?"

"Yes."

"So from this point of view too we are agreed that morality is keeping one's own property and keeping to one's own occupation."

"True."

"See if you agree with me on this as well: if a joiner tried to do a shoemaker's job, or a shoemaker a carpenter's, or if they swapped tools or status, or even if the same person tried to do both jobs, with all the tools and so on of both jobs switched around, do you think that much harm would come to the community?"

"Not really," he said.

"On the other hand, when someone whom nature has equipped to be an artisan or to work for money in some capacity or other gets so puffed up by his wealth or popularity or strength or some such factor that he tries to enter the military class, or when a member of the militia tries to enter the class of policy-makers and guardians when he's not qualified to do so, and they swap tools and status, or when a single person tries to do all these jobs simultaneously, then I'm sure you'll agree that these interchanges and intrusions are disastrous for the community."

"Absolutely."

"There's nothing more disastrous for the community, then, than the intrusion of any of the three classes into either of the other two, and the interchange of roles among them, and there could be no more correct context for using the term 'criminal.'"

"Indubitably."

"And when someone commits the worst crime against his own community, wouldn't you describe this as immorality?"

"Of course."

"Then this is what immorality is. Here's an alternative way of putting it. Isn't it the case (to put it the other way around) that when each of the three classes—the one that works for a living, the auxiliaries, and the guardians—performs its proper function and does its own job in the community, then this is morality and makes the community a moral one?"

"Yes, I think that's exactly right," he said.

WRITING AND REASONING   CHAPTER 4

---

1. What is Plato's theory of Forms? What elements do you find most plausible? Least plausible?

2. What is Plato's distinction between opinion and knowledge? Is it the case that any proposition based on sense experience cannot count as knowledge? Explain.

3. According to Plato, science can give us only opinions, not knowledge. Do you agree? Why or why not?

4. Consider Plato's view that we do not actually learn anything for the first time; we just recollect what we knew from a previous life. (Remember, he attempted a demonstration of this idea in *Meno* with the slave boy.) Is he right about this? Which is the better explanation of our knowledge: (1) that when we learn, we acquire knowledge for the first time; or (2) that we remember what we used to know previously? Why?

5. What lesson is Plato trying to teach with his allegory of the cave? Suppose the allegory is a metaphor for the search for wisdom through philosophy. What would the various aspects of the story stand for?

REVIEW NOTES

4.1 PLATO'S LIFE AND TIMES

- Plato has had a tremendous influence on Western thought and religion. He is rightly called the Father of Western Philosophy because most of its branches of inquiry can trace their beginnings to him, and they cannot be deemed complete without taking him into account.

- Plato was born in fifth-century BCE Athens. His life and his thinking were changed by three major events: his introduction to Socrates, his witnessing the trial and death of Socrates, and his subsequent travels to meet other philosophers.

- In 387 BCE, he founded the Academy in Athens, a college and research center often regarded as the first university. In various forms, the Academy endured for hundreds of years until it was abolished by Justinian I. The Academy's most distinguished student was Aristotle.

4.2 KNOWLEDGE AND REALITY

- Plato rejected the relativism and the skepticism of the Sophists and others, and he provided an important analysis of knowledge as justified true belief.

- Plato thinks that we can acquire knowledge, that knowledge is objectively true, and that the objects of knowledge are real things.

- For Plato, reality comprises two worlds: the fleeting world of the physical accessed through sense experience; and the eternal, nonphysical, changeless world of genuine knowledge accessed only through reason.
- The central notion of his philosophy is the Forms, the objectively real, eternal abstract entities that serve as models or universals of higher knowledge.

4.3 ALLEGORY OF THE CAVE

- The most famous tale in Western philosophy is probably the "Allegory of the Cave," a story that Plato tells to illustrate facets of his theories of knowledge and metaphysics.
- The most obvious interpretation centers on the individual's struggle to acquire the highest form of knowledge, the Forms, and on the opposition by the unenlightened to this wisdom.

4.4 IMMORTALITY, MORALITY, AND THE SOUL

- The early Greeks held diverse ideas about the soul and immortality—from the notion of the soul as merely an indication of life or as an insubstantial shadow to the soul as the seat of emotions, thinking, or moral values.
- Plato offers several arguments for the immortality of the soul, including the recollection and affinity arguments.
- Plato accepted the mind-body theory known as dualism but also argued that the soul consisted of three aspects or parts: appetite, spirit, and reason.
- Plato says that a person is moral and behaves morally when the three parts of the soul act in harmony and fulfill their purpose—that is, when each part performs its proper function well.

4.5 THE INDIVIDUAL AND THE STATE

- Plato declares that the only kind of society that can ensure people get their due is a meritocracy, a system of rule by those most qualified to govern. In his view, democratic rule is mob rule, the reign of a rabble too easily swayed by emotional appeals and bad arguments.
- Plato maintains that just as the moral person is a well-balanced composite of the three parts of the soul, a society consists of three types of people, each one identified according to which of the soul's components predominates. Thus, a just society has producers, auxiliaries, and guardians.
- Plato's ideal society has been criticized for its inequality, its authoritarianism, and its subordination of individual liberty to the needs of the community.

KEY TERMS

aristocracy	empiricism	meritocracy	rationalism
democracy	Forms	Platonism	skepticism
dualism			

Notes

1. Alfred North Whitehead, *Process and Reality* (New York: Free Press, 1979), 39.
2. Bertrand Russell, *A History of Western Philosophy* (New York: Simon and Schuster, 1945), 104.
3. Bernard Williams, *Plato: The Invention of Philosophy* (Abingdon-on-Thames, UK: Routledge, 1998).
4. Plato, "Meno," 98a, *The Collected Works of Plato*, trans. W. K. C. Guthrie, eds. Edith Hamilton and Huntington Cairns (Princeton, NJ: Princeton University Press, 1961), 381.
5. Plato, *Phaedo*, trans. David Gallop (Oxford: Oxford University Press, 1993), 65b–65c.
6. Plato, *Meno*, *The Dialogues of Plato*, trans. B. Jowett, vol. 3 (New York: Hearst's International Library, 1914), 34–36.
7. Plato, *The Republic*, Book VII, *The Dialogues of Plato*, trans. B. Jowett (New York: Hearst's International Library, 1914), 265–269.
8. G. M. A. Grube, *Plato's Thought* (Indianapolis: Hackett, 1980), 120–121.
9. Plato, *Phaedo*, trans. Gallop, 78a–84b.
10. Plato, *Republic*, trans. Robin Waterfield (Oxford: Oxford University Press, 1993), 436b.
11. Plato, *Republic*, trans. Waterfield, 439e–440a.
12. Julia Annas, *An Introduction to Plato's Republic* (Oxford: Oxford University Press, 1981), 126.
13. Plato, *Republic*, trans. Waterfield, 343d, 344c.
14. Plato, *Republic*, trans. Waterfield, 443d.
15. Plato, *Republic*, trans. Waterfield, xxviii.

For Further Reading

Julia Annas, *Plato: A Very Short Introduction* (Oxford: Oxford University Press, 2003).

Julia Annas, *An Introduction to Plato's Republic* (Oxford: Oxford University Press, 1981).

David Gallop, trans., *Plato: Defence of Socrates, Euthyphro, Crito* (Oxford: Oxford University Press, 1997).

G. M. A. Grube, *Plato's Thought* (Indianapolis: Hackett, 1980).

W. K. C. Guthrie, *Plato: The Man and His Dialogues—Earlier Period* (Cambridge: Cambridge University Press, 1975).

R. M. Hare, *Plato* (Oxford: Oxford University Press, 1996).

Ted Honderich, ed., *The Oxford Companion to Philosophy* (Oxford: Oxford University Press, 1995).

Christopher Janaway, "Ancient Greek Philosophy I: The Pre-Socratics and Plato," *Philosophy I: A Guide through the Subject*, ed. A. C. Grayling (Oxford: Oxford University Press, 1995).

C. J. Rowe, *Plato* (Brighton, UK: Harvester Press, 1984).

Mary Ellen Waithe, ed., *A History of Women Philosophers*, vol. 1, 600 BC–500 AD (Dordrecht: Martinus Nijhoff, 1987).

Robin Waterfield, trans., *Plato: Republic* (Oxford: Oxford University Press, 1993).

Online Resources

Biography.com, "Plato," video and notes, https://www.biography.com/scholar/plato

Philosophy Talk Podcasts, "Plato," https://www.philosophytalk.org/shows/plato

Stanford Encyclopedia of Philosophy, "Plato," https://plato.stanford.edu/entries/plato

Internet Encyclopedia of Philosophy, "Plato (427-347 BCE)," https://www.iep.utm.edu/plato

History of Philosophy (without Any Gaps) Podcast, https://historyofphilosophy.net

The Perseus Digital Library, http://www.perseus.tufts.edu/hopper

Philosophy Pages, "Socrates: Philosophical Life," http://www.philosophypages.com/hy/2d.htm

CHAPTER 5

Aristotle: Reason and Nature

CHAPTER OBJECTIVES

5.1 THE LIFE OF ARISTOTLE

- Appreciate why Aristotle's works, even after nearly two and one-half millennia, are still relevant to many areas of study, and why his influence on Western thought has been so pervasive.
- Recount the main events in Aristotle's life, including those surrounding his connections to Plato, Alexander, and the Lyceum.

5.2 LOGIC, KNOWLEDGE, AND TRUTH

- Explain how Aristotle and Plato differ in their views on sense experience, the everyday world, and the acquisition of knowledge.
- Define *deductive argument*, *valid*, *invalid*, *syllogism*, *demonstration*, and *necessary truth*.
- Explain Aristotle's view of how the primary premises or axioms of science can be known.
- Be aware of some of Aristotle's most important contributions to modern science.

5.3 PHYSICS AND METAPHYSICS

- Understand Aristotle's concepts of *substance*, *change*, and *cause*.
- Define and provide examples of *form*, *material cause*, *formal cause*, *efficient cause*, and *final cause*.
- Explain Aristotle's notion of purpose and teleology in nature.
- Recount Aristotle's reasoning that leads him to believe in an Unmoved Mover.

5.4 HAPPINESS, VIRTUE, AND THE GOOD

- Define *virtue*, *instrumental good*, and *intrinsic good*.
- Explain Aristotle's line of reasoning in determining the highest good for a human being.
- Know how Aristotle defines *happiness* and *the good life*.
- Explain how Aristotle identifies specific virtues and vices.
- Understand Aristotle's concept of soul and how it differs from Plato's.

Figure 5.1 Aristotle (384–322 BCE).

Upon hearing about the life and work of Aristotle for the first time, a man or woman of the twenty-first century could very well find the whole story hard to believe. Which is understandable: Aristotle's soaring achievements in numerous fields, his massive output of philosophical masterpieces, and his immense influence down through the ages do seem to verge on the incredible. Fortunately, it's all real.

His interests were wide-ranging, and his thinking and writing covered nearly every topic in philosophy. He laid the foundation stones for several disciplines that now make up the curriculum of the modern university, and his intellectual fingerprints can be found on ideas and issues that are still debated today. He wrote treatises on zoology, biology, chemistry, astronomy, physics, anatomy, music, theology, mathematics, sociology, history of thought, law, ethics, politics, language, rhetoric, and the arts. For many of these, he produced the first systematic analysis and exposition, and in some subject areas his writings are still the best introduction available. After almost two and one-half millennia, his discourses on politics, ethics, and poetry remain must-reads in those fields. His empirical investigations in biology were relevant and authoritative until the eighteenth century, and his astronomical theories were gospel until Galileo's telescope raised doubts about them.

Aristotle also invented formal logic, an achievement that was considered the first and last word on the subject until the twentieth century when new logical systems were added. In the process, he devised the handy method of using letters to represent arguments, an invaluable innovation that helped make further progress in logic possible. Through a winding historical path, the influence of his logic can be traced to modern applications, the most important being computer science.

Aristotle's philosophical and literary output seems all the more astonishing when we consider that most of his works are now lost, with only thirty-one surviving, and these alone are impressively voluminous. Unfortunately, the lost ones were of high literary quality, while the extant compositions seem to be less graceful lecture notes or compilations. His works on ethics include *Nicomachean Ethics* and *Politics*; on general questions about reality, *Metaphysics*; on physics, *Physics* and *On the Heavens*; on psychology, *On the Soul*; on natural history, *On the Generation of Animals* and *On the Movement of Animals*; and on logic, *Categories*, *Topics*, *Prior Analytics*, and *Posterior Analytics*.

Writing without the benefit of hundreds of years of scientific and technological advancement, Aristotle was bound to get some facts wrong. (He thought, for example, that the universe was Earth-centered and that some animals generated spontaneously from dew and mud.) But these errors cannot undermine what scholars say is most valuable in Aristotle's works: his systematic and logical ways of clarifying, analyzing, and answering philosophical questions. His arguments, even when they arrive at wrong conclusions, are often provocative and revealing. This is how one eminent scholar describes Aristotle's methods:

J. L. Ackrill: *Aristotle the Philosopher*

In working out his views on a philosophical problem Aristotle likes to start by assembling all the puzzles and difficulties, along with the main lines of argument on both sides of every question. As he goes on to clear things up, he continues to operate dialectically, that is, by trying out objections to what he has himself said, and by raising new questions. He often recognizes that obscurities remain, that what has been said is perhaps true enough, but not yet clear. He has a keen eye for difficulties and an insatiable appetite for argument, and he is never disposed to rest on his oars.[1]

5.1 The Life of Aristotle

In 384 BCE Aristotle was born in the small town of Stagira in Macedonia (now northeastern Greece), the son of a physician, Nicomachus, who served the Macedonian king. The young Aristotle probably learned anatomy from his father and was expected to take up his father's profession, but he followed another path instead. At age seventeen or eighteen, he entered Plato's famous Academy in Athens and remained there for twenty years.

We know little or nothing about Aristotle's deportment and appearance in his Academy years, and ancient sources that offer such information are of dubious reliability. Here's one such description of Aristotle given by Diogenes Laertius, a Greek biographer:

"What really characterizes Aristotle as a philosopher is not the number and weight of his conclusions (his 'doctrines'), but the number and power and subtlety of his arguments and ideas and analyses."
—J. L. Ackrill

Diogenes Laertius: *Lives of the Philosophers*

He had a lisping voice, as is asserted by Timotheus the Athenian, in his *Lives*. He had also very thin legs, they say, and small eyes; but he used to indulge in very conspicuous garments and rings, and he used to dress his hair carefully.[2]

Aristotle loved and admired Plato, but during his career he also sometimes departed from the master's doctrines, putting forth his own theories and critiquing Plato's. On this point he is thought to have said that he cherishes Plato but cherishes the truth more.

Around the time of Plato's death in 347 BCE, Aristotle left Athens for Assos on the western shores of Asia Minor (now Turkey). There he did philosophy and

Figure 5.2 Remnants of ancient Athens.

"[Aristotle] bestrode antiquity like an intellectual colossus. No man before him had contributed so much to learning. No man after him might aspire to rival his achievements."
—Jonathan Barnes

Lyceum Aristotle's school of philosophy and science, named after its location, a grove just outside Athens dedicated to the god Apollo Lyceus.

conducted research in marine biology. Later he relocated to Lesbos, an island near Assos, where he carried out more biological investigations, married a woman named Pythias, and had a daughter by her.

In 343 or 342 BCE, Philip, the king of Macedonia, offered Aristotle a tutoring job in Pella, the capital of the Macedonian kingdom. The student was none other than the king's son, thirteen-year-old Alexander, later known as Alexander the Great. This position probably lasted two or three years. What, if anything, Alexander learned from Aristotle and what Aristotle thought of his famous pupil is unclear. At any rate, within six or seven years Alexander was crowned ruler, and he began his quest to conquer the known world.

In 335 BCE, after being away from Athens for twelve years, Aristotle returned to found a school of philosophy and science called the **Lyceum**, named after its location, a grove just outside Athens dedicated to the god Apollo Lyceus. In this period Aristotle lectured, wrote many of his treatises, instituted research programs, and established the first major library of antiquity. During this time, Pythias died, and Aristotle formed a relationship with another woman, Herpyllis, who gave him a son, Nicomachus.

In the meantime, under Alexander's leadership Macedonia was exerting considerable influence over Athens, a trend that many Athenians resented. In 323 BCE, after the death of Alexander, Athens revolted against Macedonian domination, and Aristotle became an object of suspicion because of his ties to Macedonia. Athenians soon charged him with impiety, as they had Socrates, but Aristotle left Athens before they could act against him. Aristotle, being well aware of what Athenians had done

PORTRAIT

Aristotle and Alexander

We know that for a while, the young Alexander of Macedonia (later to become Alexander the Great, 356–323 BCE) was tutored by Aristotle. Through the centuries the relationship between these two has been the subject of wild speculation, tall tales, and forgeries. The truth is, we know scarcely anything about it. Bertrand Russell, twentieth-century philosopher and the author of *A History of Western Philosophy*, mentions the few shreds we have:

Figure 5.3 Aristotle teaching Alexander.

> As to Aristotle's influence on [Alexander], we are left free to conjecture whatever seems to us most plausible. For my part, I should suppose it *nil*. Alexander was an ambitious and passionate boy, on bad terms with his father, and presumably impatient of schooling. . . . I cannot imagine [Aristotle's] pupil regarding him as anything but a prosy old pedant, set over him by his father to keep him out of mischief. . . .
>
> It is more surprising that Alexander had so little influence on Aristotle, whose speculations on politics were blandly oblivious of the fact that the era of City States had given way to the era of empires. I suspect that Aristotle, to the end, thought of him as "that idle and headstrong boy, who never could understand anything of philosophy."

Bertrand Russell, *A History of Western Philosophy* (New York: Simon and Schuster, 1945), 160–161.

to Socrates, is supposed to have said that he would not allow Athens to "sin twice against philosophy." So he went into exile in the town of Chalcis on the Aegean island of Euboea. A year later, at the age of sixty-two, he died there.

5.2 Logic, Knowledge, and Truth

Plato declares that we can come to know things, that these things are objectively real, but that they are not the objects of sense experience. The truly real things, he says, are abstract objects of the mind existing in a realm beyond the reach of sense experience. Sensory properties are not reliable indicators of reality. The truly real are the independently existing Forms, and these eternal objects are more real than anything detected by our senses. Plato is the original, through-and-through rationalist.

Aristotle, however, is not. He believes that knowledge is possible, that we can grasp objective truths about reality, but that our knowing begins with sense

1. How do Aristotle and Plato differ in their attitudes toward sense experience?

experience. Here is one philosopher's elegant way of drawing the distinction between the two ways of viewing the world:

Anthony Gottlieb: *The Dream of Reason: A History of Philosophy from the Greeks to the Renaissance*

What Aristotle says in praise of his favourite study, zoology, illustrates the fundamental difference between him and Plato. Plato had a pessimistic attitude to the everyday world. Everything in it seemed to him to fall pathetically short of the standards set by the ideal Forms. The philosopher's job was to convince people of this depressing fact and persuade them to transcend this world, at least in their own minds, and learn to love the Forms instead. Aristotle, by contrast, was an optimist. While Plato wanted to leave the dark Cave of physical reality and find something better, Aristotle said that the Cave was not so bad once you turned the lights on—particularly if you started dissecting the animals in it. The beauty which Plato appreciated best in unrealized, unworldly ideals, Aristotle saw all around him.[3]

> "How many a dispute could have been deflated into a single paragraph if the disputants had dared to define their terms."
> —Aristotle

And here is Aristotle explaining that our sense experience gives us the raw materials for reliable knowledge:

Aristotle: *Metaphysics*

Figure 5.4 A section of Raphael's painting *The School of Athens* (c. 1510–1512) showing Plato and Aristotle conversing, with Plato pointing upward to suggest the higher realm of the Forms, and Aristotle pointing downward alluding to earthly, sensory things.

All men by nature desire to know. An indication of this is the delight we take in our senses; for even apart from their usefulness they are loved for themselves....

The animals other than man live by appearances and memories, and have but little of connected experience; but the human race lives also by art [practical and creative action] and reasonings. And from memory experience is produced in men; for many memories of the same thing produce finally the capacity for a single experience.... [S]cience and art come to men *through* experience.... Again, we do not regard any of the senses as wisdom; yet surely these give the most authoritative knowledge of particulars.[4]

But how exactly do the raw data of our senses lead to knowledge? As noted in the last chapter, we possess knowledge when we have a true belief supported by reasons. This is also Aristotle's view, but he is not content to leave it at that. He wants to clarify and systematize our acquisition of knowledge, and to do that he invents the field of logic, the study of correct reasoning (see Chapter 1). Specifically, he devises the first system of deductive inference or argument. Recall that an argument is a group of statements in which one of them (the conclusion) is supported by the others (the premises).

A **deductive argument** is intended to provide logically conclusive support for its conclusion so that if the premises are true, the conclusion must be true. If it succeeds in providing such support, it is **valid**; if it fails, it is **invalid**. Aristotle recognizes that logic is a potent tool that can be used in every area of knowledge and every rational inquiry. His main concern, however, is to develop principles of logic to facilitate the search for knowledge in the sciences.

His achievement is monumental; for a millennium, scholars swore by his system and assumed it was both perfect and complete. That assessment, however, was overblown. Aristotle's logic may very well be perfect as far as it goes, but modern logicians have shown that it does not go far enough. They have proved that there are more forms of deductive inference than Aristotle realized.

In any case, to understand how Aristotle's logic is used in the quest for knowledge, we need to understand some of the basics. The heart of his system is a precisely stated form of deductive argument called a **syllogism**, another Aristotelian invention. A syllogism is a three-statement argument in which two premises support a conclusion. For example:

1. All dogs are animals.
2. All animals are mortal.
3. Therefore, all dogs are mortal.

The words that name classes, or categories, of things (like *dogs*) are called **terms**. Each statement has both a subject term and a predicate term. For instance, the subject term in "all dogs are animals" is *dogs*; the predicate term is *animals*. Aristotle thought up a way to lay bare the logical structure of a syllogism by using letters (variables) to stand for the terms. This is how our syllogism is represented:

1. All A are B.
2. All B are C.
3. Therefore, all A are C.

Aristotle realized that it is an argument's inner structure that determines whether it is valid. Notice that our syllogism is valid because if all A are B, and all B are C, it *must* be the case that all A are C. Given the form or pattern of the argument, the conclusion follows inexorably. This means that in a valid argument, *if* the premises are true, the conclusion has to be true. But the truth of the premises is entirely unrelated to validity. We can plug any terms we want into our syllogism, and insert either true or false statements—and the argument would remain valid. (See Chapter 1 on these points.)

deductive argument An argument intended to give logically conclusive support to its conclusion.

valid argument A deductive argument that succeeds in providing conclusive support for its conclusion.

invalid argument A deductive argument that fails to provide conclusive support for its conclusion.

syllogism A deductive argument made up of three statements—two premises and a conclusion.

Figure 5.5 A copy of Aristotle's *Logic*, published in Lyon in 1570.

term A word that names a class, or category, of things in a deductive argument.

With his ingenious way of representing statements, Aristotle could make and examine a large variety of syllogisms, some valid and some not (some exemplifying correct reasoning, and some incorrect). He thought all the important statements found in science could be reduced to just four patterns—usually written like this: All S are P; No S are P; Some S are P; and Some S are not P. By inserting various combinations of these four statements into syllogistic form, we get 256 distinct valid and invalid arguments (only fourteen are valid). Together they constitute a compendium of possible arguments to use or avoid. With the syllogism and these four statement patterns, Aristotle believes he has found the tools he needs to acquire and systematize all scientific knowledge.

2. What is the relationship between truth and validity in a deductive argument? Can a valid argument have false premises?

To him, scientific knowledge (what he calls *episteme*) is not so much knowing *that* something is true, but knowing *why* it is true—knowing the explanation for a phenomenon. He holds that the perfect vehicle for acquiring such knowledge is the syllogism because its premises provide the explanation or reason for the state of affairs described in the conclusion. If the premises are true, and the form is valid, the conclusion will state a scientific truth. Thus Aristotle's logic allows us to evaluate whether a proposed explanation for a phenomenon is correct.

He gives us this example:

"It is the mark of an educated mind to be able to entertain a thought without accepting it."
—Aristotle

1. The planets are near (to the Earth).
2. Near celestial bodies do not twinkle (as the stars do).
3. Therefore, the planets do not twinkle.

Figure 5.6 The remains of Aristotle's Lyceum.

The phenomenon to be explained is that the planets do not twinkle. Using the syllogistic form, we can arrive at the correct explanation: nearby celestial bodies do not twinkle, and the planets are nearby celestial bodies.

In Aristotle's system, the syllogism is a proof, much like a proof in mathematics. The premises are essentially axioms from which a theorem, the conclusion, is derived. Such a proof is called a *demonstration* because it shows what the conclusion is based on (true premises) and that the conclusion follows deductively. To say a statement is demonstrable is to say it is derived logically from legitimate starting points. To say it is not demonstrable is to say it cannot be derived that way.

Aristotle also insists that all the statements in his syllogism be **necessarily** true—that is, they must be the kind of statements that could not have been false. To him, scientific knowledge cannot be otherwise than it is. Science is made up of logical sequences of necessarily true explanations from which are derived necessarily true claims about the world.

But at this point Aristotle's demonstrative syllogism seems to have a problem. We know that the necessarily true conclusion is supposed to be based on necessarily true premises. The conclusion, in other words, is the result of a proof. That gives us reason to believe it. But what are the premises based on? Where is *their* proof? It won't do to say a premise must be deduced from other premises, from another proof. If that's the case, the sequence of deductions would go on forever. Aristotle admits that it's not possible to supply a proof for everything. Not every statement is demonstrable. His answer is that the primary premises or axioms of science can be known intuitively by an immediate apprehension of the mind. These axioms are fundamental and grasped directly without the help of intervening statements and inferences. As Aristotle says:

> "Aristotle is the first to write like a professor: his treatises are systematic, his discussions are divided into heads, he is a professional teacher, not an inspired prophet."
> —Bertrand Russell

necessary truth A truth that could not have been false.

3. Is "George is taller than Mary" necessarily true? Why or why not?

> "To say that what is is not, or that what is not is, is false and to say that what is is, or that what is not is not, is true."
> —Aristotle

Aristotle: *Posterior Analytics*

[W]e do know through demonstration. By demonstration I mean a scientific deduction; and by scientific deduction I mean one in virtue of which, by having it, we understand something.

If, then, understanding is as we posited, it is necessary for demonstrative understanding in particular to depend on things which are true and primitive and immediate and more familiar than and prior to and explanatory of the conclusion (for in this way the principles will also be appropriate to what is being proved). For there will be deduction even without these conditions, but there will not be demonstration; for it will not produce understanding.[5]

Aristotle and Modern Science

Figure 5.7 A 1661 depiction of the geocentric (Earth-centered) model of the universe accepted by Aristotle (and many others before and after him). The stars and planets are fixed to translucent concentric spheres rotating in perfect circles.

From Aristotle, modern science has inherited a systematized set of remarkable ideas—some right, some wrong, many astonishingly influential, many not, and almost all useful in one way or another. Because he lacked the technical and conceptual tools of today's science and started (in some cases) from dubious assumptions, a number of his theories and analyses are very wide of the mark. For example, he erred in his claims about the movement of the stars and planets, his beliefs and theories about biology (remember, Darwin postdated Aristotle by over two millennia), and his assessment of the completeness and application of his logic. But none of this detracts from his most important contributions to contemporary science. A distinguished scholar explains:

> The concepts and the terminology of the Lyceum provided the medium within which philosophy and science developed. . . . When today we talk of matter and form, of species and genera, of energy and potentiality, of substance of quality, of accident and essence, we unwittingly speak the language of Aristotle. . . .
>
> It is worth noting that our modern notion of scientific method is roughly Aristotelian. Scientific empiricism—the idea that abstract argument must be subordinate to factual evidence, that theory is to be judged before the strict tribunal of observation—now seems a commonplace; but it was not always so, and it is largely due to Aristotle that we understand science to be an empirical pursuit.

Would Aristotle be likely to accept the findings of modern science? For example, would he accept data that show he was wrong about planetary motion? Explain.

Jonathan Barnes, *Aristotle: A Very Short Introduction* (Oxford: Oxford University Press, 2000), 137.

5.3 Physics and Metaphysics

As we've seen, the early Greek philosophers were interested in the world at its most fundamental level. They asked: What is the universe made of? What things exist? How are they structured? The first philosophers, in other words, tried to plumb the deepest waters of metaphysics (the study of reality in the broadest sense). Aristotle was well aware of their thinking and set out to critically examine their theories, which he mostly found wanting. He also countered their views with theories of his own—clearer, more insightful, more sophisticated theories. Countless philosophers, scientists, and other thinkers have been taking the measure of these ideas ever since.

"Aristotle was the best educated man that ever walked on the surface of this earth. He is still, as he was in Dante's time, the 'master of those that know.'"

—Thomas Davidson

Substance

For Aristotle, and for many other serious thinkers both before and after him, the most important question in metaphysics is one that has been asked in several different ways. The most general way (and perhaps least helpful) is, What is *being*? But there is also: What is real? What fundamental realities exist? What is it that underlies everything that *is*? What basic existing things do all other things depend on for their existence? To Aristotle, the answer that all these questions are looking for is *substance*. As he says:

Aristotle: *Metaphysics*

There are several senses in which a thing may be said to 'be', as we pointed out previously in our book on the various senses of words; for in one sense the 'being' meant is 'what a thing is' or a 'this', and in another sense it means a quality or quantity or one of the other things that are predicated as these are. While 'being' has all these senses, obviously that which 'is' primarily is the 'what', which indicates the substance of the thing. For when we say of what quality a thing is, we say that it is good or bad, not that it is three cubits long or that it is a man; but when we say what it is, we do not say 'white' or 'hot' or 'three cubits long', but 'a man' or 'a 'god'. And all other things are said to be because they are, some of them, quantities of that which is in this primary sense, others qualities of it, others affections of it, and others some other determination of it. And so one might even raise the question whether the words 'to walk', 'to be healthy', 'to sit' imply that each of these things is existent, and similarly in any other case of this sort; for none of them is either self-subsistent or capable of being separated from substance, but rather, if anything, it is that which walks or sits or is healthy that is an existent thing. Now these are seen to be more real because there is something definite which underlies them (i.e. the substance or individual), which is implied in such a predicate; for we never use the word 'good' or 'sitting' without implying this. Clearly then it is in virtue of this category that each of the others also is. Therefore that which is primarily, i.e. not in a qualified sense but without qualification, must be substance.

Now there are several senses in which a thing is said to be first; yet substance is first in every sense: (1) in definition, (2) in order of knowledge, (3) in time. For (3) of the other categories none can exist independently, but only substance. And (1) in definition also this is first; for in the definition of each term the definition of its substance must be present. And (2) we think we know each thing most fully, when we know what it is, e.g. what man is or what fire is, rather than when we know its quality, its quantity, or its place; since we know each of these predicates also, only when we know what the quantity or the quality is.[6]

But why does such a general, abstract question matter at all? For one thing, people seek understanding for its own sake. We are stuck with reality as it is, and we want to know if it is as we think it is. Many grand attempts to see reality clearly have begun out of fear that our commonsense picture of the world is a delusion. For another, whatever view of the world's primary elements is adopted, it's sure to affect how and why science is done. What would a scientist study if she thinks reality consists of nothing but numbers, or prime matter without any characteristics, or Plato's transcendent Forms?

In *Metaphysics*, Aristotle reviews several substance theories and rejects them on various grounds. For instance, the theory of the ancient atomists is that the fundamental stuff of which everything is composed is atoms. The objects around us are insubstantial, fleeting amalgams of atoms, which are the real, eternal things that make up (and help us make sense of) the world. A few other possibilities:

Aristotle: Metaphysics

Some think the limits of body [geometric properties], that is surface, line, point, and unit, are substances, and more so than body or the solid. Further, some do not think there is anything substantial besides sensible things [objects of sense experience], but others think there are eternal substances which are more in number and more real, for example, Plato posited two kinds of substance—the Forms and the objects of mathematics—as well as a third kind, namely the substance of sensible bodies. And Speusippus made still more kinds of substance, beginning with the One, and making principles for each kind of substance, one for numbers, another for spatial magnitudes, and then another for the soul; and in this way he multiplies the kinds of substance. And some say Forms and numbers have the same nature, and other things come after them, for example lines and planes, until we come to the substance of the heavens and to sensible bodies.[7]

"All men by nature desire to know."

—Aristotle

Aristotle wants to clear up all the confusion, but he does so in a roundabout way, systematically defining substance from different perspectives. He begins by pointing out a linguistic fact that suggests a truth about substance. Propositions state something about a subject, indicating that it is of a certain quality, quantity, size, shape, or some other characteristic. These characterizations, or predicates, tell us about the subject, but they are meaningless unless we know what subject is being referred to. What we most need to know is an answer to this question: *What is it*? And it is this answer that identifies the substance. It is in virtue of the subject, that which is being described, that each of the predicates *is*, Aristotle says. "Therefore that which is primarily and *is* simply (not is something) must be substance . . . [Substance] is that which is not predicated of a subject, but of which all else is predicated."[8] Substance is that which fundamentally *is*; everything else is parasitic on it.

4. Why does Aristotle reject the "pincushion" view of substance?

Does this mean substance is like a pincushion, a blank substratum that is merely the bearer of properties (pins)? Aristotle says absolutely not. What happens when all the pins are taken out of the pincushion, when all the properties are removed? If anything remains at all, it would be without any features and entirely beyond our ken. (Philosophers call such featureless stuff "prime matter.") Aristotle asserts that a nebulous nothing cannot be substance, and he rejects the notion that we can have no knowledge of the fundamental underlayment of reality.

form The shape, pattern, or function of material stuff.

If featureless matter cannot constitute substance, perhaps **form** can (not to be confused with Plato's Forms). The term means the shape, pattern, or function of material stuff. The matter of a bronze statue is the bronze; the form is the shape imparted to the bronze by the sculptor. Can form alone be substance, the primary being of the world? Aristotle again says no and insists that matter without form and form without matter (like Plato's Forms) are equally improbable.

But he does argue that a *composite* of form and matter can constitute substance, with form being the essential element that makes matter more than amorphous stuff. The sort of form Aristotle has in mind, however, goes deeper than mere shape or pattern. His kind of form is the *essence* of a thing. A thing's essence is its nature—the features without which it could not be what it is. A dog's features can vary in many ways (hair color, breed, weight, etc.), and he will still be a dog—as long as his essential characteristics (the features that make him a dog) remain. If he loses those, he will cease to be a dog. For Aristotle, then, matter plus form-as-essence equals substance:

> The essence of each thing is what it is said to be in virtue of itself. For being you is not being musical; for you are not musical in virtue of yourself. What, then, you are in virtue of yourself is your essence. . . . [W]hy are these materials a house? Because that which was the essence of a house is present. And why is this individual thing, or this body in this state, a man? Therefore what we seek is the cause, that is, the form, by reason of which the matter is some definite thing; and this is the substance of the thing.[9]

Aristotle: *Metaphysics*

Change

Aristotle's view of substance helps him counter the theories of early philosophers who hold that apparent changes in the world are illusions. Parmenides, for example, argues that the universe does not consist of numerous objects and forces; it is actually just one thing—solid, uniform, and unchanging. We might think the world is a place of movement, multiplicity, and transition, but we would be wrong. Aristotle sees that if those who deny the possibility of change are right, there can be no need and no reason for science, the empirical enterprise that Aristotle tries so hard to establish.

The change deniers backed their position with a simple argument: Either change is (1) a transition from something to that same something (because the new something is present in the original something), or (2) a transition from nothing to something. If (1), then no real change takes place. If (2), then the something would arise out of nothing, which is absurd. Change, therefore, is not possible. Aristotle debunks this view and sets out to show that change is not only possible but commonplace. In the process, he produced the West's first plausible analysis of change.

He begins his examination of change by noting something that seems intuitively obvious to most: when a thing changes, there is always something that continues, that persists through the process. Something is different, and something is not. There are, as Aristotle notes, three components to every change: the subject of change (that which persists through the change); the prechange situation (before modification); and the postchange situation (after modification). It's the first item that is the key to explaining how an object of change can change while not changing.

Figure 5.8 When is a dog a dog? Aristotle says its features may vary dramatically, but it will still be a dog if it possesses a dog's essence—the form of a dog.

Aristotle says that whether the change is an alteration of a thing's properties or the coming to be of a new thing, "there must be something underlying" the process. There is either a persisting thing whose properties change, or a thing out of which a new thing arises.

In terms of matter and form, Aristotle says, change works like this: When a new thing arises (as when gold is shaped into a statue), the persisting element is the matter (the gold) from which the statue is fashioned. Substance comes into being, a new blend of matter and form. When a thing undergoes a change of minor properties (as when a man dyes his hair red), the persisting element is the substance *man*, which experiences a change in nonessential properties, an alteration in matter but not in form.

Cause

Aristotle seeks to put science on a solid intellectual footing, and to do that he has to develop a theory of causal explanation. Explicating change and substance is not enough. He thinks any science worth the name should be able to search for and find answers to this question: Why? Why is something the way it is? More precisely, what is the explanation for a phenomenon's characteristics? As Aristotle asks, "On account of what?" He points out that the early Greek philosophers thought there was only one way to answer this, and that was to tell what something is made of. The explanation for everything is that it is composed of water, air, or some other material thing. Aristotle insists that the material composition of a thing is just one kind of explanation; actually there are three others. His translators have named them four "causes" (and tradition has gone along with that), but a more accurate label is the four "becauses" or "explanatory factors."

material cause A thing's material composition.

The explanation that cites material composition is known as the **material cause**. Why is this earthen jar the way it is? Because it's made of clay. "[T]hat out of which as a constituent a thing comes to be is called a cause," Aristotle says, "for example, the bronze and the silver and their genera would be the causes respectively of a statue and a loving-cup."[10] The **formal cause** explains why something is the way it is by citing its *form*, that is, the structure and properties that make it what it is. Why is this animal a horse? Because it has the properties that constitute the form of a horse. To use Aristotle's example: Why is this an octave? Because it has a ratio of two to one (the form of an octave). The **efficient cause** explains the main source or initiator of a change. What has produced this result, or sparked this sequence of events, or instigated this state of affairs? This type of explanation is akin to what most people think of as a cause of something. As Aristotle says:

formal cause A thing's structure and properties that make it what it is.

efficient cause The main source or initiator of a change.

Aristotle: *Physics*

Again, there is the primary source of the change or the staying unchanged: for example, the man who has deliberated is a cause, the father is a cause of the child, and in general that which makes something of that which is made, and that which changes something of that which is changed.[11]

The **final cause** explains what a thing is for or for what purpose it exists. Aristotle says this explanatory factor tells us "that for the sake of which." Such an explanation is easy enough to grasp when the something in question is an artifact. For what purpose was this statue sculpted? To honor a fallen hero. For what reason was this bridge built? To span the gorge. We humans have purposes, and we manipulate nature with those purposes in mind. And the intelligent behavior of nonhuman animals can also involve purposes when it is goal directed, as when a hound pursues a fox or an eagle searches a field for mice. But is there purpose in nonmental natural processes—in the development or functioning of feathers, fins, eyes, teeth, leaves, and roots?

Purpose

Aristotle thinks so. In *Physics* he rejects the mechanistic view that every natural event happens by chance and without purpose. He offers several arguments for his stance, including this one: The physical features of animals provide benefits to them (to help them eat, hunt, avoid danger, etc.); they enable functions that are useful to the animals. These beneficial functions arise with regularity, not haphazardly or randomly. If this is true, then the mechanistic view must be false—the features of animals can develop toward inherent ends or goals. Eyes develop for seeing; claws for hunting or digging; teeth for killing and eating. The development of such features is, as Aristotle says, "for something." Here he is making the point:

The things mentioned, and all things which are due to nature, come to be as they do always or for the most part, and nothing which is the outcome of luck or an automatic outcome does that. We do not think that it is the outcome of luck or coincidence that there is a lot of rain in winter, but only if there is a lot of rain in August; nor that there are heatwaves in August, but only if there is a heatwave in winter. If, then, things seem to be either a coincidental outcome or for something, and the things we are discussing cannot be either a coincidental or an automatic outcome, they must be for something. But all such things are due to nature, as the authors of the view under discussion themselves admit. The 'for something,' then, is present in things which are and come to be due to nature.[12]

Aristotle: *Physics*

So for Aristotle, the primary explanation (the final cause) for the development of all living things is **teleology**—the existence of purpose or ends inherent in persons or things. The development of living things is directed toward a natural goal or objective (*telos*), toward the realization of the form inherent in them. Development is pointed toward particular outcomes, and in this way it unfolds according to a purpose—not purpose in the sense of intentional action or deliberation, but purpose as an internal goal toward which nature strives. Final cause explanations are accounts of living things developing or growing toward "the good"—the particular good for the things themselves. Since wolves have sharp teeth "for the sake of" killing prey—that is, sharp teeth are good for wolves—it is good for wolves to have sharp teeth. And what's good for a creature is that which is essential to them, the

final cause What a thing is for or for what purpose it exists.

5. What is a *final cause*? Does it make sense to ask what a human being's final cause is? Why or why not?

"I do not agree with Plato, but if anything could make me do so, it would be Aristotle's arguments against him."
—Bertrand Russell

teleology The existence of purpose or ends inherent in persons or things.

6. According to Aristotle, do living things (trees, cats, tulips) have *intentions*? Do they have *purpose*?

DETAILS

Aristotle's God

The traditional God of major Western religions (Christianity, Judaism, Islam) is thought to be the creator of the world; the source of all that exists; and the divine, but involved, father deeply interested in the affairs of his human children. This is not Aristotle's God. In fact, he would think the term *God* hopelessly misleading as a label for his notion of the divine (although his translators have usually employed the word). He thinks his way, argument by argument, to a divinity who is essentially an "Unmoved Mover"—a being that is the source of motion and change in the universe but does not itself move or change.

Aristotle begins with what he thinks are reasonable premises: the universe is eternal (it has always existed), and everything that moves (or changes) is moved (or changed) by something. So what has caused the movement (and change) that we see all around us?

Aristotle reasons that movement could not have

Figure 5.9 Aristotle's eternal Unmoved Mover makes everything move and change without moving or changing itself.

been started by a first cause, because there can be no first cause in a universe that has always existed. But there has to be some sort of ultimate cause of movement or else nothing would be moving now, which is absurd. And this ultimate mover must itself be unmoved or else something would have to move it, and something would have to move *that*, and on and on to infinity—another absurdity. Thus, things move because an ultimate, Unmoved Mover makes it so.

Through an impressive series of arguments, Aristotle derives a clearer picture of this motionless mover. It is a living, eternal, single substance, unchanging, indestructible, without shape or size, and perfect. It is, in Aristotle's language of causes, a *final cause* of everything. As a final cause, it compels movement through a teleological relationship—by being the object of desire (or love) of things in the world; the end that everything else ultimately aims at or strives for. By being such an object, it causes movement in the universe without itself moving. As Aristotle says:

> [The Unmoved Mover] produces motion by being loved, and it moves the other moving things. . . . The first mover, then, of necessity exists; and in so far as it is necessary, it is good, and in this sense a first principle. . . . On such a principle, then, depend the heavens and the world of nature.

Do you think Aristotle's God is plausible? Are Aristotle's starting assumptions true? Explain.

Aristotle, *Metaphysics*, XII.7, W. D. Ross, 347–348.

properties that make them the kind of thing they are. Thus final causes are about a thing's form. Sharp teeth are not only good for a wolf; they are part of what makes a wolf a wolf.

5.4 Happiness, Virtue, and the Good

Teleology is the heart not only of Aristotle's physics and metaphysics but of his ethics as well. Whatever we do, he says, we aim at some end or object, and this goal is something good, otherwise we would not strive for it. In gardening, our aim is the healthy growth of plants. In medicine, our aim is the cure or prevention of disease. In each case, our objective is to obtain some good. But notice: Some things are good because they are a means to other goods; these are **instrumental goods**. And some things are good in themselves, for their own sake; these are **intrinsic goods**. Because intrinsic goods are what all our actions are ultimately pointed toward, they are the highest goods.

With this distinction in mind, Aristotle asks what he believes is the foundational question of ethics: What is the highest good for a human being? Here is his answer:

instrumental good Something good because it helps us attain something else good; something good for the sake of something else.

intrinsic good Something good in itself; something good for its own sake.

Aristotle: *Nicomachean Ethics*

Every art and every inquiry, and similarly every action and choice, is thought to aim at some good; and for this reason the good has rightly been declared to be that at which all things aim. . . . If, then, there is some end of the things we do, which we desire for its own sake (everything else being desired for the sake of this), and if we do not choose everything for the sake of something else (for at that rate the process would go on to infinity, so that our desire would be empty and vain), clearly this must be the good and the chief good. Will not the knowledge of it, then, have a great influence on life? Shall we not, like archers who have a mark to aim at, be more likely to hit upon what we should? If so, we must try, in outline at least, to determine what it is. . . .

Now we call that which is in itself worthy of pursuit more complete than that which is worthy of pursuit for the sake of something else, and that which is never desirable for the sake of something else more complete than the things that are desirable both in them-selves and for the sake of that other thing, and therefore we call complete without qualifi-cation that which is always desirable in itself and never for the sake of something else.

Now such a thing happiness, above all else, is held to be; for this we choose always for itself and never for the sake of something else, but honour, pleasure, reason, and every excellence we choose indeed for themselves (for if nothing resulted from them we should still choose each of them), but we choose them also for the sake of happiness, judging that through them we shall be happy. Happiness, on the other hand, no one chooses for the sake of these, nor, in general, for anything other than itself. . . .

"Happiness depends upon ourselves."
—Aristotle

7. To Aristotle, is happi-ness subjective (some-thing only in one's mind) or objective (something that has characteristics regardless of how one feels)?

8. According to Aristotle, what is the good for humans? Through what line of reasoning does he arrive at the answer?

9. What does Aristotle mean by "human good turns out to be activity of soul in conformity with excellence"?

Happiness, then, is something complete and self-sufficient, and is the end of action. . . .

Presumably, however, to say that happiness is the chief good seems a platitude, and a clearer account of what it is, is still desired. This might perhaps be given, if we could first ascertain the function of man. For just as for a flute-player, a sculptor, or any artist, and, in general, for all things that have a function or activity, the good and the "well" is thought to reside in the function, so would it seem to be for man, if he has a function. Have the carpenter, then, and the tanner certain functions or activities, and has man none? Is he naturally functionless? Or as eye, hand, foot, and in general each of the parts evidently has a function, may one lay it down that man similarly has a function apart from all these? What then can this be? Life seems to be common even to plants, but we are seeking what is peculiar to man. Let us exclude, therefore, the life of nutrition and growth. Next there would be a life of perception, but it also seems to be common even to the horse, the ox, and every animal. There remains, then, an active life of the element that has a rational principle. . . . Now if the function of man is an activity of soul in accordance with, or not without, rational principle, and if we say a so-and-so and a good so-and-so have a function which is the same in kind, e.g. a lyre-player and a good lyre-player, and so without qualification in all cases, eminence in respect of excellence being added to the function (for the function of a lyre-player is to play the lyre, and that of a good lyre-player is to do so well): if this is the case, and we state the function of man to be a certain kind of life, and this to be an activity or actions of the soul implying a rational principle, and the function of a good man to be the good and noble performance of these, and if any action is well performed when it is performed in accordance with the appropriate excellence: if this is the case, human good turns out to be activity of soul in conformity with excellence.[13]

Figure 5.10 A copy of Aristotle's *Nicomachean Ethics*, handwritten in colorful, ornate calligraphy in 1496.

virtue A disposition to behave in line with a standard of excellence.

> "We are not concerned to know what goodness is, but how we are to become good men, for this alone gives the study [of ethics] its practical value."
>
> —Aristotle

Aristotle: *Nicomachean Ethics*

Aristotle argues that the good life—a life attaining the highest good—is one lived according to the light of reason and is therefore marked by true happiness. It is to live rationally and to do so excellently; an achievement that results in a rich and satisfying life. To live this way, he says, is to possess the moral and intellectual virtues in full. A **virtue** is a disposition to behave in line with a standard of excellence—for example, honesty, compassion, loyalty, benevolence, temperance, and fairness. Virtues, in other words, are excellences of character. They are neither pure emotions nor the product of our genes. They are, as Aristotle says, a choice for which we can be praised or blamed.

They are also excellences that we learn through practice:

[B]y abstaining from pleasures we become temperate [behaving in moderation], and it is when we become so that we are most able to abstain from them; and similarly too in the case of courage; for by being habituated to despise things that are terrible and to stand our ground against them we become brave, and it is when we have become so that we shall be most able to stand our ground against them.[14]

How do we recognize the virtues (and vices) when we see them? Aristotle holds that a virtue is the midpoint (the "golden mean") between the extremes of excess and deficit, and the extremes are the vices. Courage, for example, is the virtue that comes midway between the vices of cowardice (too much fear) and rashness (too little fear).

In everything that is continuous and divisible it is possible to take more, less, or an equal amount, and that either in terms of the thing itself or relatively to us; and the equal is an intermediate between excess and defect. By the intermediate in the object I mean that which is equidistant from each of the extremes, which is one and the same for all men; by the intermediate relatively to us that which is neither too much nor too little—and this is not one, nor the same for all. . . .

Thus a master of any art avoids excess and defect, but seeks the intermediate and chooses this—the intermediate not in the object but relatively to us.

If it is thus, then, that every art does its work well—by looking to the intermediate and judging its works by this standard (so that we often say of good works of the art that it is not possible either to take away or to add anything, implying that excess and defect destroy the goodness of works of art, while the mean preserves it; and good artists, as we say, look to this in their work), and if, further, excellence is more exact and better than any art, as nature also is, then it must have the quality of aiming at the intermediate. I mean moral excellence; for it is this that is concerned with passions and actions, and in these there is excess, defect, and the intermediate. For instance, both fear and confidence and appetite and anger and pity and in general pleasure and pain may be felt both too much and too little, and in both cases not well; but to feel them at the right times, with reference to the right objects, towards the right people, with the right aim, and in the right way, is what is both intermediate and best, and this is characteristic of excellence. Similarly with regard to actions also there is excess, defect, and the intermediate. Now excellence is concerned with passions and actions, in which excess is a form of failure, and so is defect, while the intermediate is praised and is a form of success; and both these things are characteristics of excellence. Therefore excellence is a kind of mean, since it aims at what is intermediate. . . .

We must, however, not only make this general statement, but also apply it to the individual facts. . . . With regard to feelings of fear and confidence courage is the mean; of the people who exceed, he who exceeds in fearlessness has no name (many of the states have no name), while the man who exceeds in confidence is rash, and he who exceeds in fear and falls short in confidence is a coward. With regard to pleasures and pains—not all of them, and not so much with regard to the pains—the mean is temperance, the excess self-indulgence. Persons deficient with regard to the pleasures are not often found; hence such persons also have received no name. But let us call them 'insensible.'[15]

Aristotle: *Nicomachean Ethics*

10. Is Aristotle's notion of virtue (the mean between two extremes) coherent? Can all virtues be considered a mean?

Unlike some other theories of morality, Aristotle's doctrine is aspirational. It asks us to do much more than just observe minimal moral rules—it insists that we *aspire to moral excellence*, that we cultivate the virtues that will make us better persons. In this sense, his theory is goal-directed, not rule-guided. The moral virtues are ideals that we must ever strive to realize. In Aristotle's view, character is not static. We can become more virtuous by reflecting on our lives and those of others and practicing virtuous behavior.

"We become just by performing just action, temperate by performing temperate actions, brave by performing brave action."

—Aristotle

DETAILS

Aristotle's Soul

Plato has an otherworldly view of the soul: the soul is the immaterial essence of a human being, a separate entity, existing before it is imprisoned in the body and living on after the body dies. Aristotle, however, rejects this view, arguing instead for a thoroughly naturalistic soul. In his most general account of the concept, he says the soul is *the form of the body*—the characteristic way the body functions. One scholar expresses Aristotle's view like this:

Figure 5.11 According to Aristotle, the soul is not a wispy spirit dwelling in the mortal coil; it's the characteristic functions and capacities of the body. The soul is a natural object, not a paranormal or supernatural entity.

> [F]or a thing to have a soul is for it to be a natural organic body actually capable of functioning. . . . Thus Aristotle's souls are not pieces of living things, nor are they bits of spiritual stuff placed inside physical bodies; rather, they are sets of powers, sets of capacities or faculties. Possessing a soul is like possessing a skill. A carpenter's skill is not some part of him, responsible for his skilled acts; similarly, a living creature's animator or soul is not part of it, responsible for its living activities.

Accordingly we needn't ask if the soul and body are one, just as we needn't ask if ears and hearing are one, or (to use Aristotle's example) if a piece of wax and the wax's shape are one. And the perennial philosophical question of how the body and soul interact is moot.

What are some of the key differences between the soul as conceived of in the major Western religions and Aristotle's soul?

Jonathan Barnes, *Aristotle: A Very Short Introduction* (Oxford: Oxford University Press, 2000), 106–107.

WRITING AND REASONING	CHAPTER 5

1. How does Aristotle's theory of knowledge differ from Plato's? In each theory, what is the role of sense experience? What are Plato's and Aristotle's attitudes toward the everyday world? Which attitude is more reasonable? Why?

2. What is a virtue? According to Aristotle, how can we identify virtues? How are virtues related to the aim of living a good life? Do virtuous people generally live more satisfying lives than those without virtue? Explain.

3. How has Aristotle influenced modern science? Did Plato affect contemporary science in a similar way? Why or why not?

4. What is Aristotle's notion of substance? How is substance related to form and matter? Why does he reject the "pincushion" view of substance? Do you agree with him?

5. What are Aristotle's four causes? How would he characterize the four causes of a house? Do you think a horse has a final cause? Why or why not?

REVIEW NOTES

5.1 THE LIFE OF ARISTOTLE

- Aristotle was born in Stagira in Macedonia, the son of a physician, Nicomachus, who served the Macedonian king. At age seventeen or eighteen, he entered Plato's famous Academy in Athens and remained there for twenty years.
- Around the time Plato died (347 BCE), Aristotle left Athens for the western shores of Asia Minor, where he did philosophy, conducted research in marine biology, and married a woman named Pythias by whom he had a daughter.
- In 335 BCE, after being away from Athens for twelve years, he returned to found a school of philosophy and science called the Lyceum. In 323 BCE he became an object of suspicion because of his ties to Macedonia, so he fled Athens, going into exile on the Aegean island of Euboea, where he died at the age of sixty-two.

5.2 LOGIC, KNOWLEDGE, AND TRUTH

- Aristotle believes that knowledge is possible and that we can grasp objective truths about reality, but unlike Plato he thinks knowing begins with sense experience.
- With the invention of logic, Aristotle tries to clarify and systematize our acquisition of knowledge, and the heart of his deductive system is a precisely stated form of argument called the syllogism. To aid the analysis of arguments, he devised a way to lay bare the logical structure of a syllogism by using letters (variables) to stand for the terms.
- To Aristotle, scientific knowledge is not so much knowing that something is true, but knowing why it is true—knowing the explanation for a phenomenon. He says the perfect vehicle for acquiring such knowledge is the syllogism because its premises (axioms) provide the explanation or reason for the state of affairs described in

the conclusion. The axioms can be known intuitively by an immediate apprehension of the mind. Thus Aristotle's logic helps us evaluate whether a proposed explanation for a phenomenon is correct.

5.3 PHYSICS AND METAPHYSICS

• For Aristotle, the most important question in metaphysics is, What basic existing things do all other things depend on for their existence? To him, the answer must be *substance*.

• He reviews and rejects several substance theories, including the notion that substance is a featureless prime matter. He asserts that a nebulous nothing cannot be substance, and he refutes the notion that we can have no knowledge of the fundamental underlayment of reality. Ultimately, he accepts that a composite of form and matter can constitute substance, with form being the essential element that makes matter more than amorphous stuff. His kind of form is the essence of a thing.

• Aristotle argues that change is not only possible but commonplace. He says that whether change is an alteration of a thing's properties or the coming to be of a new thing, "there must be something underlying" the process. There is either a persisting thing whose properties change, or a thing out of which a new thing arises.

• Aristotle identifies four kinds of causes: material cause (a thing's material composition), formal cause (a thing's properties that make it what it is), efficient cause (the main source or initiator of a change), and final cause (what a thing is for or for what purpose it exists).

• For Aristotle, the primary explanation (the final cause) for the development of all living things is teleological—that is, the development is directed toward a natural goal or objective. Development is pointed toward particular outcomes, and in this way it unfolds according to a purpose—not purpose in the sense of intentional action or deliberation, but purpose as an internal goal toward which nature strives.

5.4 HAPPINESS, VIRTUE, AND THE GOOD

• Aristotle argues that the good life is one lived according to the light of reason and is therefore marked by true happiness. It is to live rationally and to do so excellently. To live this way, he says, is to possess the moral and intellectual virtues in full. A virtue is a disposition to behave in line with a standard of excellence; it is a choice for which we can be praised or blamed.

• He holds that a virtue is the midpoint (the "golden mean") between the extremes of excess and deficit, and the extremes are the vices. Courage, for example, is the virtue that comes midway between the vices of cowardice (too much fear) and rashness (too little fear).

KEY TERMS

deductive	formal cause	material cause	valid argument
argument	instrumental good	necessary truth	virtue
efficient cause	intrinsic good	syllogism	
final cause	invalid argument	teleology	
form	Lyceum	terms	

Notes

1. J. L. Ackrill, *Aristotle the Philosopher* (Oxford: Clarendon Press, 1981), 11.
2. Diogenes Laertius, *Lives of the Philosophers*, vol. 2, in trans. R. D. Hicks, *Diogenes Laertius* (Cambridge, MA: 1972).
3. Anthony Gottlieb, *The Dream of Reason: A History of Philosophy from the Greeks to the Renaissance* (New York: W. W. Norton, 2000), 233.
4. Aristotle, *Metaphysics* 1.1, *A New Aristotle Reader*, ed. J. L. Ackrill (Princeton, NJ: Princeton University Press, 1987), 255–256.
5. Aristotle, *Posterior Analytics* I.2.71b9, in Ackrill, *A New Aristotle Reader*, 40.
6. Aristotle, *Metaphysics*, VII.1, W. D. Ross, trans., revised by J. Barnes (Revised Oxford Aristotle, 1984), text: W. D. Ross (Oxford: Oxford University Press, 1924).
7. Aristotle, *Metaphysics*, VII.1–2, trans. Ross.
8. Aristotle, *Metaphysics*, VII.1, 3, trans. Ross.
9. Aristotle, *Metaphysics*, VII.4, 17, trans. Ross.
10. Aristotle, *Physics*, II.3, 194b23–26, Ackrill, *A New Aristotle Reader*, 98.
11. Aristotle, *Physics*, II.3, 194b29–33, Ackrill, *A New Aristotle Reader*, 98.
12. Aristotle, *Physics*, II.8, 198b34–199a9, Ackrill, *A New Aristotle Reader*, 107.
13. Aristotle, *Nicomachean Ethics*, trans. W. D. Ross (Oxford: Oxford University Press, 1908), Bk. I, chs. 1, 2, 7.
14. Aristotle, *Nicomachean Ethics*, trans. Ross, Bk. 2, ch. 2.
15. Aristotle, *Nicomachean Ethics*, trans. Ross, Bk. 2, chs. 6–7.

For Further Reading

J. L. Ackrill, *Aristotle the Philosopher* (Oxford: Oxford University Press, 1981).

J. L. Ackrill, *A New Aristotle Reader* (Princeton, NJ: Princeton University Press, 1987).

Jonathan Barnes, *Aristotle: A Very Short Introduction* (Oxford: Oxford University Press, 2000).

Jonathan Barnes, *Aristotle* [Past Masters Series] (Oxford: Oxford University Press, 1982).

Sarah Broadie and Christopher Rowe, trans., *Aristotle: Nicomachean Ethics* (Oxford: Oxford University Press, 2002).

Ted Honderich, ed., *The Oxford Companion to Philosophy* (Oxford: Oxford University Press, 1995).

Hugh Lawson-Tancred, "Ancient Greek Philosophy II: Aristotle," *Philosophy I: A Guide through the Subject*, ed. A. C. Grayling (Oxford: Oxford University Press, 1995).

Christopher Shields, ed., *The Oxford Handbook of Aristotle* (Oxford: Oxford University Press, 2012).

Mary Ellen Waithe, ed., *A History of Women Philosophers*, vol. 1, 600 BC–500 AD (Dordrecht: Martinus Nijhoff, 1987).

Online Resources

Biography.com, "Aristotle," video and notes, https://www.biography.com/scholar/aristotle

Philosophy Talk Podcasts, "Aristotle," https://www.philosophytalk.org/shows/aristotle

The Philosophy of Aristotle: Will Durant, video, https://www.youtube.com/watch?v=Yn89Jdp4mc0

Stanford Encyclopedia of Philosophy, "Aristotle," https://plato.stanford.edu/entries/aristotle

Internet Encyclopedia of Philosophy, "Aristotle (384-322 BCE)," https://www.iep.utm.edu/aristotl

History of Philosophy (without Any Gaps) Podcast, https://historyofphilosophy.net

The Perseus Digital Library, http://www.perseus.tufts.edu/hopper

CHAPTER 6

Eastern Thought

CHAPTER OBJECTIVES

6.1 HINDUISM

- Understand how Hinduism arose in India.
- Define *brahmin*, *samsara*, *atman*, *karma*, and *Brahman*.
- Identify the structure of the *Vedas* and its main components.
- Summarize the main themes of the *Upanishads*, and explain the process of *samara* and *karma* and how they relate to *atman*, *Brahman*, and *moksha*.
- Explain what the *Bhagavad-Gita* is and how it differs in content from the *Upanishads*.
- Explain the principal differences between the Hindu philosophies known as *Vedanta* and *Samkhya*.
- Discuss some of the ways that modernity has affected Hinduism.

6.2 BUDDHISM

- Discuss the main ways that the Buddha's views differed from the orthodox beliefs of the times.
- Explain the Buddha's Four Noble Truths.
- Define *anatta*, *dukkha*, *ahimsa*, and *anicca*.
- Explain the concept of nirvana and how Buddhism says it can be attained.

6.3 DAOISM

- Explain how the concept of the Dao parallels certain ideas in Western philosophy.
- Discuss the concept of *wu-wei* and how some Daoists try to integrate it into their lives.

6.4 CONFUCIANISM

- Know why Confucianism is called a humanistic doctrine, and explain what Confucius hoped his teachings would do.
- Define *li* and *ren*, and explain how these concepts fit into Confucianism.
- Define filial piety and what it means in practice to Confucians.
- Understand the Confucian attitude toward family and community, personal freedom, and individual rights.

Among the great religions of the East—Hinduism, Buddhism, Confucianism, Daoism, and others—we find just what we would expect in religious traditions: sacred texts, spiritual journeys, mystical symbols, otherworldly stories, inspired devotees, and saintly leaders. But if we look closer, we can see something else: a vibrant tradition of philosophical inquiry. The major religions of the West have had their share of philosophers, and so have the main religious traditions of the East.

Throughout the centuries Asian thinkers working inside (or alongside) their religion have addressed problems in epistemology, ethics, metaphysics, philosophy of language, and logic—all standard areas of study found in Western philosophy. The result is that, laboring independently, they have tried to provide answers to large questions that also happen to be subjects of intellectual exploration in the West. Remarkably, many of their answers parallel those given by their Western counterparts, or they entail philosophically interesting alternatives, or they challenge theories or perspectives that are widely accepted outside Asia. The Buddha taught that the self is merely a collection of attributes (not a persisting substance or soul); so did the British empiricist David Hume. Hindu thinkers have debated the worth of arguments for and against the existence of the divine; the Western philosophers Thomas Aquinas and Immanuel Kant have done the same. Confucius defended a theory of ethics and politics; Aristotle and John Locke have sailed in the same waters.

6.1 HINDUISM

Hinduism can claim to be the world's oldest living religion (dating back 3,000 years) and the third largest (with about one billion adherents). Many observers are amazed that it boasts of no common creed, founder, text, or deity. It comprises not one mode of devotion but a confounding diversity of them. Offerings to deity images, the chanting of mantras, temple worship, sensual rites, mystical experiences, ascetic privations, animal sacrifices—such practices may be embraced by some Hindus and ignored by others, but the broad tent of Hinduism accommodates them all. The sacred texts range from hymns to instructions for conducting rituals to philosophical treatises, and these are revered or disregarded to varying degrees by thousands of discrete religious groups. A Hindu may bow to many gods (polytheism), one supreme God (monotheism), one god among a whole pantheon (henotheism), or no gods whatsoever (atheism). And Hinduism's gods are said to number over a million.

The Western traditions of Christianity, Judaism, and Islam are generally faithful to a core of more or less coherent doctrines. Hinduism is different. It's a large, unwieldy family of beliefs and practices that seem reasonable and practical to Hindus but perplexing and contradictory to outsiders. Yet in the twenty-first century, this family thrives both in its mother country (India) and in foreign soil, has devotees in both the East and West, and influences the worldviews of persons high and low. And among this cacophony of views, systems of philosophical reflection and even scriptures containing philosophical speculation have their say.

"The great secret of true success, of true happiness, is this: the man or woman who asks for no return, the perfectly unselfish person, is the most successful."
—Swami Vivekananda

"In the morning I bathe my intellect in the stupendous and cosmogonal philosophy of the *Bhagavad-Gita*, in comparison with which our modern world and its literature seems puny and trivial."
—Henry David Thoreau

Beginnings

Hinduism began in northwest India, emerging from a blend of native religions and the religious traditions of an Indo-European people who migrated there from central Asia. The indigenous populace established an advanced civilization that flourished in the Indus River region and beyond as early as 2500 BCE. This Indus Valley civilization, as it is called, rivaled in many ways the Roman Empire, which was to come later. It devised a writing system, erected planned cities, and built impressive structures small and large—two-story houses, civic centers, porticos, baths, bathrooms, stairways, drainage systems, and worship halls.

Based on artifacts found in the region, scholars have hypothesized that the people were polytheistic and that some of their gods may have been forerunners of present-day Hindu deities. Many sculptures seem to have been used in worship of both gods and goddesses, and a few of these were depicted as half-human and half-animal. Evidence suggests that the inhabitants made animal sacrifices, performed ritual ablutions with water, and conducted rites where fire was the central element.

Around 1500 BCE, the migrating Indo-Europeans, called *Aryans*, moved into northwest India, carrying their distinctive culture with them. Most importantly, they brought their speech from which was derived the ancient language of Sanskrit, the medium of Hindu scripture. They too were polytheistic, worshiping gods that were thought to embody powerful elements of nature such as the sun, moon, and fire. And they sacrificed animals (including horses) and animal byproducts (such as butter and milk) as offerings to these gods.

Figure 6.1 Statue of one of India's more popular deities—Ganesha, the elephant-headed god.

Aryan culture was partitioned into four social classes called *varnas*. From these, the hereditary *caste system* was developed in Hindu society and is still holding sway in modern India, although it has been refined into thousands of subdivisions based on social and occupational criteria. Traditionally the dominant class consisted of **brahmins**, the priests and teachers who alone could study and teach scripture. Brahmins still play a priestly role and are prevalent among India's professionals and civil servants.

1. What is the caste system? Why is its existence in modern India controversial?

brahmin A priest or teacher; a man of the priestly caste.

The *Vedas*

For Hinduism, the most important result of the melding of Aryan and Indus River cultures was a set of sacred compositions known as the **Vedas** (knowledge), regarded by almost all Hindus as eternal scripture and the essential reference point for all forms of Hinduism. They were produced by the Aryans between 1500 and 600 BCE (what has been called the Vedic era), which makes these compositions India's oldest

Vedas Early Hindu scriptures, developed between 1500 and 600 BCE.

existing literature. For thousands of years the *Vedas* were transmitted orally from brahmin to brahmin until they were finally put into writing. They are said to be *sruti* (that which was heard)—revealed directly to Hindu seers (*rishis*) and presumed to be without human or divine authorship. Later scriptures are thought to be *smriti* (what is remembered)—of human authorship. These consist of commentaries and elaborations on the *sruti*. Hindus revere the *Vedas*, even though the majority of adherents are ignorant of their content, and their meanings are studied mostly by the educated. In fact, most Hindu devotional practices are derived not from the *Vedas*, but from the sacred texts that came later.

2. What is the difference between *sruti* and *smriti*? Does the difference matter much to Hindus?

The *Vedas* consist of four collections, or books, of writings, each made up of four sections. The four books are the *Rig-Veda*, the *Yajur-Veda*, the *Sama-Veda*, and

THEN AND NOW

The Caste System

Figure 6.2 Sisters who belong to the *dalit* caste in India.

Much of the social and religious landscape of modern India has been shaped by two-thousand-year-old Hindu treatises on religious, legal, and moral duty (*dharma*), the most famous being *the Laws of Manu*. (In legend, all humans are descended from Manu, the original man.) Completed by around the first century of the Common Era, the *Laws* provided the basic outlines of India's caste system, laid down a code of conduct for each social class, and marked out the four stages of life for upper-class Indian men. The *Laws*, in effect, defined the ideal Hindu society, which served as a reference point for modern laws and social rules in India today.

India's premodern Aryan culture was divided into four hierarchical classes called *varnas*, which became the basis of the four main castes of Hinduism. In later eras these divisions were refined into myriad subdivisions and hardened to forbid social movement in one's lifetime from one class to another. In modern India both the four classes and the hundreds of subdivisions are referred to as *castes*; the subdivisions are also sometimes called *jatis*. These subcastes are based on occupation, kinship, geography, even sectarian affiliation; and they are especially influential in rural areas of India. In general, caste protocol forbids members of one caste to marry members of another, and interactions with people from another caste are often restricted.

the *Atharva-Veda*. The sections are (1) *samhitas*: hymns, or chants, of praise or in-vocation to the gods (including many Aryan deities), mostly to be uttered publicly during sacrifices; (2) *brahmanas*: treatises on and how-to instructions for rituals; (3) *Aranyakas*: "forest treatises" for those who seek a reclusive religious life; and (4) the **Upanishads**: philosophical and religious speculations.

The oldest book is the *Rig-Veda*, which contains a section of over one thousand ancient hymns, each one invoking a particular god or goddess—for example, Indra (the ruler of heaven), Agni (the god of fire), and Varuna (the god of moral order in the universe). Most of the hymns in the other books are taken from the *Rig-Veda*.

There are 123 *Upanishads*, but only thirteen or fourteen (called the principal *Upanishads*) are revered by all Hindus. The *Upanishads* were added to the *Vedas* last,

Upanishads Vedic litera-ture concerning the self, Brahman, *samsara*, and liberation.

In ancient India the concepts of *dharma* and karma were central to the caste system, and the same is true today. Each caste is prescribed a *dharma*, a set of duties mandated for that caste. Theoretically no upward movement is possible during one's lifetime, but diligently performing one's *dharma* could lead to better karma and a higher-level rebirth in the next life.

Eventually the caste system was modified to include a fifth group—the "untouchables," or *dalits* (oppressed ones), who are thought to be "too polluting" to be included in any of the higher castes. This group comprises those who do "polluting" work such as sweep-ing streets; cleaning toilets; and handling leather, human waste, or dead bodies. The term "untouchables" comes from the traditional Hindu idea that upper-class persons who touch someone from the lowest class will be polluted and must therefore perform rituals to cleanse themselves. For generations *dalits* have been subjected to violence and discrimination—and they still are even in modern India and even though the untouchable class has been officially outlawed. Mohandas Gandhi called the *dalits* "the children of God" and advocated for their rights and their equal status in society.

In recent years the caste system has drawn the fire of many critics. The main complaint is that the system is inherently unfair. The plight of the *dalits* is just one example. *The Laws of Manu* mandate a lower status for the lowest class, and caste hierarchy itself implies that some people are inherently less worthy than others, or that some deserve better treatment under the law than others, or that the highest classes are privileged and therefore should get special treatment. In practice, caste rules are not as rigid, and adherence to caste rules is not as widespread as their advocates might prefer. The influence of caste in people's daily lives is weak in urban areas and much stronger in the countryside.

What do you think civil rights leader Martin Luther King, Jr. would say about India's caste system and the treatment of the *dalits*? Do you think the caste system is morally wrong? If so, what are your reasons?

Figure 6.3 Reading the Vedic texts.

"I must confess to you that when doubt haunts me, when disappointments stare me in the face, and when I see not one ray of light on the horizon, I turn to the Bhagavad Gita and find a verse to comfort me; and I immediately begin to smile in the midst of overwhelming sorrow."
—Mahatma Gandhi

samsara One's cycle of repeated deaths and rebirths.

atman One's soul or self.

karma The universal principle that governs the characteristics and quality of each rebirth, or future life.

Brahman The impersonal, all-pervading spirit that is the universe yet transcends all space and time.

asceticism The denial of physical comfort or pleasures for religious ends.

composed primarily from about 900 to 400 BCE during a time of intellectual and religious unease. The ancient certainties—the authority of the brahmins, the status of the *Vedas*, the caste system, the sacrificial rites, and the nature of the deities—were being called into question. The *Upanishads* put these issues in a different light and worked out some philosophical doctrines that became fundamental to Hinduism right up to the twenty-first century.

In the early *Vedas*, there is an emphasis on improving one's lot in life through religious practice and faith in the gods. But in the *Upanishads*, the central aim is release from this world. Specifically, the goal is liberation from **samsara**, one's repeating cycle of deaths and rebirths. The essential Hindu belief is that at death, one's soul or self (**atman**) departs from the lifeless body and is reborn into a new body, residing for a time until death, then being reborn in yet another physical form—a dreary sequence that may repeat for thousands of lifetimes. (Westerners call this the doctrine of reincarnation.) And with each new incarnation comes the pain of living and reliving all the miseries of mortal existence.

The force that regulates *samsara* is **karma**, the universal principle that governs the characteristics and quality of each rebirth, or future life. Karma is like a law of nature; it is simply the way the world works. It dictates that people's actions and intentions form their present character and determine the general nature of their future lives. Good deeds (good karma) lead to more pleasant rebirths; bad deeds (bad karma) beget less pleasant, even appalling, rebirths. Depending on karma, the *atman* may be reborn into a human, an animal, an insect, or some other lowly creature. This repeating pattern of rebirth–death–rebirth continues because humans are ignorant of the true nature of reality, of what is real and what is merely appearance. They are enslaved by illusion (*maya*) and act accordingly, with predictable results.

According to the *Upanishads*, this ignorance and its painful consequences can only be ended, and liberation (*moksha*) from *samsara* and karma can only be won, through the freeing power of an ultimate, transcendent wisdom. This wisdom comes when an *atman* realizes that the soul is not separate from the world or from other souls but is one with the impersonal, all-pervading spirit known as **Brahman**. Brahman is the universe, yet Brahman transcends all space and time.

Brahman is eternal and thus so is the *atman*. Brahman is Absolute Reality, and the *atman* is Brahman—a fact expressed in the famous adage "You are that [Brahman]," or "You are divine." The essential realization, then, is the oneness of Brahman and *atman*. Once an individual fully understands this ultimate unity, *moksha* occurs, *samsara* stops, and the *atman* attains full union with Brahman.

Achieving *moksha* is difficult, requiring great effort and involving many lifetimes through long expanses of time. The *Upanishads* stress that Brahman is ineffable—it cannot be described in words and must therefore be experienced directly through several means: meditation, various forms of yoga (both mental and physical disciplines), and **asceticism** (the denial of physical comfort or pleasures for religious ends). The aim of these practices is to look inward and discern the true nature of *atman* and its unity with Brahman. The rituals and sacrifices of the early *Vedas* are deemed superfluous.

After the *Vedas*

As noted earlier, the *sruti* scriptures of the Vedic period (roughly 1500 to 600 BCE) are thought to be of divine origin, revealed to the *rishis* who received them via an intuitive or mystical experience. Hindus regard these (the *Vedas*) as authoritative, eternal, and fixed. This canon remains as it was written, without further revelations or later emendations. But after the Vedic period, the human-authored *smriti* scriptures appeared. They too are venerated yet are considered less authoritative than the *Vedas*. They are also open-ended, a sacred work in progress. Over the centuries revered figures have added to them and continue to do so. But these facts have not diminished the influence of the *smriti* scriptures, which have probably had a greater impact on Hindu life than the *Vedas* have.

In Hindu scripture, newer writings generally do not supersede the old; they are added to the ever-expanding canon. Thus many ideas and practices found in both the *Vedas* and the post-Vedic scriptures are still relevant to contemporary Hinduism. Likewise, the ancient Vedic gods and goddesses were never entirely replaced by deities that came later in history. The pantheon was simply enlarged. Today many of the old gods are ignored or deemphasized, while some of them are still revered.

The *smriti* material is voluminous and wide-ranging. It consists mainly of (1) the epics (the *Mahabharata* and the *Ramayana*), (2) myths and legends (the *Puranas*), and (3) legal and moral codes (the *Laws of Manu*).

The great epics have served Indian and Hindu civilization much as Homer's *Iliad* and *Odyssey* served the ancient Greek and Hellenistic world: the stories express the culture's virtues, heroes, philosophy, and spiritual lessons. With eighteen voluminous chapters (or books) and one hundred thousand verses, the *Mahabharata* is the longest poem in existence, many times more extensive than the Christian Bible. Composed between 400 BCE and 400 CE, the epic recounts the ancient conflict between two great families, both descendants of the ruler of Bharata (northern India). Their struggle culminates in a fateful battle at Kurukshetra. Among the warriors who are to fight there is the war hero Arjuna, who has serious misgivings about a battle that will pit brothers against brothers and cousins against cousins. Before the fight begins, as Arjuna contemplates the bloody fratricide to come, he throws down his bow in anguish and despair. He turns to his charioteer, Krishna—who in fact is God incarnate—and asks whether it is right to fight against his own kin in such a massive bloodletting. The conversation that then takes place between Krishna and Arjuna constitutes the most famous part of the *Mahabharata*: the *Bhagavad-Gita*, the most highly venerated and influential book in Hinduism.

The seven-hundred-verse **Bhagavad-Gita** (*Song of the Lord*) is no mere war story. In dramatic fashion, it confronts the moral and philosophical questions and conflicts that arise in Hindu concepts and practice—devotion to the gods, the caste system, obligations to family, duties in time of war, the nature of the soul, the concept of Brahman, and the correct paths toward *moksha*.

3. What is the difference between the main goal in life as presented in the early *Vedas* and life's central aim as discussed in the *Upanishads*?

"The apparent multiplication of gods is bewildering at the first glance, but you soon discover that they are the same GOD. There is always one uttermost God who defies personification. This makes Hinduism the most tolerant religion in the world, because its one transcendent God includes all possible gods. In fact Hinduism is so elastic and so subtle that the most profound Methodist, and crudest idolater, are equally at home with it."

—George Bernard Shaw

4. What is the relationship between Brahman and *atman*? How are *moksha* and *samsara* related to Brahman?

Bhagavad-Gita The most highly venerated and influential scriptures in Hinduism.

Figure 6.4 A wooden statue of Krishna.

5. What is the story recounted in the *Bhagavad-Gita*? What is the *Gita's* message about the path to liberation?

"In the great books of India, an empire spoke to us, nothing small or unworthy, but large, serene, consistent, the voice of an old intelligence, which in another age and climate had pondered and thus disposed of the questions that exercise us."

—Ralph Waldo Emerson

Krishna tells Arjuna to join the battle, for a war fought for a righteous reason is permissible, even a war against one's own brothers. Arjuna has a duty to fight, Krishna says, for he must follow the dictates of his caste. A central tenet of Hinduism is that to avoid the demerits of karma, humans must do their duty according to their place in society. As a member of the warrior caste, Arjuna is obligated to take up arms.

In the *Gita*, we get a new account of the nature of God. In the *Upanishads*, Brahman is the impersonal Ultimate Reality, or World-Soul, pervading and constituting the universe but aloof from humans and their concerns. But Krishna turns out to be the Supreme Being incarnate, a personal deity who loves and cares for humans and who often takes human form to help them.

Throughout history, many Hindus have believed there is only one path to liberation—solely through meditation or only through asceticism, for example. But in the *Gita*, Krishna insists that several paths (*marga*) can lead to *moksha*, a view that fits well with modern Hinduism. (Since these paths amount to spiritual disciplines, they are also referred to as forms of *yoga*.) Today there is a general awareness of multiple paths to liberation, each appropriate for a particular kind of person.

Krishna teaches Arjuna that one path to salvation is the way of unselfish action done for duty's sake (*karma-marga*). As human beings, we cannot avoid acting. But when we do, only actions done without regard to rewards, punishments, praise, or blame can lead to liberation and union with God. We must act with detachment from these motives. Our deeds should be done with the right intention—the intention to do our duty only because it is our duty.

Another option, Krishna says, is the way of knowledge (*jnana-marga*), a path followed by those who are inclined toward intellectual pursuits. This spiritual knowledge, he says, is attained by seeing clearly into the true nature of the universe, the soul, and the Supreme Reality. It is the realization that Brahman and the human soul are in fact the same, that despite surface appearances, there is no difference between the self and Brahman, and between Brahman and the world. The self (*atman*) and the Supreme Self (*Atman*) are a unity, just as drops of water and the ocean can be a unity. The lives of humans who gain this ultimate knowledge are said to be transformed, and liberation from the cycle of death and rebirth becomes a reality. To grasp this insight, aspirants practice meditation, plunge into deep reflection, or study scripture and the words of sages.

The path to liberation that Krishna speaks of most often is devotion to a personal god (*bhakti-marga*), the path chosen by most Hindus. *Bhakti-marga* entails overwhelming love and adoration of one's favored manifestation of God. The candidates for adoration are many—Krishna, Vishnu, Shiva, Varuna, Indra, Ganesha, Kali, and many other deities. The Hindu view of *bhakti* is that to love one of these finite manifestations of God is to move closer to the infinite God of everything. Brahman is supreme but impersonal. It is difficult to adore the all-encompassing essence of all that is; it is easier to love one of God's incarnations represented in countless earthly images. Thus a Hindu may bring an offering of flowers to a stone image of Krishna and pray for help or healing, expecting that Krishna himself will be pleased and perhaps answer the plea. The devotee will feel that *moksha* is a little closer and that Brahman is a little nearer.

Hindu Philosophies

Hinduism contains complex systems, or schools (*darshana*), of philosophical reflection expressed by ancient sages and commentators. To immerse oneself in one of these is to follow the path of knowledge (*jnana-marga*), a route taken by only a minority of Hindus. The schools include six major orthodox ones, some of which appeared as far back as 500 BCE: *Samkhya* (probably the oldest), *Yoga*, *Nyaya*, *Vaisesika*, *Mimamsa*, and *Vedanta*. They all differ in important ways but presuppose the authority of the *Vedas*, accept the doctrines of reincarnation (the cycle of birth and death) and *moksha* (liberation), and set forth their doctrines in discourses, or books (*sutras*). Consider these four:

Vedanta. The term *Vedanta* means "the end of the *Vedas*" or the "culmination of the *Vedas*," suggesting that this philosophical system is based heavily on the last part of the *Vedas*, the *Upanishads*. An influential outlook in this school is known as *Advaita Vedanta*. It maintains a thoroughgoing monism (nondualism, *advaita*), claiming that reality consists not of two kinds of essential stuff (as the dualistic Samkhya school holds), but only one kind, and this kind is Brahman, who alone is real. Brahman is all, and the self is identical to Brahman. The most influential proponent of this view is Shankara (788–820 CE). He argues that people persist in believing they are separate from Brahman because of *maya*—illusion. Only by shattering this ignorance with knowledge of true reality can they escape the torturous cycle of death and rebirth.

Shankara's view is not the only Vedanta philosophy. Other early philosophers criticized Shankara's perspective and taught that separate selves have a dualistic relationship with Brahman—and yet somehow they and Brahman are a unity. Some thinkers went further, declaring that the human self and Brahman were entirely discrete entities.

Nyaya. This school has focused on developing a theory of knowledge (epistemology) and a system of logical proof that would yield indubitable truths. Nyaya thinkers applied their learning to try to discover the true nature of the universe, the self, and God. Gautama (known by some as the Aristotle of India) established the Nyaya school in ancient times and produced its foundational text, the *Nyaya Sutra*. Some early Nyaya scholars were atheistic (as was Gautama), but later ones added the concept of a supreme divinity.

"India has two million gods, and worships them all. In religion all other countries are paupers; India is the only millionaire."

—Mark Twain

Samkhya. The Samkhya school sees the world as dualistic—that is, consisting of two kinds of stuff or essences: spirit and matter. In its earlier forms, the school was atheistic in that it rejected the notion of a personal god; theistic elements were introduced later. The central concern is that myriad souls are lodged in matter and to be dislodged is to attain blissful liberation.

6. Contrast the metaphysics of the Vedanta school of philosophy with that of the Samkhya. Which one strikes you as more plausible—a monistic or dualistic world? Why?

Yoga. The Yoga school accepts the philosophical outlook of Samkhya regarding spirit, matter, and liberation but goes further in emphasizing meditative and physical techniques for binding the spirit to Brahman and thus achieving *moksha*. It also makes room for a qualified theism.

Many forms of yoga exist, the classic one being *raja* yoga, which involves working through several stages of physical, spiritual, and meditative discipline to reach a

DETAILS

Figure 6.5 The modern versus the traditional: Indian women shopping at the largest mall in India.

Hinduism and Modernity

Like other religions, Hinduism has had to contend with the forces of modernity—secularism, religious liberalism, modern values (including human rights, women's rights, free inquiry, and individual freedom), scientific progress, modern technology (including mass media), urbanization, and religious and cultural pluralism. These trends are powerful, and they have helped liberating state of consciousness. The adepts in *raja* yoga are said to be capable of extraordinary physical and mental feats. Most Westerners, however, understand yoga as *hatha* yoga, the use of physical techniques and postures for mastering the body. But this physical discipline is just one facet of liberation-oriented yoga.

6.2 BUDDHISM

Buddhism was virtually unheard of in Europe and North America until the mid-1800s, and it did not attract significant numbers of adherents in the West until the twentieth century. Now with 460 million adherents worldwide, it is the fourth-largest world religion and one of the fastest-growing religious traditions in America.

change Hinduism at its edges, but their impact has generally been less pronounced in Hinduism than in many other religions.

For example, a slow slide toward secularism is evident in the lives of some Hindus in India (especially in the large cities), but the fundamental attitudes and core values of most Hindus are probably unaffected by it. One general definition of secularism is this: the tendency of people to see their lives as not completely defined or consumed by otherworldly or supernatural concerns. Westerners generally assume that religion is only part of their lives, that important endeavors and interests exist outside the purview of religion. But to millions of Hindus, this seems wrong. Their lives and their identity are defined by their religion.

One issue that has vigorously challenged orthodox Hinduism in modern society is the role and standing of women. Hindu attitudes toward them are complicated and contradictory, and this was the case hundreds of years ago as well as today. The *Laws of Manu* say women are to be honored as spiritually powerful and auspicious goddesses who bring divine blessings to husband and home. Yet a wife's duty, or dharma, is to be faithful to her husband whom she is to worship as a god, even if he is an unfaithful lout. She must obey him, submit to his will, endure any abuse, bear him sons, and never remarry even if she is widowed. She is to be entirely dependent on him.

The rules laid down in the *Laws of Manu* were directed toward upper-caste women and were taken less seriously by the lower castes. Even among the former, some women did not adhere to Manu's decrees, choosing instead to exercise artistic, literary, religious, and financial freedom. Today many women in India have bypassed the rules to achieve extraordinary political and professional success or to chart a different understanding of their social and religious obligations. Nevertheless, the norms endorsed in the *Laws* continue to influence how Hindu society views the behavior and status of contemporary women.

Do you think the treatment of women as dictated by the *Laws of Manu* is just or unjust? Why?

It offers several metaphysical, epistemological, and moral theories and has become for many people a source of values relevant to debates about war, animal rights, the environment, capital punishment, and other issues.

Buddhist Complexities

The term *Buddhism* disguises the religion's complexities. Although Buddhists everywhere may hold in common some teachings of the Buddha, these core beliefs are few, allowing a great many meandering trails within a broad doctrinal highway. Buddhism therefore has no single set of authorized practices or a common compilation of doctrines or a universal statement of the articles of faith. Instead, there are many schools of thought and practice in Buddhism (some would say *Buddhisms*); Zen Buddhism and Tibetan Buddhism are the most familiar.

In some respects, Buddhism is the antithesis of what most people in the West think of as a religion. It posits no creator God, no all-powerful, all-knowing deity that rules the universe, takes an interest in humans, or answers prayers. It teaches that the Buddha himself was neither God nor the child of a God. He was instead the ultimate teacher and an example for all Buddhists to follow. In accordance with the Buddha's wishes, Buddhism has no central religious authority. There is no Buddhist pope; there are only the Buddha's teachings. An individual achieves salvation not through faith in God but primarily through his or her own efforts, by self-discipline and self-transformation. Buddhists must work out their own salvation.

Figure 6.6 The Great Buddha in Kamakura, Tokyo.

"Do not dwell in the past, do not dream of the future, concentrate the mind on the present moment."

—The Buddha

According to Buddhist sources, the teachings of the Buddha astonished many of his day who were used to the doctrines and practices of Indian religions. In contrast to the orthodoxies of the time, the Buddha rejected the caste system, extreme asceticism, the practice of animal sacrifice, the authority of the *Vedas*, submission to the brahmins as priests, and the existence of the soul (a permanent, unchanging identity). Contradicting the Hindu social conventions, he taught that women should not be barred from the spiritual life he proposed—they too could attain enlightenment. Contrary to doctrines of the major Western religious traditions, he was nontheistic in the sense that he had no use for the idea of a personal creator God. He believed that gods, goddesses, and demons exist, but that they are—like all other living things—finite, vulnerable, and mortal. They are trapped in the cycle of death and rebirth just as humans are. He therefore renounced religious devotion to any deity.

Buddhist scriptures point out that on some deep questions about the nature of reality—questions that most religions try to address—the Buddha was silent. He refused to conjecture about what happens after death, whether the universe was

Figure 6.7 Buddhist monks praying.

eternal, whether it was infinite, whether body and soul were the same thing, and what constitutes the divine. He taught that such speculations were pointless since they overlooked what was truly important in existence: the fact of suffering and the path of liberation from it. A person who spends his time trying to answer these imponderable questions, he said, is like a man struck by an arrow who will not pull it out until he has determined all the mundane facts about the arrow, bow, and archer—and dies needlessly while gathering the information.

7. How were the Buddha's teachings different from those in India's past?

The Buddha's Teachings

The sacred writings say the Buddha meant his teachings to be useful—to be a realistic, accurate appraisal of our burdensome existence and how to rise above it. To a surprising degree, some aspects of his approach were rational and empirical. He tried to provide a reasonable explanation for the problem of existence and offer a plausible solution. Generally he thought people should not accept his views on faith but test them through their own experience in everyday life. The Buddha declares:

Kalama Sutra

Do not believe in anything simply because you have heard it. Do not believe in traditions simply because they have been handed down for many generations. Do not believe in anything simply because it is spoken and rumored by many. Do not believe in anything simply

Kalama Sutra

because it is found written in your religious books. Do not believe in anything merely on the authority of your teachers and elders. But when, after observation and analysis, you find anything that agrees with reason, and is conducive to the good and benefit of one and all, then accept it and live up to it.[1]

Here the Buddha sounds like a philosophical skeptic and agnostic—not at all what we would expect from a religious leader.

The Buddha's system of teachings about the true nature of reality and how to live correctly to transcend it is known as the *dharma*, the heart of which is the Four Noble Truths:

1. Life is suffering.
2. Suffering is caused by desires ("craving" or "thirst").
3. To banish suffering, banish desires.
4. Banish desires and end suffering by following the Noble Eightfold Path.

The First Noble Truth is that living brings suffering and dissatisfaction, or **dukkha**. In the traditional Buddhist way of putting it, "birth is painful, old age is painful, sickness is painful, death is painful, sorrow, lamentation, dejection, and despair are painful. Contact with unpleasant things is painful, not getting what one wishes is painful."[2] *Dukkha* comes in small and large doses—from mild stress and frustration to the agonies of devastating disease and the heartbreak of overwhelming loss and grief. But in any dose, suffering and dissatisfaction are inherent in living: an inescapable cost of existence.

A fundamental element of *dukkha* is impermanence (**anicca**)—the fact that things do not last, that whatever pleasures we enjoy soon fade, that whatever we possess we eventually lose, that whatever we do will be undone by time. The very transitory nature of life brings suffering, dissatisfaction, and pain.

Dukkha also arises because of another fact of life: **anatta**, the impermanence of the self, or not-self, or no-soul. A person—the "I" that we each refer to—is merely an ever-changing, fleeting assemblage of mental states or processes. It's the belief in a permanent self that spawns "craving," greed, selfishness, and egocentrism, and these lead to misery. But facing up to the fact of no-self makes room for selflessness and compassion for the rest of the world.

The thought of not-self frightens people, but to most Buddhists, *anatta* is a very soothing doctrine. As one Buddhist monk says:

"Learning to let go should be learned before learning to get. Life should be touched, not strangled. You've got to relax, let it happen at times, and at others move forward with it."

—Ray Bradbury

dukkha The inevitable suffering and dissatisfaction inherent in existence.

anicca Impermanence; the ephemeral nature of everything.

anatta The impermanence of the self; or not-self, or no-soul.

Ajahn Sumedho

When you open the mind to the truth, then you realize there is nothing to fear. What arises passes away, what is born dies, and is not self—so that our sense of being caught in an identity with this human body fades out. We don't see ourselves as some isolated, alienated entity lost in a mysterious and frightening universe. We don't feel overwhelmed by it, trying to find a little piece of it that we can grasp and feel safe with, because we feel at peace with it. Then we have merged with the Truth.[3]

PORTRAIT

The Buddha

The traditional biographical account of the Buddha's life goes something like this: In perhaps 563 BCE (the exact year is debated by specialists), the man destined to become the Buddha is born a prince in the tiny kingdom of Sakya in northern India and given the name Siddhartha Gautama. Siddhartha means "he whose aim is accomplished," and Gautama is a family name. Later many would call him Sakyamuni, "the sage of Sakya." At age sixteen, he marries a princess, and thirteen years later they have a son, Rahula.

Figure 6.8 A statue representing the Buddha during his period of severe asceticism.

The story goes that Siddhartha's father, a ruler named Suddhodana, wants his son to succeed him, so he surrounds him with luxury and shields him from all evidence of misery in the outside world. If the prince learns that the world is full of suffering, he might be tempted to renounce his comfortable life and become a monk. But all of Suddhodana's designs fail, for at age twenty-nine the prince sees what are called the Four Passing Sights, and they change his life forever. As legend has it, he ventures beyond the palace walls several times and is shocked to see a decrepit old man, a diseased man, and a dead man. These three disturbing sights open his eyes to the unavoidable pain and impermanence of life and force him to question the meaning of it all. Then he encounters the fourth sight—a serene and detached *samana*, a wandering philosopher who had renounced all physical comforts to live as a beggar in search of the truth. Siddhartha decides that evening to lead such a life to pursue answers to the questions that haunt him. He leaves behind his wife, his son, his luxury, and his wealth to take up the alms bowl and begin his quest.

For six years he wanders about as a devoted *samana*, trying the spiritual regimens of renowned teachers, but none of the practices gives him the deep enlightenment for which he searches. So at age thirty-five Siddhartha begins to travel on what is known as the Middle Way to true wisdom—a path between self-gratification (which he practiced in his youth) and the self-mortification of asceticism. At one point he sits under a large fig tree (called the *Bodhi*, or enlightenment, tree) to meditate. According to legend, he remains under the tree all night, meditating more and more deeply yet becoming increasingly conscious and aware. Then he sees the true nature of suffering and death and how to end them forever. With this final insight, he reaches at dawn what he has been searching for—Enlightenment, or Awakening, the attainment of perfect understanding of the true nature of the universe, of life and death, and of suffering and liberation. After this momentous event, he is to be known by the title *The Buddha*, meaning "The Enlightened One" or "The Awakened One."

The Buddha preaches his first sermon in the Deer Park at present-day Sarnath. He preaches the dharma, Buddhism's core teachings systematized in the Four Noble Truths and the Noble Eightfold Path. He spends the next forty-five years walking the roads and paths of northern India, spreading his message. Finally, at the age of eighty, in the village of Kusinara, the Buddha lies down on a couch between two trees and dies calmly, uttering at the last, "And now, O priests, I take my leave of you; all the constituents of being are transitory; work out your salvation with diligence."

This focus on *dukkha* may seem like a dreary perspective on life, but it sets the stage for the Buddha's more optimistic views on the ultimate conquest of suffering. His message is not that we are doomed to unremitting suffering but that there is a way to escape our torment, to attain true and lasting happiness.

The Second Noble Truth is that the cause of *dukkha* is selfish desire (craving or thirst)—desire for things that cannot sate our thirst, that arise from our grasping egos, that we can never truly obtain no matter how hard we try. We desire possessions, pleasures, power, money, life, beliefs, ideals, and more. We want things to be different from what they are or to remain the way they are forever. But we can never have any of these for long because everything is ephemeral, constantly changing. We have no distinct, permanent identity; the "self" is no more than a locus of shifting, flowing energy. Such an insubstantial, transient thing can never acquire anything permanent, even if permanent objects exist. We desire this or that, but our desires are continually frustrated. The result is discontent, unhappiness, and pain—*dukkha*.

The Third Noble Truth is that suffering can be extinguished if selfish desire is extinguished: *dukkha* will end if self-centered craving ends. As the Buddha says:

8. What is the Buddha's doctrine of not-self or no-soul? Do you agree with it? Why or why not? What evidence could you point to that suggests the soul actually exists and is not an illusion?

Dhammacakkapparattana Sutta

Now this, O monks, is the noble truth concerning the destruction of suffering. Truly, it is the destruction of this very thirst. It is the laying aside of, the getting rid of, the being free from, the harboring no longer of this thirst. This, O monks, is the noble truth concerning the destruction of suffering.[4]

nirvana A state of bliss and well-being attained when one extinguishes the flames of desire and thus halts the repeating cycle of death and rebirth.

To quench selfish desires and therefore to end *dukkha* is to attain **nirvana**, the ultimate aim of all Buddhist practice and the liberation to which all the Buddha's teachings point. It is the extinguishing of the flames of desire (*nirvana* literally means *extinguish*) and all that accompanies it—greed, hatred, pride, delusion, and more. It is also the blossoming of contentment and inner peace; the "quietude of the heart." Buddhist scholar and monk Walpola Rahula describes it like this:

Walpola Rahula: *What the Buddha Taught*

He who has realized the Truth, Nirvana, is the happiest being in the world. He is free from all 'complexes' and obsessions, the worries and troubles that torment others. His mental health is perfect. He does not repent the past, nor does he brood over the future. He lives fully in the present. Therefore he appreciates and enjoys things in the purest sense without self-projections. He is joyful, exultant, enjoying the pure life, his faculties pleased, free from anxiety, serene and peaceful. As he is free from selfish desire, hatred, ignorance, conceit, pride, and all such 'defilements,' he is pure and gentle, full of universal love, compassion, kindness, sympathy, understanding and tolerance. His service to others is of the purest, for he has no thought of self. He gains nothing, accumulates nothing, not even anything spiritual, because he is free from the illusion of Self, and the 'thirst' for becoming.[5]

Nirvana is manifested both in life and at death. In life, it is—as Rahula suggests—a psychological and moral transformation and, ultimately, an enlightened way of living. At death, for an enlightened one, the continuing cycle, or wheel, of death and rebirth ends. *Dukkha*, the ever-recurring pain of existence, stops. And the controlling force behind the turning wheel—karma—ceases. So nirvana's quenching of "defilements" not only quenches *dukkha* in life, but it also terminates the

9. Do you agree with the Buddha that desire is the cause of suffering in the world? Why or why not?

THEN AND NOW

Buddhism and Science

Does Buddhism conflict with science? For several reasons, many Buddhists believe it does not. First, Buddhism is thought to be empirical, just as science is. The Buddha urged his followers to take nothing on faith but to test it out in their own experience. The current Dalai Lama has echoed this sentiment: "If there's good, strong evidence from science that such and such is the case and this is contrary to Buddhism, then we will change." In addition, some elements of Buddhist cosmology seem to agree, at least superficially, with ideas in modern science: every event has a cause, everything is connected or interdependent in some fundamental way, no eternally immutable objects exist (the whole cosmos is in flux). And of course the principles of Buddhist morality do not collide with science, because science is not in that line of work.

But philosophers of science would say something like this: Science's job is to test theories, and it judges the worth of theories according to certain criteria (including how well the theory fits with existing theories or evidence, how many assumptions it makes, and whether it has successfully predicted any novel phenomena). If a theory is not needed to explain a phenomenon (because science explains it better), the theory is discredited. Scientists would reject the theory that Zeus causes lightning because they have much better theories to explain lightning. By this measure, scientists would say, many Buddhist theories would be rejected—for example, hungry ghosts, demons, gods, spiritual realms, karma, and reincarnation or rebirth. And the evidence for such theories provided by the Buddhist's direct experience (meditation or mystical practice) must also be rejected. We can accept truths acquired through meditation or mysticism, says the scientist, only if they can be corroborated by our usual tests based on reason and evidence—and these truths fail the test.

How can a Buddhist respond to such allegations? Here are three ways: (1) the Buddhist can, on various grounds, deny the scientific view altogether (or large parts of it); (2) the Buddhist can agree with the scientists and reject Buddhism entirely; or (3) the Buddhist can embrace his or her religion but only after stripping out the scientifically dubious content. Some who take this last path may end up with a Buddhism that fits better with our scientific age, and some may arrive at a purely secular Buddhism, accepting only ideas that are supported, or at least not refuted, by science. The secular Buddhist, for example, may accept meditation for its scientifically proven physiological and psychological benefits and can embrace the ethical content for its moral guidance.

Do you believe that Buddhism is in serious conflict with modern science? Why?

"Many people think excitement is happiness. . . . But when you are excited you are not peaceful. True happiness is based on peace."

—Thich Nhat Hanh

"A man is not called wise because he talks and talks again; but if he is peaceful, loving and fearless then he is in truth called wise."

—Gautama Buddha

10. Is karma a coherent doctrine? What phenomena does it explain? What does it fail to explain?

repeating pattern of death–rebirth. And by attaining nirvana, one acquires the title of *arhat*, a Buddhist saint.

Beyond this profound release, what nirvana entails at one's death is uncertain. The Buddha insisted that nirvana is beyond description and impossible to imagine, for it is neither annihilation nor survival of a soul. He said that people should devote themselves to attaining it rather than trying to plumb its depths. Buddhist sources, however, refer to nirvana with words such as *freedom*, *absolute truth*, *peace*, and *bliss*.

In Buddhism, one's cycle of repeated deaths and rebirths—*samsara*—is a painful process that can go on for millennia unless there is release from it through nirvana. The thing that wanders from one life to the next (what we refer to as "I") is not an eternally existing, permanent soul, self, or *atman*, but an ever-changing mix of personality fragments that recombine in each new life. The Buddha's classic illustration of this point is a flame (the "I") that is transferred from one candle to another. Only one flame is passed among multiple candles, so there is some continuity from one candle to the next—but the flame itself is also different from moment to moment.

Karma in Buddhism is just as it is in Hinduism: it's the universal principle that determines the characteristics and quality of each future life. But unlike Hinduism, Buddhism does not posit an *atman* that is subject to karma. In the Buddha's view of karma, through their own moral choices and acts people are free to try to change their karma and its associated results, and no one is trapped in a given level of existence forever. There is always the hope of rising to a higher point through spiritual effort or of halting the cycle of rebirths altogether through nirvana.

The notions of rebirth and karma lead naturally to the Buddhist attitude of compassion, tolerance, and kindness for all living things. After all, every being must follow the karmic current, being reborn as many different creatures from the lowest to the highest. Each human being has an implied empathetic connection with all other beings (humans, animals, and others) because he or she is likely to have *been* such beings at one time or another and to have endured the same kind of pain and grief they have.

The Fourth Noble Truth says the way to extinguish selfish desires and to attain nirvana is to follow the Noble Eightfold Path. The path consists of eight factors or modes of practice whose purpose is the development, or perfection, of the three fundamental aspects of Buddhist life: *wisdom*, *moral conduct*, and *mental discipline*, or focus. The eight factors have been described as "steps," as if they should be done in order, but they are actually intended to be implemented in concert. Each one complements and enhances the others, and a complete life cultivates them all. Together they constitute a way of purposeful living that the Buddha is said to have discovered through his own experience—the "Middle Way" or "Middle Path" between the extremes of brutal asceticism and sensual self-indulgence. Here is the Buddhist view of the eight factors sorted into their three basic categories:

For the perfection of wisdom:

1. *Right understanding* is a deep understanding of the true nature of reality as revealed in the Four Noble Truths. This kind of wisdom refers not just to an intellectual grasp of the facts but, more importantly, also to profound insight that penetrates how things really are in themselves, insight gleaned experientially through a trained mind free of spiritual impediments. Right understanding entails deep awareness of the truth concerning the *dharma*, *samsara*, karma, and *dukkha*.

2. *Right thought* refers to the proper motivations underlying our thoughts and actions. Right motivations are selflessness, compassion, nonviolence, gentleness, and love. They are directed not toward a few but toward all living things. Selfishness, hatred, violence, and malice undermine spiritual progress and impede true wisdom.

ahimsa The principle of not harming living beings (often referred to as the non-harm or nonviolence principle).

For the perfection of moral conduct:

3. *Right speech* means refraining from lying, slander, gossip, unkind or rude words, malicious or abusive talk, and idle or misleading assertions. Right speech, then, is truthful, kind, and constructive, fostering harmony, trust, and honesty.

4. *Right action* involves following the Buddha's Five Precepts: refraining from (1) harming living beings (a principle known as ***ahimsa***, "non-harm" or "non-violence"), (2) taking what is not given (stealing), (3) engaging in misconduct regarding sexual or sensual pleasures, (4) lying or speaking falsely, and (5) impairing the mind with intoxicating substances. To the Buddhist, these precepts are not moral laws or commandments that demand strict adherence as if they were laid down by divine authority. They are moral ideals to strive for, affirmations to oneself for living a more compassionate, mindful life. (All Buddhists are expected to observe the Five Precepts; members of the *sangha*, the order of Buddhist monks, have additional precepts to follow.)

5. *Right livelihood* means avoiding jobs or professions that involve harming other living beings. These include occupations that traffic in weapons of war, intoxicants, and poisons; that entail the buying and selling of human beings; that cause harm or death to animals; and that involve greed, dishonesty, or deception.

Figure 6.9 In line with the doctrine of *ahimsa*, the Tibetan spiritual leader the Dalai Lama preached nonviolence after the September 11, 2001, attacks on the United States. In 2011 he seemed to modify his position, leaving open the possibility that sometimes violence is justified.

DETAILS

Buddhism and Violence

Figure 6.10 During the deadly sectarian conflict between Buddhists and Muslims in Myanmar, hundreds of stick-wielding Buddhists on motorcycles rode through the streets of Lashio.

In the West, Buddhism enjoys a reputation as the most peaceful of all religions, a tradition that is far gentler and kinder than the violence-prone religions of Western nations. After all,

"True change is within; leave the outside as it is."
—Dalai Lama XIV

For the perfection of mental discipline:

6. *Right effort* is cultivating wholesome states of mind and eliminating or minimizing unwholesome ones. It means fostering compassion, selflessness, empathy, and understanding and banishing selfish desire, hatred, attachment, and self-delusion.
7. *Right mindfulness* refers to the development of an extraordinary awareness of the functioning of one's own body and mind. It yields clear understanding of, and keen sensitivity to, one's bodily processes, emotional states, the attitudes and tendencies of the mind, and mental concepts that may help or hinder

Buddhism teaches peace, compassion, and nonviolence, and countless Buddhists exemplify these principles in their daily lives. But this very agreeable view of Buddhism is a Western misconception. Like the adherents of other traditions, Buddhists can be violent and militant, both sanctioning and committing aggressive acts.

In sixth-century China, for example, Buddhist soldiers were honored as saints for killing their enemies. In seventeenth-century Tibet, the Dalai Lama gave his blessing to a Mongol ruler's murderous assaults on his rivals. Before and during World War II, Japanese Buddhists fully supported Japan's jingoism and its imperialist wars against neighboring countries. In twenty-first century Thailand, Buddhist soldier-monks carry guns. And in Sri Lanka, a conflict has raged between Buddhists and Hindus, with brutal killings carried out on both sides.

Today the violence of our century has prompted some Buddhists to wonder if compassion and pacifism are entirely adequate responses to the brutal violence of terrorism, ethnic cleansing, and wholesale slaughter. A few Buddhists believe that military intervention in such tragedies may be warranted when all peaceful means of resolution fail. Other Buddhists see this attitude as a slippery slope toward general disregard of the Buddha's precept of nonviolence, with the result that followers of the Buddha may wage or support war.

Do you agree with some Buddhists that compassion and pacifism are adequate responses to terrorism? Or would you side with Buddhists who believe violence is sometimes warranted?

spiritual progress. To be intensely mindful of ourselves is to be delivered from harmful thoughts and desires, ignorance of our transient and insubstantial nature, and blind control of our minds by our impulses and senses.

8. *Right concentration* is the development through meditation of a sublime inner peace and profound mental tranquility. This state is attained by focusing and quieting the mind, thereby diminishing distracting emotions and taming selfish desires. To use the traditional metaphor, this kind of concentration turns the mind into a clear and calm forest pool that reflects the true nature of all things.

11. What attitude toward animals does the doctrine of *ahimsa* demand? How does it differ from *your* view?

Figure 6.11 Lao-Tzu, the presumed founder of Daoism, riding a water buffalo.

6.3 DAOISM

For two thousand years *Daoism* (or *Taoism*) has been molding Chinese culture and changing the character of religions in the East. It has both philosophical and religious sides, and each of these has many permutations. It gets its name from the impossible-to-define notion of **Dao**, which has been translated as the "Way" or the "Way of Nature." Daoism is said to have been founded by Lao-Tzu, the supposed author of the classical Daoist text the *Tao-te Ching* (Classic of the Way and Its Power), destined to become, along with Confucius' *Analects*, one of the two most respected books in Chinese writings. Scholars are unsure whether Lao-Tzu is a historical figure or a product of legend, but most agree that if Lao-Tzu was real, he probably lived in the sixth century BCE and may have been a contemporary of Confucius. The second most important text in philosophical Daoism is the *Chuang Tzu*, named after its presumed author. Regardless of their authorship, these two books laid the groundwork for a Daoist philosophy that influenced Chinese thinkers and nobles and shaped the worldviews of the Chinese right up to the present.

The Dao (pronounced *dow*) is the mysterious first principle of the universe: it is the eternal source of all that is real and the invisible process and underpinning of the world. It is the Way—the impersonal power that gives order and stability to the cosmos. Like the force of gravity, the Dao holds everything together, gives shape and structure to what is, and determines the way that everything must go. The *Chuang Tzu* characterizes the Dao as literally everything—it is the whole of all that exists, and we are of this whole. The *Chuang Tzu* asserts:

Dao The "Way" in Daoism, the mysterious first principle of the universe; the eternal source of all that is real and the underpinning of the world.

The *Chuang Tzu*

In the universe, all things are one. For him who can but realize his indissoluble unity with the whole, the parts of his body mean no more than so much dust and dirt, and death and life, end and beginning, are no more to him than the succession of day and night. They are powerless to disturb his tranquility.[6]

When it comes to the concept of the Dao, the West seems to parallel the East. The pre-Socratic Greek philosopher Heraclitus declared that there is a source of all that exists, the fount of rationality, a first principle of the cosmos that he called *logos*. And there are hints of a similar cosmic force elsewhere in Western thought—in Aristotle's Unmoved Mover, for example, and in Christianity's omnipotent God.

If the descriptions of the Dao seem obscure or perplexing, it cannot be otherwise, the Daoist would say. For the Dao is beyond words; it is "nameless" (unnameable) and thus can only be hinted at. As the *Tao-te Ching* says:

> "Knowing others is intelligence; knowing yourself is true wisdom. Mastering others is strength; mastering yourself is true power. If you realize that you have enough, you are truly rich."
>
> —Lao-Tzu

Tao-te Ching

The way that cannot be spoken of
Is not the constant way;
The name that can be named
Is not the constant name.
The nameless was the beginning of heaven and earth;
The named was the mother of the myriad creatures. . . .
There is a thing confusedly formed,
Born before heaven and earth.
Silent and void
It stands alone and does not change,
Goes round and does not weary.
It is capable of being the mother of the world.
I know not its name
So I style it "the way."
I give it the makeshift name of "the great."[7]

A fundamental notion in Daoism is that since everything and everyone is subject to the power of the Dao, since nothing can withstand its inexorable flow, the best human life is one lived in harmony with it. To live well is to go with the current of the Dao; to struggle against the stream is to invite discord, strife, and woe. The good Daoist, then, discerns the way of nature, the "grain of the universe," and lets the cosmic order guide his or her life.

Living in harmony with the Dao means realizing the virtue of *wu-wei*—active inaction, or effortless action. This paradoxical attitude does not amount to passivity or apathy. According to some scholars, it suggests acting effortlessly without straining or struggling and without feverish obsession with the objects of desire. To others it implies acting naturally, spontaneously, without predetermined ideas of how things should go. Thus the Daoist does not try to take charge of a problem, for that often just makes matters worse. She instead acts instinctively and efficiently, letting the solution unfold naturally, waiting for the right moment, harnessing the flow of the Dao by using the natural momentum in the situation,

12. How does Daoism differ from Confucianism?

letting change happen by doing nothing. The Daoist is wise like the fighter who rolls with a punch, using its force to come round and return the blow, expending almost no energy of her own. In either interpretation, the point is not to interfere with nature but to let nature follow its own path.

Daoists differ on exactly what practices *wu-wei* implies. To many it suggests a rejection of worldly pleasures or a disregard for society and its conventions and values (like those stressed in Confucianism). The *Tao-te Ching* makes explicit this abhorrence of regimented life:

> "A man with outward courage dares to die; a man with inner courage dares to live."
>
> —Lao-Tzu

Tao-te Ching

> Exterminate the sage, discard the wise,
> And the people will benefit a hundredfold;
> Exterminate benevolence, discard rectitude,
> And the people will again be filial;
> Exterminate ingenuity, discard profit,
> And there will be no more thieves and bandits.
> These three, being false adornments, are not enough
> And the people must have something to which they can attach themselves:
> Exhibit the unadorned and embrace the uncarved block,
> Have little thought of self and as few desires as possible.[8]

To some Daoists, *wu-wei* implies the opposite: a Daoism consistent with the demands of everyday life and Confucian values.

Lao-Tzu says that even in matters of governance, struggle and strain are useless, but *wu-wei* accomplishes much:

Tao-te Ching

> Govern the state by being straightforward;
> Wage war by being crafty;
> But win the empire by not being meddlesome.
> How do I know that it is like that?
> By means of this.
> The more taboos there are in the empire
> The poorer the people;
> The more sharpened tools the people have
> The more benighted the state;
> The more skills the people have
> The further novelties multiply;
> The better known the laws and edicts
> The more thieves and robbers there are.
> Hence the sage says,
> I take no action and the people are transformed of themselves;
> I prefer stillness and the people are rectified of themselves;
> I am not meddlesome and the people prosper of themselves;
> I am free from desire and the people of themselves become simple like the uncarved block.[9]

In the *Tao-te Ching*, *wu-wei* seems to imply a nearly invisible, hands-off, small-scale government. The job of the wise ruler is to shield the people from excessive regulation, overbearing laws and decrees, and unsettling ideas. Such policies may bring people closer to the natural order, but they have also been criticized as a recipe for despotism.

6.4 CONFUCIANISM

Confucianism is a school of thought that arose out of ancient China and, along with Daoism, has been a dominant philosophical system there for hundreds of years. Its effect on Chinese and East Asian life, culture, and government has been enormous—comparable to the influence of Christianity, Judaism, and Islam in the West. Until the early twentieth century, Confucian virtues and training were required of anyone entering Chinese civil service, and even now, under Communist rule, China holds to its Confucian roots in everyday life. Elsewhere in the East (especially in South Korea, Japan, and Vietnam), Confucian ethics and ideals have remodeled society, providing moral underpinning and guidance to social relationships at all levels.

> "By three methods we may learn wisdom: First, by reflection, which is noblest; second, by imitation, which is easiest; and third by experience, which is the bitterest."
>
> —Confucius

Part of the appeal of Confucianism is that in times of ideological confusion it has offered plausible answers to essential philosophical questions: What kind of person should I be? What kind of society is best? What are my moral obligations to my family, those who rule, and the rest of humanity? In the twenty-first century, millions of people are attracted to the answers supplied by this two-thousand-year-old tradition.

Many of the elements of Confucianism were part of Chinese culture long before Confucius arrived on the scene. In fact, he claimed merely to transmit the wisdom of the ancients to new generations, but what he transmitted plus what he added became the distinctive Confucian worldview. From early Chinese civilization came the Confucian emphasis on rituals and their correct performance; the veneration of ancestors; social and cosmic harmony; virtuous behavior and ideals; and the will of Heaven (or *Tian*), the ultimate power and organizing principle in the universe.

Into this mix of characteristically Eastern ideas and practices, there appeared in 551 BCE the renowned thinker we call Confucius (Westernized spelling), otherwise known as K'ung Ch'iu or as K'ung Fu-tzu (Master K'ung). According to legend and very sketchy information about his life, he was born to a poor family in the tiny Chinese state of Lu. He served briefly at age fifty in the Lu government as police commissioner, and during the next thirteen years he visited

Figure 6.12 Confucius (551–479 BCE).

other Chinese states trying to persuade the rulers to implement his philosophy of wise government. One leader after another turned him down. He spent the rest of his life teaching his philosophy and contributing to the Confucian works known as the *Five Classics*. He died in 479 BCE without his ideas achieving wide acceptance. Only later did his views become a major influence.

Confucianism, especially later forms of it, has always featured some religious or divine aspects. Confucius himself believed in the supreme deity Heaven, asserting that we should align ourselves with its will. But in general he veered away from the supernatural beliefs of the past, for his main interest was teaching a humanistic doctrine centered on social relationships. His aim was the creation of harmony and virtue in the world—specifically in individuals, in the way they interacted with one another, and in how they were treated by the state. He saw his teachings as a remedy

DETAILS

The Confucian Canon

Figure 6.13 Part of a Tang Dynasty manuscript of Confucius' *Analects*, discovered in 1967.

The teachings of Confucianism are found in a vast assemblage of writings that date back centuries and have probably been as revered in the East as the Bible has been in the West (although the Confucian texts are considered the work of men, not God). The heart of the canon consists of two sets of texts—the *Five Classics* and the *Four Books*. They contain Confucian teachings and perhaps some of Confucius' words, but scholars now think that even though he may have borrowed from them or edited some of them, he probably did not write them. We possess many of Confucius' sayings because we have a putative record of his conversations with his students (in the *Analects*).

for the social disorder, corruption, and inhumanity existing all around him, from the lowest levels of society to the highest.

In Confucianism, the ideal world is generated through the practice of *li* and *ren*. **Li** has several meanings, including ritual, etiquette, principle, and propriety, but its essence is conscientious behavior and right action. To follow *li* is to conduct yourself in your dealings with others according to moral and customary norms, and to act in this way is to contribute to social stability and harmony. **Ren** is about social virtues; it encompasses benevolence, sympathy, kindness, generosity, respect for others, and human-heartedness. At its core is the imperative to work for the common good and to recognize the essential worth of others regardless of their social status. The expression of these virtues is governed by the notion of reciprocity (*shu*), what has been called Confucius' (negative) golden rule: "Never do to others what you would not

li In early Confucianism, ritual, etiquette, principle, and propriety; conscientious behavior and right action.

ren The essential Confucian virtues, including benevolence, sympathy, kindness, generosity, respect for others, and human-heartedness.

The *Five Classics*:

- *The Book of History* (or *Historical Documents*)—A history of ancient Chinese rulers and their kingdoms, with commentary on moral issues and a discussion of the principles of good government.
- *The Book of Changes* (*I Ching*)—A how-to guide for the practice of divination, plus metaphysical conjecture.
- *The Book of Poetry* (or *Book of Songs*)—An ancient anthology of 305 songs, some of which were allegedly chosen by Confucius.
- *The Book of Rites*—An ancient compendium of instructions and rules regarding ceremonies for the nobility.
- *Springs and Autumns*—A history of the Chinese state of Lu, where Confucius was born, highlighting moral and political decay.

The *Four Books*:

- The *Analects*—A compilation of the sayings of Confucius and his students, focusing on virtue and harmony in individuals and society.
- The *Great Learning*—An account of the education and self-cultivation required to become a morally noble person.
- The *Doctrine of the Mean*—A philosophical discussion of how human nature is linked to the cosmos and how achieving balance in one's life aligns one with the cosmic order.
- The *Book of Mencius*—A compilation of the teachings of Mencius, a Confucian philosopher who arrived on the scene long after Confucius and who sought to produce a complete and coherent account of Confucianism.

The Confucian canon is not thought to be the inspired words of God, yet Confucianists seem to revere it as much as Christians revere the Bible. What is the best explanation of the Confucianists' devotion to their texts?

Analects Confucian text containing the conversations of Confucius and his followers.

like them to do to you."[10] (The Christian golden rule is stated positively: "Do unto others as you would have them do unto you.")

Confucius urges people not merely to try to live according to *li* and *ren* but to excel at such a life, to become a "superior person" (a *junzi*), a noble. Contrary to history and custom, Confucius' idea of nobility has nothing to do with noble blood; true nobility, he says, comes from noble virtues and wisdom, which anyone can acquire. He refers to a man who embodies this kind of nobility as a *gentleman*. We get a glimpse of the gentleman in the **Analects**, the main Confucian text:

Analects

Tzu-kung asked about the true gentleman. The Master [Confucius] said, He does not preach what he practises till he has practised what he preaches. . . .

The Master said, A gentleman can see a question from all sides without bias. The small man is biased and can see a question only from one side.

The Master said, the Ways of the true gentleman are three. I myself have met with success in none of them. For he that is really Good is never unhappy, he that is really wise is never perplexed, he that is really brave is never afraid. Tzu-kung said, That, Master, is your own Way!

Tzu-lu asked about the qualities of a true gentleman. The Master said, He cultivates in himself the capacity to be diligent in his tasks . . . The Master said, He cultivates in himself the capacity to ease the lot of other people . . . The Master said, He cultivates in himself the capacity to ease the lot of the whole populace.[11]

13. Consider the Confucian emphasis on the noble or superior person. Do you think striving to become such a person is a laudable goal? Would it decrease or increase the enjoyment of life?

"To be wealthy and honored in an unjust society is a disgrace."

—Confucius

So living by *li* and *ren* requires self-cultivation and action—learning the moral norms, understanding the virtues, and acting to apply these to the real world. Being a superior person, then, demands knowledge and judgment as well as devotion to the noblest values and virtues.

In Confucianism, individuals are not like atoms: they are not discrete, isolated units of stuff defined only by what they're made of. Individuals are part of a complex lattice of social relationships that must be taken into account. So in Confucian ethics, *ren* tells us what virtues apply to social relationships generally, and the text called the "Five Relationships" details the most important connections and the specific duties and virtues associated with particular relationships. These relationships are between parent and child, elder brother and younger brother, husband and wife, elder and junior, and ruler and subject. Harmony will pervade society, says Confucius, when (1) parents provide for their children, and children respect and obey their parents and care for them in their old age; (2) when elder brothers look after younger brothers, and the younger show deference to the elder; (3) when husbands support and protect wives, and wives obey husbands and tend to children and household; (4) when elders show consideration for the younger, and the younger respect and heed elders; and (5) when rulers care for and protect subjects, and subjects are loyal to rulers.

The relationship on which all others are based is that of parent and child or, as Confucius would have it, father and son. The son owes the father respect, obedience, and support—an obligation that Confucianism calls "filial piety." The central feature of this relationship is that it is hierarchical. Father and son are not equal partners; the son is subordinate. The other four relationships are also hierarchical, with the wife subordinate to the husband, the younger brother to the older, the junior to the elder, and the subject to the ruler. And as in filial piety, the subordinates have a duty of obedience and respect, and the superiors are obligated to treat the subordinates with kindness and authority, as a father would. Confucius believes that if everyone conscientiously assumes his or her proper role, harmony, happiness, and goodness will reign in the land.

On filial piety, Confucius had this to say:

Meng I Tzu asked about the treatment of parents. The Master said, Never disobey! When Ch'ih was driving his carriage for him, the Master said, Meng asked me about the treatment of parents and I said, Never disobey! Fan Ch'ih said, In what sense did you mean it? The Master said, While they are alive, serve them according to ritual. When they die, bury them according to ritual and sacrifice to them according to ritual. . . .

Tzu-yu asked about the treatment of parents. The Master said, 'Filial sons' nowadays are people who see to it that their parents get enough to eat. But even dogs and horses are cared for to that extent. If there is no feeling of respect, wherein lies the difference?[12]

The virtue of filial piety is still a strong force in China today, as this scholar explains:

John B. Noss: *A History of the World's Religions*

In China, loyalty to the family has been one's first loyalty. No lad in China ever comes of age, in the Western sense. It is still true that his whole service is expected to be devoted to the family until death, and he is expected to obey his father and, when his father dies, his eldest

"At fifteen I set my heart upon learning.

At thirty, I had planted my feet firm upon the ground.

At forty, I no longer suffered from perplexities.

At fifty, I knew what were the biddings of Heaven.

At sixty, I heard them with docile ear.

At seventy, I could follow the dictates of my own heart; for what I desired no longer overstepped the boundaries of right."

—Confucius

Analects

14. Is the Confucian prescription for harmony likely to be fully implemented in Western countries? That is, could there ever be a democratic, capitalist, consumer society that was also strictly Confucian?

"The noble-minded are calm and steady. Little people are forever fussing and fretting."

—Confucius

brother, with a perfect compliance. This has meant in the past that every father has a great and grave responsibility to fulfill toward his family. He must seek to produce virtue in his sons by being himself the best example of it. The fact that the present communist government speaks of making itself "father and elder brother" and claims for itself the first loyalty of every citizen has not totally invalidated the personal virtue of filial piety in the context of family life.[13]

Today the influence of the Confucian virtue of filial piety helps explain why there is in much of Asia a greater emphasis on meeting obligations to family, community, and state than on ensuring individual rights and personal freedom.

WRITING AND REASONING   CHAPTER 6

1. What kind of society would you prefer to live in—one based on the Confucian notion of filial piety or one focused on individual freedom and rights? Why?

2. What is your opinion of the Buddhist doctrines of karma and rebirth? Do they seem plausible? What is your judgment based on personal experience, faith, science, and philosophical or logical considerations?

3. Do you agree with some critics of Hinduism that the caste system is inherently unjust? Why or why not?

4. What are some of the practical implications of living according to the Four Noble Truths? In other words, what would your life be like if you based all your actions on these Truths? Would you prefer a life like this compared to your life now? Why or why not?

5. What is the ultimate goal in life according to Daoism? According to Confucianism? Which view seems more reasonable to you? Why?

REVIEW NOTES

6.1 HINDUISM

- The *Vedas* are regarded by almost all Hindus as eternal scripture and the essential reference point for all forms of Hinduism. They are India's oldest existing literature. Hindus revere the *Vedas*, even though the majority of adherents are ignorant of their content, and their meanings are studied mostly by the educated.

- In the early *Vedas*, there is an emphasis on improving one's lot in life through religious practice and faith in the gods. But in the *Upanishads*, the central aim is release from this world. Specifically, the goal is liberation from *samsara*. The essential Hindu belief is that at death, one's soul or self (*atman*) departs from the lifeless body and is reborn into a new body, residing for a time until death, then being reborn in yet another physical form—a dreary sequence that may repeat for thousands of lifetimes.

- The *Upanishads* say that release from *samsara* can only come through the freeing power of a transcendent wisdom, which comes when an *atman* realizes the soul is not separate from the world or from other souls but is one with the impersonal, all-pervading Spirit known as Brahman.

- The *Bhagavad-Gita* confronts the moral and philosophical questions and conflicts that arise in Hindu concepts and practice—devotion to the gods, the caste system, obligations to family, duties in time of war, the nature of the soul, the concept of Brahman, and the correct paths toward *moksha*. Unlike the *Upanishads*, the *Gita* insists that several paths can lead to *moksha*, a view that fits well with modern Hinduism.

6.2 BUDDHISM

- Buddhism posits no creator God, no all-powerful, all-knowing deity that rules the universe, takes an interest in humans, or answers prayers. It teaches that the Buddha himself was neither God nor the child of a God. He was instead the ultimate teacher and an example for all Buddhists to follow.

- The Buddha rejected the caste system, extreme asceticism, the practice of animal sacrifice, the authority of the *Vedas*, submission to the Brahmins as priests, and the existence of the soul (a permanent, unchanging identity). He taught that women should not be barred from the spiritual life he proposed. He was nontheistic in the sense that he had no use for the idea of a personal creator God.

- The Buddha's teachings are known as the *dharma*, the heart of which is the Four Noble Truths: (1) Life is suffering. (2) Suffering is caused by desires. (3) To banish suffering, banish desires. (4) Banish desires and end suffering by following the Noble Eightfold Path.

- The ultimate aim of all Buddhist practice and the liberation to which all the Buddha's teachings point is known as nirvana. It is the extinguishing of the flames of desire and all that accompanies it—greed, hatred, pride, delusion, and more.

6.3 DAOISM

- Daoism gets its name from the impossible-to-define notion of Dao, which has been translated as the "Way" or the "Way of Nature." Daoism is said to have been founded by Lao-Tzu, the supposed author of the classical Daoist text the *Tao-te Ching* (*Classic of the Way and Its Power*), destined to become, along with Confucius' *Analects*, one of the two most respected books in Chinese writings.

- A fundamental notion in Daoism is that since everything and everyone is subject to the power of the Dao, the best human life is one lived in harmony with it. To live well is to go with the current of the Dao; to struggle against the stream is to invite discord, strife, and woe.

- Living in harmony with the Dao means realizing the virtue of *wu-wei*—active inaction, or effortless action. It can mean acting effortlessly without straining or struggling and without feverish obsession with the objects of desire. Or it may suggest acting naturally, spontaneously, without predetermined ideas of how things should go.

6.4 CONFUCIANISM

- Confucianism is a school of thought that arose out of ancient China and, along with Daoism, has been a dominant philosophical system there for hundreds of years. Its effect on Chinese and East Asian life, culture, and government has been enormous—comparable to the influence of Christianity, Judaism, and Islam in the West.

- Confucius veered away from the supernatural beliefs of the past, for his main interest was teaching a humanistic doctrine centered on social relationships. His aim was the creation of harmony and virtue in the world—specifically in individuals, in the way they interacted with one another, and in how they were treated by the state.

- *Li* has several meanings, including ritual, etiquette, principle, and propriety, but its essence is conscientious behavior and right action. To follow *li* is to conduct yourself in your dealings with others according to moral and customary norms. *Ren* is about social virtues; it encompasses benevolence, sympathy, kindness, generosity, respect for others, and human-heartedness. At its core is the imperative to work for the common good and to recognize the essential worth of others regardless of their social status.

- Confucius urges people not merely to try to live according to *li* and *ren* but to excel at such a life, to become a "superior person," a noble. Confucius says that true nobility comes from noble virtues and wisdom, which anyone can acquire.

KEY TERMS

ahimsa	*atman*	*dukkha*	*ren*
Analects	*Bhagavad-Gita*	karma	*samsara*
anatta	Brahman	*li*	*Upanishads*
anicca	brahmins	nirvana	*Vedas*
asceticism	Dao		

Notes

1. *Anguttara Nikaya, Kalama Sutra*, in *The Book of Gradual Sayings*, 5 vols., trans. F. L. Woodward and E. M. Hare, (London: PTS), 1932–36.
2. E. J. Thomas, trans., "Pali Sermons, the First Sermon," in *Samyutta*, V, 420 (London: Kegan Paul International, 1935), 29–31.

3. Ajahn Sumedho, cited in *Buddha-Nature*, ed. Satnacitto Bhikku (London: World Wide Fund for Nature, 1989).

4. *Dhammacakapparattana Sutta*, 1–8, in *Buddhist Sutta*: *Sacred Books of the East*, trans. T. W. Rhys Davids (Oxford: Oxford University Press, 1881), 146–155.

5. Walpola Rahula, *What the Buddha Taught* (New York: Grove Press, 1979), 43.

6. *Chuang Tzu*, 7. 18b; Richard Welhelm, Dschuang Dsi (Jena: Diederichs, 1912), 158.

7. *Tao Te Ching*, 1, 25, trans. D. C. Lau (New York: Penguin Classics, 1963).

8. *Tao Te Ching*, 19, trans. Lau.

9. *Tao Te Ching*, 57, trans. Lau.

10. *Analects*, 15: 23, *The Analects of Confucius*, trans. Arthur Waley (New York: Macmillan, 1939).

11. *Analects*, 2: 13–14, 14: 30, 14: 45, trans. Waley.

12. *Analects*, 2: 5, 7, trans. Waley.

13. John B. Noss, *A History of the World's Religions* (New York: Macmillan, 1994), 323.

For Further Reading

Satnacitto Bhikku, ed., *Buddha-Nature* (London: World Wide Fund for Nature, 1989).

Herrlee G. Creel, *What Is Taoism?* (Chicago: University of Chicago Press, 1970).

Peter Harvey, *An Introduction to Buddhism*: *Teachings, History and Practices* (Cambridge: Cambridge University Press, 1990).

Christmas Humphreys, *Zen Buddhism* (New York: MacMillan, 1971).

W. J. Johnson, trans., *The Bhagavad Gita* (Oxford: Oxford University Press, 1994).

W. J. Johnson, *The Oxford Dictionary of Hinduism* (Oxford: Oxford University Press, 2009).

Damien Keown, *Buddhism*: *A Very Short Introduction* (Oxford: Oxford University Press, 1996).

Kim Knott, *Hinduism*: *A Very Short Introduction* (Oxford: Oxford University Press, 1998).

David Levinson, ed., *Religion*: *A Cross-Cultural Dictionary* (New York: Oxford University Press, 1996).

Donald W. Mitchell, *Buddhism*: *Introducing the Buddhist Experience* (New York: Oxford University Press, 2008).

Jennifer Oldstone-Moore, *Confucianism*: *Origins, Beliefs, Practices, Holy Texts, and Sacred Places* (New York: Oxford University Press, 2002).

Patrick Olivelle, trans., *Upanishads* (Oxford: Oxford University Press, 1996).

Willard G. Oxtoby, ed., *World Religions: Eastern Traditions* (Oxford: Oxford University Press, 2002).

Walpola Rahula, *What the Buddha Taught* (New York: Grove Press, 1979).

Huston Smith, *The World's Religions* (San Francisco: HarperSanFrancisco, 1991).

Robert E. Van Voorst, ed., *Anthology of World Scriptures* (Belmont, CA: Wadsworth, 2006).

Lewis Vaughn, *Anthology of World Religions* (New York: Oxford University Press, 2017).

F. L. Woodward and E. M. Hare, trans., *The Book of Gradual Sayings*, 5 vols. (London: PTS, 1932–36).

Online Resources

Hinduism Today Magazine, "What Is Hinduism?" hinduismtoday.com

Religion Facts, "Hinduism," http://www.religionfacts.com/hinduism

Buddhanet.net, "Basic Buddhism Guide," http://www.buddhanet.net/e-learning/basic-guide.htm

Internet Encyclopedia of Philosophy, "Daoist Philosophy," http://www.iep.utm.edu/daoism

Daoist Studies, "Daoism and Daoist Studies," http://www.daoiststudies.org

Internet Encyclopedia of Philosophy, "Confucianism," https://en.wikipedia.org/wiki/Confucianism

CHAPTER 7

The Hellenistic Era

CHAPTER OBJECTIVES

7.1 EPICURUS

- Define *Hellenistic era*, *hedonism*, *Epicureanism*, and *atomism*.
- Explain what Epicureanism is and how it differs from popular misconceptions of it.
- Understand Epicurus' concept of pleasure and why unrestrained pleasure is to be avoided.
- Know why Epicurus says that death and the gods are nothing to fear.
- Explain why Epicurus thinks that pleasure is our ultimate aim.

7.2 EPICTETUS

- Define *Stoicism*.
- Explain why Stoicism has been so important in the history of philosophy.
- Summarize the historical beginnings of Stoicism and the facts of Epictetus' life.
- Understand why Stoicism maintains that people of true Stoic virtue cannot be wounded by things external to their souls.
- Explain the Stoic observation that some things are and are not up to us, and how the notion supports Stoicism.
- Respond to the claim that the Stoic ideal is total impassiveness.

7.3 SEXTUS EMPIRICUS

- Define *skepticism* and *appearances*.
- Explain the distinction between appearances and reality.
- Understand how skeptics can maintain their skepticism and still live a normal life.
- Critically examine at least five of Sextus' ten arguments for skepticism.

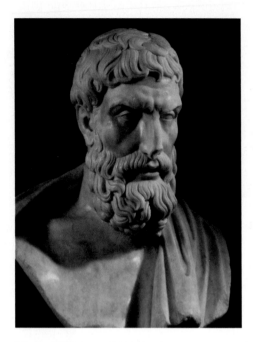

Figure 7.1 Epicurus (341–271 BCE).

Hellenistic era The period from the death of Alexander in 323 BCE to the end of the Roman Republic in 31 BCE in which Epicureanism, Stoicism, and skepticism flourished.

Epicureanism The philosophy of Epicurus; the view that life's highest aim is happiness attained through moderate pleasures and the avoidance of mental disturbance.

hedonism The doctrine that pleasure is the supreme good.

In 323 BCE Alexander the Great—the conqueror of Syria, Asia Minor, Egypt, Babylonia, Persia, the Punjab, and more—died in Babylon, leaving his vast empire without a supreme ruler. His generals divided up the conquered lands and ruled them as separate kingdoms. By scholarly agreement, Alexander's death signifies the beginning of a new age in philosophy known as the **Hellenistic era**, which ends three hundred years later in 31 BCE when the Roman Republic dissolves and the Roman Empire emerges. In this period, the language and culture of Greece that Alexander had seeded into his empire (mostly through the many cities he had founded in his name) was further propagated by his generals, suffusing all things Greek throughout the known world. Hence the name Hellenistic from *Hellene*, which means "Greek."

This age is known for the three philosophical movements that dominated philosophical debate and seeped into popular consciousness: Epicureanism, Stoicism, and skepticism. These philosophies competed with new cults from the East and the old beliefs in magic, divination, astrology, mysticism, ancestor worship, god-kings, sacred mysteries, and messiahs. But they held their own, partly because they were meant to have universal, not just local, appeal, and because they emphasized ethics and practical wisdom for living over metaphysics and logic, the lofty spheres of Plato and Aristotle. All three were philosophies of life, and all three were motivated toward the same object: peace of mind and freedom from disturbance.

7.1 EPICURUS

The Greek philosopher Epicurus (341–271 BCE) is considered the founder of **Epicureanism**, the hedonistic theory that life's highest aim is happiness attained through moderate pleasures and the avoidance of mental disturbance. **Hedonism** is the doctrine that pleasure is the supreme good, a perspective that many others after Epicurus also maintained (including, for example, the utilitarian philosophers Jeremy Bentham and John Stuart Mill). But Epicurus' hedonism is of a peculiar kind and is often misunderstood. Contrary to popular myth, he did not propose what Epicureanism has sometimes been taken to mean: recklessly sensual, overindulgent living. He believed that the true life of pleasure consists in an attitude of imperturbable emotional calm that needs only simple pleasures, a sensible diet, a prudent moral life, and good friends. As he puts it:

Epicurus: *Letter to Menoeceus*

When, therefore, we maintain that pleasure is the end, we do not mean the pleasures of profligates and those that consist in sensuality, as is supposed by some who are either

Figure 7.2 Ancient Athens. A ritual procession in which citizens bring a new robe to the goddess Athena.

ignorant or disagree with us or do not understand, but freedom from pain in the body and from trouble in the mind. For it is not continuous drinkings and revellings, nor the satisfaction of lusts, nor the enjoyment of fish and other luxuries of the wealthy table, which produce a pleasant life, but sober reasoning, searching out the motives for all choice and avoidance, and banishing mere opinions, to which are due the greatest disturbance of the spirit.[1]

1. Would Epicurus advocate gluttony? How about college keg parties? Why or why not?

Epicurus was born at Samos, went to Athens at age eighteen for military and civilian service, then spent several years setting up Epicurean communities in the Greek islands. Finally in 306 BCE he returned to Athens, where he established an Epicurean school known as the Garden. In contrast to the prejudices of the times, Epicurus opened his school to everyone—women, slaves, and aristocrats included. The Garden, however, was more than a school. It was, in fact, an Epicurean community dedicated to simple living, the study of philosophy, and friendship, as well as a withdrawal from politics. Epicurus spent all his remaining years there.

He was an impressively productive writer, perhaps penning as many as three hundred books. But very little of his work survives. We have only three letters, some maxims, and a few fragments gleaned from a deteriorated papyrus containing his greatest work, *On Nature*. What we know about his philosophy is largely based on the writings of his adherents and on the masterwork *On the Nature of Things*, a treatise in verse by the philosopher-poet Lucretius (100–55 BCE), a devoted Epicurean.

> "Do not spoil what you have by desiring what you have not; remember that what you now have was once among the things you only hoped for."
> —Epicurus

> "If God listened to the prayers of men, all men would quickly have perished: for they are forever praying for evil against one another."
> —Epicurus

2. Why does Epicurus say that pleasure is our ultimate aim?

For Epicurus, pleasure is primarily an absence of pain, rather than a quantity of satisfaction or enjoyment. A good life is a life free of trouble, and the chief aim of each person should be to attain this kind of tranquility. That pleasure is our ultimate good is plain, he says. for all people everywhere seek it:

Epicurus: *Letter to Menoeceus*

And for this cause we call pleasure the beginning and end of the blessed life. For we recognize pleasure as the first good innate in us, and from pleasure we begin every act of choice and avoidance, and to pleasure we return again, using the feeling as the standard by which we judge every good.[2]

But not all pleasures are created equal, and although all pleasures are good, they are not all to be pursued:

Epicurus: *Letter to Menoeceus*

And since pleasure is the first good and natural to us, for this very reason we do not choose every pleasure, but sometimes we pass over many pleasures, when greater discomfort accrues to us as the result of them: and similarly we think many pains better than pleasures, since a greater pleasure comes to us when we have endured pains for a long time. Every pleasure then because of its natural kinship to us is good, yet not every pleasure is to be chosen: even as every pain also is an evil, yet not all are always of a nature to be avoided. Yet by a scale of comparison and by the consideration of advantages and disadvantages we must form our judgement on all these matters. For the good on certain occasions we treat as bad, and conversely the bad as good.[3]

"Death does not concern us, because as long as we exist, death is not here. And when it does come, we no longer exist."

—Epicurus

There are physical pains and mental pains, Epicurus says, and the worst of them are mental. Specifically, the worst kind of mental pains, or disturbances of the mind, are fears engendered by false beliefs about death or the afterlife and about the gods. When these things are seen for what they really are, the fears dissolve.

As for death, Epicurus asserts that we should

Epicurus: *Letter to Menoeceus*

[b]ecome accustomed to the belief that death is nothing to us. For all good and evil consists in sensation, but death is a deprivation of sensation. And therefore a right understanding that death is nothing to us makes the mortality of life enjoyable, not because it adds to an infinite span of time, but because it takes away the craving for immortality. For there is nothing terrible in life for the man who has truly comprehended that there is nothing terrible in not living.... So death, the most terrifying of ills, is nothing to us, since so long as we exist, death is not with us; but when death comes, then we do not exist.[4]

atomism The belief that reality consists of an infinite number of minute, indivisible bits called atoms moving rapidly in an infinite void, or empty space.

Why fear death? Epicurus asks. When death is here, we're not. When we're here, death is not. This view is natural for Epicurus because he is a materialist—or more precisely, an ancient atomist. **Atomism** is the belief that reality consists of an infinite number of minute, indivisible bits called atoms moving rapidly in an infinite void, or empty space (see Chapter 2). For Epicurus, souls are also made of atoms, and

Figure 7.3 Epicureanism has become synonymous with debauchery, but that's not what Epicurus had in mind. *Romans During the Decadence*, by Thomas Couture, 1847.

at death the atoms disperse just as they do in any other material object that decays. Thus the soul is mortal, and no horrors await it after death.

As for the gods, Epicurus declares that although the gods are real, they are not the destructive meddlers in our lives that myth has made them out to be. They abide far from us in another realm and have nothing to do with us. So we need not fear the gods, nor believe the nightmarish stories and foreboding predictions offered up by the ignorant and superstitious.

So the happy life is one that is free of turmoil in body and mind, and attaining such a life requires the wisdom that philosophy can yield. For happiness requires a realistic view of both what exists and what matters.

Above all, Epicurus urges prudence in our pursuit of pleasures, in our choosing to satisfy or not to satisfy particular desires:

3. What is Epicurus' view of death? Is he right that we have nothing to fear from death? Explain.

"It is great wealth to a soul to live frugally with a contented mind."

—Lucretius

Of all this the beginning and the greatest good is prudence…for from prudence are sprung all the other virtues, and it teaches us that it is not possible to live pleasantly without living prudently and honourably and justly, nor again, to live a life of prudence, honor, and justice without living pleasantly.[5]

Epicurus: *Letter to Menoeceus*

Prudence teaches us to distinguish different sorts of desires and to choose wisely among them:

We must consider that of desires some are natural, others vain, and of the natural some are necessary and others merely natural; and of the necessary some are necessary for happiness, others for the repose of the body, and others for very life. The right

Epicurus: *Letter to Menoeceus*

Epicurus: *Letter to Menoeceus*

understanding of these facts enables us to refer all choice and avoidance to the health of the body and the soul's freedom from disturbance, since this is the aim of the life of blessedness.[6]

4. What does Epicurus say about the results of overindulging in unnecessary desires?

Epicurus says that necessary desires include those that are necessary for happiness (desires for friendship, for example), for physical comfort (desires for clothing, warmth), and for life (desires for food, water, shelter). Pain results when these desires are not satisfied, but the pain is easily removed (which brings about pleasure) by the simplest and least extravagant means. As Epicurus argues:

Epicurus: *Letter to Menoeceus*

And so plain savours bring us a pleasure equal to a luxurious diet, when all the pain due to want is removed; and bread and water produce the highest pleasure, when one who needs them puts them to his lips. To grow accustomed therefore to simple and not luxurious diet gives us health to the full, and makes a man alert for the needful employments of life, and when after long intervals we approach luxuries, disposes us better towards them, and fits us to be fearless of fortune.[7]

"If thou wilt make a man happy, add not unto his riches but take away from his desires."

—Epicurus

Those who try to satisfy necessary but outsized desires or unnecessary vain desires (that is, desires for luxurious, trendy, or prestigious things) invite pain—pain from the side effects of overindulgence, from the strain of extravagant living, from the increased strength of desires, or from the failure to satisfy insatiable desires. The proper control and moderation of our desires brings serenity, and an untroubled mind is the key to real happiness.

Stoicism The view that we can attain happiness and peace of mind if we focus on controlling only what is up to us (attitudes, intentions, perceptions, and feelings) and ignoring what is not up to us (body, reputation, property, and political office), thereby restraining our desires, cultivating virtue, and conforming our lives to Nature (or God).

7.2 EPICTETUS

Stoicism is the view that we can attain happiness and peace of mind if we focus on controlling only what is up to us (attitudes, intentions, perceptions, and feelings) and ignoring what is not up to us (body, reputation, property, and political office), thereby restraining our desires, cultivating virtue, and conforming our lives with Nature (or God). It arose in the fourth century BCE to eventually become one of the great moral systems in philosophy's history. This is how A. A. Long, a Stoicism scholar, describes its significance:

A. A. Long: *Hellenistic Philosophers: Stoics, Epicureans, and Sceptics*

Stoicism was the most important and influential development in Hellenistic philosophy. For more than four centuries it claimed the allegiance of a large number of educated men in the Graeco-Roman world, and its impact was not confined to Classical antiquity. Many of the Christian fathers were more deeply affected by Stoicism than

PORTRAIT

Lucretius

Lucretius (100–55 BCE), a Roman poet and philosopher, was a zealous adherent of Epicureanism and an admirer of Epicurus, even though the two men lived far apart in time. Through his long poem *On the Nature of Things*, Lucretius transmitted Epicurean philosophy to the West and presented a worldview that is astonishingly modern and surprisingly fervent. On the face of it, his *Nature* may seem forlorn—it paints a picture of human beings as entirely material and transitory, configurations of atoms adrift in a vast material universe of atoms, with no possibility of surviving the annihilation of the body. But Lucretius argues that we can strive to grasp the joys and pleasures of existence and be free of the fears that imprison us. This is how Stephen Greenblatt, a Lucretius scholar, characterizes the poet-philosopher's legacy:

Figure 7.4 Lucretius (100–55 BCE).

> More surprisingly, perhaps, is the sense, driven home by every page of *On the Nature of Things*, that the scientific vision of the world—a vision of atoms randomly moving in an infinite universe—was in its origins imbued with a poet's sense of wonder. Wonder did not depend on gods and demons and the dream of an afterlife; in Lucretius it welled up out of a recognition that we are made of the same matter as the stars and the oceans and all things else. And this recognition was the basis for the way he thought we should live our lives.
>
> In my view, and by no means mine alone, the culture in the wake of antiquity that best epitomized the Lucretian embrace of beauty and pleasure and propelled it forward as a legitimate and worthy human pursuit was that of the Renaissance. The pursuit was not restricted to the arts. It shaped the dress and the etiquette of courtiers; the language of the liturgy; the design and decoration of everyday objects. It suffused Leonardo da Vinci's scientific and technological explorations, Galileo's vivid dialogues on astronomy, Francis Bacon's ambitious research projects, and Richard Hooker's theology.

Stephen Greenblatt, *The Swerve: How the World Became Modern* (New York: W. W. Norton, 2011), 8.

they themselves recognized, and from the Renaissance up to modern times the effect of Stoic moral teaching on Western culture has been pervasive. Sometimes Stoic doctrines have reappeared in the work of major philosophers. Spinoza, Bishop Butler and Kant were all indebted to the Stoics....Even today, the influence persists at the most

A. A. Long:
Hellenistic Philosophers: Stoics, Epicureans, and Sceptics

mundane level. Not only the words *stoic* (uncapitalized) and *stoical* recall it. In popular language to be 'philosophical' means to show that fortitude in the face of adversity recommended by Stoic writers. This is a small, but highly significant example, of Stoicism's influence.[8]

"There is only one way to happiness and that is to cease worrying about things which are beyond the power of our will."
—Epictetus

5. According to Epictetus, what things are up to us? What things are not up to us?

In this chapter, we concentrate on Stoic moral theory, but we should keep in mind that Stoicism is more than that. The Stoics developed an impressive—and highly coherent—philosophical system comprising logic, epistemology, physics, metaphysics, linguistics, and theology. All these areas of Stoic thinking fit together well, with each one supporting and explaining others. Stoics believed, for example, that the universe is a kind of organizing being, or *logos*—a rational, all-pervading Nature, or God, that structured and directed everything. Human beings have the power of reason because they too have this *logos* within them. They are happiest and wisest when they live according to the *logos*, this inner spark of rationality, which in turn harmonizes their lives with the *logos* of Nature. The result is a good life in the most profound sense.

Stoicism began in Athens with Zeno of Citium (334–262 BCE) discoursing on his philosophy in the marketplace from a porch (a *stoa*, the root word of Stoicism).[9] Stoicism was attractive to many for a variety of reasons. First, it offered itself as an antidote for the miseries of the world: it addressed the question of how people can cope with, even surmount, all the suffering that befalls them. And in Zeno's time, and for hundreds of years after, immeasurable pain and sorrow were extraordinarily common. For the Stoic, the only real harm that can be done to a person is self-inflicted injury to the soul by a lack of virtue. Zeno and the rest of the Stoics, like the Buddhists and other followers of Eastern religions, sought virtue and inner peace through moderation or elimination of desire.

Second, the antidote was available to everyone—high and low born, slave and master, rulers and the ruled. The shining philosophies of Plato and Aristotle spoke of wisdom, truth, and virtue—but few non-philosophers could understand what all the fuss was about. Stoicism, however, could be grasped by Everyman. To receive the blessings of Stoicism, the advantages of wealth, status, and birth were not required. Virtue, a condition of the soul, was the only prerequisite, which anyone could acquire.

Third, the Stoics were the first to preach cosmopolitanism, the idea that all men—whether Roman, Athenian, or

Figure 7.5 Epictetus (c. 55–135 CE).

barbarian—are brothers. We are all, they declared, made of the same stuff, fated to travel the same mortal road, and part of the same universal community composed of humans and benign providence.

The three most widely read Stoics can also claim to have the most interesting life stories. Seneca (after 4 BCE–65 CE) was a distinguished Roman statesman whose suicide (demanded by the emperor Nero) became an exemplar of Stoic indifference to misfortune. Epictetus (c. 55–135 CE) was a former slave, maimed in captivity, who took to heart Socrates' claim that a good man cannot be harmed. Marcus Aurelius (121–180 CE) was a Roman emperor who applied Stoicism to his life in a time of cultural tumult and confusion. The views of these men on Stoicism are in remarkable agreement, despite their separation in time.

So Stoicism holds that people of true Stoic virtue cannot be wounded by things external to their souls. Trouble may swarm around them, yet they cannot be distressed or frightened or coerced or enslaved or injured. This is an astonishing claim, and the Stoics spent a lot of time explaining how it could be true. Here is Epictetus' explanation:

> "It's not what happens to you, but how you react to it that matters."
> —Epictetus

6. Why was Stoicism so attractive to people in ancient times? Would it appeal to people today?

Epictetus: *Encheiridion*

It is not things that upset people but rather ideas about things. For example, death is nothing terrible, else it would have seemed so even to Socrates; rather it is the idea that death is terrible that is terrible. So whenever we are frustrated or upset or grieved, let us not blame others, but ourselves—that is, our ideas. It is the act of a philosophically ignorant person to blame others for his troubles. One who is beginning to learn blames himself. An educated person blames neither anyone else nor himself.[10]

7. Why does Epictetus say that a virtuous person cannot be harmed?

Consider these two people in identical situations. Bailey's sunglasses have been stolen, and so have Payton's. The sunglasses are alike, and the circumstances surrounding the thefts are the same. But Bailey gets angry and remains upset all day long, while Payton is slightly annoyed but soon forgets about the incident and later buys new sunglasses. The difference between these two reactions cannot be due to anything inherent in the events themselves, because the events are the same. The difference lies in the attitudes and feelings of the persons involved. One woman is unhappy and the other happy, because they *think* about the incident differently. And that means their happiness or unhappiness is *up to them*. The power to be happy is theirs to use or not use. So it goes, says the Stoic, for everything in life. We may not be in charge of events, but we are in charge of our happiness. We may not be able to change the world, but we can change the way we think about it. Epictetus would say, as Shakespeare did, that the problem lies not in our stars but in ourselves.

> "He is a wise man who does not grieve for the things which he has not, but rejoices for those which he has."
> —Epictetus

The Stoic way of thinking about things involves observing an important difference in how things are. As Epictetus says:

Epictetus: *Encheiridion*

Some things are up to us, some are not up to us. Up to us are perception, intention, desire, aversion, and in sum, whatever are our own doings; not up to us are body, property, reputation, political office and in sum whatever are not our own doings. And the things that are up to us are naturally free, unforbidding, unimpeding, while those not up to us are weak, slavish, forbidding, alien. Remember, then, that if you think naturally slavish things are free and that alien things are your own, you will be impeded, grieved, troubled, you will blame gods and men; but if you think that what is yours is yours and what is alien is alien, as it really is, nobody will ever compel you, nobody will forbid you, you will not blame anyone, you will not complain about anything, you will not do a single thing unwillingly, you will have no enemy, no one will hurt you; for you will not suffer anything harmful.[11]

The idea of distinguishing what is up to us from what is not up to us—what belongs to us from what doesn't—is a theme that runs throughout the Stoics' writings. Here is Epictetus driving the point home:

Epictetus: *Encheiridion*

Don't seek for things to happen as you wish, but wish for things to happen as they do, and you will get on well. . . .

Never say about anything that you have "lost it," but that you have "given it back." Your child has died? It has been given back. Your wife has died? She has been given back . . .

If you want your children and your wife and friends to live forever, you are a fool; for you want what is not up to you to be up to you, and what is not yours to be yours. . . . Every person's master is the one who controls whether that person shall get what he wants and avoid what he doesn't want. Thus whoever wishes to be free should neither seek nor avoid anything that is up to others; otherwise he will necessarily be a slave. . . .

Remember that it is not the man who curses you or the man who hits you that insults you, but the idea you have of them as insulting. . . .

If someone were to hand over your body to just whomever happened along, you would be outraged. Why aren't you outraged at the fact that *you* turn over your own mind to whomever happens along—if he insults you and you let it upset you and trouble you? . . .

But don't worry about what anyone says about you; for this is not at all up to you.[12]

"Wealth consists not in having great possessions, but in having few wants."
—Epictetus

Note that the Stoic ideal is not total impassiveness, a complete lack of emotion or desire in every situation. The Stoics were not, as some ancient critics asserted, "men of stone." The ideal Stoic—the Stoic sage—is not emotionless. But he is selective about what he does and does not feel. He does not give in to excessive and "irrational" feelings—anger, fear, dread, lust, and anxiety. But he does experience "good emotional states"—kindness, generosity, joy, and goodwill. The central Stoic insight is the need to *moderate* our attitudes and feelings through reason: to ask ourselves whether things not in our control are really appropriate objects of our desires, whether our desires are in proportion to the true worth of what we seek, and whether we have attained an evenness of mind and a sense of calm regarding the ups and downs of life.

Figure 7.6 Richard Harris, left, as emperor and Stoic philosopher Marcus Aurelius, in the movie *Gladiator*.

The Stoic attitude toward suffering and tragedy is not a relic of the third century. Today it's often on display in the aftermath of disasters, although it's not called Stoicism; it's called grace. When a woman's house has been obliterated by a tornado, and she has lost every material possession she has, and she says, "We're lucky; I'm alive, and my children are alive, and we can always rebuild"—that's grace: Stoicism by another name.

In its commonsense lessons on coping with adversity, accepting what cannot be changed, and changing what is within our power, Stoicism is surprisingly modern, bearing a striking resemblance to science-based forms of psychotherapy. Psychotherapist Donald Robertson explains:

> In fact, Stoicism provides a rich armamentarium of strategies and techniques for developing psychological resilience, by changing our feelings *rationally* and *naturally* rather than simply trying to block them out by force. In a sense, ancient Stoicism was the granddaddy of all "self-help" and its ideas and techniques have inspired many modern approaches to both personal development and psychological therapy. It's generally accepted that the modern psychotherapy that most resembles ancient Stoic "remedies" for emotional problems is Cognitive Behavioural Therapy (CBT) and its precursor Rational Emotive Behavioural Therapy (REBT).[13]

"The essence of philosophy is that a man should so live that his happiness shall depend as little as possible on external things."

—Epictetus

THEN AND NOW

Stoicism Today

Is Stoicism relevant in the twenty-first century? Plenty of thoughtful people think so—including Rob Goodman and Jimmy Soni, coauthors of *Rome's Last Citizen*. In a recent *Forbes* article, they offer five reasons why Stoicism matters:

1. It was built for hard times.

Stoicism was born in a world falling apart. Invented in Athens just a few decades after Alexander the Great's conquests and premature death upended the Greek world, Stoicism took off because it offered security and peace in a time of warfare and crisis. The Stoic creed didn't promise material security or a peace in the afterlife; but it did promise an unshakable happiness in this life. . . .

Stoicism tells us that no happiness can be secure if it's rooted in changeable, destructible things. Our bank accounts can grow or shrink, our careers can prosper or falter, even our loved ones can be taken from us. There is only one place the world can't touch: our inner selves, our choice at every moment to be brave, to be reasonable, to be good.

The world might take everything from us; Stoicism tells us that we all have a fortress on the inside. The Stoic philosopher Epictetus, who was born a slave and crippled at a young age, wrote: "Where is the good? In the will. . . . If anyone is unhappy, let him remember that he is unhappy by reason of himself alone." . . .

2. Stoicism is made for globalization.

The world that gave birth to Stoicism was a parochial, often xenophobic place: most people held fast to age-old divisions of nationality, religion, and status. If openly embracing those divisions sounds strange to us, we have Stoicism to thank. It was perhaps the first Western philosophy to preach universal brotherhood. Epictetus said that each of us is a citizen of our own land, but "also a member of the great city of gods and men." The Roman emperor Marcus Aurelius, history's best-known Stoic, reminded himself daily to love the world as much as he loved his native city. . . .

3. If you're Christian, you're already part-Stoic.

Imagine a religion that stressed human brotherhood under a benevolent creator God; that told us to moderate and master our basic urges rather than giving in to them; that nevertheless insisted that all humans, because we're human, are bound to fail at this mission; and that spent a lot of time talking about "conscience" and the multiple aspects, or "persons," of a unitary God. All of that might sound familiar. But the philosophy that invented all of those ideas was not Christianity, but Stoicism. . . .

7.3 SEXTUS EMPIRICUS

skepticism The view that we lack knowledge in some fundamental way.

8. What logical pattern do Sextus' ten arguments have?

Skepticism is the view that we lack knowledge in some fundamental way. We assume we know a great many things—dogs bark, grass is green, fire is hot, the Earth is round, $2 + 2 = 4$, and a jump from a tall building may be deadly. But skeptics balk: they say we, in fact, don't know what we think we know. They may raise fundamental doubts about any knowledge claims based on sense experience or reason or both. Or they may

4. It's the unofficial philosophy of the military.

In 1965, James Stockdale's A-4E Skyhawk was shot down over Vietnam. He later remembered the moment like this: "After ejection I had about thirty seconds to make my last statement in freedom before I landed . . . And so help me, I whispered to myself: 'Five years down there, at least. I'm leaving the world of technology and entering the world of Epictetus.'"

Stockdale spent more than seven years in a Vietnamese prison, and he wrote that Stoicism saved his life. Stockdale had spent years studying Stoic thought before deploying, and he drew on those teachings to endure his captivity. . . .

5. It's a philosophy for leadership.

Stoicism teaches us that, before we try to control events, we have to control ourselves first. Our attempts to exert influence on the world are subject to chance, disappointment, and failure—but control of the self is the only kind

Figure 7.7 James Stockdale was an American pilot, a prisoner of war in Vietnam, a modern-day Stoic, and a follower of the ancient Stoic Epictetus.

that can succeed 100% of the time. From emperor Marcus Aurelius on, leaders have found that a Stoic attitude earns them respect in the face of failure, and guards against arrogance in the face of success. . . .

What is your opinion of Stoicism as a philosophy of life? Do you have Stoic qualities in your character? Explain.

Rob Goodman and Jimmy Soni, "Five Reasons Why Stoicism Matters Today," *Forbes*, September 28, 2012.

limit skepticism to particular domains such as the existence of material objects, the past and future, other minds, or God. In any case, philosophers throughout the centuries have recognized the seriousness of the skeptics' challenges, and they have been trying to counter or accommodate them ever since the rise of skeptical schools in the Hellenistic period. (See Chapters 9 and 10 for additional discussions of skepticism.)

The most influential tradition of skepticism from this era can be traced to Pyrrho of Elis (c. 365–270 BCE), an obscure figure whose ideas about skepticism

"Skepticism, like chastity, should not be relinquished too readily."

—George Santayana

DETAILS

The Self-Destruction of Skepticism

For Sextus Empiricus, skepticism is a matter of questioning whether anything can be known. This amounts to suspending judgment about the truth of knowledge claims. But he does *not* assert that "nothing can be known" or "no proposition can be known." Why? Because such statements would get him into a logical tangle. The assertion that "no proposition can be known" applies to *all* propositions—including "no proposition can be known." So if the proposition is true, it must be false, which means that it is self-refuting. No respectable skeptic would meander into such an obvious trap.

Is the statement "All truth is relative" (that is, "there is no objective truth") self-refuting? Why or why not? (See Chapter 10 for more on self-refuting propositions.)

Figure 7.8 Sextus Empiricus (fl. c. 200 CE).

appearances The way things in the world appear to us.

were preserved in the works of Sextus Empiricus (fl. c. 200 CE), a later follower. In *Outlines of Pyrrhonism*, Sextus presents the Pyrrhonist case against the "dogmatists"— philosophers such as Aristotle, Epicurus, and Epictetus who believe we can indeed come to know things about the world. He lays out ten Pyrrhonist arguments, or "modes," that purport to show that we cannot be sure whether any beliefs are true and therefore must suspend judgment about them. The suspension of judgment is a failure to attain knowledge, and the wholesale application of the arguments would spread skepticism to a wide range of beliefs.

But how could a skeptic get through the day without firm beliefs? In order to act at all, don't we have to make judgments? (An ancient canard has it that since Pyrrho didn't believe what his senses told him, he had to be continually rescued from obvious dangers by his friends.) Sextus says that skeptics manage to get through life just fine by attending to **appearances**—that is, to the way things in the world *appear* to us. We are all aware of how things *seem to be*—which is not necessarily the way things *are*. Appearances may not be reality. (Throughout philosophy's history, the relationship between appearance and reality has been explored and disputed time after time.) Sextus says that skeptics act according to how things appear without believing that the appearances reflect the actual world, without any claims to knowledge. As Sextus explains:

Sextus Empiricus: *Outlines of Pyrrhonism*

[W]hen we question whether the external object is such as it appears, we grant that it does appear, and we are not raising a question about the appearance but rather about what is said about the appearance; this is different from raising a question about the appearance itself.... Accordingly, we say that the criterion of the Skeptic Way is the appearance ... for since this appearance lies in [involuntary perception] it is not open to question.... Holding to the appearances, then, we live without beliefs but in accord with the ordinary regimen of life, since we cannot be wholly inactive.[14]

To the Pyrrhonists, living without beliefs but in conformity with the "ordinary regimen of life" means conducting daily life according to the demands of nature and of the laws and customs of society.

Like the Epicureans and the Stoics, the skeptics aim toward peace of mind. They reason that the search for genuine knowledge always involves doubt, and doubt can be a profoundly disturbing state. To rise above the inner turmoil and achieve tranquility, it is necessary to end the painful chase after knowledge and to suspend judgment on all matters. The result is *ataraxia*, imperturbability of soul.

Sextus' ten arguments for skepticism have the same general form: since there are differences or conflicts between appearances, we cannot trust any of them to reveal the truth about how things really are. The most reasonable response, then, is a suspension of judgment—a principled skepticism. Here are a few of Sextus' modes:

The first argument, as we were saying, is that according to which the same [impressions] do not arise from the same things because of the difference of animals. This we conclude from the difference in the ways animals are produced and from the variety in the structures of their bodies....

But if the same things do appear differently because of the difference of animals, then we shall be in a position to say how the external object looks to *us*, but we shall suspend judgment on how it is in nature. For we shall not be able to decide between our [impressions] and those of the other animals, since we are part of the dispute and thus are in need of someone to make the decision, rather than competent to pass judgment ourselves. Besides, we shall not be able to give preference, whether with or without proof, to our [impressions] over those of the non-rational animals....

We said that the second was the one based on the differences among human beings. ... Since, then, choice and avoidance are in pleasure and displeasure, and pleasure and displeasure lie in sense and [impressions], when the same things are chosen by some people and avoided by others it is logical for us to infer that these people are not affected alike by the same things, since if they would alike have chosen and avoided the same things. But if the same things produce different affects depending on the difference of human beings, this too would reasonably lead to suspension of judgment and we would, perhaps, be able to say what each of the external objects appears to be, relative to each difference, but we would not be able to state what it is in nature....

This [third] mode is the one that we say is based on the difference [among our] senses. That the senses differ from one another is obvious from the start. For instance, to the eye it seems

"Dogmatism and skepticism are both, in a sense, absolute philosophies; one is certain of knowing, the other of not knowing. What philosophy should dissipate is certainty, whether of knowledge or ignorance."

—Bertrand Russell

9. What is the distinction between appearances and reality? Why is it important?

Sextus Empiricus:
Outlines of Pyrrhonism

10. Are you a skeptic? What propositions can you truthfully say you know? Why?

"Education has failed in a very serious way to convey the most important lesson science can teach: skepticism."

—David Suzuki

Sextus Empiricus:
Outlines of Pyrrhonism

Figure 7.9 People see things differently. Does this show that knowledge is impossible?

that paintings have hollows and prominences, but not to the touch. And for some people honey seems pleasant to the tongue but unpleasant to the eye; consequently, it is impossible to say without qualification whether it is pleasant or unpleasant.... Hence we shall not be able to say how each of these [objects] is in its nature, but only how it appears to be in each instance....

The tenth mode, which is principally concerned with ethics, is the one depending on ways of life and on customs, laws, mythic beliefs, and dogmatic suppositions.... At any rate, since by this mode, too, so many anomalies in "the facts" have been shown, we shall not be able to say how any external object or state of affairs is in its nature, but only how it appears in relation to a given way of life or law or custom, and so forth. And so because of this mode, too, we must suspend judgment about the nature of the external "facts."[15]

WRITING AND REASONING   CHAPTER 7

1. What is Epicureanism and how is it different from pure hedonism and the unrestrained pursuit of pleasure? How does the reputation of Epicurus differ from his actual character and teachings?

2. What is Epicurus' view of the mental pains caused by fear of death, the after-life, and the gods? Why does he say that we have nothing to fear from these?

3. What is the significance of Epictetus' distinction between controlling only what is up to us and ignoring what is not up to us? According to Epictetus, what effect would focusing ourselves only on what is up to us have on our lives?

4. Why does Stoicism claim that people of true virtue cannot be wounded by things external to their souls? Do you agree? Why or why not?

5. Explain and critique at least three of Sextus' arguments for skepticism.

REVIEW NOTES

7.1 EPICURUS

- Epicurus is considered the founder of Epicureanism, the hedonistic theory that life's highest aim is happiness attained through moderate pleasures and the avoidance of mental disturbance.

- Epicureanism is not about recklessly sensual, overindulgent living. It says that the true life of pleasure consists in an attitude of imperturbable emotional calm that needs only simple pleasures, a sensible diet, a prudent moral life, and good friends.

- A good life is a life free of trouble, and the chief aim of each person should be to attain this kind of tranquility. But not all pleasures are created equal, and although all pleasures are good, they are not all to be pursued.

- Epicurus says there's no reason to fear death, because when death is here, we're not. When we're here, death is not.

- Those who try to satisfy necessary but excessive desires or unnecessary vain desires invite pain.

7.2 EPICTETUS

- Stoicism is the view that we can attain happiness and peace of mind if we focus on controlling only what is up to us and ignoring what is not up to us, thereby restraining our desires and conforming our lives with Nature, or God.

- Stoicism was attractive to many for a variety of reasons. It offered itself as an antidote for the miseries of the world, and the antidote was available to everyone—high and low born, slave and master, rulers and the ruled. The Stoics were also the first to preach cosmopolitanism, the idea that all men—whether Roman, Athenian, or barbarian—are brothers.

- For the Stoic, the only real harm that can be done to a person is self-inflicted injury to the soul by a lack of virtue. Zeno and the rest of the Stoics, like the Buddhists and other followers of Eastern religions, sought virtue and inner peace through moderation or elimination of desire.

- The power to be happy is ours to use or not use. We may not be in charge of events, but we are in charge of our happiness. We may not be able to change the world, but we can change the way we think about it.

7.3 SEXTUS EMPIRICUS

- Skepticism is the view that we lack knowledge in some fundamental way. Skeptics may raise fundamental doubts about any knowledge claims based on sense experience or reason or both. Or they may limit skepticism to particular domains such as the existence of material objects, the past and future, other minds, or God.

- In *Outlines of Pyrrhonism*, Sextus Empiricus presents the Pyrrhonist case against the "dogmatists." He lays out ten Pyrrhonist arguments, or "modes," that purport to show that we cannot be sure whether any beliefs are true and therefore must suspend judgment about them. The suspension of judgment is a failure to attain knowledge.

- Sextus says that skeptics manage to live a normal life by attending to appearances—to the way things in the world appear to us. Skeptics act according to how things appear without believing that the appearances reflect the actual world, without any claims to knowledge.

- Like the Epicureans and the Stoics, the skeptics aim toward peace of mind. They reason that the search for genuine knowledge always involves doubt, and doubt can be a profoundly disturbing state. To rise above the inner turmoil and achieve tranquility, it is necessary to end the painful chase after knowledge and to suspend judgment on all matters.

KEY TERMS

appearances	Epicureanism	Hellenistic era	Stoicism
atomism	hedonism	skepticism	

Notes

1. Epicurus, *Letter to Menoeceus*, in *The Extant Remains*, trans. Cyril Bailey (Oxford: Oxford University Press, 1926), 131–132.
2. Epicurus, *Letter to Menoeceus*, trans. Bailey, 128–129.
3. Epicurus, *Letter to Menoeceus*, trans. Bailey, 129–130.
4. Epicurus, *Letter to Menoeceus*, trans. Bailey, 124–127.
5. Epicurus, *Letter to Menoeceus*, trans. Bailey, 132.
6. Epicurus, *Letter to Menoeceus*, trans. Bailey, 127–128.
7. Epicurus, *Letter to Menoeceus*, trans. Bailey, 130–131.
8. A. A. Long, *Hellenistic Philosophers: Stoics, Epicureans, and Sceptics* (Berkeley: University of California Press, 1986), 107.
9. Not to be confused with Zeno of Elea, the purveyor of paradoxes.
10. Epictetus, *Encheiridion*, trans. Wallace I. Matson, in *Classics of Philosophy*, 3rd edition, ed. Louis P. Pojman and Lewis Vaughn (New York: Oxford University Press, 2011).
11. Epictetus, *Encheiridion*, trans. Matson.
12. Epictetus, *Encheiridion*, trans. Matson.
13. Donald Robertson, *Stoicism and the Art of Happiness* (New York: McGraw-Hill, 2018), xix.
14. Sextus Empiricus, *Outlines of Pyrrhonism*, trans. Benson Mates (Oxford: Oxford University Press, 1996).
15. Sextus Empiricus, *Outlines of Pyrrhonism*, trans. Mates.

For Further Reading

Frederick Copleston, *A History of Philosophy: Volume 1: Greece and Rome: From the Pre-Socratics to Plotinus* (New York: Doubleday, 1993).

Stephen Greenblatt, *The Swerve: How the World Became Modern* (New York: W. W. Norton, 2011).

Ted Honderich, ed., *The Oxford Companion to Philosophy*, 2nd edition (Oxford: Oxford University Press, 2005).

Anthony Kenny, *Ancient Philosophy: A New History of Western Philosophy*, vol. 1 (Oxford: Oxford University Press, 2004).

A. A. Long, *Hellenistic Philosophy: Stoics, Epicureans, and Sceptics* (Berkeley: University of California Press, 1986).

A. A. Long and D. N. Sedley, *The Hellenistic Philosophers: Translations of the Principal Sources with Philosophical Commentary*, vol. 1 (Cambridge: Cambridge University Press, 1987).

Lucretius, *The Nature of Things*, trans. A. E. Stallings (New York: Penguin Books, 2007).

Bertrand Russell, *A History of Western Philosophy* (New York: Simon and Schuster, 1945).

Seneca, *Letters from a Stoic*, trans. Robin Campbell (New York: Penguin, 1969, 2004).

Online Resources

Daily Stoic, "What Is Stoicism? A Definition and 9 Stoic Exercises to Get You Started," https://dailystoic.com/what-is-stoicism-a-definition-3-stoic-exercises-to-get-you-started

Modern Stoicism, https://modernstoicism.com

"Practical Stoicism" and other Stoicism videos, https://www.bing.com/videos/search?q=stoicism&view=detail&mid=920E3B48FED02461F9D3920E3B48FED02461F9D3&FORM=VIRE

Stanford Encyclopedia of Philosophy, "Stoicism," https://plato.stanford.edu/entries/stoicism

Internet Encyclopedia of Philosophy, "Stoicism," https://www.iep.utm.edu/stoicism

Philosophy Talk Podcasts, "Stoicism," https://www.philosophytalk.org/shows/stoicism

CHAPTER 8

The Medieval Period

CHAPTER OBJECTIVES

8.1 BETWEEN ANCIENT AND MODERN

- Understand the historical changes that led to the Middle Ages.
- Summarize the social and cultural conditions that obtained in the Dark Ages.
- Explain how philosophy and the Church were interdependent in the medieval era.

8.2 AUGUSTINE

- Recount the main events in Augustine's life from his dissolute youth to his appointment as bishop of Hippo.
- Define *Neoplatonism*, *necessary truth*, and *moral evil*.
- Explain the significance to Augustine of the biblical quotation, "Unless you believe, you shall not understand."
- Know Augustine's response to skepticism, and describe the kinds of knowledge that he thinks humans can attain.
- Summarize Augustine's doctrine of the *great chain of being*.
- Understand how Augustine explains the presence of evil in the world.

8.3 ANSELM AND AQUINAS

- Relate the premises and conclusion of Anselm's ontological argument and summarize criticisms of it.
- Explain Gaunilo's objection to Anselm's argument.
- Define *ontological argument*, *cosmological argument*, *natural law theory*, and the *doctrine of double effect*.
- Explain and evaluate Aquinas's first-cause argument.
- Explain Aquinas's objection to an infinite chain of movers, and summarize how critics have responded to it.
- Understand Aquinas's natural law theory of ethics.
- Assess the proposition that nature is teleological.

8.1 BETWEEN ANCIENT AND MODERN

By the end of the Hellenistic and Roman eras, Greek philosophy in the rigorous style of Plato and Aristotle—with its commitment to logical argument and the open-ended search for truth—had ebbed in every corner of the Western world. The grand tradition of rational inquiry that first blossomed in Athens and then spread to all the places subdued by Alexander and his Greek culture seemed to be fading away. Stoicism, Epicureanism, and Neoplatonism still had their adherents—but so did a new crop of pagan cults, oracles, superstitions, prophets, magicians, and mystics. The most powerful trend of all was the rise of Christianity from a banned cult to the official state religion dominating the political and intellectual life of the Roman Empire. In many ways, philosophy then had to answer to religion. When in 476 CE the Goths sacked Rome, the Western empire fell, and civilization itself was in general decline. But the Church emerged from the chaos as the supreme power in Europe, becoming philosophy's master, censor, and—indirectly—its patron. Philosophy had tumbled far from its pinnacle in ancient Greece, but it was far from dead, and a few thinkers in the Middle Ages (the medieval era) set about proving it.

Some experts take medieval philosophy to span a thousand years from (very roughly) 500 to 1500 CE. Before this time, ancient philosophy had flourished; after this period, modern philosophy arose. There is little agreement about these dates (or any others), but they seem at least plausible because they more or less correspond to the virtual takeover of philosophy by Christianity in the first millennium CE and the weakening of Christianity's grip during the Renaissance in the second millennium.

In any case, ancient times and the Middle Ages overlap considerably, and so do the Middle Ages and the Renaissance. Thus Augustine is traditionally thought to appear at the beginning of the period, even though he could be counted as a figure of late antiquity, living before 500 CE. And toward the end of the era, we encounter the renowned philosopher William of Ockham (of "Ockham's razor" fame), who died in 1349, over a hundred and fifty years before the supposed beginning of the Renaissance.

Scholars used to contend that no philosophy worth reading came out of the medieval period. Histories of philosophy typically skipped the period altogether and focused on the philosophical achievements of the ancients and the moderns. Now we know that this attitude was understandable but unjustified.

It's true that civilization fell under a shadow of ignorance when the Roman Empire was undone. Progress in everything from astronomy to physics was all but halted, and culture stagnated. For good reason, experts label this time the Dark Ages, a period stretching from around 500 to 1000 CE. Almost all of the great works of the ancient philosophers were inaccessible, either because the original texts were lost or because very few people knew how to read Greek or to translate the texts into Latin. (Around the same time in the Arab world, the original Greek texts were being rescued from oblivion and studied by Islamic scholars from India to Spain.) It's also true that philosophy became a servant of the medieval Church, being relegated mostly to the role of explaining or commenting on Church dogma. Philosophy had to be careful not to directly challenge received doctrine: deviation was officially condemned, and transgressors could be excommunicated or imprisoned.

Figure 8.1 A medieval castle at night against a stormy sky.

But all this is only half the story. The Church may have placed shackles on philosophy, but philosophy also had its hooks in the Church. The latter needed philosophy to work out the details of doctrine or to make sense of the Church's teachings or to show that there was no real conflict between religion and reason. Little wonder that countless clerics and Church officials studied philosophy. The inevitable result of this mingling of philosophy and religion was that some good philosophical work got done. Cleric-philosophers were free to delve into philosophical topics that did not infringe on religious doctrine, and they eagerly applied their philosophical expertise to theological puzzles that the Church had trouble unraveling. This environment produced an occasional beacon in the dim medieval light: Augustine, Boethius, Anselm, Avicenna, Maimonides, Hildegard, William of Ockham, and—perhaps the greatest medieval thinker of all— Thomas Aquinas.

8.2 AUGUSTINE

Augustine (354–430 CE) was a Christian philosopher and theologian who had an enormous influence on Christian thought and on the West's appreciation of Plato and Aristotle. He affected Christian theology more than any other early Christian author, introduced Plato to generations of thinkers, and forced philosophers in every epoch to reckon with his ideas and authority. Pascal, Luther, Wittgenstein, and others had to take Augustine into account. He was the pivot point between Greco-pagan and Christian thinking, a transition that would change both the Church and future philosophy.

Augustine was born to a Christian mother (St. Monica) and pagan father (Patricius) in Roman North Africa (now Algeria). In his autobiography *Confessions*, he describes an idle youth spent in an uninhibited romp through sensuality:

Figure 8.2 *St. Augustine Subdues Heresy with Lightning Bolts from His Pen*, Joseph Hartmann, 1740s or 1770s.

"Grant me chastity and continence, but not yet."
—Augustine

Augustine: *Confessions*

The single desire that dominated my search for delight was simply to love and to be loved. But no restraint was imposed by the exchange of mind with mind, which marks the brightly lit pathway of friendship. Clouds of muddy carnal concupiscence [strong desire] filled the air. The bubbling impulses of puberty befogged and obscured my heart so that it could not see the difference between love's serenity and lust's darkness. Confusion of the two things boiled within me. It seized hold of my youthful weakness sweeping me through the precipitous rocks of desire to submerge me in a whirlpool of vice. . . . Where was I in the sixteenth year of the age of my flesh? 'Far away in exile from the pleasures of your [God's] house.' (Mic. 2:9) Sensual folly assumed domination over me, and I gave myself totally to it in acts allowed by shameful humanity but under your laws illicit.[1]

"[T]he cause of moral evil is not the Creator but the created will."
—Augustine

Figure 8.3 The consecration of St. Augustine.

Neoplatonism The philosophical view consisting of a blend of Plato's metaphysics (primarily concerning the theory of the Forms) and other nonmaterialist or religious ideas.

1. In what ways do the ideas in the "Platonic books" echo Christian doctrines?

2. What is the Christian explanation for why evil exists? How does evil enter into the Manicheanist worldview?

Augustine was trained in rhetoric at Carthage and developed an intense interest in philosophy after being exposed to some classical philosophy from Cicero. Later he became an adherent of the religion of Manicheanism, which held that the world is not ruled by a benevolent God, but by two great competing forces, one good and one evil. Augustine thought Manicheanism offered a better explanation of why evil exists than Christianity did. In 383 he left for Rome to teach rhetoric, and a year later he sailed to Milan for the same reason. In Rome his belief in Manicheanism weakened considerably, and in Milan he was impressed by the sermons of St. Ambrose, bishop of Milan. He also became intrigued by a doctrine that seemed to shine new light on Christianity: **Neoplatonism**. This view is a blend of Plato's metaphysics (primarily concerning the theory of Forms) and other nonmaterialist or religious ideas. In the "Platonic books," Augustine found musings about an immaterial transcendent realm, about high and low levels of reality, about a supreme entity (the One in Plato), and about the possibility of knowledge of all these things. Moreover, Augustine thought he saw analogs of these concepts in the Christian worldview. After a very long, anguished struggle with these ideas, he finally converted to Christianity in 386 at age thirty-one and was baptized by St. Ambrose on Easter Day.

In 388 Augustine returned to Africa, and in 395 or 396 he became the bishop of Hippo (now the city of Annaba in Algeria), a post he kept for the rest of his life. During his long journey from reprobate to learned Christian bishop, he produced a vast trove of writings—about five million words. The most renowned of these include *Confessions* (an autobiography cum meditation), *City of God* (a synthesis of Christian and classical philosophy), *On the Trinity* (a commentary on the mysterious doctrine of the unity of three persons in one Godhead), and *On Free Will* (a dialogue about human choice).

From both classical and Christian threads, Augustine wove a distinctive set of doctrines about God, the world, knowledge, ethics, and existence. In epistemology, metaphysics, and moral philosophy, he shaped new doctrines from old ideas and original analyses. Along the way, he found that in his search for wisdom there was a place for both faith and reason, both belief and understanding. He thought that to attain wisdom belief had to come first, then understanding. On this point, a verse from the Bible spoke volumes to him: "Unless you believe, you shall not understand." So he came to believe in the Christian God, but he wanted more: he wanted to *understand* God and how He relates to the world and to him. And he was prepared by his faith to finally receive the truth with the help of philosophy. (Centuries later, Thomas Aquinas and countless other philosopher-theologians would also see faith and reason as partners, not enemies.)

Truth

But could Augustine or anyone else *know* anything at all? The skeptics from Plato's time said no, and for a while Augustine wonders whether they might be right. He finally reasons his way out of his doubts in much the same way that Descartes does in the seventeenth century (Descartes declared, "I think, therefore I am"). The skeptics say we can know nothing because we can always be mistaken. But Augustine replies, "'If I am mistaken, I exist.' A nonexistent being cannot be mistaken; therefore I must exist, if I am mistaken."[2] And he asserts that if he has this proof that he exists, he cannot be mistaken in thinking that he exists. He therefore knows he exists. And if he is glad of these two facts, he can add a third fact—he knows he is glad. So Augustine knows at least that he exists, that he knows it, and that he is glad. In fact, he can know the contents of his direct experience, his subjective sensory impressions. About these he cannot be mistaken, just as the man who says "this tastes sweet to me" cannot be mistaken. So, contrary to the skeptic's view, Augustine says, there is such a thing as truth. But can we trust our senses to give us knowledge about the world (not just our inner subjective experience)? Complete skepticism, says Augustine, is not justified. That we are sometimes mistaken about the objects of our sense experience is no reason to be an extreme skeptic.

In addition to these propositions, Augustine thinks he also knows mathematical truths. Seven plus three equals ten, now and forever, and for anyone who thinks about it. Likewise we can know logical truths: for example, that either it is raining or not raining; that the world either exists or it does not exist. Moreover, we can know particular value statements. We know for example that good is better than evil and that the eternal is better than the temporal. Of all these mathematical, logical, and evaluative truths, we can have certain knowledge; they are eternal, changeless, and necessary. They are not truths that we concoct; they are not dependent on our minds for their existence. As Augustine says, "You will never be able to say that [truth] belongs particularly to you or to me or to any man, for it is available and offers itself to be shared by all who discern things immutably true."[3] Augustine concludes that **necessary truth** (a truth that could not have been false) is extremely precious—more valuable even than rationality ("superior to our minds," Augustine says), which is our means for discovering such truth. It is valuable precisely because it has the superlative properties of immutability, timelessness, and necessity. Necessary truth is a candidate for being the very highest good, the best of things, and the zenith of the intrinsically valuable.

From this notion of necessary truth, Augustine argues for the existence of God. He reasons that if truth is the highest good, then truth must be God, because God is the highest good, the most excellent of all things. If an entity is higher and more excellent than truth, then *that* entity must be God. Either way, God must exist. By starting with an understanding of truth and with the concept of God as the highest good, Augustine reasons that whether God is truth, or God is higher than truth, God *is*. "Whether there is or is not such a higher thing," says Augustine, "you cannot deny that God exists."[4] (In the next section, you will see that Anselm makes a similar but more nuanced argument.)

The Hierarchy of Being

From Plato and Neoplatonists, Augustine derived a view of the world as an all-encompassing hierarchy of existing things and their value. Recall that Plato had

3. What is Augustine's argument against skepticism?

necessary truth A truth that could not have been false.

"Augustine's *Confessions* will always rank among the greater masterpieces of Western literature. Like Rousseau's book with the same title . . . the work has a perennial power to speak, even though written virtually sixteen centuries ago and certainly a book rooted in antiquity."

—Henry Chadwick

Figure 8.4 A page from the manuscript of Augustine's *City of God*.

insisted that reality consists of two worlds: the ordinary world of sense experience and the world of the independently existing Forms, or Ideas. The former is fleeting, physical, and imperfect; the latter is perfect, eternal, nonphysical, and changeless. The Forms are the ideals, or standards, that we can first come to know through reason and then use to understand the objects of everyday experience. The imperfect world is a mere shadow of the world of the Forms: the Forms are *more real* than physical objects. And greatest of the Forms is the Form of the Good, the ultimate source of all that is.

For Augustine, the Good is God—the ultimate reality, the source and creator of everything that is. Like Plato's Good, God is eternal, immutable, and perfect. All that exists is God and what he creates out of nothing (*ex nihilo*). Creation out of nothing means that God did not take existing primordial materials and fashion the world; there were no preexisting primordial materials. He brought the world into existence from nonexistence. Moreover, since God is all-good, everything he creates is also good. But he is the supreme good, and everything else is less good. All these things fit into a hierarchy of goodness, with God (the highest possible good) at the summit and everything else varying by degrees of value from higher good to lowest good. This ranking of existing things—what has been called the *great chain of being*—ranges from material objects (the least good entities), to the simplest living organisms, to animals possessing a degree of consciousness, to thinking and feeling human souls (with good souls higher than bad ones), to angels, and to (at a great distance from everything else) God.

Like Plato, Augustine also ranks things according to degrees of being—that is, by *how real they are*. And he correlates gradations of being with gradations of goodness: the more real something is, the greater its goodness. So God, the supremely good, is the most fully real. Everything else is much less real, with their reality (and goodness) extending from nothingness up to a higher level of reality (and goodness) below God, the supreme reality.

> "Faith is to believe what you do not see; the reward of this faith is to see what you believe."
>
> —Augustine

4. How does Augustine's idea of degrees of being and value resemble Plato's view of reality?

> "If you believe what you like in the gospels, and reject what you don't like, it is not the gospel you believe, but yourself."
>
> —Augustine

Good and Evil

Augustine's hierarchy of being has interesting implications for the concepts of good and evil. If goodness is correlated with being, then anything that exists must be good. If something has zero goodness, then it must have zero being; it must not exist at all. So nothing in God's creation can be absolutely evil. Pure evil is not. That is, evil as a discrete reality does not exist; it is not a thing or an object to be removed or diluted. We cannot point to an entity in creation and say, "That's evil" or "That evil should be cast out." Augustine says that what we typically call evil is a deficiency of goodness, a *privation of good*. He reports that he once mistakenly "believed that evil is a kind of material substance with its own foul and misshapen mass . . . [The Manicheans] imagine it to be a malignant mind creeping through the earth."[5]

This notion of evil allows Augustine to assert, contrary to the Manicheans, that the world is not a battleground in which good and evil struggle against each other in perpetual conflict. There is no evil deity contending against an all-good God. Furthermore, God, the creator of all things, is not the source of evil. God creates only good. God created good things and set them in proper order. It is only when this order is upended that we see a privation of the good.

But what about the evil that comes from human choices and actions—what philosophers call **moral evil**? According to Augustine, this too is a deprivation of God's good. It is God who creates human will, and it is God who endows it with the power of free choice. So the will itself can only be good. But through their free choices, humans cause disorder: they turn away from God's high and immutable good toward the low and fading goods of mortal life. As Augustine says:

moral evil Evil that comes from human choices and actions.

Augustine: *On Free Will*

But the will which turns from the unchangeable and common good and turns to its own private good or to anything exterior or inferior, sins. It turns to its private good, when it wills to be governed by its own authority; to what is exterior, when it is eager to know what belongs to others and not to itself; to inferior things, when it loves bodily pleasure. In these ways a man becomes proud, inquisitive, licentious, and is taken captive by another kind of life which, when compared to the life we have just described, is really death. . . . So it happens that the good things sought by sinners cannot in any way be bad, nor can free will be bad. . . . What is bad is its turning away from the unchangeable good and its turning to changeable goods.[6]

5. How does Augustine explain the presence of evil in the world?

8.3 ANSELM AND AQUINAS

After Augustine, philosophers in the Middle Ages increased their efforts to reconcile faith with reason and to integrate Christian doctrine with classical Greek ideas. Augustine had been preoccupied with these projects, but to many later thinkers his contribution seemed inadequate or at least incomplete. He had tried to meld Plato to Christianity, but philosophers who came after him (especially Aquinas) thought Aristotle shed more light on Christian beliefs. And Augustine's style of doing philosophy—with its heavy emphasis on scripture, church fathers, and creative theorizing—was mostly abandoned by many other thinkers (notably Anselm and Aquinas) who relied more on logic and argumentation.

"For I do not seek to understand in order to believe, but I believe in order to understand. For I believe this: unless I believe, I will not understand."

—Augustine

Anselm

St. Anselm (1033–1109) was born in northern Italy, became a Benedictine monk, and was eventually appointed archbishop of Canterbury. He championed both the prerogatives of the Church and the application of reason in theology. He is most famous (and influential) for an attempted proof of the existence of God known as an

Figure 8.5 St. Anselm (1033–1109).

ontological argument. He was the first to articulate a precise statement of such an argument, and, ever since, other philosophers have been offering their own versions.

Some arguments for the existence of God appeal to the evidence of experience—either to the empirical facts about the cosmos (cosmological arguments) or to the apparent signs of design or purposeful creation in the world (**teleological arguments**). But **ontological arguments** appeal not to observations of the universe but to the concept of God itself. From the definition of God, we prove with logic alone that a supreme deity is a reality. In Anselm's ontological argument, he first posits a definition of God as the greatest possible being. This assertion, Anselm says, implies that God must actually exist, because if he did not exist in reality (and only existed in our minds), he would not be the greatest possible being. (Existing in reality is thought to make something greater than if it exists merely in someone's mind.) Therefore, God exists. Here is the argument in Anselm's own words:

Anselm: *Proslogium*

teleological arguments
Arguments that reason from apparent signs of design or purposeful creation in the world to the existence of a supreme designer.

ontological arguments
Arguments that reason from the concept of God to the existence of God.

6. Does existence always add greatness to an entity? That is, is it always greater to exist than not to exist? Why or why not?

And so, Lord, do thou, who dost give understanding to faith, give me, so far as thou knowest it to be profitable, to understand that thou art as we believe; and that thou art that which we believe. And, indeed, we believe that thou art a being than which nothing greater can be conceived. Or is there no such nature, since the fool hath said in his heart, there is no God? (Psalms xiv.1). But, at any rate, this very fool, when he hears of this being of which I speak—a being than which nothing greater can be conceived—understands what he hears, and what he understands is in his understanding; although he does not understand it to exist.

For, it is one thing for an object to be in the understanding, and another to understand that the object exists. When a painter first conceives of what he will afterwards perform, he has it in his understanding, but he does not yet understand it to be, because he has not yet performed it. But after he has made the painting, he both has it in his understanding, and he understands that it exists, because he has made it.

Hence, even the fool is convinced that something exists in the understanding, at least, than which nothing greater can be conceived. For, when he hears of this, he understands it. And whatever is understood, exists in the understanding. And assuredly that, than which nothing greater can be conceived, cannot exist in the understanding alone. For, suppose it exists in the understanding alone: then it can be conceived to exist in reality; which is greater.

Therefore, if that, than which nothing greater can be conceived, exists in the understanding alone, the very being, than which nothing greater can be conceived, is one, than which a greater can be conceived. But obviously this is impossible. Hence, there is no doubt that there exists a being, than which nothing greater can be conceived, and it exists both in the understanding and in reality.

And it assuredly exists so truly, that it cannot be conceived not to exist. For, it is possible to conceive of a being which cannot be conceived not to exist; and this is greater than one which can be conceived not to exist. Hence, if that, than which nothing greater can be conceived, can be conceived not to exist, it is not that, than which nothing greater can be conceived. But this is an irreconcilable contradiction. There is, then, so truly a being than which nothing greater can be conceived to exist, that it cannot even be conceived not to exist; and this being thou art, O Lord, our God.

So truly, therefore, dost thou exist, O Lord, my God, that thou canst not be conceived not to exist; and rightly. For, if a mind could conceive of a being better than thee, the creature would rise above the Creator; and this is most absurd. And, indeed, whatever else there is, except thee alone, can be conceived not to exist. To thee alone, therefore, it belongs to exist more truly than all other beings, and hence in a higher degree than all others. For, whatever else exists does not exist so truly, and hence in a less degree it belongs to it to exist. Why, then, has the fool said in his heart, there is no God (Psalms xiv.l), since it is so evident, to a rational mind, that thou dost exist in the highest degree of all? Why, except that he is dull and a fool?[7]

> **7.** What is the most plausible meaning of "exists in the understanding alone"? Could it mean that the concept of the greatest being possible is not actually exemplified, that it does not refer to anything existing in reality? If so, how would such an interpretation affect Anselm's argument?

Here's the argument stated more formally:

1. God, by definition, is the greatest being possible.
2. Suppose the greatest being possible exists only in the understanding (in the mind, as a mental object).
3. Then a greater being than the greatest being possible can be conceived, one existing not just in the understanding but also in reality (for a being is greater if it exists in reality than if it exists only in the understanding).
4. But this yields a contradiction, for a being greater than the greatest being possible is impossible.
5. Therefore, God, the greatest being possible, must exist in reality, not just in the understanding.

Many have found fault with this line of reasoning. The first major criticism came from an eleventh-century monk named Gaunilo, who thought that Anselm was trying to define God into existence. He maintained that if Anselm's argument were a good piece of reasoning, we could use it to prove the existence of many things that obviously do not exist—for instance, the greatest island possible. We could argue that the greatest island possible must actually exist because if it existed only in the understanding, there could conceivably be an island that is greater, namely, one that exists in reality as well as in the understanding.

Anselm replied that his reasoning does not pertain to things like Gaunilo's island, but only to God, the greatest being possible. Others have suggested that Gaunilo's critique fails because his island is not a possibility. To them it seems that for any island thought to be the greatest possible, we can always imagine how it can be greater by enhancing its properties. Such an island could therefore never be the greatest. Critics have rejected both of these suggestions, and some have countered that Anselm's line could prove the existence of absurd things other than a perfect island—like a supremely evil super being.

> "If God did not exist, it would be necessary to invent him."
>
> —Voltaire

Figure 8.6 Could there be such a thing as the greatest possible island?

In putting forth his argument, Anselm makes two assumptions: (1) existence makes something greater (that is, something is greater if it exists in the world than if it exists only in the mind as an idea), and (2) existence can be a defining property. Critics have questioned both of these. On the first count, they contend that there is no good reason to think that existence adds to the value of an entity. After all, it is not obvious that it is better for, say, a thoroughly evil being to exist than not to exist. On the second count, they doubt that existence can be any kind of defining property at all. Anselm assumes that one thing can be greater than another thing even though they have exactly the same properties, differing only in that the first thing exists and the second does not. On his view, existence is another defining property—the essential attribute that the one thing has and the other lacks. But is this plausible? Suppose you imagine an incredibly beautiful beach, detailing in your mind its every property (white sand, lovely palm trees, blue water, etc.). Then you add one more attribute—actual existence. Does this last step change the defining properties of your beach—or does it simply indicate that the beach with all its defining properties is actual? Many philosophers, including Immanuel Kant (1724–1804), would choose the latter. As Kant says:

Immanuel Kant: *Critique of Pure Reason*

"Being" is obviously not a real predicate [term designating a property]; that is, it is not a concept of something which could be added to the concept of a thing. It is merely the positing

of a thing, or of certain determinations, as existing in themselves. . . . By whatever and by however many predicates we may think a thing—even if we completely determine it—we do not make the least addition to the thing when we further declare that this thing *is*.[8]

In any case, some detractors think the weakest link in Anselm's chain of reasoning is premise 2, the supposition that the greatest being possible exists only in the understanding. This claim gives rise to the contradiction that a greater being than the greatest being possible can be conceived (one existing in reality). But they argue that the contradiction dissolves if we take premise 2 to mean not that the greatest being possible exists in some sense in the mind (the view that Anselm seems to take), but simply that the concept of the greatest being possible does not refer to any actually existing thing. The latter, they insist, is the more reasonable reading of "exists only in the understanding," and it does not yield any contradictions about the nature of God. With this reading of premise 2, Anselm's argument does not go through.

"Faith seeking reason."
—Anselm

8. According to critics, what is the weakest link in Anselm's chain of reasoning? Do you agree with them? Why or why not?

Aquinas

St. Thomas Aquinas (1225–1274) was born into a noble family in Southern Italy to eventually become the greatest philosopher of the medieval period and, to this day, the official theologian of the Roman Catholic Church. Because his family had decided that he should be a great church leader, they packed him off before the age of six to the Benedictine monastery of Monte Cassino for training. At fourteen, he was sent to the University of Naples for further study, and there his life took what his family considered a radical turn. At age twenty, he joined the scholarly Dominican order and pursued, not a leadership position in the church, but the rarefied life of the intellect.

Becoming alarmed at Aquinas's change of plans, his family had him kidnapped and locked in the family castle for several months. When it became clear that he was not going to relinquish his scholarly ambitions, they released him, and he continued his studies and his writing at the University of Paris and in Cologne, Rome, Naples, Viterbo, and Orvieto.

Aquinas's great contribution to both philosophy and Christianity was his fusion of Aristotle's philosophy with Christian doctrines. In theology he distinguished between reason and faith, giving each its own domain of inquiry. Reason can be used to prove the existence of God, he says, but only through faith can we know such mysteries as the incarnation and the trinity.

Aquinas produced significant works in many areas of philosophy, including logic, epistemology, ethics, and philosophy of religion. Nowadays he is most famous for his arguments for the existence of God and for his system of ethics known as *natural law theory*.

"A man has free choice to the extent that he is rational."
—Aquinas

Figure 8.7 St. Thomas Aquinas (1225–1274).

cosmological arguments Arguments that reason from the existence of the universe, or cosmos (or some fundamental feature of it), to the conclusion that God exists.

Aquinas's Five Ways. As mentioned earlier, **cosmological arguments** reason from the existence of the universe, or cosmos (or some fundamental feature of it), to the conclusion that God exists. They can boast a long lineage, having been set out by many theorists besides Aquinas—from Aristotle, Plato, Ghazali, Averroës, and Spinoza to contemporary philosophers such as Richard Swinburne and William Lane Craig. The arguments all begin with the empirical fact that the universe, or one of its essential properties, exists—and end with the conclusion that only God could be responsible for this fact. In his masterpiece *Summa Theologica*, Aquinas offers five "proofs" (his famous "Five Ways") of God's existence, the first three of which are cosmological arguments. This is how Aquinas lays out the first two:

Thomas Aquinas: *Summa Theologica*

The existence of God can be shown in five ways.

The first and more manifest way is the argument from motion. It is certain, and evident to our senses, that in the world some things are in motion. Now whatever is in motion is put in motion by another, for nothing can be in motion except it is in potentiality to that towards which it is in motion; whereas a thing moves inasmuch as it is in actuality.

For motion is nothing else than the reduction of something from potentiality to actuality. But nothing can be reduced from potentiality to actuality, except by something in a state of actuality. Thus that which is actually hot, as fire, makes wood, which is potentially hot, to be actually hot, and thereby moves and changes it. Now it is not possible that the same thing should be at once in actuality and potentiality in the same respect, but only in different respects. For what is actually hot cannot simultaneously be potentially hot; but it is simultaneously potentially cold. It is therefore impossible that in the same respect and in the same way a thing should be both mover and moved, i.e. that it should move itself.

9. Why does Aquinas think there cannot be an infinite chain of movers? Do you accept his reasons for this? Can you conceive of a series of movers stretching infinitely into the past? If so, can you detect any contradictions inherent in your conception?

Figure 8.8 Must there be a first cause to the long chain of causes?

Therefore, whatever is in motion must be put in motion by another. If that by which it is put in motion be itself put in motion, then this also must needs be put in motion by another, and that by another again. But this cannot go on to infinity, because then there would be no first mover, and, consequently, no other mover; seeing that subsequent movers move only inasmuch as they are put in motion by the first mover; as the staff moves only because it is put in motion by the hand. Therefore it is necessary to arrive at a first mover, put in motion by no other; and this everyone understands to be God.

The second way is from the nature of the efficient cause. In the world of sense we find there is an order of efficient causes. There is no case known (neither is it, indeed, possible) in which a thing is found to be the efficient cause of itself; for so it would be prior to itself, which is impossible. Now in efficient causes it is not possible to go on to infinity, because in all efficient causes following in order, the first is the cause of the intermediate cause, and the intermediate is the cause of the ultimate cause, whether the intermediate cause be several, or only one. Now to take away the cause is to take away the effect. Therefore, if there be no first cause among efficient causes, there will be no ultimate, nor any intermediate cause. But if in efficient causes it is possible to go on to infinity, there will be no first efficient cause, neither will there be an ultimate effect, nor any intermediate efficient causes; all of which is plainly false. Therefore it is necessary to admit a first efficient cause, to which everyone gives the name of God.[9]

10. Why does Aquinas insist that there must be a first cause? Does his argument show that the first cause is in fact God? Does it show, for example, that the first cause could not be an evil demon or an impersonal force?

Aquinas's *argument from motion* (his first way) goes like this: It is obvious that some things in the universe are moving (that is, changing), and if they are moving, something else must have caused them to move. And this "something else" must also have been moving, set in motion by yet another thing that was moving, and this thing set in motion by another moving thing, and so on. But this series of things-moving-other-things cannot go on forever, to infinity, because then there would not be something that started all the moving. There must therefore be an initial mover (a first mover), an extraordinary being that started the universe moving but is not itself moved by anything else—and this being we call God.

Aquinas's second way is his famous *first-cause argument*. He maintains that everything we can observe has a cause, and it is clear that nothing can cause itself. For something to cause itself, it would have to exist *prior to* itself, which is impossible. Neither can something be caused by an infinite regress of causes—that is, a series of causes stretching to infinity. In any series of causes, Aquinas says, there must be a first cause, which causes the second, which causes the third, and so on. But in an infinite series of causes, there would be no first cause and thus no subsequent causes, including causes existing now. So infinite regresses make no sense. Therefore, there must be a first cause of everything, and this first cause we call God. (Here Aquinas is not thinking of a first cause of a *temporal* series of causes, as in a sequence of falling dominoes, but of a first cause that sustains the whole series of causes, like the bottom building block that holds up all the others in a stack.)

Against these two arguments, philosophers have lodged several criticisms. One of the strongest takes aim at Aquinas's claim that an infinite regress is not possible. Aquinas thinks that a chain of causes must have a first cause; otherwise there would be no subsequent causes in the world. In an infinite regress of causes, he contends,

"To one who has faith, no explanation is necessary. To one without faith, no explanation is possible."

—Aquinas

DETAILS

Science and the Uncaused Universe

The notion that some events in the universe are entirely uncaused is now widely accepted among quantum physicists, the scientists who study the realm of subatomic particles (such as electrons,

Figure 8.9 If some events are uncaused, does that refute Aquinas's first-cause argument?

there would be no first cause and therefore no subsequent causes. Critics reply that just because an infinite chain of causes has no first cause, that doesn't mean that the chain of causes has no cause at all: in an infinite chain of causes, *every* link has a cause. Many philosophers, including David Hume (1711–1776), see no logical contradiction in the idea of an infinite regress. They hold that the universe need not have had a beginning; it may be eternal, without beginning, and without a first cause or a first mover. The universe may have simply *always been*.

Some claim that the worst problem with Aquinas's arguments is that at best they prove only that the universe had a first mover or first cause—but not that the first mover or first cause is God. For all the arguments show, the first mover or first cause could be an impersonal substance or energy, or several minor deities, or a supreme but evil demon. Perhaps the universe is, as many scientists and philosophers allege, simply an eternal, uncaused brute fact.

positrons, and quarks). According to quantum physics, subatomic particles frequently pop in and out of existence randomly—that is, they appear and disappear uncaused out of a perfect vacuum. From these findings, some scientists have speculated that the universe itself may have arisen uncaused. This is how two physicists describe the phenomenon:

> [T]he idea of a First Cause sounds somewhat fishy in light of the modern theory of quantum mechanics. According to the most commonly accepted interpretation of quantum mechanics, individual subatomic particles can behave in unpredictable ways and there are numerous random, uncaused events.
>
> —Richard Morris, *Achilles in the Quantum World*, 1997

> [Q]uantum electrodynamics reveals that an electron, positron, and photon occasionally emerge spontaneously in a perfect vacuum. When this happens, the three particles exist for a brief time, and then annihilate each other, leaving no trace behind. . . . The spontaneous, temporary emergence of particles from a vacuum is called a vacuum fluctuation, and it is utterly commonplace in quantum field theory.
>
> —Edward Tryon, "Is the Universe a Vacuum Fluctuation?" *Nature*, 1973

Suppose some subatomic events are uncaused. Does this show that the universe is uncaused? What bearing does the phenomenon have on Aquinas's first-cause argument?

Aquinas's fifth way is a teleological argument (an argument from design). He contends that since the world shows signs of order and purposeful design—since things in nature act toward ends even though they lack intelligence or awareness—the world must be purposefully designed by an intelligent being, which we call God. As Aquinas puts it,

> The fifth way is taken from the governance of the world. We see that things which lack knowledge, such as natural bodies, act for an end, and this is evident from their acting always, or nearly always, in the same way, so as to obtain the best result. Hence it is plain that they achieve their end, not fortuitously, but designedly. Now whatever lacks knowledge cannot move towards an end, unless it is directed by some being endowed with knowledge and intelligence; as the arrow is directed by the

archer. Therefore some intelligent being exists by whom all natural things are directed to their end; and this being we call God.[10]

Some modern philosophers have cast this sort of design argument as an inference to the best explanation, an argument form that we use every day and that science relies on heavily. It says the best explanation for a state of affairs is most likely to be true. So Aquinas's argument can be expressed like this: The universe exhibits order and purposeful design; the best explanation for this order and purposeful design is that the universe was designed by God; therefore, it is probably true that the universe was designed by God.

But philosophers deny this conclusion. They argue that naturalistic (nontheistic) explanations are better. For one thing, such explanations are simpler—that is, they are based on fewer assumptions. The God explanation, however, assumes an unknown entity (God) with unknown powers and unknown properties. Naturalistic explanations do not leap to such assumptions. A case in point is the question of what best explains the apparent design of biological life. Science maintains that the best explanation for the apparent design of biological life is the theory of evolution, which says living things, in all their variety and complexity, arose through natural processes.

Aquinas's Moral Philosophy. From ancient times to the present day, many people have thought that the outlines of the moral law are plain to see because they are written large and true in nature itself. This basic notion has been developed over the centuries into what is known as **natural law theory**, the view that right actions are those that conform to moral standards discerned in nature through human reason. Undergirding this doctrine is the belief that all of nature (including humankind) is teleological, that it is somehow directed toward particular goals or ends, and that humans achieve their highest good when they follow their true, natural inclinations leading to these goals or ends. (Recall that this was also Aristotle's view.) There is, in other words, a way things *are*—natural processes and functions that accord with the natural law—and how things are shows how things *should be*. The prime duty of humans, then, is to guide their lives toward these natural ends, acting in accordance with the requirements of natural law.

Implicit in all this is the element of rationality. According to natural law theory, humans are rational beings empowered by reason to perceive the workings of nature, determine the natural inclinations of humans, and recognize the implications therein for morally permissible actions. That is, reason enables human beings to ascertain the moral law implicit in nature and to apply that objective, universal standard to their lives.

Though natural law theory has both religious and nonreligious forms, Aquinas's theistic formulation has been the theory's dominant version. It is not only the official moral outlook of the Roman Catholic Church, but it has also been the intellectual starting point for many contemporary variations of the theory, secular and otherwise. For Aquinas, God is the author of the natural law who gave humans the gift of reason to discern the law for themselves and live accordingly. Aquinas argues that

natural law theory The view that right actions are those that conform to moral standards discerned in nature through human reason.

"All that I have written seems like straw to me."
—Aquinas

human beings naturally tend toward—and therefore have a duty of—preserving human life and health (and so must not kill the innocent), producing and raising children, seeking knowledge (including knowledge of God), and cultivating cooperative social relationships. In all this, Aquinas says, the overarching aim is to do and promote good and avoid evil.

Natural law theory does not provide a relevant moral rule covering every situation, but it does offer guidance through general moral principles, some of which are thought to apply universally and absolutely (admitting no exceptions). Among these principles are absolutist prohibitions against directly killing the innocent, lying, and using contraceptives. In his list of acts considered wrong no matter what, Aquinas includes adultery, blasphemy, and sodomy.

Of course, moral principles or rules often conflict, demanding that we fulfill two or more incompatible duties. We may be forced, for example, to either tell a lie and save people's lives or tell the truth and cause their death—but we cannot do both. Some moral theories address these problems by saying that all duties are prima facie: when duties conflict, we must decide which ones override the others. Theories that posit absolute duties—natural law theory being a prime example—often do not have this option. How does the natural law tradition resolve such dilemmas? Among other resources, it uses the **doctrine of double effect**, a principle derived partly from Aquinas's discussion of the morality of self-defense.

This principle, now a cornerstone of Roman Catholic ethics, affirms that performing a bad action to bring about a good effect is never morally acceptable but that performing a good action may sometimes be acceptable even if it produces a bad effect. More precisely, the principle says it is always wrong to intentionally perform

11. Is nature teleological? Is it directed toward particular goals or ends? Why or why not?

doctrine of double effect The moral principle that performing a bad action to bring about a good effect is never morally acceptable but that performing a good action may sometimes be acceptable even if it produces a bad effect.

Figure 8.10 Is each part of nature directed toward particular aims or goals?

a bad action to produce a good effect, but doing a good action that results in a bad effect may be permissible if the bad effect is not intended although foreseen. In the former case, a bad thing is said to be directly intended; in the latter, a bad thing is not directly intended.

These requirements have been detailed in four "tests" that an action must pass to be judged morally permissible. We can express a traditional version of these tests like this:

1. The action itself must be morally permissible.
2. Causing a bad effect must not be used to obtain a good effect (the end does not justify the means).
3. Whatever the outcome of an action, the intention must be to cause only a good effect. (The bad effect can be foreseen but never intended.)
4. The bad effect of an action must not be greater in importance than the good effect.

Consider the application of these tests to euthanasia. Suppose an eighty-year-old, hopelessly ill patient is in continuous, unbearable pain and begs to be put out of her misery. Is it morally permissible to grant her request (either by giving a lethal injection or ending all ordinary life-sustaining measures)? If we apply the doctrine of double effect as outlined earlier, we must conclude that the answer is *no*: euthanasia—either active or passive—is not a morally permissible option here. (In the Roman Catholic view, all forms of euthanasia are wrong, although it is permissible not to treat a hope-lessly ill person for whom ordinary life-sustaining treatments are useless.) Failing even one of the tests would render an action impermissible, but in this case let us run through all four as a natural law theorist might:

1. Taking steps to terminate someone's life is a clear violation of test 1. Whatever its effects, the action of taking a life is in itself immoral, a violation of the cardinal duty to preserve innocent life.
2. Ending the woman's life to save her from terrible suffering is an instance of causing a bad effect (the woman's death) as a means of achieving a good effect (cessation of pain)—a failure of test 2.
3. The death of the woman is intended; it is not merely a tragic side effect of the attempt solely to ease her pain. So the action fails test 3.
4. Causing the death of an innocent person is a great evil that cannot be counter-balanced by the good of pain relief. So the action does not pass test 4.

The verdict in such a case would be different, however, if the patient's death were not intentionally caused but unintentionally brought about. Suppose, for example, that the physician sees that the woman is in agony and gives her a large injection of morphine to minimize her suffering—knowing full well that the dose will also probably speed her death. In this scenario, the act of easing the woman's pain is itself morally permissible (test 1). Her death is not a means to achieve some greater good; the goal is to ease her suffering (test 2). Her death is not intended; the intention is to alleviate her pain, though the unintended (but foreseen) side effect is her hastened death (test 3). Finally, the good effect of an easier death seems more or less equivalent in importance to the bad effect of a hastened death. Therefore, unintentionally but knowingly bringing about the woman's death in this way is morally permissible.

12. What is the doctrine of double effect? Is it a plausible principle for dealing with conflicts between moral principles? Explain.

8.4 AVICENNA AND MAIMONIDES

As we've seen, in the early Middle Ages, access to classical Greek learning was limited. The works of the great Greek thinkers were generally unavailable in the West—while many of the surviving manuscripts were being translated, preserved, and studied in the Arab world. As a result, there arose in later medieval times several brilliant philosophers who were *not* Christians. Some came out of Islam and some Judaism. The brightest star from the former is Avicenna, and the greatest figure from the latter is Maimonides.

> "The world is divided into men who have wit and no religion and men who have religion and no wit."
> —Avicenna

Avicenna

Known in the Arab world as Ibn Sina, the Persian philosopher and physician Avicenna (980–1037) was a prodigy and polymath who made extraordinary contributions to both philosophy and science. He was born in present-day Uzbekistan (then Persia) and educated in mathematics, medicine, physics, and logic, purportedly mastering these subjects in his teens. By age sixteen he was a practicing physician, and by age twenty he had published an encyclopedia. In his life he wrote approximately two hundred books in both Arabic and Persian, including the *Canon of Medicine* (a medical textbook used in the West for hundreds of years) and the philosophical works *Metaphysics, The Healing,* and *Deliverance.* He advanced important distinctions in ontology (the study of being, or existence), discovered useful relationships in logic, and made unique contributions to the field of medical diagnosis.

In philosophy Avicenna developed a systematic and comprehensive metaphysics—that is, a view of the fundamental nature of reality. Constructing this metaphysics was his greatest achievement: he combined his own interpretation of Aristotelian concepts with Neoplatonism and reconciled the whole with a version of Islamic theology. For him, there was no conflict between truth acquired through religion and truth arrived at through reason and argument. Truth is truth wherever it is found.

Avicenna is esteemed by Western readers for having devised a new argument for the existence of the soul. He asks us to imagine a fellow (a "flying man") suspended in empty space, unable to detect his body or to receive any sensations from any sense organs. Despite the man's inability to have sense experience or to even tell whether he has a body, the man would know that he exists, that he is a being. (Descartes offered a similar argument in the seventeenth century.) And since a body is not necessary to determine whether he exists, says Avicenna, the man must be essentially an immaterial being—in other words, a soul.

He also developed a sophisticated cosmological argument, one that Aquinas would use two hundred years later. It depends on the philosophical concepts of necessity and contingency. A contingent being is one that is possible but not necessary: it

Figure 8.11 The image of Avicenna (980–1037) on a Polish postage stamp.

13. What is Avicenna's argument for the existence of the soul? Is it sound?

"Do not consider it proof just because it is written in books, for a liar who will deceive with his tongue will not hesitate to do the same with his pen."
—Maimonides

"You must accept the truth from whatever source it comes."
—Maimonides

14. What is Maimonides's attitude toward reason and religion? How does he propose that we deal with apparent conflicts between reason and scripture?

Figure 8.12 Maimonides (1138–1204).

could have failed to exist. A horse is a contingent being, because it is possible for it to never have come into existence. A necessary being is one that could *not* have failed to exist; it is impossible for it not to exist. Avicenna argues that reality consists of beings (entities) arranged in a hierarchy in which each thing causes a subordinate thing to exist. Since each being is caused (sustained) by something else (and the chain of causes cannot go on forever), all such beings must be contingent, and their ultimate cause must be a necessary being—that is, God.

Maimonides

Moses Maimonides (Moses ben Maimon, 1138–1204) is an unsurpassed scholar of Jewish law and the most important Jewish philosopher in history. His comprehensive attempt to reconcile religious tradition with philosophy, especially Aristotelian thought, engages thinkers to this day.

Maimonides was born in Cordova, Spain, a Muslim-ruled city whose intellectual life was among the liveliest and most permissive of the medieval world. That atmosphere changed in 1148 when the Muslim Almohads conquered Cordova and demanded that non-Muslims immediately convert or submit to exile or death. Having little choice, Maimonides and his family fled the city, traveling about for years, seeking refuge in Morocco, Palestine, and finally Egypt.

In Cairo, he served as court physician and Egypt's foremost rabbinic leader, all the while writing the works that would influence generations to come. His preeminent authority as a rabbinic jurist was forever established by his *Book of the Commandments*; the *Commentary on the Mishnah*; and the fourteen-volume *Code of Jewish Law*, the *Mishneh Torah*. His credentials as a philosopher were secured by his masterpiece, *The Guide for the Perplexed*.

Like ancient Greek thinkers and some philosophers of his day (including a few Arabic scholars), Maimonides sought truth through reason and tried to apply rational methods of inquiry not just to philosophy and science but also to religious and biblical beliefs. This approach led him to argue in his *Guide for the Perplexed* that biblical and rabbinic writings embody, in figurative language, truths that can be discovered and demonstrated by philosophy. There can be no contradiction between religious texts and the deliverances of reason, although the former must be interpreted figuratively to agree with the latter. To interpret scripture literally is to fall into error. For example, scriptural language seems to suggest that God is corporeal and that he possesses essential attributes. But, Maimonides says, philosophy shows that these literal understandings are false, so the passages must be given a figurative meaning. God has no body and cannot be conceived of or described at all. We can only characterize God negatively (for instance, "God does not lack power" instead of "God is powerful"), which is simply a way of acknowledging that God is beyond our comprehension.

PORTRAIT

Averroës

Averroës, or Ibn Rushd (1126–1198), was an eminent Islamic philosopher who wrote renowned commentaries on Aristotle and defended philosophy as a Koran-sanctioned method to reflect on God's (Allah's) design. He was born in Cordoba, studied science and Islamic law, became a judge in Seville, and finally died in Marrakesh, Morocco. He argues for the legitimacy of philosophy in *The Decisive Treatise* and for naturalism in his *Incoherence of the Incoherence*.

In several works he departs from Muslim orthodoxy, a move that resulted, at one point, in his being persecuted by the authorities. He rejected ideas in Neoplatonism, took a skeptical view of Platonic Forms, and attacked Avicenna's cosmological argument. He also arrived at some non-Christian views, holding that the world is eternal (not created at a moment in time) and that all minds are one and eternal (as opposed to being individual immortal souls). He insists that if the Koran appears to contain contradictions, the discrepancies can be reconciled via a better grasp of philosophy.

Figure 8.13 Averroës (1126–1198).

8.5 HILDEGARD OF BINGEN

As we've seen, after the fall of Rome, philosophy was practiced under the auspices of the Church, and philosophy was largely a Christian affair. It was also a male affair. Both culture and religion said it must be so. Generally only men could get a good education, which could be acquired only through the Church—and without education, no one was likely to do philosophy. In such an inhospitable environment, what chance did a woman have of doing philosophy? Slim, perhaps—but a few women nevertheless beat the odds and produced important philosophical writings that deserve much more scholarly attention than they have received so far.

Probably the most remarkable woman philosopher-theologian of the era was Hildegard of Bingen (1098–1179). She was one of the first religious mystics in the West, and her endeavors and writings (including her philosophy) were often inspired and guided by her lifelong involvement in Christian mysticism. (**Mysticism** is belief in the alleged ability to access, through trances or visions, divine knowledge that is unattainable through sense experience or reason.)

She was born in a small town in Germany to a noble German family, the tenth of ten children. At eight years old, she was given over to the Church, where she received a religious education, including training in Latin. She later wrote that it was as a young girl that she started to experience visions. Some scholarship suggests that her

mysticism The belief in the alleged ability to access, through trances or visions, divine knowledge that is unattainable through sense experience or reason.

Sv.
Hilde
garda·

Figure 8.14 Hildegard of Bingen (1098–1179).

visions arose from migraines, a serious ailment known to produce some of the kinds of visual effects and physical symptoms that Hildegard described. In any case, the extraordinary experiences led Hildegard to the philosophical and theological insights that she wrote down and preached.

Perhaps her main contribution in philosophy is in ethics, but like many other thinkers of the past she also wrote about natural science and medicine. She composed poetry and liturgical music, wrote a musical morality play, and established two convents where ancient philosophical manuscripts were copied and women learned Latin. In a time when female intellects were generally ignored by Church officials, Hildegard earned the respect of monks, archbishops, emperors, and even popes. She preached publicly (even going on preaching tours), corresponded prolifically, and attracted followers, including some fanatical ones. (The movie *Visions* depicts her life, and her music is now available on CD.)

Most of her important writings are found in three major works. In the first, *Scivias* ("Know the Ways of the Lord"), she elaborates Christian cosmology and Church doctrine. In the second, "The Book of Life's Merits," she presents her theory of ethics as an allegorical conflict between thirty-five vices and their associated virtues, detailing penance and punishment for each. In her allegory, vices are hideous but tempting, while virtues are wise and powerful, exhorting us to overcome temptation. The third, "Book of Divine Works," is simultaneously a treatise on Christian cosmology and man's relationship to God. The central metaphor is man as a microcosm reflecting the glory and intricacy of the macrocosmic universe.

We might expect that since Hildegard lived in the Church-dominated, sin-obsessed Middle Ages, she would take a prudish nun's view of sexuality. She didn't. She had a much more favorable opinion of sex than we would expect, and she—like a liberated woman—wrote about women's sexual pleasure. She may even have given us the first written account of the female orgasm:

Hildegard: *Causae et Curae*

When a woman is making love with a man, a sense of heat in her brain, which brings with it sensual delight, communicates the taste of that delight during the act and summons forth the emission of the man's seed. And when the seed has fallen into its place, that vehement heat descending from her brain draws the seed to itself and holds it, and soon the woman's sexual organs contract, and all the parts that are ready to open up during the time of menstruation now close, in the same way as a strong man can hold something in his fist.[11]

In 2012 Pope Benedict XVI declared Hildegard a saint and gave her writings the same lofty status as those produced by such luminaries as St. Augustine and St. Thomas Aquinas.

8.6 WILLIAM OF OCKHAM

William of Ockham (c. 1285–1347) was an English philosopher and theologian who, like a few other philosophers in the late Middle Ages, was willing to challenge the views of the Church and the venerated philosophers of the past. He brought new ideas and fresh insights to logic, metaphysics, epistemology, and language—and in the process was excommunicated for heresy.

Ockham was born in the English village of Ockham, joined the Franciscan order when he was young, and studied philosophy in London and theology in Oxford. He lectured in philosophy and wrote a logic textbook, commentaries on Aristotle, and several works on current philosophical controversies. Because of his writings, he was involved in numerous philosophical and theological disputes with critics (including the pope). Inevitably he was accused of heresy. The last straw came in 1328 when he argued that the pope's view on the Church's ownership of property was wrong, contrary to scripture, and in conflict with the positions of previous popes. The papal reaction was excommunication. Ockham had to flee to Munich and live under the protection of the emperor of Bavaria. He remained there, writing treatises, until his death, possibly caused by the Black Death.

Aside from Ockham's quarrels over Church doctrine, he is best remembered for the *principle of parsimony* (also called "Ockham's razor") and for his strong stand against the possibility of real universals (which earned him the title of the "father of nominalism"). In defining the principle of parsimony, he is often quoted as saying, "Entities are not to be multiplied beyond necessity"—something he never actually said. The principle, which became associated with him because of his style of philosophy, admonishes that in devising explanations or theories to explain a phenomenon, we should prefer the simpler theory over the more complex. The principle is widely applied in science and everyday life and is often formulated as a requirement to prefer theories that, all things considered, make the fewest assumptions.

His rejection of universals concerns a philosophical controversy that feverishly preoccupied philosophers and theologians throughout the late Middle Ages. A universal is a term (such as a noun) that refers to several particular things—for example, "man" or "triangle." "Man" does not apply to a particular man, but to the many individuals that make up humankind. "Socrates," on the other hand, applies to just one particular thing, the philosopher Socrates. The debate over universals has

15. What is Ockham's principle of parsimony? How might a scientist use it to judge which of two theories concerning the same phenomenon is better?

Figure 8.15 William of Ockham (c. 1285–1347).

THEN AND NOW

Modern Realism about Universals

Probably most people today would not have gone along with Ockham's nominalism. Common sense and modern science prefer some form of realism regarding universals. One eminent thinker who took this realist stand was the twentieth-century philosopher Bertrand Russell (1872–1970). He gave one of the clearest defenses of the realist position, focusing on universals that denote relations (such as "over" or "beside") and arguing that they are neither mental nor material but nevertheless real:

> Consider such a proposition as 'Edinburgh is north of London'. Here we have a relation between two places, and it seems plain that the relation subsists independently of our knowledge of it. When we come to know that Edinburgh is north of London, we come to know something which has to do only with Edinburgh and London: we do not cause the truth of the proposition by coming to know it, on the contrary we merely apprehend a fact which was there before we knew it. The part of the earth's surface where Edinburgh stands would be north of the part where London stands, even if there were no human being to know about north and south, and even if there were no minds at all in the universe. . . . Hence we must admit that the relation ["north of"], like the terms it relates, is not dependent on thought, but belongs to the independent world which thought apprehends but does not create.

Ockham would probably say that the notion "north of" is just a concept in our minds and does not refer to any independently existing reality. Do you agree? Why or why not?

Bertrand Russell, *The Problems of Philosophy* (Oxford: Oxford University Press, 1912, 1959), 97–98.

16. Is nominalism plausible? Why or why not?

been ongoing and complex, but in its simplest form it amounts to this: On one side are the *realists*, who believe, as Plato does, that universals exist outside the mind, that they somehow have an actual existence beyond our thinking of them. For Plato, universals are the Forms, existing independently of the mind in a perfect, timeless realm that is more real than material reality. For realists, however, it's possible to deny the existence of Plato's Forms and still believe that universals somehow correspond to real things. The opposing view is taken by the *nominalists*, who claim that universals do not apply to anything really existing but are merely names or concepts representing many things. Ockham's position on the matter has been called nominalist, even though his view is more subtle than the one presented here.

It's easy to dismiss the medieval scholars' obsession with universals as pedantry run amok. But the implications of realism or nominalism are far-reaching. The philosopher Frederick Copleston explains one of the difficulties like this:

Frederick Copleston: *A History of Philosophy, Volume II: Medieval Philosophy: From Augustine to Duns Scotus*

The scientist expresses his knowledge in abstract and universal terms (for example, he does not make a statement about this particular electron, but about electrons in general), and if these terms have no foundation in extramental reality, his science is an arbitrary construction, which has no relation to reality. In so far indeed as human judgements are of a universal character or involve universal concepts, as in the statement that this rose is red, the problem would extend to human knowledge in general, and if the question as to the existence of an extramental foundation of a universal concept is answered in the negative, skepticism would result.[12]

WRITING AND REASONING   **CHAPTER 8**

1. What were some of the most important contributions that Augustine made to Christianity?

2. What are Aquinas's Five Ways? What criticisms have been launched against them by philosophers? Do you accept any of the Ways? Why?

3. What is Avicenna's argument for the existence of the soul? Is his argument sound? Why?

4. What is Anselm's ontological argument? What are two assumptions that Anselm makes in putting forth his famous argument? Are these assumptions well founded? Explain.

5. What is Ockham's razor? Provide an example of how the principle can be applied in science or everyday life.

REVIEW NOTES

8.1 BETWEEN ANCIENT AND MODERN

- At the beginning of the Middle Ages, the tradition of rational inquiry that first blossomed in Athens and then spread to all the places subdued by Alexander and his Greek culture was fading.

- There was a virtual takeover of philosophy by Christianity in the first millennium CE and a weakening of Christianity's grip during the Renaissance in the second millennium. In the first millennium, the Church dominated philosophy, but it also needed philosophy to work out the details of doctrine or to make sense of the Church's teachings or to show that there was no real conflict between religion and reason. Countless clerics and Church officials studied philosophy. The inevitable result of this mingling of philosophy and religion was that some good philosophical work was achieved.

8.2 AUGUSTINE

- Augustine (354–430 CE) was a Christian philosopher and theologian who had an enormous influence on Christian thought and on the West's appreciation of Plato and Aristotle. He affected Christian theology more than any other early Christian author, introduced Plato to generations of thinkers, and forced philosophers in every epoch to reckon with his ideas and authority.

- From both classical and Christian threads, Augustine wove a distinctive set of doctrines about God, the world, knowledge, ethics, and existence. In epistemology, metaphysics, and moral philosophy, he shaped new doctrines from old ideas and original analyses. Along the way, he found that in his search for wisdom there was a place for both faith and reason, both belief and understanding. He thought that to attain wisdom, belief had to come first, then understanding.

- Augustine rejects skepticism and insists that regarding mathematical, logical, and evaluative truths, we can have certain knowledge; they are eternal, changeless, and necessary.

- From his notion of necessary truths, Augustine argues for the existence of God. He reasons that if truth is the highest good, then truth must be God, because God is the highest good, the most excellent of all things. If an entity is higher and more excellent than truth, then *that* entity must be God.

- From Plato and Neoplatonists, Augustine derives a view of the world as an all-encompassing hierarchy of existing things and their value—a great chain of being.

- Augustine reasons that evil as a discrete reality does not exist; it is not a thing or an object to be removed or diluted. We cannot point to an entity in creation and say, "That's evil" or "That evil should be cast out." He says that what we typically call evil is a deficiency of goodness, a privation of good. Moral evil arises through the free choices of humans. They cause disorder: they turn away from God's high and immutable good toward the low and fading goods of mortal life.

8.3 ANSELM AND AQUINAS

- Anselm is famous for his ontological argument. He first posits a definition of God as the greatest possible being. This assertion, he says, implies that God must actually exist, because if he did not exist in reality (and only existed in our minds), he would not be the greatest possible being. (Existing in reality is thought to make something greater than if it exists merely in someone's mind.) Therefore, God exists. Detractors think the weakest link in Anselm's chain of reasoning is premise 2, the supposition that the greatest being possible exists only in the understanding.

- Aquinas presents a first-cause argument. He maintains that everything we can observe has a cause, and it is clear that nothing can cause itself. For something to cause itself, it would have to exist *prior to* itself, which is impossible. Neither can something be caused by an infinite regress of causes—that is, a series of causes stretching to infinity. In any series of causes, Aquinas says, there must be a first cause, which causes the second, which causes the third, and so on. Therefore, there must be a first cause of everything, and this first cause is God.

- Aquinas argues for the natural law theory of ethics, the view that right actions are those that conform to moral standards discerned in nature through human reason.

Undergirding this doctrine is the belief that all of nature is directed toward particular goals or ends, and that humans achieve their highest good when they follow their true, natural inclinations leading to these goals or ends. There is, in other words, a way things *are*—natural processes and functions that accord with the natural law—and how things are shows how things *should be*. The prime duty of humans, then, is to guide their lives toward these natural ends, acting in accordance with the requirements of natural law.

8.4 AVICENNA AND MAIMONIDES

- Avicenna, a Persian philosopher and physician, was a prodigy and polymath who made extraordinary contributions to both philosophy and science.

- Avicenna is famous for devising a new argument for the existence of the soul. He asks us to imagine a fellow (a "flying man") suspended in empty space, unable to detect his body or to receive any sensations from any sense organs. Despite the man's inability to have sense experience or to even tell whether he has a body, the man would know that he exists, that he is a being. And since a body is not necessary to determine whether he exists, says Avicenna, the man must be essentially an immaterial being—a soul.

- Moses Maimonides was an unsurpassed scholar of Jewish law and the most important Jewish philosopher in history. His comprehensive attempt to reconcile religious tradition with philosophy, especially Aristotelian thought, engages thinkers to this day.

- Maimonides sought truth through reason and tried to apply rational methods of inquiry not just to philosophy and science but also to religious and biblical beliefs. There can be no contradiction between religious texts and the deliverances of reason, he says, although the former must be interpreted figuratively to agree with the latter. To interpret scripture literally is to fall into error.

8.5 HILDEGARD OF BINGEN

- Hildegard of Bingen was one of the first religious mystics in the West, and her endeavors and writings (including her philosophy) were often inspired and guided by her lifelong involvement in Christian mysticism.

- Contrary to the culture and Christian order of the times, Hildegard earned the respect of monks, archbishops, emperors, and even popes. She preached publicly (even going on preaching tours), corresponded prolifically, and attracted followers.

- Hildegard presents her theory of ethics as an allegorical conflict between thirty-five vices and their associated virtues. The vices are depicted as hideous but tempting, while virtues are wise and powerful, exhorting us to overcome temptation.

8.6 WILLIAM OF OCKHAM

- William of Ockham was an English philosopher and theologian who, like a few other philosophers in the late Middle Ages, was willing to challenge the views of the Church and the venerated philosophers of the past. He brought new ideas and fresh insights to logic, metaphysics, epistemology, and language.

- Because of his writings, he was involved in numerous philosophical and theological disputes with critics (including the pope). Inevitably he was accused of heresy. Ockham had to flee to Munich and live under the protection of the emperor of Bavaria. He remained there, writing treatises, until his death, possibly caused by the Black Death.

- He is best remembered for the principle of parsimony (also called "Ockham's razor") and for his strong stand against the possibility of real universals. The principle, which became associated with him because of his style of philosophy, admonishes that in devising explanations or theories to explain a phenomenon, we should prefer the simpler theory over the more complex. The principle is widely applied in science and everyday life and is often formulated as a requirement to prefer theories that, all things considered, make the fewest assumptions.

- Ockham's rejection of universals concerns a philosophical controversy that feverishly preoccupied thinkers throughout the late Middle Ages. The debate over universals has been ongoing and complex. On one side are the *realists*, who believe, as Plato does, that universals exist outside the mind, that they somehow have an actual existence beyond our thinking of them. The opposing view is taken by the *nominalists*, who claim that universals do not apply to anything really existing but are merely names or concepts representing many things. Ockham's position on the matter has been called nominalist, even though his view is more subtle than the one presented here.

KEY TERMS

cosmological arguments	moral evil mysticism	Neoplatonism ontological arguments	teleological arguments
doctrine of double effect	natural law theory necessary truth		

Notes

1. Augustine, *Confessions*, II.2, 4, trans. Henry Chadwick (Oxford: Oxford University Press, 1992).
2. Augustine, *City of God*, 11.27, trans. Henry Bettenson (Harmondsworth, Middlesex, England: Penguin Books, 1972).
3. Augustine, *On Free Will*, 2.12, 33, *Augustine: Earlier Writings*, trans. John H. S. Burleigh (London: SCM Press, 1953).
4. Augustine, *On Free Will*, 2.15, 39, trans. Burleigh.
5. Augustine, *Confessions*, V. 20, trans. Chadwick.
6. Augustine, *On Free Will*, 2.53, trans. Burleigh.
7. Anselm, *Proslogium*, chs. II–III (La Salle, IL: Open Court, 1962), 53–55.
8. Immanuel Kant, *Critique of Pure Reason* (London: Macmillan and St. Martin's Press, 1929), 504–505.
9. Thomas Aquinas, *Summa Theologica*, Question 2, "Whether God Exists," trans. Anton C. Pegis, *Basic Writings of St. Thomas Aquinas* (New York: Random House, 1944), 22.
10. Thomas Aquinas, *Summa Theologica*, "Whether God Exists," trans. Anton C. Pegis, *Basic Writings of St. Thomas Aquinas* (New York: Random House, 1944), 23.
11. *Hildegardis Causae et Curae*, ed. Paul Kaiser (Leipzig: Teubner, 1903).
12. Frederick Copleston, *A History of Philosophy, Volume II: Medieval Philosophy: From Augustine to Duns Scotus* (New York: Doubleday, 1962), 139.

For Further Reading

Anselm, *St. Anselm: Basic Writings*, trans. S. N. Deane (New York: Open Court, 1966).

Thomas Aquinas, *Summa Theologica, Basic Writings of St. Thomas Aquinas*, trans. A. C. Pegis (New York: Random House, 1945).

Augustine, *Confessions*, trans. Henry Chadwick (Oxford: Oxford University Press, 1991).

Stephen Buckle, "Natural Law," in *A Companion to Ethics*, ed. Peter Singer (Cambridge: Blackwell, 1993), 161–174.

Joseph Buijs, ed., *Maimonides: A Collection of Critical Essays* (Notre Dame, IN: University of Notre Dame Press, 1988).

Henry Chadwick, *Augustine: A Very Short Introduction* (Oxford: Oxford University Press, 1986).

Frederick Copleston, *A History of Philosophy, Volume II: Medieval Philosophy* (New York: Doubleday, 1962).

Herbert Davidson, *Maimonides: The Man and His Works* (Oxford: Oxford University Press, 2005).

Brian Davies and Eleonore Stump, ed., *The Oxford Handbook of Aquinas* (Oxford: Oxford University Press, 2012).

John Finnis, *Natural Law and Natural Rights* (New York: Oxford University Press, 1980).

M. Friedlander, trans., *The Guide for the Perplexed* (New York: Dover, 1956).

Richard M. Gale, *On the Nature and Existence of God* (Cambridge: Cambridge University Press, 1991).

Anthony Kenny, *Medieval Philosophy: A New History of Western Philosophy* (Oxford: Oxford University Press, 2005).

J. Kraemered, *Perspectives on Maimonides* (Oxford University Press, 1991).

Michael Peterson, William Hasker, Bruce Reichenbach, and David Basinger, *Reason and Religious Belief* (New York: Oxford University Press, 2003).

S. Pines, trans., *The Guide of the Perplexed* (Chicago: University of Chicago Press, 1929).

Online Resources

Stanford Encyclopedia of Philosophy, "Saint Thomas Aquinas," https://plato.stanford.edu/entries/aquinas

Internet Encyclopedia of Philosophy, "Thomas Aquinas (1224/6-1274)" https://www.iep.utm.edu/aquinas

Biography.com, "Saint Thomas Aquinas," https://www.biography.com/religious-figure/saint-thomas-aquinas

History of Philosophy (without Any Gaps) Podcast, https://historyofphilosophy.net

The Perseus Digital Library, http://www.perseus.tufts.edu/hopper

Crash Course, "Aquinas' 5 Arguments for the Existence of God," video, https://www.youtube.com/watch?v=TgisehuGOyY

CHAPTER 9

Descartes: Doubt and Certainty

CHAPTER OBJECTIVES

9.1 THE PURSUIT OF KNOWLEDGE

- Understand the nature of propositional knowledge.
- Explain the difference between rationalism and empiricism.
- Define *epistemology*, *skepticism*, *a priori*, and *a posteriori*.

9.2 PLATO'S RATIONALISM

- Understand Plato's reasons for believing that we possess knowledge.
- Explain Plato's notion of the Forms.
- Explain the doctrine of innate ideas, how rationalists and empiricists differ on the issue, and what role it plays in arguments for rationalism.

9.3 DESCARTES' DOUBT

- Understand Descartes' dream and evil-genius arguments and why they lead to skepticism.
- Know how such thought experiments as the brain in a vat and the Matrix relate to Descartes' skepticism arguments.

9.4 DESCARTES' CERTAINTY

- Articulate Descartes' argument for knowledge and the significance of his slogan "I think, therefore I am."
- Understand how the concept of God saves Descartes from complete skepticism.
- Explain Descartes' use of the idea of "clear and distinct" ideas.

9.1 THE PURSUIT OF KNOWLEDGE

In René Descartes' time, the world must have seemed to many to be turning upside down. Time-honored ideas, established religious doctrines, and traditional attitudes were being called into question both by new discoveries in science and by radically different religious outlooks on the Continent. This was the era of Galileo, Copernicus, Kepler, Bacon, Newton, and Martin Luther—thinkers who were dismantling the old ideological structures piece by piece. These were unsettling signs that the modern world—the world we inherited—was being born. Into this crucible of upheaval and change came the brilliant Descartes (1596–1650)—the inventor of analytic geometry and founder of modern philosophy. He was determined to see if there could be any epistemological certainties in an age of doubt. He hoped that knowledge could be given a foundation as sturdy as that which buttressed mathematics. If only knowledge of the world could be as certain as knowledge of geometry! Thus Descartes chose bravely to wrestle with a very old and difficult issue: whether it was possible for anyone to possess knowledge.

Figure 9.1 René Descartes (1596–1650).

But isn't it obvious that we do in fact *know* things? Many philosophers who have looked deeply into the question have thought the answer is not obvious at all. They ask—quite seriously—this question and several others: If you have knowledge, how did you attain it? And if you possess it, how much do you possess— that is, what is the extent of your knowledge? Do you know only the contents of your own mind or only mathematical or logical truths? Do you *know* that there is a God, that ordinary physical objects exist, that there is an external world (one existing independently of your mind), that unobservable entities such as electrons are real, that other minds besides your own exist, that events have occurred before the present moment?

Do these questions seem odd, even absurd, to you? Among serious thinkers, they are neither. Trying to find good answers to these is the main business of **epistemology**, the philosophical study of knowledge (see Chapter 1). It is the branch of philosophy that systematically investigates whether, how, and to what extent we know things. For well over two thousand years, philosophers have been searching for answers because both the asking and the answering have theoretical and practical value. We value knowledge for its own sake, regardless of what we can do with it. When we are at our best, we crave the light simply because it is the light. But we also value knowledge because it can guide us to our goals, steer us away from error, and help us succeed in life, however we define success. Knowledge is power. Whatever our reply to the epistemological questions, if we take them seriously, they surely will affect how we see the world and what we do in it.

Knowledge comes in different forms, and philosophy is usually concerned with only one of them. Knowing *what* something feels like (for example, what influenza

"If you would be a real seeker after truth, it is necessary that at least once in your life you doubt, as far as possible, all things."

—Descartes

epistemology The philosophical study of knowledge.

THEN AND NOW

The Scientific (and Philosophical) Revolution

Figure 9.2 Copernicus's sun-centered model of the universe, from his *De revolutionibus orbium coelestium*, 1543.

At the center of the universe, the stationary Earth—the focus of all God's attention—reigns as a perfect sphere, nested in the exact center of a series of other perfect hollow spheres, like an onion. On each sphere rests one of the planets, the sun, the moon, or stars, every sphere turning around the Earth producing the familiar movements of these heavenly bodies. The spheres are not only perfect but changeless and eternal. Beyond the sphere of the stars is heaven, the realm of light where God abides and human souls go to their reward.

This view of cosmic reality is roughly what

propositional knowledge
Knowledge of a proposition.

feels like) constitutes one form of knowledge. Knowing *how* to do something (for example, how to throw a ball) constitutes another. Knowing *that* something is the case (such as knowing that an elm tree grows in the quad) is **propositional knowledge**—knowledge of a proposition. A proposition is a statement that is either true or false, an assertion that something is or is not a fact. This kind of knowledge has been the main focus of philosophers.

As we saw in Chapter 4, thinkers going back as far as Plato have said that propositional knowledge has three necessary and sufficient conditions: to know a proposition, (1) you must *believe* it, (2) it must be *true*, and (3) you must have good *reasons* for—be justified in—believing it true. On this traditional account, merely believing something is not enough; what you believe must be true. But a mere true belief is not knowledge either, because you can have a true belief and yet not genuinely know. To have knowledge, your belief must be true, and you must have good reasons to believe it true. Knowledge, then, is true belief that is justified.

Most philosophers believe we have some knowledge but differ on its extent. They may insist that we possess knowledge of the existence of an external world, other

1. Do questions—such as "Is it raining?"—count as propositions?

millions of people believed and never questioned in ancient and medieval times. It was said to be derived from unimpeachable authorities—from Aristotle and Christian scripture or dogma. But the scientific revolution (dating roughly from the late sixteenth through the eighteenth centuries) upended the medieval worldview and ushered in a host of new ideas both in society and philosophy. The combined work of Copernicus (1473–1543), Kepler (1571–1630), Galileo (1564–1642), and others showed that the Earth rotated around the sun, not the other way around; that the movements of the heavens could be precisely described through mathematics; that the old notion of spheres was unfounded; that (thanks to Galileo's telescope) the heavenly bodies are not perfect but have obvious imperfections; and that teleological explanations (those assuming that everything is guided to an end or goal) are inaccurate and uninformative.

Descartes was influenced by, and influenced, the scientific revolution, which in turn affected his contributions to philosophy. He was the genius who founded analytic geometry (remember Cartesian coordinates?), advanced the science of optics, wrote treatises on meteorology, and discovered how rainbows work. In philosophy he insisted that a radically different perspective was required. In light of the methods and findings of the "new sciences," he saw that the old ideas had to go and that a new mechanistic and mathematical view of the world had to take its place. In fact, he deemed mathematics a model for human understanding. He declared that the simple mathematical steps used to derive very complicated proofs "gave me occasion to suppose that all things which fall within the scope of human understanding are interconnected in the same way" (*Discourse on Method*, Part II).

What do you think contemporary scientists would say about Descartes' rationalism? Is it through our rational faculties that we discover scientific truths?

minds, physical objects, the past and future, or self-evident truths. But some philosophers embrace **skepticism**, the view that we lack knowledge in some fundamental way. They hold that many or all of our beliefs are false or unfounded.

skepticism The view that we lack knowledge in some fundamental way.

Some skeptics argue that we lack knowledge because we have no way of distinguishing between beliefs that we think constitute knowledge from beliefs that clearly do *not* constitute knowledge. For all we know, we could be hallucinating, dreaming, in the grips of an illusion, or mistaken for some other reason. How do we know that we are not hallucinating or dreaming right now? Hallucinations and dreams can seem as real as our "normal" experience. If we cannot distinguish these two, the skeptic says, then we cannot have knowledge.

Other skeptics raise doubts about the *reliability* of what we take to be our normal sources of knowledge—perception, memory, introspection, and reasoning. We realize that all these sources are fallible, that they sometimes lead us into error. But skeptics ask how we know that these sources are not *always* in error. If all these sources are suspect, we cannot use one to check another. We cannot, for example, use our sense of sight to check the reliability of our sense of touch. And if we think one mode

"The first precept was never to accept a thing as true until I knew it as such without a single doubt."
—Descartes

"I think, therefore I am."
—Descartes

"I feel, therefore I exist."
—Thomas Jefferson

Figure 9.3 Sometimes we are mistaken about what we perceive. Does that mean we can never know anything? (In this common optical trick, a man is standing several yards behind the woman in the foreground—who looks like a giant devouring the man.)

2. Are you a skeptic? What propositions can you truthfully say you know?

a priori Knowledge gained independently of or prior to sense experience.

a posteriori Knowledge that depends entirely on sense experience.

rationalists Those who believe that some or all of our knowledge about the world is gained independently of sense experience.

empiricists Those who believe that our knowledge of the world comes solely from sense experience.

of perception is more trustworthy than the others, how do we know that? We seem forced once again into skepticism.

Philosophers distinguish two ways to acquire knowledge: through reason and through sense experience. The former is called **a priori**; it yields knowledge gained independently of or prior to sense experience. The latter is known as **a posteriori**; it gives us knowledge that depends entirely on sense experience. We can come to know many propositions a priori—for example, that all bachelors are unmarried, that all triangles have three sides, that $2 + 3 = 5$, and that something is either a cat or not a cat. We need not do a survey of bachelors to see if they really are all unmarried; we can know this just by thinking about it. And we know that the statement "something is either a cat or not a cat" is true; it is a simple logical truth—and we know it without having to observe any cats. It seems that we can also come to know many propositions a posteriori—for instance, John the bachelor has red hair, that he just drew a triangle on paper, that he is holding five pencils, and that Tabby the cat is on the mat. To know these things, we must rely on our senses.

Through the centuries, philosophers have debated whether our knowledge of the world is fundamentally a priori or a posteriori (if indeed we have knowledge), and these arguments continue today in many forms in both philosophy and science. On one side of this divide are the **rationalists**, who believe that some or all of our knowledge about the world is gained independently of sense experience. That is, they maintain that some or all of our knowledge is a priori. On the other side are the **empiricists**, who contend that our knowledge of the world comes solely from sense experience. We acquire knowledge entirely a posteriori. We may come to know logical and mathematical truths through reason, but we can know nothing about the world unless we use our senses.

At this point, you may find yourself being more sympathetic to the empiricists than to the rationalists. After all, you seem to acquire an enormous amount of information via your five senses. Through them, you grasp that the grass is green, the stove is hot, the music is loud, the lime is tart, and the sugar is sweet. But what can you know through reason alone? Rationalists like Descartes would say that you can know a great deal. Without making any empirical observations, mathematicians can not only discover new mathematical truths but also develop mathematical models that can accurately describe the empirical world. They can, for example, accurately predict the existence of astronomical objects and their movements without once looking through a telescope. Likewise we know the fundamental truths of logic, without which reasoning itself would be impossible. We know, for example, that nothing can both have a property and lack it at the same time, and that for any particular property, everything either has it or lacks it. Thus we know without looking that nothing can both be a dog and not be a dog at the same time, there are no square circles, and married bachelors don't exist. Some rationalists have gone further and asserted that reason alone can reveal the most important, basic truths about the world—such as "every event has a cause" and "the shortest distance between two points is a straight line."

Many of the greatest thinkers in history have taken the rationalist approach to knowledge, most notably Plato and Descartes. Descartes, espousing the most influential rationalist theory, thinks sense experience is an unreliable source of knowledge, so he looks to reason to give all our knowledge a foundation as firm as that which supports unshakeable mathematical truths. Through reason he hopes to defeat skepticism. His method is first to doubt everything that he cannot be certain of, a process that leaves him knowing hardly anything. But through reason alone he soon uncovers what he considers to be self-evident; certain truths from which he derives other indubitable propositions. In this way he tries to build an edifice of knowledge that, like an inverted pyramid, rests on one or two rock-solid foundation stones that support all the others.

The empiricist view of knowledge has been advanced most famously by the British empiricists John Locke (1632–1704), George Berkeley (1685–1753), and David Hume (1711–1776) (see Chapter 10). They want to turn Descartes' pyramid right side up, resting all knowledge on a vast foundation of sense data (the content of our experience) that supports the upper stones. Among these thinkers, Hume probably has been most influential, arguing for an uncompromising **empiricism** that leads to a far-reaching skepticism that not all empiricists have shared. He holds that all our knowledge (aside from purely logical truths) is derived from sense perceptions or ideas about those perceptions. Like other empiricists, he believes that the mind is empty—a blank slate—until experience gives it content. We can have knowledge of something only if it can be sensed, and any proposition that does not refer to what can be sensed is meaningless. Guided by this latter empiricist principle, Hume is driven to skepticism about many things that others have taken for granted, including the existence of the external world, causation, a continuing self, religious doctrines, and inductive reasoning. His skepticism arises because he thinks that even though

"All that we see or seem is but a dream within a dream."

—Edgar Allan Poe

empiricism The view that our knowledge of the world comes solely from sense experience.

all our knowledge is based on sense experience, we cannot know how the objects of our sense experience are related. We cannot know, for example, that there is a cause-and-effect relationship between associated objects. To infer such a connection is to go beyond what our senses tell us. Our notions of causal connections are merely matters of custom and habit.

3. What facts about the world can we know based solely on our reasoning?

9.2 PLATO'S RATIONALISM

rationalism The view that some or all of our knowledge about the world is gained independently of sense experience.

"There is thus, in all philosophy derived from Descartes, a tendency to subjectivism, and to regarding matter as something only knowable, if at all, by inference from what is known of mind."

—Bertrand Russell

The great-grandfather of modern **rationalism** is Plato. As noted in Chapter 4, Plato maintained that sense experience alone could not be the source of knowledge, although many of his contemporaries claimed otherwise. Some of them assumed that since knowledge must be based on sense experience, and since sense experience can vary from person to person or culture to culture, relativism must be true. If one person says a grape is sour, and another says it's sweet, there must be no objective fact of the matter, just truth relative to different persons. Other thinkers thought that since our perceptions are often illusory, distorted, or otherwise mistaken, sense experience is not a reliable source of knowledge. And since our perceptions are the only possible route to knowledge, we must not know anything. Thus skepticism, they said, is the proper epistemological attitude. Plato thought that our perceptions were just as unreliable a guide to genuine knowledge as the relativists and skeptics assumed. But he argued that since we clearly do have knowledge, we must derive it from a reliable source—and that source has to be reason.

Plato deduced that we must be able to acquire knowledge because we can identify false beliefs, and we obviously possess knowledge because we can grasp, through reason, mathematical, conceptual, and logical truths. We know that $2 + 5 = 7$; that a triangle has three sides; and that if A is larger than B, and B is larger than C, then A is larger than C. Plato pointed out that these truths are objective: they are true regardless of what we think. We do not invent them out of our imaginations; we discover them. No matter how hard we try we cannot make $2 + 5 = 9$. Plato reasoned that if such truths are objective, they must also be about real things. They must refer to an independently existing, immaterial reality that is beyond sense experience. In addition, he insisted, these truths must also be immutable and eternal, existing in the immaterial realm unchanged for all time. Only through our powers of reason can we reach beyond the physical world to take hold of real knowledge of fundamental truths. Sense experience, in contrast, can yield only transitory, ever-changing information—mere opinion that is vastly inferior to everlasting truths.

4. Is the number *five* an objective entity? Is the preposition *over* objectively real? Explain your reasons. Do your answers to these questions give any support to Plato's notion of the Forms?

So for Plato, reality comprises two worlds: the fleeting world of the physical accessed through sense experience; and the eternal, nonphysical, changeless world of genuine knowledge accessed only through reason. In spelling out the contents of the latter, Plato articulates his notion of the *Forms*. As discussed earlier, the Forms (also called Ideas) are perfect conceptual models for every existing thing, residing only in the eternal world penetrated by reason alone. They are the ideals, or standards, that we can first come to know and then use to assess the notions and objects we encounter in our lives. Through reason, we can access the Form of "table" and thus know

DETAILS

Innate Ideas

Rationalists like Plato and Descartes typically accept the doctrine of innate ideas—the notion that we are born with some general ideas already in our minds. Ideas such as God, freedom, the laws of logic, the truths of mathematics, moral principles, and causality (specifically, that every event has cause) are supposed to be hidden in our minds until we are cognitively mature enough to see that they are self-evident. Rationalists believe that the theory of innate ideas is the best explanation of why we can know some concepts a priori—that is, without ever experiencing them. We understand the idea of *perfection*, for example, even though we have never encountered a perfect object.

Figure 9.4 Are babies born with knowledge of mathematics, moral principles, or . . . computer skills?

Most philosophers reject the doctrine, but in contemporary life, advocates of the view are not hard to find. The linguist Noam Chomsky, for instance, argues that children come into the world possessing a universal grammar that enables them to learn a first language—an achievement that Chomsky thinks would not be possible without some innate grammatical ideas.

Critics of innate ideas ask how we can possess knowledge that we are not aware of. Innate ideas are not learned; the mind is supposed to somehow always have them. But if we are unaware of them, how can they be or become knowledge?

Empiricists admit that our minds do possess innate cognitive *capacities* to learn certain concepts, but they maintain that having these capacities is a long way from having innate *knowledge*.

Do you believe that people possess innate ideas? If so, why? If not, why not? How do you explain our seemingly a priori idea of perfection or 2 + 2 = 4?

the ideal template of "table." With this knowledge we can understand the essence of a table and use this understanding to make judgments about all physical tables. Likewise when we access the Form "courage," we know what the ideal of courage is and can use this knowledge to appraise a particular instance of courage. As Plato sees it, the truly real world is the world of the Forms—the domain of the perfect and everlasting. With knowledge of the really real, we can understand the "less real" realm of the imperfect and transitory.

How is it, Plato asks, that we seem to have knowledge of the Forms, however dimly, even though our senses can tell us nothing about them? Our sense experience can acquaint us only with material objects, but the Forms are not material. It's as if these universals were already in our minds waiting to be uncovered. Plato's answer—and the answer of most other rationalists—is the doctrine of *innate knowledge*: at birth our minds come equipped with conceptual content, ideas about the world that we can know a priori. In Plato's version of this view, knowledge of the Forms is present at the very beginning of our lives, inscribed in our minds (our immortal souls) in a previous existence. We are born with this knowledge. Accessing this knowledge then is a matter of using reason to *recall* what we previously knew in another life.

Many thinkers reject Plato's notion of a preexisting state in which we acquire knowledge, and they are skeptical of the claim that we are born with knowledge. But the idea of innate knowledge in some form is still attractive to rationalist philosophers, for it would explain how we could possess knowledge without relying on sense experience. In any case, both rationalists and empiricists must provide an explanation of how we seem to know logical and mathematical truths (and perhaps scientific truths) that we do not arrive at through our senses.

9.3 DESCARTES' DOUBT

Oddly enough, Descartes begins his quest for knowledge by first plunging into skepticism. He sees that a great many things he thought he knew appear now to be false. So he decides to "raze everything to the ground and begin again" from a firm foundation, doubting all beliefs except those that are "certain and indubitable," beliefs that cannot possibly be false. Only beliefs that are certain can count as knowledge, he says. If he has reason to doubt any of them, they are not knowledge. Here he is at the start of his quest:

> "[T]o have recourse to the veracity of the supreme Being, in order to prove the veracity of our senses, is surely making a very unexpected circuit."
> —David Hume

> "Common sense is the most fairly distributed thing in the world, for each one thinks he is so well-endowed with it that even those who are hardest to satisfy in all other matters are not in the habit of desiring more of it than they already have."
> —Descartes

> "Hamlet did think a great many things; does it follow that he existed?"
> —Jaako Hintikka

René Descartes: *Meditations on First Philosophy*

It is now some years since I detected how many were the false beliefs that I had from my earliest youth admitted as true, and how doubtful was everything I had since constructed on this basis; and from that time I was convinced that I must once for all seriously undertake to rid myself of all the opinions which I had formerly accepted, and commence to build anew from the foundation, if I wanted to establish any firm and permanent structure in the sciences. But as this enterprise appeared to be a very great one, I waited until I had attained an age so mature that I could not hope that at any later date I should be better fitted to execute my design. This reason caused me to delay so long that I should feel that I was doing wrong were I to occupy in deliberation the time that yet remains to me for action. To-day, then, since very opportunely for the plan I have in view I have delivered my mind from every care [and am happily agitated by no passions] and since I have procured for myself an assured leisure in a peaceable retirement, I shall at last seriously and freely address myself to the general upheaval of all my former opinions.

Now for this object it is not necessary that I should show that all of these are false—I shall perhaps never arrive at this end. But inasmuch as reason already persuades me that I ought no less carefully to withhold my assent from matters which are not entirely certain and indubitable than from those which appear to me manifestly to be false, if I am able to find in each one some reason to doubt, this will suffice to justify my rejecting the whole. And for that end it will not be requisite that I should examine each in particular, which would be an endless undertaking; for owing to the fact that the destruction of the foundations of necessity brings with it the downfall of the rest of the edifice, I shall only in the first place attack those principles upon which all my former opinions rested.[1]

> "All our knowledge has its origins in our perceptions."
> —Leonardo da Vinci

Descartes soon finds reason to doubt all beliefs based on sense experience, arriving at this conclusion via his famous dream argument. He notes that "there are no certain indications by which we may clearly distinguish wakefulness from asleep."[2] Our dreams can seem like reality, and in dreams we often don't know we are dreaming. So it is possible that we are dreaming now, he says, and that what we take to be the real world is in fact not real at all. More to the point, it is possible that our sense experience—by which we presume to know material reality—is just a dream. If so, we can't be certain about anything we think we know through our senses. Therefore, sense experience can yield no knowledge.

All that up to the present time I have accepted as most true and certain I have learned either from the senses or through the senses; but it is sometimes proved to me that these senses are deceptive, and it is wiser not to trust entirely to any thing by which we have once been deceived.

But it may be that although the senses sometimes deceive us concerning things which are hardly perceptible, or very far away, there are yet many others to be met with as to which we cannot reasonably have any doubt, although we recognise them by their means. For example, there is the fact that I am here, seated by the fire, attired in a dressing gown, having this paper in my hands and other similar matters. . . .

At the same time I must remember that I am a man, and that consequently I am in the habit of sleeping, and in my dreams representing to myself the same things or sometimes even less probable things, than do those who are insane in their waking moments. How often has it happened to me that in the night I dreamt that I found myself in this particular place, that I was dressed and seated near the fire, whilst in reality I was lying undressed in bed! At this moment it does indeed seem to me that it is with eyes awake that I am looking at this paper; that this head which I move is not asleep, that it is deliberately and of set purpose that I extend my hand and perceive it; what happens in sleep does not appear so clear nor so distinct as does all this. But in thinking over this I remind myself that on many occasions I have in sleep been deceived by similar illusions, and in dwelling carefully on this reflection I see so manifestly that there are no certain indications by which we may clearly distinguish wakefulness from sleep that I am lost in astonishment. And my astonishment is such that it is almost capable of persuading me that I now dream.[3]

René Descartes:
Meditations on First Philosophy

5. Is there any way you can tell whether you are awake or dreaming? Is Descartes right that he cannot tell the difference? Explain.

6. Is there any way you can determine whether you are living in the Matrix? Can you tell whether an evil genius is systematically deceiving you? Why or why not?

After this insight, Descartes discovers that his skepticism goes even deeper. Suppose, he says, that an evil genius or god has set out to systematically deceive me. This being could delude me about every kind of thought I could possibly have. I can't be sure that this is not the case. I can't be certain that all my thoughts are not the work of an evil entity that infuses my mind with false sensations and ideas, making an

DETAILS

Living in the Matrix

Descartes' evil-genius scenario is the forerunner of some similar what-if tales told by philosophers and others in our own times. In one of them, you are not at the mercy of a malicious demon; you are instead a brain in a vat of chemicals in a laboratory. Your brain is hardwired to a computer, which a brilliant (but probably crazy) scientist is using to give you experiences that are indistinguishable from those you might have if you were not a wired-up marinating brain. The question is, How could you ever be certain that you are not such a brain in a vat?

The same sort of question arises about the predicament of humans in the movie *The Matrix*. Intelligent computers have enslaved the human race, encasing everyone in pods and electronically feeding simulations of the real world into their brains. As Christopher Grau says:

> These creatures have fed Neo [the movie's protagonist] a simulation that he couldn't possibly help but take as the real thing. What's worse, it isn't clear how any of us can know with certainty that we are not in a position similar to Neo before his "rebirth." . . . A viewer of *The Matrix* is naturally led to wonder: how do I know I am not in the Matrix?

Figure 9.5 The movie *The Matrix* raises troubling questions about the real and the unreal and whether we can distinguish the two.

Some philosophers think the skeptical implications of Matrix-type scenarios can be countered through an argument based on inference to the best explanation. What would such an argument look like? Do you agree that it can successfully counter the skeptical scenarios?

Christopher Grau, "Bad Dreams, Evil Demons, and the Experience Machine: Philosophy and *The Matrix*," in *Philosophers Explore the Matrix* (New York: Oxford University Press, 2005), 10–23.

external reality appear to exist. And if I am not certain of this, I can't know anything that I previously thought I knew, including such seemingly obvious things as the truths of mathematics.

Nevertheless I have long had fixed in my mind the belief that an all-powerful God existed by whom I have been created such as I am. But how do I know that He has not brought it to pass that there is no earth, no heaven, no extended body, no magnitude, no place, and that nevertheless [I possess the perceptions of all these things and that] they seem to me to exist just exactly as I now see them? And, besides, as I sometimes imagine that others deceive themselves in the things which they think they know best, how do I know that I am not deceived every time that I add two and three, or count the sides of a square, or judge of things yet simpler can be imagined?[4]

René Descartes: *Meditations on First Philosophy*

As we have seen, Descartes' assumption is that knowledge requires certainty. He holds that for beliefs to count as knowledge, we must be certain of them—they must be so well supported as to be beyond all possible doubt. But some philosophers claim that this requirement for knowledge sets the bar too high. They reject Descartes' skeptical arguments because they are convinced that knowledge demands not beyond-all-doubt certainty but only reasonable grounds for believing. After all, they say, we often claim to know many propositions that are not certain. We insist that we know that grass grows, that some dogs have fleas, that Africa exists, and that Abraham Lincoln lived and died in America—yet none of these statements are beyond all possible doubt.

"If a man will begin with certainties, he shall end in doubts. But if he will be content to begin with doubts, he shall end in certainties."

—Francis Bacon

9.4 DESCARTES' CERTAINTY

Adrift in doubt, Descartes wonders whether there is anything at all he can know. But just when it seems that he can know nothing, he comes upon a truth that he cannot possibly doubt: he exists.

René Descartes: *Meditations on First Philosophy*

The Meditation of yesterday filled my mind with so many doubts that it is no longer in my power to forget them. And yet I do not see in what manner I can resolve them; and, just as if I had all of a sudden fallen into very deep water, I am so disconcerted that I can neither make certain of setting my feet on the bottom, nor can I swim and so support myself on the surface. I shall nevertheless make an effort and follow anew the same path as that on which I yesterday entered, i.e. I shall proceed by setting aside all that in which the least doubt could be supposed to exist, just as if I had discovered that it was absolutely false; and I shall ever follow in this road until I have met with something which is certain, or at least, if I can do

René Descartes:
*Meditations on First
Philosophy*

nothing else, until I have learned for certain that there is nothing in the world that is certain. Archimedes, in order that he might draw the terrestrial globe out of its place, and transport it elsewhere, demanded only that one point should be fixed and immoveable; in the same way I shall have the right to conceive high hopes if I am happy enough to discover one thing only which is certain and indubitable.

I suppose, then, that all the things that I see are false; I persuade myself that nothing has ever existed of all that my fallacious memory represents to me. I consider that I possess no senses; I imagine that body, figure, extension, movement and place are but the fictions of my mind. What, then, can be esteemed as true? Perhaps nothing at all, unless that there is nothing in the world that is certain. . . .

But how can I know there is not something different from those things that I have just considered, of which one cannot have the slightest doubt? Is there not some God, or some other being by whatever name we call it, who puts these reflections into my mind? That is not necessary, for is it not possible that I am capable of producing them myself? I myself, am I not at least something? But I have already denied that I had senses and body. Yet I hesitate, for what follows from that? Am I so dependent on body and senses that I cannot exist without these?

But I was persuaded that there was nothing in all the world, that there was no heaven, no earth, that there were no minds, nor any bodies: was I not then likewise persuaded that I did not exist? Not at all; of a surety I myself did exist since I persuaded myself of something [or merely because I thought of something]. But there is some deceiver or other, very powerful and very cunning, who ever employs his ingenuity in deceiving me. Then without doubt I exist also if he deceives me, and let him deceive me as much as he will, he can never cause me to be nothing so long as I think that I am something. So that after having reflected well and carefully examined all things, we must come to the definite conclusion that this proposition: I am, I exist, is necessarily true each time that I pronounce it, or that I mentally conceive it.[5]

"I am indeed amazed
when I consider how
weak my mind is and how
prone to error."

—Descartes

Descartes concludes that if he can persuade himself of something, if he can have thoughts, he must exist. Even an evil genius cannot rob him of this knowledge. In the very act of doubting, or of experiencing something contrived by the evil genius, Descartes finds unshakeable proof that he himself exists: "I think, therefore I am."

But can he know any more than this? He holds that he can indeed. He believes that he has discovered a first principle by which he can acquire knowledge despite his obvious fallibility:

René Descartes:
*Meditations on First
Philosophy*

[I]t seems to me that already I can establish as a general rule that all things which I perceive very clearly and very distinctly are true.[6]

He declares that if he perceives something clearly and distinctly, he must know it with certainty. Armed with this principle of knowledge acquisition, he thinks he can know a great many things about the world. If he seems to perceive a flower, and his perception is clear and distinct, then the flower must exist and be very much as it appears to be.

But why does Descartes think this principle is sound? He argues that in his mind he has a clear and distinct notion of perfection, which must have a cause. The cause of the idea of perfection, he says, must also be perfect, and this perfect cause can only be a perfect God. A perfect God is no deceiver; such a God would not allow him to be deceived when he correctly applies his God-given ability to achieve knowledge—that is, when he follows the principle of clarity and distinctness. Therefore, when he perceives something clearly and distinctly, he knows it beyond all doubt. He has knowledge, and skepticism is defeated.

But after I have recognised that there is a God—because at the same time I have also recognised that all things depend upon Him, and that He is not a deceiver, and from that have inferred that what I perceive clearly and distinctly cannot fail to be true—although I no longer pay attention to the reasons for which I have judged this to be true, provided that I recollect having clearly and distinctly perceived it no contrary reason can be brought forward which could ever cause me to doubt of its truth; and thus I have a true and certain knowledge of it. And this same knowledge extends likewise to all other things which I recollect having formerly demonstrated, such as the truths of geometry and the like; for what can be alleged against them to cause me to place them in doubt? Will it be said that my nature is such as to cause me to be frequently deceived? But I already know that I cannot be deceived in the judgment whose grounds I know clearly. Will it be said that I formerly held many things to be true and certain which I have afterwards recognised to be false? But I had not had any clear and distinct knowledge of these things, and not as yet knowing the rule whereby I assure myself of the truth, I had been impelled to give my assent from reasons which I have since recognised to be less strong than I had at the time imagined them to be. What further objection can then be raised? That possibly I am dreaming (an objection I myself made a little while ago), or that all the thoughts which I now have are no more true than the phantasies of my dreams? But even though I slept the case would be the same, for all that is clearly present to my mind is absolutely true.[7]

René Descartes:
Meditations on First Philosophy

7. How does Descartes try to show that the principle of clear and distinct ideas is justified? Does he, as his critics assert, argue in a circle?

Being a thoroughgoing rationalist, Descartes believes that he apprehends substantial truths about the world through reason. He would admit that through perception he learns simple facts such as the color of a flower and the position of the sun in the sky. But in many other cases, he says, knowledge of the external world is obtained through an "intuition of the mind," not sense data. Here is Descartes explaining this point:

Let us begin by considering the commonest matters, those which we believe to be the most distinctly comprehended, to wit, the bodies which we touch and see; not indeed bodies in general, for these general ideas are usually a little more confused, but let us consider one body in particular. Let us take, for example, this piece of wax: it has been taken quite freshly from the hive, and it has not yet lost the sweetness of the honey which it contains; it still retains somewhat of the odour of the flowers from which it has been culled; its colour, its figure, its size are apparent; it is hard, cold, easily handled, and if you strike it with the finger, it will emit a sound. Finally all the things which are requisite to cause us distinctly to recognise a body, are met with in it. But notice that while I speak and approach the fire what remained of the taste is exhaled, the smell evaporates, the colour alters, the figure is destroyed, the size increases, it becomes liquid, it heats, scarcely can one handle it, and when one strikes it, no sound is emitted. Does the same wax remain after this change? We must

René Descartes:
Meditations on First Philosophy

PORTRAIT

René Descartes

Descartes (1596–1650) did his philosophical work in a time of intellectual, scientific, and religious change; an era of revolutionary new thinking that would eventually transform the Western world. He was a contemporary of Galileo and Kepler, coming along after Copernicus did his work and before Newton did his. While trying to reconcile the old ideas with the new, he sparked a quiet revolution of his own and became the "father of modern philosophy."

He was born in La Haye, France, educated in philosophy and mathematics at the Jesuit College of La Fleche in Anjou, and trained in the law at Pontiers. He served for a while in the Dutch army, where he did much of his early philosophical thinking, supposedly inspired by dreams he had while sleeping in a "stove-heated room."

Figure 9.6 Descartes in writing mode.

He was such a bright student that he easily advanced beyond his teachers, and he quickly realized that their arguments and reasoning were defective. Knowledge in general, he thought, is on very shaky ground, and that state of affairs is intolerable. So he set out on his long quest for knowledge that was as logical and certain as a mathematical proof. Along the way, he reshaped mathematics by inventing coordinate geometry.

He developed a rationalistic theory of knowledge whose starting point was a recognition of personal existence ("I think, therefore I am"). Reason is the source of substantial knowledge, and sense experience has only a subordinate role. His epistemology would be influential and controversial for centuries to come. His metaphysics has also affected succeeding generations. He posited a stark division between mind and matter, with the two somehow interacting (an interaction that he could not adequately explain). His *Discourse on Method* was published in 1637, *Meditations on First Philosophy* in 1641, *Principles of Philosophy* in 1644, and *The Passions of the Soul* in 1649.

In 1649 he agreed to tutor the philosophically minded Queen Kristina of Sweden. But the work demanded an unpleasant departure from his usual routine of sleeping in: he was asked to begin lessons at 5:00 a.m.! The change allegedly caused his demise; he contracted pneumonia and died. Another notable philosopher, Grotius, had visited Kristina in 1644 and suffered an identical fate. Kristina seems to have been very tough on famous philosophers.

René Descartes: *Meditations on First Philosophy*

confess that it remains; none would judge otherwise. What then did I know so distinctly in this piece of wax ? It could certainly be nothing of all that the senses brought to my notice, since all these things which fall under taste, smell, sight, touch, and hearing, are found to be changed, and yet the same wax remains.

. . . We must then grant that . . . it is my mind alone which perceives . . . this piece of wax. . . . But what is this piece of wax which cannot be understood excepting by the [understanding or] mind? It is certainly the same that I see, touch, imagine, and finally it is the same which I have always believed it to be from the beginning. But what must particularly be observed is that its perception is neither an act of vision, nor of touch, nor of imagination . . . but only an intuition of the mind.[8]

René Descartes:
Meditations on First Philosophy

Descartes points out that although our senses tell us that the wax has changed through melting—that it has become a completely different object than it was before—our minds know better. Through a rational intuition, our minds understand that the wax, though radically altered, remains a piece of wax. If we relied only on sense experience to inform us about the wax, we would have to conclude that the original object no longer exists.

For three and a half centuries, Descartes' case for knowledge has been both commended and criticized. Many reject a key part of his argument, the premise asserting the existence of God. They doubt that Descartes—or anyone else—can infer the existence of God merely from the concept of God. Some also charge Descartes with begging the question, the fallacy of trying to establish the conclusion of an argument by using that conclusion as a premise (also known as arguing in a circle). Through his principle of clarity and distinctness, he tries to demonstrate that God exists. But then he attempts to establish the legitimacy of the principle by citing the existence of God. (Descartes' pattern of argument here has become known as the *Cartesian circle*.) Not everyone agrees that Descartes falls into this fallacy, but few doubt the ingenuity of his effort to rout the skeptic.

8. Does Descartes succeed in showing that knowledge of the external world is gained by an intuition of the mind? Does his argument show that empiricism is false? Why or why not?

"So, my soul, it is time to part."
—Descartes, his last words

WRITING AND REASONING	**CHAPTER 9**

1. Do you agree with Descartes (and skeptics) that only propositions that are beyond all doubt can be knowledge? How would you argue against this view?

2. The skeptic argues that if we are sometimes mistaken about our beliefs, then it is logically possible that we are always mistaken and that we therefore do not have knowledge. Evaluate this argument.

3. Are you living in the Matrix right now? What argument can you offer to show that you are not in the Matrix? What kind of argument would Descartes offer?

4. Consider this statement: All triangles have three sides. Explain how you know it is true even though you haven't examined all triangles in existence.

5. Consider the skeptic's charge that we can never be confident about the reliability of our normal sources of knowledge (perception, memory, introspection, and reasoning). Does it follow from the fact that we are sometimes mistaken when we rely on these sources that we are *always* mistaken? How would you respond to the skeptic?

REVIEW NOTES

9.1 THE PURSUIT OF KNOWLEDGE

- The main question in epistemology is whether we have propositional knowledge and, if we do, how much we have.

- Propositional knowledge has three necessary and sufficient conditions: to know a proposition, (1) you must *believe* it, (2) it must be *true*, and (3) you must have good *reasons* for—be justified in—believing it true.

- Some philosophers embrace skepticism, the view that we lack knowledge in some fundamental way. Skeptics may deny that we have knowledge in all areas of inquiry or maintain that we lack knowledge in only some of them. In any case, they hold that many or all our beliefs are false or unfounded.

- Philosophers distinguish two ways to acquire knowledge: through reason and through sense experience. The former is called *a priori*; it yields knowledge gained independently of or prior to sense experience. The latter is known as *a posteriori*; it gives us knowledge that depends entirely on sense experience.

- Rationalists believe that some or all of our knowledge about the world is gained independently of sense experience. Empiricists contend that our knowledge of the empirical world comes solely from sense experience.

9.2 PLATO'S RATIONALISM

- Plato believes that the source of our knowledge is reason. He says that we must be able to acquire knowledge because we can identify false beliefs, and we obviously possess knowledge because we can grasp, through reason, mathematical, conceptual, and logical truths.

- For Plato, reality comprises two worlds: the fleeting world of the physical accessed through sense experience; and the eternal, nonphysical, changeless world of genuine knowledge accessed only through reason. This nonphysical world contains the *Forms*, which are perfect conceptual models for every existing thing, residing only in the eternal world penetrated by reason alone.

- Plato believes in innate knowledge—the idea that knowledge of the Forms is already present at birth, inscribed in our minds in a previous existence.

9.3 DESCARTES' DOUBT

- Descartes initially finds reason to doubt all beliefs based on sense experience, arriving at this conclusion via his dream and evil-genius arguments.

- Descartes pulls himself out of skepticism by realizing that he cannot possibly doubt that he exists—for if he can have thoughts, he must exist ("I think, therefore I am").

9.4 DESCARTES' CERTAINTY

- From "I think, therefore I am," Descartes goes on to discover another principle of knowledge acquisition: If he perceives something clearly and distinctly, he must know it with certainty. He must know it with certainty because a perfect God would not allow him to be deceived.

- With his wax thought experiment, Descartes argues for his rationalism. He says that although our senses tell us that the wax has changed through melting—that it has become a completely different object than it was before—our minds know better. Through a rational intuition, our minds understand that the wax, though radically altered, remains a piece of wax. If we relied only on sense experience to inform us about the wax, we would have to conclude that the original object no longer exists.

KEY TERMS

a posteriori
a priori
empiricism

empiricists
epistemology

propositional
   knowledge
rationalism

rationalists
skepticism

Notes

1. René Descartes, "Meditation One," in *Meditations on First Philosophy*, vol. 1, *The Philosophical Works of Descartes*, trans. Elizabeth S. Haldane and G. R. T. Ross (Cambridge: Cambridge University Press, 1911), 144–145.
2. René Descartes, "Meditation One," *Meditations on First Philosophy*, vol. 1, trans. Elizabeth S. Haldane and G. R. T. Ross (Cambridge: Dover, 1931), 146.
3. Descartes, "Meditation One," trans. Haldane and Ross, 1931, 145–146.
4. Descartes, "Meditation One," trans. Haldane and Ross, 1931, 147.
5. Descartes, "Meditation Two," trans. Haldane and Ross, 1931, 149–150.
6. Descartes, "Meditation One," trans. Haldane and Ross, 1931, 158.
7. Descartes, "Meditation Five," trans. Haldane and Ross, 1931, 184–185.
8. Descartes, "Meditation Two," trans. Haldane and Ross, 1931, 154–155.

For Further Reading

Robert Audi, *Belief, Justification, and Knowledge* (Belmont, CA: Wadsworth, 1988).

Paul Boghossian, *Fear of Knowledge* (Oxford: Oxford University Press, 2006).

Lorraine Code, *What Can She Know?* (Ithaca, NY: Cornell University Press, 1991).

Eve Browning Cole, *Philosophy and Feminist Criticism: An Introduction* (New York: Paragon House, 1993). A readable introduction to feminist criticism of traditional philosophy.

René Descartes, "Meditation One," *Meditations on First Philosophy*, trans. Elizabeth S. Haldane and G. R. T. Ross (Cambridge: Dover, 1931).

Christopher Grau, ed., *Philosophers Explore the Matrix* (New York: Oxford University Press, 2005).

Jean-Luc Marion, *On Descartes' Metaphysical Prism: The Constitution and the Limits of Onto-Theo-Logy in Cartesian Thought* (Chicago: University of Chicago Press, 1999).

Paul K. Moser, Dwayne H. Mulder, and J. D. Trout, *The Theory of Knowledge: A Thematic Introduction* (New York: Oxford University Press, 1998).

Bertrand Russell, *The Problems of Philosophy* (London: Oxford University Press, 1912, 1959).

Online Resources

Crash Course, "Cartesian Skepticism," video, https://www.youtube.com/watch?v=MLKrmw906TM

Stanford Encyclopedia of Philosophy, "Rene Descartes," https://plato.stanford.edu/entries/descartes

Internet Encyclopedia of Philosophy, "Rene Descartes (1596–1650)," https://www.iep.utm.edu/descarte/#H11

Biography.com, "Rene Descartes," https://www.biography.com/scholar/rene-descartes

History of Philosophy (without Any Gaps) Podcast, https://historyofphilosophy.net

The Perseus Digital Library, http://www.perseus.tufts.edu/hopper

CHAPTER 10

From Hobbes to Hume

CHAPTER OBJECTIVES

10.1 HOBBES

- Define *justice*, *distributive justice*, and *social contract theory*.
- Summarize the main features of Hobbes's social contract theory.
- Understand Hobbes's view of human nature.
- Explain Hobbes's definition of justice and how justice can come into being as the Leviathan assumes power.
- Know the three main similarities between Hobbes's and Locke's social contract theories, and enumerate the dissimilarities.

10.2 LOCKE

- Summarize Locke's arguments against the notion of innate ideas.
- Explain Locke's reference to the mind as unmarked "white paper."
- Explain in what way Locke is an empiricist.
- Understand the misgivings that philosophers have about cognitive relativism.
- Summarize the main criticism that both rationalists and empiricists have of Locke's theory of knowledge.

10.3 BERKELEY

- Know the meaning of Berkeley's famous phrase, "to be is to be perceived."
- Explain how Berkeley's theory of knowledge differs from Locke's.
- Understand why Berkeley asserts that there are no material objects.
- State and evaluate Berkeley's logical argument that material objects cannot exist.
- Understand how Berkeley brings in the concept of God to explain how knowledge is possible.

10.4 HUME

- Define *principle of induction*.
- Explain Hume's distinction between relations of ideas and matters of fact.

- Explain why Hume concludes that theological and metaphysical speculations are worthless.
- Trace Hume's reasoning that ultimately leads him to strong skepticism.
- State Hume's argument against the principle of induction.

10.5 SPINOZA

- Define *pantheism.*
- Understand what Spinoza attempts to do by laying out his arguments in "geometrical order."
- Grasp Spinoza's reason for thinking that humans can have free will.
- Understand why Spinoza's view has been labeled a form of pantheism.

10.6 LEIBNIZ

- Understand Leibniz's reasoning that led him to conclude that monads exist.
- Explain the meaning of Leibniz's notion about our wills being inclined by God but not necessitated.
- State and evaluate Leibniz's belief that this world is the best of all possible worlds.

Remember: the luminous career of René Descartes (1596–1650) marks the beginning of the modern world with its new ideas, new science, new philosophy, and new questioning of religious values. In the seventeenth century, not only did Descartes start his epistemological revolution, but an impressive array of brilliant minds launched philosophical rebellions of their own. In the space of a hundred years, four British empiricists and two rationalists from the Continent veered from the path laid down by Aristotle, Descartes, the Church, and the reigning powers of the day. What they found along the way helped shape the intellectual and scientific future of the West.

10.1 HOBBES

"The source of every crime, is some defect of the understanding; or some error in reasoning; or some sudden force of the passions. Defect in the understanding is ignorance; in reasoning, erroneous opinion."
—Thomas Hobbes

Thomas Hobbes (1588–1679) was an eminent English philosopher whose ideas influenced all the English moral and political thinkers who came after him. He was also a linguist, poet, classical scholar, translator, logician, critic, and mathematical tutor to Charles II.

He was born into a poor religious family and liked to say that when his mother was pregnant with him, she went into labor on hearing that the Spanish Armada was threatening England. He joked that "fear and I were born twins together." He was educated at Oxford and spent most of his years as secretary and tutor to the family of the third earl of Devonshire. During this employment, he met the foremost European thinkers (Galileo and Francis Bacon among them) and wrote on a wide range of issues, both scientific and philosophical. Many of these works were extremely controversial. His political philosophy was offensive to both sides in the English Civil War; the Roman Catholic Church and Oxford University forbade the reading of his books; and he went against the grain of his era by advancing materialism, egoism, and (what some considered) heresy.

His best-known and most influential creation is *Leviathan* (1651), a sweeping treatise on political theory. His other writings include *Philosophical Rudiments Concerning Government and Society* (1651), *On the Body* (1655), and *On Man* (1658).

In *Leviathan*, Hobbes sets forth a new theory of **distributive justice**, or social justice. In its broadest sense, **justice** refers to people getting what is fair or what is their due, and the core principle that defines a person's due is *equals should be treated equally*. Distributive justice is about the fair distribution of society's benefits and burdens (its material and nonmaterial goods)—such things as jobs, income, property, liberties, rights, welfare aid, taxes, and public service. How these goods are distributed among the citizens of a state

Figure 10.1 Thomas Hobbes (1588–1679).

is a function of how the state is structured, how its social and political institutions are arranged. It's this kind of justice that is the focus of political philosophers and their theories of justice.

Hobbes's understanding of distributive justice is a **social contract theory**, which says that justice is secured, and the state is made legitimate, through an agreement among citizens of the state. The people consent explicitly or implicitly to be governed—to be subject to the dictates and the power of the state—in exchange for the state's providing security, rights, and liberties. The state's existence is justified by the binding contract that all parties accept. This idea about the role and justification of the state was incorporated into the Constitution of the United States, and in the twenty-first century, the wisdom of social contracts is taken for granted by much of the world.

Theories of justice embody principles that define fair distributions, that explain what people are due and why. A utilitarian theory of justice, for example, says that the distribution of goods should be based on the principle of *utility*. Society's institutions must be arranged so that its benefits and burdens are allocated to maximize some measure of society's welfare (total happiness, for example). This is a popular scheme of distribution, although some think it is inconsistent with our commonsense notions of justice and equality. As you might guess, the utilitarian philosopher John Stuart Mill favors the view.

Some theories of justice insist on distributions according to *merit*, or *desert* (what people deserve). Plato took this tack, arguing that because people differ in their talents and achievements, they should be given a station in life that reflects

distributive justice (or social justice) The fair distribution of society's benefits and burdens—such things as jobs, income, property, liberties, rights, welfare aid, taxes, and public service.

justice The idea that people should get what is fair or what is their due.

social contract theory The view that justice is secured, and the state is made legitimate, through an agreement among citizens of the state or between the citizens and the rulers of the state.

"Hell is truth seen too late."

—Thomas Hobbes

1. Hobbes is a pessimist about human nature; he thinks people are basically greedy and treacherous. Do you think he's right about this? Or are people fundamentally sociable, cooperative, and good? Explain your reasoning.

"It is not wisdom but Authority that makes a law."

—Thomas Hobbes

this difference. Some people have superior capacities and therefore should receive a superior share of society's goods; some possess few capacities and should get a smaller share. As you can see, Plato's view is strongly antidemocratic.

Hobbes was the first philosopher in modern times to systematically articulate a social contract theory. It was a major departure from received views about society, and that fact alone was enough to infuriate many. It also contained a rejection of both the divine right of kings and the notion of a divinely established moral law— points that gave his critics even more reasons to attack him.

Hobbes contends that a social contract is necessary in human affairs because living without one would be a horrific nightmare of existence. He begins by assuming a pessimistic view of human beings: at their core, he says, they are selfish, treacherous, dishonest, and violent. He argues that when these tendencies are left unchecked by enforced laws or agreements, humans sink into a "state of nature"—a "war of every man against every man." In the state of nature, there is no code, culture, or comfort. There is no justice. There is only "continual fear, and danger of violent death; and the life of man [is] solitary, poor, nasty, brutish, and short."[1]

But, Hobbes says, humankind also has a strong instinct for self-interest and self-preservation, and fortunately this impulse is coupled with the power of reason. Through reason, he says, people see that the only way to escape this "war of all against all" is to enter into a social contract with one another. In the name of self-interest, they agree to turn over much of their autonomy, freedom, and power to an absolute sovereign that will forcibly keep the peace, restrain antisocial actions, and compel people to keep their agreements. Hobbes calls this sovereign the *Leviathan* (the name of a sea monster mentioned in the Bible), which symbolizes great power and evil. Its authority over those bound by the social contract is absolute, and its power is fearsome (enough to deter any tendency to disorder). Once power is given up to this despot, there is no going back, and there is always the chance that the sovereign will create an environment worse than the state of nature. But that is the chance people must take.

So the state's authority is justified by a social contract, and justice comes into being as the Leviathan assumes power. For Hobbes, justice is a matter of keeping covenants (contracts), and the only way to ensure that covenants are kept is to let the Leviathan reign. Without the Leviathan to enforce covenants, there is no justice. As Hobbes says, "Where there is no common power, there is no law; where no law no injustice."[2]

Here is Hobbes arguing for his theory:

Thomas Hobbes: *Leviathan*

CHAPTER 13. OF THE NATURAL CONDITION OF MANKIND AS CONCERNING THEIR FELICITY, AND MISERY

Nature hath made men so equal, in the faculties of body, and mind; as that though there be found one man sometimes manifestly stronger in body, or of quicker mind than another; yet when all is reckoned together, the difference between man, and man, is not so considerable, as that one man can thereupon claim to himself any benefit, to which another may not pretend, as well as he. For as to the strength of body, the weakest has strength enough to kill the strongest, either by secret machination, or by confederacy with others, that are in the same danger with himself.

And as to the faculties of the mind (setting aside the arts grounded upon words, and especially that skill of proceeding upon general, and infallible rules, called science; which very few have, and but in few things; as being not a native faculty, born with us; nor attained, [as prudence], while we look after somewhat else), I find yet a greater equality amongst men, than that of strength. For prudence, is but experience; which equal time, equally bestows on all men, in those things they equally apply themselves unto. That which may perhaps make such equality incredible, is but a vain conceit of one's own wisdom, which almost all men think they have in a greater degree, than the vulgar; that is, than all men but themselves, and a few others, whom by fame, or for concurring with themselves, they approve. For such is the nature of men, that howsoever they may acknowledge many others to be more witty, or more eloquent, or more learned; yet they will hardly believe there be many so wise as themselves: For they see their own wit at hand, and other men's at a distance. But this proves rather that men are in that point equal, than unequal. For there is not ordinarily a greater sign of the equal distribution of any thing, than that every man is contented with his share.

From this equality of ability, arises equality of hope in the attaining of our ends. And therefore if any two men desire the same thing, which nevertheless they cannot both enjoy, they become enemies; and in the way to their end (which is principally their own conservation, and sometimes their delectation only), endeavor to destroy, or subdue one another. And from hence it comes to pass, that where an invader hath no more to fear, than another man's single power; if one plant, sow, build, or possess a convenient seat, others may probably be expected to come prepared with forces united, to dispossess, and deprive him, not only of the fruit of his labour, but also of his life, or liberty. And the invader again is in the like danger of another.

And from this diffidence of one another, there is no way for any man to secure himself, so reasonable, as anticipation; that is, by force, or wiles, to master the persons of all men he can, so long, till he see no other power great enough to endanger him: and this is no more than his own conservation requires, and is generally allowed. Also because there be some, that taking pleasure in contemplating their own power in the acts of conquest, which they pursue farther than their security requires; if others, that otherwise would be glad to be at ease within modest bounds, should not by invasion increase their power, they would not be able, long time, by standing only on their defence, to subsist. And by consequence, such augmentation of dominion over men, being necessary to a man's conservation, it ought to be allowed him.

Again, men have no pleasure (but on the contrary a great deal of grief) in keeping company, where there is no power able to over-awe them all. For every man looks that his companion should value him, at the same rate he sets upon himself: and upon all signs of contempt, or undervaluing, naturally endeavors, as far as he dares (which amongst them that have no common power to keep them in quiet, is far enough to make them destroy each other), to extort a greater value from his condemners, by damage; and from others, by the example.

So that in the nature of man, we find three principal causes of quarrel. First, competition; secondly, diffidence [distrust]; thirdly, glory.

The first, maketh men invade for gain; the second, for safety; and the third, for reputation. The first use violence, to make themselves masters of other men's persons, wives,

Thomas Hobbes:
Leviathan

2. Do you think Hobbes is right about humans being roughly equal physically and mentally? Why or why not?

3. Does the existence of stable democracies in the twenty-first century show that Hobbes is wrong about human nature?

Figure 10.2 Title page from Hobbes's *Leviathan*, 1651.

4. Suppose the world is suddenly left with no governmental authority anywhere; no formal restraints on human behavior exist. Speculate on how you think people would act. Would chaos and savagery ensue, or would people more or less live in peace and harmony?

children, and cattle; the second to defend them; the third, for trifles, as a word, a smile, a different opinion, and any other sign of undervalue, either direct in their persons, or by reflection in their kindred, their friends, their nation, their profession, or their name.

Hereby it is manifest, that during the time men live without a common power to keep them all in awe, they are in that condition which is called war; and such a war, as is of every man, against every man. For WAR, consists not in battle only, or the act of fighting; but in a tract of time, wherein the will to contend by battle is sufficiently known: and therefore the notion of time, is to be considered in the nature of war; as it is in the nature of weather. For as the nature of foul weather, lies not in a shower or two of rain; but in an inclination thereto of many days together: so the nature of war, consists not in actual fighting; but in the known disposition thereto, during all the time there is no assurance to the contrary. All other time is PEACE.

Whatsoever therefore is consequent to a time of war, where every man is enemy to every man; the same is consequent to the time; wherein men live without other security, than what their own strength, and their own invention shall furnish them withal. In such condition, there is no place for industry; because the fruit thereof is uncertain: and consequently no culture of the earth; no navigation, nor use of the commodities that may be imported by sea; no commodious building; no instruments of moving, and removing such things as require much force; no knowledge of the face of the earth; no account of time; no arts; no letters; no society; and which is worst of all, continual fear, and danger of violent death; and the life of man, solitary, poor, nasty, brutish, and short. . . .

To this war of every man against every man, this also is consequent; that nothing can be unjust. The notions of right and wrong, justice and injustice have there no place. Where there is no common power, there is no law: where no law no injustice. Force, and fraud, are in war the two cardinal virtues. Justice, and injustice are none of the faculties neither of the body, nor mind. If they were, they might be in a man that were alone in the world, as well as his senses, and passions. They are qualities, that relate to men in society, not in solitude. It is consequent also to the same condition, that there be no propriety, no dominion, no mine and thine distinct; but only that to be every man's, that he can get; and for so long, as he can keep it. And thus much for the ill condition, which man by mere nature is actually placed in; though with a possibility to come out of it, consisting partly in the passions, partly in his reason.

The passions that incline men to peace, are fear of death; desire of such things as are necessary to commodious living; and a hope by their industry to obtain them. And reason suggests convenient articles of peace, upon which men may be drawn to agreement. These articles, are they, which otherwise are called the Laws of Nature. . . .

CHAPTER 14. OF THE FIRST AND SECOND NATURAL LAW'S,
AND OF CONTRACTS

The RIGHT OF NATURE, which writers commonly call *jus naturale*, is the liberty each man hath, to use his own power, as he will himself, for the preservation of his own nature; that is to say, of his own life; and consequently, of doing any thing, which in his own judgment, and reason, he shall conceive to be the aptest means thereunto.

By LIBERTY, is understood, according to the proper signification of the word, the absence of external impediments: which impediments, may oft take away part of a man's power to do what he would; but cannot hinder him from using the power left him, according as his judgment, and reason shall dictate to him.

A LAW OF NATURE (*lex naturalis*), is a precept, or general rule, found out by reason, by which a man is forbidden to do that, which is destructive of his life, or taketh away the means of preserving the same; and to omit that, by which he thinks it may be best preserved. For though they that speak of this subject, use to confound jus, and lex, right and law; yet they ought to be distinguished; because RIGHT, consists in liberty to do, or to forbear; whereas LAW, determines, and binds to one of them: so that law, and right, differ as much, as obligation, and liberty; which in one and the same matter are inconsistent.

And because the condition of man (as hath been declared in the precedent chapter) is a condition of war of every one against every one; in which case every one is governed by his own reason; and there is nothing he can make use of that may not be a help unto him, in preserving his life against his enemies; it followeth, that in such a condition, every man has a right to every thing; even to one another's body. And therefore, as long as this natural right of every man to every thing endures, there can be no security to any man (how strong or wise soever he be) of living out the time, which nature ordinarily allows men to live. And consequently it is a precept, or general rule of reason, that every man, ought to endeavor peace, as far as he has hope of obtaining it; and when he cannot obtain it, that he may seek, and use, all helps, and advantages of war. The first branch of which rule, containeth the first, and fundamental law of nature; which is, to seek peace, and follow it. The second, the sum of the right of nature; which is, by all means we can, to defend ourselves.

From this fundamental law of nature, by which men are commanded to endeavor peace, is derived this second law; that a man be willing, when others are so too, as far-forth, as for peace, and defence of himself he shall think it necessary, to lay down this right to all things; and be contented with so much liberty against other men, as he would allow other men against himself. For as long as every man holds this right, of doing any thing he likes; so long are all men in the condition of war. But if other men will not lay down their right, as well as he; then there is no reason for any one, to divest himself of his: for that were to expose himself to prey (which no man is bound to) rather than to dispose himself to peace. This is that law of the Gospel; whatsoever you require that others should do to you, that do ye to them. And that law of all men, [what you would not have done to you, do not do to others]. . . .

CHAPTER 15. OF OTHER LAWS OF NATURE

From that law of nature, by which we are obliged to transfer to another, such rights, as being retained, hinder the peace of mankind, there followeth a third; which is this, that men

Thomas Hobbes: *Leviathan*

Figure 10.3 Hobbes's state of nature is a "war of all against all." Depicted here is the massacre at Magdeburg during the Thirty Years' War, a partly religious conflict that raged during Hobbes's lifetime.

"The condition of man . . . is a condition of war of everyone against everyone."

—Thomas Hobbes

5. Is ceding all power to a Leviathan the only way for people to achieve peace, security, and cooperation in a society? Explain.

perform their covenants made: without which, covenants are in vain, and but empty words; and the right of all men to all things remaining, we are still in the condition of war.

And in this law of nature, consists the fountain and original of JUSTICE. For where no covenant hath proceeded, there hath no right been transferred, and every man has right to every thing; and consequently, no action can be unjust. But when a covenant is made, then to break it is unjust: and the definition of INJUSTICE, is no other than the not performance of covenant. And whatsoever is not unjust, is just.

But because covenants of mutual trust, where there is a fear of not performance on either part (as hath been said in the former chapter), are invalid; though the original of justice be the making of covenants; yet injustice actually there can be none, till the cause of such fear be taken away; which while men are in the natural condition of war, cannot be done. Therefore before the names of just, and unjust can have place, there must be some coercive power, to compel men equally to the performance of their covenants, by the terror of some punishment, greater than the benefit they expect by the breach of their covenant; and to make good that propriety, which by mutual contract men acquire, in recompense of the universal right they abandon: and such power there is none before the erection of a commonwealth. And this is also to be gathered out of the ordinary definition of justice in the Schools: for they say, that justice is the constant will of giving to every man his own. And therefore where there is no own, that is, no propriety, there is no injustice; and where there is no coercive power erected, that is, where there is no commonwealth, there is no propriety; all men having right to all things: therefore where there is no commonwealth, there nothing is unjust. So that the nature of justice, consists in keeping of valid covenants: but the validity of covenants begins not but with the constitution of a civil power, sufficient to compel men to keep them: and then it is also that propriety begins.[3]

The philosopher John Locke (1632–1704), a contemporary of Hobbes, devised a different kind of social contract theory. It has some points in common with Hobbes's—but also much that Hobbes would have rejected outright. Both Hobbes and Locke assert that (1) reason enables people to see the wisdom of forming a state through a social contract, (2) people must freely consent to be bound by the contract (not be coerced into accepting it), and (3) the state's authority is justified by this consent of the governed. Beyond these matters, Hobbes and Locke part company.

For one thing, they have very different ideas about the "state of nature," the world in which no civil society exists. For Hobbes, to be in the state of nature is to be in a "war of all against all," where morality is nonexistent, and the only laws are commonsense rules for survival and self-interest. For Locke, on the other hand, the state of nature is considerably less nasty and brutish, for even there, natural moral laws apply and help regulate people's behavior. Those living in the state of nature are free, sociable, equal, and (mostly) at peace.

Hobbes contends that, generally, justice and rights do not come into being until the state is established. People surrender their lives and liberties to the Leviathan in exchange for security and peace, and he can do what he wants with his subjects. But Locke argues that humans have inherent, God-given rights whether or not a government is around to guarantee them. Chief among these is the right to property—not just land but your own body and any object that you change through work (with which you "mix your labor"). These rights are inalienable: they cannot be transferred

"I have always thought the actions of men the best interpreters of their thoughts."

—John Locke

to the government or any other entity. Humans create the government and cede some power to it; in return it protects their rights and liberties. The state serves the people (not the other way round), directing all its power "to no other end but the peace, safety, and public good of the people."

But what exactly does the state do to preserve liberties and promote the common good? Locke identifies three functions that people need the state to perform. First, citizens need the natural moral law to be set out in clearly expressed laws of the land. Unwritten natural laws are clear to humans, but people are apt to misconstrue them in line with their biases. Second, there needs to be impartial judges who can settle disputes concerning the application of the laws. Third, there needs to be power in the state to enforce the laws. Otherwise people will be able to take justice into their own hands.

Suppose, however, that the state abuses its power by repeatedly and arbitrarily trampling on the people's rights and liberties. Hobbes says once you cede power to the Leviathan, he is free to treat you as he will. But Locke says if the government violates the rights of citizens, it is no longer legitimate, obligations to it are voided, and the people have a right to dissolve it—to initiate rebellion. Locke's insistence on the right to rebel against a government that misuses its power is echoed clearly in the Declaration of Independence:

> We hold these truths to be self-evident, that all men are created equal, that they are endowed by their Creator with certain unalienable Rights, that among these are Life, Liberty and the pursuit of Happiness.—That to secure these rights, Governments are instituted among Men, deriving their just powers from the consent of the governed,—That whenever any Form of Government becomes destructive of these ends, it is the Right of the People to alter or abolish it, and to institute a new Government.[4]

10.2 LOCKE

In addition to his political writing, John Locke also advanced a theory of knowledge, taking an empiricist approach, as do two other British empiricists—George Berkeley and David Hume. Like most empiricists, Locke and Berkeley reject skepticism while denying rationalist claims (such as the doctrine of innate ideas), building their theories of knowledge on the supposed firmer ground of sense experience. (See Descartes' rationalist view in Chapter 9.) But the differences among these seminal thinkers are stark. Locke argues that we can know much about things external to our minds; Berkeley agrees that we can have knowledge but denies the reality of material objects; and Hume insists that the scope of our knowledge is much narrower than most people realize, raising skeptical doubts about the existence of the external world and the inductive methodology of science.

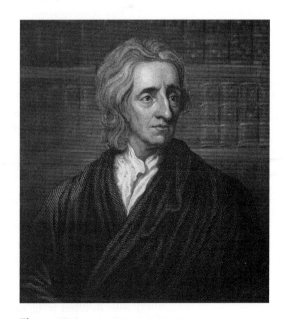

Figure 10.4 John Locke (1632–1704).

"Reading furnishes the mind only with materials of knowledge; it is thinking that makes what we read ours."

—John Locke

In Locke's philosophical masterwork, *An Essay Concerning Human Understanding* (1689), he builds a case against rationalism and for a thoroughgoing empiricism. First he contends that the rationalist notion that we are born with knowledge ("innate principles," as he says) already imprinted on our minds is unfounded. The rationalist argues, says Locke, that since all people seem to possess knowledge of certain universal principles (such as truths of logic), this knowledge must be inborn. How else could everyone have come by this knowledge? Locke replies that there are no such universal principles, and even if there were, they could have easily arisen through sense experience. They need not be present at birth. Here is Locke's critique of innate ideas:

John Locke: *An Essay Concerning Human Understanding*

1. The way shown how we come by any knowledge, sufficient to prove it not innate. It is an established opinion amongst some men, that there are in the understanding certain innate principles; some primary notions, characters, as it were, stamped upon the mind of man, which the soul receives in its very first being; and brings into the world with it. It would be sufficient to convince unprejudiced readers of the falseness of this supposition, if I should only shew (as I hope I shall in the following parts of this discourse) how men, barely by the use of their natural faculties, may attain to all the knowledge they have, without the help of any innate impressions; and may arrive at certainty, without any such original notions or principles. For I imagine any one will easily grant, that it would be impertinent to suppose, the ideas of colours innate in a creature, to whom God hath given sight, and a power to receive them by the eyes, from external objects: And no less unreasonable would it be to attribute several truths to the impressions of nature, and innate characters, when we may observe in ourselves faculties, fit to attain as easy and certain knowledge of them, as if they were originally imprinted on the mind.

But because a man is not permitted without censure to follow his own thoughts in the search of truth, when they lead him ever so little out of the common road; I shall set down the reasons that made me doubt of the truth of that opinion, as an excuse for my mistake, if I be in one; which I leave to be considered by those who, with me, dispose themselves to embrace truth, wherever they find it.

2. General assent, the great argument. There is nothing more commonly taken for granted, than that there are certain principles, both speculative and practical, (for they speak of both), universally agreed upon by all mankind: Which therefore, they argue, must needs be the constant impressions, which the souls of men receive in their first beings, and which they bring into the world with them, as necessarily and really as they do any of their inherent faculties.

3. Universal consent proves nothing. This argument, drawn from universal consent, has this misfortune in it, that if it were true in matter of fact, that there were certain truths wherein all mankind agreed, it would not prove them innate, if there can be any other way shewn how men may come to that universal agreement, in the things they do consent in, which I presume may be done.

4. What is, is; and it is impossible for the same thing to be, and not to be; not universally assented to. But, which is worse, this argument of universal consent, which is

6. Locke says that universal agreement on principles does not prove that they are innate. Why does he say this? Is he right?

made use of to prove innate principles, seems to me a demonstration that there are none such; because there are none to which all mankind give an universal assent. I shall begin with the speculative, and instance in those magnified principles of demonstration; "Whatsoever is, is;" and "It is impossible for the same thing to be and not to be;" which, of all others, I think have the most allowed title to innate. These have so settled a reputation of maxims universally received, that it will, no doubt, be thought strange, if any one should seem to question it. But yet I take liberty to say, that these propositions are so far from having an universal assent, that there are a great part of mankind to whom they are not so much as known.

5. Not on the mind naturally imprinted, because not known to children, idiots, etc. For, first, it is evident, that all children and idiots have not the least apprehension or thought of them; and the want of that is enough to destroy that universal assent, which must needs be the necessary concomitant of all innate truths: It seeming to me near a contradiction, to say, that there are truths imprinted on the soul, which it perceives or understands not; imprinting if it signify any thing, being nothing else, but the making certain truths to be perceived. For to imprint any thing on the mind, without the mind's perceiving it seems to me hardly intelligible. If therefore children and idiots have souls, have minds, with those impressions upon them, they must unavoidably perceive them, and necessarily know and assent to these truths: Which since they do not, it is evident that there are no such impressions.[5]

John Locke: An Essay Concerning Human Understanding

7. In response to Locke's point about children, suppose a rationalist insists that children's minds are not fully developed and so cannot yet have knowledge of innate principles—therefore, their lack of innate knowledge does not prove anything. Is this a good argument?

For Locke, the mind does not come into the world already inscribed with ideas or knowledge. On the contrary, he says, the mind is unmarked "white paper" void of any ideas until sense experience gives it content. From where does the mind obtain "all the *materials* of reason and knowledge"? he asks. "To this I answer, in one word, from *experience*. In that all our knowledge is founded."[6]

Rationalists like Descartes would say that our most important items of knowledge must be innate because they could not possibly have come from sense experience. They would maintain, for example, that our knowledge of the concept "infinity" and of the proposition "every event has a cause" must be prenatally imprinted on our minds because we can never observe instances of these in reality. Through sense experience we can become acquainted only with finite things, not an infinity of things; and we can observe only a limited number of events, not all events. Locke, however, holds that we can grasp such ideas by first having sense experience related to them and then extrapolating the ideas from the sense data. We can, for example, have the concept of infinity by experiencing finite things and multiplying and extending them in our imagination until we approach the idea of the infinite.

Locke tries to defeat the skeptic by showing how our sense experience can reveal the existence of an external world. He says we must distinguish between the objects of our experience (external objects) and the experience of those objects (sensations, or sense data). Physical objects cause sensations in us, and we are directly aware only of those sensations (or ideas, as Locke calls them). So we have direct knowledge not of external objects,

Figure 10.5 Title page of Locke's *Essay Concerning Human Understanding*.

8. Evaluate Locke's point about extrapolating ideas from sense data. Is it plausible? Is it a good response to the rationalist?

but of the sense data that seem to be external objects. But if all we ever really know are sense data, how can we be sure they give us an accurate picture of the external world?

Locke's answer is that sensations caused by external objects somehow represent those objects and thereby give us knowledge of them. Sensations are, Locke says, "resemblances" of external things. But he points out that not all of our sensations faithfully reflect reality. He distinguishes between two kinds of properties that external objects can have. *Primary qualities* are objective properties such as size, solidity, and mobility. They are *in material objects*, independent of our senses, and would be possessed by the objects even if no one was around to sense anything. *Secondary qualities* are subjective properties such as the color red or the smell of roses. They are *in the mind* in that they depend on the operation of the senses. They exist only when someone experiences them. For Locke, we can have objective knowledge of material objects because some of our sense data represent the objects' primary qualities, which are objective characteristics of them.

THEN AND NOW

The Defeat of Relativism

Like Plato and many other philosophers, Locke rejected the doctrine of *relativism*. Recall that relativism is a view about knowledge that has been controversial since Socrates' time. (It's surprisingly common today, especially among college students.) It's the doctrine that the truth about something depends on what persons or cultures believe. The notion that truth depends on what a person believes is known as *subjective relativism*, and the idea that truth depends on what a culture believes is called *cultural relativism*.

As we've seen, we normally assume that truth is objective—that it depends on the way the world is. When we assert a proposition, we generally believe that the proposition is true if and only if it says the way things are in reality. But the relativist rejects this view, believing instead that truth is relative to what a person or culture accepts as true. Truth is a matter of what a person or culture believes—not a matter of how the world is. Most philosophers have rejected relativism because the doctrine implies several absurdities that render it implausible. They point out, for example, that if we could make a statement true just by believing it to be true, we could never be in error; we would be infallible.

But relativism in all its forms has a bigger problem: it is self-defeating. It defeats itself because its truth implies its falsity. The relativist says, "All truth is relative." If this statement is objectively true, then it refutes itself because if it is objectively true that "all truth is relative," then the statement itself is an example of an objective truth. So if "all truth is relative" is objectively true, it is objectively false.

Are you a relativist? Why or why not?

Locke's theory of knowledge, however, has been sharply criticized by both ratio-nalists and empiricists. The main criticism is that Locke has not given us any good reason to think that our sense data are proof of the existence of an external reality. After all, according to Locke, we directly experience only our sensations, or ideas; we do not directly perceive external objects. We have no way of jumping out of our subjective point of view to compare our sense experience with the objective world. For all we know, our sense data present a radically distorted or thoroughly false picture of reality.

Here is Locke's answer to this charge:

1. Is to be had only by sensation. The knowledge of our own being we have by intuition. The existence of a God reason clearly makes known to us, as has been shown.

The knowledge of the existence of any other thing, we can have only by sensation: For there being no necessary connexion of real existence with any idea a man hath in his memory, nor of any other existence but that of God, with the existence of any particular man; no particular man can know the existence of any other being, but only when by actual operating upon him, it makes itself perceived by him.

For the having the idea of any thing in our mind, no more proves the existence of that thing, than the picture of a man evidences his being in the world, or the visions of a dream make thereby a true history.

2. Instance, whiteness of this paper. It is therefore the actual receiving of ideas from without [outside], that gives us notice of the existence of other things, and makes us know that something doth exist at that time without us, which causes that idea in us, though perhaps we neither know nor consider how it does it. For it takes not from the certainty of our senses, the ideas we receive by them, that we know not the manner wherein they are produced: V. g. whilst I write this, I have, by the paper affecting my eyes, that idea produced in my mind, which whatever object causes, I call white; by which I know that that quality or accident (i.e. whose appearance before my eyes always causes that idea) doth really exist, and hath a being without me. And of this, the greatest assurance I can possibly have, and to which my faculties can attain, is the testimony of my eyes, which are the proper and sole judges of this thing, whose testimony I have reason to rely on as so certain, that I can no more doubt, whilst I write this, that I see white and black, and that something really exists, that causes that sensation in me, than that I write or move my hand; which is a certainty as great as human nature is capable of, concerning the existence of any thing, but a man's self alone, and of God.

3. This, though not so certain as demonstration, yet may be called knowledge, and proves the existence of things without us. The notice we have by our senses, of the existing of things without us, though it be not altogether so certain as our intuitive knowl-edge, or the deductions of our reason employed about the clear abstract ideas of our own minds; yet it is an assurance that deserves the name of knowledge. If we persuade our-selves, that our faculties act and inform us right, concerning the existence of those objects that affect them, it cannot pass for an ill-grounded confidence: For I think nobody can, in earnest, be so sceptical, as to be uncertain of the existence of those things which he sees and feels. At least, he that can doubt so far (whatever he may have with his own thoughts) will never have any controversy with me; since he can never be sure I say any thing contrary to his own opinion. As to myself, I think God has given me assurance enough of the exis-tence of things without me; since by their different application I can produce in myself both

"One unerring mark of the love of truth is not entertaining any proposi-tion with greater assur-ance than the proofs it is built upon will warrant."

—John Locke

John Locke: *An Essay Concerning Human Understanding*

9. Has Locke provided good reasons to think that our sense data prove the existence of an external world? Evaluate his attempt to answer his critics on this point.

pleasure and pain, which is one great concernment of my present state. This is certain; the confidence that our faculties do not herein deceive us is the greatest assurance we are capable of, concerning the existence of material beings. For we cannot act any thing but by our faculties; nor talk of knowledge itself, but by the help of those faculties, which are fitted to apprehend even what knowledge is. But besides the assurance we have from our senses themselves, that they do not err in the information they give us, of the existence of things without us, when they are affected by them, we are farther confirmed in this assurance by other concurrent reasons.

4. Because we cannot have them but by the inlets of the senses. First, it is plain those perceptions are produced in us by exterior causes affecting our senses; because those that want [lack] the organs of any sense, never can have the ideas belonging to that sense produced in their minds. This is too evident to be doubted: And therefore we cannot but be assured, that they come in by the organs of that sense, and no other way. The organs themselves, it is plain, do not produce them, for then the eyes of a man in the dark would produce colors, and his nose smell roses in the winter: But we see nobody gets the relish of a pine-apple, till he goes to the Indies, where it is, and tastes it.

5. Because an idea from actual sensation, and another from memory, are very distinct perceptions. Secondly, because sometimes I find, that I cannot avoid the having those ideas produced in my mind. For though when my eyes are shut, or windows fast, I can at pleasure recall to my mind the ideas of light, or the sun, which former sensations had lodged in my memory; so I can at pleasure lay by that idea, and take into my view that of the smell of a rose, or taste of sugar. But, if I turn my eyes at noon towards the sun, I cannot avoid the ideas, which the light, or sun, then produces in me. So that there is a manifest difference between the ideas laid up in my memory, (over which, if they were there only, I should have constantly the same power to dispose of them, and lay them by at pleasure) and those which force themselves upon me, and I cannot avoid having. And therefore it must needs be some exterior cause, and the brisk acting of some objects without me, whose efficacy I cannot resist, that produces those ideas in my mind, whether I will or no. Besides, there is nobody who doth not perceive the difference in himself between contemplating the sun, as he hath the idea of it in his memory, and actually looking upon it: Of which two, his perception is so distinct, that few of his ideas are more distinguishable one from another. And therefore he hath certain knowledge that they are not both memory, or the actions of his mind, and fancies only within him; but that actual seeing hath a cause without.

6. Pleasure and Pain, which accompanies actual sensation, accompanies not the returning of those ideas, without the external objects. Thirdly, add to this, that many of those ideas are produced in us with pain, which afterwards we remember without the least offence. Thus the pain of heat or cold, when the idea of it is revived in our minds, gives us no disturbance; which, when felt, was very troublesome, and is again, when actually repeated; which is occasioned by the disorder the external object causes in our bodies when applied to it. And we remember the pains of hunger, thirst, or the head-ache, without any pain at all; which would either never disturb us, or else constantly do it, as often as we thought of it, were there nothing more but ideas floating in our minds, and appearances entertaining our fancies, without the real existence of things affecting us from abroad. The same may be said of pleasure, accompanying several actual sensations: And though mathematical demonstration depends not upon sense, yet the examining them by diagrams gives great credit to the evidence of our sight, and seems to give it a certainty approaching to that of demonstration itself. For it would be very strange, that a man should allow it for an undeniable truth, that two angles of a figure, which he measures by lines and angles of a diagram, should be bigger one than the other; and yet doubt of the existence of those lines and angles, which by looking on he makes use of to measure that by. . . .

8. This certainty is as great as our condition needs. But yet, if after all this any one will be so sceptical, as to distrust his senses, and to affirm that all we see and hear, feel and taste, think and do, during our whole being, is but the series and deluding appearances of a long dream, whereof there is reality; and therefore will question the existence of all things, or our knowledge of any thing; I must desire him to consider, that if all be a dream, then he doth but dream, that he makes the question; and so it is not much matter, that a waking man should answer him. But yet, if he pleases, he may dream that I make him this answer, that the certainty of things existing in *rerum natura*, when we have the testimony of our senses for it, is not only as great as our frame can attain to, but as our condition needs. For our faculties ties being suited not to the full extent of being, nor to a perfect, clear, comprehensive knowledge of things free from all doubt and scruple; but to the preservation of us, in whom they are; and accommodated to the use of life; they serve to our purpose well enough, if they will but give us certain notice of those things, which are convenient or inconvenient to us. For he that sees a candle burning, and hath experimented the force of its flame, by putting his finger in it, will little doubt that this is something existing without him, which does him harm, and puts him to great pain: Which is assurance enough, when no man requires greater certainty to govern his actions by, than what is as certain as his actions themselves. And if our dreamer pleases to try, whether the glowing heat of a glass furnace be barely a wandering imagination in a drowsy man's fancy; by putting his hand into it, he may perhaps be wakened into a certainty greater than he could wish, that it is something more than bare imagination. So that this evidence is as great as we can desire, being as certain to us as our pleasure or pain, i.e. happiness or misery; beyond which we have no concernment, either of knowing or being. Such an assurance of the existence of things without us is sufficient to direct us in the attaining the good, and avoiding the evil, which is caused by them; which is the important concernment we have of being made acquainted with them.[7]

> John Locke: *An Essay Concerning Human Understanding*

> **10.** Is Locke's argument (an inference to the best explanation) successful? Evaluate its strengths and weaknesses.

Locke asks, in effect: What could possibly cause our sense experience if not external objects? His answer is that we know that external objects are real (and not a dream or delusion) because the theory that they exist is the best explanation for the sensations we have. External objects cause our sensations, and this is a much better explanation for our experience than that an evil genius or our own minds create a fantasy world that we take to be real.

> "Hunting after arguments to make good one side of a question, and wholly to refuse those which favour the other, is so far from giving truth its due value, that it wholly debases it."
> —John Locke

10.3 BERKELEY

Like Locke, George Berkeley (1685–1753) is an empiricist who rejects skepticism. He believes that we can indeed acquire knowledge and that the only path to it is through sense experience. But beyond these points of agreement, Berkeley veers sharply from Locke's view and from the theories of most other empiricists. (Caution: At first glance, you may think Berkeley's theory of knowledge is both bizarre and

Figure 10.6 George Berkeley (1685–1753).

wrong. But he provides plausible, and unsettling, arguments for his view, and generations of philosophers—whether they agreed with Berkeley or not—have been forced to take his theory seriously.)

For Berkeley, there are no material objects, no things that exist in the external world. There are objects to be sure, but they exist only as sensations (what Berkeley calls *ideas*) in some mind. They are real only because they are perceived by someone. Thus he declares in his famous phrase, *esse est percipi,* "to be is to be perceived." What we usually call physical objects, then, are simply compilations of sense data, and reality consists only of ideas and the minds that perceive them. Our sense experience does not represent an external reality as Locke thought; our sense experience *is* reality. Locke's view is vulnerable to skeptical criticism because he admits that there is a gap between our sensations and reality. Berkeley, however, tries to defeat skepticism by doing away with the gap entirely. He contends that there is no gap, because material objects do not exist; only ideas exist along with the minds that perceive them.

Let's allow Berkeley to make his case:

George Berkeley: *Of the Principles of Human Knowledge*

I. It is evident to any one who takes a survey of the objects of human knowledge, that they are either ideas actually imprinted on the senses, or else such as are perceived by attending to the passions and operations of the mind, or lastly, ideas formed by help of memory and imagination, either compounding, dividing, or barely representing those originally perceived in the aforesaid ways. By sight I have the ideas of light and colours with their several degrees and variations. By touch I perceive, for example, hard and soft, heat and cold, motion and resistance, and of all these more and less either as to quantity or degree. Smelling furnishes me with odours; the palate with tastes; and hearing conveys sounds to the mind in all their variety of tone and composition. And as several of these are observed to accompany each other, they come to be marked by one name, and so to be reputed as one thing. Thus, for example, a certain colour, taste, smell, figure, and consistence having been observed to go together, are accounted one distinct thing, signified by the name apple. Other collections of ideas constitute a stone, a tree, a book, and the like sensible things; which, as they are pleasing or disagreeable, excite the passions of love, hatred, joy, grief, and so forth.

II. But besides all that endless variety of ideas or objects of knowledge, there is likewise something which knows or perceives them, and exercises divers operations, as willing, imagining, remembering about them. This perceiving, active being is what I call mind, spirit, soul, or myself. By which words I do not denote any one of my ideas, but a thing entirely distinct from them, wherein they exist, or, which is the same thing, whereby they are perceived; for the existence of an idea consists in being perceived.

III. That neither our thoughts, nor passions, nor ideas formed by the imagination, exist without the mind, is what every body will allow. And (to me) it seems no less evident that the various sensations or ideas imprinted on the sense, however blended or combined together (that is, whatever objects they compose), cannot exist otherwise than in a mind perceiving them. I think an intuitive knowledge may be obtained of this, by any one that shall attend to what is meant by the term exist, when applied to sensible things. The table I write on, I say, exists, that is, I see and feel it; and if I were out of my study I should say it existed, meaning thereby that if I was in my study I might perceive it, or that some other spirit actually does perceive it. There was an odour, that is, it was smelled; there was a sound, that is to say, it was heard; a colour or figure, and it was perceived by sight or touch. This is all that I can understand by these and the like expressions. For as to what is said of the absolute existence of unthinking things without any relation to their being perceived, that seems perfectly unintelligible. Their *esse est percipi*, nor is it possible they should have any existence, out of the minds or thinking things which perceive them.

IV. It is indeed an opinion strangely prevailing amongst men, that houses, mountains, rivers, and in a word sensible objects have an existence natural or real, distinct from their being perceived by the understanding. But with how great an assurance and acquiescence soever this principle may be entertained in the world; yet whoever shall find in his heart to call it in question, may, if I mistake not, perceive it to involve a manifest contradiction. For what are the forementioned objects but the things we perceive by sense, and what do we perceive besides our own ideas or sensations; and is it not plainly repugnant that any one of these or any combination of them should exist unperceived? . . .

VI. Some truths there are so near and obvious to the mind, that a man need only open his eyes to see them. Such I take this important one to be, to wit, that all the choir of heaven and furniture of the earth, in a word all those bodies which compose the mighty frame of the world, have not any subsistence without a mind, that their being (*esse*) is to be perceived or known; that consequently so long as they are not actually perceived by me, or do not exist in my mind or that of any other created spirit, they must either have no existence at all, or else subsist in the mind of some eternal spirit: it being perfectly unintelligible and involving all the absurdity of abstraction, to attribute to any single part of them an existence independent of a spirit. To be convinced of which, the reader need only reflect and try to separate in his own thoughts the being of a sensible thing from its being perceived. . . .[8]

To provide further support for his theory, Berkeley takes aim at Locke's distinction between primary and secondary qualities. He claims that primary qualities are just as mind dependent as secondary qualities are, for primary qualities can also vary according to the state of our senses, and primary qualities are inseparable from secondary qualities.

IX. Some there are who make a distinction betwixt primary and secondary qualities: by the former, they mean extension, figure, motion, rest, solidity or impenetrability, and number: by the latter they denote all other sensible qualities, as colours, sounds, tastes, and so forth. The ideas we have of these they acknowledge not to be the resemblances of any

---

George Berkeley: *Of the Principles of Human Knowledge*

11. Is Berkeley right that belief in material objects involves a logical contradiction? Explain.

"All the choir of heaven and furniture of earth—in a word, all those bodies which compose the frame of the world—have not any subsistence without a mind."

—George Berkeley

George Berkeley: *Of the Principles of Human Knowledge*

thing existing without the mind or unperceived; but they will have our ideas of the primary qualities to be patterns or images of things which exist without the mind, in an unthinking substance which they call matter. By matter therefore we are to understand an inert, senseless substance, in which extension, figure and motion, do actually subsist. But it is evident from what we have already shown, that extension, figure, and motion, are only ideas existing in the mind, and that an idea can be like nothing but another idea, and that consequently neither they nor their archetypes can exist in an unperceiving substance. Hence it is plain, that the very notion of what is called matter, or corporeal substance, involves a contradiction in it.

X. They who assert that figure, motion, and the rest of the primary or original qualities, do exist without the mind, in unthinking substances, do at the same time acknowledge that colours, sounds , heat, cold, and such like secondary qualities, do not, which they tell us are sensations existing in the mind alone, that depend on and are occasioned by the different size, texture, and motion of the minute particles of matter. This they take for an undoubted truth, which they can demonstrate beyond all exception. Now if it be certain, that those original qualities are inseparably united with the other sensible qualities, and not, even in thought, capable of being abstracted from them, it plainly follows that they exist only in the mind. But I desire any one to reflect and try, whether he can, by any abstraction of thought, conceive the extension and motion of a body, without all other sensible qualities. For my own part, I see evidently that it is not in my power to frame an idea of a body extended and moved, but I must withal give it some colour or other sensible quality which is acknowledged to exist only in the mind. In short, extension, figure, and motion, abstracted from all other qualities, are inconceivable. Where therefore the other sensible qualities are, there must these be also, to wit, in the mind and nowhere else. . . .

XV. In short, let any one consider those arguments which are thought manifestly to prove that colours and tastes exist only in the mind, and he shall find they may with equal force be brought to prove the same thing of extension, figure, and motion. Though it must be confessed, this method of arguing doth not so much prove that there is no extension or colour in an outward object, as that we do not know by sense which is the true extension or colour of the object. But the arguments foregoing plainly show it to be impossible that any colour or extension at all or other sensible quality whatsoever, should exist in an unthinking subject without the mind, or in truth, that there should be any such thing as an outward object.[9]

12. Do you think there is no substantial difference between primary and secondary qualities? Why or why not?

"The possession of knowledge does not kill the sense of wonder and mystery. There is always more mystery."
—Anaïs Nin

Berkeley's most interesting argument against the existence of material objects is a purely logical one: he contends that they cannot exist because their existence would be logically absurd. The commonsense view is that material objects *continue to be* even when no one has them in mind. But, says Berkeley, this would mean that they can be conceived of as existing unconceived, that we can think about things that no one is thinking about—a logical contradiction. Therefore, Berkeley concludes, the claim that material objects exist is false.

Critics have taken issue with this argument. They agree that in one sense it is impossible to conceive of something unconceived: it is impossible to contemplate a thing that is at the same time not being contemplated. But they maintain that there is no incoherence in believing the assertion that an entity exists unconceived. No contradiction lurks here. If so, the concept of a material object is not, as Berkeley charges, "a manifest repugnancy."

Some have faulted Berkeley's theory in another way. They ask, Why do patterns of sensations present themselves to us as if they were entirely independent of our minds? That is, why do the configurations of sense data behave like material objects, seemingly existing unperceived and beyond our control? Berkeley's answer is that things are never unperceived, for God continually perceives them and thus causes them to be as they are. God inserts a grand, intricate panoply of ideas into our minds—sensations that constitute for us a real world of God's making. What we think of as material objects are instead repeating patterns of sense experience caused by God.

Like the rationalist Descartes, Berkeley the empiricist ultimately brings in God to explain how knowledge is possible. But to many, his explanation of the peculiar nature of our sense experience is not as good by far as the commonsense explanation: material objects exist independently of us and cause the patterns of our sensations. They think the God theory leaves too much unexplained; to them the material-object theory seems simpler and more consistent with scientific understanding of perception. As Bertrand Russell says:

> [E]very principle of simplicity urges us to adopt the natural view, that there really are objects other than ourselves and our sense-data which have an existence not dependent upon our perceiving them.[10]

10.4 HUME

So, in their own ways, Locke and Berkeley wrestled with the great epistemological questions: Do we have knowledge? And if so, what exactly do we know? In the end they all concluded that we do indeed have knowledge, but they differed on its extent. In contrast, David Hume—the renowned Enlightenment thinker and preeminent British philosopher—argued for a thoroughly consistent empiricism that led him to a skepticism so extensive that few others dared follow his lead.

Hume insists that whatever knowledge we have is of two kinds: "relations of ideas" and "matters of fact." The former includes truths of mathematics and truths of logic (such as "either it's raining or it's not raining" and "no bachelors are married"); they are derived from reason. The latter consists of information about the world and is based entirely on sense experience. We can come to know relations of ideas with certainty, but they are not informative about reality. We know that "either it's raining or it's not raining" is true, but the proposition tells us nothing about whether it is actually raining. It simply states an obvious logical truth. Matters of fact, on the other hand, are informative about the world, but they cannot be known with certainty. So contrary to the rationalists, Hume maintains that reason is not a source of knowledge about the world. In line with the empiricists, he holds that knowledge about the world can be acquired only through experience.

"Reason is, and ought only to be the slave of the passions, and can never pretend to any other office than to serve and obey them."

—David Hume

13. How does Hume's empiricism differ from Locke's and Berkeley's?

But how much can we really know through experience alone? That is, what can we know about matters of fact? Hume's answer: very little. He says that the information derived from experience—what he calls *perceptions*—consists of sense data (such as sights, odors, and sounds) and inner psychological states (such as hate, fear, love, and desire). Perceptions are of two types: *impressions* and *ideas*. Impressions are what we directly and vividly experience, the raw sense data and psychological states. Ideas are our less vivid thoughts and reflections about impressions. The experience of a bright red color when you look at a rose is an impression. Your thoughts or imaginings about the original rose experience is an idea. Hume uses this terminology to make his central point: For something to count as knowledge, it must be based on impressions or on ideas derived from impressions. And for a statement to be meaningful, it must ultimately refer to impressions. Here is Hume outlining these distinctions:

David Hume: *An Enquiry Concerning Human Understanding*

Every one will readily allow, that there is a considerable difference between the perceptions of the mind, when a man feels the pain of excessive heat, or the pleasure of moderate warmth, and when he afterwards recalls to his memory this sensation, or anticipates it by his imagination. These faculties may mimic or copy the perceptions of the senses; but they never can entirely reach the force and vivacity of the original sentiment. The utmost we say of them, even when they operate with greatest vigor, is, that they represent their object in so lively a manner, that we could almost say we feel or see it: But, except the mind be disordered by disease or madness, they never can arrive at such a pitch of vivacity, as to render these perceptions altogether undistinguishable. All the colours of poetry, however splendid, can never paint natural objects in such a manner as to make the description be taken for a real landscape. The most lively thought is still inferior to the dullest sensation.

We may observe a like distinction to run through all the other perceptions of the mind. A man in a fit of anger, is actuated in a very different manner from one who only thinks of that emotion. If you tell me, that any person is in love, I easily understand your meaning, and form a just conception of his situation; but never can mistake that conception for the real disorders and agitations of the passion. When we reflect on our past sentiments and affections, our thought is a faithful mirror, and copies its objects truly; but the colours which it employs are faint and dull, in comparison of those in which our original perceptions were clothed. It requires no nice discernment or metaphysical head to mark the distinction between them.

Here therefore we may divide all the perceptions of the mind into two classes or species, which are distinguished by their different degrees of force and vivacity. The less forcible and lively are commonly denominated Thoughts or Ideas. The other species want a name in our language, and in most others; I suppose, because it was not requisite for any, but philosophical purposes, to rank them under a general term or appellation. Let us, therefore, use a little

14. Hume thinks that all knowledge must be traced back to perceptions; otherwise assertions of knowledge are meaningless. From this he concludes that all theological and metaphysical speculations are worthless. Do you agree with him? Why or why not?

PORTRAIT

David Hume

During his lifetime, David Hume (1711–1776) earned a reputation as one of Britain's premier men of letters and garnered fame as the author of the six-volume *History of England*. In our time, he is regarded as a key figure in the Enlightenment, the most influential of the British empiricists, and possibly Britain's greatest philosopher.

He was born in Edinburgh, Scotland, educated at its university, and spent most of his literary career in the city of his birth. By age sixteen he was already well versed in classical literature, logic, metaphysics, philosophy, and ethics. Later, in a three-year period, he read, in his words, "most of the celebrated Books in Latin, French & English."

Figure 10.7 David Hume (1711–1776).

He wrote essays on politics, ethics, and economics as well as major philosophical treatises. The first (and some say the greatest) of the latter was *A Treatise of Human Nature* (1739), followed by *An Enquiry Concerning Human Understanding* (1748) and *An Enquiry Concerning the Principles of Morals* (1751). In *An Enquiry Concerning Human Understanding*, his masterpiece in epistemology, he argued for a stronger and more encompassing skepticism than any other major philosopher dared embrace. His skepticism extended to induction, causation, the external world, the self, miracles, and the existence of God. (His *Dialogues Concerning Natural Religion* was such a scorching attack on religious belief that he delayed its publication until after his death.) His doubts about all these ideas sprang naturally from his consistent and thoroughgoing empiricism in which assertions can count as knowledge only if they can be traced back to experience. He boldly declared, "When we run over libraries, persuaded of these [empiricist] principles, what havoc must we make? If we take in our hand any volume; of divinity or school metaphysics, for instance, let us ask, *Does it contain any abstract reasoning concerning quantity or number*? No. *Does it contain any experimental reasoning concerning matter of fact and existence*? No. Commit it then to the flames: for it can contain nothing but sophistry and illusion."

Despite his tough-minded philosophy, Hume was blessed with a cheerful disposition, which probably helped him cope with the gloomy skepticism of his studies. He said that reason could not cure his melancholy but distraction and recreation could. As he put it, "I dine, I play a game of backgammon, I converse, and am merry with my friends; and when after three or four hours' amusement, I would return to these speculations, they appear so cold, and strained, and ridiculous, that I cannot find in my heart to enter into them any farther." But he did enter into them again many times—and so laid down a challenge to future thinkers to try to answer his philosophical doubts.

By all accounts, Hume was a decent, generous, and honorable person, admired and liked by everyone who knew him. A contemporary of Hume's, Adam Smith, the renowned philosopher and economist, said of Hume that "upon the whole, I have always considered him, both in his life-time and since his death, as approaching as nearly to the idea of a perfectly wise and virtuous man, as perhaps the nature of human frailty will admit."

David Hume: *An Enquiry Concerning Human Understanding*

freedom, and call them Impressions; employing that word in a sense somewhat different from the usual. By the term impression, then, I mean all our more lively perceptions, when we hear, or see, or feel, or love, or hate, or desire, or will. And impressions are distinguished from ideas, which are the less lively perceptions, of which we are conscious, when we reflect on any of those sensations or movements above mentioned. . . .

All the objects of human reason or enquiry may naturally be divided into two kinds, to wit, Relations of Ideas, and Matters of Fact. Of the first kind are the sciences of Geometry, Algebra, and Arithmetic; and in short, every affirmation, which is either intuitively or demonstratively certain. That the square of the hypothenuse [*sic*] is equal to the squares of the two sides, is a proposition, which expresses a relation between these figures. That three times five is equal to the half of thirty, expresses a relation between these numbers. Propositions of this kind are discoverable by the mere operation of thought, without dependence on what is any where existent in the universe. Though there never were a circle or triangle in nature, the truths, demonstrated by Euclid, would for ever retain their certainty and evidence.

Matters of fact, which are the second objects of human reason, are not ascertained in the same manner; nor is our evidence of their truth, however great, of a like nature with the foregoing. The contrary of every matter of fact is still possible; because it can never imply a contradiction, and is conceived by the mind with the same facility and distinctness, as if ever so conformable to reality. That the sun will not rise to-morrow is no less intelligible a proposition, and implies no more contradiction, than the affirmation, that it will rise. We should in vain, therefore, attempt to demonstrate its falsehood. Were it demonstratively false, it would imply a contradiction, and could never be distinctly conceived by the mind.[11]

Hume not only argues that whatever we know about the world must be grounded in our perceptions but also that we can be sure *only* of those perceptions. We know just our experience and can only guess what lies beyond it. It's as if we are locked in a windowless room and must speculate about what it's like outside based on a video we can watch indoors. The video may or may not resemble the outside world, but it's the only information we have.

Hume's strict empiricism leads naturally to skepticism about a notion that we usually assume without question: causality. We believe the world is filled with causes and effects; we think one thing causes another, and the two are somehow physically linked. Every day of our lives we draw countless conclusions based on our assumptions about cause-and-effect relationships. But Hume argues that we have no good grounds for believing that causes and effects are related the way we think they are.

"Generally speaking, the errors in religion are dangerous; those in philosophy only ridiculous."
—David Hume

David Hume: *An Enquiry Concerning Human Understanding*

To be fully acquainted, therefore, with the idea of power or necessary connexion, let us examine its impression; and in order to find the impression with greater certainty, let us search for it in all the sources, from which it may possibly be derived.

When we look about us towards external objects, and consider the operation of causes, we are never able, in a single instance, to discover any power or necessary connexion; any quality, which binds the effect to the cause, and renders the one an infallible consequence of the other. We only find, that the one does actually, in fact, follow the other. The impulse of one billiard-ball is attended with motion in the second. This is the whole that appears to the outward senses. The mind feels no sentiment or inward impression from this succession of objects: Consequently, there is not, in any single, particular instance of cause and effect, any thing which can suggest the idea of power or necessary connexion.

From the first appearance of an object, we never can conjecture what effect will result from it. But were the power or energy of any cause discoverable by the mind, we could foresee the effect, even without experience; and might, at first, pronounce with certainty concerning it, by the mere dint of thought and reasoning. . . .

But to hasten to a conclusion of this argument, which is already drawn out to too great a length: We have sought in vain for an idea of power or necessary connexion, in all the sources from which we could suppose it to be derived. It appears, that, in single instances of the operation of bodies, we never can, by our utmost scrutiny, discover any thing but one event following another; without being able to comprehend any force or power, by which the cause operates, or any connexion between it and its supposed effect.[12]

Hume asserts that neither reason nor experience can provide us with evidence that causal relationships exist. We can observe no power or force that enables causes to produce events. Our perceptions do not give us any reason to believe that one thing makes another thing happen. All we observe, says Hume, is one event associated with another, and when we repeatedly see such a pairing, we jump to the conclusion that the events are causally connected. We make these inferences out of habit, not logic or empirical evidence.

In making judgments about causes and effects, we reason inductively. That is, we assume that events that followed one another in the past will do the same in the future, that the future will be like the past. We presuppose, in other words, the **principle of induction**. Because of previous experience, we expect night to follow day, fire to burn, bread to nourish, and dogs to bark. Likewise the whole scientific enterprise runs on this principle, with scientists making inferences from empirical regularities to predictions about events to come. At first glance, it might seem that no one would seriously question the legitimacy of inductive reasoning. But Hume does:

As to past Experience, it can be allowed to give direct and certain information of those precise objects only, and that precise period of time, which fell under its cognizance: But why this experience should be extended to future times, and to other objects, which for aught we know, may be only in appearance similar; this is the main question on which I would insist. The bread, which I formerly eat, nourished me; that is, a body of such sensible qualities, was, at that time, endued with such secret powers: But does it follow, that other bread must also nourish me at another time, and that like sensible qualities must always be attended with like secret powers? The consequence seems nowise necessary. At least, it must be acknowledged, that there is here a consequence drawn by the mind; that there is a certain step taken; a process of thought, and an inference, which wants to be explained. These two propositions are far from being the same, I have found that such an object has always been attended with such an effect, and I foresee, that other objects, which are, in appearance, similar, will be attended with similar effects. I shall allow, if you please, that the one proposition may justly be inferred from the other: I know in fact, that it always is inferred. But if you insist, that the inference is made by a chain of reasoning,

David Hume: *An Enquiry Concerning Human Understanding*

15. Why does Hume conclude that we have no evidence for causal relationships between events? Do you agree with him? Why or why not?

"We have limited knowledge, or else science and philosophy would not be necessary."

—Ivan Urlaub

principle of induction The presumption that events that followed one another in the past will do the same in the future, that the future will be like the past.

David Hume: *An Enquiry Concerning Human Understanding*

I desire you to produce that reasoning. The connexion between these propositions is not intuitive. There is required a medium, which may enable the mind to draw such an inference, if indeed it be drawn by reasoning and argument. What that medium is, I must confess, passes my comprehension; and it is incumbent on those to produce it, who assert, that it really exists, and is the origin of all our conclusions concerning matter of fact.[13]

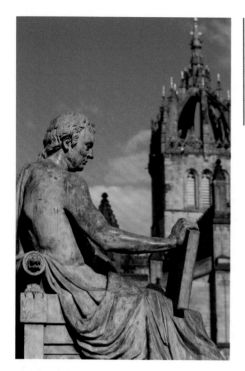

Figure 10.8 A statue of David Hume in his home city, Edinburgh, Scotland.

16. What is Hume's argument against the principle of induction? Does his view imply that we must discard all inductive reasoning or scientific research? Why or why not?

"A wise man proportions his belief to the evidence."
—David Hume

Hume asks, Do we have any grounds whatsoever for believing the principle of induction? What justifies our assumption that the future will be like the past? He argues that the principle cannot be an a priori truth, and it cannot be an a posteriori fact. It cannot be the former because the denial of an a priori truth (such as "all bachelors are unmarried") is self-contradictory, and the denial of the principle of induction is not like that. It cannot be the latter because no amount of empirical evidence can show it to be true. Why? As Hume observes, to maintain that the principle of induction is an a posteriori fact is to say that it can be established by experience (that is, inductively). That is equivalent to saying that the principle of induction can be proved by the principle of induction—which is to beg the question. Arguing in a circle like this offers no support to the principle at all.

This difficulty of justifying the assumption that the future will be like the past is known as the *problem of induction*, and it has incited generations of thinkers to try to solve it. They have explored whether there are grounds for believing that the inductive principle—so indispensable in science and daily life—is true. All the while we use the principle to make all kinds of inferences and predictions, which usually serve us well.

Hume, for his part, holds that we rely on the principle of induction not because it is an established truth but because it is a habit of mind. Because of our long experience of seeing one event repeatedly follow another, we develop a feeling of expectation that they will always follow one another.

By now you probably know that Hume's skepticism extends beyond causality and induction to the existence of the external world. He reasons that because all we can directly know is our experience, we can never be sure that an external world exists beyond our internal perceptions:

David Hume: *An Enquiry Concerning Human Understanding*

It is a question of fact, whether the perceptions of the senses be produced by external objects, resembling them: how shall this question be determined? By experience surely; as all other questions of a like nature. But here experience is, and must be entirely silent. The mind has never any thing present to it but the perceptions, and cannot possibly reach any experience of their connexion with objects. The supposition of such a connexion is, therefore, without any foundation in reasoning.[14]

Provoked by Hume's radical skepticism, philosophers have expended a great deal of energy trying to show that his views on causality, induction, and the external world are partly or wholly unfounded. But the brilliant Hume has put forward some compelling arguments, and they have proven hard to counter.

10.5 SPINOZA

Baruch (Benedictus) Spinoza (1632–1677) was one of the three greatest rationalist philosophers of the seventeenth century (the others were Descartes and Leibniz), ultimately constructing an imposing metaphysical and epistemological system that has been studied and debated for three centuries. In his lifetime he earned the devotion of friends and followers and the disdain of enemies and critics. In the latter camp, he was both reviled as an atheist and characterized as "a god-intoxicated" man. Among those who were affected by him we can count Nietzsche, Freud, Russell, and Einstein, and among the most influential books of Western philosophy we can include his masterpiece the *Ethics*.

Spinoza was born into a well-to-do Jewish family living in Amsterdam, Holland, where they had fled to escape religious persecution in Portugal. He received a Jewish education in Hebrew and studied the works of Jewish and Arabic theologians and philosophers (including Maimonides). But as he became familiar with secular and Christian thought and with Descartes' philosophical and scientific thinking, he turned away from his orthodox upbringing and adopted heretical views. Thus in 1656, at age twenty-four, he was excommunicated from the Jewish community, whose members were enjoined to cease all contact with him. To earn an income, he ground lenses for spectacles and telescopes, and this money (plus modest financial support from friends) allowed him to pursue a life of philosophical reflection and writing without formal attachments to the academic world. He did, however, engage in frequent correspondence with several eminent thinkers of the day.

In 1663 Spinoza published his first book, *Principles of Descartes's Philosophy*, a rendering of Descartes' *Principles of Philosophy* in strict "geometrical order"—that is, in the form of a deductive geometry proof consisting of definitions, axioms, and derived propositions. In 1670 Spinoza published—anonymously—his *Theological-Political Treatise*, an argument for free inquiry, tolerance, religious liberty, and open-minded biblical criticism. The work was first condemned, then banned, by the Reformed Church. His greatest work, the *Ethics*, was published posthumously. It too is set out in geometrical fashion, comprising five parts: "Concerning God," "On the Nature and Origin of the Mind," "Concerning the Origin and Nature of the Emotions," "Of Human Bondage, or the Strength of the Emotions," and "Of the Power of the Intellect, or of Human Freedom."

The heart of Spinoza's metaphysics is his concept of *substance*. To ask what is substance in the philosophical sense is to ask, What is being? or What fundamental realities exist? (Such questions, of course, are central concerns in any mature

"Do not weep; do not wax indignant. Understand."
—Baruch Spinoza

Figure 10.9 Baruch Spinoza (1632–1677).

"Be not astonished at new ideas; for it is well known to you that a thing does not therefore cease to be true because it is not accepted by many."
—Baruch Spinoza

pantheism The view that God is identical with everything.

17. How does pantheism differ from polytheism? Why might pantheism be attractive to a scientist like Einstein?

metaphysics, from Aristotle to the present.) Descartes declares that there are two kinds of substances—matter and mind (the material and mental)—and this dichotomy is what constitutes his dualism. But for Spinoza, there is only one substance, and this substance is God (or Nature), and all material and mental things are attributes of God (who also has an infinite number of other attributes). So entities in the world are features of the one eternal, divine substance. A human being is a finite feature of the infinite God, a feature that can be conceived as either material or mental. Spinoza's view then is a form of **pantheism**, the notion that God is identical with everything. Thus his God is infinite, eternal, and immanent but is not a person, not a being that interacts with the world as the West's traditional God is supposed to.

Spinoza uses the notion of substance to try to prove the existence of his God through an ontological argument. Anthony Kenny summarizes it like this:

A substance *A* cannot be brought into existence by some other thing *B*; for if it could, the notion of *B* would be essential to the concept of *A*; and therefore *A* would not satisfy the definition of substance given above. So any substance must be its own cause and contain its own explanation; existence must be part of its essence. Suppose now that God does not exist. In that case his essence does not involve existence, and therefore he is not a substance. But that is absurd, since God is a substance by definition. Therefore, by *reductio ad absurdum*, God exists.[15]

Spinoza argues that God not only exists, but exists necessarily: God could not have failed to exist, nor could he have existed with any other attributes than what he has. And if God exists necessarily, then everything that arises from his nature arises necessarily.

If everything behaves by necessity, it would seem that neither God nor humans can act freely. But Spinoza maintains God is nevertheless free because his actions are determined by his own nature. God cannot act in any way other than how he must act, but how he must act is determined by him. Humans too can have a kind of freedom. As aspects of a determined God, they are ultimately determined, but they can still act freely if they themselves are in control of their choices, if they can do what they choose to do, rather than have their choices dictated to them by forces beyond their control. They lack freedom when their choices are ruled by, for example, unconstrained emotions, hidden motivations, and irrational thinking. They can act freely when they are fully aware of these factors and choose in the light of reason.

DETAILS

Russell on Spinoza

The English philosopher Bertrand Russell was one of the twentieth century's greatest minds and a world-famous symbol of philosophy itself. He wrote about every area of philosophy and penned several histories of philosophy in the West. He also wrote about other philosophers and had biting criticisms of many of them. Here's Russell's assessment of Spinoza and Leibniz:

Figure 10.10 Bertrand Russell (1872–1970).

> Spinoza . . . is the noblest and most lovable of the great philosophers. Intellectually, some others have surpassed him, but ethically he is supreme. As a natural consequence, he was considered, during his lifetime and for a century after his death, a man of appalling wickedness. He was born a Jew, but the Jews excommunicated him. Christians abhorred him equally; although his whole philosophy is dominated by the idea of God, the orthodox accused him of atheism. Leibniz, who owed much to him, concealed his debt, and carefully abstained from saying a word in his praise; he even went so far as to lie about the extent of his personal acquaintance with the heretic Jew.

Russell obviously regards the treatment of Spinoza by the Jews, Christians, and Leibniz as unfair. Assuming Russell's account is correct, do you agree that the Jews and Christians treated Spinoza shabbily? Suppose their religious beliefs dictated their behavior. Would that change your mind about the morality of what they did? Should Russell's assessment of Leibniz's character affect your opinion of Leibniz's philosophy?

Bertrand Russell, *A History of Western Philosophy* (New York: Simon and Schuster, 1945), 569.

Figure 10.11 G. W. Leibniz (1646–1716).

10.6 LEIBNIZ

Gottfried Wilhelm Leibniz (1646–1716) was not only one of the great rationalist philosophers of the seventeenth century but also the most impressive polymath of all the philosophers in the modern era. He was an innovator and leader in mathematics, jurisprudence, history, politics, theology, science, and technology. He independently discovered the infinitesimal calculus (he didn't know that earlier Newton had also discovered it). He invented a calculating machine that could handle many of the functions that electronic calculators do now. He founded learned societies (the Society of the Sciences in Berlin, for example), undertook diplomatic missions, tried to reconcile Christian denominations, devised a plan to unite the Christian states of Europe, and corresponded with most of the great thinkers of his day, including Spinoza. In philosophy he made his mark in logic, ethics, metaphysics, epistemology, and the philosophies of mind, religion, and science.

Leibniz was born in Leipzig, Germany, where his father taught philosophy at the university. By the time he entered that school at age fifteen, he had already fully imbibed metaphysics and the Greek and medieval classics. During his college years, he studied mathematics, law, and the works of Descartes, Bacon, Hobbes, Galileo, and others. In 1667, at age twenty-one, he took his doctorate in law at the University of Altdorf and was offered a professorship there, which he declined.

In the same year, he began working for the archbishop-elector of Mainz, systematizing German law and later leading a diplomatic mission to Paris. Over the following decade, he was tutored in mathematics by the physicist and astronomer Christian Huygens, studied Descartes and Spinoza, met scientific and philosophical luminaries in Paris and England, and invented his infinitesimal calculus, a feat that engendered a long-running controversy over whether he or Newton was first to make the discovery. He spent the last two decades of his life in Hanover.

Like Spinoza, Leibniz developed a metaphysical system built largely on the fundamental notion of *substance.* As with Spinoza, Leibniz's urgent question is, What is being? Any stable metaphysics, thinks Leibniz, must begin there. He believes that for lack of a plausible understanding of substance, the philosophies of Descartes, Spinoza, and Locke ran into trouble.

While Descartes maintains that there are two kinds of substances, and Spinoza insists that there is only one, Leibniz argues that there are many. The reasoning goes like this: A substance must be simple (having no parts). Material (extended) objects cannot be substances because they are not simple: they can always be divided into many separate pieces. Simple substances make up compound material objects. As Leibniz says, "There must be simple substances, since there are compound substances, for the compound is only a collection or *aggregatum* of simple substances."[16]

"I hold that the mark of a genuine idea is that its possibility can be proved, either a priori by conceiving its cause or reason, or a posteriori when experience teaches us that it is in fact in nature."

—G. W. Leibniz

18. Which perspective on substance seems most plausible to you—the view of Descartes, Spinoza, or Leibniz? Why?

But simple substances cannot be extended. They must instead be immaterial, mind-like existents. Leibniz calls these existents **monads**. They are, he says, "the true atoms of nature and, in a word, the elements of things."[17] They are, however, more like souls than tiny bits of matter.

Monads are strange, to say the least, but for Leibniz, they are the only things that make sense as substances. Frederick Copleston explains some other implications that Leibniz draws from his odd concept:

> The use of the word "atom" must not be taken to mean that the Leib-nizian monad resembles the atoms of Democritus or Epicurus. The monad, being without parts, does not possess extension, figure or divisibility. A thing cannot possess figure or shape unless it is extended; nor can it be divisible unless it possesses extension. But a simple thing cannot be extended; for simplicity and extension are incompatible. This means that monads cannot come into existence in any other way than by creation. Nor can they perish in any other way than by annihilation. Compound substances can, of course, come into existence and perish by aggregation and dissolution of monads; but the latter, being simple, do not admit of these processes.[18]

Monads are not full-blown minds but are centers of rudimentary mental processes—specifically, perceptions and their changes. Through its perceptions, each monad mirrors the entire cosmos in its own distinctive fashion and from its own perspective. Each is "windowless," meaning that nothing can enter or leave it, nothing from outside can causally affect it. Its perceptions—its mirror images of the world—are supplied and coordinated by God. It is God who manages the monads and arranges them into a harmonious, intelligible reality. In fact, monads behave according to a *pre-established* harmony laid down by God from eternity. Thus monads are like cells of the body—each one independent of, and distinct from, the others yet behaving in perfect accord with them, each one containing a representation of the whole (a perceptual representation in monads; a genetic representation in cells).

In the Leibnizian universe, everything seems to follow its natural course by necessity. But if necessity reigns, humans would have no free will, for everything would happen according to a pre-established harmony that no one except God has any control over. Leibniz says that even in God's well-ordered world, humans are free to act as they see fit:

monads Leibniz's term for the only true substances—immaterial, mental entities that constitute reality.

"This is the best of all possible worlds."
—G. W. Leibniz

Gottfried Wilhelm Leibniz: *Discourse on Metaphysics*

In his ordinary concourse with our actions, God only follows the laws which he has established; that is to say, he continually conserves and continually produces our being in such a way that our thoughts occur spontaneously and freely in the order laid down by the notion of our individual substance, in which they could be foreseen from all eternity. Furthermore, he determines our will to choose what appears best, yet without necessitating it. This is in virtue of his decision that our will should always tend to the apparent good, thus expressing or imitating the will of God in certain particular areas, with respect to which this apparent good always has some truth in it. For speaking absolutely, our will is in a state of indifference, in so far as indifference is opposed to necessity, and it has the power to do otherwise, or to suspend its action altogether, both alternatives being and remaining possible.[19]

Leibniz's view is that God may *incline* our wills one way or another but does not *necessitate* them. Our thoughts are our own, occurring "spontaneously and freely." In this way, Leibniz says, determinism and free will coexist in human actions and choices.

According to Leibniz, God also has free will. He had the freedom to select among many possible worlds this one world we now inhabit and to make that world actual. In fact, Leibniz says, God—acting in the light of reason and through his own goodness—chose this world because *it is the best of all possible worlds.*

From this view, the question naturally arises: Is this "best of all possible worlds" really the best that God could do? How can the best possible world contain so much evil and imperfection? Leibniz's answer is that for God, the best possible world is one in which humans have freedom to choose good or evil. A universe full of obedient, sinless automatons is not God's idea of perfection. And if humans have such freedom, they will inevitably err, engendering evil. As Leibniz says:

19. What is Leibniz's solution to the problem of evil?

Gottfried Wilhelm Leibniz: *Discourse on Metaphysics*

God sees from all time that there will be a certain Judas whose notion or idea, which God has, contains that future [sinful] free action. The only remaining question therefore is why such a Judas, the traitor, who in God's idea is merely possible, actually exists. But to that question there is no reply to be expected on this earth, except that in general we should say that since God found it good that he should exist, despite the sin which he foresaw, it must be that this evil is repaid with interest somewhere in the universe, that God will derive some greater good from it, and all in all that it will turn out that the sequence of things which includes the existence of this sinner is the most perfect out of all the other possible ways. . . . It is, however, clear that God is not the cause of evil.[20]

The idea that we now live in the best possible world, however, has struck some critics as preposterous. Voltaire, for example, satirized Leibniz's notion in his novella *Candide.* In the book, the character Dr. Pangloss reacts to woes and misfortunes with an optimistic, "All is for the best in the best of all possible worlds."

| **WRITING AND REASONING** | **CHAPTER 10** |

1. Hobbes believes that there is no such thing as justice until the Leviathan is established. This means that justice does not exist independently of an authority to define and enforce it. Explain why you agree or disagree with this view.

2. Assess Locke's argument that we can have knowledge of an external world despite our being directly aware only of sense data. Do you agree with him, or do you side with his critics who say that we can know only the contents of our minds?

3. Suppose someone claims that he can easily refute Berkeley's idealism by simply kicking a rock or eating an apple. Does this demonstration show that Berkeley's view is false? Explain.

4. Do you agree with Hume that any belief not based on perceptions (which includes all theological and metaphysical beliefs) cannot be knowledge and is completely meaningless? Give reasons for your view.

5. What is Leibniz's argument that there are an infinite number of substances? Do you think the argument sound? Why or why not? Are any premises questionable?

REVIEW NOTES

10.1 HOBBES

- Social contract theory is the view that justice is secured, and the state is made legitimate, through an agreement among citizens of the state or between the citizens and the rulers of the state. The people consent explicitly or implicitly to be governed—to be subject to the dictates and the power of the state—in exchange for the state's providing security, rights, and liberties. The state's existence is justified by the binding contract that all parties accept.

- Hobbes says that people are basically selfish, dishonest, and violent, but they also have a strong instinct for self-interest and self-preservation. Without a social contract, they would devolve into a state of nature—a "war of every man against every man."

- Hobbes argues that through reason, people can see that the only way to escape the "war of all against all" is to enter into a social contract with one another. In the name of self-interest, they agree to turn over much of their autonomy, freedom, and power to an absolute sovereign—a Leviathan—that will forcibly keep the peace, restrain antisocial actions, and compel people to keep their agreements. Its authority over those bound by the social contract is absolute. For Hobbes, justice is a matter of the keeping of covenants (contracts), and the only way to ensure that covenants are kept is to let the Leviathan reign. Without the Leviathan to enforce covenants, there is no justice.

- Hobbes and Locke differ about social contract theory on many points. For one thing, Hobbes contends that justice and rights do not come into being until the state is established. People surrender their lives and liberties to the Leviathan in exchange for security and peace, and he can do what he wants with his subjects. But Locke argues that humans have inherent, God-given rights whether or not a government is around to guarantee them.

10.2 LOCKE

- Locke argues against rationalism, maintaining, among other things, that there are no innate ideas. He says that the mind does not come into the world already inscribed with ideas or knowledge. On the contrary, the mind is unmarked "white paper" void of any ideas until sense experience gives it content.

- Locke thinks that our sense experience can reveal the existence of an external world. We must distinguish between the objects of our experience (external objects) and the experience of those objects (sensations, or sense data). Physical objects cause sensations in us, and we are directly aware only of those sensations (or ideas, as Locke calls them). So we have direct knowledge not of external objects, but of the sense data related to those objects.

- Critics have lambasted this view, but Locke asks, what could possibly cause our sense experience if not external objects? His answer is that we know that external objects are real (and not a dream or delusion) because the theory that they exist is the best explanation for the sensations we have.

10.3 BERKELEY

- For Berkeley, there are no material objects, no things that exist in the external world. There are objects to be sure, but they exist only as sensations (what Berkeley calls *ideas*) in some mind. They are real only because they are perceived by someone: "to be is to be perceived."

- Berkeley argues that Locke's distinction between primary and secondary qualities is bogus, for primary qualities are just as mind dependent as secondary qualities are.

- Berkeley contends that material objects cannot exist because their existence would be logically absurd. The commonsense view is that material objects *continue to be* even when no one has them in mind. But, says Berkeley, this would mean that they can be conceived of as existing unconceived, that we can think about things that no one is thinking about—a logical contradiction. Critics of this argument insist that it's based on logical confusion.

10.4 HUME

- Hume says that whatever knowledge we have is of two kinds: "relations of ideas" and "matters of fact." The former includes truths of mathematics and truths of logic; they are derived from reason. The latter consists of information about the world and is based entirely on sense experience. We can come to know relations of ideas with certainty, but they are not informative about reality. Matters of fact, on the other hand, are informative about the world, but they cannot be known with certainty. So, contrary to the rationalists, Hume maintains that reason is not a source of knowledge about the world.

- Hume thinks that all knowledge must be traced back to perceptions; otherwise assertions of knowledge are meaningless. From this he concludes that all theological and metaphysical speculations are worthless.

- Hume asserts that neither reason nor experience can provide us with evidence that causal relationships exist. Our perceptions do not give us any reason to believe that one thing makes another thing happen. All we observe, says Hume, is one event associated with another, and when we repeatedly see such a pairing, we jump to the conclusion that the events are causally connected. We make these inferences out of habit, not logic or empirical evidence. For Hume, the principle of induction is unfounded.

10.5 SPINOZA

- The heart of Spinoza's metaphysics is his concept of *substance*. Descartes declares that there are two kinds of substances—matter and mind (the material and mental). But for Spinoza, there is only one substance, and this substance is God (or Nature), and all material and mental things are attributes of God (who also has an infinite number of other attributes). So entities in the world are features of the one eternal, divine substance. A human being is a finite feature of the infinite God, a feature that can be conceived as either material or mental. Spinoza's view then is a form of *pantheism*, the notion that God is identical with everything.

- Spinoza argues that God not only exists but exists necessarily: God could not have failed to exist, nor could he have existed with any other attributes than what he has. And if God exists necessarily, then everything that arises from his nature arises necessarily.

- For Spinoza, God is free because his actions are determined by his own nature. Humans too can have a kind of freedom. As aspects of a determined God, they are ultimately determined, but they can still act freely if they themselves are in control of their choices, if they can do what they choose to do, rather than have their choices dictated to them by forces beyond their control.

10.6 LEIBNIZ

- While Descartes maintains that there are two kinds of substances, and Spinoza insists that there is only one, Leibniz argues that there are an infinite number. Simple substances must exist and make up compound material objects. They must be immaterial, mind-like existents—*monads*.

- Monads are not full-blown minds but are centers of rudimentary mental processes—perceptions and their changes. Through its perceptions, each monad mirrors the entire cosmos in its own distinctive fashion. Each is "windowless," meaning that nothing can enter or leave it, nothing from outside can causally affect it. Its perceptions—its mirror images of the world—are supplied and coordinated by God. It is God who manages the monads and arranges them into a harmonious, intelligible reality. Monads behave according to a pre-established harmony laid down by God from eternity.

• Leibniz's view is that God may incline our wills one way or another but does not necessitate them. God also has free will. He had the freedom to select, among many possible worlds, this one world we now inhabit and to make that world actual. In fact, Leibniz says, God—acting in the light of reason and through his own goodness—chose this world because it is the best of all possible worlds.

KEY TERMS

distributive justice	monads	principle of	social contract
justice	pantheism	induction	theory

Notes

1. Thomas Hobbes, *Leviathan*, 1651.
2. Hobbes, *Leviathan*.
3. Hobbes, *Leviathan*.
4. *Declaration of Independence*, July 4, 1776.
5. John Locke, *An Essay Concerning Human Understanding*, book I, ch. 2 (1689).
6. Locke, *An Essay Concerning Human Understanding*, book II, ch. 1, part 2.
7. Locke, *An Essay Concerning Human Understanding*, book IV, ch. 11, parts 1–9.
8. George Berkeley, *Of the Principles of Human Knowledge*, in *Principles of Human Knowledge and Three Dialogues*, part I, sec. 1–4, 6, 8 (Oxford: Oxford University Press, 1999).
9. Berkeley, *Of the Principles of Human Knowledge*, part I, sec. 9–10, 14–15.
10. Bertrand Russell, *The Problems of Philosophy* (London: Oxford University Press, 1912, 1959), 24.
11. David Hume, *An Enquiry Concerning Human Understanding*, sec. 2 and 4, ed. Peter Millican (New York: Oxford University Press, 2008).
12. Hume, *An Enquiry Concerning Human Understanding*, sec. 7, parts I and II.
13. Hume, *An Enquiry Concerning Human Understanding*, sec. 4, part II.
14. Hume, *An Enquiry Concerning Human Understanding*, sec. 12, part I.
15. Anthony Kenny, *The Oxford Illustrated History of Western Philosophy* (Oxford: Oxford University Press, 1994), 149.
16. G. W. Leibniz, *Monadology*, 2; G., 6, 607; D., p. 218.
17. Leibniz, *Monadology*, 3; G., 6, 607; D., p. 218.
18. Frederick Copleston, *A History of Philosophy*, *Volume IV: Modern Philosophy from Descartes to Leibniz* (New York: Doubleday, 1994), 1994.
19. G. W. Leibniz, *Discourse on Metaphysics*, trans. and ed. R. S. Woolhouse and Richard Francks (Oxford: Oxford University Press, 1998), 81.
20. Leibniz, *Discourse on Metaphysics*, Woolhouse and Francks, 81–82.

For Further Reading

Robert Audi, *Belief, Justification, and Knowledge* (Belmont, CA: Wadsworth, 1988).

A. J. Ayer, *Hume: A Very Short Introduction* (Oxford: Oxford University Press, 1980).

Paul Boghossian, *Fear of Knowledge* (Oxford: Oxford University Press, 2006).

Steven M. Cahn, ed., *Political Philosophy: The Essentials* (New York: Oxford University Press, 2011).

Frederick Copleston, *A History of Philosophy, Volume IV: Modern Philosophy from Descartes to Leibniz* (New York: Doubleday, 1994).

Frederick Copleston, *A History of Philosophy, Volume V: Modern Philosophy—the British Philosophers from Hobbes to Hume* (New York: Doubleday, 1994).

Anthony Kenny, *The Rise of Modern Philosophy*, vol. 3 (Oxford: Oxford University Press, 2006).

G. W. Leibniz, *Philosophical Texts*, trans. and ed. R. S. Woolhouse and Richard Francks (Oxford: Oxford University Press, 1998).

David Miller, *Political Philosophy: A Very Short Introduction* (Oxford: Oxford University Press, 2003).

Paul K. Moser, *Knowledge and Evidence* (Cambridge: Cambridge University Press, 1989).

Robert Nozick, *Anarchy, State, and Utopia* (New York: Basic Books, 1974).

John Rawls, *A Theory of Justice* (Cambridge, MA: Harvard University Press, 1999).

Bertrand Russell, *The Problems of Philosophy* (London: Oxford University Press, 1912, 1959).

Roger Scruton, *Spinoza: A Very Short Introduction* (Oxford: Oxford University Press, 2002).

John Simmons, *Political Philosophy* (New York: Oxford University Press, 2008).

Benedict de Spinoza, *A Spinoza Reader*, trans. and ed. Edwin Curley (Princeton, NJ: Princeton University Press, 1994).

Roger Trigg, *Reason and Commitment* (Cambridge: Cambridge University Press, 1973).

Jonathan Wolff, *An Introduction to Political Philosophy* (Oxford: Oxford University Press, 2006).

Online Resources

Crash Course, Philosophy, videos, https://www.youtube.com/playlist?list=PL8dPuua LjXtNgK6MZucdYldNkMybYIHKR

Stanford Encyclopedia of Philosophy, "Thomas Hobbes," "John Locke," "George Berkeley," "David Hume," "Baruch Spinoza," "Gottfried Wilhelm Leibniz," https:// plato.stanford.edu

Internet Encyclopedia of Philosophy, "Thomas Hobbes," "John Locke," "George Berkeley," "David Hume," "Baruch Spinoza," "Gottfried Wilhelm Leibniz," https://www.iep.utm.edu

Encyclopedia Britannica, "Thomas Hobbes," "John Locke," "George Berkeley," "David Hume," "Baruch Spinoza," "Gottfried Wilhelm Leibniz," https://www.britannica.com

Biography.com, "Thomas Hobbes," "John Locke"

History of Philosophy (without Any Gaps) Podcast, https://historyofphilosophy.net

The Perseus Digital Library, http://www.perseus.tufts.edu/hopper

CHAPTER 11

Kant's Revolution

CHAPTER OBJECTIVES

11.1 THE SMALL-TOWN GENIUS

- Understand why Kant is considered a philosophical revolutionary.
- Appreciate the contrast between Kant's plain and regimented life and his achievements in science, epistemology, and ethics.

11.2 THE KNOWLEDGE REVOLUTION

- Define *analytic statement* and *synthetic statement*.
- Explain the disagreement between Kant and Hume and how their theories of knowledge conflict.
- Explain how Kant's theory of knowledge has both empiricist and rationalist elements.
- Summarize Kant's explanation of how synthetic a priori knowledge is possible.
- Understand Kant's insight about conceptualized experience and how it is reflected in modern psychology.

11.3 THE MORAL LAW

- Define *ethics*, *morality*, *moral theory*, *consequentialist theory*, *deontological theory*, *utilitarianism*, and *categorical imperative*.
- Understand the distinction between ethics and morality, and know the basic elements that make morality a unique normative enterprise.
- Distinguish between moral objectivism, moral absolutism, moral relativism, subjective relativism, and cultural relativism.
- Summarize some of the main objections to cultural relativism.
- Know the essential differences between utilitarianism and Kant's theory.
- Articulate the main features of Kant's moral theory and of his two versions of the categorical imperative.

Figure 11.1 Immanuel Kant (1724–1804).

"Science is organized knowledge. Wisdom is organized life."

—Immanuel Kant

11.1 THE SMALL-TOWN GENIUS

Immanuel Kant (1724–1804), a small-town man of conventional living, launched a revolution in epistemology and charted a major new route in ethics. For these feats, he earned the title of the greatest philosopher of the last three hundred years.

A superficial look at his life would lead many to think he was about as dull and as unimaginative as one could get. He was born, lived all his life, and died in Königsberg, East Prussia (now Kaliningrad). His habits were so regimented that the good folk of his town could set their watches to his punctual, daily stroll.

But appearances can be deceiving. Kant had many friends, was charming and interesting in conversation, participated in many of the scholarly debates of his time, and made exciting discoveries in both science and philosophy. Early in his career, he wrote about physics and astronomy and predicted the existence of the planet Uranus, which was discovered three-quarters of a century after his death.

Kant studied at the University of Königsberg for six years; later served as a private tutor; and then in 1755 began lecturing at the university, an appointment that lasted over forty years. He taught physics, mathematics, geography, philosophy (all the main areas of study), and more. Most of his writings reflected his relentless search for the proper philosophical foundations or methods in science, metaphysics, and ethics.

In epistemology, he effected an intellectual revolution as dramatic and as influential as any advance in science up to that time. To the astonishment of many thinkers of the day, he turned the conventional assumptions about knowledge upside down. To acquire knowledge, he said, the mind does not conform to reality—rather, reality conforms to the mind. Thus he found what he thought was a third path to knowledge between empiricism and rationalism, extracting from each their grains of truth and changing epistemology forever.

In ethics, he fashioned a powerful answer to consequentialist moral theories (utilitarianism and ethical egoism, for example) and to anyone who thinks morality must be based on desires, feelings, and other contingencies instead of solid, unvarying reason.

He published his greatest work, *The Critique of Pure Reason*, in 1781. After that came an extraordinary procession of other influential writings, including *Prolegomena to Any Future Metaphysics* (1783), the *Groundwork of the Metaphysic of Morals* (1785), *Metaphysical Foundations of Natural Science* (1786), the *Critique of Practical Reason* (1788), and *Religion within the Limits of Reason Alone* (1793).

Since Kant, anyone who seeks a full understanding of theories of knowledge and moral philosophy must submit to lessons taught by this modest, small-town genius.

11.2 THE KNOWLEDGE REVOLUTION

Kant began his forays into epistemology after being scandalized by David Hume's radical skepticism (Chapter 10). Kant was sure that knowledge was possible and that we can know many things about the world, most notably countless propositions in mathematics and science. But Hume had raised serious doubts about the possibility of scientific knowledge, and his extreme skepticism shocked Kant into trying to show that Hume was wrong. Kant declares:

Immanuel Kant: *Prolegomena to Any Future Metaphysics*

I openly confess, the suggestion of David Hume was the very thing, which many years ago first interrupted my dogmatic slumber, and gave my investigations in the field of speculative philosophy a quite new direction. I was far from following him in the conclusions at which he arrived.[1]

Recall that Hume had maintained that knowledge of the world comes entirely from experience; we know nothing unless our knowledge can be traced back to perceptions (sense data and internal states). Moreover, he had insisted that we have access *only* to these inner experiences. We have direct awareness of our own perceptions but not of the world beyond them. This means that the empirical laws and principles of science, which scientists regard as universal and changeless, cannot be known. They cannot be known because they assert more than experience is capable of establishing. This skeptical conclusion, Hume had argued, applies even to the principle at the heart of the scientific enterprise—the law of cause and effect. He had maintained that our experience cannot reveal to us any causal connections, for all we can actually perceive is some events following other events. And even if we could repeatedly observe a particular sequence of cause and effect, we still could not conclude that the sequence will happen the same way in the future. We may drop a baseball from the roof of a house and watch it fall downward, and we may repeat this little experiment a hundred times with the same result. But according to Hume, we have no basis for inferring—and therefore do not know—that exactly the same thing will happen on the hundred-and-first try. So Hume's view meant that scientists could never legitimately conclude that they had discovered a universal, changeless law of nature. They could not know what they thought they knew. This was the conclusion that so exasperated Kant—and that set him on his quest to disprove it.

To map out the epistemological differences between Hume and Kant, we can apply some terms that Kant himself used. Two of these terms we have already met: a priori statements (statements known independently of or prior to experience) and a posteriori statements (statements that depend entirely on sense experience). Two new terms are analytic and synthetic. An **analytic statement** is a logical truth whose denial results in a contradiction. For example, "All brothers are male" is analytic. To

"Always treat people as ends in themselves, never as means to an end."
—Immanuel Kant

analytic statement A logical truth whose denial results in a contradiction.

Figure 11.2 Contrary to Kant and most scientists in history, some events on the quantum level (the domain of subatomic particles) have no cause.

synthetic statement A statement that is not analytic.

deny it—to say that "it is not the case that all brothers are male"—is to say that some males are not males, which is a contradiction. Or consider, "All bodies are extended [occupying space]." To deny this is to say that something extended is not extended—another contradiction. Analytic statements are necessarily true (cannot be false) but trivially so. They are true but tell us nothing about the world. The statement about brothers is obviously true but does not tell us whether any brothers exist. A **synthetic statement** is one that is not analytic. It does tell us something about the world, and denying it does not yield a contradiction. Science specializes in synthetic statements, and so do we in our everyday lives. Examples include: every event has a cause, the planets orbit around the sun, from nothing comes nothing, water boils at 100 degrees Celsius at sea level, and Abraham Lincoln was born in the United States.

Both Hume and Kant agree that we can know analytic statements without appealing to experience (that is, a priori). (Remember, Hume refers to such statements as "relations of ideas.") Through reason alone we can come to know such analytic a priori propositions as "all brothers are male" and "all bodies are extended." But Hume also holds that we can know synthetic propositions (those that are informative about the world) *only* a posteriori (only through experience). And this synthetic a posteriori knowledge ("matters of fact") is limited: we cannot know what our perceptions cannot detect. According to Hume, we are not able to directly observe causality at work, and we cannot infer universal propositions or laws based on limited, local observations. The empiricist path to knowledge, then, is detoured by skepticism. Kant, on the other hand, insists that synthetic a priori knowledge is possible. We can indeed know things about the world, and we can know them independently or prior to experience. Because this knowledge is a priori, it is both necessarily true and universally applicable, a far cry from Hume's extensive skepticism. Kant says we can know that every event has a cause (a synthetic truth), and we can acquire this knowledge a priori, through our powers of reason:

Immanuel Kant: *Critique of Pure Reason*

"The Copernican revolution brought about by Kant was, I think, the most important single turning point in the history of philosophy."

—Bryan Magee

[I]f we seek an example from the understanding in its quite ordinary employment, the proposition, 'every alteration must have a cause,' will serve our purpose. In the latter case, indeed, the very concept of a cause so manifestly contains the concept of a necessity of connection with an effect and of the strict universality of the rule, that the concept would be altogether lost if we attempted to derive it, as Hume has done, from a repeated association of that which happens with that which precedes, and from a custom of connecting representations, a custom originating in this repeated association, and constituting therefore a merely subjective necessity.[2]

So Kant's epistemology is neither entirely empiricist nor fully rationalist. He departs radically from tradition by finding a third way—one that sees merit and error in both theories of knowledge. In line with the empiricists, he holds that all knowledge has its origins in experience, but that doesn't mean experience alone is the source of all our knowledge. With a nod to the rationalists, he maintains that experience by itself is blind, but that doesn't mean we can acquire knowledge of the world through reason alone. Kant says that Plato took this latter route and, like a dove trying to fly in empty space with no air resistance, found himself trying to reason about reality with no raw material (experience) to reason about:

There can be no doubt that all our knowledge begins with experience. For how should our faculty of knowledge be awakened into action did not objects affecting our senses partly of themselves produce representations, partly arouse the activity of our understanding to compare these representations, and, by combining or separating them, work up the raw material of the sensible impressions into that knowledge of objects which is entitled experience? In the order of time, therefore, we have no knowledge antecedent to experience, and with experience all our knowledge begins.

But though all our knowledge begins with experience, it does not follow that it all arises out of experience. For it may well be that even our empirical knowledge is made up of what we receive through impressions and of what our own faculty of knowledge (sensible impressions serving merely as the occasion) supplies from itself. If our faculty of knowledge makes any such addition, it may be that we are not in a position to distinguish it from the raw material, until with long practice of attention we have become skilled in separating it.

This, then, is a question which at least calls for closer examination, and does not allow of any off-hand answer:—whether there is any knowledge that is thus independent of experience and even of all impressions of the senses. Such knowledge is entitled *a priori*, and distinguished from the *empirical*, which has its sources *a posteriori*, that is, in experience. . . . Mathematics gives us a shining example of how far, independently of experience, we can progress in *a priori* knowledge. . . . Misled by such a proof of the power of reason, the demand for the extension of knowledge recognises no limits. The light dove, cleaving the air in her free flight, and feeling its resistance, might imagine that its flight would be still easier in empty space. It was thus that Plato left the world of the senses, as setting too narrow limits to the understanding, and ventured out beyond it on the wings of the ideas, in the empty space of the pure understanding. He did not observe that with all his efforts he made no advance—meeting no resistance that might, as it were, serve as a support upon which he could take a stand; to which he could apply his powers, and so set his understanding in motion.[3]

But Kant cannot simply assert that synthetic a priori knowledge is possible and leave it at that. He must show *how* it's possible. His starting point is the premise (which he thought obvious) that science and mathematics do give us necessary, universal knowledge about the world. From there he argues that something must therefore be fundamentally wrong with both empiricism and rationalism because these theories fail to explain how this kind of knowledge is possible. In Hume's empiricism, he says, sense experience can shine no light on the outer

1. Contemporary scientists assert that in the realm of subatomic particles, some events are *not* caused. Does this fact give the lie to Kant's claim that the law of cause and effect is a synthetic a priori truth?

Immanuel Kant: *Critique of Pure Reason*

"The wish to talk to God is absurd. We cannot talk to one we cannot comprehend—and we cannot comprehend God; we can only believe in him."

—Immanuel Kant

2. What is the point Kant is making with the example of a dove flying in empty space? Who do you think is closer to the truth regarding the nature of a priori truth—Plato or Kant?

3. What is Kant's Copernican revolution? Is his theory of knowledge more plausible than rationalism or empiricism? Explain.

Immanuel Kant:
Critique of Pure Reason

world, leaving in profound doubt the existence of external objects, causality, and scientific laws. And rationalism promises access to synthetic knowledge while ignoring sense experience, where such knowledge begins. To Kant, only a drastically different approach could demonstrate how synthetic a priori knowledge could be justified.

Actually, to call Kant's approach drastically different is an understatement, for what he proposed was a far-reaching transformation in epistemology that he thought was comparable to the Copernican revolution in science. At a time when the prevailing (and Church-sanctioned) belief was that the sun orbited the earth, Nicolaus Copernicus (1473–1543) thought the better theory was that the earth orbited the sun. Copernicus turned out to be right, and he arrived at his answer through a stunning reversal of the received view. In similar fashion, Kant thought he had instigated his own revolution by turning the traditional perspective on knowledge upside down. For centuries the conventional view was that knowledge is acquired when the mind *conforms to objects*—that is, when the mind tracks the external world. But Kant proposed the opposite: *objects conform to the mind.* He argued that sense experience can match reality because the mind stamps a structure and organization on sense experience. Synthetic a priori knowledge is possible, he said, because the mind's concepts force an (a priori) order onto (synthetic) experience. The idea is not that our minds literally create the world, but that our minds organize our experience so we perceive it as recognizable objects. The empiricists see the mind as a passive absorber of sense information, but Kant says the mind is an active shaper of experience into objects that we can know a priori. As he says:

Hitherto it has been assumed that all our knowledge must conform to objects. But all attempts to extend our knowledge of objects by establishing something in regard to them *a priori*, by means of concepts, have, on this assumption, ended in failure. We must therefore make trial whether we may not have more success in the tasks of metaphysics, if we suppose that objects must conform to our knowledge. This would agree better with what is desired, namely, that it should be possible to have knowledge of objects *a priori*, determining something in regard to them prior to their being given.... If intuition must conform to the constitution of the objects, I do not see how we could know anything of the latter *a priori*; but if the object (as object of the senses) must conform to the constitution of our faculty of intuition, I have no difficulty in conceiving such a possibility.[4]

According to Kant, the mind shapes raw experience by organizing it in accordance with certain fundamental concepts, such as time, space, and causality. All our experience is sifted and sorted through the mind's "conceptual processor," without which we could make no sense of the bewildering flow of sights, sounds, smells, and other perceptions. Our raw sense data may consist of a blur of red, for example, but by interpreting this information in light of basic concepts (roundness, space, time, past experience, etc.), our minds perceive a red rose. We therefore know the world only as conceptualized sense data, a world that Kant calls *phenomena*. What the world is *in itself* outside our experience Kant calls *noumena*, a reality forever beyond our ken.

:

PORTRAIT

Copernicus

Until the scientific work of the Polish astronomer Nicolaus Copernicus in the sixteenth century, most of the Western world believed in the geocentric (Earth-centered) theory of the universe. After all, the doctrine had come down from Aristotle and had been refined by the great astronomer and mathematician Ptolemy, who flourished in Alexandria between 146 and 170 CE. But Copernicus thought the Ptolemaic system was a monstrosity, a complex patchwork of components propped up by numerous assumptions for the purpose of making the theory fit the data. He proposed a heliocentric theory in which Earth and the other planets orbit the sun, the true center of the universe. In doing so, he greatly simplified both the picture of the heavens and the calculations required to predict the positions of planets—and thus launched what came to be known as the Copernican revolution.

Figure 11.3 The great astronomers: Aristotle, Ptolemy, and Nicolaus Copernicus.

Copernicus's theory was simpler than Ptolemy's on many counts, but one of the most impressive was retrograde motion, a phenomenon that had stumped astronomers for centuries. From time to time, certain planets seem to reverse their customary direction of travel across the skies—to move backward! Ptolemy explained this retrograde motion by positing yet more epicycles, asserting that planets orbiting Earth will often orbit around a point on the larger orbital path. Seeing these orbits within orbits from Earth, an observer would naturally see the planets sometimes backing up.

But the Copernican theory could easily explain retrograde motion without all those complicated epicycles. As the outer planets (Mars, Jupiter, Saturn) orbit the sun, so does Earth, one of the inner planets. The outer planets, though, move much slower than Earth does. On its own orbital track, Earth sometimes passes the outer planets as they lumber along on their orbital track, just as a train passes a slower train on a parallel track. When this happens, the planets appear to move backward, just as the slower train seems to reverse course when the faster train overtakes it.

One test implication of the Copernican theory is the phenomenon known as parallax. Critics of the heliocentric view claimed that if the theory were true, then as Earth moved through its orbit, stars closest to it should seem to shift their position relative to stars farther away. There should, in other words, be parallax. But no one had observed parallax. Copernicus and his followers responded to this criticism by saying that stars were too far away for parallax to occur. As it turned out, they were right about this, but confirmation didn't come until 1832 when parallax was observed with more powerful telescopes.

Another test implication seemed to conflict with the heliocentric model. Copernicus reasoned that if the planets rotate around the sun, then they should show phases just as the moon shows phases due to the light of the sun falling on it at different times. But in Copernicus's day, no one could see any such planetary phases. Fifty years later, though, Galileo used his new telescope to confirm that Venus had phases.

Ultimately, scientists accepted the Copernican model over Ptolemy's because of its simplicity—despite what seemed at the time like evidence against the theory.

Figure 11.4 An Immanuel Kant stamp from Germany.

Kant's insight about conceptualized experience might sound odd, but he was on the right track, anticipating findings in modern science by two centuries. Research in developmental and cognitive psychology shows that our perceptions are not the result of the mind's passive recording of sensations. Our perceptions are, to a large degree, *constructed*; they originate with our unfiltered sense experience and then are interpreted by the mind according to our preexisting ideas. For example, our experience may consist only of red sensations in dim light, but because we have reason to believe we are looking at a red rose and already have in mind the relevant concepts, we perceive a red rose. We hear only a muffled sound in the next room, but because of our expectations, we perceive the sound as a telephone ring. When we look at a car in the far distance, the image we see is tiny. But because of previous experience and our understanding of how the size of objects stays constant, we perceive the car as having normal dimensions and is actually much larger than we are.

This is how Kant explains the role of sense experience and concepts in our perception of reality:

Immanuel Kant:
Critique of Pure Reason

Our knowledge springs from two fundamental sources of the mind; the first is the capacity of receiving representations (receptivity for impressions), the second is the power of knowing an object through these representations (spontaneity [in the production] of concepts). Through the first an object is *given* to us, through the second the object is *thought* in relation to that [given] representation (which is a mere determination of the mind). Intuition [raw sense data] and concepts constitute, therefore, the elements of all our knowledge, so that neither concepts without an intuition in some way corresponding to them, nor intuition without concepts, can yield knowledge.... Our nature is so constituted that our *intuition* can never be other than sensible; that is, it contains only the mode in which we are affected by objects. The faculty, on the other hand, which enables us to *think* the object of sensible intuition is the understanding. To neither of these powers may a preference be given over the other. Without sensibility no object would be given to us, without understanding no object would be thought. Thoughts without content are empty, intuitions without concepts are blind. It is, therefore, just as necessary to make our concepts sensible, that is, to add the object to them in intuition, as to make our intuitions intelligible, that is, to bring them under concepts. These two powers or capacities cannot exchange their functions. The understanding can intuit nothing, the senses can think nothing. Only through their union can knowledge arise.[5]

4. What does Kant mean by "thoughts without content are empty, intuitions without concepts are blind"? Do you agree that at least some of your perceptions are conceptualized?

Kant thought his theory of knowledge corrected the errors of rationalism and empiricism and expelled the skepticism that these views engendered. In their theories the rationalists had bet heavily on reason as the key to knowledge; the empiricists had bet everything on experience. Kant tried to show that genuine knowledge

THEN AND NOW

Conceptualizing the World

Figure 11.5 What do you see here—a duck or a rabbit? Although the image does not change, your interpretation can vary so you see either a duck or a rabbit (but not both at the same time). If you change your interpretation of the image, you see something different.

Figure 11.6 Depending on how you conceptualize this figure, you will see a young woman or an old woman.

Kant's view of the mind as an actively constructive faculty is echoed in contemporary psychological research, which shows that our minds constantly construct and interpret our perceptions. That is, our senses are not mere recorders of perceptual information; instead our minds take the raw data of experience and rework them in light of the concepts and beliefs already in our heads. Our minds must "conceptualize" the raw sensory input so we can understand it. We do this so often and so extensively that we are hardly aware of the process. Consider these three examples of "ambiguous figures." In each case, it's possible to see the figure in two ways—even though the visual input is the same in both.

Do these examples prove Kant's constructivist theory of knowledge? Or do they just show that much of our sensory input is conceptualized? Do they show that our conceptualized experience is nothing like what is actually "out there"?

Figure 11.7 Do you see a woman's face here—or the silhouette of a saxophone player?

is a synthesis of both reason and experience. He argued that we can know many things about the world—cause-and-effect relationships, the truths of mathematics, the laws of science—and we can know they are necessarily, universally, and a priori true. We can, in other words, take hold of synthetic a priori knowledge. We can obtain it because our thinking is framed by fundamental concepts that guarantee our experience will take a predetermined form. And we can be sure the truths we discover are universal because all our minds possess the same cognitive structure determined by the same set of innate concepts. In short, Kant's answer to the rationalists, empiricists, and skeptics is that we know the world because we, in effect, constitute it.

After Kant, epistemology was never the same. Anyone who has seriously tried to fathom the nature and extent of our knowledge has had to contend with his insights and arguments. That is not to say that everyone who has delved deeply into Kant has agreed with him. Some philosophers doubt that everyone uses the same set of basic concepts to make sense of the empirical world. They point to anthropological and psychological research showing that not every culture uses the same set of concepts (the same conceptual scheme) to interpret and organize their experience. Other critics have argued that Kant's theory does not adequately explain our certainty that facts about the world must be consistent with logic and mathematics. We think that truths of logic and mathematics are true necessarily and universally *regardless of the structure of our minds*. But Kant wants us to believe that logical and mathematical concepts *do* depend on the innate structure of our minds. This implies that the structure of our minds could possibly change to make 5 + 12 = 13, or make the statement "all brothers are male" false.

These and many other criticisms of Kant's work will be debated for generations to come—which is proof of his lasting influence.

5. Do you think logical and mathematical truths depend on the structure of our minds—or are such propositions true regardless of how our minds are organized? Can you imagine the world changing so that 2 + 2 = 5? Explain.

11.3 THE MORAL LAW

To understand Kant's achievement in ethics, we need to step back and take a broad view of the field. Ethics is part of philosophy; it is also part of life—a very large, vital, inevitable part of life. You cannot avoid thinking about right and wrong, judging people as good or bad, wondering what kind of life is worthwhile, debating others about moral issues, accepting or rejecting the moral beliefs of your family or culture, or coming to some general understanding (a moral theory) about the nature of morality itself. When you do these things, you are in the realm of ethics.

Ethics and Morality

ethics (moral philosophy) The study of morality using the methods of philosophy.

morality Beliefs about right and wrong actions and good and bad persons or character.

Ethics, or moral philosophy, is the study of morality using the methods of philosophy, and **morality** consists of our beliefs about right and wrong actions and good and bad persons or character. Morality has to do with our moral judgments, principles, values, and theories; ethics is the careful, philosophical examination of these.

Ethics applies critical reasoning to questions about what we should do and what is of value, questions that pervade our lives and demand reasonable answers.

Morality is a *normative* enterprise, which means that it provides us with norms, or standards, for judging actions and persons—standards usually in the form of moral principles or theories. With moral standards in hand, we decide whether an action is morally right or wrong, whether a person is morally good or bad, and whether we are living a good or bad life. The main business of morality is therefore not to describe how things are but *to prescribe how things should be*. There are of course other normative spheres (art and law, for example), but these are interested in applying *nonmoral* norms (aesthetic and legal norms, for instance) to judge the worth or correctness of things. When we participate in ethics, we are typically either applying or evaluating moral norms and using the tools of philosophy to do it.

Morality stands out among other normative spheres because of its distinctive set of properties. One of these is that moral norms have a much stronger hold on us than nonmoral ones do. The former are thought to dominate the latter, possessing a property that philosophers call *overridingness*. For example, we would think that a moral norm mandating that everyone be treated fairly should override a legal norm (a law) that enjoined one group to discriminate against another. If a law commanded us to commit a seriously immoral act, we would probably think the law illegitimate and might even flout it in an act of civil disobedience. Moral norms are generally stronger and more important than nonmoral norms.

"Two things fill the mind with ever new and increasing admiration and awe, the more often and steadily we reflect upon them: the starry heavens above me and the moral law within me."

—Immanuel Kant

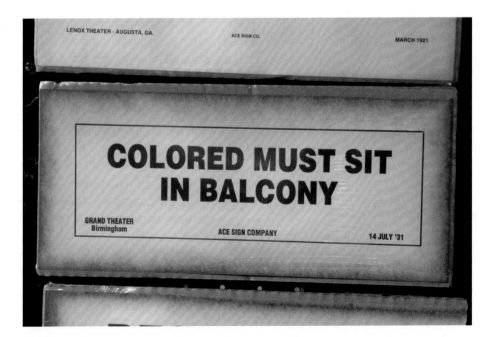

Figure 11.8 Morality demands impartiality. Equals must be treated equally unless there is a morally relevant reason to treat them differently.

6. How is discrimination against a group of people contrary to morality's demand for impartiality? Can there ever be reasons for treating equals *unequally*? If so, what kind of reasons?

"Morality is not the doctrine of how we may make ourselves happy, but how we may make ourselves worthy of happiness."
—Immanuel Kant

7. Can you think of examples in history or literature in which people let their conscience be their guide and ended up committing immoral acts? Is it possible that Hitler's conscience told him to murder six million Jews?

"All that any of us has to do in this world is his simple duty."
—H. C. Trumbull

In addition, moral norms have *impartiality:* they apply to everyone equally. Morality demands that everyone be considered of equal moral worth and that each person's interests be given equal weight. Morality, in other words, says that equals should be treated equally unless there is a morally relevant reason to treat them differently. We would consider it unjust to apply a moral norm to some people but not to others when there is no morally relevant difference between them.

Moral norms, like nonmoral ones, also possess the property of *universality*: they apply not just in a single case, but in all cases that are relevantly similar. Logic tells us that we cannot reasonably regard an action performed by one person as morally wrong while believing that the same action performed in an almost identical situation by another person is morally right. Morality demands consistency among similar cases.

Finally, morality is *reason based.* To be fully involved in the moral life and to make informed moral judgments is to engage in moral reasoning. To do moral reasoning is to try to ensure that our moral judgments are not wrought out of thin air or concocted from prejudice or blind emotion—but are supported by good reasons. We would think it preposterous for someone to assert that killing innocent children is morally permissible (or impermissible)—and that he has no reasons whatsoever for believing this. In science, medicine, law, business, and every other area of intellectual life, we want and expect claims to be backed by good reasons. Morality is no different. And ethics—the systematic search for moral understanding—can be successful only through careful reflection and the sifting of reasons for belief. Critical reasoning is the main engine that drives ethical inquiry.

But what about emotions—what role do they play in ethics? Feelings are an essential and inevitable part of the moral life. They can help us empathize with others and enlarge our understanding of the stakes involved in moral decisions. But they can also blind us. Our feelings are too often the product of our psychological needs, cultural conditioning, and selfish motivations. Critical reasoning is the corrective, giving us the power to examine and guide our feelings to achieve a more balanced view.

Some people believe that conscience, not ethics, is the best guide to plausible moral judgments. At times, it seems to speak to us in an imaginary though authoritative voice, telling us to do or not to do something. But conscience is no infallible indicator of moral truth. It is conditioned by our upbringing, cultural background, and other factors, and, like our feelings, it may be the result of irrelevant influences. Nevertheless the voice of conscience should not be ignored; it can often alert us to something of moral importance. But we must submit its promptings to critical examination before we can have any confidence in them.

The moral life, then, is about grappling with a distinctive class of norms, which can include moral principles, rules, theories, and judgments. We apply these norms to two distinct spheres of our moral experience—to both moral *obligations* and to moral *values*. Moral obligations concern our duty, what we are obligated to do. That is, obligations are about conduct, how we ought or ought not behave. In this sphere, we talk primarily about *actions*. We may look to moral principles or rules to guide our actions, or study a moral theory that purports to explain right actions, or make judgments about right or wrong actions. Moral values, on the other hand, generally concern those things that we judge to be morally good, bad, praiseworthy, or blame-worthy. Normally we use such words to describe persons (as in "he is a good person" or "she is to blame for hurting them"), their character ("he is virtuous" or "she is honest"), or their motives ("she did wrong but did not mean to"). Note that we also attribute *nonmoral* value to things. If we say that a book or bicycle or vacation is good, we mean good in a nonmoral sense. Such things in themselves cannot have *moral* value.

Strictly speaking, only actions are morally *right* or *wrong*, but persons are morally *good* or *bad* (or some degree of goodness or badness). With this distinction we can acknowledge a simple fact of the moral life: A good person can do something wrong, and a bad person can do something right.

A large part of ethics and the moral life consists of devising and evaluating moral theories. That is, we do moral theorizing. In science, theories help us under-stand the empirical world by explaining the causes of events, why things are the way they are. The germ theory of disease explains how particular diseases arise and spread in a human population. The heliocentric (sun-centered) theory of planetary motion explains why the planets in our solar system behave the way they do. In ethics, moral theories have a similar explanatory role. A **moral theory** explains not why one event causes another but why an action is right or wrong or why a person or a person's character is good or bad. A moral theory tells us what it is about an action that *makes it right* or what it is about a person that *makes him or her good*. The divine command theory of morality, for example, says that right actions are those commanded or willed by God. Traditional utilitarianism says that right ac-tions are those that produce the best balance of happiness over unhappiness for all concerned. These and other moral theories are attempts to define rightness or good-ness. In this way, they are both more general and more basic than moral principles or other general norms.

Two types of theories have been of the greatest interest to philosophers. **Consequentialist theories** insist that the rightness of actions depends solely on their consequences or results. The key question is what or how much good the actions pro-duce, however *good* is defined. **Deontological** (or nonconsequentialist) **theories** say that the rightness of actions is determined not solely by their consequences but partly or entirely by their intrinsic nature. For some or all actions, rightness depends on the kind of actions they are, not on how much good they produce. A consequentialist theory, then, may say that stealing is wrong because it causes more harm than good. But a deontological theory may contend that stealing is inherently wrong regardless of its consequences, good or bad.

The most influential consequentialist theory is **utilitarianism** (discussed in Chapter 13), the view that right actions are those that maximize the overall well-being of everyone involved. Or to put it another way, we should do what re-sults in the greatest balance of good over bad, everyone considered. Various forms of utilitarianism differ in how they define the good, with some equating it with happiness or pleasure (the hedonistic view), others with satisfaction of preferences or desires or some other intrinsically valuable things or states such as knowledge or perfection.

"Do not do unto others as you would they should do unto you. Their tastes may not be the same."
—George Bernard Shaw

moral theory A theory that explains why an action is right or wrong or why a person or a person's character is good or bad.

consequentialist theory A moral theory in which the rightness of actions depends solely on their consequences or results.

deontological (or nonconsequentialist) **theory** A moral theory in which the rightness of actions is determined not solely by their consequences but partly or entirely by their intrinsic nature.

utilitarianism The view that right actions are those that result in the most beneficial bal-ance of good over bad consequences for everyone involved.

8. Do you generally judge the rightness or wrongness of an action by its consequences? By the nature of the action itself? By some other measure of rightness?

DETAILS

Moral Relativism

Recall that Socrates, Plato, and Aristotle are opposed to relativism, including the form known as *moral relativism*—and so is Kant. (See Chapter 2.) As we've seen, moral relativism is the view that moral standards are not objective but are relative to what individuals or cultures believe. But moral relativism seems to have as many unpalatable implications as generic relativism.

Without thinking much about it, most people accept a view of morality known as *moral objectivism*, the idea that at least some moral norms or principles are objectively valid or true for everyone. (Moral objectivism, however, is distinct from *moral absolutism*, the belief that objective moral principles allow no exceptions or must be applied the same way in all cases and cultures.) But some reject moral objectivism in favor of moral relativism. To them, morality is not an objective fact; it's a human invention, dependent entirely on what people believe.

Figure 11.9 Cultural relativism implies that if a culture approves of a pogrom or the ethnic cleansing of millions of people, then the horrendous slaughter is morally right. The Memorial to the Murdered Jews of Europe (Holocaust Memorial) in Berlin.

Critics point out that subjective moral relativism (moral relativism that applies to individuals) implies that each person is morally infallible. An action is morally right for someone if he approves of it—if he sincerely believes it to be right. His approval makes the action right, and—if his approval is genuine—he cannot be mistaken. His believing it to be right makes it right, and that's the end of it. But our commonsense moral experience suggests that this relativist account must be mistaken. Our judgments about moral matters—actions, principles, and people—are often wide of the mark. We are morally fallible, and we are rightly suspicious of anyone who claims to be otherwise. The same criticism can be launched

Kant's Theory

The most sophisticated and influential deontological theory comes from Kant. His theory is profoundly opposed to consequentialism on numerous counts. Utilitarians insist that the morality of an action depends entirely on its effects—whether it maximizes human well-being. No action whatsoever is *inherently* right or wrong;

against cultural moral relativism. If a culture genuinely approves of an action, then there can be no question about the action's moral rightness: it is right, and that's that. But is it at all plausible that cultures cannot be wrong about morality? Throughout history, cultures have approved of ethnic cleansing, slavery, racism, holocausts, massacres, mass rape, torture of innocents, burning of heretics, and much more. Is it reasonable to conclude that the cultures that approved of such deeds could not have been mistaken?

Related to the infallibility problem is this difficulty: moral relativism implies that we cannot legitimately criticize others for immorality. They are all beyond criticism. Cultural relativism, for example, says if a culture approves of its actions, then those actions are morally right—and it does not matter one bit whether another culture disapproves of them. Remember, there is no objective moral code to appeal to. Each society is its own maker of the moral law. What this would mean is that if the people of Germany approved of the extermination of millions of Jews, Gypsies, and others during World War II, then the extermination was morally right.

Moral relativism also seems to rule out the possibility of moral progress. As a society we sometimes compare our past moral beliefs with those of the present and judge our views to be morally better than they used to be. We no longer countenance such horrors as massacres of native peoples, slavery, lynching, and racial discrimination, and we think these changes are signs of moral progress. But cultural relativism implies that there can be no such thing. To legitimately claim that there has been moral progress, there must be an objective, transcultural standard for comparing cultures of the past and present. But according to moral relativism, there are no objective moral standards, just norms relative to each culture. If over time a culture goes from condoning racial discrimination to condemning it, that does not represent moral progress. That is just a change from one set of moral attitudes to another; each one just as plausible as the other. The two are different, but one is not superior to the other. On the other hand, if there is such a thing as moral progress, then there must be objective moral standards.

Defenders of moral relativism assert that it promotes tolerance of other societies. The idea is that if the values of one culture are no better or worse than those of another, then there is no basis for hatred or hostility toward any culture anywhere. But do tolerance and relativism necessarily go together? If there are intolerant cultures (and there surely are), then since cultures make rightness, intolerance in those cultures is morally right. What is the relationship between cultural relativism and intolerance?

only its costs and benefits make it so. Kant will have none of this. He maintains that right actions do not depend on their consequences, the production of happiness, people's motives, or their desires and feelings. Right actions are those that are right *in themselves* because they are consistent with universal moral rules derived from reason, and the actions have moral worth only if we do them out of a sense of duty, simply because *they are our duty*. Our motives are irrelevant. For Kant, the moral law cannot be something contingent, changeable, or relative. The moral law is absolute, unchangeable, and universal; a rock-solid structure built on eternal reason.

Here is Kant on the subject:

Immanuel Kant: *Groundwork of the Metaphysic of Morals*

"History is a voice forever sounding across the centuries the laws of right and wrong. Opinions alter, creeds rise and fall, but the moral law is written on the tablets of eternity."

—James A. Froude

9. What does Kant mean by his assertion that morality cannot have an empirical basis? Is he right about this?

As my concern here is with moral philosophy, I limit the question suggested to this: Whether it is not of the utmost necessity to construct a pure moral philosophy, perfectly cleared of everything which is only empirical, and which belongs to anthropology? For that such a philosophy must be possible is evident from the common idea of duty and of the moral laws. Everyone must admit that if a law is to have moral force, *i.e.*, to be the basis of an obligation, it must carry with it absolute necessity; that, for example, the precept, "Thou shall not lie," is not valid for men alone, as if other rational beings had no need to observe it; and so with all the other moral laws properly so called; that, therefore, the basis of obligation must not be sought in the nature of man, or in the circumstances in the world in which he is placed, but *a priori* simply in the conception of pure reason; and although any other precept which is founded on principles of mere experience may be in certain respects universal, yet in as far as it rests even in the least degree on an empirical basis, perhaps only as to a motive, such a precept, while it may be a practical rule, can never be called a moral law. . . .

Nothing can possibly be conceived in the world, or even out of it, which can be called good, without qualification, except a Good Will. Intelligence, wit, judgment, and the other *talents* of the mind, however they may be named, or courage, resolution, perseverance, as qualities of temperament, are undoubtedly good and desirable in many respects; but these gifts of nature may also become extremely bad and mischievous if the will which is to make use of them, and which, therefore, constitutes what is called *character*, is not good. It is the same with the *gifts of fortune*. Power, riches, honour, even health, and the general well-being and contentment with one's conditions which is called *happiness*, inspire pride, and, often presumption, if there is not a good will to correct the influence of these on the mind, and with this also to rectify the whole principle of acting, and adapt it to its end. The sight of a being who is not adorned with a single feature of a pure and good will, enjoying unbroken prosperity, can never give pleasure to an impartial rational spectator. Thus a good will appears to constitute the indispensable condition even of being worthy of happiness.

There are even some qualities which are of service to this good will itself, and may facilitate its action, yet which have no intrinsic unconditional value, but always presuppose a good will, and this qualifies the esteem that we justly have for them, and does not permit us to regard them as absolutely good. Moderation in the affections and passions, self-control, and calm deliberation are not only good in many respects, but even seem to constitute part of the intrinsic worth of the person; but they are far from deserving to be called good without qualification, although they have been so unconditionally praised by the ancients. For without the principles of a good will, they may become extremely bad; and the coolness of a villain not only makes him far more dangerous, but also directly makes him more abominable in our eyes than he would have been without it.

A good will is good not because of what it performs or effects, not by its aptness for the attainment of some proposed end, but simply by virtue of the volition, that is, it is good in itself, and considered by itself to be esteemed much higher than all that can be brought about by it in favour of any inclination, nay, even of the sum-total of all inclinations. Even if it should happen that, owing to special disfavour of fortune, or the niggardly provision of a step-motherly nature, this will should wholly lack power to accomplish its purpose, if with its greatest efforts it should yet achieve nothing, and there should remain only the good will (not, to be sure, a mere wish, but the summoning of all means in our power), then, like a jewel, it would still shine by its own light, as a thing which has its whole value in itself. Its usefulness or fruitlessness can neither add to nor take away anything from this value. It would be, as it were, only the setting to enable us to handle it the more conveniently in common commerce, or to attract to it the attention of those who are not yet connoisseurs, but not to recommend it to true connoisseurs, or to determine its value.[6]

> **10.** What is Kant's argument for his view that nothing can be good without qualification except a good will? Is his argument sound?

In Kant's system, all our moral duties are expressed in the form of *categorical imperatives.* An imperative is a command to do something; it is categorical if it applies without exception and without regard for particular needs or purposes. A categorical imperative says, "Do this—regardless." In contrast, a *hypothetical imperative* is a command to do something if we want to achieve particular aims, as in "if you want good pay, work hard." The moral law, then, rests on absolute directives that do not depend on the contingencies of desire or utility.

Kant says that through reason and reflection we can derive our duties from a single moral principle, what he calls *the* **categorical imperative**. He formulates it in different ways, the first one being: "I am never to act otherwise than so *that I could also will that my maxim should become a universal law*."[7] For Kant, our actions have

> **categorical imperative**
> Kant's fundamental moral principle, which he formulates as (1) "I am never to act otherwise than so *that I could also will that my maxim should become a universal law*," and (2) "So act as to treat humanity, whether in thine own person or in that of any other, in every case as an end withal, never as a means only."

Figure 11.10 German and Polish prime ministers paying their respects at the tomb of Immanuel Kant in Kaliningrad Cathedral, 2011.

logical implications—they imply general rules, or maxims, of conduct. If you tell a lie for financial gain, you are in effect acting according to a maxim like "it's okay to lie to someone when doing so benefits you financially." The question is whether the maxim corresponding to an action is a legitimate moral law. To find out, we must ask if we could consistently will that the maxim become a universal law applicable to everyone—that is, if everyone could consistently act on the maxim and we would be willing to have them do so. If we could do this, then the action described by the maxim is morally permissible; if not, it is prohibited. Thus moral laws embody two characteristics thought to be essential to morality itself: universality and impartiality.

To show us how to apply this formulation of the categorical imperative to a specific situation, Kant uses the example of a lying promise. Suppose you need to borrow money from a friend, but you know you could never pay her back. So to get the loan, you decide to lie, falsely promising to repay the money. To find out if such a lying promise is morally permissible, Kant would have you ask if you could consistently will the maxim of your action to become a universal law, to ask, in effect, "What would happen if everyone did this?" The maxim is "whenever you need to borrow money you cannot pay back, make a lying promise to repay." So what *would* happen if everyone in need of a loan acted in accordance with this maxim? People would make lying promises to obtain loans, but everyone would also know that such promises were worthless, and the custom of loaning money on promises would disappear. So willing the maxim to be a universal law involves a contradiction: If everyone made lying promises, promise making would be no more; you cannot consistently will the maxim to become a universal law. Therefore, your duty is clear: making a lying promise to borrow money is morally wrong.

Kant's first formulation of the categorical imperative yields several other important duties. He argues that there is an absolute moral prohibition against killing the innocent, lying, committing suicide, and failing to help others when feasible.

Perhaps the most renowned formulation of the categorical imperative is the principle of respect for persons (a formulation distinct from the first one, though Kant thought them equivalent). As he expresses it, "So act as to treat humanity, whether in thine own person or in that of any other, in every case as an end withal, never as a means only."[8] People must never be treated as if they were mere instruments for achieving some further end, for people are ends in themselves, possessors of ultimate inherent worth. People have ultimate value because they are the ultimate source of value for other things. They bestow value; they do not have it bestowed upon them. So we should treat both ourselves and other persons with the respect that all inherently valuable beings deserve.

> "It is not necessary that whilst I live I live happily; but it is necessary that so long as I live I should live honourably."
>
> —Immanuel Kant

> "Nothing can possibly be conceived in the world, or even out of it, which can be called good without qualification, except a *good will*."
>
> —Immanuel Kant

Immanuel Kant:
Groundwork of the Metaphysic of Morals

Now I say: man and generally any rational being *exists* as an end in himself, *not merely as a means* to be arbitrarily used by this or that will, but in all his actions, whether they concern himself or other rational beings, must be always regarded at the same time as an end. All objects of the inclinations have only a conditional worth; for if the inclinations and the wants founded on them did not exist, then their object would be without value. But the inclinations themselves being sources of want are so far from having an absolute worth for which they should be desired, that, on the contrary, it must be the universal wish of every rational being to be wholly free from them. Thus the worth of any object which is *to be acquired* by our action is always conditional. Beings whose existence depends not on our will but on nature's, have nevertheless, if they are nonrational beings, only a relative value as means, and are therefore called *things*; rational beings, on the contrary, are called *persons*, because their very nature points them out as ends in themselves, that is as something which must not be used merely as means, and so far therefore restricts freedom of action (and is an object of respect). These, therefore, are not merely subjective ends whose existence has a worth *for us* as an effect of our action, but *objective ends*, that is things whose existence is an end in itself: an end moreover for which no other can be substituted, which they should subserve *merely* as means, for otherwise nothing whatever would possess *absolute worth*; but if all worth were conditioned and therefore contingent, then there would be no supreme practical principle of reason whatever.

If then there is a supreme practical principle or, in respect of the human will, a categorical imperative, it must be one which, being drawn from the conception of that which is necessarily an end for everyone because it is *an end in itself*, constitutes an *objective* principle of will, and can therefore serve as a universal practical law. The foundation of this principle is: *rational nature exists as an end in itself*. Man necessarily conceives his own existence as being so: so far then this is a *subjective* principle of human actions. But every other rational being regards its existence similarly, just on the same rational principle that holds for me: so that it is at the same time an objective principle, from which as a supreme practical law all laws of the will must be capable of being deduced. Accordingly the practical imperative will be as follows: *So act as to treat humanity, whether in thine own person or in that of any other, in every case as an end withal, never as a means only.*[9]

11. In these passages, does Kant make clear how we are supposed to apply his principle of respect for persons? For example, how exactly do you show respect for a person who is terminally ill and in great pain who begs you to help him end his life?

According to Kant, the inherent worth of persons derives from their nature as autonomous, rational beings capable of directing their own lives, determining their own ends, and decreeing their own rules by which to live. Thus, the inherent value of persons does not depend in any way on their social status, wealth, talent, race, or culture. Moreover, inherent value is something that all persons possess equally. Each person deserves the same measure of respect as any other.

Kant explains that we treat people merely as a means instead of an end-in-themselves if we disregard these characteristics of personhood—if we thwart people's freely chosen actions by coercing them, undermine their rational decision-making by lying to them, or discount their equality by discriminating against them.

Notice that this formulation of the categorical imperative does not actually prohibit treating a person as a means but forbids treating a person *simply*, or *merely*, as a means—as nothing but a means. Kant recognizes that in daily life we often must use people to achieve our various ends. To buy milk we use the cashier; to find books we use the librarian; to get well we use the doctor. But because their actions are freely chosen and we do not undermine their status as persons, we do not use them *solely* as instruments of our will.

Kant's principle of respect for persons captures what seems to most people an essential part of morality itself—the notion that some things must not be done to a person even if they increase the well-being of others. People have certain rights, and these rights cannot be violated merely for the sake of an overall increase in utility. We tend to think that there is something terribly wrong with jailing an innocent person just because her imprisonment would make a lot of other people very happy or with

"The death of dogma is the birth of morality."

—Immanuel Kant

Figure 11.11 Imagine that in 1944 you own the house where the young Anne Frank and her family are hiding from the Nazis, and the Nazis ask you if anyone lives there. You can lie and save Anne and her family from death in a concentration camp, or you can tell the truth and doom them. Kant would have you tell the truth no matter what. Is he right? (In 1944 in the Netherlands, the authorities did in fact discover the hiding place of Anne and the other members of her family. They were all shipped off to concentration camps; only Anne's father survived.)

12. Is Kant's view clearly superior to utilitarianism? Or is utilitarianism the superior one? Or does each theory offer something of value that should be part of any adequate system of morality?

seizing a person's possessions and giving them to the poor to maximize overall happiness or with enslaving a race of people so the rest of the world can have a higher standard of living. Over the principle of respect for persons, Kantians and utilitarians part company. Utilitarians reject the concept of rights, or they define rights in terms of utility. Kantians take respecting rights to be central to the moral life.

Kant's theory, however, does have its detractors. Many philosophers argue that it is not consistent with our considered moral judgments. A major cause of the problem, they say, is Kant's insistence that we have absolute (or "perfect") duties—obligations that must be honored without exception. Thus in Kantian ethics, we have an absolute duty not to lie or to break a promise or to kill the innocent, come what may. Imagine that a band of killers wants to murder an innocent man who has taken refuge in your house, and the killers come to your door and ask you point blank if he is in your house. To say no is to lie; to answer truthfully is to guarantee the man's death. What should you do? In a case like this, says Kant, you must *do your duty*—you must tell the truth though murder is the result and a lie would save a life. But in this case such devotion to moral absolutes seems completely askew, for saving an innocent life seems far more important morally than blindly obeying a rule. Moral common sense suggests that sometimes the consequences of our actions *do* matter more than adherence to the letter of the law, even if the law is generally worthy of our respect and obedience.

Some have thought that Kant's theory can yield implausible results for another reason. Recall that the first formulation of the categorical imperative says that an action is permissible if persons could consistently act on the relevant maxim, and we would be willing to have them do so. This requirement seems to make sense if the maxim in question is something like "do not kill the innocent" or "treat equals equally." But what if the maxim is "enslave all Christians" or "kill all Ethiopians"? We could—without contradiction—will either one of these precepts to become a universal law. And if we were so inclined, we could be willing for everyone to act accordingly, even if we ourselves were Christians or Ethiopians. So by Kantian lights, these actions could very well be morally permissible, and their permissibility would depend on whether someone was willing to have them apply universally. Critics conclude that because the first formulation of the categorical imperative seems to sanction such obviously immoral acts, the theory is deeply flawed. Defenders of Kant's theory, on the other hand, view the problems as repairable and have proposed revisions.

This apparent arbitrariness in the first formulation can significantly lessen the theory's usefulness. The categorical imperative is supposed to help us discern moral directives that are rational, universal, and objective. But if it is subjective in the way just described, its helpfulness as a guide for living morally is dubious. There may be remedies for this difficulty, but Kant's theory in its original form seems problematic.

13. In Kant's view, is lying to someone to spare her feelings morally permissible? Do you think it is permissible?

"Nothing is divine but what is agreeable to reason."

—Immanuel Kant

WRITING AND REASONING	**CHAPTER 11**

1. How does Kant's moral theory differ from consequentialism? Are the two theories in conflict in particular cases? Explain.

2. What is Kant's revolution in epistemology? According to his theory of knowledge, how is it that sense experience can match reality?

3. Is Kant a moral objectivist or a moral relativist? According to him, can the moral law be contingent or changeable? Explain.

4. For Kant, what does it mean to treat someone as an end and never as a means only? Provide a scenario in which a person is treated merely as a means, and give an example of a person being treated as an end.

5. What is the categorical imperative? Explain how Kant applies the categorical imperative to the example of the lying promise. Does he think that a lying promise is ever morally permissible? Explain.

REVIEW NOTES

11.1 THE SMALL-TOWN GENIUS

- Immanuel Kant, a modest man of conventional living, launched a revolution in epistemology and charted a major new route in ethics. He is regarded as the greatest philosopher of the last three hundred years.

- In epistemology, he effected an intellectual revolution as dramatic and as influential as any advance in science up to that time. He turned the conventional assumptions about knowledge upside down.

- In ethics, he fashioned a powerful answer to consequentialist moral theories and to anyone who thinks morality must be based on desires, feelings, and other contingencies instead of solid, unvarying reason.

11.2 THE KNOWLEDGE REVOLUTION

- An *analytic statement* is a logical truth whose denial results in a contradiction. A *synthetic statement* is one that is not analytic. It does tell us something about the world, and denying it does not yield a contradiction.

- Kant brought about a Copernican revolution in epistemology. Just as Copernicus revolutionized astronomy by reversing the traditional theory, so Kant brought forth a radically different theory of knowledge by arguing for an analogous reversal. Instead of accepting the conventional view that knowledge is acquired when the mind conforms to objects, he argued that objects conform to the mind.

- Kant argued that sense experience can match reality because the mind stamps a structure and organization on sense experience. Synthetic a priori knowledge is possible because the mind's concepts force an (a priori) order onto (synthetic) experience.

11.3 THE MORAL LAW

- *Ethics*, or moral philosophy, is the study of morality using the methods of philosophy, and *morality* consists of our beliefs about right and wrong actions and good and bad persons or character. Morality has to do with our moral judgments, principles, values, and theories; ethics is the careful, philosophical examination of these. A *consequentialist theory* is a moral theory in which the rightness of actions depends solely on their consequences or results. A *deontological theory* is a moral theory in which the rightness of actions is determined not solely by their consequences but partly or entirely by their intrinsic nature. *Utilitarianism* is the view that right actions are those that maximize the overall well-being of everyone involved.

- *Moral objectivism* is the view that at least some moral norms or principles are objectively valid or true for everyone. *Moral relativism* says that moral standards are not objective but are relative to what individuals or cultures believe. Moral relativism pertaining to individuals is known as *subjective relativism*, more precisely stated as the view that right actions are those sanctioned by a person. Moral relativism regarding cultures is called *cultural relativism*, the view that right actions are those sanctioned by one's culture. Both forms of relativism face serious difficulties.

- The *categorical imperative* is Kant's fundamental moral principle, formulated in two ways: (1) "I am never to act otherwise than so *that I could also will that my maxim should become a universal law*," and (2) "So act as to treat humanity, whether in thine own person or in that of any other, in every case as an end withal, never as a means only."

- Kant's theory says that right actions are those that are right in themselves because they are consistent with universal moral rules derived from reason, and the actions have moral worth only if we do them out of a sense of duty. Kant's central moral tenet is the categorical imperative. For Kant, the moral law cannot be something contingent, changeable, or relative. The moral law is absolute, unchangeable, and universal; a rock-solid structure built on eternal reason.

KEY TERMS

analytic statement	consequentialist	ethics	synthetic statement
categorical	theory	morality	utilitarianism
imperative	deontological theory	moral theory	

Notes

1. Immanuel Kant, *Prolegomena to Any Future Metaphysics*, trans. Paul Carus (New York: Open Court, 1912).
2. Immanuel Kant, *Critique of Pure Reason*, trans. Norman Kemp Smith (New York: Humanities Press, 1929), 44.
3. Kant, *Critique of Pure Reason*, trans. Smith, 41–42, 46–47.
4. Kant, *Critique of Pure Reason*, trans. Smith, 22.
5. Kant, *Critique of Pure Reason*, trans. Smith, 92–93.
6. Immanuel Kant, *Groundwork of the Metaphysic of Morals*, trans. T. K. Abbott (London: Longmans, Green, 1909, 1873), 3–4, 9–10.
7. Kant, *Groundwork*, trans. Abbott, 18.
8. Kant, *Groundwork*, trans. Abbott, 311.
9. Kant, *Groundwork*, trans. Abbott, 46–47.

For Further Reading

Robert Audi, *Belief, Justification, and Knowledge* (Belmont, CA: Wadsworth, 1988).

Paul Boghossian, *Fear of Knowledge* (Oxford: Oxford University Press, 2006). Concise and powerful critique of relativism and constructionism.

Steven M. Cahn and Joram G. Haber, *Twentieth Century Ethical Theory* (Upper Saddle River, NJ: Prentice-Hall, 1995).

Eve Browning Cole, *Philosophy and Feminist Criticism: An Introduction* (New York: Paragon House, 1993).

C. E. Harris, *Applying Moral Theories* (Belmont, CA: Wadsworth, 1997).

Paul K. Moser, *Knowledge and Evidence* (Cambridge: Cambridge University Press, 1989).

Kai Nielsen, *Ethics without God* (Buffalo, NY: Prometheus, 1973).

Onora O'Neill, "Kantian Ethics," in *A Companion to Ethics*, ed. Peter Singer (Cambridge: Blackwell, 1993), 175–185.

James Rachels, *The Elements of Moral Philosophy*, 4th edition (New York: McGraw-Hill, 2003).

Russ Shafer-Landau, *Whatever Happened to Good and Evil?* (New York: Oxford University Press, 2004).

Roger Trigg, *Reason and Commitment* (Cambridge: Cambridge University Press, 1973).

Lewis Vaughn, *Contemporary Moral Arguments: Readings in Ethical Issues*, 2nd edition (New York: Oxford University Press, 2010).

Online Resources

Stanford Encyclopedia of Philosophy, "Immanuel Kant," https://plato.stanford.edu/entries/kant

Internet Encyclopedia of Philosophy, "Immanuel Kant," https://www.iep.utm.edu/kantview

Philosophy Talk Podcasts, "Karl Marx," https://www.philosophytalk.org/shows/karl-marx

Encyclopedia Britannica, "Immanuel Kant," https://www.britannica.com/biography/Immanuel-Kant

ThoughtCo, "Kantian Ethics in a Nutshell: The Moral Philosophy of Immanuel Kant," https://www.thoughtco.com/kantian-ethics-moral-philosophy-immanuel-kant-4045398

Biography.com, "Immanuel Kant," https://www.biography.com/scholar/immanuel-kant

History of Philosophy (without Any Gaps) Podcast, https://historyofphilosophy.net

Works of Immanuel Kant, Internet Archive, https://archive.org/search.php?query=immanuel%20kant

CHAPTER 12

John Stuart Mill and Utilitarianism

CHAPTER OBJECTIVES

12.1 THE PHILOSOPHER-REFORMER

- Appreciate that Mill was an empiricist philosopher dedicated to seeing that his liberal and utilitarian ideals be used for the betterment of society. He became one of the greatest social reformers of his day, advocating individual liberty, freedom of expression, social tolerance, aid to the poor, the abolition of slavery, humane treatment of prisoners, and women's rights.

- Know that after suffering a mental breakdown at age twenty, Mill recovered, having gained a new perspective on his life and on his previous way of thinking. He remained a utilitarian, but he left behind many of the less desirable features of Jeremy Bentham's theory.

- Appreciate that Mill earned a prestigious place in the pantheon of respected philosophers for his work in epistemology, deductive and inductive logic, political thought, and ethics. Among other works, he wrote *System of Logic* (1843), *On Liberty* (1860), and *Utilitarianism* (1861).

12.2 MILL'S UTILITARIANISM

- Understand that utilitarians judge the morality of conduct by a single standard, the *principle of utility*: right actions are those that result in greater overall well-being (or *utility*) for the people involved than any other possible actions.

- Explain the two main forms of utilitarianism and be able to apply them to sample cases.

- Know that the classic version of utilitarianism, devised by Bentham and given more plausibility by Mill, is hedonistic in that the utility to be maximized is pleasure, broadly termed happiness, the only intrinsic good.

- Explain how Mill and Bentham differ in their conceptions of happiness, and understand why Mill says, "It is better to be a human being dissatisfied than a pig satisfied; better to be Socrates dissatisfied than a fool satisfied."

- Understand classic utilitarianism's emphasis on impartiality, the maximization of total net happiness, and the method for determining the quality of happiness.

12.3 CRITIQUES OF THE THEORY

- Understand the concept of our considered moral judgments and how critics use it to suggest that utilitarianism is a flawed theory.
- Know how utilitarians have replied to such criticism.

As we've seen (Chapter 11), in deontological moral theories, the rightness or wrongness of an action is based on its nature, not on the consequences that follow from it. But consequentialist theories say the effects of an action are all that matter; our only duty is to ensure that the effects are a maximization of the good. The good is whatever has intrinsic value—whatever is valuable for its own sake—which can include such things as pleasure, happiness, virtue, knowledge, autonomy, and the satisfaction of desires. In consequentialist ethics, then, the ends (the results) justify the means (the actions). Utilitarianism is the foremost theory of this kind, built on the notion that the only thing of intrinsic value is well-being, governed by the proposition that the rightness or wrongness of an action is to be judged by its impact on the people involved. John Stuart Mill (1806–1873) is the theory's greatest champion, the sharpest thinker to explain it, and the most compelling example (after Bentham) of a utilitarian applying the ideal creed to reality.

12.1 THE PHILOSOPHER-REFORMER

Mill was an unusual blend—an empiricist philosopher dedicated to the practical endeavor of seeing that his liberal and utilitarian ideas were used for the betterment of society. He was born in London and given a rigorous education by his father, James Mill, a philosopher in his own right. James was a strong proponent of the utilitarianism of Jeremy Bentham (English philosopher and intellectual father of the theory), and he was determined to raise John Stuart according to utilitarian principles. John Stuart turned out to be an extremely precocious and bright student, beginning the study of Greek at age three and Plato and Latin at eight. In his teens, he dutifully absorbed his father's philosophical and political views, worked for the East India Company, and went abroad to learn French and study chemistry and mathematics.

At age twenty, his life took an unexpected turn. He suffered a mental breakdown and fell into a dark depression, a condition that he later said was due to his strict upbringing and exacting education. After a few months, he recovered, having gained a new perspective on his life and on his previous way of thinking. He remained a utilitarian, but he left behind many of the less desirable features of Bentham's theory. He developed a deep friendship with the feminist Harriet Taylor, whom he married years later after her husband died. She had a profound effect on his view of the world and was a major influence on the ideas he expressed in *The Subjection of Women* (1869).

Mill went on to earn a prestigious place in the pantheon of respected philosophers for his work in epistemology, deductive and inductive logic, political thought, and ethics. Among other works, he wrote *System of Logic* (1843), *On Liberty* (1860), and *Utilitarianism* (1861).

He became one of the greatest social reformers of his day, advocating individual liberty, freedom of expression, social tolerance, aid to the poor, the abolition of slavery, humane treatment of prisoners, and women's rights. Such views were radical notions at the time, clashing violently with social forces that had little patience for talk of personal freedom, rights, and concern for the oppressed.

Figure 12.1 John Stuart Mill (1806–1873).

12.2 MILL'S UTILITARIANISM

Utilitarians judge the morality of conduct by a single standard, the *principle of utility*: right actions are those that result in greater overall well-being (or *utility*) for the people involved than any other possible actions. We are duty bound to maximize the utility of everyone affected, regardless of the contrary urgings of moral rules or unbending moral principles. In some moral theories (Kant's, for example), moral rules are absolute, allowing no exceptions even in exceptional cases. But in utilitarianism, there are no absolute prohibitions or mandates (except for the principle of utility itself). There is only the goal of maximizing well-being. Thus utilitarianism is not bothered by unusual circumstances, nor is it hobbled by conflicting moral principles or rules that demand a uniform response to extraordinary situations.

In applying the utilitarian moral standard, some moral philosophers concentrate on specific acts and some on rules covering kinds of acts. The former approach is called **act-utilitarianism**, the idea that the rightness of actions depends solely on the overall well-being produced by *individual actions*. An act is right if in a particular situation it produces a greater balance of well-being over suffering than any alternative acts; determining rightness is a matter of weighing the effects of each possible act. The latter approach, known as **rule-utilitarianism**, avoids judging rightness by specific acts and focuses instead on *rules governing categories of acts*. It says a right action is one that conforms to a rule that, if followed consistently, would create for everyone involved the most beneficial balance of well-being over suffering. We are to adhere to the rules because, in the long run, they maximize well-being for everyone considered—even though a given act may produce bad effects in a particular situation.

"There are in nature neither rewards nor punishments, there are consequences."

—Robert Ingersoll

act-utilitarianism The idea that the rightness of actions depends solely on the overall well-being produced by *individual actions.*

rule-utilitarianism The doctrine that a right action is one that conforms to a rule that, if followed consistently, would create for everyone involved the most beneficial balance of well-being over suffering.

DETAILS

Harriet Taylor, Champion of Liberty

Credit for producing *On Liberty* and *The Subjection of Women* does not belong to Mill alone. He had help—or, more accurately as modern scholars attest, he had a coauthor and a co-champion of political and social liberty in Harriet Taylor (1807–1858). Here is an account by the writer Adam Gopnik:

> When I think about the liberal tradition I wanted to show my daughter, my inner vision kept returning to a simple scene, one that had delighted me for a long time. It's of the nineteenth-century philosopher and his lover, collaborator, and (as he always insisted) his most important teacher, the writer Harriet Taylor. Desperately in love, they were courting clandestinely, and they would meet secretly at the rhino's cage at the London Zoo. "Our old friend Rhino," Taylor called him in a note. It was a place where they could safely meet and talk without fear of being seen by too many people, everyone's attention being engaged by the enormous exotic animal.
>
> They were pained, uncertain, contemplating adultery, if not yet having committed it—opinions vary; they had been in Paris together—and yet in those conversations began the material of "On Liberty," one of the greatest books of political theory ever written, and "On the Subjection of Women," one of the first great feminist manifestos and one of the most explosive books ever written. (One of the most successful, too, inasmuch as almost all of its dreams for female equality have been achieved, at least legally, in our lifetime.)
>
> Throughout his life, Mill said, emphatically and clearly and unambiguously, that Taylor was the smartest person he had ever met and the greatest influence on his work he had ever known. . . . Fortunately, newer generations of scholars, less blinded by prejudice, have begun to "recover" Harriet Taylor for us, and her role in the making of modern liberalism seems just as large and her mind as fine as her husband always asserted it was. . . .
>
> Mill and Taylor, in their later collaborations, most famously in that 1889 "The Subjection of Women," published after her death but with her imprint all over it, weren't content to show that women would be happier if freer; they went right to the ground and asked what reason we have for thinking that *any* restraint on women's freedom is just. Mill and Taylor together make the point again and again that no one can possibly know what women are or are not "naturally" good at, since their opportunities have been so vanishingly small compared with the length of their oppression. . . .
>
> Taylor and Mill believed in complete equality of the sexes before anyone else did, just as he believed in the absolute moral evil of slavery while others in Britain were temporizing.

Adam Gopnik, *A Thousand Small Sanities* (New York: Basic Books, 2019), 7–8, 1–12.

Consider how these two forms of utilitarianism could apply to the moral issue of euthanasia, or mercy killing, the taking of someone's life for his or her own sake. Suppose a woman is terminally ill and suffering horrible, inescapable pain, and she asks to be put out of her misery. An act-utilitarian might conclude that euthanasia would be the right course of action because it would result in the least amount of suffering for everyone concerned. Allowing the current situation to continue would cause enormous pain and anguish—the woman's own physical agony, the misery of her distraught family, and the distress and frustration of the physician and nurses who can do little more than stand by as she withers away. Administering a lethal injection to her, however, would immediately end her pain and prevent future suffering. Her family would grieve for her but would at least find some relief—and perhaps peace—in knowing that her torture was over. The medical staff would probably also be relieved for the same reason. There would, of course, also be possible negative consequences to take into account. In administering the lethal injection, her physician would be risking both professional censure and criminal prosecution. If his actions were to become public, people might begin to mistrust physicians who treat severely impaired children, undermining the whole medical profession. Perhaps the physician's action would lead to a general devaluing of the lives of disabled or elderly people everywhere. These dire consequences, however, would probably not be very likely if the physician acted discreetly. On balance, the act-utilitarian might say, greater net well-being (positive amounts of well-being minus negative influences on well-being) would result from the mercy killing, which would therefore be the morally right course.

On the other hand, a rule-utilitarian might insist that more net well-being would be produced by consistently following a rule that disallowed euthanasia. The argument would be that permitting mercy killings would have terrible consequences overall—increases in involuntary euthanasia (mercy killing without the patient's consent), erosion of respect for the medical profession, and a weakening of society's abhorrence of homicide.

Notice that in either kind of utilitarianism, getting direct answers to a difficult moral problem is straightforward. The facts of the case may be difficult to ascertain, but the procedure for discerning the morally right course of action is theoretically simple: determine which action best maximizes well-being. Such simplicity makes utilitarianism an appealing theory, especially when compared to others that require the use of abstract principles or elusive moral concepts.

The classic version of utilitarianism was devised by Bentham (1748–1832) and given more detail and plausibility by Mill. Classic utilitarianism is hedonistic in that the utility to be maximized is pleasure, broadly termed happiness, the only intrinsic good. A right action produces more net happiness (amounts of happiness minus unhappiness) than any alternative action, everyone considered.

Bentham and Mill had different ideas about what happiness entailed, as do many philosophers today. Bentham thinks that happiness is one-dimensional: it is pleasure, pure and simple, something that varies only in the amount that an agent can experience. On this scheme, it seems that the moral ideal would be to experience

1. How might a deontological theorist judge a case of euthanasia? Do you think this approach is better than the utilitarian's? Why or why not?

"I have learned to seek my happiness by limiting my desires, rather than in attempting to satisfy them."
—John Stuart Mill

PORTRAIT

Jeremy Bentham

Few in the English-speaking world have had as much influence on law, ethics, and social policy as Jeremy Bentham (1748–1832). Born in London and educated at Oxford, he became a philosopher preoccupied early in his life with the injustice and harm that he thought was being perpetrated by the law and mores of the times. He spent most of his career developing his ideas about ethics and society and trying to apply them to the world around him. His answer to the problems he saw was a moral theory he called utilitarianism, spelled out in his *Introduction to the Principles of Morals and Legislation* (1789).

Figure 12.2 Not just any mummy: the embalmed corpse of Jeremy Bentham at University College, London.

For Bentham, the result of applying misguided ideas and half-baked theories to society was a vast amount of human suffering. He complained that in traditional law and morality, harmless actions were condemned and harmful actions were promoted. Freedom of speech and freedom of action were constrained or eliminated altogether in the name of traditional, religious, or subjective morals. Worst of all, as Bentham saw it, policies and laws were laid down without any consideration of human happiness.

His utilitarianism, on the other hand, made human happiness the crux and measure of a good society. His famous utilitarian formula sums it up: the goal of actions should be the greatest happiness for the greatest number. With this theoretical underpinning, Bentham campaigned for equal rights for women, the reform of prisons, the elimination of imprisonment for debtors, more democratic government, the relaxation of laws against certain kinds of sexual behavior, and the abolition of what he called moral fictions such as "natural rights."

Bentham died in 1832, but he is still hanging around University College in London, which he helped found. Actually it's his embalmed body that is still on display there—fully clothed, sporting a wax model of his head, looking as if he were ready to make an important point. This strange state of affairs was mandated in his will. Apparently Bentham had an odd sense of humor.

2. Which view of the nature of happiness seems more plausible to you—Bentham's or Mill's? Why?

maximum amounts of pleasure, as does the glutton or the debauchee. But Mill thinks that pleasures can vary in quality as well as quantity. For him, there are lower and higher pleasures—the lower and inferior ones indulged in by the glutton and his ilk and the higher and more satisfying ones found in such experiences as the search for knowledge and the appreciation of art and music. Mill famously sums up this contrast by saying, "It is better to be a human being dissatisfied than a pig satisfied; better to be Socrates dissatisfied than a fool satisfied."[1]

Like all forms of utilitarianism, the classic formulation demands a strong sense of impartiality. When promoting happiness, we must not only take into account the happiness of everyone affected, but also give everyone's needs or interests equal weight. Mill explains:

John Stuart Mill: *Utilitarianism*

[The] happiness which forms the utilitarian standard of what is right conduct, is not the agent's own happiness, but that of all concerned. As between his own happiness and that of others, utilitarianism requires him to be as strictly impartial as a disinterested and benevolent spectator.[2]

This moral even-handedness is an attractive feature of utilitarianism. As we have seen, impartiality is a fundamental characteristic of morality itself. Despite our differences in social status, race, gender, religion, and wealth, we are all equal before the moral law. Early utilitarians such as Bentham and Mill took moral equality seriously, crusading for social changes that were based on strict adherence to the impartiality principle.

In classic utilitarianism, the emphasis is on maximizing the total quantity of net happiness, not ensuring that it is rationed in any particular amounts among the people involved. This means that an action resulting in one thousand units of happiness for ten people is better than an action yielding only nine hundred units of happiness for those same ten people—regardless of how the units of happiness are distributed among them. Classic utilitarians *do* want to allocate the total amount of happiness among as many people as possible (thus their motto, "the greatest happiness for the greatest number"). But maximizing total happiness is the fundamental concern whether everyone gets an equal portion or one person gets the lion's share.

This is how Mill defends his brand of utilitarianism:

The creed which accepts as the foundation of morals, Utility, or the Greatest Happiness Principle, holds that actions are right in proportion as they tend to promote happiness, wrong as they tend to produce the reverse of happiness. By happiness is intended pleasure, and the absence of pain; by unhappiness, pain, and the privation of pleasure. To give a clear view of the moral standard set up by the theory, much more requires to be said; in particular, what things it includes in the ideas of pain and pleasure; and to what extent this is left an open question. But these supplementary explanations do not affect the theory of life on which this theory of morality is grounded—namely, that pleasure, and freedom from pain, are the only things desirable as ends; and that all desirable things (which are as numerous in the utilitarian as in any other scheme) are desirable either for the pleasure inherent in themselves, or as a means to the promotion of pleasure and the prevention of pain.

Now, such a theory of life excites in many minds, and among them in some of the most estimable in feeling and purpose, inveterate dislike. To suppose that life has (as they express it)

John Stuart Mill: *Utilitarianism*

DETAILS

Utilitarianism and the Golden Rule

Probably much to the dismay of his religious critics, John Stuart Mill defended his radical doctrine of utilitarianism by arguing that it was entirely consistent with a fundamental Christian teaching:

> In the golden rule of Jesus of Nazareth, we read the complete spirit of the ethics of utility. To do as one would be done by, and to love one's neighbour as oneself, constitute the ideal perfection of utilitarian morality. As the means of making the nearest approach to this ideal, utility would enjoin, first, that laws and social arrangements should place the happiness, or (as speaking practically it may be called) the interest, of every individual, as nearly as possible in harmony with the interest of the whole; and secondly, that education and opinion, which have so vast a power over human character, should so use that power as to establish in the mind of every individual an indissoluble association between his own happiness and the good of the whole; especially between his own happiness and the practice of such modes of conduct, negative and positive, as regard for the universal happiness prescribes: so that not only he may be unable to conceive the possibility of happiness to himself, consistently with conduct opposed to the general good, but also that a direct impulse to promote the general good may be in every individual one of the habitual motives of action, and the sentiments connected therewith may fill a large and prominent place in every human being's sentient existence.

Do you think utilitarianism is really equivalent to the Golden Rule? If so, why? If not, what are the chief differences between the two?

John Stuart Mill, "What Utilitarianism Is," *Utilitarianism* (1861).

John Stuart Mill:
Utilitarianism

no higher end than pleasure—no better and nobler object of desire and pursuit—they designate as utterly mean and groveling; as a doctrine worthy only of swine, to whom the followers of Epicurus were, at a very early period, contemptuously likened; and modern holders of the doctrine are occasionally made the subject of equally polite comparisons by its German, French, and English assailants.

When thus attacked, the Epicureans have always answered, that it is not they, but their accusers, who represent human nature in a degrading light; since the accusation supposes human beings to be capable of no pleasures except those of which swine are capable. If this supposition were true, the charge could not be gainsaid, but would then be no longer an imputation; for if the sources of pleasure were precisely the same to human beings and to swine, the rule of life which is good enough for the one would be good enough for the other. The comparison of the Epicurean life to that of beasts is felt as degrading, precisely because a beast's pleasures do not satisfy a human being's conception of happiness. Human beings have faculties more elevated than the animal appetites, and when once made conscious of them, do not regard anything as happiness which does not include their gratification. I do not, indeed, consider the Epicureans to have been by any means faultless in drawing out their scheme of consequences from the utilitarian principle. To do this in any sufficient manner, many Stoic, as well as Christian elements require to be included. But there is no known Epicurean theory of life which does not assign to the pleasures of the intellect, of the feelings and imagination, and of the moral sentiments, a much higher value as pleasures than to those of mere sensation. It must be admitted, however, that utilitarian writers in general have placed the superiority of mental over bodily pleasures chiefly in the greater permanency, safety, uncostliness, etc., of the former—that is, in their circumstantial advantages rather than in their intrinsic nature. And on all these points utilitarians have fully proved their case; but they might have taken the other, and, as it may be called, higher ground, with entire consistency. It is quite compatible with the principle of utility to recognise the fact, that some *kinds* of pleasure are more desirable and more valuable than others. It would be absurd that while, in estimating all other things, quality is considered as well as quantity, the estimation of pleasures should be supposed to depend on quantity alone.

If I am asked, what I mean by difference of quality in pleasures, or what makes one pleasure more valuable than another, merely as a pleasure, except its being greater in amount, there is but one possible answer. Of two pleasures, if there be one which all or almost all who have experience of both give a decided preference, irrespective of any feeling of moral obligation to prefer it, that is the more desirable pleasure. If one of the two is, by those who are competently acquainted with both, placed so far above the other that they prefer it, even though knowing it to be attended with a great amount of discontent, and would not resign it for any quantity of the other pleasure which their nature is capable of, we are justified in ascribing to the preferred enjoyment a superiority in quality, so far outweighing quantity as to render it, in comparison, of small account.

Now it is an unquestionable fact that those who are equally acquainted with, and equally capable of appreciating and enjoying, both, do give a most marked preference to the manner of existence which employs their higher faculties. Few human creatures would consent to be changed into any of the lower animals, for a promise of the fullest allowance of a beast's pleasures; no intelligent human being would consent to be a fool, no instructed person would be an ignoramus, no person of feeling and conscience would be selfish and base, even though they should be persuaded that the fool, the dunce, or the rascal is better satisfied with his lot than they are with theirs. They would not resign what they possess more than he for the most complete satisfaction of all the desires which they have in common with him. If they ever fancy they would, it is only in cases of unhappiness so extreme, that to escape from it they would exchange their lot for almost any other, however undesirable in their own eyes. A being of higher faculties requires more to make him happy, is capable probably of more acute suffering, and certainly accessible to it at more points, than one of an inferior type; but in spite of these liabilities, he can never really wish to sink into what he feels to be a lower grade of existence. We may give what explanation we please of this unwillingness; we may attribute it to pride, a name which is given indiscriminately to some of the most and to some of the least estimable feelings of which mankind are capable; we may refer it to the love of liberty and personal independence, an appeal to which was with the Stoics one of the most effective means for the inculcation of it; to the love of power, or to the love of excitement, both of which do really enter into and

3. Is the utilitarian view of morality based on the promotion of happiness demeaning? Is there more to life than the pursuit of happiness (as Mill defines it)?

"The despotism of custom is everywhere the standing hindrance to human advancement."

—John Stuart Mill

contribute to it: but its most appropriate appellation is a sense of dignity, which all human beings possess in one form or another, and in some, though by no means in exact, proportion to their higher faculties, and which is so essential a part of the happiness of those in whom it is strong, that nothing which conflicts with it could be, otherwise than momentarily, an object of desire to them. Whoever supposes that this preference takes place at a sacrifice of happiness—that the superior being, in anything like equal circumstances, is not happier than the inferior—confounds the two very different ideas, of happiness, and content. It is indisputable that the being whose capacities of enjoyment are low, has the greatest chance of having them fully satisfied; and a highly endowed being will always feel that any happiness which he can look for, as the world is constituted, is imperfect. But he can learn to bear its imperfections, if they are at all bearable; and they will not make him envy the being who is indeed unconscious of the imperfections, but only because he feels not at all the good which those imperfections qualify. It is better to be a human being dissatisfied than a pig satisfied; better to be Socrates dissatisfied than a fool satisfied. And if the fool, or the pig, are of a different opinion, it is because they only know their own side of the question. The other party to the comparison knows both sides....

From this verdict of the only competent judges, I apprehend there can be no appeal. On a question which is the best worth having of two pleasures, or which of two modes of existence is the most grateful to the feelings, apart from its moral attributes and from its consequences, the judgment of those who are qualified by knowledge of both, or, if they differ, that of the majority among them, must be admitted as final. And there needs to be the less hesitation to accept this judgment respecting the quality of pleasures, since there is no other tribunal to be referred to even on the question of quantity. What means are there of determining which is the acutest of two pains, or the intensest of two pleasurable sensations, except the general suffrage of those who are familiar with both? Neither pains nor pleasures are homogeneous, and pain is always heterogeneous with pleasure. What is there to decide whether a particular pleasure is worth purchasing at the cost of a particular pain, except the feelings and judgment of the experienced? When, therefore, those feelings and judgment declare the pleasures derived from the higher faculties to be preferable in *kind*, apart from the question of intensity, to those of which the animal nature, disjoined from the higher faculties, is susceptible, they are entitled on this subject to the same regard.

I have dwelt on this point, as being a necessary part of a perfectly just conception of Utility or Happiness, considered as the directive rule of human conduct. But it is by no means an indispensable condition to the acceptance of the utilitarian standard; for that standard is not the agent's own greatest happiness, but the greatest amount of happiness altogether; and if it may possibly be doubted whether a noble character is always the happier for its nobleness, there can be no doubt that it makes other people happier, and that the world in general is immensely a gainer by it. Utilitarianism, therefore, could only attain its end by the general cultivation of nobleness of character, even if each individual were only benefited by the nobleness of others, and his own, so far as happiness is concerned, were a sheer deduction from the benefit. But the bare enunciation of such an absurdity as this last, renders refutation superfluous.

According to the Greatest Happiness Principle, as above explained, the ultimate end, with reference to and for the sake of which all other things are desirable (whether we are considering our own good or that of other people), is an existence exempt as far as possible from pain, and as rich as possible in enjoyments, both in point of quantity and quality; the test of quality, and the rule for measuring it against quantity, being the preference felt by those who in their opportunities of experience, to which must be added their habits of self-consciousness and self-observation, are best furnished with the means of comparison. This, being, according to the utilitarian opinion, the end of human action, is necessarily also the standard of morality; which may accordingly be defined, the rules and precepts for human conduct, by the observance of which an existence such as has been described might be, to the greatest extent possible, secured to all mankind; and not to them only, but, so far as the nature of things admits, to the whole sentient creation. . . .

The objectors to utilitarianism cannot always be charged with representing it in a discreditable light. On the contrary, those among them who entertain anything like a just idea of its disinterested character, sometimes find fault with its standard as being too high for humanity. They say it is exacting too much to require that people shall always act from the inducement of promoting the general interests of society. But this is to mistake the very meaning of a standard of morals, and confound the rule of action with the motive of it. It is the business of ethics to tell us what are our duties, or by what test we may know them; but no system of ethics requires that the sole motive of all we do shall be a feeling of duty; on the contrary, ninety-nine hundredths of all our actions are done from other motives, and rightly so done, if the rule of duty does not condemn them. It is the more unjust to utilitarianism that this particular misapprehension should be made a ground of objection to it, inasmuch as utilitarian moralists have gone beyond almost all others in affirming that the motive has nothing to do with the morality of the action, though much with the worth of the agent. . . .

It has already been remarked, that questions of ultimate ends do not admit of proof, in the ordinary acceptation of the term. To be incapable of proof by reasoning is common to all first principles; to the first premises of our knowledge, as well as to those of our conduct. But the former, being matters of fact, may be the subject of a direct appeal to the faculties which judge of fact—namely, our senses, and our internal consciousness. Can an appeal be made to the same faculties on questions of practical ends? Or by what other faculty is cognisance taken of them?

Questions about ends are, in other words, questions about what things are desirable. The utilitarian doctrine is, that happiness is desirable, and the only thing desirable, as an end; all other things being only desirable as means to that end. What ought to be required of this doctrine—what conditions is it requisite that the doctrine should fulfill—to make good its claim to be believed? The only proof capable of being given that an object is visible, is that people actually see it.

The only proof that a sound is audible, is that people hear it: and so of the other sources of our experience. In like manner, I apprehend, the sole evidence it is possible to produce that anything is desirable, is that people do actually desire it. If the end which the utilitarian doctrine proposes to itself were not, in theory and in practice, acknowledged to be an end, nothing could ever convince any person that it was so. No reason can be given why the general happiness is desirable, except that each person, so far as he believes it to be attainable, desires his own happiness. This, however, being a fact, we have not only all the proof which the case admits of, but all which it is possible to require, that happiness is a good: that each person's happiness is a good to that person, and the general happiness, therefore, a good to the aggregate of all persons. Happiness, has made out its title as *one* of the ends of conduct, and consequently one of the criteria of morality.

But it has not; by this alone, proved itself to be the sole criterion. To do that, it would seem, by the same rule, necessary to show, not only that people desire happiness, but that they never desire anything else. . . .

"He who lives only to benefit himself confers on the world a benefit when he dies."

—Tertullian

We have now, then, an answer to the question, of what sort of proof the principle of utility is susceptible. If the opinion which I have now stated is psychologically true—if human nature is so constituted as to desire nothing which is not either a part of happiness or a means of happiness, we can have no other proof, and we require no other, that these are the only things desirable. If so, happiness is the sole end of human action, and the promotion of it the test by which to judge of all human conduct; from whence it necessarily follows that it must be the criterion of morality, since a part is included in the whole.

And now to decide whether this is really so; whether mankind does desire nothing for itself but that which is a pleasure to them, or of which the absence is a pain; we have

THEN AND NOW

Utilitarianism and the Death Penalty

Figure 12.3 In debates on capital punishment, which matters most: rights or utility?

Utilitarianism is alive and well in contemporary debates about personal morality, institutional policy, and government programs. It plays an especially big role in arguments over capital punishment—officially sanctioned punishment by death for very grievous (capital) crimes. On one side of this dispute are the *abolitionists*, those who want to do away with capital punishment and who believe the death penalty is never justified. On the other side are the *retentionists*, those who want to retain the death penalty as part of a system of legal punishment and who believe that sometimes capital punishment is warranted. Both camps in the debate argue their cases on utilitarian grounds (as well as on the basis of deontological principles).

Many retentionists take the utilitarian path by arguing that the death penalty has positive effects on society—specifically that it either *prevents* criminals from harming others again or *deters* would-be offenders from capital crimes. Executing hardened murderers, say retentionists, is the best way to prevent them from killing other inmates or escaping and killing innocent people. Abolitionists respond that life in prison without parole (and with appropriate security measures) is as effective as execution in preventing inmates from repeating their crimes. To make their arguments stick, both sides in this dispute have to support their nonmoral claims with empirical evidence, but definitive evidence for the effectiveness of the evidently arrived at a question of fact and experience, dependent, like all similar questions, upon evidence. It can only be determined by practised self-consciousness and self-observation, assisted by observation of others. I believe that these sources of evidence, impartially consulted, will declare that desiring a thing and finding it pleasant, aversion to it and thinking of it as painful, are phenomena entirely inseparable, or rather two parts of the same phenomenon; in strictness of language, two different modes of naming the same psychological fact: that to think of an object as desirable (unless for the sake of its consequences), and to think of it as pleasant, are one and the same thing; and that to desire anything, except in proportion as the idea of it is pleasant, is a physical and metaphysical possibility.[3]

4. Does the fact that people desire happiness prove that it should be desired, that achieving it should be the ultimate goal of the moral life?

two prevention strategies is hard to come by. Each side can challenge the other to produce evidence to back their assertions.

Retentionists often maintain that the most powerful deterrent against murder is the threat of the ultimate punishment, death. Several sociological studies seem to support this claim, but they have been the subject of a good deal of critical scrutiny and debate, a fact that abolitionists are quick to point out. Some retentionists argue that common sense tells us that the death penalty is a better deterrent than life in prison. It seems obvious, they say, that the more severe the punishment, the more it deters potential offenders. Abolitionists reply that there are reasons to think the commonsense view is mistaken.

(Some retentionists take the deontological path through *retributivism*, the doctrine that people should be punished simply because they deserve it and that the punishment should be proportional to the crime. Kant argued for this view. Many abolitionists reject the retributivist theory of punishment and thus reject the retentionist argument that it supports. But some of them accept it, arguing that although offenders should get the punishment they deserve, no one deserves the death penalty.)

Like retentionists, abolitionists also try to make their case on utilitarian grounds. They may contend that life in prison for murderers results in greater overall happiness or goodness for society than sentencing them to death. For one thing, if human life has great value, then preserving it by forgoing the death penalty must maximize the good. Abolitionists also insist that the death penalty brings with it some drawbacks that life sentences avoid. They may assert that the monetary costs involved in capital punishment exceed the costs of life sentences without parole, that the chances of unintentionally executing the innocent are great, or that the execution of offenders may actually provoke murders or have an overall dehumanizing effect on society. Retentionists may dispute these claims by questioning the evidence for them, or they may take a retributivist line by arguing that the consequences are beside the point.

Do you accept or reject the use of the death penalty? What are your grounds for doing so? Are your grounds utilitarian, deontological, or both?

12.3 CRITIQUES OF THE THEORY

So there is much to like about utilitarianism. Its simplicity, its straightforward application to moral problems, and its insistence on moral impartiality have helped to make it one of the most influential moral theories in modern history.

Still it has drawn many criticisms, the most serious one being that the theory flies in the face of our *considered moral judgments*, especially regarding issues of duty, rights, and justice. Our considered moral judgments, what some call our moral common sense, are our moral opinions that we arrive at after careful deliberation that is as free of bias, self-interest, and other distorting influences as possible. Moral philosophers grant them considerable respect and try to take them into account in their moral theorizing. These judgments are fallible, and they are often revised under pressure from trustworthy principles or theories. But we are entitled to trust them unless we have good reason to doubt them. Therefore, any moral theory that is seriously inconsistent with our most basic considered judgments must generally be regarded as flawed, perhaps fatally so, and in need of revision. Our considered judgments, for example, tell us that slavery, murder, rape, and genocide are wrong. A moral theory that implies otherwise fails this criterion and is a candidate for revision or rejection. That equals should be treated equally, that there must be good reasons to deliberately cause harm to others, that justice is an essential part of the moral life—these and other considered judgments are among the many that good moral theories must account for. Some critics have accused utilitarianism of running afoul of this important criterion.

Suppose you promise a friend that you will help her prepare for a big exam. You know the subject inside and out, but she constantly struggles with it. At the last minute, you decide that you would rather stay home and watch a movie. You calculate that the satisfaction you get from watching the movie outweighs whatever dissatisfaction your friend feels because you broke your promise. By utilitarian lights, you should stay home and watch the movie, for your only obligation is to maximize utility. But this view of the matter seems mistaken. When we make a promise, we impose a duty on ourselves, and such duties seem to carry weight in our moral deliberations that is independent of considerations of utility. Sometimes when a large measure of well-being hangs in the balance, breaking a promise or forsaking some other duty may seem justified. But our considered judgments suggest that such duties as promise keeping cannot be easily or automatically overridden by calculations of utility.

Now consider the case of a man arrested for murder who is in fact innocent of the crime. Angry citizens demand that he be lynched immediately, and they threaten riots and reprisal killings against the man's family. The local police chief knows that by lynching the man, the overall happiness of the people would be increased far more than if the man got a fair trial—the mob would be satisfied, lives would be saved, and property would be spared destruction. So the chief lets the town string the man up. Did the chief do what is right? The utilitarian seems obliged to say yes. But our considered judgment would likely be that the chief did wrong by violating

5. Is breaking the promise really wrong in this case? What would you have done? Why?

6. How do you think Mill would respond to this criticism?

Figure 12.4 If lynching an innocent man will prevent other killings, is the lynching justified? The utilitarian answer might be yes.

the man's rights and perpetrating an injustice. According to utilitarianism's critics, this shows that the theory is inadequate. The requirements of justice and individual rights must be taken into account; utility is not the only thing that matters.

Some utilitarians have replied to such criticisms by saying that scenarios like the one just presented are unrealistic and misleading. In the real world, they say, actions that seem to conflict with our moral intuitions almost always produce consequences so dire that the actions cannot be justified even on utilitarian grounds. Once *all* the possible consequences are taken into account, it becomes clear that the proposed actions do not maximize happiness and that commonsense morality and utilitarianism coincide.

Critics reply that many times the judgments of commonsense morality and utilitarianism do in fact coincide when all the facts are known—but not always. They insist that even the utilitarian must admit that there could be cases in which actions that maximize utility do clash with our considered moral judgments, and this possibility raises doubts about the utilitarian standard.

"All action is for the sake of some end; and rules of action, it seems natural to suppose, must take their whole character and color from the end to which they are subservient."

—John Stuart Mill

DETAILS

Mill's View of Personal Freedom

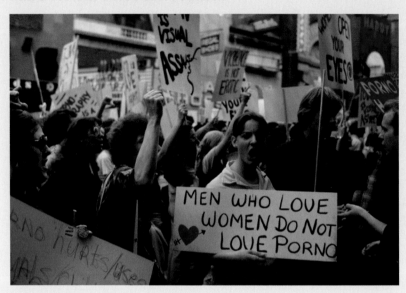

Figure 12.5 If pornography gives offense, should it be banned? What would Mill say?

John Stuart Mill makes one of the more memorable cases for individual liberty and thus inspires many contemporary arguments against government attempts to curtail freedom of speech and action:

WRITING AND REASONING   **CHAPTER 12**

1. How does Mill respond to the charge that utilitarianism is a pig philosophy? What is meant by "better to be a human being dissatisfied than a pig satisfied"? Do you agree with this ordering of values?

2. What is Mill's "proof" of the truth of utilitarianism? Is it a good argument? Explain.

3. Suppose that by killing one innocent person you can greatly increase the health and well-being of a thousand. Would it be morally permissible to kill that person? How might a utilitarian decide this question?

4. Do you believe that the quantity of happiness is more important than its quality? What are your reasons for choosing one over the other?

5. Are you a utilitarian? Why or why not?

[T]he only purpose for which power can be rightfully exercised over any member of a civilized community, against his will, is to prevent harm to others. His own good, either physical or moral, is not a sufficient warrant. He cannot rightfully be compelled to do or forbear because it will be better for him to do so, because it will make him happier, because, in the opinion of others, to do so would be wise or even right. These are good reasons for remonstrating with him, or reasoning with him, or persuading him, or entreating him, but not for compelling him, or visiting him with any evil in case he do otherwise. To justify that, the conduct from which it is desired to deter him, must be calculated to produce evil to someone else. The only part of the conduct of any one for which he is amenable to society, is that which concerns others. In the part which merely concerns himself, his independence is, of right, absolute. . . . The only freedom which deserves the name, is that of pursuing our own good in our own way, so long as we do not attempt to deprive others of theirs, or impede their efforts to obtain it.

Legal moralism is the view that a community's basic moral standards should be enshrined in law and enforced by the state. Considering Mill's position on individual liberty, would he be for or against this doctrine? What would be his grounds?

John Stuart Mill, *On Liberty* (Indianapolis, IN: Hackett, 1859, 1978).

REVIEW NOTES

12.1 THE PHILOSOPHER-REFORMER

- Mill was an empiricist philosopher dedicated to seeing that his liberal and utilitarian ideals be used for the betterment of society. He became one of the greatest social reformers of his day, advocating individual liberty, freedom of expression, social tolerance, aid to the poor, the abolition of slavery, humane treatment of prisoners, and women's rights.

- After suffering a mental breakdown at age twenty, Mill recovered, having gained a new perspective on his life and on his previous way of thinking. He remained a utilitarian, but he left behind many of the less desirable features of Bentham's theory. He married the feminist Harriet Taylor, who was a major influence on the ideas he expressed in *The Subjection of Women* (1869).

- Mill earned a prestigious place in the pantheon of respected philosophers for his work in epistemology, deductive and inductive logic, political thought, and ethics. Among other works, he wrote *System of Logic* (1843), *On Liberty* (1860), and *Utilitarianism* (1861).

12.2 MILL'S UTILITARIANISM

- Utilitarians judge the morality of conduct by a single standard, the *principle of utility*: right actions are those that result in greater overall well-being (or *utility*) for the people involved than any other possible actions.

- There are two main forms of utilitarianism: (1) *act-utilitarianism* is the view that the rightness of actions depends solely on the overall well-being produced by individual actions and (2) *rule-utilitarianism* is the doctrine that a right action is one that conforms to a rule that, if followed consistently, would create for everyone involved the most beneficial balance of well-being over suffering.

- The classic version of utilitarianism, devised by Jeremy Bentham and given more plausibility by Mill, is hedonistic in that the utility to be maximized is pleasure, broadly termed happiness, the only intrinsic good.

- Bentham thinks happiness is one-dimensional: it is pleasure, pure and simple, something that varies only in the amount that an agent can experience. But Mill contends that pleasures can vary in quality as well as quantity. Mill famously remarks, "It is better to be a human being dissatisfied than a pig satisfied; better to be Socrates dissatisfied than a fool satisfied."

- Classic utilitarianism features a strong sense of impartiality, and its emphasis is on maximizing the total quantity of net happiness, not ensuring that it is rationed in any particular amounts among the people involved.

12.3 CRITIQUES OF THE THEORY

- Utilitarianism has drawn many criticisms, the most serious one being that the theory conflicts with our considered moral judgments, especially regarding issues of duty, rights, and justice. Our considered moral judgments are our moral opinions that we arrive at after careful deliberation that is as free of bias, self-interest, and other distorting influences as possible. Any moral theory that is seriously inconsistent with our most basic considered judgments must generally be regarded as flawed, perhaps fatally so, and in need of revision. Critics have constructed scenarios that seem to show that utilitarianism conflicts with our strongest moral intuitions.

- Some utilitarians have replied to such criticisms by saying that the scenarios are unrealistic and misleading. Critics reply that many times the judgments of commonsense morality and utilitarianism do in fact coincide when all the facts are known—but not always.

KEY TERMS

act-utilitarianism   rule-utilitarianism

Notes

1. John Stuart Mill, "What Utilitarianism Is," *Utilitarianism* (1861).
2. Mill, "What Utilitarianism Is."
3. Mill, "What Utilitarianism Is."

For Further Reading

Jeremy Bentham, "Of the Principle of Utility," *An Introduction to the Principles of Morals and Legislation* (Oxford: Clarendon Press, 1879), 1–7.

William K. Frankena, *Ethics*, 2nd edition (Englewood Cliffs, NJ: Prentice-Hall, 1973). A highly regarded, concise introduction to ethics.

Kai Nielsen, "A Defense of Utilitarianism," *Ethics* 82 (1972): 113–124.

Louis P. Pojman, *Ethics: Discovering Right and Wrong*, 4th edition (Belmont, CA: Wadsworth, 2002). An introduction to ethics that lays out a case for objective morality.

James Rachels, *The Elements of Moral Philosophy*, 4th edition (New York: McGraw-Hill, 2003). A concise guide to ethics and ethical theories.

Russ Shafer-Landau, *Whatever Happened to Good and Evil?* (New York: Oxford University Press, 2004). A readable, carefully crafted defense of objective ethics.

Peter Singer, ed., *A Companion to Ethics* (Cambridge: Blackwell, 1993). A topical anthology covering many issues, including moral theory, theory applications, and challenges to commonsense ethics.

J. J. C. Smart, "Extreme and Restricted Utilitarianism," in *Essays Metaphysical and Moral* (Oxford: Blackwell, 1987).

Lewis Vaughn, *Contemporary Moral Arguments: Readings in Ethical Issues* (New York: Oxford University Press, 2010). A moral-issues anthology organized by topics and by influential, classic arguments.

Bernard Williams, "A Critique of Utilitarianism," in *Utilitarianism: For and Against*, eds. J. J. C. Smart and Bernard Williams (New York: Cambridge University Press, 1973).

Online Resources

Stanford Encyclopedia of Philosophy, "John Stuart Mill," "Harriet Taylor Mill," "Mill's Moral and Political Philosophy," https://plato.stanford.edu

Internet Encyclopedia of Philosophy, "John Stuart Mill (1806–1873)," https://www.iep.utm.edu/milljs

Utilitarianism.com, "Utilitarianism Resources," https://www.utilitarianism.com/index.htm

Philosophy Talk Podcasts, "J.S. Mill and the Good Life," https://www.philosophytalk.org/shows/mill-and-good-life

Encyclopedia Britannica, "John Stuart Mill," https://www.britannica.com/biography/John-Stuart-Mill

ThoughtCo, "About John Stuart Mill, a Male Feminist and Philosopher" https://www.thoughtco.com/john-stuart-mill-male-feminist-3530510

Biography.com, "John Stuart Mill," https://www.biography.com/scholar/john-stuart-mill

History of Philosophy (without Any Gaps) Podcast, https://historyofphilosophy.net

Works of John Stuart Mill, Internet Archive, https://archive.org/search.php?query=john%20stuart%20mill

CHAPTER 13

Hegel and Marx

CHAPTER OBJECTIVES

13.1 HEGEL

- Define *absolute idealism* and *panentheism*.
- Explain Hegel's concept of Spirit and the notion of universal self-consciousness.
- Understand the basic steps in the process that Hegel calls dialectic.

13.2 MARX

- Define *socialism*, *communism*, and *capitalism*.
- Understand the meaning of Marx's phrase, "From each according to his ability, to each according to his needs."
- Articulate the main social and political differences between the proletariat and the bourgeoisie.
- Explain Marx's comment that the bourgeoisie produce their own gravediggers.
- Summarize the main criticisms that have been lodged against socialist systems.
- Understand how Marx applies the concept of dialectic to the rise of socialism.

The nineteenth century was a time of social and political upheaval as well as remarkable philosophical debate and innovation. The former had several sources. First, the scientific awakening of the previous century led to trailblazing discoveries in biology, chemistry, and other fields, and a widespread expectation of human progress came with them. Second, the Industrial Revolution transformed social and economic systems that previously had seemed unshakeable. It filled up the cities, changed the relationship between people and their labors, and produced equal measures of prosperity and woe. Third, political turmoil swept the Continent as wars and revolutions spread, and great empires rose and declined. In Europe the greatest emissaries of philosophical change were G. W. F. Hegel, Søren Kierkegaard, Karl Marx, and Friedrich Nietzsche. They criticized the theories of revered philosophers while disagreeing with each other on important issues. But they all left their mark, influenced the future of ideas, and—in the case of Hegel and Marx—helped shape a large share of the world's social and political landscape.

13.1 HEGEL

Hegel belongs to a tradition in philosophy characterized less by sustained rational argument than by the construction of grand systems of thought, vast worldviews that attempt to grasp the whole of reality in every significant aspect. The core of Hegel's system is a kind of **absolute idealism**, the doctrine that the universe is an objective reality consisting of ideas in the universal mind, what Hegel calls Spirit or Absolute. This Spirit (which has also been called God) is not merely the sum of all human minds and their ideas; it is certainly that, but everything else as well. Spirit is all, but it is also at the same time distinct from humanity, with its own self-awareness and its own plans to be worked out through the actions and thinking of human beings. Spirit is a spiritual organism encompassing the whole universe, evolving and developing according to its own internal principles toward its destiny. Hegel's view, then, is a form of **panentheism**, the view that God is in every part of the universe (as in *pantheism*) but is also *more* than the universe, just as cells in an organism constitute the organism yet are not identical with it (the organism is more than a collection of its cells). Hegel declares:

absolute idealism The doctrine that the universe is an objective reality consisting of ideas in the universal mind.

panentheism The view that God is in every part of the universe but is also more than the universe.

Hegel: *Lectures on the History of Philosophy*

Spirit is not to be considered only as individual, finite, consciousness, but as that Spirit which is universal and concrete within itself . . . Spirit's intelligent comprehension of itself is at the same time the progression of the total evolving reality. This progression is not one that takes its course through the thought of an individual and exhibits itself in a single consciousness, for it shows itself to be universal Spirit presenting itself in the history of the world in all the richness of its form.[1]

This reference to history is significant, for Hegel sees the history of the world as the continual development of Spirit toward greater self-consciousness and rationality, greater cognizance of itself as a free, self-determining being. The ultimate goal and

1. Does Hegel accept the Judeo-Christian notion of God—an all-knowing, all-good, all-powerful deity?

PORTRAIT

Hegel

Georg Wilhelm Friedrich Hegel (1770–1831) was born in Stuttgart in what is now Germany, the eldest son of a low-level government officer and a housewife, who died when Hegel was eleven. He attended the University at Tübingen and, after graduation in 1793, held tutoring positions in Bern and Frankfurt. He later moved to Jena, where he lectured in philosophy and coedited the journal *The Critical Journal of Philosophy*. In 1816 he secured a chair in philosophy at the University of Heidelberg, and he remained there until his death from cholera in 1831.

Figure 13.1 Georg Wilhelm Friedrich Hegel (1770–1831).

In his career he produced a prodigious amount of work, including many seminal but ponderous volumes on metaphysics, philosophy of history, philosophy of religion, ethics, and aesthetics. His most important and influential books are *The Phenomenology of Mind* (or *The Phenomenology of Spirit*), *The Science of Logic*, and *The Philosophy of Right*. Through his lectures and writings, he became the most important thinker of nineteenth-century Germany and the biggest philosophical influence on Karl Marx and his collaborator Friedrich Engels.

"We do not need to be shoemakers to know if our shoes fit, and just as little have we any need to be professionals to acquire knowledge of matters of universal interest."

—G. W. F. Hegel

2. What are the most important attributes of Hegel's Spirit?

"The history of the world is none other than the progress of the consciousness of freedom."

—G. W. F. Hegel

final stage of this cosmic development is total self-consciousness and self-knowledge. This final moment is the culmination of history; it is the goal toward which the world inevitably progresses. As individuals and nations become increasingly aware of themselves and their freedom, Spirit—the whole of existence—also achieves greater self-consciousness and progresses further along the path to the final objective.

Hegel holds that both Spirit and humanity move toward ultimate self-consciousness through stages of history, through epochs that unfold by logical and historical necessity. And he thinks he knows the repeating pattern of development that history embodies. He calls it *dialectic*, and it always goes like this: First there is a historical starting point (the *thesis*), which eventually produces a state of affairs directly opposed to it (the *antithesis*), and the conflict yields a new situation (the *synthesis*). Then the pattern repeats, beginning with the synthesis as the new thesis. Thus Hegel believes that the repeating cycle is rational and inevitable and that history is going in a positive direction—that is, there is continual progress toward a better future.

13.2 MARX

Karl Marx (1818–1883) was in his early teens when Hegel died. But by the time Marx attended the university, Hegel was all the rage in German intellectual circles.

Marx soon became a young, radical Hegelian, reading and discussing Hegel at every opportunity. He admired Hegel and incorporated some of Hegel's ideas into his own philosophical writings. Marx accepted Hegel's view that history unfolds in stages according to a rational pattern and that this pattern takes the form of Hegel's dialectic (thesis, antithesis, and synthesis). And he agreed with Hegel's optimistic view that history is a story of human progress; there are winners and losers in history, but the overall trend points to a positive end. But Marx parted ways with Hegel on his idealism. Hegel thought the forces that guide history are essentially spiritual; history advances as Spirit strives toward self-consciousness and freedom. But for Marx history is the result of the material conditions of society (principally economic and social conditions). From this odd blend of Hegelian views and Marx's brand of materialism came socialism.

Socialism is the political and economic doctrine that the means of production (property, factories, businesses) should be owned or controlled by the people, either communally or through the state. Socialism can accommodate liberal democratic forms of government and can even retain some elements of market capitalism. **Communism** usually implies socialism within a totalitarian system.

Figure 13.2 Karl Marx (1818–1883).

The guiding principle of the socialist view is equality: the wealth of society should be shared by all. The ideal distribution of goods usually follows the classic formula laid down by Marx, the father of modern socialism: "From each according to his ability, to each according to his needs." People should do work that fits their

socialism The political and economic view that the means of production (property, factories, businesses) should be owned and controlled by the state for the general welfare.

communism A term broadly synonymous with socialism but associated with nominally Marxist countries such as the Soviet Union in the twentieth century.

3. What is Hegel's dialectic? How does Marx make use of it?

4. Is Marx correct in saying that a society's means of production shape its political and philosophical ideas? What about religion, culture, social reformers—can any of these influence a society's thinking?

Figure 13.3 Grave of Karl Marx at Highgate Cemetery in London.

capitalism A socioeconomic system in which wealth goes to anyone who can acquire it in a free marketplace.

abilities, and they should reap rewards that match their needs. Generally, liberal societies let the means of production accrue to fewer people through the workings of a free market—that is, through **capitalism**. In such a system, wealth goes to anyone who can acquire it in the marketplace, but in a socialist system wealth is controlled by the state, which allocates it for the good of the people generally.

DETAILS

Einstein on Socialism

Albert Einstein (1879–1955), the world-famous scientist and discoverer of the theory of relativity, had strong philosophical and social interests, which he often expressed in his writings. This is what he had to say about the relative merits of capitalism and socialism:

> [In capitalism] production is carried on for profit, not for use. There is no provision that all those able and willing to work will always be in a position to find employment; an "army of unemployed" almost always exists. The worker is constantly in fear of losing his job. Since unemployed and poorly paid workers do not provide a profitable market, the production of consumers' goods is restricted, and great hardship is the consequence. Technological progress frequently results in more unemployment rather than in an easing of the burden of work for all. The profit motive, in conjunction with competition among capitalists, is responsible for an instability in the accumulation and utilization of capital which leads to increasingly severe depressions. Unlimited competition leads to a huge waste of labor, and to that crippling of the social consciousness of individuals which I mentioned before.
>
> This crippling of individuals I consider the worst evil of capitalism. Our whole educational system suffers from this evil. An exaggerated competitive attitude is inculcated into the student, who is trained to worship acquisitive success as a preparation for his future career.
>
> I am convinced there is only one way to eliminate these grave evils, namely through the establishment of a socialist economy, accompanied by an educational system which would be oriented toward social goals. In such an economy, the means of production are owned by society itself and are utilized in a planned fashion. A planned economy, which adjusts production to the needs of the community, would distribute the work to be done among all those able to work and would guarantee a livelihood to every man, woman, and child. The education of the individual, in addition to promoting his own innate abilities, would attempt to develop in him a sense of responsibility for his fellow men in place of the glorification of power and success in our present society.

Do you agree with Einstein's argument for socialism? Why or why not?

Albert Einstein, "Why Socialism," *Monthly Review*, May 1949.

Few philosophers have had as much influence on the world as Marx has—who, ironically, did not consider himself a philosopher and did not believe that ideas alone could have much of an impact on history. He thinks that what drives philosophy, history, society, law, government, and morality is economics. It is the dominant system of economics in every age, he says, that determines how society is structured and how history will go. A society's system of economics is defined by its means of production—by its economic and technological ways of meeting people's physical and social needs. The means of production, Marx says, shape social relationships, class structure, technological tools, and political and philosophical ideas. Those who own and control the means of production make up the dominant class, possess most of the wealth, wield most of the political power, and exploit the lower class. Their ideas—political, philosophical, or social—are the ruling ideas. The rest of the people own no property and occupy the lowest rungs of society, selling their labor to the ruling class, the property owners. The two camps, then, are forever at odds.

Marx maintains that this pattern of opposition—this class struggle—repeats itself throughout history via Hegel's dialectic process. He thinks the dialectic struggle in modern times is between those who own the means of production (the *bourgeoisie*, or capitalists) and those who do not (the *proletariat*). The bourgeoisie are few but own all the factories and other means of production (thesis); the proletariat are many but own nothing, serving only as workers in the capitalist system (antithesis). To increase their profits, the bourgeoisie hire more and more workers but pay them less and less, replacing workers with machines whenever possible. The workers' wages decline, more become unemployed, and their exploitation by the capitalists continues. As their situation worsens, Marx observes, they have an increased sense of *alienation*: they are no longer valued as persons, for they have become mere cogs in the capitalist machinery; and they can no longer take pride in their work, for it has been downgraded into mindless assembly-line motions. But ultimately the success of the bourgeoisie proves to be their undoing. They produce, as Marx says, their own gravediggers. They unwittingly create a large, poor, angry proletarian class that has had enough of capitalism and the woes that come with it. A proletarian revolution sweeps the old order away and eventually ushers in a classless society (synthesis) in which the means of production belong to everyone, and wealth is shared equally among equals.

A frequent criticism of socialism is that a distribution of goods according to needs and abilities would require coercion by the state. For socialism to work, people must be forced to do the jobs that match their skills, not the jobs they prefer. And they must be compelled to accept the benefits (monetary or otherwise) that match their needs, not the benefits they most desire.

Critics also accuse socialist systems of providing no incentive for people to excel at their jobs. Under socialism, people are rewarded according to their needs, not by how well or how hard they work. So what inducement is there to be more ambitious or efficient?

"History repeats itself, first as tragedy, second as farce."

—Karl Marx

5. Do ideas affect history? Marx says no. But his socialist ideas seem to have affected history profoundly. Does this fact disprove Marx's claim?

"From each according to his abilities, to each according to his needs."

—Karl Marx

Figure 13.4 Early twentieth-century German socialist propaganda. The caption reads: "The workers have nothing to lose but their chains. They have a world to win. Proletarians of all lands unite."

Marx conveyed his views over many years and in several writings, the best-known being the *Manifesto of the Communist Party* (1848), which he coauthored with his colleague Friedrich Engels:

Marx: *The Communist Manifesto*

A specter is haunting Europe—the specter of communism. All the powers of old Europe have entered into a holy alliance to exorcise this specter: Pope and Czar, Metternich and Guizot, French radicals and German police spies.

Where is the party in opposition that has not been decried as communistic by its opponents in power? Where the opposition that has not hurled back the branding reproach of communism against the more advanced opposition parties, as well as against its reactionary adversaries?

Two things result from this fact:

I. Communism is already acknowledged by all European powers to be itself a power.

II. It is high time that communists should openly, in the face of the whole world, publish their views, their aims, their tendencies, and meet this nursery tale of the specter of communism with a Manifesto of the party itself.

To this end, communists of various nationalities have assembled in London and sketched the following Manifesto, to be published in the English, French, German, Italian, Flemish, and Danish languages.

The history of all hitherto existing society is the history of class struggles.

Free man and slave, patrician and plebeian, lord and serf, guild master and journeyman, in a word, oppressor and oppressed, stood in constant opposition to one another, carried on an uninterrupted, now hidden, now open fight, a fight that each time ended either in a revolutionary reconstitution of society at large or in the common ruin of the contending classes.

In the earlier epochs of history we find almost everywhere a complicated arrangement of society into various orders, a manifold gradation of social rank. In ancient Rome we have patricians, knights, plebeians, slaves; in the Middle Ages, feudal lords, vassals, guild masters, journeymen, apprentices, serfs; in almost all of these classes, again, subordinate gradations.

The modern bourgeois [capitalist] society that has sprouted from the ruins of feudal society has not done away with class antagonisms. It has but established new classes, new conditions of oppression, new forms of struggle in place of the old ones.

Our epoch, the epoch of the bourgeoisie, possesses, however, this distinctive feature: it has simplified the class antagonisms. Society as a whole is more and more splitting up into two great hostile camps, into two great classes directly facing each other: bourgeoisie and proletariat. . . .

The bourgeoisie cannot exist without constantly revolutionizing the instruments of production, and thereby the relations of production, and with them the whole relations of society. Conservation of the old modes of production in unaltered form was, on the contrary, the first condition of existence for all earlier industrial classes. Constant revolutionizing of production, uninterrupted disturbance of all social conditions, everlasting uncertainty and agitation distinguish the bourgeois epoch from all earlier ones. All fixed, fast-frozen relations, with their train of ancient and venerable prejudices and opinions, are

"Religion is the impotence of the human mind to deal with occurrences it cannot understand."

—Karl Marx

6. Many countries have developed a large middle class that doesn't seem to fit into Marx's two-class scheme. Is this fact a counterexample to his theory?

swept away, all new-formed ones become antiquated before they can ossify. All that is solid melts into air, all that is holy is profaned, and man is at last compelled to face with sober senses his real conditions of life and his relations with his kind.

The need of a constantly expanding market for its products chases the bourgeoisie over the whole surface of the globe. It must nestle everywhere, settle everywhere, establish connections everywhere. . . .

The bourgeoisie, by the rapid improvement of all instruments of production, by the immensely facilitated means of communication, draws all, even the most barbarian, nations into civilization. The cheap prices of its commodities are the heavy artillery with which it batters down all Chinese walls, with which it forces the barbarians' intensely obstinate hatred of foreigners to capitulate. It compels all nations, on pain of extinction, to adopt the bourgeois mode of production: it compels them to introduce what it calls civilization into their midst, i.e., to become bourgeois themselves. In one word, it creates a world after its own image. . . .

But not only has the bourgeoisie forged the weapons that bring death to itself; it has also called into existence the men who are to wield those weapons—the modern working class—the proletarians.

In proportion as the bourgeoisie, i.e., capital, is developed, in the same proportion is the proletariat, the modern working class developed—a class of laborers, who live only so long as they find work, and who find work only so long as their labor increases capital. These laborers, who must sell themselves piecemeal, are a commodity, like every other article of commerce, and are consequently exposed to all the vicissitudes of competition, to all the fluctuations of the market.

Owing to the extensive use of machinery and to division of labor, the work of the proletarians has lost all individual character and, consequently, all charm for the workman. He becomes an appendage of the machine, and it is only the simplest, most monotonous,

> "Capital is dead labor, which, vampire-like, lives only by sucking living labor, and lives the more, the more labor it sucks."
> —Karl Marx

7. Marx lists the many technological and civic innovations brought about by capitalism, things that seem beneficial to society. Do they counterbalance the many bad things about capitalism that Marx details?

> "If anything is certain, it is that I myself am not a Marxist."
> —Karl Marx

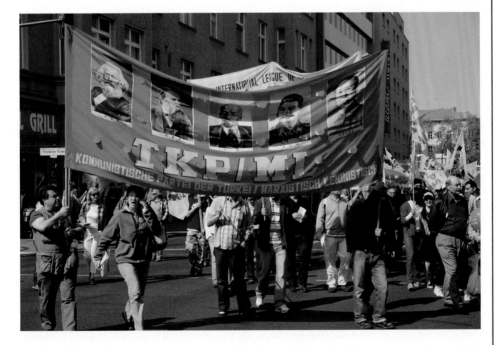

Figure 13.5 In Berlin, protesters and supporters of socialist parties participate in a march on Labor Day 2009.

Is the United States a Socialist Country?

To many Americans, socialism is a dirty word. President Obama had been accused of trying to turn the United States into a socialist country like those in Europe. To score points with the electorate, politicians label their opponents socialists. Some political theorists say that a little socialism won't hurt and might help, and a few declare that the debate is silly because the United States is already a socialist country. Is it?

It depends on your definition of socialism. Some people (including a few television commentators) say that a government is socialist if it runs social programs that otherwise could be left to the marketplace—programs like public education, prisons, aid to the poor, and Medicare. By this standard, the United States is indeed socialist. But the traditional definition is more like the one

Figure 13.6 A poster linking President Barack Obama with socialism.

given at the beginning of this section: socialism is the doctrine that the *means of production* (property, factories, businesses) should be owned or controlled by the people, either communally or through the state. The programs just mentioned are generally not considered means of production. Neither are such things as police and fire protection, national defense, and income redistribution. Welfare programs are examples not of socialism but of welfare liberalism. So even though the United States may have some socialist elements (such as partial ownership and control of the banking industry), it's not predominantly socialist—and calling it that would be an exaggeration.

Suppose the government owns and runs all technology companies, half the farms, and the entire steel industry. Would the United States then be properly called socialist? What would be the advantages or disadvantages of such a scheme?

Marx: The Communist Manifesto

and most easily acquired knack that is required of him. Hence the cost of production of a workman is restricted, almost entirely, to the means of subsistence that he requires for his maintenance and for the propagation of his race. But the price of a commodity, and therefore also of labor, is equal to its cost of production. In proportion, therefore, as the repulsiveness of the work increases, the wage decreases. Nay, more, in proportion as the use of machinery and division of labor increases, in the same proportion the burden of toil also increases, whether by prolongation of the working hours, by increase of the work exacted in a given time, or by increased speed of the machinery, etc.

Modern industry has converted the little workshop of the patriarchal master into the great factory of the industrial capitalist. Masses of laborers, crowded into the factory, are organized like soldiers. As privates of the industrial army they are placed under the command of a perfect hierarchy of officers and sergeants. Not only are they slaves of the bourgeois class, and of the bourgeois state; they are daily and hourly enslaved by the machine, by the overlooker, and, above all, by the individual bourgeois manufacturer himself. The more openly this despotism proclaims gain to be its end and aim, the more petty, the more hateful, and the more embittering it is. . . .

But with the development of industry the proletariat not only increases in number; it becomes concentrated in greater masses, its strength grows, and it feels that strength more. The various interests and conditions of life within the ranks of the proletariat are more and more equalized, in proportion as machinery obliterates all distinctions of labor and nearly everywhere reduces wages to the same low level. The growing competition among the bourgeois and the resulting commercial crises make the wages of the workers ever more fluctuating. The unceasing improvement of machinery, ever more rapidly developing, makes their livelihood more and more precarious; the collisions between individual workmen and individual bourgeois take more and more the character of collisions between two classes. Thereupon the workers begin to form combinations (trade unions) against the bourgeois; they club together in order to keep up the rate of wages; they found permanent associations in order to make provision beforehand for these occasional revolts. Here and there the contest breaks out into riots.

Now and then the workers are victorious, but only for a time. The real fruit of their battles lies not in the immediate result, but in the ever expanding union of the workers. This union is helped on by the improved means of communication that are created by modern industry and that place the workers of different localities in contact with one another. . . .

The essential condition for the existence, and for the sway of the bourgeois class, is the formation and augmentation of capital; the condition for capital is wage labor. Wage labor rests exclusively on competition between the laborers. The advance of industry, whose involuntary promoter is the bourgeoisie, replaces the isolation of the laborers, due to competition, by their revolutionary combination, due to association. The development of modern industry, therefore, cuts from under its feet the very foundation on which the bourgeoisie produces and appropriates products. What the bourgeoisie, therefore, produces, above all, is its own gravediggers. Its fall and the victory of the proletariat are equally inevitable. . . .

All property relations in the past have continually been subject to historical change consequent upon the change in historical conditions.

The French Revolution, for example, abolished feudal property in favor of bourgeois property.

The distinguishing feature of communism is not the abolition of property generally, but the abolition of bourgeoisie property. But modern bourgeois private property is the final and most complete expression of the system of producing and appropriating products that is based on antagonisms, on the exploitation of the many by the few.

In this sense the theory of the communists may be summed up in the single sentence: Abolition of private property.

We communists have been reproached with the desire of abolishing the right of personally acquired property as the fruit of a man's own labor, which property is alleged to be the groundwork of all personal freedom, activity, and dependence.

Hard-won, serf-acquired, serf-earned property! Do you mean the property of the petty artisan and of the small peasant, a form of property that preceded the bourgeois form? There is no need to abolish that; the development of industry has to a great extent already destroyed it and is still destroying it daily. . . .

8. In capitalist societies, Marx predicts worker alienation, oppression and exploitation of workers, and general misery among those who do not control the means of production. Many societies today, including the United States, are capitalist, but they do not seem to be following Marx's pattern. Does this show that Marx's views are wrong?

"The state is nothing but an instrument of oppression of one class by another—no less so in a democratic republic than in a monarchy."

—Friedrich Engels

9. Many Western countries have been strongly committed to private property for decades, yet no proletarian revolution has erupted or is likely to erupt. Why is this? Does it show that Marx's socialism is mistaken?

"All history has been a history of class struggles between dominated classes at various stages of social development."
—Friedrich Engels

The charges against communism made from a religious, a philosophical, and, generally, from an ideological standpoint are not deserving of serious examination.

Does it require deep intuition to comprehend that man's ideas, views, and conceptions, in one word, man's consciousness, change with every change in the conditions of his material existence, in his social relations, and in his social life?

What else does the history of ideas prove than that intellectual production changes its character in proportion as material production is changed? The ruling ideas of each age have ever been the ideas of its ruling class.

When people speak of ideas that revolutionize society they do but express the fact that within the old society the elements of a new one have been created, and that the dissolution of the old ideas keeps even pace with the dissolution of the old conditions of existence. . . .

We have seen above that the first step in the revolution by the working class is to raise the proletariat to the position of ruling class, to win the battle of democracy.

The proletariat will use its political supremacy to wrest, by degrees, all capital from the bourgeoisie, to centralize all instruments of production in the hands of the state, i.e., of the proletariat organized as the ruling class, and to increase the total of productive forces as rapidly as possible.

Of course, in the beginning this cannot be effected except by means of despotic inroads on the rights of property and on the conditions of bourgeois production; by means of measures, therefore, which appear economically insufficient and untenable, but which, in the course of the movement, outstrip themselves, necessitate further inroads upon the old social order, and are unavoidable as a means of entirely revolutionizing the mode of production.

These measures will of course be different in different countries.

Nevertheless, in the most advanced countries the following will be pretty generally applicable:

1. Abolition of property in land and application of all rents of land to public purposes.
2. A heavy progressive or graduated income tax.
3. Abolition of all right of inheritance.
4. Confiscation of the property of all emigrants and rebels.
5. Centralization of credit in the hands of the state, by means of a national bank with state capital and an exclusive monopoly.
6. Centralization of the means of communication and transport in the hands of the state.
7. Extension of factories and instruments of production owned by the state; the bringing into cultivation of wastelands, and the improvement of the soil generally in accordance with a common plan.
8. Equal liability of all labor. Establishment of industrial armies, especially for agriculture.
9. Combination of agriculture with manufacturing industries; gradual abolition of the distinction between town and country, by a more equable distribution of the population over the country.
10. Free education for all children in public schools. Abolition of children's factory labor in its present form. Combination of education with industrial production, etc.

When, in the course of development, class distinctions have disappeared and all production has been concentrated in the hands of a vast association of the whole nation, the public power will lose its political character. Political power, properly so called, is merely the organized power of one class for oppressing another. If the proletariat during its contest with the bourgeoisie is compelled, by the force of circumstances, to organize itself as a class, if by means of a revolution, it makes itself the ruling class and, as such, sweeps away by force the old conditions of production, then it will, along with these conditions, have swept away the conditions for the existence of class antagonisms and of classes generally, and will thereby have abolished its own supremacy as a class.

In place of the old bourgeois society, with its classes and class antagonisms, we shall have an association in which the free development of each is the condition for the free development of all. . . .

The communists disdain to conceal their views and aims. They openly declare that their ends can be attained only by the forcible overthrow of all existing social conditions. Let the ruling classes tremble at a communistic revolution. The proletarians have nothing to lose but their chains. They have a world to win.

WORKING MEN OF ALL COUNTRIES UNITE![2]

Writing and Reasoning	**CHAPTER 13**

1. Critique the doctrine of absolute idealism. Do you think it plausible? Why or why not?

2. A classical liberal might say to a Marxist that liberty and rights are the most important values in a society, and Marxist societies have few if any liberties. The Marxist might reply that liberties and rights don't mean much if people are too poor and oppressed to enjoy them. Which view seems more reasonable to you? Which society would you be willing to live in—classical liberal or Marxist? Why?

3. Suppose the state compelled you to work in a factory for the rest of your life, and it arranged for your salary to be based solely on what the state thinks you need. Would these actions be a violation of your autonomy? If they would improve the general welfare, would they be morally justified?

4. Suppose all resources in the United States were distributed according to Marx's dictum: from each according to his ability, to each according to his need. What would such a society look like? Would it be better than the system that exists now? Why or why not?

5. Does alienation as described by Marx exist today in modern capitalist societies? Explain.

REVIEW NOTES

13.1 HEGEL

- Hegel became the most important thinker of nineteenth-century Germany and the biggest philosophical influence on Karl Marx and his collaborator Friedrich Engels.

- The core of Hegel's system is his absolute idealism, the doctrine that the universe is an objective reality consisting of ideas in the universal mind, what Hegel calls Spirit or Absolute.

- Hegel sees the history of the world as the continual development of Spirit toward greater self-consciousness and rationality, greater cognizance of itself as a free, self-determining being.

13.2 MARX

- Socialism is the political and economic doctrine that the means of production (property, factories, businesses) should be owned or controlled by the people, either communally or through the state.

- The guiding principle of the socialist view is equality: the wealth of society should be shared by all. The ideal distribution of goods usually follows Marx's formula: "From each according to his ability, to each according to his needs."

- Marx thinks that what drives philosophy, history, society, law, government, and morality is economics. It is the dominant system of economics in every age that determines how society is structured and how history will go.

- Marx says that class struggle repeats itself throughout history via Hegel's dialectic process. He thinks the dialectic struggle in modern times is between those who own the means of production (the *bourgeoisie*, or capitalists) and those who do not (the *proletariat*).

- Marx holds that the bourgeoisie produce their own gravediggers. They unwittingly create a large, poor, angry proletarian class that has had enough of capitalism and the woes that come with it. A proletarian revolution sweeps the old order away and eventually ushers in a classless society.

KEY TERMS

absolute idealism	communism	panentheism	socialism
capitalism			

Notes

1. G. W. F. Hegel, *Lectures on the History of Philosophy*, I. 33, trans. Elizabeth S. Haldane and Frances H. Simpson (San Bernadino, CA: Ulan Press, 2012).
2. Karl Marx and Friedrich Engels, *Manifesto of the Communist Party*, trans. Samuel Moore, 1888.

For Further Reading

Steven M. Cahn, ed., *Political Philosophy: The Essentials* (New York: Oxford University Press, 2011).

Frederick Copleston, *A History of Philosophy, Volume VII*: *Modern Philosophy from the Post-Kantian Idealists to Marx, Kierkegaard, and Nietzsche* (New York: Doubleday, 1994).

C. Stephen Evans, *Kierkegaard*: *An Introduction* (Cambridge: Cambridge University Press, 2009).

Michael Allen Fox, *The Accessible Hegel* (Amherst, NY: Humanity Books, 2005).

Patrick Gardiner, *Kierkegaard*: *A Very Short Introduction* (Oxford: Oxford University Press, 1988).

Ted Honderich, ed., *The Oxford Companion to Philosophy*, 2nd edition (Oxford: Oxford University Press, 2005).

Walter Kaufmann, trans., *The Portable Nietzsche* (New York: Penguin Books, 1977).

Anthony Kenny, *The Rise of Modern Philosophy*: *A New History of Western Philosophy*, vol. 3 (Oxford: Oxford University Press, 2006).

Anthony Kenny, *The Rise of Modern Philosophy*: *A New History of Western Philosophy*, vol. 4 (Oxford: Oxford University Press, 2007).

Bertrand Russell, *A History of Western Philosophy* (New York: Simon and Schuster, 1945).

Richard Schacht, *Making Sense of Nietzsche*: *Reflections Timely and Untimely* (Chicago: University of Illinois Press, 1995).

John Simmons, *Political Philosophy* (New York: Oxford University Press, 2008).

Peter Singer, *Hegel*: *A Very Short Introduction* (Oxford: Oxford University Press, 1983).

Robert C. Solomon and Kathleen M. Higgins, *What Nietzsche Really Said* (New York: Schocken, 2001).

Michael Tanner, *Nietzsche*: *A Very Short Introduction* (Oxford: Oxford University Press, 2001).

Jonathan Wolff, *An Introduction to Political Philosophy* (Oxford: Oxford University Press, 2006).

Online Resources

Stanford Encyclopedia of Philosophy, "Karl Marx," "Georg Wilhelm Friedrich Hegel," "Socialism," https://plato.stanford.edu

BBC, History, "Karl Marx (1818–1883)," http://www.bbc.co.uk/history/historic_figures/marx_karl.shtml

Encyclopedia Britannica, "Marxism," https://www.britannica.com/topic/Marxism

Internet Encyclopedia of Philosophy, "Socialism" https://www.iep.utm.edu/socialis

Biography.com, "Karl Marx," https://www.biography.com/scholar/karl-marx

History of Philosophy (without Any Gaps) Podcast, https://historyofphilosophy.net

CHAPTER 14

Existentialism

CHAPTER OBJECTIVES

14.1 THE EXISTENTIAL TONE

- Define *existentialism*.
- Know the five themes that existentialists explore in their work.

14.2 KIERKEGAARD

- Define *fideism*, and explain why Kierkegaard's view is thought to be an example of it.
- Understand how, according to Kierkegaard, society is crushing individuality.
- State Kierkegaard's idea about the paradox of Christian belief, and explain his view that an absurd belief is necessary for a leap of faith.
- State and evaluate Kierkegaard's claim that subjective truth can become objective truth.

14.3 NIETZSCHE

- Understand Nietzsche's doctrine of the will to power, and explain how this phenomenon is supposed to manifest itself in philosophy and science.
- Explain what Nietzsche means by his assertion that "God is dead."
- Critically evaluate three myths about Nietzsche.
- Summarize Nietzsche's distinction between master morality and slave morality.
- Understand why Nietzsche maintains that slave morality is manifested in Christianity and belief in God.

14.4 HEIDEGGER

- Define *phenomenology*.
- Summarize key events in Heidegger's life and explain why he has been both admired and reviled by other philosophers.
- Understand Heidegger's notion of being.
- Explain the three fundamental aspects of *Dasein* discussed by Heidegger.

14.5 SARTRE

- Explain Sartre's notion of radical freedom and why he thinks we are entirely responsible for who we are.
- Explain Sartre's concept of "existence precedes essence."
- Understand why Sartre believes that our radical freedom is both a blessing and a curse.
- Know Sartre's views on God and human nature.
- Explain why Sartre thinks human life is characterized by anguish and despair.

14.6 CAMUS

- Define existential *absurdity*.
- Understand why Camus thinks human existence is absurd.
- Recount the myth of Sisyphus, and explain what it symbolizes for Camus.
- Explain what Camus means by "there is no fate that cannot be surmounted by scorn."

14.1 THE EXISTENTIAL TONE

Philosophers regard Søren Kierkegaard (1813–1855) as the father of modern existentialism, and they judge Jean-Paul Sartre (1905–1980) to be the last great existentialist thinker. In this span of over a hundred years, existentialism spread throughout Europe, reaching the height of its appeal among intellectuals and the general public after World War II. It became not just a viewpoint, but also a movement whose attitudes and style spilled over into art, literature, psychology, and other fields. Today the existentialist spirit is still alive, with both philosophers and nonphilosophers identifying their outlooks on life as existentialist.

In one sense, however, existentialism is not new. Like Socrates, it has little or no interest in metaphysical theories, scientific facts, or abstract truths. It focuses instead, as he did, on answering the ultimate question—*how should a person live*? That is, how can an individual live a meaningful life? Kierkegaard says the answers can be found only in the realm of the personal and subjective—only in the "existing individual." From this reference to unique human existence comes the term *existentialism*.

Existentialism is an inexact label for different philosophies that share themes about the uniqueness of each human being, about the central importance of choice, and about the individual's response to an indifferent, absurd universe. The philosophers who embrace these ideas may differ among themselves on other important issues, on their approach to philosophical questions, or even on whether the term *existentialist* applies to them. But in their own way, they explore many of these basic concerns and try to show how they relate to flesh-and-blood individuals. From the

"Life can only be understood backwards; but it must be lived forwards."
—Søren Kierkegaard

existentialism A term applied to different philosophies that share themes about the uniqueness of each human being, the central importance of choice, and the individual's response to an indifferent, absurd universe.

Christian Kierkegaard we can trace the existentialist thread to the atheistic philosophers Friedrich Nietzsche, Martin Heidegger, Jean-Paul Sartre, and Simone de Beauvoir; to the theologians Karl Barth and Paul Tillich; and to the literary figures Fyodor Dostoevsky and Albert Camus.

The main existentialist themes are as follows:

- **Individualism and subjectivity.** Existentialism is centered on the individual, not on abstract principles or universal generalizations. It is the solitary, unique person who must come to terms with the world, who must choose how to live and how to die, who must take responsibility for the actions that define his or her existence. Rules and generalities and one-size-fits-all morality are of little help.

- **Freedom and responsibility.** The heart of existentialism is its emphasis on the freedom of the individual—freedom *from* deterministic forces and freedom *to* make choices that shape who he or she is. But with freedom comes the momentous responsibility to choose and to accept what follows. However we choose, we have no one to blame or thank but ourselves.

- **Existence and essence.** The traditional view is that we have a human nature, an essence given to us by God or nature, and this essence defines us, explains us. In other words, our essence is present when we begin to exist, and it is not up to us. But existentialists demur. They insist that—in Sartre's famous phrase—"existence precedes essence." We first exist, and then *we* make our own essence. We can decide what and who we are by the choices we make in life. For better or worse, we create ourselves. We are born with a blank slate, and we are responsible for filling it in.

- **Anguish and absurdity.** The existential predicament—the conditions just described—engenders existential emotions when the implications of the predicament are recognized. We feel anguish (*angst*) or a sense of absurdity when we realize that we are totally free to create ourselves, that we and we alone are responsible for the direction of our lives, or that life is meaningless unless we give it meaning through our choices.

- **Authenticity.** To be *authentic* is to realize that you are an individual whose essence is up to you and that you are responsible for choosing the kind of individual you want to be. To be authentic is to choose your own path. To be *inauthentic*—to act in "bad faith," as Sartre says—is to run from this responsibility, to accept whatever the world has already decided you should be. In inauthenticity, you believe you are stuck with the traits that nature or God gave you, that you simply cannot change. Or you lie to yourself, pretending that all your choices are free when in fact they are weighted down with determining factors from the past.

> "You are the music while the music lasts."
> —T. S. Eliot

14.2 KIERKEGAARD

The Danish philosopher and theologian Søren Aabye Kierkegaard (1813–1855) is the acknowledged father of modern existentialism and the champion of a radical form of **fideism**, the notion that religious belief is grounded in faith, not reason. He was an intellectual rebel who challenged the attitudes and values of his times and tried to jolt his contemporaries into soul-searching and truth-seeking. He relentlessly criticized the church for what he considered its insipid version of Christianity, and he rejected the system-building philosophy of Hegel that was in vogue at the time. Much of his writing is controversial, but few who have studied him would doubt the depth and breadth of his thinking. Unlike some philosophers, he is a fine writer; and like Socrates, he is preoccupied with the vital questions: How should I live? What should I believe? What is important?

He was born in Copenhagen into a family of pious Lutherans, the youngest of seven children, five of whom died before he reached twenty-one. His father, Michael, a successful businessman, was extremely devout and mysteriously weighed down by enormous gloom and guilt, both of which he transmitted to his children through his harsh and unyielding form of Christianity. Søren was haunted by this dark inheritance his whole life.

Figure 14.1 Søren Aabye Kierkegaard (1813–1855).

In 1830 he entered the University of Copenhagen, where he worked toward a degree in theology. He eventually developed a distaste for his chosen field of study, however, and lapsed into the life of a cultivated and dissolute man about town. He believed, as young adults sometimes do, that his existence was empty, devoid of a worldview or grand commitment that would give meaning to his life. But after his father died in 1838, his attitude changed. He devoted himself again to his studies and finally in 1840 earned his theology degree. Shortly afterward, he became engaged to Regine Olsen, the daughter of a local official, but quickly regretted the decision. For reasons that are not entirely clear, he called off the engagement. For the rest of his life, he dedicated himself to his writing, producing an amazing number of books and essays on an impressive range of subjects.

fideism The notion that religious belief is grounded in faith, not reason.

He penned many of his works under a variety of pseudonyms, sometimes making a point by letting the fictitious authors present different sides of an issue and even disagree with one another. Most of his more important works appeared in the 1840s: *Either/Or* (1843), *Fear and Trembling* (1843), *Philosophical Fragments* (1844), *The Concept of Anxiety* (1844), *Concluding Unscientific Postscript* (1846), and *The Sickness unto Death* (1849).

"Faith is the highest passion in a human being. Many in every generation may not come that far, but none comes further."
—Søren Kierkegaard

In October 1855, at age forty-two, he crumpled to the street, was struck with paralysis, and never recovered. He died in a hospital on November 11, 1855. Despite his scathing attacks on establishment Christianity, he was given a funeral service in Copenhagen Cathedral.

1. What is the nature of Kierkegaard's fideism? Would you be comfortable basing your belief in God entirely on such fideism? Why or why not?

A central concern of Kierkegaard's work is the nature and status of the *individual*, an "existing human being." Armed with his distinctive view of what genuine individuality amounts to, he launches one assault after another on the pretensions of society, on the ideal of objectivity (mainly in science and philosophy), on organized religion, and on the concepts of objective and subjective truth in religion.

Kierkegaard charges that society is crushing individuals, diluting their personal identity, and replacing them with people who have "forgotten what it means to *exist*," to live as authentic, passionate human beings. Here is philosopher Patrick Gardiner's description of what Kierkegaard has in mind:

Patrick Gardiner: *Kierkegaard: A Very Short Introduction*

Thus [Kierkegaard] considered that [his contemporaries] had succumbed to an impersonal and anonymous mode of consciousness which precluded spontaneous feeling and was devoid of a secure sense of self-identity. Everything tended to be seen in 'abstract' terms, as theoretical possibilities which could be contemplated and compared but to the concrete realization of which people were unwilling to commit themselves. If they attended to their own attitudes or emotions it was through a thick haze of pseudo-scientific expressions or cliché-ridden phrases which they had picked up from books or newspapers rather than in the direct light of their own inner experience. Living had become a matter of knowing rather than doing, accumulating information and learning things by rote as opposed to taking decisions that bore the stamp of individual passion or conviction. What this led to was the formation of an outlook in which everything was approached through the medium of set responses and automatic reactions; people knew what they were supposed to say, but they no longer attached any real significance to the words they used.[1]

And here is Kierkegaard's own denunciation of society's plague of conformity and groupthink:

Søren Kierkegaard: *Either/Or*

Let others complain that the age is wicked; my complaint is that it is wretched, for it lacks passion. Men's thoughts are thin and flimsy like lace, they are themselves pitiable like lace-makers. The thoughts of their hearts are too paltry to be sinful. For a worm it might be regarded as a sin to harbor such thoughts, but not for a being made in the image of God. Their lusts are dull and sluggish, their passions sleepy. They do their duty, these shopkeeping souls, but they clip the coin a trifle . . . ; they think that even if the Lord keeps ever so careful a set of books, they may still cheat Him a little. Out upon them! This is the reason my soul always turns back to the Old Testament and to Shakespeare. I feel that those who speak there are at least human beings: they hate, they love, they murder their enemies, and curse their descendants throughout all generations, they sin.[2]

In the crowd—the opposite of the individual—there is a danger of losing the person, Kierkegaard says:

Søren Kierkegaard: *The Point of View*

A crowd—not this crowd or that, the crowd now living or the crowd deceased, a crowd of humble people or of superior people, of rich or of poor, etc.—a crowd in its very concept is the untruth, by reason of the fact that it renders the individual completely impenitent and irresponsible, or at least weakens his sense of responsibility by reducing it to a fraction.[3]

Objective knowledge has its place, says Kierkegaard, but it cannot give someone the truth—the real and immediate truth of personal experience, where the individual uncovers the meaning of his or her life. Objective facts are just that—cold, abstract, impersonal, impartial truths that are relevant only within the realm of theoretical speculation and empirical generalities. Only subjective truth—the realities of concrete, lived experience—can show the individual what really matters in life and how that life can be lived. Kierkegaard asks:

2. Is Kierkegaard's "truth is subjectivity" view the same thing as subjective relativism? If people accepted this theory of truth, would it be possible for them to use it to support their belief in the existence of Zeus or Apollo? Satan?

Søren Kierkegaard: *Journal*

For what would it profit me if I found the so-called 'objective truth,' if I worked through all the systems of philosophy and were able to analyze them and expose their inconsistencies ... what would it profit me if I developed the correct interpretation of Christianity in which I resolved all the internal problems, if it had no deeper significance *for me and for my life* ... ?[4]

Kierkegaard thinks of himself as an authentic Christian, one whose own individuality and subjectivity has embraced (or tried to embrace) all the implications of his austere brand of Christianity. For him, being a genuine Christian means resisting the anemic values of conventional society and expressing personal faith through one's life, not through mere belief in a set of abstract principles or through the perfunctory performance of prescribed behavior. A real Christian is a radical, a person who lives life in opposition to socially acceptable conduct, as Christ did. For a real Christian, Christianity is intensely personal, an extreme commitment with no guarantees, an inner transforming experience that needs no justifying reasons, no phony assurances or blessings or endorsements from the church.

Figure 14.2 Statue of Kierkegaard in the garden of the Old Royal Library in Copenhagen.

"Man is something to be surpassed."

—Nietzsche

But to Kierkegaard, the organized Christianity of his day (what he contemptuously calls "Christendom") fails utterly to live up to biblical standards—as he says, "the Christianity of the New Testament no longer exists." Christendom does not oppose conventional society; instead it tries to identify itself with conventional society. It avoids giving offense or disquieting the casual Christian. It is worldly and hypocritical. It has watered down genuine Christianity by ignoring its implications for the individual Christian in everyday life.

Kierkegaard insists that attempts to make religion conform to reason—to prove it objectively, to offer evidence or arguments in its favor—are doomed to fail. First, from an objective standpoint, the belief in, say, the incarnation of Christ is absurd. No scientific or philosophical investigations could ever prove it. Second, even with the best of reasons supporting a religious belief, its truth is still only a matter of thin probabilities, dry uncertainties, or approximations. And humans cannot base their lives on probabilities. Kierkegaard gives us a paradox: Christian belief is absurd, but only such an absurd belief can be believed. Believing the absurd requires an extreme, passionate "leap of faith," and only an absurd belief—a belief contrary to all objective evidence—can provoke such passionate belief. What this intense kind of belief can yield, and what objectivity can never give, is a deeply fulfilling subjective certainty, a personally meaningful truth. Great absurdities (such as Christianity's central story) require great, passionate faith.

Kierkegaard maintains that *what is believed* has to do with objective truth, and *how it is believed* has to do with subjective truth. Subjective truth is an objectively uncertain belief "held fast in an appropriation process of the most passionate inwardness." And subjective truth is "the highest truth available for an existing person."[5] In fact, Kierkegaard says, if the *how* of faith is present (in the "most passionate inwardness"), then the *what* of objectivity will also be present. That is, subjective truth becomes objective truth:

3. Is it possible to prove the existence of God through reason and argument? Why or why not?

Søren Kierkegaard: *Concluding Unscientific Postscript*

At its maximum this inward *how* is the passion of infinity and the passion of the infinite is itself the truth. But since the passion of the infinite is exactly subjectivity, subjectivity is the truth.[6]

14.3 NIETZSCHE

Friedrich Wilhelm Nietzsche (1844–1900) lived in the nineteenth century, but his ideas echoed loudest throughout the twentieth, and they resound still, over a hundred years after his passing. Today he is both reviled and embraced, and he has outraged many—including exponents of Christianity, contemporary culture, traditional morality, democratic socialism, and Western philosophy. Among those who have claimed to be inspired by his words are Marxists, postmodernists, atheists, anarchists, feminists, reactionaries, vegetarians, and Nazis. Some have claimed him as one of their own, even though he has given them no explicit reason to (as in the case of the Nazis). The divergent perspectives on his work are due in part to his writing style, which is mostly brilliant but by turns opaque, poetic, aphoristic, vague, and ironic. But most debate is over the substance of his views, of which the most famous (or notorious) are his doctrine of the will to power, his notion of the mighty human being known as the *Übermensch* (Overman or Superman), and his claim that "God is dead."

Nietzsche was born in Prussian Saxony to pious Lutherans. His father, a Lutheran pastor, died insane in 1849, so the boy was raised in a household of women: his mother and grandmother, his sister, and two aunts. He studied classical philology at the Universities of Bonn and Leipzig, demonstrating such brilliance that at age twenty-four he was given a professorship at Basel

Figure 14.3 Friedrich Wilhelm Nietzsche (1844–1900).

University, even though he had not met the doctoral requirements. He was heavily influenced by Arthur Schopenhauer's famous book *The World as Will and Idea* and by Richard Wagner's musical dramas, especially *Tristan und Isolde*. This dual influence showed in Nietzsche's first book, *The Birth of Tragedy*, published in 1872, whose theme was the rise and fall of Greek tragedy, killed by the rationalism of Socrates.

From 1873 to 1876 Nietzsche produced *Untimely Meditations* (actually four essays under the single title). In 1879 he resigned his post at the university because of his failing health and spent the following decade writing and wandering about Italy and Switzerland, lonely and in great physical pain. Out of this period came, among others, *The Wanderer and His Shadow* (1880), *Daybreak* (1881), *The Gay Science* or *Joyful Wisdom* (1882), *Beyond Good and Evil* (1887), and *The Genealogy of Morals* (1887). *Thus Spake Zarathustra*, his well-known masterpiece, appeared in the years 1883 to 1885.

In 1889, on a street in Turin, Nietzsche collapsed after seeing a horse being whipped. He spent the remaining ten years of his life insane, dying in August 1900. By the time of his death, he was world renowned, and his writings were the subject of extensive scholarship and controversy.

A central concept of Nietzsche's is the **will to power**, the fundamental nature of existence as a drive to control and dominate. The will to power is not the real world behind appearances (as in Descartes), nor ideas in the universal mind (as in Hegel), nor the will to live, nor the conscious will of God or humans. It *is* life, striving to

4. Does Nietzsche think the "will to power" is a conscious being? How does it fit in his view of reality?

"Morality is herd instinct in the individual."
—Nietzsche

will to power The fundamental nature of existence as a drive to control and dominate.

DETAILS

Nietzsche: Myths and Rumors

In *What Nietzsche Really Said*, Robert C. Solomon and Kathleen M. Higgins debunk many of the fables and misreadings surrounding one of the most mythologized and misunderstood thinkers of the modern period. Here's a sampling:

1. **Nietzsche was crazy**. Not quite. "Nietzsche may have been 'crazy,' in the vernacular sense, in the last years of his life, but this does not mean that he was mentally ill before 1889."

2. **Nietzsche was a Nazi.** False. "[W]e can say with confidence, that Nietzsche was no Nazi and that he shared virtually none of the Nazis' vicious ideas about the 'Thousand Year Reich' and the superiority of the German race."

3. **Nietzsche hated Jews**. False. "Nietzsche was no anti-Semite. . . . Nietzsche is sharply critical not only of Judaism but of the entire sweep of Western history that followed. For Jews themselves, Nietzsche shows no malice but a strange fascination."

4. **Nietzsche was a drunk, and he took drugs**. "Nietzsche spent most of his adult life sick and in pain. . . . Accordingly, he kept something of a pharmacy on hand, including some powerful painkillers and sedatives to allow him a few pain-free hours of sleep. . . . But Nietzsche, unlike some of his French contemporaries (notably Baudelaire), had no use for recreational drugs, and he generally avoided alcohol."

Suppose someone argues like this: "Nietzsche's view of God is bunk; after all, he was crazy." Is this a valid argument? Why or why not?

Robert C. Solomon and Kathleen M. Higgins, *What Nietzsche Really Said* (New York: Schocken Books, 2000).

overcome, to rule, to break out. All human struggles and striving are manifestations of the will to power. As Nietzsche's Zarathustra says:

Friedrich Nietzsche: *Thus Spake Zarathustra*

Where I found the living, there I found will to power; and even in the will of those who serve I found the will to be master. . . . And where men make sacrifices and serve and cast amorous glances, there too is the will to be master. Along stealthy paths the weaker steals into the castle and into the very heart of the more powerful—and there steals power.

And life itself confided this secret to me: "Behold," it said, "I am *that which must always overcome itself*. Indeed, you call it a will to procreate or a drive to an end, to something higher, farther, more manifold: but all this is one, and one secret.

"Rather would I perish than forswear this; and verily, where there is perishing and a falling of leaves, behold, there life sacrifices itself—for power. . . .

"Whatever I create and however much I love it—soon I must oppose it and my love; thus my will wills it. And you too, lover of knowledge, are only a path and footprint of my will; verily, my will to power walks also on the heels of your will to truth."[7]

To Nietzsche, the will to power is evident in humankind's search for knowledge, especially in science, philosophy, and religion. "Knowledge," he says, "is an instrument of power." The will to know arises from the will to power—from the desire to master and control a particular domain of reality. Reality is in flux, a kaleidoscope of sense data and concepts, and on this chaos we try to impose order, theory, and pattern so we can turn reality to our advantage. We do not seek truth for truth's sake. There is only the will to power that impels us to try to make sense of the muddle.

A belief, says Nietzsche, may be necessary for the survival of humankind, but it has nothing to do with the truth:

> "God is dead! God remains dead! And we have killed him."
>
> —Nietzsche

Friedrich Nietzsche: *Beyond Good and Evil*

The falseness of a judgment is for us not necessarily an objection to a judgment; in this respect our new language may sound strangest. The question is to what extent it is life-promoting, life-preserving, species-preserving, perhaps even species-cultivating. And we are fundamentally inclined to claim that the falsest judgments (which include the synthetic judgments *a priori*) are the most indispensible for us; that without accepting the fictions of logic, without measuring reality against the purely invented world of the unconditional and self-identical, without a constant falsification of the world by means of numbers, man could not live—that renouncing false judgments would mean renouncing life and a denial of life.[8]

Even philosophers, he says, do not pursue the truth; they strive to satisfy their own inner needs by creating a world in their own image. They use reasons after the fact to defend their cognitive creations. Their real, hidden agenda is the satisfaction of their irresistible urge to "truth." Philosophy, Nietzsche says, is this "tyrannical drive itself, the most spiritual will to power, to the 'creation of the world.'"[9]

We can also see the pulse of the will to power in morality, says Nietzsche. For him, there are two sorts of morality: *master morality* and *slave morality*. Master morality is the morality of the powerful, the superior, the proud, the aristocrats, the rich, the conquerors. They are the proud, independent, select few. In master morality, the masters define themselves as the *good*. So *good* means powerful, aristocratic,

5. For Nietzsche, what is the difference between master morality and slave morality? Why does he think Christianity is an example of slave morality? Do you agree with him?

PORTRAIT

Schopenhauer

Arthur Schopenhauer (1788–1860) ranks among the great Continental philosophers who built elaborate systems of thought and developed ideas that influence generations of readers and writers. He was a major influence on Nietzsche, providing him with a new perspective on the world and introducing him to the fundamental notion of will. He was born in Danzig to wealthy, cosmopolitan parents—a successful merchant father with Enlightenment views and varied cultural interests, and an author mother who was, for a time, more famous than her son. Unlike most other thinkers of his day, he was from a young age exposed to a variety of cultures and ideas. He was educated in France, Britain, and Germany; was fluent in several modern and classical languages; and studied not only philosophy but also science, Hinduism, and Buddhism.

Figure 14.4 Arthur Schopenhauer (1788–1860).

On several counts, Schopenhauer was a maverick and an eccentric. Contrary to the great rationalist philosophers preceding him, he thinks the will more fundamental than reason. Against their belief in the possibility of achieving some ultimate good in this life or the next, he posits a universe of suffering and illusion, a troubled reality from which the only true escape is extinction. He is renowned for his pessimism, which seems all the darker when contrasted with the more affirmative thinkers in the Western tradition. Putting no stock in the West's strong Christian ethic, he instead looks to the East to nontheistic Buddhism and to asceticism (although in practice he was hardly ascetic).

Some famous philosophers (David Hume and Baruch Spinoza, for example) are admired for their social virtues and goodness of character. Not so Schopenhauer. On one hand, he was obviously a brilliant intellectual and gifted writer, but he was also a conceited, dour man given to selfishness, pettiness, and quarrels. Once he was irritated by an elderly woman's chatting outside his apartment door, so he hurled her down the stairs. She sustained permanent injuries, for which a court ordered Schopenhauer to pay her an allowance for the rest of her life. When she died years later, he wrote on her death certificate in Latin, "The old woman is dead, the burden departs."

noble—the characteristics of the superior people of the "first rank." For the masters, *bad* refers to those who are none of these things: the lowly, the vile, the common, the pathetic, the slaves. The bad people are unworthy, and the good masters can use them or abuse them as they see fit.

Slave morality, on the other hand, is concerned not with good and bad but with good and evil. For the slave, the masters are dangerous monsters; they are *evil*. The slaves define themselves as the *good*; the good are the weak, meek, powerless, and downtrodden. Good qualities are those that advance the interests of the good ones, the slaves—qualities such as love, kindness, and sympathy. From such slave values the modern world has derived the ideals of equality, human dignity, equal rights, socialism, and democracy.

But despite their revered status, Nietzsche says, these are still slave values, which amount to *herd* morality, the morality of weakness, inferior existence, and degradation. And in slave morality, he thinks he clearly sees Judeo-Christian roots. Didn't Jesus reserve his blessings for the poor, humble, meek, and weak? Christian morality is slave morality. And this morality of weakness and otherworldliness, says Nietzsche, looks at this life and sees only pessimism and hopelessness.

Nietzsche holds out the hope that herd morality can be transcended by a rising champion of a much greater morality, a higher form of human life: the Overman (or Superman). The Overman is the superior man of the future. Zarathustra, the prophet of the Overman, declares:

> "There is something infantile in the presumption that somebody else has a responsibility to give your life meaning and point . . . The truly adult view, by contrast, is that our life is as meaningful, as full and as wonderful as we choose to make it."
> —Richard Dawkins

Friedrich Nietzsche: *Thus Spake Zarathustra*

I teach you the overman. Man is something that shall be overcome. . . . Behold, I teach you the overman. The overman is the meaning of the earth. Let your will say: the overman *shall be* the meaning of the earth! I beseech you, my brothers, *remain faithful to the earth*, and do not believe those who speak of otherworldly hopes![10]

Zarathustra says that someday man will be surpassed by the Overman—the future of mortal human life. In the meantime, look to *this* world, this earthly, material existence, for answers, and do not be deceived by those who would have you put your faith in the supernatural or otherworldly. The Overman himself will remain faithful to the Earth, this world. He will be his own master and the giver of his own rules, his own creator of his own higher morality.

Nietzsche maintains that slaves are weak and fearful—and slave morality helps keep them that way—largely because of religion. To believe in God, he says, is to accept the morality of the herd (and to assume the role of a sheep), to live not for this world but for a hereafter, to see humans as sinful and inadequate, and to view this life with pessimism and hopelessness. Thus for Nietzsche, the death of God would be good news—and he believes this great event has already occurred! He proclaims that "God is dead" in the sense that belief in the Christian God is now weaker and less common than ever before. Science, technology, secularism, and worldly pursuits now reign, and these have put a stake in God's heart. But humankind has not yet fully grasped this epic event; the news, however, is slowly sinking in. Nietzsche says, "The greatest recent event—that 'God is dead,' that the belief in the Christian God has ceased to be believable—is even now beginning to cast its first shadows over Europe." He expresses this idea (shocking in his day and less so in ours) in a well-known parable:

Friedrich Nietzsche: *The Gay Science*

The Madman. Have you not heard of that madman who lit a lantern in the bright morning hours, ran to the market place, and cried incessantly, "I seek God! I seek God!" As many of those who do not believe in God were standing around just then, he provoked much laughter. Why, did he get lost? said one. Did he lose his way like a child? said another. Or is he hiding? Is he afraid of us? Has he gone on a voyage? or emigrated? Thus they yelled and laughed. The madman jumped into their midst and pierced them with his glances.

"Whither is God?" he cried. "I shall tell you. *We have killed him*—you and I. All of us are his murderers. But how have we done this? How were we able to drink up the sea? Who gave us the sponge to wipe away the entire horizon? What did we do when we unchained this earth from its sun? Whither is it moving now? Whither are we moving now? Away from all suns? Are we not plunging continually? Backward, sideward, forward, in all directions? Is there any up or down left? Are we not straying as through an infinite nothing? Do we not feel the breath of empty space? Has it not become colder? Is not night and more night coming on all the while? Must not lanterns be lit in the morning? Do we not hear anything yet of the noise of the gravediggers who are burying God? Do we not smell anything yet of God's decomposition? Gods too decompose. God is dead. God remains dead. And we have killed him. How shall we, the murderers of all murderers, comfort ourselves? What was holiest and most powerful of all that the world has yet owned has bled to death under our knives. Who will wipe this blood off us? What water is there for us to clean ourselves? What festivals of atonement, what sacred games shall we have to invent? Is not the greatness of this deed too great for us? Must not we ourselves become gods simply to seem worthy of it? There has never been a greater deed; and whoever will be born after us—for the sake of this deed he will be part of a higher history than all history hitherto."

Here the madman fell silent and looked again at his listeners; and they too were silent and stared at him in astonishment. At last he threw his lantern on the ground, and it broke and went out. "I come too early," he said then; "my time has not come yet. This tremendous event is still on its way, still wandering—it has not yet reached the ears of man. Lightning and thunder require time, the light of the stars requires time, deeds require time even after they are done, before they can be seen and heard. This deed is still more distant from them than the most distant stars—*and yet they have done it themselves*."

It has been related further that on that same day the madman entered divers churches and there sang his *requiem aeternam deo*. Led out and called to account, he is said to have replied each time, "What are these churches now if they are not the tombs and sepulchers of God?"[11]

6. Who or what is the Overman? What are his main characteristics? Would you want beings like the Overman to be in control of the world? Why or why not?

7. What does the claim "God is dead" mean? Does it mean that God used to exist but now does not? Suppose you reject Nietzsche's theory about the death of God. How would you refute it?

14.4 HEIDEGGER

According to some observers, Martin Heidegger (1889–1976) was the greatest philosopher of the twentieth century; according to others, he was the most overrated and despicable. The former opinion derives partly from the perceived profundity of his ideas, his obvious genius, and his undeniable influence on modern philosophy, especially on existentialism. The latter opinion is likely a reaction to his murky, exasperating prose and his sympathy for the Nazi cause in Germany.

He was born in the Black Forest region of Germany and set out in his youth to become a priest. He attended high school in Freiburg, where his reading of some books by German philosophers got him thinking about philosophy as a subject of serious study. Not long after entering Freiburg University he gave up once and for all the idea of becoming a priest, and from then on philosophy was his main interest. He graduated in 1913, married in 1917, and became a lecturer at Freiburg in 1918. Later he was appointed professor of philosophy at Marburg University, lecturing on a wide range of subjects, from Aristotle and Plato to Kant and Leibniz. It wasn't until 1927 while at Marburg that he published his masterpiece, *Being and Time* (*Sein und Zeit*).

Eventually Heidegger was given the philosophy chair at Freiburg, and in 1933 he became the university's rector. At the same time, he joined the Nazi party and, while rector, cooperated with the Nazi government. In 1934 he resigned his position at Freiburg but not his party membership. He spent most of the rest of his life lecturing and writing.

Throughout his philosophical career, Heidegger was consumed with what he calls the most pressing and most important question a person could ask: the question of *being*, or existence. Heidegger asks, What is it for something to *be*? What is it for a stone or pen or human to exist? He doesn't mean by *being* what philosophers of the past have usually meant. The question of being is not about a particular being, an existing thing (such as a dog or a desk), or even about everything. It's not synonymous with the properties or essence or substance of something. And it's not about *the* Being, the God or *logos* or supreme entity that creates or sustains the world. Being concerns

Figure 14.5 Edvard Munch's conception of Friedrich Nietzsche, painted in 1906, appearing on a 1998 Guinea postage stamp.

Figure 14.6 Martin Heidegger (1889–1976).

what we might call "pure existence"—not *how* an object exists or *what* it is that exists but *existence itself.* Heidegger explains it like this:

Martin Heidegger: *The Basic Problems of Phenomenology*

Can something like being be imagined? If we try to do this, doesn't our head start to swim? Indeed, at first we are baffled and find ourselves clutching thin air. A being, yes, indeed— but being? . . . We think being . . . on innumerable occasions, whether aloud or silently, we say "This *is* such and such," "That other is *not* so," "That *was*," "It *will be.*" In each use of a verb we have already thought, and have always in some way understood, being. We understand immediately "Today is Saturday; the sun is up." We understand the "is" we use in speaking, although we do not comprehend it conceptually. The meaning of this "is" remains closed to us. . . . If philosophy is the science of being, then the first and last and basic problem of philosophy must be, What does being signify?[12]

"If I take death into my life, acknowledge it, and face it squarely, I will free myself from the anxiety of death and the pettiness of life—and only then will I be free to become myself."
—Martin Heidegger

phenomenology A way of painstakingly describing the data of consciousness without the distortions of preconceived ideas.

8. Can insights about subjective consciousness gleaned from phenomenology yield truths about metaphysics—that is, about free will, idealism and realism, causality, or substance?

Heidegger recognized that investigating being directly would be difficult, so he decided that to fathom being, he would need to examine one particular type of being—the self-conscious kind called human, the "entity for which being is an issue." His name for this kind is *Dasein*, German for "existence" or "being there." The idea is that by understanding the being of *Dasein*, we may be able to grasp the meaning of being itself.

But how can we study *Dasein*? Science, Heidegger believes, is no help here. He thinks another approach is far more useful—a method for plumbing the depths of *Dasein* that he learned from his teacher, the famous German philosopher Edmund Husserl (1859–1938). The technique is called **phenomenology**. It's a way of painstakingly describing the data of consciousness without the distortions of preconceived ideas.

Heidegger says that through his phenomenological study, he was able to learn a great deal about *Dasein*, and therefore about *being*. For one thing, *Dasein* is necessarily *in the world* (Heidegger's word for this aspect of being is, not surprisingly, *being-in-the-world*). *Dasein* is not something that exists independently of the universe. For Plato and Descartes there are two realms of existence, but for Heidegger there is only one reality or being. *Dasein's* being-in-the-world is expressed through its involvement in, or concern for, the world by actions—doing things, producing things, accomplishing things, exploring things, and the like.

Like Sartre and others, Heidegger denies that we come into the world with an assigned essence. We are instead what we make of ourselves. *Dasein* is the *happening* of its life in its journey from birth to death. *Dasein* is a becoming, not a soul or substance.

According to Heidegger, *Dasein's* being is characterized by three "existentials," or fundamental aspects. First there is *thrownness*: *Dasein* is thrown into the world without its consent. We had no say in the where and when of our birth and no

Figure 14.7 Freiburg University, where Heidegger was rector.

choice about our parents, our nationality, our race, our gender, our economic situation, or anything else. Yet we unavoidably care about the world into which we are thrown. Second, there is the element of *projection*, the notion that *Dasein* is forced to define itself by actions that shape its present and future. Each action undertaken now changes future possibilities and thus our lives, and actions help form who we are now. Third, we have the concept of *fallenness*, the erosion of *Dasein's* individuality by falling away from its true self and into the world. This falling happens when we dim our understanding of the world through idle, ambiguous, and vacuous thinking. The distinction here, Heidegger says, is between the *authentic* and *inauthentic* self. As the Heidegger scholar Thomas Flynn notes,

"Thinking begins only when we have come to know that reason, glorified for centuries, is the stiff-necked adversary of thought."

—Martin Heidegger

Thomas R. Flynn: *Existentialism: A Very Short Introduction*

One is no more born an individual (in the existentialist sense) than one is born authentic. To be truly authentic is to have realized one's individuality and vice versa. Both existential 'individuality' and 'authenticity' are achievement words. The person who avoids choice, who becomes a mere face in the crowd or cog in the bureaucratic machine, has failed to become authentic. So we can now describe the person who lives his or her life as 'they' command or expect as inauthentic.[13]

Figure 14.8 Jean-Paul Sartre (1905–1980).

"Everything has been figured out, except how to live."

—Jean-Paul Sartre

9. Sartre reasons from his lived experience to his theory of free will. Does his experience provide adequate support for his assertions?

14.5 SARTRE

Jean-Paul Sartre (1905–1980), the famed existentialist philosopher and novelist, was the chief proponent of existentialism after World War II. He was a student of Hegel, Husserl, and Heidegger and was steeped in psychology and phenomenology. But in many ways he surpassed all these men. His greatest work—*Being and Nothingness*—examined the central theme of his philosophy: freedom of the individual. Humans, he says, are profoundly free to create their own lives and thus are entirely responsible for defining the meaning and moral relevance of their existence.

From reflections on his own lived experience, Sartre arrives at what he takes to be some basic truths about human beings and their existential predicament. Unlike almost every philosopher before him, he not only believes that we are free but also insists that we are *radically* free. We may be influenced by the factors of nature and nurture (heredity and environment), but ultimately we are not determined by them. We are totally free—free to define ourselves by our own lights and capable of resisting the physical, psychological, and social forces that will thoroughly shape us if we let them. We are determined only if we allow ourselves to be determined.

Most people assume, Sartre says, that "essence precedes existence"—that before we come into existence, our fundamental characteristics (our essence) as humans are already set. They think that our psychological makeup, choices, desires, and ideas are, in a sense, locked in before we can say our first words. Our destiny is mapped out beforehand through the workings of a creator God or a universal human nature or some unalterable social structure. But according to Sartre, this kind of "essence precedes existence" thinking is tragically mistaken. It prevents us from seeing a future of open possibilities, saps our creativity, limits our freedom, and weakens our sense of our moral responsibility. The truth, says Sartre, is the opposite of the received view: "existence precedes essence"—we first come into being and then we define ourselves. He declares, "Man is nothing else but what he makes of himself."

And what is this radical freedom that we all possess? It is both a blessing and a curse. As Sartre says, "We are condemned to be free." The blessing is that as free persons, we have the power to set our own goals, live our own lives, and create ourselves as we go. The curse is that as free beings, we can look to no one but ourselves to decide how we should live. We carry this burden alone. We must bear the awesome moral responsibility of deciding how we should live, how we should treat others, and what values we should prescribe for the rest of the world through our actions. We can celebrate our capacity to create our essence and live by our own rules, but because

PORTRAIT

Sartre

Jean-Paul Sartre (1905–1980) was born in Paris and educated in both France and Germany (in Germany he studied under Husserl and Heidegger). His first novel, *Nausea*, appeared in 1938, and his other books and essays were published throughout the 1940s and 1950s. His most important philosophical work, *Being and Nothingness*, was published in 1956. In World War II he served in the French army and in 1940 was captured by the Germans and imprisoned. When he was set free a year later, he continued his writing. Throughout his career, his lifelong partner Simone de Beauvoir, a well-known feminist philosopher, helped shape and stimulate his work.

Figure 14.9 Jean-Paul Sartre and Simone de Beauvoir, 1964.

Sartre was political. He led and energized leftist thought, and he even tried to form his own political party. He was a Marxist, but his relationship with the Communist Party was complicated and contentious. He joined the party in the early 1950s but withdrew from it in 1956.

In 1964 he was awarded the Nobel Prize for literature, which he refused to accept. At his funeral, fifty thousand people came to honor him.

we are utterly alone in bearing this monumental burden, we are also condemned to experience great anguish, despair, and a sense of abandonment.

Here is how Sartre explained this existentialist freedom in a famous lecture:

Jean-Paul Sartre: *Existentialism*

What [existentialists] have in common is that they think that existence precedes essence, or, if you prefer, that subjectivity must be the starting point.

Just what does that mean? Let us consider some object that is manufactured, for example, a book or a paper-cutter: here is an object which has been made by an artisan whose inspiration came from a concept. He referred to the concept of what a paper-cutter is and likewise to a known method of production, which is part of the concept, something which is, by and large, a routine. Thus, the paper-cutter is at once an object produced in a certain way and, on the other hand, one having a specific use; and one cannot postulate a man who produces a paper-cutter but does not know what it is used for. Therefore, let us say that, for the paper-cutter, essence—that is, the ensemble of both the production routines and the properties which enable it to be both produced and defined—precedes existence.

> "Man is condemned to be free; because once thrown into the world, he is responsible for everything he does."
>
> —Jean-Paul Sartre

Jean-Paul Sartre:
Existentialism

"Hell is other people."
—Jean-Paul Sartre

10. Is Sartre exaggerating the extent to which people can define themselves when "existence precedes essence"?

Thus, the presence of the paper-cutter or book in front of me is determined. Therefore, we have here a technical view of the world whereby it can be said that production precedes existence.

When we conceive God as the Creator, He is generally thought of as a superior sort of artisan. Whatever doctrine we may be considering, whether one like that of Descartes or that of Leibnitz, we always grant that will more or less follows understanding or, at the very least, accompanies it, and that when God creates He knows exactly what He is creating. Thus, the concept of man in the mind of God is comparable to the concept of paper-cutter in the mind of the manufacturer, and, following certain techniques and a conception, God produces man, just as the artisan, following a definition and a technique, makes a paper-cutter. Thus, the individual man is the realization of a certain concept in the divine intelligence.

In the eighteenth century, the atheism of the *philosophes* discarded the idea of God, but not so much for the notion that essence precedes existence. To a certain extent, this idea is found everywhere; we find it in Diderot, in Voltaire, and even in Kant. Man has a human nature; this human nature, which is the concept of the human, is found in all men, which means that each man is a particular example of a universal concept, man. In Kant, the result of this universality is that the wild-man, the natural man, as well as the bourgeois, are circumscribed by the same definition and have the same basic qualities. Thus, here too the essence of man precedes the historical existence that we find in nature.

Atheistic existentialism, which I represent, is more coherent. It states that if God does not exist, there is at least one being in whom existence precedes essence, a being who exists before he can be defined by any concept, and that this being is man, or, as Heidegger says, human reality. What is meant here by saying that existence precedes essence? It means that, first of all, man exists, turns up, appears on the scene, and, only afterwards, defines himself. If man, as the existentialist conceives him, is indefinable, it is because at first he is nothing. Only afterward will he be something, and he himself will have made what he will be. Thus, there is no human nature, since there is no God to conceive it. Not only is man what he conceives himself to be, but he is also only what he wills himself to be after this thrust toward existence.

Man is nothing else but what he makes of himself. Such is the first principle of existentialism. It is also what is called subjectivity, the name we are labeled with when charges are brought against us. But what do we mean by this, if not that man has a greater dignity than a stone or table? For we mean that man first exists, that is, that man first of all is the being in the future. Man is at the start a plan which is aware of itself, rather than a patch of moss, a piece of garbage, or a cauliflower; nothing exists prior to this plan; there is nothing in heaven; man will be what he will have planned to be. Not what he will want to be. Because by the word "will" we generally mean a conscious decision, which is subsequent to what we have already made of ourselves. I may want to belong to a political party, write a book, get married; but all that is only a manifestation of an earlier, more spontaneous choice that is called "will." But if existence really does precede essence, man is responsible for what he is. Thus, existentialism's first move is to make every man aware of what he is and to make the full responsibility of his existence rest on him. And when we say that a man is responsible for himself, we do not only mean that he is responsible for his own individuality, but that he is responsible for all men. . . .

This helps us understand what the actual content is of such rather grandiloquent words as anguish, forlornness, despair. As you will see, it's all quite simple.

First, what is meant by anguish? The existentialists say at once that man is anguish. What that means is this: the man who involves himself and who realizes that he is not only the person he chooses to be, but also a law-maker who is, at the same time, choosing all mankind as well as himself, cannot help escape the feeling of his total and deep responsibility. Of course, there are many people who are not anxious; but we claim that they are hiding their anxiety, that they are fleeing from it. Certainly, many people believe that when they do something, they themselves are the only ones involved, and when someone says to them, "What if everyone acted that way?" they shrug their shoulders and answer, "Everyone doesn't act that way." But really, one should always ask himself, "What would happen if everybody looked at things that way?" There is no escaping this disturbing thought except by a kind of double-dealing. . . .

When we speak of forlornness, a term Heidegger was fond of, we mean only that God does not exist and that we have to face all the consequences of this. The existentialist is strongly opposed to a certain kind of secular ethics which would like to abolish God with the least possible expense. . . .

The existentialist, on the contrary, thinks it very distressing that God does not exist, because all possibility of finding values in a heaven of ideas disappears along with Him; there can be no longer an *a priori* Good, since there is no infinite and perfect consciousness to think it. Nowhere is it written that the Good exists, that we must be honest, that we must not lie; because the fact is we are on a plane where there are only men. Dostoevsky said, "If God didn't exist, everything would be possible." That is the very starting point of existentialism. Indeed, everything is permissible if God does not exist, and as a result man is forlorn, because neither within him nor without does he find anything to cling to. He can't start making excuses for himself.

If existence really does precede essence, there is no explaining things away by reference to a fixed and given human nature. In other words, there is no determinism, man is free, man is freedom. On the other hand, if God does not exist, we find no values or commands to turn to which legitimize our conduct. So, in the bright realm of values, we have no excuse behind us, no justification before us. We are alone, with no excuses.

That is the idea I shall try to convey when I say that man is condemned to be free. Condemned, because he did not create himself, yet, in other respects is free; because, once thrown into the world, he is responsible for everything he does. . . .

As for despair, the term has a very simple meaning. It means that we shall confine ourselves to reckoning only with what depends upon our will, or on the ensemble of probabilities which make our action possible. When we want something, we always have to reckon with probabilities. I may be counting on the arrival of a friend. The friend is coming by rail or street-car; this supposes that the train will arrive on schedule, or that the street-car will not jump the track. I am left in the realm of possibility; but possibilities are to be reckoned with only to the point where my action comports with the ensemble of these possibilities, and no further. The moment the possibilities I am considering are not rigorously involved by my action, I ought to disengage myself from them, because no God, no scheme, can adapt the world and its possibilities to my will. When Descartes said, "Conquer yourself rather than the world," he meant essentially the same thing.[14]

---

11. Are people wholly responsible for the kind of persons they become?

"I do not believe in God; his existence has been disproved by Science. But in the concentration camp, I learned to believe in men."

—Jean-Paul Sartre

12. Is it true that if God does not exist, there are no objective moral standards? What would utilitarians and others who prefer secular theories of morality have to say about this claim?

"As far as men go, it is not what they are that interests me, but what they can become."

—Jean-Paul Sartre

DETAILS

The Stir Caused by Sartre

In his lifetime, Jean-Paul Sartre achieved rock-star status. Today it may be hard to imagine a philosopher causing as much excitement throughout society as Sartre did in post–World War II France. Here's a description of the commotion Sartre caused when he gave a public lecture.

Figure 14.10 Parisians celebrating the end of the war, May 16, 1945.

[On October 29, 1945, shortly after the end of the war], at the Club Maintenant, Jean-Paul Sartre delivered a lecture, "Existentialism Is a Humanism." Here was the new Paris. This occasion . . . was packed. Men and women fainted, fought for chairs, smashing thirty of them, shouted and barracked. It coincided with the launching of Sartre's new review, *Les Temps Modernes*, in which he argued that literary culture, plus the haute couture of the fashion shops, were the only things France now had left—a symbol of Europe really—and he produced Existentialism to give people a bit of dignity and to preserve their individuality in the midst of degradation and absurdity. The response was overwhelming. As his consort, Simone de Beauvoir, put it, "We were astounded by the furor we caused." Existentialism was remarkably un-Gallic; hence perhaps, its attractiveness. Sartre was half-Alsacian (Albert Schweitzer was his cousin) and he was brought up in the house of his grandfather, Karl Schweitzer. His culture was as German as French. He was essentially a product of the Berlin school and especially Heidegger, from whom most of his ideas derived. . . . Thus Existentialism was a French cultural import, which Paris then reexported to Germany, its country of origin, in a sophisticated and vastly more attractive guise.

What aspects of Sartre's philosophy do you think appealed most to a mass audience? Why?

Paul Johnson, *Modern Times* (New York: Harper & Row, 1983), 575.

14.6 CAMUS

As we've seen, existentialism does not offer rules or principles to guide moral action. Instead, it provides a broad analysis of the individual's predicament in an uncaring universe and explains how to find meaning in such a forlorn world. Thus, a central existentialist theme is that our existence is **absurd**: there is an unbearable conflict between our need for meaning and purpose in life and the meaningless, indifferent universe. Our situation is impossible, and there is no higher power or governing principle to help us make sense of it. There is just us and the cold, silent cosmos, which cares nothing about our needs and desires. Moreover, our condition is terminal; our death is guaranteed. So we must

Figure 14.11 Albert Camus (1913–1960) on a Swedish postage stamp, 1990.

live an absurd existence, and at the last we get no answers, just an ending. The responsibility of self-definition rests heavily upon us. To many, the weight is terrifying. But those who accept their responsibility and freedom, who recognize that they alone are the ultimate designers of their lives, who are brave enough to make the best of an absurd existence—they are living *authentically*. Those who allow society, religion, history, mass culture, or their own fear to define them are living inauthentically.

No one has dealt with the issue of absurdity more forcefully and vividly than the French novelist and essayist Albert Camus (1913–1960). For his efforts, he was awarded the Nobel Prize for literature in 1957. In his writings, he drew from his experiences as a young Frenchman coming of age in war-ravaged North Africa; as a journalist, editor, and playwright in Algiers; and as a member of the French resistance against Nazi Germany. Absurdity is the dominant theme in his novels (notably *The Stranger* and *The Plague*) and in his essays (especially "The Myth of Sisyphus").

In "The Myth of Sisyphus," Camus dramatizes the absurdity of human existence by likening it to that of the mythical Sisyphus, who is forced by the gods to repeat a pointless task for all eternity: push a boulder to the top of a mountain only to have it tumble down to the bottom. Yet Sisyphus finds meaning in this seemingly meaningless burden by courageously embracing it and refusing to be overwhelmed by despair. The implication for humans is that we too can live meaningfully and bravely by accepting our freedom and shaping our own lives through free choices. To Camus, Sisyphus is a hero because he accepts his fate and valiantly pushes on anyway. Likewise, humans too can be heroic by carrying on with life even though it has no inherent meaning and will soon be over.

absurdity In existentialism, a sense of meaninglessness and irrationality in the world arising from the conflict between our need for meaning in life and the meaningless, indifferent universe.

"The struggle itself towards the heights is enough to fill a man's heart. One must imagine Sisyphus happy."

—Albert Camus

13. Is Camus right about the absurdity of existence? Is the universe meaningless?

Albert Camus: *The Myth of Sisyphus*

The gods had condemned Sisyphus to ceaselessly rolling a rock to the top of a mountain, whence the stone would fall back of its own weight. They had thought with some reason that there is no more dreadful punishment than futile and hopeless labor.

If one believes Homer, Sisyphus was the wisest and most prudent of mortals. According to another tradition, however, he was disposed to practice the profession of highwayman. I see no contradiction in this. Opinions differ as to the reasons why he became the futile laborer of the underworld. To begin with, he is accused of a certain levity in regard to the gods. He stole their secrets. Ægina, the daughter of Æsopus, was carried off by Jupiter. The father was shocked by that disappearance and complained to Sisyphus. He, who knew of the abduction, offered to tell about it on condition that Æsopus would give water to the citadel of Corinth. To the celestial thunderbolts he preferred the benediction of water. He was punished for this in the underworld. Homer tells us also that Sisyphus had put Death in chains. Pluto could not endure the sight of his deserted, silent empire. He dispatched the god of war, who liberated Death from the hands of her conqueror.

It is said also that Sisyphus, being near to death, rashly wanted to test his wife's love. He ordered her to cast his unburied body into the middle of the public square. Sisyphus woke up in the underworld. And there, annoyed by an obedience so contrary to human love, he obtained from Pluto permission to return to earth in order to chastise his wife. But when he had seen again the face of this world, enjoyed water and sun, warm stones and the sea, he no longer wanted to go back to the infernal darkness. Recalls, signs of anger, warnings were of no avail. Many years more he lived facing the curve of the gulf, the sparkling sea, and the smiles of earth. A decree of the gods was necessary. Mercury came and seized the impudent man by the collar and, snatching him from his joys, led him forcibly back to the underworld, where his rock was ready for him.

You have already grasped that Sisyphus is the absurd hero. He is, as much through his passions as through his torture. His scorn of the gods, his hatred of death, and his passion for life won him that unspeakable penalty in which the whole being is exerted toward accomplishing nothing. This is the price that must be paid for the passions of this earth. Nothing is told us about Sisyphus in the underworld. Myths are made for the imagination to breathe life into them. As for this myth, one sees merely the whole effort of a body straining to raise the huge stone, to roll it and push it up a slope a hundred times over; one sees the face screwed up, the cheek tight against the stone, the shoulder bracing the clay-covered mass, the foot wedging it, the fresh start with arms outstretched, the wholly human security of two earth-clotted hands. At the very end of his long effort measured by skyless space and time without depth, the purpose is achieved. Then Sisyphus watches the stone rush down in a few moments toward that lower world whence he will have to push it up again towards the summit. He goes back down to the plain.

It is during that return, that pause, that Sisyphus interests me. A face that toils so close to stones is already stone itself! I see that man going back down with a heavy yet measured step toward that torment of which he will never know the end. That hour like a breathing-space which returns as surely as his suffering, that is the hour of consciousness. At each of those moments when he leaves the heights and gradually sinks toward the lairs of the gods, he is superior to his fate. He is stronger than his rock.

> "The only way to deal with an unfree world is to become so absolutely free that your very existence is an act of rebellion."
>
> —Albert Camus

If this myth is tragic, that is because its hero is conscious. Where would his torture be, indeed, if at every step the hope of succeeding upheld him? The workman of today works every day in his life at the same tasks, and this fate is no less absurd. But it is tragic only at the rare moments when it becomes conscious. Sisyphus, proletarian of the gods, powerless and rebellious, knows the whole extent of his wretched condition: it is what he thinks of during his descent. The lucidity that was to constitute his torture at the same time crowns his victory. There is no fate that cannot be surmounted by scorn.

If the descent is thus sometimes performed in sorrow, it can also take place in joy. This word is not too much. Again I fancy Sisyphus returning toward his rock, and the sorrow was in the beginning. When the images of earth cling too tightly to memory, when the call of happiness becomes too insistent, it happens that melancholy rises in man's heart: this is the rock's victory, this is the rock itself. The boundless grief is too heavy to bear. These are our nights of Gethsemane. But crushing truths perish from being acknowledged. Thus, Œdipus at the outset obeys fate without knowing it. But from the moment he knows, his tragedy begins. Yet at the same moment, blind and desperate, he realizes that the only bond linking him to the world is the cool hand of a girl. Then a tremendous remark rings out: "Despite so many ordeals, my advanced age and the nobility of my soul make me conclude that all is well." Sophocles' Œdipus, like Dostoevsky's Kirilov, thus gives the recipe for the absurd victory. Ancient wisdom confirms modern heroism.

One does not discover the absurd without being tempted to write a manual of happiness. "What! by such narrow ways—?" There is but one world, however. Happiness and the absurd are two sons of the same earth. They are inseparable. It would be a mistake to say that happiness necessarily springs from the absurd discovery. It happens as well that the feeling of the absurd springs from happiness. "I conclude that all is well," says Œdipus, and that remark is sacred. It echoes in the wild and limited universe of man. It teaches that all is not, has not been, exhausted. It drives out of this world a god who had come into it with dissatisfaction and a preference for futile sufferings. It makes of fate a human matter, which must be settled among men.

All Sisyphus' silent joy is contained therein. His fate belongs to him. His rock is his thing. Likewise, the absurd man when he contemplates his torment, silences all the idols. In the universe suddenly restored to its silence, the myriad wondering little voices of the earth rise up. Unconscious, secret calls, invitations from all the faces, they are the necessary reverse and price of victory. There is no sun without shadow, and it is essential to know the night. The absurd man says yes and his effort will henceforth be unceasing. If there is a personal fate, there is no higher destiny, or at least there is but one which he concludes is inevitable and despicable. For the rest, he knows himself to be the master of his days. At that subtle moment when man glances backward over his life, Sisyphus returning toward his rock, in that slight pivoting he contemplates that series of unrelated actions which becomes his fate, created by him, combined under his memory's eye and soon sealed by his death. Thus, convinced of the wholly human origin of all that is human, a blind man eager to see who knows that the night has no end, he is still on the go. The rock is still rolling.

I leave Sisyphus at the foot of the mountain! One always finds one's burden again. But Sisyphus teaches the higher fidelity that negates the gods and raises rocks. He too concludes that all is well. This universe henceforth without a master seems to him neither sterile nor futile. Each atom of that stone, each mineral flake of that night-filled mountain, in itself forms a world. The struggle itself toward the heights is enough to fill a man's heart. One must imagine Sisyphus happy.[15]

"Man stands face to face with the irrational. He feels within him his longing for happiness and for reason. The absurd is born of this confrontation between the human need and the unreasonable silence of the world."

—Albert Camus

14. Does Camus' perspective leave open the possibility of moral relativism? If we have absolute freedom of choice, does that mean we can make any moral choice at all? Does Camus set any limits on moral decisions?

"The absurd is the essential concept and the first truth."

—Albert Camus

"Man is something to be surpassed."

—Nietzsche

THEN AND NOW

Existentialism in Literature and Film

Figure 14.12 Bill Murray in the movie *Groundhog Day*.

Existentialism lives. Among short stories and novels, you'll find existentialist themes in Camus' *The Stranger* (1942), *The Plague* (1947), and *The Fall* (1956); Sartre's *Nausea* (1938) and *No Exit* (1943); Franz Kafka's *The Trial* (1925); Fyodor Dostoyevsky's "Notes from the Underground" (1864); Samuel Beckett's *Waiting for Godot* (1953); and Kurt Vonnegut's *Slaughterhouse-Five* (1969).

In movies: David Fincher's *Fight Club* (1999); Milos Forman's *One Flew Over the Cuckoo's Nest* (1975); Stanley Kubrick's *Paths of Glory* (1957) and *A Clockwork Orange* (1971); Francis Ford Coppola's *Apocalypse Now* (1979); and Ridley Scott's *Blade Runner* (1982).

And here are a reviewer's synopses of three movies that appear on his list of the "Top 10 Existential Movies of All Time":

• ***American Beauty*** (1999) takes a very literal look at modern life and the human struggle to find contentment and meaning. The film follows the mid-life crisis of Lester

Burnham, a suburban husband and father who is emerging from the sleepy malaise that has come to define his life. It's through the lens of Burnham's existential crisis that we see the true inanity of the modern lifestyle along with the emptiness and banality of the lives of those around him. The film reveals the ludicrousness of conformist society while at the same time suggesting that we can still discover and enjoy the small pleasures in life.

- *The Truman Show* (1998) chronicles the life of a man, Truman Burbank, whose existence is not what it appears to be—at least not to him. Truman lives happily in an island community but eventually discovers that he is the star of an all-day TV soap opera, and that his wife, friends and neighbors are all acting their parts. There are many layers to peel back: the film serves as a commentary on the all-controlling media, the pervasiveness of television in today's society and how everybody wants to appear on it. There's a postmodernist angle as well, with the entire construct of society being portrayed as a facade that can be stripped down and revealed as an illusion. . . .

- *Groundhog Day* (1993) . . . has come to be recognized as a highly innovative treatise on the human condition, the meaning of life, personal responsibility, and the seemingly endless repetition that characterizes our lives. By having the main character, Phil, re-live the same wintry and overcast Groundhog day over and over again, the film explores a host of life issues. As Phil struggles to come to grips with his predicament he goes through a number of phases: disbelief, shock, hedonism, scheming, nihilism, depression (including numerous suicide attempts) and social detachment. Ultimately, he learns that his happiness is only attainable through acceptance of his situation and constructive behavior that furthers his own life and those around him. Once Phil gets his personal act together he is able to snap the cycle—a theme that is very closely aligned with Buddhism and its notions of samsara and the endless cycle of re-birth.

Why do you think existentialist issues appear so often in literature and film? What existentialist themes run through many of the movies and literature listed here?

From *Sentient Developments*, "The Top 10 Existential Movies of All Time," June 7, 2009, sentientdevelopments.com/2009/06/top-10-existential-movies-of-all-time.html.

WRITING AND REASONING	CHAPTER 14

1. Is Sartre right about free will being the main factor that determines who you are—or do such things as genetics and society have the greatest impact on how you turn out?

2. What is your reaction to Sartre's perspective on freedom? Do you find his view liberating and inspiring, or do you think it is disheartening and forlorn?

3. Is life absurd, as Camus insists? Does Camus give good reasons for this claim? What leads him to this pessimistic conclusion?

4. What is Kierkegaard's theory about truth and subjectivity? In his view, how does subjective truth become objective truth? Do you accept his view? Why or why not?

5. Is God dead, as Nietzsche says? Give reasons for or against the idea.

REVIEW NOTES

14.1 THE EXISTENTIAL TONE

- The term *existentialism* is applied to different philosophies that share themes about the uniqueness of each human being, the central importance of choice, and the individual's response to an indifferent, absurd universe.

- Existentialist themes include individualism and subjectivity, freedom and responsibility, existence and essence, anguish and absurdity, and authenticity.

14.2 KIERKEGAARD

- Kierkegaard is the acknowledged father of modern existentialism and the champion of a radical form of fideism.

- Kierkegaard charges that society is crushing individuals, diluting their personal identity, and replacing them with people who have "forgotten what it means to *exist*," to live as authentic, passionate human beings.

- Kierkegaard asserts that attempts to make religion conform to reason are doomed to fail. From an objective standpoint, the belief in Christian doctrine is absurd. Even with the best of reasons supporting a religious belief, its truth is still only a matter of thin probabilities, dry uncertainties. And humans cannot base their lives on probabilities.

- Kierkegaard says that the paradox of Christian belief is that such belief is absurd, but only an absurd belief can be believed. Believing the absurd requires an extreme, passionate "leap of faith," and only an absurd belief can provoke such passionate belief.

- Kierkegaard claims that subjective truth is an objectively uncertain belief "held fast in an appropriation process of the most passionate inwardness." And subjective truth is "the highest truth available for an existing person." Subjective truth can become objective truth.

14.3 NIETZSCHE

- A central concept of Nietzsche's is the will to power, the fundamental nature of existence as a drive to control and dominate. It is life in toto striving to overcome, to rule, to break out. All human struggles and striving are manifestations of the will to power.

- To Nietzsche, the will to power is evident in humankind's search for knowledge, especially in science, philosophy, and religion. The will to know arises from the will to power—from the desire to master and control a particular domain of reality.

- Nietzsche says that there are two sorts of morality: master morality and slave morality. Master morality is the morality of the powerful, the superior, the proud, the aristocrats, the rich, the conquerors.

- Slave morality is herd morality. For the slave, the masters are dangerous monsters; they are evil. The slaves define themselves as the good; the good are the weak, meek, powerless, and downtrodden. Good qualities are those that advance the interests of the good ones, the slaves—qualities such as love, kindness, and sympathy.

- Nietzsche holds out the hope that herd morality can be transcended by a rising champion of a much greater morality, a higher form of human life: the Overman. The Overman is the superior man of the future.

- To believe in God, Nietzsche says, is to accept the morality of the herd, to live not for this world but for a hereafter, to see humans as sinful and inadequate, and to view this life with pessimism and hopelessness. For Nietzsche, the death of God would be good news—and he believes this great event has already occurred.

14.4 HEIDEGGER

- Martin Heidegger is regarded by some as the greatest philosopher of the twentieth century, and by others as overrated and despicable. These contrasting opinions derive mostly from the perceived profundity of his ideas, his undeniable influence on modern philosophy, his murky, exasperating prose, and his sympathy for the Nazi cause in Germany.

- Heidegger was consumed with what he calls the most pressing and most important question a person could ask: the question of *being*, or existence. Heidegger asks, What is it for something to be? What is it for a stone or pen or human to exist? For Heidegger, being concerns what we might call "pure existence"—not how an object exists or what it is that exists but existence itself.

- To explore the nature of *Dasein* (the self-conscious human being), Heidegger uses the technique called phenomenology—a way of painstakingly describing the data of consciousness without the distortions of preconceived ideas.

- Heidegger claims that *Dasein* has three important aspects: thrownness, projection, and fallenness (marked by authenticity or inauthenticity).

14.5 SARTRE

- From reflections on his own lived experience, Sartre arrives at what he takes to be some basic truths about human beings and their existential predicament, the most important truth being that humans are radically free.

- Sartre argues that the "essence precedes existence" kind of thinking is tragically mistaken. The truth is the opposite of the received view: "existence precedes essence"—we first come into being and then we define ourselves. He declares, "Man is nothing else but what he makes of himself."

- Sartre says, "We are condemned to be free," and our freedom is both a blessing and a curse. The blessing is that as free persons, we have the power to set our own goals, live our own lives, and create ourselves as we go. The curse is that as free beings, we can look to no one but ourselves to decide how we should live. We can celebrate our capacity to create our essence and live by our own rules, but because we are utterly alone in bearing this monumental burden, we are also condemned to experience great anguish, despair, and a sense of abandonment.

14.6 CAMUS

- A central existentialist theme is that our existence is *absurd*: there is an unbearable conflict between our need for meaning and purpose in life and the meaningless, indifferent universe. Our situation is impossible, and there is no higher power or governing principle to help us make sense of it.

- Those who accept their responsibility and freedom, who recognize that they alone are the ultimate designers of their lives, who are brave enough to make the best of an absurd existence—they are living authentically. Those who allow society, religion, history, mass culture, or their own fear to define them are living inauthentically.

- In "The Myth of Sisyphus," Camus dramatizes the absurdity of human existence by likening it to the story of Sisyphus, who is forced by the gods to repeat a pointless task for all eternity: push a boulder to the top of a mountain only to have it tumble down to the bottom. Yet Sisyphus finds meaning in this seemingly meaningless burden by courageously embracing it and refusing to be overwhelmed by despair.

KEY TERMS

absurdity	fideism	phenomenology	will to power
existentialism			

Notes

1. Patrick Gardiner, *Kierkegaard: A Very Short Introduction* (Oxford: Oxford University Press, 1998, 2002), 39.
2. Søren Kierkegaard, *Either/Or*, vol. 1: *Diapsalmata*, trans. D. F. Swenson, L. M. Swenson, and W. K. Lowrie, in *A Kierkegaard Anthology* (Princeton, NJ: Princeton University Press, 1946), 33.
3. Søren Kierkegaard, *The Point of View*, trans. W. Lowrie (London, 1939), 114.
4. Søren Kierkegaard, *Journal*, trans. Louis P. Pojman, in *The Classics of Philosophy*, ed. Louis P. Pojman and Lewis Vaughn (New York: Oxford University Press, 2011), 942.
5. Søren Kierkegaard, *Concluding Unscientific Postscript*, trans. Louis P. Pojman, in *The Classics of Philosophy*, eds. Pojman and Vaughn, 950.
6. Kierkegaard, *Concluding Unscientific Postscript*, trans. Pojman, 950.
7. Friedrich Nietzsche, *Thus Spake Zarathustra*, trans. Walter Kaufmann, in *The Portable Nietzsche* (New York: Penguin Books, 1954, 1982), 226–227.
8. Friedrich Nietzsche, *Beyond Good and Evil*, trans. Walter Kaufmann (New York: Vantage Books, 1989), 11–12.
9. Nietzsche, *Beyond Good and Evil*, trans. Kaufmann, 16.
10. Nietzsche, *Thus Spake Zarathustra*, trans. Kaufmann, 125.
11. Friedrich Nietzsche, *The Gay Science*, trans. Walter Kaufmann in *The Portable Nietzsche*.
12. Martin Heidegger, *The Basic Problems of Phenomenology* (Bloomington: Indiana University Press, 1975), 13–14.
13. Thomas R. Flynn, *Existentialism: A Very Short Introduction* (Oxford: Oxford University Press, 2006), 74–75.
14. Jean-Paul Sartre, *Existentialism*, trans. Bernard Frechtman (New York: Philosophical Library, 1947), 15–28, 34–35.
15. Albert Camus, *The Myth of Sisyphus and Other Essays*, trans. J. O'Brien (New York: Alfred A. Knopf, 1983), 119–123.

For Further Reading

Albert Camus, *Myth of Sisyphus and Other Essays* (New York: Random House, 1959).

Frederick Copleston, *A History of Philosophy, Vol. IX: Modern Philosophy from the French Revolution to Sartre, Camus, and Levi-Straus* (New York: Doubleday, 1994).

Simon Critchley, *Continental Philosophy: A Very Short Introduction* (Oxford: Oxford University Press, 2001).

Thomas R. Flynn, *Existentialism: A Very Short Introduction* (Oxford: Oxford University Press, 2006).

Michael Inwood, *Heidegger: A Very Short Introduction* (Oxford: Oxford University Press, 1997).

Richard Kearny, ed., *Continental Philosophy in the Twentieth Century* (New York: Blackwell, 1994).

Anthony Kenny, *The Rise of Modern Philosophy: A New History of Western Philosophy*, vol. 4 (Oxford: Oxford University Press, 2008).

Brian Leiter and Michael Rosen, eds., *The Oxford Companion to Continental Philosophy* (Oxford: Oxford University Press, 2007).

Robert C. Solomon, *Existentialism* (New York: Oxford University Press, 2005).

Mary Warnock, *Existentialism* (Oxford: Oxford University Press, 1970).

Online Resources

Stanford Encyclopedia of Philosophy, "Existentialism," "Jean-Paul Sartre," "Simone de Beauvoir," "Albert Camus," https://plato.stanford.edu

Internet Encyclopedia of Philosophy, "Existentialism," "Albert Camus," "Jean-Paul Sartre," "Soren Kierkegaard," https://www.iep.utm.edu/existent

Philosophy Now, "Existentialism," by Anja Steinbauer, https://philosophynow.org/issues/32/Existentialism

Crash Course, "Existentialism," video, https://www.youtube.com/watch?v=YaDvRdLMkHs

Biography.com, "Jean-Paul Sartre," "Albert Camus," https://www.biography.com

Philosophy Talk, "Sartre's Existentialism," podcast, https://www.philosophytalk.org/blog/sartres-existentialism

History of Philosophy (without Any Gaps) Podcast, https://historyofphilosophy.net

CHAPTER 15

The Pragmatists: Peirce and James

CHAPTER OBJECTIVES

15.1 THE PRAGMATIST WAY

- Define *pragmatism*.
- Know how a pragmatist might explicate the meaning of terms such as *hard*, *wet*, and *sharp*.
- Understand the main complaint that James and Peirce lodge against traditional metaphysics.

15.2 PEIRCE

- Define *fallibilism*.
- Explain Peirce's theory of meaning.
- Evaluate Peirce's notion of truth, a converging of opinions by competent investigators.

15.3 JAMES

- Define *evidentialism*.
- Explain what James means by his claim that the "truth works."
- Evaluate James's argument for the view that sometimes we may be justified in making a leap of faith to embrace a belief that is unsupported by evidence.
- Understand what James means by a "genuine option."

15.1 THE PRAGMATIST WAY

As we've seen, philosophy in nineteenth-century Europe was dominated by the subversive ideas of four great agents of change: Hegel, Marx, Kierkegaard, and Nietzsche. On the Continent, the prevailing view was German idealism, and the preferred philosophical approach was the building of sprawling systems of thought (in Hegel, Schopenhauer, and Nietzsche, for example). In these imposing structures, sustained argumentation mattered less than the sweeping vision of the system. In Britain, German idealism also took root, and various versions of it flourished throughout the century. But British empiricism also spread, with the utilitarianism of Jeremy Bentham and John Stuart Mill being the most obvious examples. Meanwhile in the United States, a uniquely American kind of philosophy sprang up, developing into a robust strain of empiricist thought that is influential still. This way of looking at the world is known as *pragmatism*.

pragmatism The doctrine that the meaning or truth of a belief is synonymous with the practical results of accepting it.

Pragmatism is the doctrine that the meaning or truth of a belief is synonymous with the practical results of accepting it. So to pragmatists the meaning of a term is defined by its consequences in the real world. What does it mean to say that a thing is *hard*? The meaning, as a pragmatist might see it, is that the thing cannot be scratched by other materials, or that when the thing is pressed, it will not give easily. The sum of such effects is the full sense of *hard*.

The pragmatic take on truth is similar. Is the doctrine of idealism true? What of rationalism or empiricism? The truth of these views depends on their practical effects. The view of the pragmatist philosopher William James is that these practical results should affect our personal lives:

William James: "Pragmatism"

Pragmatism ... asks its usual question. "Grant an idea or belief to be true," it says, "what concrete difference will its being true make in any one's actual life? How will the truth be realized? What experiences will be different from those which would obtain if the belief were false? What, in short, is the truth's cash-value in experiential terms?"

The moment pragmatism asks this question, it sees the answer: *True ideas are those that we can assimilate, validate, corroborate and verify. False ideas are those that we cannot.*[1]

For James and Charles S. Peirce, the two most important nineteenth-century pragmatists, pragmatism was in part a reaction to the ethereal metaphysics of past philosophizing. They were repelled by the otherworldly belief systems, the theories of the Absolute, the a priori musings, and the unsupported speculations. To them, these were philosophical castles in the sky—both meaningless and worthless. Philosophy should be *useful*, an instrument for better living. They asked: What do any of these abstractions have to do with our lives? How do they help us cope with day-to-day, life-and-death reality? James says it best:

The pragmatic method is primarily a method of settling metaphysical disputes that otherwise might be interminable. Is the world one or many?—fated or free?—material or spiritual?—here are notions either of which may or may not hold good of the world; and disputes over such notions are unending. The pragmatic method in such cases is to try to interpret each notion by tracing its respective practical consequences. What difference would it practically make to any one if this notion rather than that notion were true? If no practical difference whatever can be traced, the alternatives mean practically the same thing, and all dispute is idle. Whenever a dispute is serious, we ought to be able to show some practical difference that must follow from one side or the other's being right.[2]

William James: "Pragmatism"

"In all the works on pedagogy that ever I read—and they have been many, big, and heavy—I don't remember that any one has advocated a system of teaching by practical jokes, mostly cruel. That, however, describes the method of our great teacher, Experience."

—Charles S. Peirce

15.2 PEIRCE

Charles Sanders Peirce (1839–1914), America's most original philosopher and the founder of pragmatism, demonstrated by his work that historically significant philosophy in the United States had finally arrived. Before he came along, philosophy in the West was almost exclusively a European and British affair.

He was born in Cambridge, Massachusetts, to a highly regarded professor of mathematics at Harvard, where in 1863 he earned a degree in chemistry, *summa cum laude*. From 1861 to 1891 he worked off and on for the U.S. Coast and Geodetic Survey while sometimes teaching logic and the history of science at Harvard and lecturing in logic at Johns Hopkins University. He published no books in philosophy (his only published book is about astronomy), but he wrote several journal articles that set out his views on his notion of **fallibilism** (the idea that our claims to knowledge may turn out to be false), the "principle of pragmatism," metaphysics, and philosophy of mind. He wrote much more than this, but most of his papers went unpublished in his lifetime and appeared in print only in the twentieth century.

Although Peirce laid the groundwork for pragmatism, the world paid little heed to him, reserving its attention for James, who wrote in a more popular vein about the doctrine. James admired Peirce, befriended him, and tried to help him out of his financial woes. Nevertheless Peirce died of cancer in 1914, impoverished, generally unappreciated, and almost unknown.

Peirce was the first to articulate pragmatism's classic theory of meaning. The meaning of a concept equals its real-world effects:

Figure 15.1 Charles Sanders Peirce (1839–1914).

Charles Sanders Peirce: "How to Make Our Ideas Clear"

[C]onsider what effects, which might conceivably have practical bearings, we conceive the object of our conception to have. Then, our conception of these effects is the whole of our conception of the object. . . .

fallibilism The view that our claims to knowledge may turn out to be false.

DETAILS

Four Ways to Fix Belief

Peirce asserts that doubt "causes a struggle to attain a state of belief," and this struggle is an inquiry whose goal is to substitute a settled belief for doubt. But not every method of inquiry is useful. He mentions four methods, only one of which (the fourth one) is satisfactory:

Figure 15.2 Iranians in Tehran walk past a billboard showing an image of Iran's supreme leader. When deciding what to believe, how often do we defer to political or religious authority? Should we *ever* defer?

1. In the **method of tenacity**, we accept any available answer and hold onto it against all reason and all alternatives. But, says Peirce, this approach doesn't work. It "will be unable to hold its ground in practice. . . . The man who adopts it will find that other men think differently from him, and it will be apt to occur to him, in some saner moment, that their opinions are quite as good as his own, and this will shake his confidence in his belief."

2. In the **method of authority**, we defer to powerful persons or institutions and let them dictate our beliefs and prevent contrary opinions. But this procedure can lead to the realization that the sanctioning of some beliefs and not others is arbitrary—which again will lead to doubts about the "correct" beliefs.

3. In the **a priori method**, we base our beliefs not on any experience or observed facts but on our ungrounded inclinations toward particular opinions. But this scheme too is arbitrary and subjective.

4. In the **method of science**, we judge beliefs by a standard outside ourselves. It says, "There are Real things, whose characters are entirely independent of our opinions about them; those Reals affect our senses according to regular laws, and, though our sensations are as different as our relations to the objects, yet, by taking advantage of the laws of perception, we can ascertain by reasoning how things really and truly are."

What's wrong with the method of tenacity? the method of authority? How does the method of science differ from other methods of fixing belief?

Charles Sanders Peirce, "The Fixation of Belief," *Popular Science Monthly*, 1877.

Let us next seek a clear idea of Weight. This is another very easy case. To say that a body is heavy means simply that, in the absence of opposing force, it will fall. This (neglecting certain specifications of how it will fall, etc., which exist in the mind of the physicist who uses the word) is evidently the whole concept of weight.[3]

Peirce's idea of truth also appeals to practical consequences, but he gives it an interesting twist. A true belief is one that is destined to be converged on by competent investigators if they have an unlimited amount of time to reach their conclusion. Peirce explains:

> Different minds may set out with the most antagonistic views, but the progress of investigation carries them by force outside of themselves to one and the same conclusion. This activity of thought by which we are carried, not where we wish, but to a foreordained goal, is like the operation of destiny. No modification of the point of view taken, no selection of other facts for study, no natural bent of mind even, can enable a man to escape the predestinate opinion. This great law is embodied in the conception of truth and reality. The opinion which is fated to be ultimately agreed to by all who investigate is what we mean by the truth, and the object presented in this opinion is the real. That is the way I would explain reality.[4]

So for Peirce, if a proposition is true, careful research conducted through multiple investigators over a long enough time would eventually lead to that truth. Truth is a matter of reasonable consensus, a fallible enterprise in which opinions may be true or false yet are becoming better approximations of reality. Truth, then, is something we must work to achieve, something we must aspire to.

Peirce's critics take issue with his view of truth. For one thing, they think his assumption that competent investigators will come to accept one and the same belief at the conclusion of inquiry is dubious. It's possible to devise many different hypotheses to account for the same evidence, so isn't it possible for investigators to ultimately converge on two conflicting beliefs about the same facts? If so, that would mean two conflicting beliefs could both be true—which is absurd.

15.3 JAMES

For William James (1842–1910), truth is not a matter of interpersonal consensus; it is about practical consequences for individuals. A belief is true if it is beneficial to our lives—that is, if it is useful or satisfying. The truth is "what works," and what works may mean either success in predicting events or promotion of beneficial feelings and actions:

William James: "Pragmatism"

The true is the name of whatever proves itself to be good in the way of belief, and good, too, for definite, assignable reasons.[5]

Charles Sanders Peirce: "How to Make Our Ideas Clear"

1. Are there concepts or ideas that involve no practical effects yet are meaningful? If there are such ideas, would that fact undercut Peirce's theory of meaning?

Charles Sanders Peirce: "How to Make Our Ideas Clear"

"In order to ascertain the meaning of an intellectual conception one should consider what practical consequences might conceivably result by necessity from the truth of that conception; and the sum of these consequences will constitute the entire meaning of the conception."
—Charles S. Peirce

2. Is it possible for investigators to reach an ultimate consensus on a proposition that is actually false? If so, what are the implications for Peirce's theory of truth?

This principle applies to the workaday world, to science, and even to religion:

William James: "Pragmatism"

> If theological ideas prove to have a value for concrete life, they will be true, for pragmatism, in the sense of being good for so much. For how much they are true, will depend entirely on their relations to the other truths that also have to be acknowledged.[6]

Figure 15.3 William James (1842–1910).

3. Can a false belief have good consequences? If a racist gets emotional satisfaction from believing that non-white people are inferior, does that mean his belief is true?

"Peirce wrote as a logician and James as a humanist."
—John Dewey

evidentialism The view that we are justified in believing something only if it is supported by sufficient evidence.

Contrary to his scientifically minded colleagues, James argues that sometimes we may be justified in making a leap of faith to embrace a belief—a belief that works—that is entirely unsupported by evidence. In the absence of any evidence that could help us decide an issue, and when we are presented with a true choice between opposing beliefs (a "genuine option"), believing on faith may be the rational thing to do. To James, a genuine option is one that is *live*, *forced*, and *momentous*. A live option presents someone with alternatives that he believes could possibly be actualized. A forced option is unavoidable because the two possibilities are mutually exclusive, and not deciding is the same as choosing one of the alternatives. (An example from James is "either accept this truth or go without it.") A momentous option is one that really matters, because the stakes are high, the decision is irreversible, or the choice offers a once-in-a-lifetime opportunity. When we are confronted with a genuine option with no evidence to go by, James says, we have the right to let our "passional nature"—our feelings and desires—decide.

James thus repudiates **evidentialism**, the view that we are justified in believing something only if it is supported by sufficient evidence. In James's day, the foremost champion of evidentialism was W. K. Clifford, who declared, "It is wrong always, everywhere, and for anyone, to believe anything upon insufficient evidence."[7] In other words, it is *morally wrong* to believe beyond the evidence. Against this position James asserts, "Our passional nature not only lawfully may, but must, decide an option between propositions, whenever it is a genuine option that cannot by its nature be decided on intellectual grounds."[8]

To James, the decision to believe or not to believe in a divine reality (the "religious hypothesis") is a genuine option that the intellect cannot help us decide. It is indeed momentous: "We are supposed to gain, even now, by our belief, and to lose by our nonbelief, a certain vital good."[9] The skeptic, out of fear of being wrong, would have us refrain from believing and wait until evidence tilts one way or the other. But James insists that the wiser choice—and the more advantageous—is to believe the religious hypothesis, to refuse to forfeit your "sole chance in life of getting upon the winning side." Moreover, to discover whether a divine being exists, we may first have to have faith that it does. Unless we first believe, we may not be able to confirm the truth through our own experience. One who insists on evidence before belief "might cut himself off forever from his only opportunity of making the gods' acquaintance."

This is how James makes his case:

William James: "The Will to Believe"

IV

The thesis I defend is, briefly stated, this: *Our passional nature not only lawfully may, but must, decide an option between propositions, whenever it is a genuine option that cannot by its nature be decided on intellectual grounds; for to say, under such circumstances, "Do not decide, but leave the question open," is itself a passional decision just like deciding yes or no,—and is attended with the same risk of losing the truth....*

VII

There are two ways of looking at our duty in the matter of opinion,—ways entirely different, and yet ways about whose difference the theory of knowledge seems hitherto to have shown very little concern. *We must know the truth*; and *we must avoid error*,—these are our first and great commandments as would-be knowers; but they are not two ways of stating an identical commandment, they are two separable laws. Although it may indeed happen that when we believe the truth A, we escape as an incidental consequence from believing the falsehood B, it hardly ever happens that by merely disbelieving B we necessarily believe A. We may in escaping B fall into believing other falsehoods, C or D, just as bad as B; or we may escape B by not believing anything at all, not even A.

Believe truth! Shun error!—these, we see, are two materially different laws; and by choosing between them we may end by colouring differently our whole intellectual life. We may regard the chase for truth as paramount, and the avoidance of error as secondary; or we may, on the other hand, treat the avoidance of error as more imperative, and let truth take its chance. Clifford, in the instructive passage which I have quoted, exhorts us to the latter course. Believe nothing, he tells us, keep your mind in suspense forever, rather than by closing it on insufficient evidence incur the awful risk of believing lies. You, on the other hand, may think that the risk of being in error is a very small matter when compared with the blessings of real knowledge, and be ready to be duped many times in your investigation rather than postpone indefinitely the chance of guessing true. I myself find it impossible to go with Clifford. We must remember that these feelings of our duty about either truth or error are in any case only expressions of our passional life. Biologically considered, our minds are as ready to grind out falsehood as veracity, and he who says "Better go without belief forever than believe a lie!" merely shows his own preponderant private horror of becoming a dupe. He may be critical of many of his desires and fears, but this fear he slavishly obeys. He cannot imagine anyone questioning its binding force. For my own part, I have also a horror of being duped; but I can believe that worse things than being duped may happen to a man in this world: so Clifford's exhortation has to my ears a thoroughly fantastic sound. It is like a general informing his soldiers that it is better to keep out of battle forever than to risk a single

"Believe that life is worth living and your belief will help create the fact."

—William James

4. Is it ever rational to believe something without evidence? James says yes; Clifford says no. Who is right?

William James:
"The Will to Believe"

wound. Not so are victories either over enemies or over nature gained. Our errors are surely not such awfully solemn things. In a world where we are so certain to incur them in spite of all our caution, a certain lightness of heart seems healthier than this excessive nervousness on their behalf. At any rate, it seems the fittest thing for the empiricist philosopher.

VIII

Wherever the option between losing truth and gaining it is not momentous, we can throw the chance of *gaining truth* away, and at any rate save ourselves from any chance of *believing falsehood*, by not making up our minds at all till objective evidence has come. In scientific questions, this is almost always the case; and even in human affairs in general, the need of acting is seldom so urgent that a false belief to act on is better than no belief at all. Law courts, indeed, have to decide on the best evidence attainable for the moment, because a judge's duty is to make law as well as to ascertain it, and (as a learned judge once said to me) few cases are worth spending much time over: the great thing is to have them decided on

PORTRAIT

William James

William James (1842–1910) is one of America's most influential philosophers, leaving a lasting impression on debates in epistemology, philosophy of religion, ethics, and free will. He was born in New York City and grew up in an intellectually stimulating family. His father was a philosopher of religion, and his brother Henry was the famous novelist. He studied abroad, earned a Harvard degree in medicine, and spent most of his career lecturing and writing in psychology and philosophy.

His reputation as the greatest psychologist of America and Europe was assured by the publication of his voluminous work *The Principles of Psychology* (1890). After that came numerous philosophical essays and books, including *The Will to Believe and Other Essays in Popular Philosophy* (1897); *The Varieties of Religious Experience* (1902); *Pragmatism: A New Name for Some Old Ways of Thinking* (1907); and *The Meaning of Truth* (1909).

Figure 15.4 William James (right) with his famous brother Henry, author of *The Turn of the Screw, The Portrait of a Lady,* and other works of fiction.

Through pragmatism, James came to the conclusion that religion was a legitimate and important aspect of life, because we can plausibly accept religious claims on grounds of their utility, regardless of their lack of evidence.

Ironically, James, the famous psychologist, was given to psychosomatic illness and clinical depression. Once while wrestling with the problem of free will, he fell into a devastatingly dark mood and did not recover until he had found a solution. He concluded that despite determinism, we can have free will because chance events make room for free actions.

any acceptable principle, and got out of the way. But in our dealings with objective nature we obviously are recorders, not makers, of the truth; and decisions for the mere sake of deciding promptly and getting on to the next business would be wholly out of place. Throughout the breadth of physical nature facts are what they are quite independently of us, and seldom is there any such hurry about them that the risks of being duped by believing a premature theory need be faced. The questions here are always trivial options, the hypotheses are hardly living (at any rate not living for us spectators), the choice between believing truth or falsehood is seldom forced. The attitude of sceptical balance is therefore the absolutely wise one if we would escape mistakes. . . .

The question next arises: Are there not somewhere forced options in our speculative questions, and can we (as men who may be interested at least as much in positively gaining truth as in merely escaping dupery) always wait with impunity till the coercive evidence shall have arrived? It seems *a priori* improbable that the truth should be so nicely adjusted to our needs and powers as that. In the great boardinghouse of nature, the cakes and the butter and the syrup seldom come out so even and leave the plates so clean. Indeed, we should view them with scientific suspicion if they did.

IX

Moral questions immediately present themselves as questions whose solution cannot wait for sensible proof. A moral question is a question not of what sensibly exists, but of what is good, or would be good if it did exist. Science can tell us what exists; but to compare the worths, both of what exists and of what does not exist, we must consult not science, but what Pascal calls our heart. Science herself consults her heart when she lays it down that the infinite ascertainment of fact and correction of false belief are the supreme goods for man. Challenge the statement and science can only repeat it oracularly, or else prove it by showing that such ascertainment and correction bring man all sorts of other goods which man's heart in turn declares. The question of having moral beliefs at all or not having them is decided by our will. Are our moral preferences true or false, or are they only odd biological phenomena, making things good or bad for us, but in themselves indifferent? How can your pure intellect decide? If your heart does not want a world of moral reality, your head will assuredly never make you believe in one. . . .

Turn now from these wide questions of good to a certain class of questions of fact, questions concerning personal relations, states of mind between one man and another. *Do you like me or not?*—for example. Whether you do or not depends, in countless instances, on whether I meet you halfway, am willing to assume that you must like me, and show you trust and expectation. The previous faith on my part in your liking's existence is in such cases what makes your liking come. But if I stand aloof, and refuse to budge an inch until I have objective evidence, until you shall have done something apt, as the absolutists say, *ad extorquendum assensum meum*, ten to one your liking never comes. How many women's hearts are vanquished by the mere sanguine insistence of some man that they *must* love him! He will not consent to the hypothesis that they cannot. The desire for a certain kind of truth here brings about that special truth's existence; and so it is in innumerable cases of other sorts. Who gains promotions, boons, appointments, but the man in whose life they are seen to play the part of live hypotheses, who discounts them, sacrifices other things for their sake before they have come, and takes risks for them in advance? His faith acts on the powers above him as a claim, and creates its own verification. . . .

There are, then, cases where a fact cannot come at all unless a preliminary faith exists in it coming. *And where faith in a fact can help create the fact*, that would be an insane logic

"All truth passes through three stages. First, it is ridiculed. Second, it is violently opposed. Third, it is accepted as being self-evident."

—Arthur Schopenhauer

William James:
"The Will to Believe"

which should say that faith running ahead of scientific evidence is the "lowest kind of immorality" into which a thinking being can fall. Yet such is the logic by which our scientific absolutists pretend to regulate our lives!

X

5. Are the beliefs involved in James's do-you-like-me example really groundless? Or are they backed by basic principles of human psychology?

In truths dependent on our personal action, then, faith based on desire is certainly a lawful and possibly an indispensable thing.

But now, it will be said, these are all childish human cases, and have nothing to do with great cosmical matters, like the question of religious faith. Let us then pass on to that. Religions differ so much in their accidents that in discussing the religious question we must make it very generic and broad. What then do we now mean by the religious hypothesis? Science says things are; morality says some things are better than other things; and religion says essentially two things.

First, she says that the best things are the more eternal things, the overlapping things, the things in the universe that throw the last stone, so to speak, and say the final word. "Perfection is eternal"—this phrase of Charles Secrétan seems a good way of putting this first affirmation of religion, an affirmation which obviously cannot yet be verified scientifically at all.

The second affirmation of religion is that we are better off even now if we believe her first affirmation to be true.

Now let us consider what the logical elements of this situation are *in case the religious hypothesis in both its branches be really true.* (Of course, we must admit that possibility at the outset. If we are to discuss the question at all, it must involve a living option. If for any of you religion be a hypothesis that cannot, by any living possibility be true, then you need go no farther. I speak to the 'saving remnant' alone.) So proceeding, we see, first, that religion offers itself as *a momentous* option. We are supposed to gain, even now, by our belief, and to lose by our nonbelief, a certain vital good. Secondly, religion is a *forced* option so far as that good goes. We cannot escape the issue by remaining sceptical and waiting for more light, because, although we do avoid error in that way *if religion be untrue,* we lose the good, *if it be true,* just as certainly as if we positively chose to disbelieve. It is as if a man should hesitate indefinitely to ask a certain woman to marry him because he was not perfectly sure that she would prove an angel after he brought her home. Would he not cut himself off from that particular angel-possibility as decisively as if he went and married someone else? Scepticism, then, is not avoidance of option; it is option of a certain particular kind of risk. *Better risk loss of truth than chance of error,*—that is your faith-vetoer's exact position. He is actively playing his stake as much as the believer is; he is backing the field against the religious hypothesis, just as the believer is backing the religious hypothesis against the field. To preach scepticism to us as a duty until 'sufficient evidence' for religion be found, is tantamount therefore to telling us, when in presence of the religious hypothesis, that to yield to our fear of its being error is wiser and better than to yield to our hope that it may be true. It is not intellect against all passions, then; it is only intellect with one passion laying down its law. And by what, forsooth, is the supreme wisdom of this passion warranted? Dupery for dupery, what proof is there that dupery through hope is so much worse than dupery through fear? I, for one, can see no proof; and I simply refuse obedience to the scientist's command to imitate his kind of option, in a case where my own stake is important enough to give me the right to choose my own form of risk. If religion be true and the evidence for it be still insufficient, I do not wish, by putting your extinguisher upon my nature (which feels to me as if it had after all some business in this matter), to forfeit my sole chance in life of getting upon the winning side,—that chance depending, of course, on my willingness to run the risk of acting as if my passional need of taking the world religiously might be prophetic and right.

All this is on the supposition that it really may be prophetic and right, and that, even to us who are discussing the matter, religion is a live hypothesis which may be true. Now to most of us religion comes in a still farther way that makes a veto on our active faith even more illogical. The more perfect and more eternal aspect of the universe is represented in our religions as having personal form. The universe is no longer a mere *It* to us, but a *Thou*, if we are religious; and any relation that may be possible from person to person might be possible here. For instance, although in one sense we are passive portions of the universe, in another we show a curious autonomy, as if we were small active centers on our own account. We feel, too, as if the appeal of religion to us were made to our own active good-will as if evidence might be forever withheld from us unless we met the hypothesis halfway. To take a trivial illustration: just as a man who in a company of gentlemen made no advances, asked a warrant for every concession, and believed no one's word without proof, would cut himself off by such churlishness from all the social rewards that a more trusting spirit would earn,—so here, one who should shut himself up in snarling logicality and try to make the gods extort his recognition willy-nilly, or not get it at all, might cut himself off forever from his only opportunity of making the gods' acquaintance. This feeling, forced on us we know not whence, that by obstinately believing that there are gods (although not to do so would be so easy both for our logic and our life) we are doing the universe the deepest service we can, seems part of the living essence of the religious hypothesis. If the hypothesis *were* true in all its parts, including this one, then pure intellectualism, with its veto on our making willing advances, would be an absurdity; and some participation of our sympathetic nature would be logically required. I therefore, for one, cannot see my way to accepting the agnostic rules for truth-seeking, or willfully agree to keep my willing nature out of the game. I cannot do so for this plain reason, *that a rule of thinking which would absolutely prevent me from acknowledging certain kinds of truth if those kinds of truth were really there, would be an irrational rule*. That for me is the long and short of the formal logic of the situation, no matter what the kinds of truth might materially be. . . .

When I look at the religious question as it really puts itself to concrete men, and when I think of all the possibilities which both practically and theoretically it involves, then this command that we shall put a stopper on our heart, instincts and courage, and *wait*—acting of course meanwhile more or less as if religion were *not* true—till doomsday, or till such time as our intellect and senses working together may have raked in evidence enough—this command, I say, seems to me the queerest idol ever manufactured in the philosophic cave. Were we scholastic absolutists, there might be more excuse. If we had an infallible intellect with its objective certitudes, we might feel ourselves disloyal to such a perfect organ of knowledge in not trusting to it exclusively, in not waiting for its releasing word. But if we are empiricists, if we believe that no bell in us tolls to let us know for certain when truth is in our grasp, then it seems a piece of idle fantasticality to preach so solemnly our duty of waiting for the bell. Indeed we *may* wait if we will,—I hope you do not think that I am denying that,—but if we do so, we do so at our peril as much as if we believed. In either case we *act*, taking our life in our hands. No one of us ought to issue vetoes to the other, nor should we bandy words of abuse. We ought, on the contrary, delicately and profoundly to respect one another's mental freedom—then only shall we bring about the intellectual republic; then only shall we have that spirit of inner tolerance without which all our outer tolerance is soulless, and which is empiricism's glory; then only shall we live and let live, in speculative as well as in practical things.[10]

"Belief creates the actual fact."

—William James

---

6. James assumes that we are better off in this life if we believe the religious hypothesis than if we don't. Is this assumption correct? What evidence can you bring to bear on this question?

---

7. Is it reasonable to expect that by first having faith in God you can *confirm* his existence in your experience? Would having faith before you get confirmation distort this method of inquiry and bias the results?

THEN AND NOW

James and Indeterminism

Figure 15.5 Does indeterminism on the quantum level show that some actions are not caused?

Like many philosophers and scientists today, James was gripped by the philosophical problem of free will—the challenge of reconciling determinism with our intuitions or ideas about personal freedom. *Determinism* is the doctrine that every event in the universe is determined or necessitated by preceding events and the laws of nature. It says that everything that happens must happen in an unalterable, preset fashion. But if determinism is true, how can any choices we make or any actions we perform be up to us? How can we do anything "of our own free will"? The problem of free will, then, is the challenge of reconciling determinism with our intuitions or ideas about personal freedom. *Hard determinists* believe that because determinism is true, no one has free will. James rejects this view, holding that not every event is determined by preceding events and the laws of nature (the position known as *indeterminism*) and that therefore there is room for free will in our lives. He argues that indeterminism is a feature of the universe that permits "alternative futures" and the possibility of freedom. It allows some things to happen by chance. Most importantly, James says, it allows free actions, for *free actions are chance happenings*.

Despite the eloquence of James's argument, it has many detractors. For starters, they deny his assumption that the claims of religion cannot be decided by argument and evidence. Many theists and atheists think that reason can indeed decide the issue of God's existence, and the traditional arguments are attempts to do just that.

Others doubt James's assertion that it is better to believe the religious hypothesis than not to believe it because by believing we acquire "even now . . . a certain vital good." He doesn't say what this vital good is, but if he means something like a better life, happiness, or spiritual satisfaction in this life, he seems to be on shaky ground. It is not obvious that religious believers of any sort lead better, happier, or more satisfying lives than nonbelievers.

Some have also taken issue with James's notion of verifying through our experiences the religious hypothesis by first believing it. Faith is supposed to be the prerequisite for experiences that will enable us to confirm some divine reality. But critics

> "A great many people think they are thinking when they are merely rearranging their prejudices."
> —William James

As it turns out, modern science offers evidence that indeterminism may actually be true. Quantum physics (the science of subatomic particles) provides a surprising counterexample to the notion that every event has a cause. The most widely accepted view among quantum physicists is that at the subatomic level, some events (such as the decay of radioactive particles) are random and therefore uncaused. If so, it is not the case that every event is determined by preceding events and the laws of nature. (Some hard determinists maintain that these uncaused events are mostly confined to the subatomic realm and do not significantly affect the larger world of human actions. This suggests, they say, that for all practical purposes, determinism *is* true.)

Many philosophers nowadays reject James's argument, but not because of quantum physics. The problem, they say, is that indeterminism alone does not make for free and responsible actions. They agree that indeterminism is necessary for free will, that free actions can occur only in a world where not all actions are determined by prior events and natural laws. But they also point out that if what an agent does happens by chance (that is, randomly), then she is not free to act or not act. What she does just happens, and she has nothing to do with it. Her actions are not under her control and therefore are not really *her* actions. In fact, they would not be actions at all.

Despite these complications, many today believe, on various grounds, that some of our actions are indeed free. And a few think James was right all along.

Who do you think is right about indeterminism and free will—James or those who claim that chance actions cannot be free? Why?

say that having faith first is not likely to corroborate anything. Michael Martin explains the point this way:

Michael Martin: *Atheism: A Philosophical Justification*

James talks as if believing in God and seeing whether the hypothesis that God exists is confirmed in one's experience is like an experiment. But his procedure lacks an essential element of standard experimental procedure: he does not seem to allow for the *disconfirmation* of the hypothesis by the results of the experiment. Suppose one believes in some god and yet no evidence of his existence is revealed in one's experience. James does not entertain the possibility that this failure would count against the hypothesis that this god exists.[11]

WRITING AND REASONING	CHAPTER 15

1. Evaluate this criticism of Peirce's theory of truth: It's possible to devise many different hypotheses to account for the same evidence, so it's possible for investigators to ultimately converge on two conflicting beliefs about the same facts. But this results in a contradiction, which shows that Peirce's theory of truth cannot be right.

2. Provide an example showing that a false belief can have good consequences. Then explain how this fact would undermine James's theory of truth.

3. Do you agree with James that faith in the religious hypothesis can bring about a "vital good" in one's life now? What evidence can you cite to back up your answer? For example, is there evidence showing that those who accept the religious hypothesis are happier than those who don't?

4. Suppose it is true that sometimes, as James says, "faith in a fact can help create the fact." Is the existence of God one of the facts that we can create by believing it? Explain.

5. Give reasons for why you accept or do not accept the doctrine of evidentialism. What does your position imply about James's rejection of this doctrine? Is James right or wrong?

REVIEW NOTES

15.1 THE PRAGMATIST WAY

• Pragmatism is the doctrine that the meaning or truth of a belief is synonymous with the practical results of accepting it; to pragmatists the meaning of a term is defined by its consequences in the real world.

• For James and Charles S. Peirce, pragmatism was, in part, a reaction to the metaphysics of the past. They rejected the otherworldly belief systems and the unsupported speculations.

15.2 PEIRCE

• Peirce was the first to articulate pragmatism's theory of meaning, the idea that the meaning of a concept equals its real-world effects.

• For Peirce, a true belief is one that is destined to be converged on by competent investigators if they have an unlimited amount of time to reach their conclusion.

15.3 JAMES

• James argues that truth is not a matter of interpersonal consensus but of practical consequences for individuals. A belief is true if it is beneficial to our lives: the truth is "what works," and what works may mean either success in predicting events or promotion of beneficial feelings and actions.

- James maintains that sometimes we may be justified in making a leap of faith to embrace a belief that is unsupported by evidence. He says, "Our passional nature not only lawfully may, but must, decide an option between propositions, whenever it is a genuine option that cannot by its nature be decided on intellectual grounds."

- James says that when we are presented with the unproven "religious hypothesis," the wise choice is to believe it and to refuse to forfeit our "sole chance in life of getting upon the winning side." And to discover whether a divine being exists, we may first have to have faith that it does.

KEY TERMS
evidentialism   fallibilism   pragmatism

Notes

1. William James, "Pragmatism," translated in the *Revue Philosophique* for January 1879, vol. vii.
2. James, "Pragmatism."
3. Charles Sanders Peirce, "How to Make Our Ideas Clear," *Popular Science Monthly*, 1878.
4. Peirce, "How to Make Our Ideas Clear."
5. James, "Pragmatism."
6. James, "Pragmatism."
7. W. K. Clifford, "The Ethics of Belief," *Lectures and Essays* (London: Macmillan, 1886).
8. William James, "The Will to Believe," in *The Will to Believe and Other Essays in Popular Philosophy* (New York: Longmans, Green, 1896), 11.
9. James, "The Will to Believe," 26.
10. James, "The Will to Believe," 2–30.
11. Michael Martin, *Atheism: A Philosophical Justification* (Philadelphia: Temple University Press, 1990), 246.

For Further Reading

Robert Audi, *Belief, Justification, and Knowledge* (Belmont, CA: Wadsworth, 1988).

Frederick Copleston, *A History of Philosophy, Volume VIII: Modern Philosophy: Empiricism, Idealism, and Pragmatism in Britain and America* (New York: Doubleday, 1994).

Ted Honderich, ed., *The Oxford Companion to Philosophy*, 2nd edition (Oxford: Oxford University Press, 2005).

William James, *The Varieties of Religious Experience* (New York: Barnes and Noble Classics, 1902, 2004).

Anthony Kenny, *The Rise of Modern Philosophy: A New History of Western Philosophy*, vol. 4 (Oxford: Oxford University Press, 2008).

Keith Lehrer, *Theory of Knowledge*, 2nd edition (Boulder, CO: Westview Press, 2000).

Cheryl Misak, *The American Pragmatists* (New York: Oxford University Press, 2013).

Cheryl Misak, *The Oxford Handbook of American Philosophy* (Oxford: Oxford University Press, 2008).

Paul K. Moser, *Knowledge and Evidence* (Cambridge: Cambridge University Press, 1989).

Online Resources

Stanford Encyclopedia of Philosophy, "Pragmatism," "William James," "Charles Sanders Peirce," https://plato.stanford.edu

Internet Encyclopedia of Philosophy, "Pragmatism," "William James (1842–1910)," https://www.iep.utm.edu

Biography.com, "William James," https://www.biography.com/scholar/william-james

Philosophy Talk, "William James," podcast, https://www.philosophytalk.org/shows/william-james

Encyclopedia Britannica, "William James," https://www.britannica.com/biography/William-James

CHAPTER 16

Feminist Philosophers

CHAPTER OBJECTIVES

16.1 MARY WOLLSTONECRAFT

- Summarize the basic facts of Wollstonecraft's life.
- Understand some of the ways that middle-class English women in Wollstonecraft's day were made to "exist for the sake of men."
- State the three factors that Wollstonecraft says are the source of true happiness for both men and women.
- Understand why Wollstonecraft rejects men's attempts to keep women innocent.

16.2 SIMONE DE BEAUVOIR

- Explain the distinction that Beauvoir makes between *sex* and *gender*.
- Explain what Beauvoir means by her assertion that women have been defined by men as the "Other."
- Summarize Beauvoir's central argument in *The Second Sex*.
- Understand what Beauvoir thinks "real freedom and true equality" would entail.
- Describe the two positions staked out in the debate about innate gender difference.

16.3 FEMINIST ETHICS

- Define *feminist ethics* and the *ethics of care*.
- Enumerate some of the values and experiences that some feminists say are associated with the typically male perspective.
- Describe the nature of the ethics of care, its most attractive features, and some of the criticisms that have been lodged against it.

16.4 FEMINIST PERSPECTIVES ON KNOWLEDGE

- State the central aim of feminist philosophy and of feminist epistemology.
- List some ways that, according to feminists, "dominant knowledge practices" disadvantage women.

- Summarize the principal claims of feminist empiricism, feminist standpoint theory, and feminist postmodernism.
- Understand some of the criticisms that feminists have lodged against feminist postmodernism.

Feminism, as both a movement and an approach to social and intellectual issues, is concerned with identifying and remedying harm and disadvantage arising from biases against women. Feminists argue that such prejudices are common throughout society and academia, and that they lead to the widespread discrediting of women's ideas and experiences and the relegating of women to subordinate roles. Feminist philosophy is an attempt to address the disparagement or subordination of women in philosophy and related fields, and feminist ethics and epistemology try to do the same in theories of morality and knowledge.

In philosophy, there is no single outlook that can be called feminist; rather there are several different viewpoints and approaches that deserve the name. The common thread is an emphasis on gender and on how it shapes the issues at hand. Alison Ainley, a feminist philosopher, notes the diversity of the philosophical projects:

Alison Ainley: "Feminist Philosophy"

Feminist approaches to philosophy can take place at a number of levels and from different perspectives, and indeed this has been identified as a notable strength. For example, feminists have presented philosophical critiques of philosophers' images of women, political critiques of the organization of the discipline of philosophy, critiques of philosophy as masculine, historical research into the work of past women philosophers whose work may have been unjustly disregarded, and positive contributions to philosophy from a feminist perspective. Feminist philosophers may take some or all of these approaches to be important, but, generally speaking, feminist philosophy will assume the question of sexual difference to be a philosophical issue at some level and, depending on the point of departure, produce very different ways of theorizing about this question. Although women tend to work in this area, not all women philosophers are necessarily feminist philosophers (although there may be feminist implications in their work).[1]

1. Does the fact that some famous philosophers held negative views of women impugn the nature of the philosophical enterprise? Why or why not?

Feminist thinkers have had good reason to suspect bias in the philosophical enterprise. It is easy in philosophy's history to find eminent male philosophers dismissing, devaluing, or ignoring the female intellect—even though women philosophers have been present in every age, from the classical period to modern times. (Some important male philosophers have afforded women more respect—for example, Plato and John Stuart Mill; and some have developed ideas that have been put to use in feminist writings—for example, David Hume and John Dewey.) Louise M. Antony points out some of the more notorious examples of bias:

Louise M. Antony: "Embodiment and Epistemology"

Although women were largely ignored by the major philosophers, whenever we *were* discussed, we were denigrated. Strikingly, the insult often involved a philosopher's explicitly denying to women some characteristic that that philosopher had elsewhere held to be essential to full personhood, making us, by definition, less than human. Thus Aristotle, who defined "man" as a rational animal, claimed that women's reason was defective in that it was "without the power to be effective." Locke, who thought that "man" could transcend natural power relations by means of civil agreement, still found it obvious that in case of conflict between husband and wife, "the rule . . . naturally falls to the man's share, as the abler and the stronger." Rousseau, who took freedom to be the distinguishing mark of humanity, held that it followed from the different natures of men ("active and strong") and women ("passive and weak") that "woman is made to please and be dominated" by man. Perhaps most notoriously of all, Kant, who made acting from apprehension of the categorical imperative the essence of moral agency, averred that "I hardly believe that the fair sex is capable of principles."[2]

> "Men, in general seem to employ their reason to justify prejudices, which they have imbibed, they can scarcely trace how, rather than to root them out."
>
> —Mary Wollstonecraft

16.1 MARY WOLLSTONECRAFT

Mary Wollstonecraft (1759–1797) was a political radical, a social critic with a strong egalitarian bent, a distinguished novelist, and one of the great forebears of feminist thought. What she wrote then about women's rights and women's situation in society is still relevant today—and still considered radical by many. By law and by custom, middle-class English women in her day were thought to be subordinate to men in countless ways. They lived under the weight of a damaging presumption: *women exist for the sake of men.* Women were denied property ownership, expected to defer to men in important matters, barred from almost all professions, excluded from voting and government posts, deprived of higher education, and judged by different moral standards than those applied to men. Few societies in the rest of the world treated women any better.

Wollstonecraft studied the conditions that women found themselves in, and she read what prominent men had to say about the character, duties, and education of women. Thus much of her literary output was in response to the views of

Figure 16.1 Mary Wollstonecraft (1759–1797).

the famous Edmund Burke, who wrote in support of aristocratic rights and privileges, and to Rousseau, who considered women inferior to men.

Her greatest works are *A Vindication of the Rights of Men* (1790) and *A Vindication of the Rights of Women* (1792). In the latter, she envisions a society of equals freed from the tyranny of unreason and spurious authority. Such a society requires the full development of the moral and rational faculties of both men and women. For too long, she says, women have had their powers of reason obstructed by men who believe that reason is the domain of males and who define women in ways that serve men. Men have ensured that women are uneducated, molded by male expectations, judged by appearances instead of intellect, and obliged to submit to the preferences of men instead of the dictates of reason. As Wollstonecraft puts it:

> "Every profession, in which subordination of rank constitutes its power, is highly injurious to morality."
>
> —Mary Wollstonecraft

Mary Wollstonecraft: *A Vindication of the Rights of Women*

I have turned over various books written on the subject of education, and patiently observed the conduct of parents and the management of schools; but what has been the result?—a profound conviction that the neglected education of my fellow-creatures is the grand source of the misery I deplore; and that women, in particular, are rendered weak and wretched by a variety of concurring causes, originating from one hasty conclusion. The conduct and manners of women, in fact, evidently prove that their minds are not in a healthy state; for, like the flowers which are planted in too rich a soil, strength and usefulness are sacrificed to beauty; and the flaunting leaves, after having pleased a fastidious eye, fade, disregarded on the stalk, long before the season when they ought to have arrived at maturity.—One cause of this barren blooming I attribute to a false system of education, gathered from the books written on this subject by men who, considering females rather as women than human creatures, have been more anxious to make them alluring mistresses than affectionate wives and rational mothers; and the understanding of the sex has been so bubbled [deluded] by this specious homage, that the civilized women of the present century, with a few exceptions, are only anxious to inspire love, when they ought to cherish a nobler ambition, and by their abilities and virtues exact respect.[3]

> "How grossly do they insult us who thus advise us only to render ourselves gentle, domestic brutes!"
>
> —Mary Wollstonecraft

Wollstonecraft argues that humanity's true happiness and ultimate perfection lie in the development of reason, virtue, and knowledge. Yet in women, these human capacities have been deliberately stunted, and the result is a deformity of the soul that society must correct. If women have souls just as men do, they can—and should—aspire to possess these same qualities and in the same measure.

> Mary Wollstonecraft: *A Vindication of the Rights of Women*

To account for, and excuse the tyranny of man, many ingenious arguments have been brought forward to prove, that the two sexes, in the achievement of virtue, ought to aim at attaining a very different character: or, to speak explicitly, women are not allowed to have sufficient strength of mind to acquire what really deserves the name of virtue. Yet it should seem, allowing them to have souls, that there is but one way appointed by Providence to lead *mankind* to either virtue or happiness.

PORTRAIT

Figure 16.2 Mary Woll-stonecraft's gravestone in St. Pancras Gardens, London.

Wollstonecraft

Mary Wollstonecraft (1759–1797) was born in London to a fi-nancially strapped family, one of seven children, only one of whom (her brother Edward) received a formal education. She was mostly self-taught and very well read, eventually showing herself to be an astute social critic and an insightful moral, philosophi-cal, and political writer. She expressed her ideas in several forms, including books, essays, reviews, translations, stories, and novels.

Her literary and philosophical achievements are remarkable in themselves, but they seem all the more extraordinary con-sidering that she produced them during a short life filled with grief and disappointment. To support herself she worked as a schoolteacher, a companion to a lady, and a governess—almost the only jobs open to women in her situation. She had to aban-don her own plans to care for her dying mother, and she had to come to the aid of her sister Eliza, who suffered a breakdown that Mary believed resulted from mistreatment by Eliza's husband. In 1784 she opened a progressive school, but it failed within two years and became a major cause of misery to her, both financially and otherwise. In 1785 she left for Lisbon to be with her best friend, Fanny Blood, who was soon to have a baby. Fanny had been described as the "ruling passion" of Mary's mind. Unfortunately, when Mary arrived, Fanny was already in premature labor and died in Mary's arms, with the baby soon to follow.

Despite these woes, she managed to produce several important works, including *Thoughts on the Education of Daughters* (1786); *Mary, A Fiction* (her first novel, 1788); *Original Stories from Real Life* (1788); *A Vindication of the Rights of Men* (1790); *A Vindication of the Rights of Women* (1792); and *An Historical and Moral View of the Origin and Progress of the French Revolution* (1794).

In the early 1790s, she had a miserable affair with an American author named Gilbert Imlay. They never married, and she had a child by him. She ended the affair in 1796 and later that year fell in love with William Godwin, whom she married in 1797. They soon had a daughter—later known as Mary Shelley, the author of *Frankenstein* and the wife of the famous poet Percy Bysshe Shelley. But the delivery was complicated, and ten days after the birth, Mary Wollstonecraft was dead at age thirty-eight.

If then women are not a swarm of ephemeron [short-lived] triflers, why should they be kept in ignorance under the specious name of innocence? Men complain, and with reason, of the follies and caprices of our sex, when they do not keenly satirize our headstrong and groveling vice.—Behold, I should answer, the natural effect of ignorance! The mind will ever be unstable that has only prejudices to rest on, and the current will run with destruc-tive fury when there are not barriers to break its force. Women are told from their infancy, and taught by the example of their mothers, that a little knowledge of human weakness,

Mary Wollstonecraft:
A Vindication of the Rights of Women

---

2. What specifically is morally wrong about the kind of education that Wollstonecraft says leaves women ignorant and weak? Is it a violation of rights, a lack of respect for persons, a case of producing more bad than good, or something else?

"[According to the dominant view] woman was created to be the toy of man, his rattle, and it must jingle in his ears whenever, dismissing reason, he chooses to be amused."

—Mary Wollstonecraft

justly termed cunning, softness of temper, *outward* obedience, and a scrupulous attention to a puerile kind of propriety, will obtain for them the protection of man; and should they be beautiful, every thing else is needless, for, at least twenty years of their lives. . . .

Men, indeed, appear to me to act in a very unphilosophical manner when they try to secure the good conduct of women by attempting to keep them always in a state of childhood. Rousseau was more consistent when he wished to stop the progress of reason in both sexes, for if men eat of the tree of knowledge, women will come in for a taste; but, from the imperfect cultivation which their understandings now receive, they only attain a knowledge of evil. . . .

Consequently, the most perfect education, in my opinion, is such an exercise of the understanding as is best calculated to strengthen the body and form the heart. Or, in other words, to enable the individual to attain such habits of virtue as will render it independent. In fact, it is a farce to call any being virtuous whose virtues do not result from the exercise of its own reason. This was Rousseau's opinion respecting men: I extend it to women. . . .

Youth is the season for love in both sexes; but in those days of thoughtless enjoyment provision should be made for the more important years of life, when reflection takes place of sensation. But Rousseau, and most of the male writers who have followed his steps, have warmly inculcated that the whole tendency of female education ought to be directed to one point:—to render them pleasing. . . .

[T]hough moralists have agreed that the tenor of life seems to prove that *man* is prepared by various circumstances for a future state, they constantly concur in advising *woman* only to provide for the present. Gentleness, docility, and a spaniel-like affection are, on this ground, consistently recommended as the cardinal virtues of the sex; and, disregarding the arbitrary economy of nature, one writer has declared that it is masculine for a woman to be melancholy. She was created to be the toy of man, his rattle, and it must jingle in his ears whenever, dismissing reason, he chooses to be amused. . . .

Figure 16.3 A U.S. postage stamp commemorating three early suffragettes. American women did not get the vote until 1920; British women, 1918.

It is time to effect a revolution in female manners—time to restore to them their lost dignity—and make them, as part of the human species, labour by reforming themselves to reform the world.[4]

16.2 SIMONE DE BEAUVOIR

In the last sixty years, the world's attitudes toward women, and women's attitudes toward themselves, have changed (mostly for the better) in ways that probably would have shocked even Mary Wollstonecraft. Much of this alteration in outlook can be traced back to the French philosopher, novelist, and feminist Simone de Beauvoir (1908–1986). The writer Judith Thurman sums up Beauvoir's influence like this:

> "If woman discovers herself as the inessential and never turns into the essential, it is because she does not bring about this transformation herself."
> —Simone de Beauvoir

Judith Thurman: Introduction to *The Second Sex* by Simone de Beauvoir

While no one individual or her work is responsible for that seismic shift in laws and attitudes, the millions of young women who now confidently assume that their entitlement to work, pleasure, and autonomy is equal to that of their brothers owe a measure of their freedom to Beauvoir.[5]

Beauvoir was born in Paris, schooled in the Sorbonne, and known as the lover and companion of the renowned Jean-Paul Sartre. She was his devoted colleague, a fellow existentialist, and she also served as his most astute critic and influenced him more than her own critics realized. She wrote essays, philosophical works, novels, and biography, and became renowned in her own right with the publication of *The Second Sex* (1949), her influential study of the inequality and injustice that defines the female condition. In her writings she ranged far and wide, examining radical freedom, the nature of evil, the use of violence, sex and gender, existentialism, good and bad faith, and moral responsibility.

Beauvoir begins *The Second Sex* by asking a seemingly inane question: What is a woman? The answer is not at all obvious to men and women, she says. To clarify, she makes a distinction that has become central to feminist thought: biological sexual difference (male, female) is not the same as gender, which is mostly (or entirely) a socially determined characteristic. So she declares, "one is not born, but rather becomes, a woman." And this socially determined *becoming* is shaped by male expectations and prerogative.

Figure 16.4 Simone de Beauvoir (1908–1986).

Thus woman has been defined by a male-skewed society as the *Other* (another important concept introduced by Beauvoir). Throughout history the male human has been thought of as the epitome of a human, as the embodiment of humanity—the One. Woman, however, has been cast as the Other, a creature defined in relation to man. Women are secondary; men are primary.

Here is Beauvoir making her case:

Simone de Beauvoir: *The Second Sex*

If the female function is not enough to define woman, and if we also reject the explanation of the "eternal feminine," but if we accept, even temporarily, that there are women on earth, we then have to ask: What is a woman?

Merely stating the problem suggests an immediate answer to me. It is significant that I pose it. It would never occur to a man to write a book on the singular situation of males in humanity. If I want to define myself, I first have to say, "I am a woman"; all other assertions will arise from this basic truth. A man never begins by positing himself as an individual of a certain sex: that he is a man is obvious. The categories masculine and feminine appear as symmetrical in a formal way on town hall records or identification papers. The relation of the two sexes is not that of two electrical poles: the man represents both the positive and the neuter to such an extent that in French *hommes* designates human beings, the particular meaning of the word *vir* being assimilated into the general meaning of the word "homo." Woman is the negative, to such a point that any determination is imputed to her as a limitation, without reciprocity. I used to get annoyed in abstract discussions to hear men tell me: "You think such and such a thing because you're a woman." But I know my only defense is to answer, "I think it because it is true," thereby eliminating my subjectivity; it was out of the question to answer, "And you think the contrary because you are a man," because it is understood that being a man is not a particularity; a man is in his right by virtue of being man; it is the woman who is in the wrong. In fact, just as for the ancients there was an absolute vertical that defined the oblique, there is an absolute human type that is masculine. Woman has ovaries and a uterus; such are the particular conditions that lock her in her subjectivity; some even say she thinks with her hormones. Man vainly forgets that his anatomy also includes hormones and testicles. He grasps his body as a direct and normal link with the world that he believes he apprehends in all objectivity, whereas he considers woman's body an obstacle, a prison, burdened by everything that particularizes it. "The female is female by virtue of a certain *lack* of qualities," Aristotle said. "We should regard women's nature as suffering from natural defectiveness." And Saint Thomas in his turn decreed that woman was an "incomplete man," an "incidental" being. This is what the Genesis story symbolizes, where Eve appears as if drawn from Adam's "supernumerary" bone, in Bossuet's words. Humanity is male, and man defines woman, not in herself, but in relation to himself; she is not considered an autonomous being. "Woman, the relative being," writes Michelet. Thus Monsieur Benda declares in [Uriel's Report]: "A man's body has meaning by itself, disregarding the body of the woman, whereas the woman's body seems devoid of meaning without reference to the male. Man thinks himself without woman. Woman does not think herself without man." And she is nothing other than what man decides; she is thus called "the sex," meaning that the male sees her essentially as a sexed being; for him she is sex, so she is it in the absolute. She is determined and differentiated in relation to man, while he is not in relation to her; she is the inessential in front of the essential. He is the Subject; he is the Absolute. She is the Other.

The category of *Other* is as original as consciousness itself. The duality between Self and Other can be found in the most primitive societies. . . . No group ever defines itself as One without immediately setting up the Other opposite itself. . . .

Now, woman has always been, if not man's slave, at least his vassal; the two sexes have never divided the world up equally; and still today, even though her condition is changing, woman is heavily handicapped. In no country is her legal status identical to man's, and often it puts her at a considerable disadvantage. Even when her rights are recognized abstractly, long-standing habit keeps them from being concretely manifested in customs. Economically, men and women almost form two castes; all things being equal, the former have better jobs, higher wages, and greater chances to succeed than their new female competitors; they occupy many more places in industry, in politics, and so forth, and they hold the most important positions. . . . At the moment that women are beginning to share in the making of the world, this world still belongs to men: men have no doubt about this, and women barely doubt it. . . . The man who sets the woman up as an *Other* will thus find her in deep complicity. Hence woman makes no claim for herself as subject because she lacks the concrete means, because she senses the necessary link

3. Do you agree with Beauvoir that women have been defined as the Other? If so, in what ways? What are the ramifications for women of being so defined?

Figure 16.5 The headstone for Jean-Paul Sartre and Simone de Beauvoir in Montparnasse Cemetery, Paris.

Simone de Beauvoir:
The Second Sex

connecting her to man without positing its reciprocity, and because she often derives satisfaction from her role as *Other*. . . .

[T]he very fact that woman is *Other* challenges all the justifications that men have ever given: these were only too clearly dictated by their own interest. "Everything that men have written about women should be viewed with suspicion, because they are both judge and party," wrote Poulain de la Barre, a little-known seventeenth-century feminist. . . . Among the blessings Plato thanked the gods for was, first, being born free and not a slave and, second, a man and not a woman. . . . Lawmakers, priests, philosophers, writers, and scholars have gone to great lengths to prove that women's subordinate condition was willed in heaven and profitable on earth.[6]

"No one is more arrogant toward women, more aggressive or more disdainful, than a man anxious about his own virility."
—Simone de Beauvoir

Lifting this oppression, says Beauvoir, requires real freedom and true equality of both men and women—equality in education, working conditions and salaries, sexuality, marriage, motherhood, the care of children, and more. But can men and women become peers, she asks, just by changing institutions, customs, and social systems? No: a deeper transformation must first occur.

THEN AND NOW

Innate Gender Differences?

In 1949 Simone de Beauvoir declared in *The Second Sex* that "one is not born, but rather becomes, a woman." In other words, gender is not innate—it's *learned*. It's a product of the continually reinforced male perspective. In the twenty-first century the question of innate gender differences has arisen in several forms. One popular version is, "Are females hard-wired to be worse at math than males?" Many people believe the answer is yes. They assume that males are inherently better at math and that biology (hormones, genetics, etc.) accounts for the male/female differences that researchers have uncovered. (The issue matters because people who assume that boys are naturally better at math may end up treating boys and girls accordingly, expecting less from girls and more from boys.) But is biology the reason for a male/female math gap?

Of course there are obvious sex differences between men and women (genitals and breasts). There are also subtle biological differences (brain size and neural activity patterns, for example), but so far these differences seem not to have much effect on cognition. In the past decade, scientific research has shown that cognitive differences between girls and boys come mostly from bias, culture, and education systems. Studies consisting of hundreds of thousands of students in dozens of countries have failed to find a strong link between math skills and biology, but they have found clear correlations between math skills and

"Women will always be women," say the skeptics; other seers prophesy that in shedding their femininity, they will not succeed in changing into men and will become monsters. This would mean that today's woman is nature's creation; it must be repeated again that within the human collectivity nothing is natural, and woman, among others, is a product developed by civilization.... Woman is defined neither by her hormones nor by mysterious instincts but by the way she grasps, through foreign consciousnesses, her body and her relation to the world; the abyss that separates adolescent girls from adolescent boys was purposely dug out from early infancy; later, it would be impossible to keep woman from being what she *was made*, and she will always trail this past behind her; if the weight of this past is accurately measured, it is obvious that her destiny is not fixed in eternity. One must certainly not think that modifying her economic situation is enough to transform woman: this factor has been and remains the primordial factor of her development, but until it brings about the moral, social, and cultural consequences it heralds and requires, the new woman cannot appear.... The same drama of flesh and spirit, and of finitude and transcendence, plays itself out in both sexes; both are eaten away by time, stalked by death, they have the same essential need of the other; and they can take the same glory from their freedom; if they knew how to savor it, they would no longer be tempted to contend for false privileges; and fraternity could then be born between them.[7]

Simone de Beauvoir:
The Second Sex

sociological and psychological factors. Here is a typical account from the American Psychological Association:

> Girls around the world are not worse at math than boys, even though boys are more confident in their math abilities, and girls from countries where gender equity is more prevalent are more likely to perform better on mathematics assessment tests, according to a new analysis of international research.
>
> "Stereotypes about female inferiority in mathematics are a distinct contrast to the actual scientific data," said Nicole Else-Quest, PhD, a psychology professor at Villanova University, and lead author of the meta-analysis. "These results show that girls will perform at the same level as the boys when they are given the right educational tools and have visible female role models excelling in mathematics."

Beauvoir's assertions about sociological male influences shaping women's self-image are empirical claims. But in her day there was little or no empirical evidence to back them up. Was she justified in making such claims?

American Psychological Association, "Worldwide Study Finds Few Gender Differences in Math Abilities," January 5, 2010, http://www.apa.org/news/press/releases/2010/01/gender-math.aspx.

16.3 FEMINIST ETHICS

feminist ethics An approach to morality aimed at advancing women's interests, underscoring their distinctive experiences and characteristics, and advancing the obvious truth that women and men are morally equal.

In recent decades, an important development has challenged the traditional theories and concepts of moral philosophy: the rise of **feminist ethics**. Feminist ethics is an approach to morality aimed at advancing women's interests, underscoring their distinctive experiences and characteristics, and advancing the obvious truth that women and men are morally equal. It is defined by a distinctive focus on these issues, rather than by a set of doctrines or common ideology among feminists, many of whom may disagree on the nature of feminist ethics or on particular moral issues.

Feminist ethics generally downplays the role of moral principles and traditional ethical concepts, insisting instead that moral reflection must take into account the social realities—the relevant social practices, relationships, institutions, and power arrangements. Many feminists think that the familiar principles of Western ethics—autonomy, utility, freedom, equality, and the like—are too broad and abstract to help us make moral judgments about specific persons who are enmeshed in concrete social situations. It is not enough, for example, to respect a woman's decision to have an abortion if she is too poor to have one, or if her culture is so oppressive (or oppressed) as to make abortion impossible to obtain, or if social conditioning leads her to believe that she has no choice or that her views don't count. Theoretical autonomy does not mean much if it is so thoroughly undermined in reality.

4. Is there such a thing as "the female perspective"? That is, do all women have the same basic outlook or style of reasoning?

Many feminist writers maintain that the values and virtues inherent in most traditional moral theories reflect a typically masculine perspective—and thus offer a one-sided (or wrong-sided) view of the moral life. What's needed, they say, is a moral outlook that takes into account values and experiences that usually have been identified with women. According to one feminist philosopher, feminists claim that traditional ethics favors the

Alison Jaggar: "Feminist Ethics"

. . . supposedly masculine or male-associated values of independence, autonomy, intellect, will, wariness, hierarchy, domination, culture, transcendence, product, asceticism, war and death over the supposedly feminine or female-associated values of interdependence, community, connection, sharing, emotion, body, trust, absence of hierarchy, nature, immanence, process, joy, peace and life.[8]

Some proponents of feminist ethics also reject the traditional concept of the moral agent. Jan Crosthwaite says that the old notion is that of "abstract individuals as fundamentally autonomous agents, aware of their own preferences and values, and motivated by rational self-interest (though not necessarily selfish)."[9] But, she says, many feminists

Jan Crosthwaite: "Gender and Bioethics"

... present a richer conception of persons as historically and culturally located, socially related and essentially embodied. Individuals are located in and formed by specific relationships (chosen and unchosen) and ties of affection and responsibility.... Such a conception of socially embedded selves refocuses thinking about autonomy, shifting the emphasis from independent self-determination towards ideals of integrity within relatedness.... Respecting autonomy becomes less a matter of protecting individuals from "coercive" influences than one of positive empowerment, recognizing people's interdependence and supporting individuals' development of their own understanding of their situation and options.[10]

Many of these themes run through the **ethics of care**, a moral perspective that arose out of feminist concerns and grew to challenge core elements of most other moral theories. Generally those theories emphasize abstract principles, general duties, individual rights, justice, utility, impartial judgments, and deliberative reasoning. But the ethics of care shifts the focus to the unique demands of specific situations and to the virtues and feelings that are central to close personal relationships—empathy, compassion, love, sympathy, and fidelity. The heart of the moral life is feeling for and caring for those with whom you have a special, intimate connection.

ethics of care A moral perspective that emphasizes the unique demands of specific situations and the virtues and feelings that are central to close personal relationships.

Early on, the ethics of care drew inspiration from the notion that men and women have dramatically different styles of moral decision-making, with men seizing on principles, duties, and rights, and women homing in on personal relationships, caring, and empathy. This difference was highlighted in research done by psychologist Carol Gilligan and published in her 1982 book *In a Different Voice*.[11] Typically men recognize an ethic of justice and rights, she says, and women are guided by an ethic of compassion and care. In her view the latter is as legitimate as the former, and both have their place in ethics.

"A system of morality which is based on relative emotional values is a mere illusion, a thoroughly vulgar conception which has nothing sound in it and nothing true."

—Socrates

Other research has suggested that the differences between men and women in styles of moral thinking may not be as great as Gilligan suggests. But the credibility of the empirical claim does not affect the larger insight that the research seemed to some writers to suggest: caring is an essential part of morality, and the most influential theories have not fully taken it into account.

These points get support along several lines. First, many philosophers—from Aristotle to contemporary thinkers—hold that virtues are part of the moral life. If caring is viewed as a virtue—in the form of compassion, empathy, or kindness—then caring too must be an element of morality. A moral theory then would be deficient if it made no room for care.

Moreover, many argue that unlike the ethics of care, most moral theories push the principle of impartiality too far. Recall that impartiality in morality requires us to consider everyone as equal, counting everyone's interests the same. The principle applies widely, especially in matters of public justice, but less so in personal relationships of love, family, friendship, and the like. We seem to have special obligations (partiality) to close friends, family members, and others we care for, duties that we do not have to strangers or to universal humanity.

Most moral theories emphasize duties and downplay the role of emotions, attitudes, and motivations. Kant, for example, would have us do our duty for duty's sake, whatever our feelings. For him, to be a morally good parent, we need only act from duty. But taking care of our children as a matter of moral obligation alone seems an empty exercise. Surely being a morally good parent also involves having feelings of love and attitudes of caring. The ethics of care eagerly takes these emotional elements into account.

The feminist philosopher Virginia Held offers this synopsis of the main elements of the ethics of care:

Virginia Held: *The Ethics of Care*

I think one can discern among various versions of the ethics of care a number of major features.

First, the central focus of the ethics of care is on the compelling moral salience of attending to and meeting the needs of the particular others for whom we take responsibility. Caring for one's child, for instance, may well and defensibly be at the forefront of a person's moral concerns. The ethics of care recognizes that human beings are dependent for many years of their lives, that the moral claim of those dependent on us for the care they need is pressing, and that there are highly important moral aspects in developing the relations of caring that enable human beings to live and progress. All persons need care for at least their early years. Prospects for human progress and flourishing hinge fundamentally on the care that those needing it receive, and the ethics of care stresses the moral force of the responsibility to respond to the needs of the dependent. Many persons will become ill and dependent for some periods of their later lives, including in frail old age, and some who are permanently disabled will need care the whole of their lives. Moralities built on the image of the independent, autonomous, rational individual largely overlook the reality of human dependence and the morality for which it calls. The ethics of care attends to this central concern of human life and delineates the moral values involved. It refuses to relegate care to a realm "outside morality." . . .

Second, in the epistemological process of trying to understand what morality would recommend and what it would be morally best for us to do and to be, the ethics of care values emotion rather than rejects it. Not all emotion is valued, of course, but in contrast with the dominant rationalist approaches, such emotions as sympathy, empathy, sensitivity, and responsiveness are seen as the kind of moral emotions that need to be cultivated not only to help in the implementation of the dictates of reason but to better ascertain what morality recommends. Even anger may be a component of the moral indignation that should be felt when people are treated unjustly or inhumanely, and it may contribute to (rather than interfere with) an appropriate interpretation of the moral wrong. This is not to say that raw emotion can be a guide to morality; feelings need to be reflected on and educated. But from the care perspective, moral inquiries that rely entirely on reason and rationalistic deductions or calculations are seen as deficient. . . .

Third, the ethics of care rejects the view of the dominant moral theories that the more abstract the reasoning about a moral problem the better because the more likely to avoid bias and arbitrariness, the more nearly to achieve impartiality. The ethics of care respects rather than removes itself from the claims of particular others with whom we share actual relationships. It calls into question the universalistic and abstract rules of the dominant theories. When the latter consider such actual relations as between a parent and child, if they say anything about them at all, they may see them as permitted and cultivating them a preference that a person may have. Or they may recognize a universal obligation for all parents to care for their children. But they do not permit actual relations ever to take priority over the requirements of impartiality. . . .

To most advocates of the ethics of care, the compelling moral claim of the particular other may be valid even when it conflicts with the requirement usually made by moral theories that moral judgments be universalizeable, and this is of fundamental moral importance.

Dominant moral theories tend to interpret moral problems as if they were conflicts between egoistic individual interests on the one hand, and universal moral principles on the other. The extremes of "selfish individual" and "humanity" are recognized, but what lies between these is often overlooked. The ethics of care, in contrast, focuses especially on the area between these extremes. Those who conscientiously care for others are not seeking primarily to further their own *individual* interests; their interests are intertwined with the persons they care for. Neither are they acting for the sake of *all others* or *humanity in general*; they seek instead to preserve or promote an actual human relation between themselves and *particular others*. Persons in caring relations are acting for self-and-other together. Their characteristic stance is neither egoistic nor altruistic; these are the options in a conflictual situation, but the well-being of a caring relation involves the cooperative well-being of those in the relation and the well-being of the relation itself. . . .

A fourth characteristic of the ethics of care is that like much feminist thought in many areas, it reconceptualizes traditional notions about the public and the private. The traditional view, built into the dominant moral theories, is that the household is a private sphere beyond politics into which government, based on consent, should not intrude. . . .

Dominant moral theories have seen "public" life as relevant to morality while missing the moral significance of the "private" domains of family and friendship. Thus the dominant theories have assumed that morality should be sought for unrelated, independent, and mutually indifferent individuals assumed to be equal. They have posited an abstract, fully rational "agent as such" from which to construct morality, while missing the moral issues that arise between interconnected persons in the contexts of family, friendship, and social groups. In the context of the family, it is typical for relations to be between persons with highly unequal power who did not choose the ties and obligations in which they find themselves enmeshed. For instance, no child can choose her parents yet she may well have obligations to care for them. Relations of this kind are standardly noncontractual, and

5. Does Held suggest a way to decide which emotions to heed and which to ignore? If the ethics of care cannot help us sort out our emotions, should we consider it a bad theory?

"Two things fill the mind with ever new and increasing admiration and awe: the starry heavens above and the moral law within."

—Immanuel Kant

Virginia Held:
The Ethics of Care

conceptualizing them as contractual would often undermine or at least obscure the trust on which their worth depends. The ethics of care addresses rather than neglects moral issues arising in relations among the unequal and dependent, relations that are often laden with emotion and involuntary, and then notices how often these attributes apply not only in the household but in the wider society as well. . . .

A fifth characteristic of the ethics of care is the conception of persons with which it begins. . . . The ethics of care usually works with a conception of persons as relational, rather than as the self-sufficient independent individuals of the dominant moral theories.[12]

"The ethics of care confirms the priority that we naturally give to our family and friends, and so it seems a more plausible conception."

—James Rachels

Many philosophers, including some who favor traditional theories, think the ethics of care is surely right about certain aspects of the moral life. Caring, they say, is indeed a vital part of morality. Sometimes the most important factor in moral decision-making is not justice, utility, or rights, but compassionate consideration. Impartiality is a basic requirement of morality, an ideal that guides us to fairness and justice and away from prejudice and inequality. But it often does not apply in our relationships with friends and loved ones, for to those close to us we may have special obligations that we do not have toward others. And, contrary to Kant, feelings do matter. They can alert us to important moral issues and give us a deeper understanding of morality's point and purpose. True, reason must hold the reins of our emotions, but there can be no denying that they have a legitimate place in the moral life.

DETAILS

Ethics Terminology

ethics (moral philosophy) The study of morality using the methods of philosophy. (Chapter 11)

morality Beliefs about right and wrong actions and good and bad persons or character. (Chapter 11)

moral theory A theory that explains why an action is right or wrong or why a person or a person's character is good or bad. (Chapter 11)

virtue A disposition to behave in line with a standard of excellence. (Chapter 5)

deontological (or nonconsequentialist) **theory** A moral theory in which the rightness of actions is determined not solely by their consequences but partly or entirely by their intrinsic nature. (Chapter 11)

consequentialist theory A moral theory in which the rightness of actions depends solely on their consequences or results. (Chapter 11)

utilitarianism The consequentialist view that right actions are those that result in the most beneficial balance of good over bad consequences for everyone involved. (Chapter 13)

To these concessions many moral philosophers would add a cautionary note: the ethics of care is not the whole of morality, and to view it that way is a mistake. To decide on the right action, we often cannot avoid applying the concepts of justice and rights. Sometimes impartiality is the best (or only) policy, without which our moral decisions would be misguided, even tragic. And abstract principles or rules, though unwieldy in many cases, may be essential to reconciling conflicting obligations or intuitions.

So should plausible moral theories try to accommodate *both* an ethic of obligation and an ethic of care? Many theorists, including several writing from a feminist perspective, think so. Annette Baier, for example, says that

Annette C. Baier: "The Need for More Than Justice"

...the best moral theory has to be a cooperative product of women and men, has to harmonize justice and care. The morality it theorizes about is after all for all persons, for men and for women, and will need their combined insights. As Gilligan said, what we need now is a 'marriage' of the old male and the newly articulated female insights.[13]

16.4 FEMINIST PERSPECTIVES ON KNOWLEDGE

Feminist epistemology focuses most of its attention on the "situated knower" and "situated knowledge"—that is, on how knowledge arises from the unique perspectives and practices of those involved in knowing. The basic claim is that gender has skewed traditional epistemology toward the dominant male perspective and has thus adversely affected women and other disadvantaged groups. Feminist philosophers say the remedy is to develop theories of knowledge based on alternative conceptions of gender and power, banishing the ill effects of the traditional view in the process. According to Elizabeth Anderson:

"The most important human endeavor is the striving for morality in our actions. Our inner balance and even our very existence depend on it. Only morality in our actions can give beauty and dignity to life."

—Albert Einstein

Elizabeth Anderson: "Feminist Epistemology and Philosophy of Science"

Various practitioners of feminist epistemology and philosophy of science argue that dominant knowledge practices disadvantage women by (1) excluding them from inquiry, (2) denying them epistemic authority, (3) denigrating their "feminine" cognitive styles and modes of knowledge, (4) producing theories of women that represent them as inferior, deviant, or significant only in the ways they serve male interests, (5) producing theories of social phenomena that render women's activities and interests, or gendered power relations, invisible, and (6) producing knowledge (science and technology) that is not useful for people in subordinate positions, or that reinforces gender and other social hierarchies.[14]

Eve Browning Cole, another feminist philosopher, characterizes traditional epistemology like this:

Eve Browning Cole: *Philosophy and Feminist Criticism*

[T]here is widespread agreement that the dominant theories of knowledge provided by the Western philosophical tradition have focused on a specific *kind* of knowledge which is, as Lorraine Code has described it, "a commodity of privilege." Asking such questions as "How do I know that there is a cat on the mat?" assumes that any "I" might be substituted for any other, that conditions of knowing are homogeneous and can be generally specified. All potential knowers have a presumed equal access to the view of the cat, and the epistemologist's job is to explain what is going on in their viewing and whether it amounts to knowledge or something else. But the fact of the matter is that ideal viewing conditions simply do not obtain for all potential viewers; in our society, knowledge conditions are vastly different for members of groups differentiated by gender, race, class, age, economic status, and so forth. An aged woman who cannot get out to see her social worker, or who fears going downtown on the bus alone, will be ignorant of important benefits to which she may be entitled; in this sense, she will not be in a position to view that particular cat on its mat. Traditional epistemologies have not regarded such situations as problematic or interesting; they have not regarded them at all. Yet surely these are situations in which the social and situational *differences* among knowers are crucial for determining the kind of knowing that can take place. Epistemologies that do not have room for these differences doom themselves to irrelevance at best, and at worst they perpetuate injustice—for, as we have already stressed, knowledge *is* power.[15]

6. What is Cole's main point in the preceding passage? Do you agree with her?

To develop alternatives to traditional theories of knowledge, feminist thinkers have explored three epistemological paths: *feminist empiricism*, *feminist standpoint theory*, and *feminist postmodernism*. Feminist empiricism is probably the least controversial. It doesn't want to abolish established theories; instead, it calls for a deeper, more rigorous application of empiricism, a theory with a long history. As Cole says:

Eve Browning Cole: *Philosophy and Feminist Criticism*

One way to react to all this is that prescribed by the feminist empiricist, who suggests that philosophy's shortcomings with regard to white women, to women and men of color, to lesbians, and to all the nonprivileged, can be remedied by a more careful adherence to what is after all philosophy's stated mission: the pursuit of wisdom, the search for truth. What has produced the lamentably flawed history of philosophy has been a pattern of failures to live up to the basic scenario of empiricist knowing: the unbiased observation of the face of the universe. Prejudice and bias have been all too clearly present, clouding the judgment of the philosopher and skewing the resultant description.

To give just one famous example: Aristotle, whose allegiance to careful empirical observation is stated and evinced everywhere in his work, is incorrect about the number of teeth women have. He asserts that the adult man has thirty-two teeth but the adult woman only twenty-eight. Now, this cannot have been a function of the difficulty of observation, as women with countable teeth existed in plenty then as now. Rather, scholars have hypothesized that Aristotle counted the teeth in the male jaw and, in the grip of a powerful prejudice, subtracted four to arrive at the number in a woman's (smaller) jaw. Another possibility is that he observed the dentition of a woman who had no wisdom teeth. In either case, Aristotle's mistake is a result of failing to be a *good enough empiricist* rather than something endemic to the method of observation itself.

The feminist empiricist maintains that philosophers and scientists need to be told to "Look again!" rather than to find a wholly new way of looking. The prospects for a better philosophical understanding of human existence and its surroundings will improve as larger numbers of women enter the domains in which "received knowledge" is processed: universities, laboratories, publishing houses, journal editorial boards, and funding agencies. These women will be placed well to point out mistakes in the observations of their colleagues and to set up research agendas that promise to avoid the mistakes of the past.[16]

"I myself have never been able to find out precisely what feminism is: I only know that people call me a feminist whenever I express sentiments that differentiate me from a doormat."

—Rebecca West

Feminist standpoint theory says that different social groups have distinctive kinds of knowledge acquired through unique experiences and that some of these groups may enjoy epistemological advantages over others. In particular, the type of knowledge derived from women's experiences may be just as good as or better than knowledge acquired by the dominant knowledge-producing group—that is, white, middle-class men of science. Cole explains:

We noted . . . that philosophy's history has issued predominantly from the minds of privileged white males. It was suggested that their position, their standpoint, has had a decisive influence on the shape history has taken. Though many philosophers have presumed to speak for all "mankind," for "Reason itself," or even for "Absolute Spirit," and to be discussing the general "Nature of Mind," "conditions for knowledge," and "the human good," feminist critics have shown and continue to show the limitations of such spuriously universal discourse, and to point out large portions of human experience as yet undreamt of in their philosophy.

This specificity of the traditional standpoint has led some feminist philosophers to explore the potential of basing an epistemology in a feminist (sometimes in a women's) standpoint. The basic assumption, originating in a Hegelian or Marxian view that the human self is essentially shaped by its material activities and situation, is that women's lives have differed from men's lives in ways that would construct clear differences in their respective world views and self-concepts. Since the making and transmitting of knowledge are crucially important human activities, women's "ways of knowing" may be expected to be no less real than men's, but they are also quite likely to be very different from what traditional epistemology has supplied from the white men's standpoint.

Feminist-standpoint epistemologies seek to uncover and describe women's knowledge-making activities as these have originated in and been shaped by women's daily work and women's values. . . .

Now, standpoint theorists in feminist epistemology look at how these different work situations (women's dual-sphere work responsibilities, men's single-sphere work responsibilities) shape personality and character along gender-specific lines. Women, to be

Eve Browning Cole:
Philosophy and Feminist Criticism

proficient workers in both their domains, must become conversant with two different sets of behavior prescriptions: those appropriate to the domestic, personal situations in which they are caregivers and maintainers of life, and those appropriate to the more public and male-dominated locations in which they also labor. Behaviorally, then, and epistemically, they must be able to speak two languages, avail themselves of two different repertoires of rules dictating appropriate activity. . . .

This brings out an important point concerning standpoint theories. Those who advocate the construction of a feminist-standpoint epistemology do not merely maintain that "adding in" this standpoint, derived from women's experiences and practices traditionally excluded from philosophy's purview, will produce better philosophy, science, politics, etc.; they go further and argue that the feminist standpoint has certain inherent epistemic advantages over androcentric [male-centered] epistemologies which make it a better place to stand, so to speak, when engaged in the making of knowledge.[17]

"And seeing ignorance is the curse of God, Knowledge the wing wherewith we fly to heaven."
—William Shakespeare

7. Which view strikes you as more plausible—feminist empiricism or feminist standpoint theory? Explain.

Critics, however, have argued that standpoint theory undermines itself. The theory says that the feminist perspective is privileged (for example, better than traditional theories) and that every perspective is both limited and validated by a group's experiences. But there are many different groups and perspectives—how then can the feminist view be better or less limited than any other?

In philosophy, postmodernism is a distrust or rejection of some of the most influential epistemological ideas of modernity: objective or scientific truth, objective reality or fact, universal propositions, foundational knowledge, ultimate justification, and traditional conceptions of rationality. Feminist postmodernism is similarly skeptical of these notions and sets about systematically "deconstructing" them (critically analyzing and debunking them). Feminist postmodernists refuse to accept a basic tenet of feminist standpoint theory: that there can be a single privileged perspective from which to acquire knowledge. Instead, they insist on the existence of countless perspectives, a plurality of viewpoints, with none able to claim any epistemological advantage over the others. None can be called objectively true, because there is no perspective-neutral standard by which to judge objective truth. Cole characterizes feminist postmodernism like this:

Feminist postmodern epistemologies are thus essentially critical. Only through a thoroughgoing deconstruction of "our intellectual heritage" (every word of which phrase should be questioned), an abjuring of privileged standpoints and claims to objective truth, and a relentless critique of the relation between knowledge-making and power-guarding can a liberatory feminist thinking and practice proceed.

In the absence of objective truth, epistemically privileged standpoints, methodologies legitimated by experts, and all the other apparatus of traditional knowledge-seeking, what will make any knowledge claim more reliable than any other? Is this epistemic anarchism, a situation in which all claims, no matter how bizarre or contradictory, are equally valid? Postmodern feminist epistemologies maintain that knowledge claims will find all the legitimation they need in "localized practices," in the application they find in contexts socially and historically specific, for which they were designed. Thus what will emerge is a kind of *epistemic pluralism*, similar to that seen in [lesbian epistemologies]; the knowledge I need will be made by me, and those immediately surrounding me, in the work we do; it will be circulated to the extent that others' practices encourage such interaction, and will grow or change in this interactive process. What I must not do is dictate in advance the shape this knowledge must take (rational, empirical, justifiable under counterfactual test, etc.) or impose this knowledge on anyone else in some kind of intellectual imperialist frenzy.[18]

Cole also notes the criticisms that have been lodged against the theory by feminists themselves:

Some feminist philosophers express serious concerns about postmodernism as a viable basis for epistemology or for feminist politics in general. If a radical deconstruction of gender categories is carried out, where is the basis for the claim that women as such have anything in common? If gender identity is revealed to be an entirely social construct, a myth told to serve the interests of the lords of culture, where is the basis for feminist thinking? Sisterhood is *not* powerful if it is merely a bad dream caused by some foul cognitive substance we ingested last millennium.

Sandra Harding has expressed concern that the willingness to resign objectivity and individual autonomy to the dustbin of outmoded obsessions is perhaps a luxury many feminists would not afford. Western academic women have "had access to the benefits of the Enlightenment" and thus might give them up more easily than other women, especially third-world women, who have yet to achieve the political autonomy, suffrage and legal rights, and degree of access to the benefits of science their Western sisters enjoy. Thus it is all too easy for Western feminists to criticize the philosophical foundations on which liberalism and modern science rest; such critical latitude is born of privilege.

There are also good reasons for caution about the relinquishing of the concept of objectivity as understood by Western science. Many of the most significant advances in women's political history have been achieved through successfully putting across the argument that barriers to women's freedom are based only on prejudice, a mistaken and subjective attitude. Appeals to fairness, justice, and dispassionate objectivity have been powerful elements in this argument. Most of us believe that sexism, racism, heterosexism, and other pernicious attitudes are not objectively defensible, are based in part on false beliefs and bad faith or moral inconsistency. If we no longer have a standpoint from which to make these claims, with what justification can we continue to decry the attitudes? We ought rather to seek to reconceive the notions of objectivity, justice, and truth than to discard them and leave ourselves rhetorically helpless.[19]

Eve Browning Cole:
*Philosophy and
Feminist Criticism*

8. Do you think feminist postmodernism undermines itself in the ways that Cole suggests?

WRITING AND REASONING   **CHAPTER 16**

1. What kind of education for women did the men of Mary Wollstone-craft's day prefer? According to her, what were the results of such an education? Do you agree with her analysis? Explain.

2. Do you think women should be granted the same rights, privileges, and opportunities that men have—or do you believe women should be treated differently and provided with opportunities that are more fitting to their gender? Justify your answer.

3. Do you agree with Beauvoir that *woman* has been defined by a male-skewed society as the Other and that this has had a damaging effect on women? Why or why not?

4. What features of the ethics of care do you find plausible? Are there any important elements missing? If so, what elements?

5. Do you think there are innate differences between men and women in the ways they think about morality or moral issues? Are there culturally engrained differences in moral thinking?

REVIEW NOTES

16.1 MARY WOLLSTONECRAFT

- Mary Wollstonecraft was an early feminist and social critic who wrote about women's rights and rejected the common assumption that "women exist for the sake of men."

- In *A Vindication of the Rights of Women* she envisions a society of equals freed from the tyranny of unreason and spurious authority. Such a society requires the full development of the moral and rational faculties of both men and women. For too long, she says, women have had their powers of reason obstructed by men who believe that reason is the domain of males and who define women in ways that serve men.

- Wollstonecraft argues that humanity's true happiness and ultimate perfection lie in the development of reason, virtue, and knowledge. In women, however, these human capacities have been deliberately stunted.

16.2 SIMONE DE BEAUVOIR

- Many of the changes in modern society's attitudes toward women can be traced back to the French philosopher, novelist, and feminist Simone de Beauvoir.

- She wrote essays, philosophical works, novels, and biography, and became famous with the publication of *The Second Sex*, her influential study of the inequality and injustice that defines the female condition.

- She asserts that "one is not born, but rather becomes, a woman" and that this socially determined becoming is shaped by male expectations and prerogative. Thus woman has been defined by a male-skewed society as the *Other*. Throughout history the male has been thought of as the epitome of a human, as the embodiment of humanity—the One. Woman, however, has been cast as the Other, a creature defined in relation to man.

- Beauvoir says that eradicating the oppression of women requires real freedom and true equality of both men and women—equality in education, working conditions and salaries, sexuality, marriage, motherhood, the care of children, and more.

16.3 FEMINIST ETHICS

- Feminist ethics is an approach to morality aimed at advancing women's interests, underscoring their distinctive experiences and characteristics, and advancing the obvious truth that women and men are morally equal. It is defined by a distinctive focus on these issues, rather than by a set of doctrines or common ideology among feminists.

- Feminist ethics generally downplays the role of moral principles and traditional ethical concepts, insisting instead that moral reflection must take into account social realities—the relevant social practices, relationships, institutions, and power arrangements.

- The ethics of care is a moral perspective that arose out of feminist concerns and grew to challenge core elements of most other moral theories. This approach shifts the focus from abstract principles and rules to the unique demands of specific situations and to the virtues and feelings that are central to close personal relationships. The heart of the moral life is feeling for and caring for those with whom you have a special, intimate connection.

16.4 FEMINIST PERSPECTIVES ON KNOWLEDGE

- Feminist philosophy is an attempt to address the disparagement or subordination of women in philosophy and related fields, and feminist epistemology tries to do the same in theories of knowledge.

- According to Eve Browning Cole, feminists believe that dominant knowledge practices disadvantage women by (1) excluding them from inquiry, (2) denying them epistemic authority, (3) denigrating their "feminine" cognitive styles, (4) producing theories of women that represent them as inferior, deviant, or significant only in the ways they serve male interests, (5) producing theories of social phenomena that render women's activities and interests invisible, and (6) producing knowledge (science and technology) that is not useful for people in subordinate positions or that reinforces gender and other social hierarchies.

- Feminist empiricism calls for a deeper, more rigorous application of empiricism. Feminist standpoint theory says that different social groups have distinctive kinds of knowledge acquired through unique experiences and that some of these groups may enjoy epistemological advantages over others. Feminist postmodernism is skeptical of such notions as objective or scientific truth, objective reality or fact, universal propositions, foundational knowledge, ultimate justification, and traditional conceptions of rationality. Feminist postmodernists are devoted to deconstructing these ideas.

- Some feminists worry that a deconstruction of traditional assumptions about knowledge and truth could undermine feminist philosophy itself and take away an important tool for dismantling barriers to women's freedom.

KEY TERMS
ethics of care   feminist ethics

Notes

1. Alison Ainley, "Feminist Philosophy," *The Oxford Companion to Philosophy*, ed. Ted Honderich (Oxford: Oxford University Press, 1995), 273.
2. Louise M. Antony, "Embodiment and Epistemology," *The Oxford Handbook of Epistemology* (New York: Oxford University Press, 2002), 465.
3. Mary Wollstonecraft, *A Vindication of the Rights of Women*, ed. Deidre Shauna Lynch (New York: W. W. Norton, 2009), 8–9.
4. Wollstonecraft, *A Vindication of the Rights of Women*, 21–24, 37, 49.
5. Judith Thurman, Introduction to *The Second Sex*, by Simone de Beauvoir (New York: Vintage Books, 2011), ix.
6. Simone de Beauvoir, *The Second Sex* (New York: Vintage Books, 2011), 4–6, 9–11.
7. Beauvoir, *The Second Sex*, 760–761, 763.
8. Alison Jaggar, "Feminist Ethics," in *Encyclopedia of Ethics*, ed. Lawrence Becker and Charlotte Becker (New York: Garland, 1992), 364.
9. Jan Crosthwaite, "Gender and Bioethics," in *A Companion to Bioethics*, eds. Helga Kuhse and Peter Singer (Malden, MA: Blackwell, 2001), 32–40.
10. Crosthwaite, "Gender and Bioethics," 37.
11. Carol Gilligan, *In a Different Voice*: *Psychological Theory and Women's Development* (Cambridge, MA: Harvard University Press, 1982).
12. Virginia Held, *The Ethics of Care* (Oxford: Oxford University Press, 2006), 10–13.
13. Annette C. Baier, "The Need for More Than Justice," *Canadian Journal of Philosophy*, suppl. vol. 13 (1988): 56.
14. Elizabeth Anderson, "Feminist Epistemology and Philosophy of Science," *The Stanford Encyclopedia of Philosophy* (Spring 2011), ed. Edward N. Zalta, http://plato.stanford.edu/archives/spr2011/entries/feminism-epistemology/.
15. Eve Browning Cole, *Philosophy and Feminist Criticism*: *An Introduction* (New York: Paragon House, 1993), 83–84.
16. Cole, *Philosophy and Feminist Criticism*, 84–85.
17. Cole, *Philosophy and Feminist Criticism*, 88–90.
18. Cole, *Philosophy and Feminist Criticism*, 94–95.
19. Cole, *Philosophy and Feminist Criticism*, 95–96.

For Further Reading

G. E. M. Anscombe, "Modern Moral Philosophy," *Philosophy* 33, no. 124 (January 1958).

Simone de Beauvoir, *The Second Sex* (New York: Bantam, 1961).

Paul Boghossian, *Fear of Knowledge* (Oxford: Oxford University Press, 2006).

Eve Browning Cole, *Philosophy and Feminist Criticism: An Introduction* (New York: Paragon House, 1993).

Philippa Foot, "Virtues and Vices," in *Virtues and Vices and Other Essays in Moral Philosophy* (Berkeley: University of California Press, 1979).

Gary Gutting, "Feminism and the Future of Philosophy," *New York Times*, September 18, 2017.

Virginia Held, ed., *Justice and Care: Essential Readings in Feminist Ethics* (Oxford: Westview Press, 1995).

Paul K. Moser, *Knowledge and Evidence* (Cambridge: Cambridge University Press, 1989).

Onora O'Neill, "Kantian Ethics," in *A Companion to Ethics*, ed. Peter Singer (Cambridge: Blackwell, 1993), 175–185.

Russ Shafer-Landau, *Whatever Happened to Good and Evil?* (New York: Oxford University Press, 2004).

Margaret A. Simons, ed., *Simone de Beauvoir: Philosophical Writings* (Chicago: University of Illinois, 2004).

Claire Tomalin, *The Life and Death of Mary Wollstonecraft* (New York: Harcourt, Brace, Jovanovich, 1974).

Lewis Vaughn, *Contemporary Moral Arguments: Readings in Ethical Issues* (New York: Oxford University Press, 2010).

Mary Wollstonecraft, *A Vindication of the Rights of Women* (New York: W. W. Norton, 2009).

Online Resources

Stanford Encyclopedia of Philosophy, "Feminist Perspective on Power," "Liberal Feminism," "Analytic Feminism," "Pragmatic Feminism," "Continental Feminism," https://plato.stanford.edu

Routledge Encyclopedia of Philosophy, "Feminist Philosophy," https://www.rep.routledge.com/articles/thematic/feminist-philosophy/v-1

Hypatia: A Journal of Feminist Philosophy, http://hypatiaphilosophy.org

Internet Encyclopedia of Philosophy, "Feminist Epistemology," Feminist Ethics and Narrative Ethics," "Feminism and Race in the United States," https://www.iep.utm.edu/existent

PhilPapers, "Feminist Philosophy," https://philpapers.org/browse/feminist-philosophy

ThoughtCo, "Feminism: Ideas, Beliefs, and Movements," https://www.thoughtco.com/what-is-feminism-3528958

CHAPTER 17

The Contemporary Period

CHAPTER OBJECTIVES

17.1 APPIAH: COSMOPOLITANISM

- Define *cosmopolitanism* and *cultural relativism*.
- Understand why Appiah thinks cosmopolitanism may help answer the social and ethical questions that arise from the differences among cultures.
- State and evaluate Appiah's views on cultural relativism.
- Explain why Appiah insists that we shouldn't expect everyone to become cosmopolitan.

17.2 NUSSBAUM: RELIGIOUS TOLERANCE

- Understand Nussbaum's principle of equal moral respect for all individuals, and illustrate how she applies it to the problem of religious intolerance.
- Give examples of religious prejudice and fear that have arisen in the United States.
- Summarize the three ingredients that Nussbaum believes should be part of our approach to religious tolerance and intolerance.

17.3 BLUM: RACISM

- Know the two beliefs that Blum identifies as essential to racism.
- Understand why Blum is concerned about the "conceptual inflation" of the words *racist* and *racism*.
- Explain Blum's three categories of racism.
- Know why Blum rejects the view of racism as solely systemic.

17.4 MARTIN LUTHER KING, JR.: CIVIL RIGHTS

- Give an overview of the segregationist South in the 1960s, and detail some of its civil rights abuses.
- Tell the story of Rosa Parks's courageous stand against racial segregation and discrimination.
- Review King's philosophy of nonviolent protest, explaining its key features.

17.5 CHALMERS: CONSCIOUSNESS AND ZOMBIES

- Know how Chalmers defines consciousness.
- Define the "hard problem" of consciousness.
- Explain Chalmers's zombie argument against reductionist accounts of consciousness. That is, explain why he says that if it is logically possibly that his zombie could exist, then physical states must not be essential to conscious experience.

17.6 GARDINER: CLIMATE CHANGE

- Explain Gardiner's idea of the "real global environmental tragedy" and why he believes it is mostly an ethical failure.
- Understand the three "storms" that hinder our ability to behave ethically.
- Explain the "tyranny of the contemporary" and why it is above all a moral question.

17.7 DERRIDA AND CIXOUS: DECONSTRUCTION

- Define Derrida's notion of *logocentrism*.
- Explain his concept of deconstruction and what deconstructing texts is meant to disclose.
- Understand the process of dismantling "binary oppositions."
- Know what Cixous means by "feminine writing" and why she thinks it's important.

If you have read most of this book from the beginning, then you know that philosophy has come a long way in its 2,500-year history. You may also have guessed that philosophy has come a long way *recently*—in the last one hundred years or so. In this span some major theories have arisen, and some have fallen. The big, difficult questions (God, mind, freedom, morality, knowledge, etc.) have endured, although philosophers have refined them, weeded out some of the weakest answers, and offered better analyses of the problems. Philosophy has expanded its scope, diversifying its subject areas and becoming more specialized in all its branches.

It has also taken on some of the most pressing, complex issues of twenty-first century life—from racism and religious intolerance to climate change and immigration to the depths of consciousness and artificial intelligence.

We cannot hope to cover all this ground in one book or even a thousand books. But we can survey a small, diverse sample of philosophers who have recently added their voices to this vexing, inspiring, unsettling, enlightening conversation known as philosophy.

Figure 17.1 Kwame Anthony Appiah.

"In philosophy we often find that what we normally take for granted—the 'commonsense' point of view—gets in the way of a proper understanding of the issues."

—Kwame Anthony Appiah

cosmopolitanism The idea that we have moral duties to all persons, even those outside our family and community.

17.1 APPIAH: COSMOPOLITANISM

As we have seen, philosophy can be abstract and theoretical (as in, say, Plato and Wittgenstein), and it can be more concrete and readily applicable to everyday life (as in, for example, Epictetus and John Stuart Mill). In contemporary philosophy, good work is being done all along this continuum, from the abstruse technicalities in philosophy of mind to the real-life problems of applied ethics. Some philosophers excel in both the technical and the practical and are broadening the focus of philosophy in the process. A good example is Kwame Anthony Appiah (b. 1957).

He was born in London, reared in Ghana, and educated mostly in Britain, ultimately taking his BA and PhD degrees in philosophy at Cambridge University in England. He began his philosophy career at the deep end, exploring recondite problems in the philosophy of language (specifically, probabilistic semantics) and in the philosophy of mind. This work led to the publication of *Assertion and Conditionals* (2008) and *For Truth in Semantics* (1986). His interests broadened gradually from theory to practice as he wrote about African and African-American cultural life and the ethics of identity, culture, race, politics, and global citizenship. On this path he wrote an introduction to philosophy (*Thinking It Through*), co-edited the *Dictionary of Global Culture*, and published three novels (*Avenging Angel*, *Nobody Likes Letitia*, and *Another Death in Venice*). He is now a professor of philosophy and law at New York University.

A major focus of Appiah's work is the social and ethical questions that arise from the collision of cultures in a shrinking world. Answers are imperative because globalism is upon us, because countries, communities, tribes, and clans often chafe against each other. Their differences bringing a high risk of mutual misunderstandings, mistrust, intolerance, and violence. His prescription for the inevitable friction that comes from six billion strangers trying to coexist is **cosmopolitanism**. The word comes from the Cynics and Stoics of the ancient world who took *cosmopolitan* to mean "citizen of the cosmos," a recognition of the oneness of humanity, of universal kinship beyond the narrow concerns of a single group. For Appiah, cosmopolitanism is the idea that we have significant moral duties to all persons, even those outside our family and community. As he says:

Kwame Anthony Appiah: *Cosmopolitanism: Ethics in a World of Strangers*

[W]e have obligations to others, obligations that stretch beyond those to whom we are related by the ties of kith and kind, or even the moral formal ties of a shared citizenship.... [W]e take seriously the value not just of human life but of particular human lives, which means taking an interest in the practices and beliefs that lend them significance.[1]

Cosmopolitanism in this sense, however, has had its detractors, Appiah says. Some have declared their love of humanity in the abstract while renouncing all local loyalties and commitments. Others—including many murderous tyrants—have demanded exclusive allegiance to their preferred slice of the human race, disdaining any cosmopolitan sentiments. Both these views are unfounded. Regarding the latter, Appiah says that "the one thought that cosmopolitans share is that no local loyalty can ever justify forgetting that each human being has responsibilities to every other."[2]

So cosmopolitans see humankind as one family with common interests, but they also respect human differences:

Cosmopolitanism is an adventure and an ideal: but you can't have any respect for human diversity and expect everyone to become cosmopolitan. The obligations of those who wish to exercise their legitimate freedom to associate with their own kind—to keep the rest of the world away as the Amish do in the United States—are only the same as the basic obligations we all have: to do for others what morality requires. Still, a world in which communities are neatly hived off from one another seems no longer a serious option, if it ever was.[3]

For many, the notion of respecting other cultures and their differences leads naturally to **cultural relativism**, the view that the truth about something depends on what cultures believe. Cultures, in other words, make truth. But Appiah thinks this is a mistake.

As I'll be arguing, it is an error—to which we dwellers in a scientific age are peculiarly prone—to resist talk of "objective" values. . . . I want to hold on to at least one important aspect of the objectivity of values: that there are some values that are, and should be, universal, just as there are lots of values that are, and must be, local. . . .

For if relativism about ethics and morality were true, then, at the end of many discussions, we would each have to end up saying, "From where I stand, I am right. From where you stand, you are right." And there would be nothing further to say. From our different perspectives, we would be living effectively in different worlds. And without a shared world, what is there to discuss? People often recommend relativism because they think it will lead to tolerance. But if we cannot learn from one another what it is right to think and feel and do, then conversation between us will be pointless. Relativism of that sort isn't a way to encourage conversation; it's just a reason to fall silent.[4]

17.2 NUSSBAUM: RELIGIOUS TOLERANCE

Among contemporary philosophers, there are few who are as thought-provoking, erudite, and distinctive as Martha Nussbaum (b. 1947). She has been called "the most prominent female philosopher in America," but because of her intellectual accomplishments and her impact on debates in both everyday life and academia, she has become more than that: she is one of America's most important thinkers.

She began her academic career in theater and the classics at New York University but was soon drawn into philosophy and went on to teach at Harvard, Brown, and Oxford. Today she is a professor of law and ethics in the law school and philosophy

---

1. Do you think cultural relativism is true? Do you think it entails social tolerance? Why or why not?

Kwame Anthony Appiah: *Cosmopolitanism: Ethics in a World of Strangers*

cultural relativism The view that the truth about something depends on what cultures believe.

Kwame Anthony Appiah: *Cosmopolitanism: Ethics in a World of Strangers*

"Each person you know about and can affect is someone to whom you have responsibilities: to say this is just to affirm the very idea of morality."

—Kwame Anthony Appiah

Figure 17.2 Martha Nussbaum.

2. Do you believe we have moral obligations to people living in Africa? If so, what kind of moral obligations? If not, why not?

"[P]rejudice and occasional violence have never been absent from the U.S. scene."

—Martha Nussbaum

"Fear is implicated in most bad behavior in the area of religion."

—Martha Nussbaum

department of the University of Chicago. She is also an associate professor in the divinity school and the political science and classics departments.

Despite these lofty affiliations, she is no ivory-tower academic. She believes that philosophy should be honest, well argued, and—especially—*applicable to real life*. It's supposed to be genuinely useful in the hard and necessary work of making sense of social and moral issues. She says, "For any view you put forward, the next question simply has to be, 'What would the world be like if this idea were actually taken up?' . . . It's what happens in the long haul that really matters. You just never know where or how your ideals will be realized."[5]

So she has taken on some of the most serious social concerns of our times—sex and social justice, feminism, religious intolerance, gay rights, race and international development, moral relativism, democracy, education, and others. And she has also not been shy about debating these issues in magazines and journals with other well-known writers, including Allan Bloom, Noam Chomsky, John Rawls, Michel Foucault, Judith Butler, and Susan Moller Okin.

Compared to most other philosophers, her range of interests is extraordinarily wide, as we can see from the titles of some of her books: *The Fragility of Goodness*: *Luck and Ethics in Greek Tragedy and Philosophy* (1986); *For Love of Country* (1996); *Cultivating Humanity*: *A Classical Defense of Reform in Liberal Education* (1997); *Women and Human Development* (2000); *Upheavals of Thought*: *The Intelligence of Emotions* (2001); *Frontiers of Justice*: *Disability, Nationality, Species Membership* (2006); *Liberty of Conscience*: *In Defense of America's Tradition of Religious Equality* (2008); *From Disgust to Humanity*: *Sexual Orientation and Constitutional Law* (2010); and *Creating Capabilities*: *The Human Development Approach* (2011).

A theme that runs through much of Nussbaum's work is the overriding importance of equal moral respect for all individuals, regardless of the attributes bestowed on them by biology and society (such as race, class, and gender). Nussbaum declares that

Martha Nussbaum: *The New Religious Intolerance*

. . . all human beings possess human dignity, and with respect to that dignity, they are equal. People may be unequal in wealth, class, talent, strength, achievement, or moral character—but all are equal as bearers of an inalienable basic human dignity that cannot be lost or forfeited.[6]

In *The New Religious Intolerance*, she applies this principle to the worldwide problem of prejudice and hatred toward religions, all of which are feared and misunderstood by some group or other. This loathsome problem, she says, is real, prevalent, and dangerous, and Western countries (including the United States) have long been guilty of this kind of intolerance:

[N]o reasonable person could deny that religious prejudice and fear, in the form of anti-Catholicism and "nativism," anti-Semitism, and a host of other prejudices against "strange" minorities, have been a persistent blot on our society. We need only remember, for example, that not until the 1970s did "white-shoe" law firms begin to hire Jews in any significant numbers, and that only in very recent times could a majority of the Supreme Court be composed of Roman Catholics without public outrage, in order to feel humility about our own record as an allegedly tolerant and respectful culture. Still, the self-image of U.S. citizens in recent years has been that we are a welcoming and diversity-friendly society that has outgrown the prejudices of the past.

Today we have many reasons to doubt this complacent self-assessment. Our situation calls urgently for searching critical self-examination, as we try to uncover the roots of ugly fears and suspicions that currently disfigure all Western societies.[7]

Martha Nussbaum:
The New Religious Intolerance

Nussbaum points out that many recent cases of religious intolerance have involved anti-Muslim sentiments. For example, some European countries have banned in public places the wearing of the *burqa* and *niqab* (face and body coverings worn by some Muslim women). A few communities in the United States, thinking that Muslim sharia law could be imposed on them, have introduced legislation against that possibility. And in New York City, numerous protests were launched against the building of an alleged mosque near Ground Zero. Yet, she says, all these reactions to Muslim interests are based on misunderstandings, misinformation, and poor reasoning.

To the equal-respect principle, she adds some important qualifications:

3. Upon what moral principle does Nussbaum base her view of religious tolerance?

Whatever else governments do, they may not violate that equal dignity, and in general they ought to show *respect* for our equality and dignity. The whole idea that governments may not violate basic human rights is an elaborated form of this premise. . . .

We now add a further premise: that the faculty with which people search for life's ultimate meaning—frequently called "conscience"—is a very important part of people, closely related to their dignity, or an aspect of it. . . . In other words, to violate conscience is to conduct an assault on human dignity. . . .

We then add one further premise, which we might call the vulnerability premise: this faculty can be seriously impeded by bad worldly conditions. It can be stopped from becoming active, and it can even be violated or damaged within. (The first sort of damage, which seventeenth-century American philosopher Roger Williams compared to imprisonment, occurs when people are prevented from conducting outward observances required by their beliefs. The second sort, which Williams called "soul rape," occurs when people are forced to affirm convictions that they may not hold.) . . .

The vulnerability premise, then, means that giving equal respect to conscience requires tailoring worldly conditions so as to protect both freedom of belief and freedom of expression and practice. It also suggests that freedom should be quite ample: being able to whisper prayers in your home is hardly enough for genuine religious liberty, and we judge, rightly, that a society like China, which forces many religious people to keep their religious beliefs and acts hidden, has not adequately protected religious freedom, even though we know that many Chinese people do hold religious beliefs, and very likely act on them in the privacy of their homes, insofar as they have privacy.[8]

Martha Nussbaum:
The New Religious Intolerance

4. Do you think it likely that Nussbaum would approve of any kind of racial profiling? If so, under what circumstances would she be likely to do this? If not, on what grounds would she disapprove?

Can philosophy help free us from these evils? Nussbaum thinks so:

Martha Nussbaum:
*The New Religious
Intolerance*

At this time we badly need an approach inspired by ethical philosophy in the spirit of Socrates, an approach that combines three ingredients:

- Political principles expressing equal respect for all citizens, and an understanding of what these principles entail for today's confrontations with religious difference. (These principles already inhere in the political traditions of both Europe and, especially, the United States.)
- Rigorous critical thinking that ferrets out and criticizes inconsistencies, particularly those that take the form of making an exception for oneself, noting the "mote" in someone's else's eye while failing to note the large plank in one's own eye.
- A systematic cultivation of the "inner eyes," the imaginative capacity that makes it possible for us to see how the world looks from the point of view of a person different in religion or ethnicity.[9]

"By itself, fear contracts the spirit."
—Martha Nussbaum

17.3 BLUM: RACISM

Philosophers have been doing good work on some of the weightiest issues of our time, and few issues are harder to tackle than racism. Racism is a monstrous evil to dispel from society and is often a hard topic to discuss without raising voices and elevating blood pressures. What can philosophy possibly say about this issue that could be helpful or enlightening?

Apparently, a great deal. One of several philosophers working in this field is Lawrence Blum, a distinguished professor at the University of Massachusetts and author of the book *"I'm Not a Racist But . . . ."* He and other philosophers point out that racism begins with the belief that races exist and can be differentiated by significant moral, intellectual, or cultural characteristics. This (scientifically dubious) supposition of readily identifiable racial differences, however, is not in itself racism, no more than simply identifying someone's race is racism. According to Blum, what transforms this assumption about race into racism is the addition of the belief that (1) some races are inferior to others in important respects or (2) some races deserve disdain, hatred, or hostility. Blum labels these two factors *inferiorization* and *antipathy*:

Inferiorization is linked to historical racist doctrine and racist social systems. Slavery, segregation, imperialism, apartheid, and Nazism all treated certain groups as inferior to other groups . . . .

"Not every instance of racial conflict, insensitivity, discomfort, miscommunication, exclusion, injustice, or ignorance should be called 'racist.'"
—Lawrence Blum

Though race-based antipathy is less related to the original concept of "racism," today the term unequivocally encompasses racial bigotry, hostility, and hatred. Indeed, the racial bigot is many people's paradigm image of a "racist." . . .

Historical systems of racism did of course inevitably involve racial antipathy as well as inferiorization. Hatred of Jews was central to Nazi philosophy; and it is impossible to understand American racism without seeing hostility to blacks and Native Americans as integral to the nexus of attitudes and emotions that shored up slavery and segregation.[10]

But if inferiorization and antipathy are the heart of racism, then many actions, attitudes, institutions, and people that are being called racist don't deserve the label. No serious observer of contemporary society believes that racism no longer exists, and it seems clear that racism in the United States is far more prevalent and insidious today than most people realize. But Blum and other scholars are concerned about the "conceptual inflation" of the words *racist* and *racism*. Because the terms are so often overused and misapplied, they are losing their moral importance and their ability to shame. As Blum says,

> Some feel that the word [racist] is thrown around so much that anything involving "race" that someone does not like is liable to castigation as "racist." . . . A local newspaper called certain blacks "racist" for criticizing other blacks who supported a white over a black candidate for mayor. A white girl in Virginia said that it was "racist" for an African American teacher in her school to wear African attire. . . . Merely mentioning someone's race (or racial designation), using the word "Oriental" for Asians without recognizing its origins and its capacity for insult, or socializing only with members of one's own racial group are called "racist." . . .
>
> Not every instance of racial conflict, insensitivity, discomfort, miscommunication, exclusion, injustice, or ignorance should be called "racist." Not all *racial* incidents are *racist* incidents. We need a more varied and nuanced moral vocabulary for talking about the domain of race. . . . All forms of racial ills should elicit concern from responsible individuals. If someone displays racial insensitivity, but not racism, people should be able to see that for what it is.[11]

Blum is careful to point out that we can't conclude from this "conceptual inflation" that racism and inequality have been overstated. Indirect or veiled racism, he says, is likely worse than we might think.

He distinguishes three categories of racial inferiorization or antipathy:

> *Personal racism* consists in racist acts, beliefs, attitudes, and behavior on the part of individual persons. *Social* (or sociocultural) *racism* comprises racist beliefs, attitudes, and stereotypes widely shared within a given population and expressed in cultural and social modes such as religion, popular entertainment, advertisements, and other media. *Institutional racism* refers to racial inferiorizing or antipathy perpetrated by specific social institutions such as schools, corporations, hospitals, or the criminal justice system as a totality. . . . The people who work in such systems may or may not be guilty of racial prejudice or discrimination, but the systems themselves encourage or cause the negative outcomes.[12]

Blum says that these three can interact with each other in complex ways but that there is a danger in conflating them.

5. Why does Blum reject the idea that racism is solely systemic?

Some contemporary writing has attempted to reduce one of these forms to another, or to demote it in importance. For instance, in some influential writing on racism, the True-Hamilton notion of racism as a *system* of injustice and unequal advantage or power has almost entirely eclipsed the earlier Allportian focus on individual attitude and behavior.

The view of racism as solely systemic substitutes one partial conception of racism for another. For instance, suppose a white person hates black people, but the white person is relatively isolated and powerless, does not come into contact with blacks, and generally does not even express his or her feelings to others. This hatred is unquestionably racist, yet it contributes virtually nothing to a system of unjust advantage based on race. If racism were only systemic, then such an individual would not be racist and, indeed, individuals can never be racist. It is revealing, however, that adherents of the view in question seldom follow that logic exclusively. Generally they at least implicitly acknowledge that individual actions and persons may be "racist." They imply, however, that when an individual acts in what would ordinarily be called a racist manner, the action is to be condemned as racist only insofar as it contributes to a system of unjust racial advantage.[13]

17.4 MARTIN LUTHER KING, JR.: CIVIL RIGHTS

Martin Luther King, Jr. (1929–1968) is known for his central, galvanizing role in the American civil rights movement and for his compelling calls for justice and equality, pleas that challenged the country to live up to its democratic ideals. He is also recognized for developing the philosophical underpinnings of his nonviolent activism. His speeches and writings often had a religious flavor (he was a minister and the son and grandson of a minister), but he directed his arguments to the religious and nonreligious alike and appealed to what he took to be universal values. He alluded to biblical stories and metaphors while citing the moral courage and insight of Socrates, Aquinas, and Augustine. He was inspired by the work and words of Gandhi, the modern world's greatest and most successful practitioner of nonviolent activism, and he in turn inspired future generations who would seek social change through peaceful means.

He was born in Atlanta and attended elementary and secondary schools there, skipped two grades in high school, and attended Morehouse College, earning a bachelor's degree in sociology. He went on to get a bachelor's degree from Crozer Theological Seminary in Pennsylvania and earned his doctorate in theology from Boston University. In 1954 he became the pastor of a prestigious Baptist church in Montgomery, Alabama.

Figure 17.3 Martin Luther King, Jr (1929–1968).

King's achievement seems all the more remarkable when we consider the powerful social forces that he was up against. He concentrated most of his efforts in the South, where the norm was segregation, an entrenched system that was invariably accompanied by unequal and abusive treatment of African-Americans in countless areas of life. In response to those who thought he should indefinitely postpone attempts to change the status quo, King presented a sad litany of such injustices:

Martin Luther King, Jr., in *A Testament of Hope*

But when you have seen vicious mobs lynch your mothers and fathers at will and drown your sisters and brothers at whim; when you have seen hate-filled policemen curse, kick, brutalize and even kill your black brothers and sisters with impunity; when you see the vast majority of your twenty million Negro brothers smothering in an airtight cage of poverty in the midst of an affluent society; when you suddenly find your tongue twisted and your speech stammering as you seek to explain to your six-year-old daughter why she can't go to the public amusement park that has just been advertised on television, and see tears welling up in her little eyes when she is told that Funtown is closed to colored children, and see the depressing clouds of inferiority begin to form in her little mental sky, and see her begin to distort her little personality by unconsciously developing a bitterness toward white people; when you have to concoct an answer for a five-year-old son asking in agonizing pathos: "Daddy, why do white people treat colored people so mean?"; when you take a cross-country drive and find it necessary to sleep night after night in the uncomfortable corners of your automobile because no motel will accept you; when you are humiliated day in and day out by nagging signs reading "white" and "colored"; when your first name becomes "nigger" and your middle name becomes "boy" (however old you are) and your last name becomes "John," and when your wife and mother are never given the respected title "Mrs."; when you are harried by day and haunted by night by the fact that you are a Negro, living constantly at tiptoe stance never quite knowing what to expect next, and plagued with inner fears and outer resentments; when you are forever fighting a degenerating sense of "nobodiness"; then you will understand why we find it difficult to wait.[14]

"It is difficult to appreciate King's achievement if we do not understand that his dilemma was that he saw both the need for and the danger of nationalism."
—James Melvin Washington

Martin Luther King, Jr.: in *A Testament of Hope*

In 1954 in the case of *Brown v. Board of Education*, the U.S. Supreme Court ruled that public schools throughout the land must be desegregated. The backlash in the South was immediate and ferocious. The Ku Klux Klan (KKK) and other racist groups stepped up violence against blacks, and several African-American males were lynched, including—in the most infamous case—a fourteen-year-old boy named Emmett Till.

A year later in Birmingham, Alabama, a black seamstress and activist named Rosa Parks became a symbol of courageous resistance to racial segregation and discrimination. On a public bus, she was ordered by the bus driver to give up her seat to a white man, in accordance with Alabama and Birmingham law. She refused. So she was arrested, booked, and jailed, and her ordeal became the rallying cry of the 1960s civil rights movement. For 381 days, King and his followers staged a nonviolent

6. On what moral principles does King base his objections to segregation?

Figure 17.4 Martin Luther King, Jr. in the Birmingham jail.

"Violence solves no social problems; it merely creates new and more complicated ones."

—Martin Luther King, Jr.

boycott against Montgomery's public bus system. Ultimately they won: in 1956 the Supreme Court affirmed a decision of a lower court that had ruled against the Alabama segregation laws. But winning in the courts did not ensure victory in the cities and towns. Seven years went by before buses in the South were desegregated.

Through the next decade, King and his followers participated in many other boycotts, sit-ins, prayer pilgrimages, mass marches, and mass meetings—all of them nonviolent in accordance with King's philosophy of nonviolent direct action. Like the struggle for desegregated buses, these protests were harrowing and risky, often drawing the outrage, ridicule, and hatred of whites. Frequently protesters were subjected to beatings, arrests, threats, bombings, and arson. King was threatened many times, his house was bombed, and he was stabbed. Progress was slow: it took years for courtroom successes to affect the racial segregation and discrimination in people's lives. It was not until 1964 that Congress passed the Civil Rights Act; even then the struggle was far from over.

On August 28, 1963, King gave his historic "I Have a Dream" speech to hundreds of thousands who attended the March on Washington (and to thousands more who watched the event on television). In 1964 he was awarded the Nobel Peace Prize. And on April 4, 1968, during a visit to Memphis, Tennessee, to give support and encouragement to striking sanitation workers, he was assassinated.

King's philosophy of nonviolent protest is coherent and thorough. He argues that nonviolent direct action is the wise middle road between the paths of militant violence and nonviolent inaction. The nonviolent way works, and "violence solves no social problems; it merely creates new and more complicated ones."[15]

Martin Luther King, Jr.: "Nonviolence and Racial Justice"

The alternative to violence is nonviolent resistance. This method was made famous by Mohandas K. Gandhi, who used it to free India from the domination of the British empire. Five points can be made concerning nonviolence as a method in bringing about better racial conditions.

First, this is not a method for cowards: it *does* resist. The nonviolent resister is just as strongly opposed to the evil against which he protests as is the person who uses violence. His method is passive or nonaggressive in the sense that he is not physically aggressive toward his opponent. But his mind and emotions are always active, constantly seeking to persuade the opponent that he is mistaken. This method is passive physically but strongly active spiritually; it is nonaggressive physically but dynamically aggressive spiritually.

A second point is that nonviolent resistance does not seek to defeat or humiliate the opponent, but to win his friendship and understanding. The nonviolent resister must often express his protest through noncooperation or boycotts, but he realizes that

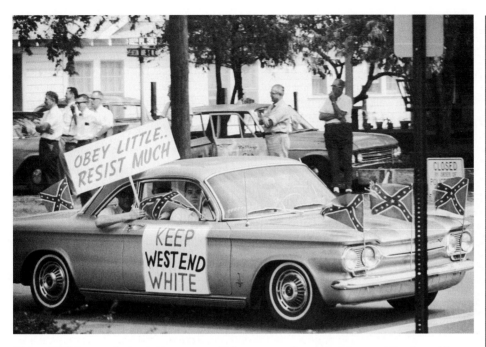

Figure 17.5 Segregationists in Montgomery, Alabama, protesting against desegregating the public schools, 1963.

noncooperation and boycotts are not ends themselves; they are merely means to awaken a sense of moral shame in the opponent. The end is redemption and reconciliation. The aftermath of nonviolence is the creation of the beloved community, while the aftermath of violence is tragic bitterness.

A third characteristic of this method is that the attack is directed against forces of evil rather than against persons who are caught in those forces. It is evil we are seeking to defeat, not the persons victimized by evil. Those of us who struggle against racial injustice must come to see that the basic tension is not between races. As I like to say to the people in Montgomery, Alabama: "The tension in this city is not between white people and Negro people. The tension is at bottom between justice and injustice, between the forces of light and the forces of darkness. And if there is a victory it will be a victory not merely for fifty thousand Negroes, but a victory for justice and the forces of light. We are out to defeat injustice and not white persons who may happen to be unjust."

A fourth point that must be brought out concerning nonviolent resistance is that it avoids not only external physical violence but also internal violence of spirit. At the center of nonviolence stands the principle of love. In struggling for human dignity the oppressed people of the world must not allow themselves to become bitter or indulge in hate campaigns. To retaliate with hate and bitterness would do nothing but intensify the hate in the world. Along the way of life, someone must have sense enough and morality enough to cut off the chain of hate. This can be done only by projecting the ethics of love to the center of our lives. . . .

Finally, the method of nonviolence is based on the conviction that the universe is on the side of justice. It is this deep faith in the future that causes the nonviolent resister to accept suffering without retaliation. He knows that in his struggle for justice he has cosmic companionship. This belief that God is on the side of truth and justice comes down to us

7. Is King a moral relativist? Why or why not? Does he believe in universal values? If so, what values does he think are universal?

Martin Luther King, Jr.: "Nonviolence and Racial Justice"

Martin Luther King, Jr.: "Nonviolence and Racial Justice"

from the long tradition of our Christian faith. There is something at the very center of our faith which reminds us that Good Friday may reign for a day, but ultimately it must give way to the triumphant beat of the Easter drums. Evil may so shape events that Caesar will occupy a palace and Christ a cross, but one day that same Christ will rise up and split history into A.D. and B.C., so that even the life of Caesar must be dated by his name. So in Montgomery we can walk and never get weary, because we know that there will be a great camp meeting in the promised land of freedom and justice.[16]

8. What is King's theory of civil disobedience? Explain why you think his theory is sound (or unsound).

In 1963 King was jailed in Birmingham for taking part in nonviolent demonstrations. While incarcerated, he wrote his famous essay, "Letter from a Birmingham Jail," to respond to white clergymen who had urged him to let the courts handle the question of racial integration and to stop his nonviolent protests. In this section of the "Letter," King defends the theory and practice of civil disobedience:

Martin Luther King, Jr.: "Letter from a Birmingham Jail"

You express a great deal of anxiety over our willingness to break laws. This is certainly a legitimate concern. Since we so diligently urge people to obey the Supreme Court's decision outlawing segregation in the public schools, it is rather strange and paradoxical to find us consciously breaking laws. One may well ask, "How can you advocate breaking some laws and obeying others?" The answer is found in the fact that there are two types of laws: there are *just* laws and there are *unjust* laws. I would agree with Saint Augustine that "An unjust law is no law at all."

Now what is the difference between the two? How does one determine when a law is just or unjust? A just law is a manmade code that squares with the moral law or the law of God. An unjust law is a code that is out of harmony with the moral law. Any law that uplifts human personality is just. Any law that degrades human personality is unjust. All segregation statutes are unjust because segregation distorts the soul and damages the personality. It gives the segregator a false sense of superiority, and the segregated a false sense of inferiority. To use the words of Martin Buber, the great Jewish philosopher, segregation substitutes an "I-it" relationship for the "I-thou" relationship, and ends up relegating persons to the status of things. So segregation is not only politically, economically and sociologically unsound, but it is morally wrong and sinful. Paul Tillich has said that sin is separation. Isn't segregation an existential expression of man's tragic separation, an expression of his awful estrangement, his terrible sinfulness? So I can urge men to disobey segregation ordinances because they are morally wrong. . . .

I hope you can see the distinction I am trying to point out. In no sense do I advocate evading or defying the law as the rabid segregationist would do. This would be anarchy. One who breaks an unjust law must do it *openly*, *lovingly* (not hatefully as the white mothers did in New Orleans when they were seen on television screaming, "nigger, nigger, nigger"), and with a willingness to accept the penalty. I submit that an individual who breaks a law that conscience tells him is unjust, and willingly accepts the penalty by staying in jail to arouse the conscience of the community over its injustice, is in reality expressing the very highest respect for the law.[17]

17.5 CHALMERS: CONSCIOUSNESS AND ZOMBIES

Some of the most exciting work in philosophy today is happening in the philosophy of mind, specifically on what is called the "hard problem" of consciousness. David Chalmers, professor of philosophy and neuroscience at New York University, invented that phrase and has been a leader and impetus in the recent explosion of research in that area. No adequate definition of consciousness exists, but Chalmers characterizes it as

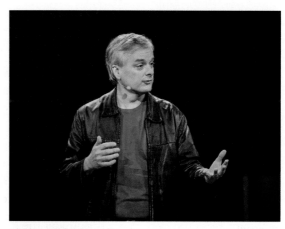

Figure 17.6 David Chalmers.

"the subjective quality of experience." When we perceive, think, and act, there is a whir of causation and information processing, but this processing does not usually go on in the dark. There is also an internal aspect; there is something it feels like to be a cognitive agent. This internal aspect is conscious experience. . . .

We can say that a being is conscious if there is *something it is like* to be that being. . . . To put it another way, we can say that a mental state is conscious if it has a *qualitative feel*—an associated quality of experience.[18]

The hard problem of consciousness is the problem of explaining why we have conscious experience at all.

Many books and articles on consciousness have appeared in the past few years, and one might think that we are making progress. But on a closer look, most of this work leaves the hardest problems about consciousness untouched. Often, such work addresses what might be called the "easy" problems of consciousness: How does the brain process environmental stimulation? How does it integrate information? How do we produce reports on internal states? These are important questions, but to answer them is not to solve the hard problem: Why is all this processing accompanied by an experience of inner life?[19]

Contrary to Chalmers, some theorists believe the hard problem is not so hard. They think consciousness can be explained entirely in terms of physical elements and their states, structures, or functions. Consciousness can be reduced to physics and chemistry. One such "reductive," or materialist, view is the mind-body identity theory, which says that mind states are brain states. Our apparent sensations, thoughts, perceptions, and emotions (so-called phenomenal consciousness) are not immaterial phenomena distinct from the material brain. These mental states are *identical to* physical brain states, just as lightning is identical to an electrical discharge. A pain or a perception is nothing more than a certain process going on in the brain's neurons.

"No explanation given wholly in physical terms can ever account for the emergence of conscious experience."

—David Chalmers

But according to Chalmers,

> Almost everything in the world can be explained in physical terms; it is natural to hope that consciousness might be explained this way, too. . . . I will argue that consciousness escapes the net of reductive explanation. No explanation given wholly in physical terms can ever account for the emergence of conscious experience.[20]

Chalmers's now famous argument against reductionist accounts of consciousness is based on, of all things, the possibility of zombies:

> . . . [C]onsider the logical possibility of a *zombie*: someone or something physically identical to me (or to any other conscious being), but lacking conscious experiences altogether. At the global level, we can consider the logical possibility of a *zombie world*: a world physically identical to ours, but in which there are no conscious experiences at all. In such a world, everybody is a zombie.
>
> So let us consider my zombie twin. This creature is molecule for molecule identical to me, and identical in all the low-level properties postulated by a completed physics, but he lacks conscious experience entirely. (Some might prefer to call a zombie "it," but I use the personal pronoun; I have grown quite fond of my zombie twin.) To fix ideas, we can imagine that right now I am gazing out the window, experiencing some nice green sensations from seeing the trees outside, having pleasant taste experiences through munching on a chocolate bar, and feeling a dull aching sensation in my right shoulder.
>
> What is going on in my zombie twin? He is physically identical to me, and we may as well suppose that he is embedded in an identical environment. He will certainly be identical to me *functionally*: he will be processing the same sort of information, reacting in a similar way to inputs, with his internal configurations being modified appropriately and with indistinguishable behavior resulting. He will be *psychologically* identical to me. . . . He will be perceiving the trees outside, in the functional sense, and tasting the chocolate, in the psychological sense. All of this follows logically from the fact that he is physically identical to me, by virtue of the functional analyses of psychological notions. He will even be "conscious" in the functional senses described earlier—he will be awake, able to report the contents of his internal states, able to focus attention in various places, and so on. It is just that none of this functioning will be accompanied by any real conscious experience. There will be no phenomenal feel. There is nothing it is like to be a zombie.[21]

Chalmers asserts that it is conceivable that such a zombie could exist. That is, it is conceivable that there could be a creature physically identical to him in every way but lacking the mental states that constitute conscious experience. If this zombie is conceivable, he says, then it is logically possible that the zombie could exist. If it is logically possible that the zombie could exist, then physical states must not be essential to conscious experience. Materialism, therefore, must be false.

This is how Chalmers outlines the argument:

1. It is conceivable that there be zombies.
2. If it is conceivable that there be zombies, it is metaphysically possible that there be zombies.
3. If it is metaphysically possible that there be zombies, then consciousness is nonphysical.
4. Consciousness is nonphysical.[22]

How might a materialist respond to this argument? One way is to charge that Chalmers is mistaken, that his zombies are actually inconceivable and therefore not logically possible. Many people, however, would probably disagree. Can you imagine an android like *Star Trek*'s Mr. Data that is physically identical to you but lacking any trace of internal conscious experience?

> **9.** Do you agree that the possibility of zombies shows that consciousness is nonphysical? Why or why not?

17.6 GARDINER: CLIMATE CHANGE

Climate change is usually thought of as a scientific, political, or technical issue, but it is also a profoundly important *ethical* issue. So say many philosophers, most notably Stephen Gardiner, professor of philosophy at the University of Washington and author of *A Perfect Moral Storm*: *The Ethical Tragedy of Climate Change*. Most actively publishing climate scientists—97 percent—affirm that global warming is happening now and that humans are causing it, and eighteen American scientific societies and eleven international science academies concur.[23] But the question of what we should do about this fact is ethical—and dangerously difficult to answer. Gardiner explains:

> My concern is with why, given that the relevant facts are known, effective action is so difficult, and indeed has so far eluded us. This is the real global environmental tragedy, and it is what needs to be explained.
>
> In my view, the global environmental tragedy is most centrally an ethical failure, and one that implicates our institutions, our moral and political theories, and ultimately ourselves, considered as moral agents.[24]

To explain this ethical failure, Gardiner uses the metaphor of "a perfect moral storm," a phrase borrowed from the book *A Perfect Storm* (and the movie) that tells the true story of a fishing boat, the *Andrea Gail*, destroyed at sea when three violent storms strangely converged.

"We do not 'solve' the climate problem if we inflict catastrophe on future generations, or facilitate genocide against poor nations, or rapidly accelerate the pace of mass extinction."

—Stephen Gardiner

[T]he three problems (or "storms") are all obstacles to our ability to behave ethically. Like the *Andrea Gail*, we are beset by forces that are likely at least to throw us off course, and may even sink us into the bargain.

Each of the first two storms involves a serious asymmetry of power, where the possibility of some taking undue advantage of others is pronounced. The first storm is global. Its key feature is that the world's most affluent nations, and especially the rich within those nations, have considerable power to shape what is done, and to do so in ways which favor their own concerns, especially over those of the world's poorer nations, and poor people within those nations.

The second storm is intergenerational. Its key feature is that the current generation has similar, but more pronounced, asymmetric power over the prospects of future generations: roughly speaking, earlier generations can affect the prospects of future generations, but not vice versa. In my view, the intergenerational storm is the most prominent of the three. Here the possibilities for taking advantage are deep.

The third storm is theoretical. In dealing with the first two storms, it would be nice if we had robust general theories to guide us. Unfortunately, this is not the case. In particular, existing theories are extremely underdeveloped in many of the relevant areas, including intergenerational ethics, international justice, scientific uncertainty, and the human relationship to animals and the rest of nature. This not only complicates the task of behaving well, but also renders us more vulnerable to the first two storms.[25]

Gardiner argues that a huge portion of the perfect moral storm is what he calls the "tyranny of the contemporary"—a "problem in which earlier generations exploit the future by taking modest benefits for themselves now while passing on potentially catastrophic costs later." However we decide this tyranny question, we will be deciding a moral question using our moral framework, and the implications are grave.

Suppose, for example, one were deciding where to set a global ceiling on emissions.

At one extreme, we might give absolute priority to the future. It is *technically* feasible for us all to reduce our emissions by 50 to 80 percent tomorrow, or even eliminate them. We could, after all, just turn off our electricity, refuse to drive, and so on. The problem is not that this cannot be done; it is that the implications are bleak. Given our current infrastructure, a very rapid reduction would probably cause social and economic chaos, including humanitarian disaster and severe dislocation for the current generation. If this is correct, we are justified in dismissing such drastic measures. However, that justification is ethical: A policy that demanded those measures would be profoundly unjust, violate important rights and be deeply harmful to human welfare.

Still, the acknowledgement of those limits has its own implications. Even if any emissions cuts would be disruptive to some extent, presumably at some point the risks imposed on future generations are severe enough to outweigh them. Where is this point? That is an ethical question. So far, we do not seem very interested in answering it.

Perhaps this is because up until now we have been acting as if our answer is closer to the other extreme—giving absolute priority to our own short-term interests. Over the past 25 years—since the first Intergovernmental Panel on Climate Change report—we have continued to allow high levels of emissions, suggesting that we are giving the future no weight at all. Given the threat of a tyranny of the contemporary, this bias is highly predictable. Yet it also appears grossly unethical. . . .

The real climate challenge is ethical, and ethical considerations of justice, rights, welfare, virtue, political legitimacy, community and humanity's relationship to nature are at the heart of the policy decisions to be made. We do not "solve" the climate problem if we inflict catastrophe on future generations, or facilitate genocide against poor nations, or rapidly accelerate the pace of mass extinction. If public policy neglects such concerns, its account of the challenge we face is impoverished, and the associated solutions quickly become grossly inadequate. Ongoing political inertia surrounding climate action suggests that so far, we are failing the ethical test.[26]

> **10.** What is the "theoretical storm" that Gardiner identifies?

17.7 DERRIDA AND CIXOUS: DECONSTRUCTION

Jacques Derrida (1930–2004) was a French philosopher whose ideas greatly influenced philosophy in Europe and profoundly altered literary criticism in the English-speaking world. He was born in Algeria, a French colony at the time, and attended school in Paris, where he studied philosophy at the distinguished École Normale Supérieure. He published his most important works between 1967 and 1972, including his best-known book *Of Grammatology*.

Derrida is most famous for his method of dissecting language known as **deconstruction**. It's a way of unpacking a text (philosophical, literary, or other) to reveal hidden assumptions and contradictions that subvert the ostensible meaning. Although deconstructionists may pore over particular literary or philosophical works, their ultimate target is what Derrida terms *logocentrism*, the preoccupation with truth, logic, and rationality that characterizes the Western intellectual tradition.

What is it about language that deconstruction is supposed to disclose? Derrida says it reveals that, contrary to what most of us assume, the meanings we think are in the words we use are not static or fixed. Language is fluid, meanings are slippery, ephemeral. Words and their meanings are not firmly moored to the world; they are free-floating and changeable. So there can be no final or conclusive interpretation of a text; there can be no stable, changeless linguistic system. The problem is that

"There is nothing outside the text."

—Jacques Derrida

deconstruction A way of unpacking a text (philosophical, literary, or other) to reveal hidden assumptions and contradictions that subvert the ostensible meaning.

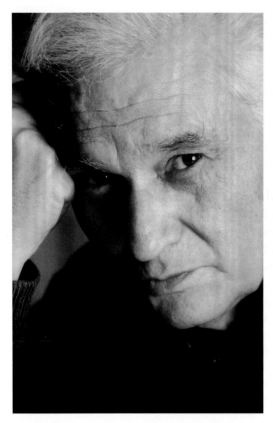

Figure 17.7 Jacques Derrida (1930–2004).

a word's meaning arises out of a web of relationships with similar words, related objects in the world, human activity, and all the situations in which the word is used. A word's meaning, Derrida says, is shaped continually by *traces* of all these relationships. From these fleeting residues, meaning arises and changes, and we can never pin it down or lock it in place. And because our understanding and thinking depend on language, they too fall into a web of relationships that undercuts definitive meaning.

Deconstruction can be done in many ways. One well-known strategy is to dismantle the "binary oppositions" that Derrida believes have for centuries warped Western thought. They are, he says, the handiwork of logocentrism: male/female, master/slave, white/black, truth/fiction, reality/appearance, speech/writing, literal/metaphorical, and others. In the Western tradition, the left-hand term is supposed to be primary or superior ("privileged"), and the right-hand term is secondary and inferior, dependent on the first. The deconstructionist uncovers these pairs (implicit or explicit) in the text and tries to show that logocentrism has it wrong—that the right-hand term is actually superior or primary or somehow the true source of the left-hand term. The overall strategy is to turn a philosophical or literary text against itself.

"The question to ask about our beliefs is not whether they are about reality or merely about appearance, but simply whether they are the best habits of action for gratifying our desires."

—Richard Rorty

11. How might a deconstructionist dismantle the binary opposition of male/female?

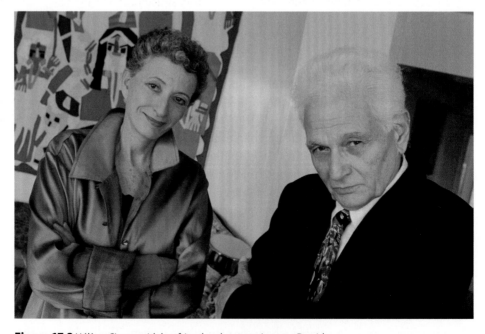

Figure 17.8 Hélène Cixous with her friend and mentor Jacques Derrida.

Derrida was not alone in trying to get the world to think differently about language and to resist the pull of logocentrism. He was mentor and friend to another thinker with similar goals, the French feminist and writer Hélène Cixous (b. 1937). Like Derrida, she was born in Algeria and came to France, where she showed herself to be an excellent student. She received her doctorate in 1968 and promptly founded Europe's first doctoral program in women's studies at the University of Paris.

Reading Cixous is a challenge because in her writing she blends genres and disciplines, often mixing philosophy, autobiography, feminist literary theory, drama, poetry, and several forms of nonfiction. Her range of topics and issues is vast, covering serious questions in philosophy, birth and death, love lost and found, internal experience, psychoanalysis, embodiment, motherhood, patriarchy, myths, and more.

A large part of her work is devoted to examining the philosophical and psychological implications of the act of writing. Cixous, for example, draws attention to a unique kind of female or bisexual writing, songlike and focused on female sexuality. Susan Sellers, also a writer and feminist, describes this aspect of Cixous's thinking:

> "Language enrobes us and inspires us and launches us beyond ourselves, it is ours and we are its, it is our master and our mistress."
>
> —Hélène Cixous

Susan Sellers: *The Hélène Cixous Reader*

Cixous' name is most often associated with that of *écriture féminine*—"feminine writing." For Cixous such a writing is feminine in two senses. First, while Cixous suggests that feminine writing is potentially the province of both sexes, she believes women are currently closer to a feminine economy [thought and behavior] than men. As a result she sees in women's writing the potential to circumvent and reformulate existing structures through the inclusion of other experience. . . . Second, since a feminine subject position refuses to appropriate or annihilate the other's difference in order to construct the self in a (masculine) position of mastery, Cixous suggests that a feminine writing will bring into existence alternative forms of relation, perception and expression. It is in this sense that Cixous believes writing is revolutionary. Not only can writing exceed the binary logic that informs our present system and thus create the framework for a new "language" and culture, but, she stresses, through its transformations, feminine writing will initiate changes in the social and political sphere to challenge the very foundation of the patriarchal and capitalist state. Feminine writing is [according to Cixous]:

> a place (. . .) which is not economically or politically indebted to all the vileness and compromise. That is not obliged to reproduce the system. That is writing. If there is a somewhere else that can escape the infernal repetition, it lies in that direction, where *it* writes itself, where *it* dreams, where *it* invents new worlds.[27]

> "[In] my own tradition I have never conceived of poetic writing as separate from philosophy.
>
> —Hélène Cixous

WRITING AND REASONING   CHAPTER 17

---

1. Do you think Appiah's cosmopolitanism is right about our social and cultural relations—that is, do we have a duty to take an interest in the practices and beliefs of people who live outside our own community? Why or why not?

2. What is Nussbaum's overriding principle of tolerance? Do you accept this principle? It would apparently allow such actions as, say, building a mosque near Ground Zero in New York City. Do you agree with this implication? Explain.

3. Using Blum's criteria for racism, offer as examples several behaviors or beliefs that are racial but not racist.

4. Do you think Chalmers's zombie argument establishes that reductive explanations of consciousness are false? Why or why not?

5. Do you agree with Gardiner that the real global environment tragedy is *ethical*? Explain.

REVIEW NOTES

17.1 APPIAH: COSMOPOLITANISM

- Appiah focuses on the social and ethical questions that arise from the collision of cultures in a shrinking world. His prescription for the inevitable friction that comes from six billion strangers trying to coexist is cosmopolitanism. For Appiah, cosmopolitanism is the idea that we have significant moral duties to all persons, even those outside our family and community. Each individual has responsibilities to every other.

- Appiah thinks cultural relativism is a mistake. He says, "there are some values that are, and should be, universal, just as there are lots of values that are, and must be, local."

17.2 NUSSBAUM: RELIGIOUS TOLERANCE

- Nussbaum stresses the overriding importance of equal moral respect for all individuals, regardless of the attributes bestowed on them by biology and society (such as race, class, and gender).

- She applies the equal-respect principle to the worldwide problem of prejudice and hatred toward religions. The problem, she says, is real, prevalent, and dangerous, and Western countries (including the United States) have long been guilty of this kind of intolerance.

- She maintains that governments must show respect for our equality and dignity; to violate conscience is to conduct an assault on human dignity. Moreover, conscience can be seriously impeded by bad worldly conditions. It can be stopped from becoming active, and it can even be violated or damaged within.

- To combat religious intolerance, she says, we need three things: (1) political principles expressing equal respect for all citizens, and an understanding of what these principles entail for today's confrontations with religious difference; (2) rigorous critical thinking that ferrets out and criticizes inconsistencies, particularly those that take the form of making an exception for oneself; and (3) a systematic cultivation of the "inner eyes," the imaginative capacity that makes it possible for us to see how the world looks from the point of view of a person different in religion or ethnicity.

17.3 BLUM: RACISM

- According to Blum, what transforms assumptions about race into racism is the addition of the belief that (1) some races are inferior to others in important respects or (2) some races deserve disdain, hatred, or hostility. Blum labels these two factors *inferiorization* and *antipathy*.

- Blum and other scholars are concerned about the "conceptual inflation" of the words *racist* and *racism*. Because the terms are so often overused and misapplied, they are losing their moral importance and their ability to shame.

- *Personal racism* consists in racist acts, beliefs, attitudes, and behavior on the part of individual persons. *Social* (or sociocultural) *racism* comprises racist beliefs, attitudes, and stereotypes widely shared within a given population and expressed in cultural and social modes such as religion, popular entertainment, advertisements, and other media. *Institutional racism* refers to racial inferiorizing or antipathy perpetrated by specific social institutions such as schools, corporations, hospitals, or the criminal justice system as a totality.

- Blum contends that the view of racism as solely systemic substitutes one partial conception of racism for another. This notion of racism is untenable.

17.4 MARTIN LUTHER KING, JR.: CIVIL RIGHTS

- In the 1960s, King's fight for justice faced very strong anti-integration prejudices. In the South, the norm was segregation; it was an entrenched system that was invariably accompanied by unequal and abusive treatment of African-Americans in countless areas of life.

- In 1955 in Birmingham, Alabama, a black seamstress and activist named Rosa Parks became a symbol of courageous resistance to racial segregation and discrimination. On a public bus, she was ordered by the bus driver to give up her seat to a white man, but she refused and was arrested and jailed. For over a year, King and his followers staged a nonviolent boycott against Montgomery's public bus system. In 1956 the Supreme Court affirmed a decision of a lower court that had ruled against the Alabama segregation laws.

- King developed a coherent philosophy of nonviolent protest. He argued that nonviolent direct action is the wise middle road between the paths of militant violence and nonviolent inaction. The nonviolent way works, and "violence solves no social problems; it merely creates new and more complicated ones."

- He maintains that nonviolent action (1) is not passive but is a way to resist; (2) does not seek to defeat or humiliate the opponent, but to win his friendship and understanding; (3) is directed against forces of evil rather than against persons who are caught in those forces; (4) avoids not only external physical violence but also internal violence of spirit; and (5) is based on the conviction that the universe is on the side of justice. It is this deep faith in the future that causes the nonviolent resister to accept suffering without retaliation.

17.5 CHALMERS: CONSCIOUSNESS AND ZOMBIES

- No completely adequate definition of consciousness exists, but Chalmers characterizes it as "the subjective quality of experience."

- Chalmers thinks that most work in this field leaves the hardest problems about consciousness untouched, addressing only the "easy problems of consciousness" such as How does the brain process environmental stimulation? How does it integrate information? How do we produce reports on internal states? "These are important questions," he says, "but to answer them is not to solve the hard problem: Why is all this processing accompanied by an experience of inner life?"

- Chalmers asserts that it is conceivable that a zombie could exist. That is, it is conceivable that there could be a creature physically identical to him in every way but lacking the mental states that constitute conscious experience. If this zombie is conceivable, he says, then it is logically possible that the zombie could exist. If it is logically possible that the zombie could exist, then physical states must not be essential to conscious experience. Materialism, therefore, must be false.

17.6 GARDINER: CLIMATE CHANGE

- Gardiner asks why, given that the relevant facts about climate change are known, effective action is so difficult, and indeed has so far eluded us. He thinks this is the real global environmental tragedy, and it is most centrally an ethical failure.

- Gardner says we are facing a "perfect moral storm"—three problems that are huge obstacles to our ability to behave ethically. He says, "We are beset by forces that are likely at least to throw us off course, and may even sink us into the bargain." The storms are global, intergenerational, and theoretical

17.7 DERRIDA AND CIXOUS: DECONSTRUCTION

- Derrida is most famous for his method of dissecting language known as deconstruction. It's a way of unpacking a text (philosophical, literary, or other) to reveal hidden assumptions and contradictions that subvert the ostensible meaning.

- Derrida's ultimate target is what he calls logocentrism, the preoccupation with truth, logic, and rationality that characterizes the Western intellectual tradition.

- A large part of Cixous's work is devoted to examining the philosophical and psychological implications of the act of writing. She draws attention to a unique kind of female or bisexual writing—"feminine writing"—songlike and focused on female sexuality.

KEY TERMS

cosmopolitanism   cultural relativism   deconstruction

Notes

1. Kwame Anthony Appiah, *Cosmopolitanism: Ethics in a World of Strangers* (New York: W. W. Norton, 2006), xv.

2. Appiah, *Cosmopolitanism*, xvi.

3. Appiah, *Cosmopolitanism*, xx.

4. Appiah, *Cosmopolitanism*, xxi, 30–31.

5. Martha Nussbaum, quoted in Robert S. Boynton, "Who Needs Philosophy?: A Profile of Martha Nussbaum," *New York Times Magazine*, November 21, 1999.

6. Martha Nussbaum, *The New Religious Intolerance* (Cambridge, MA: Harvard University Press, 2012), 61.

7. Nussbaum, *The New Religious Intolerance*, 2.

8. Nussbaum, *The New Religious Intolerance*, 67–68.

9. Nussbaum, *The New Religious Intolerance*, 2–3.

10. Lawrence Blum, *"I'm Not a Racist But . . .": The Moral Quandary of Race* (Ithaca, NY: Cornell University Press, 2002), 8–9.

11. Blum, *"I'm Not a Racist But . . ."* 1–2.

12. Blum, *"I'm Not a Racist But . . ."* 9.

13. Blum, *"I'm Not a Racist But . . ."* 9.

14. Martin Luther King, Jr., in *A Testament of Hope*, ed. James Melvin Washington (Cambridge: Harper & Row, 1986), 292–293.

15. King, Jr., "Nonviolence and Racial Justice," ed. Washington, 7.

16. King, Jr., "Nonviolence and Racial Justice," ed. Washington, 8–9.

17. King, Jr., "Letter from a Birmingham Jail," ed. Washington, 293–294.

18. David Chalmers, *The Conscious Mind* (Oxford: Oxford University Press, 1996), 4.

19. Chalmers, *The Conscious Mind*, xi–xii.

20. Chalmers, *The Conscious Mind,* 93.

21. Chalmers, *The Conscious Mind,* 94–95.

22. David Chalmers, *Philosophy of Mind: Classical and Contemporary Readings* (New York: Oxford University Press, 2002), 249.

23. National Academy of Sciences/The Royal Society, *Climate Change: Evidence and Causes*, http://dels.nas.edu/resources/static-assets/exec-office-other/climate-change-full.pdf; NASA, *Global Climate Change*, "Global Climate Change: Vital Signs of the Planet," https://climate.nasa.gov/; Intergovernmental Panel on Climate Change (IPCC), *Climate Change 2014: Synthesis Report, Summary for Policymakers*, https://www.ipcc.ch/site/assets/uploads/2018/02/AR5_SYR_FINAL_SPM.pdf.

24. Stephen Gardiner, *A Perfect Moral Storm: The Ethical Tragedy of Climate Change* (New York: Oxford University Press, 2011), 7.

25. Gardiner, *A Perfect Moral Storm*, 7.

26. Stephen Gardiner, "Why Climate Change Is an Ethical Problem," *Washington Post*, Opinions, January 9, 2016.

27. Susan Sellers, ed., *The Hélène Cixous Reader* (Oxford: Routledge, 1994), xxix.

For Further Reading

Kwame Anthony Appiah, "Racisms," in *Anatomy of Racism*, ed. David Theo Goldberg (Minneapolis: University of Minnesota Press, 1970).

Kwame Anthony Appiah, *Thinking It Through* (Oxford: Oxford University Press, 2003).

Jeffrey Bennett, *A Global Warming Primer* (Boulder, CO: Big Kid Science, 2016).

Lawrence Blum, *"I'm Not a Racist But …": The Moral Quandary of Race* (Ithaca, NY: Cornell University Press, 2002).

David Chalmers, *Philosophy of Mind: Classical and Contemporary Readings* (New York: Oxford University Press, 2002).

David Chalmers, *The Conscious Mind* (Oxford: Oxford University Press, 1996).

Frederick Copleston, *A History of Philosophy, Vol. IX: Modern Philosophy from the French Revolution to Sartre, Camus, and Levi-Straus* (New York: Doubleday, 1994).

Simon Critchley, *Continental Philosophy: A Very Short Introduction* (Oxford: Oxford University Press, 2001).

Stephen Gardiner, *A Perfect Moral Storm: The Ethical Tragedy of Climate Change* (New York: Oxford University Press, 2011).

Peggy Kamuf, ed., *A Derrida Reader: Between the Blinds* (New York: Columbia University Press, 1991).

Anthony Kenny, *Philosophy in the Modern World* (Oxford: Oxford University Press, 2007).

Brian Leiter and Michael Rosen, ed., *The Oxford Companion to Continental Philosophy* (Oxford: Oxford University Press, 2007).

Martha C. Nussbaum, *The New Religious Intolerance* (Cambridge, MA: Harvard University Press, 2012).

John R. Searle, *Mind: A Brief Introduction* (New York: Oxford University Press, 2004).

Susan Sellers, ed., *The Hélène Cixous Reader* (Oxford: Routledge, 1994).

James Melvin Washington, ed., *A Testament of Hope: The Essential Writings of Martin Luther King, Jr.* (San Francisco: Harper & Row, 1986).

Naomi Zack, *The Oxford Handbook of Philosophy and Race* (New York: Oxford University Press, 2017).

Online Resources

Michael James, "Race," in *The Stanford Encyclopedia of Philosophy*, May 25, 2020, https://plato.stanford.edu/entries/race/

S. Crowell, "Existentialism," in *The Stanford Encyclopedia of Philosophy*, June 9, 2020, https://plato.stanford.edu/entries/existentialism/

David Chalmers, blog, http://consc.net/

Rachel Aviv, "The Philosopher of Feelings," [Martha Nussbaum], *The New Yorker*, July 18, 2016, https://www.newyorker.com/magazine/2016/07/25/martha-nussbaums-moral-philosophies

Andrew Altman, "Civil Rights," in *The Stanford Encyclopedia of Philosophy*, April 28, 2017, https://plato.stanford.edu/entries/civil-rights/

CHAPTER 18

The Meaning of Life

CHAPTER OBJECTIVES

18.1 THE SEARCH FOR MEANING

- Understand why people think questions concerning the meaning of human existence are extremely important and relevant.
- Understand why and how examining the question of life's meaning is personal.
- Explain the difference between external and internal meaning.

18.2 PESSIMISM: LIFE HAS NO MEANING

- Summarize the pessimistic views of Tolstoy, Schopenhauer, and Darrow.
- Critically examine the case for pessimism and for optimism.
- Assess Baggini's charge that pessimists confuse external and internal meaning.

18.3 OPTIMISM: LIFE CAN HAVE MEANING

- Explain the religious externalist approach to life's meaning.
- Critically examine Tolstoy's view and his justification for it.
- Explain why some philosophers think the notion of a God assigning a purpose to humans should be objectionable to believers and nonbelievers alike.
- Summarize the internalist's position on life's meaning and produce an argument for or against it.
- Devise an argument for the idea that death and the ephemeral nature of human endeavors are irrelevant to the meaningfulness or meaningless of a person's existence.

18.1 THE SEARCH FOR MEANING

> "For the meaning of life differs from man to man, from day to day and from hour to hour. What matters, therefore, is not the meaning of life in general but rather the specific meaning of a person's life at a given moment."
>
> —Viktor E. Frankl

At one time or another, in one way or another, most people ask themselves if life has any meaning, any point. Many of them seem satisfied with their lives—until they begin to wonder whether it is a meaningless charade. Then "the meaning of life"—a phrase often tossed around in mock seriousness or for comedic effect—is infused with a more somber tone. A few insist that questions about the meaning of existence are themselves meaningless. But most who have contemplated such things take them to be extremely important and relevant to their lives. Many philosophers have tried to clarify the concepts involved and to give discussions of life's meaning more precision, but they too think the questions about meaningful or meaningless lives are worth asking and answering. The existentialist philosopher Albert Camus, for one, declares that "Judging whether life is or is not worth living amounts to answering the fundamental question of philosophy. All the rest—whether the world has three dimensions, whether the mind has nine or twelve categories—comes afterwards."[1]

Some people, including a fair number of students, think philosophy is *mostly* about the question of life's meaning. In a sense, they are not far wrong. Most of the philosophers and topics covered in the preceding chapters can inform your thinking about this important sort of meaning. And your conclusions about the meaningfulness of life are directly or indirectly related to your actions and beliefs regarding lifestyle, work, morality, political involvement, free will, God, and other issues. If by thinking carefully about life's meaning (or lack thereof) you decide to dramatically change your career choice, you would not be the first.

> "Life has no meaning the moment you lose the illusion of being eternal."
>
> —Jean-Paul Sartre

What, besides a course in philosophy, can push someone into this kind of serious reflection? Often the tripwire is a disturbing thought—the inevitably of death, the brevity of life, the smallness and triviality of our lives compared with the unimaginably vast universe, the shortness of our lives in the context of eternity, or the eventual obliteration of everything we have cared for or created.

Figure 18.1 People often begin their search for meaning by asking, "What is the meaning of life?" But the first step in finding answers is to understand the question.

Consider this odd fairytale based *very loosely* on a real event. A graduate student with a master's in business pays a visit to a philosophy professor. The student has come seeking something that she has so far failed to acquire in her studies: the ultimate secret, the meaning of life. The professor pauses, then answers in his best guru-like voice, "The meaning of life is . . . a big purple thing." Silence. The professor chuckles; the student doesn't know whether to laugh or sigh.

With his absurd answer the professor means to make a point, or several. There is no great secret concerning the meaning of life, no cryptic bit of knowledge that, once known, will reveal all. There is no slogan or incantation or parable that will ensure your life is worth living. Moreover, no one can simply hand you the meaning of life as if it were a gift basket. The process of examining the question of life's meaning or purpose is *personal*. You have to make that journey yourself. No one can bestow upon you what you must find for yourself, no more than a friend can tell you what your favorite foods are supposed to be.

Probably most philosophers would agree with all this. Many would also add that although there is no straight road to understanding the "big question," there are guideposts here and there that can help you find your way, some of which we discuss in the following pages.

Many people think they have an intuitive grasp of what is meant by "the meaning of life." But the concept in common usage is actually vague and slippery. So for purposes of this discussion, we can say that to ask whether your life has meaning is to ask whether it has sufficient value or worth. Through the centuries, people have claimed that such sufficient value is derived from being part of God's plan, serving the greater good of humankind, helping others, caring for and protecting family, giving and receiving love, creating art, searching for knowledge, and many other activities and states.

Philosophers have gone further and distinguished life's value or meaning from happiness and moral rightness. Someone might be continually and blissfully happy because she is, for example, taking psychotropic drugs, but few would call such a life meaningful. And some people can lead meaningful lives while being miserable because their meaningful activities are arduous or dangerous. Physicians working in a war zone treating wounded children may be sad because of the suffering they witness—and still feel their lives have meaning. Moreover, many things that people do to add meaning to their lives are also morally right, but moral rightness and meaningfulness need not go together. While creating a beautiful painting, an artist might add meaning to his life, but the act of creation seems to be morally neutral. Morality and meaningfulness are not synonymous.

Perhaps the main impediment to clear thinking about life's meaning is confusion about what *meaning* refers to. Consider the phrase "the meaning of life." For most people, these words refer to *external* meaning—meaning or purpose that comes from outside humanity. Whatever meaning people have in their lives is bestowed or assigned by God, by some metaphysical order, or by the workings of some universal principle. For Christians, to have a meaningful life is to be part of God's plan for all of humankind. But many people also speak of a different kind of meaning—what some refer to as "meaning *in* life." This is *internal* meaning—meaning or purpose that comes from inside people, that humans can give to themselves. On this view, life can be meaningful for persons if they come to see their goals or purposes as inherently valuable or worthwhile.

Many people, including those who accept a religious worldview, assume that if life has no external meaning, it has no meaning *period*. They believe humans can have a purposeful life only if God created them with a purpose. The opposing view is that even if there is no external meaning, people's lives can still be meaningful because meaning and purpose come from within. Because of these different senses of meaning, a person who states that life is meaningless may actually be asserting only that life has no external meaning but still has internal meaning. Someone who declares that life has meaning may reject the notion that humans are given a purpose by a higher power, claiming that lives are made meaningful only by human choices.

> "My life has no purpose, no direction, no aim, no meaning, and yet I'm happy. I can't figure it out. What am I doing right?"
> —Charles M. Schulz

1. When you talk about the meaning of life, which sense of the term do you use—external meaning or internal meaning?

> "Life takes on meaning when you become motivated, set goals and charge after them in an unstoppable manner."
> —Les Brown

Figure 18.2 Is a meaningful life possible only when lived in accordance with God's plan?

Unfortunately, the phrase "the meaning of life" is frequently used to refer to both external and internal meaning.

To the question of whether life holds any meaning for us, there are two principal answers: (1) life has no meaning (the *pessimist's* view) and (2) life in some sense does have meaning (the *optimist's* view). The optimist's answer can be further divided: either (1) life's meaning is external (the common religious perspective) or (2) life's meaning is internal (the view held mostly by the nonreligious or nontheistic).

18.2 PESSIMISM: LIFE HAS NO MEANING

"Life is without meaning. You bring the meaning to it. The meaning of life is whatever you ascribe it to be. Being alive is the meaning."

—Joseph Campbell

The pessimists (also called nihilists) have something in common with the religious optimists: they both believe that unless a divine entity or transcendent reality has provided the world with ultimate purpose or value, life is meaningless. In other words, life can have no meaning if external meaning is nonexistent.

Among famous pessimists we can count the renowned Russian novelist Leo Tolstoy (1828–1910). Before undergoing a Christian conversion (and becoming an optimist), he found himself at age fifty doubting the existence of God and being tortured by the thought that life was entirely without meaning or purpose. Here we can see that his agony at the loss of meaning was extreme:

Leo Tolstoy: *My Confession*

[F]ive years ago something very strange began to happen with me: I was overcome by minutes at first of perplexity and then of an arrest of life, as though I did not know how to live or what to do, and I lost myself and was dejected. But that passed, and I continued to live as before. Then those minutes of perplexity were repeated oftener and oftener, and always in one and the same form. These arrests of life found their expression in ever the same questions: "Why? Well, and then?"

At first I thought that those were simply aimless, inappropriate questions. It seemed to me that that was all well known and that if I ever wanted to busy myself with their solution, it would not cost me much labour,—that now I had no time to attend to them, but that if I wanted to I should find the proper answers. But the questions began to repeat themselves oftener and oftener, answers were demanded more and more persistently, and, like dots that fall on the same spot, these questions, without any answers, thickened into one black blotch.

There happened what happens with any person who falls ill with a mortal internal disease. At first there appear insignificant symptoms of indisposition, to which the patient pays no attention; then these symptoms are repeated more and more frequently and blend into one temporally indivisible suffering. The suffering keeps growing, and before the patient has had time to look around, he becomes conscious that what he took for an indisposition is the most significant thing in the world to him,—his death.

The same happened with me. I understood that it was not a passing indisposition, but something very important, and that, if the questions were going to repeat themselves, it would be necessary to find an answer for them. And I tried to answer them. The questions seemed to be so foolish, simple, and childish. But the moment I touched them and tried to solve them, I became convinced, in the first place, that they were not childish and foolish, but very important and profound questions in life, and, in the second, that, no matter how much I might try, I should not be able to answer them. Before attending to my Samára estate, to my son's education, or to the writing of a book, I ought to know why I should do that. So long as I did not know why, I could not do anything. I could not live. Amidst my thoughts of farming, which interested me very much during that time, there would suddenly pass through my head a question like this: "All right, you are going to have six thousand desyatínas of land in the Government of Samára, and three hundred horses,—and then?" And I completely lost my senses and did not know what to think farther. Or, when I thought of the education of my children, I said to myself: "Why?" Or, reflecting on the manner in which the masses might obtain their welfare, I suddenly said to myself: "What is that to me?" Or, thinking of the fame which my works would get me, I said to myself: "All right, you will be more famous than Gógol, Púshkin; Shakespeare, Molière, and all the writers in the world,—what of it?" And I was absolutely unable to make any reply. The questions were not waiting, and I had to answer them at once; if I did not answer them, I could not live.

I felt that what I was standing on had given way, that I had no foundation to stand on, that that which I lived by no longer existed, and that I had nothing to live by. . . .

All that happened with me when I was on every side surrounded by what is considered to be complete happiness. I had a good, loving, and beloved wife, good children, and a large estate, which grew and increased without any labour on my part. I was respected by my neighbours and friends, more than ever before, was praised by strangers, and, without any self-deception, could consider my name famous. With all that, I was not deranged or mentally unsound,—on the contrary, I was in full command of my mental and physical powers, such as I had rarely met with in people of my age: physically I could work in a field, mowing, without falling behind a peasant; mentally I could work from eight to ten hours in succession, without experiencing any consequences from the strain. And while in such condition I arrived at the conclusion that I could not live, and, fearing death, I had to use cunning against myself, in order that I might not take my life.

Leo Tolstoy:
My Confession

2. Is Tolstoy's pessimism about life's meaning a result of his objective assessment of his life, or is it merely a product of his unique personality traits?

3. What bearing, if any, does the ephemeral nature of our existence have on the question of whether life has meaning? Does the fact that we will die negate the possibility of meaning in life?

This mental condition expressed itself to me in this form: my life is a stupid, mean trick played on me by somebody. Although I did not recognize that "somebody" as having created me, the form of the conception that some one had played a mean, stupid trick on me by bringing me into the world was the most natural one that presented itself to me.

Involuntarily I imagined that there, somewhere, there was somebody who was now having fun as he looked down upon me and saw me, who had lived for thirty or forty years, learning, developing, growing in body and mind, now that I had become strengthened in mind and had reached that summit of life from which it lay all before me, standing as a complete fool on that summit and seeing clearly that there was nothing in life and never would be. And that was fun to him—

But whether there was or was not that somebody who made fun of me, did not make it easier for me. I could not ascribe any sensible meaning to a single act, or to my whole life. I was only surprised that I had not understood that from the start. All that had long ago been known to everybody. Sooner or later there would come diseases and death (they had come already) to my dear ones and to me, and there would be nothing left but stench and worms. All my affairs, no matter what they might be, would sooner or later be forgotten, and I myself should not exist. So why should I worry about all these things? How could a man fail to see that and live,—that was surprising! A person could live only so long as he was drunk; but the moment he sobered up, he could not help seeing that all that was only a deception, and a stupid deception at that! Really, there was nothing funny and ingenious about it, but only something cruel and stupid.[2]

"The sole meaning of life is to serve humanity."
—Leo Tolstoy

The German philosopher Arthur Schopenhauer (1788–1860), another famous pessimist, argues that life is so bereft of meaning, and so fraught with misery, that the nonexistence of the world is preferable to its existence.

Figure 18.3 Leo Tolstoy (1828–1910).

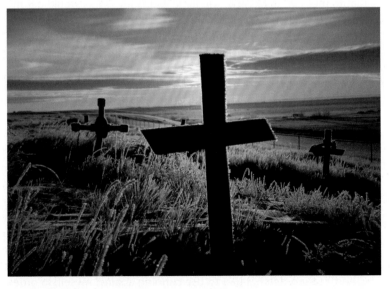

Figure 18.4 Is life any less meaningful because it is short?

Arthur Schopenhauer: *On the Sufferings of the World*

Unless *suffering* is the direct and immediate object of life, our existence must entirely fail of its aim. It is absurd to look upon the enormous amount of pain that abounds everywhere in the world, and originates in needs and necessities inseparable from life itself, as serving no purpose at all and the result of mere chance. Each separate misfortune, as it comes, seems, no doubt, to be something exceptional; but misfortune in general is the rule . . .

The best consolation in misfortune or affliction of any kind will be the thought of other people who are in a still worse plight than yourself; and this is a form of consolation open to every one. But what an awful fate this means for mankind as a whole!

We are like lambs in a field, disporting themselves under the eye of the butcher, who chooses out first one and then another for his prey. So it is that in our good days we are all unconscious of the evil Fate may have presently in store for us—sickness, poverty, mutilation, loss of sight or reason.

No little part of the torment of existence lies in this, that Time is continually pressing upon us, never letting us take breath, but always coming after us, like a taskmaster with a whip. If at any moment Time stays his hand, it is only when we are delivered over to the misery of boredom. . . .

Certain it is that *work*, *worry*, *labor* and *trouble*, form the lot of almost all men their whole life long. But if all wishes were fulfilled as soon as they arose, how would men occupy their lives? what would they do with their time? If the world were a paradise of luxury and ease, a land flowing with milk and honey, where every Jack obtained his Jill at once and without any difficulty, men would either die of boredom or hang themselves; or there would be wars, massacres, and murders; so that in the end mankind would inflict more suffering on itself than it has now to accept at the hands of Nature. . . .

Again, you may look upon life as an unprofitable episode, disturbing the blessed calm of non-existence. And, in any case, even though things have gone with you tolerably well, the longer you live the more clearly you will feel that, on the whole, life is a *disappointment*, *nay*, *a cheat*. . . .

If children were brought into the world by an act of pure reason alone, would the human race continue to exist? Would not a man rather have so much sympathy with the coming generation as to spare it the burden of existence? or at any rate not take it upon himself to impose that burden upon it in cold blood.[3]

The distinguished atheist lawyer Clarence Darrow (1857–1938), defense attorney in the famous Scopes "monkey trial," came to the same conclusion that Tolstoy and Schopenhauer did: life is not worthwhile. "Life is like a ship on the sea," he says, "tossed by every wave and by every wind; a ship headed for no port and no harbor, with no rudder, no compass, no pilot; simply floating for a time, then lost in the waves."[4]

4. Is Schopenhauer right about the meaninglessness of life? Does the wretchedness of our existence show that life has no meaning?

5. What is Schopenhauer's argument for the meaninglessness of life? Is his assessment of life based on objective facts or on his distinctive frame of mind?

"I have always believed, and I still believe, that whatever good or bad fortune may come our way we can always give it meaning and transform it into something of value."
—Hermann Hesse

Figure 18.5 Arthur Schopenhauer (1788–1860).

Against the pessimists, it has been argued that most of them have been guilty of perpetrating the confusion mentioned earlier—mixing up the two senses of *meaning*. Contemporary philosopher Julian Baggini explains:

Julian Baggini: *What's It All About?*

It seems to me that when most people say that life is meaningless, they are talking about meaning in one or both of these senses. They are saying—rightly, in my view—that our lives were not created with any purpose or goal in mind and that there is nothing beyond or after life that can provide a purpose for what we do in this life. But to conclude that 'therefore life is meaningless' is simply to ignore the many other ways in which life can be meaningful. . . .

What is missing is the recognition that life can be meaningful if we find it worth living for its own sake, without recourse to further aims, goals or purposes. . . .

The same kinds of consideration apply when dealing with [existentialist Albert] Camus's question about how we can live life if it is absurd and meaningless. Again it is only 'meaningless' in certain particular senses of the word. . . . Almost all deniers of meaning in life really seem to be rejecting only the idea that life has a specific kind of meaning: one determined by agents, purposes or principles somehow external to this world. This does not justify the conclusion that life has no meaning at all. Their pronouncement that 'life is meaningless' thus just appears to be a kind of hyperbole.[5]

6. Do you think many people who say that life is meaningless are assuming that *meaning* refers to external meaning?

7. If we reject the religious view of meaning in life, are we forced to conclude that life is meaningless?

"Faith consists in being vitally concerned with that ultimate reality to which I give the symbolical name of God. Whoever reflects earnestly on the meaning of life is on the verge of an act of faith."

—Paul Tillich

18.3 OPTIMISM: LIFE CAN HAVE MEANING

Optimists say human existence can be meaningful but are divided on how this meaning is possible. As noted earlier, some believe life's meaning has an external source, and some think it arises internally.

Meaning from Above

Most of those who take the externalist approach view the matter from a religious standpoint. Typically the central doctrine is that a human life has meaning only because it is part of God's plan, a grand cosmic order that encompasses every entity in the universe. As participants in this plan, people have a preeminent role to play and a purpose preordained by God. To have a meaningful existence is to align your life with God's plan, either by performing certain duties or being a particular kind of person. To live contrary to God's plan is to live a meaningless life. And, of course, if there is no God, there is no point to living.

Tolstoy not only gave us a glimpse of his fall into pessimism, he also wrote about his gradual acceptance of a deeply religious understanding of life's meaning:

DETAILS

Is Religion Necessary for a Meaningful Life?

Rick Warren, author of *The Purpose-Driven Life* and the pastor who delivered the invocation at Barack Obama's inauguration ceremony, maintains that religion is required if your life is to have meaning. "You were made by God and for God," he says, "and until you understand that, life will never make sense." Is that true?

The results of a Gallup poll raise doubts about it. The pollsters surveyed thousands of people in eighty-four countries. They concluded that "There is some support in Gallup's data for Warren's premise that religious involvement makes devotees more likely to feel their lives have a purpose. On the other hand, the results also suggest that religious involvement is not *necessary* for most people to feel that way." Here are some of the results.

Do you feel your life has an important meaning or purpose?
Among those claiming any religious affiliation: 92% yes; 6% no.
Among those claiming to be secular, nonreligious, atheist, or agnostic: 83% yes; 14% no.

Do you feel your life has an important meaning or purpose?
Percentage answering yes: Christian: 93%; Hindu: 92%; Muslim: 91%; Buddhist: 90%; Other: 89%; Jewish: 88%; Secular/atheist/agnostic: 83%.

Do you feel your life has an important meaning or purpose?
Percentage answering yes: Elementary education or less: 88%; Secondary education up to 3 years of tertiary education: 91%; At least 4 years of tertiary education: 91%; Have a job: 92%; Do not have a job: 89%.

Do these results surprise you, or are they what you would expect? Do they corroborate the idea that people can have a meaningful life without religion? Do they show that meaning in life can arise internally? Explain.

Gallup survey, 2007, data from 1,000 adults per country across 84 populations; ±4 percentage points sampling error.

Leo Tolstoy: *My Confession*

Long ago has been told the Eastern story about the traveller who in the steppe is overtaken by an infuriated beast. Trying to save himself from the animal, the traveller jumps into a waterless well, but at its bottom he sees a dragon who opens his jaws in order to swallow him. And the unfortunate man does not dare climb out, lest he perish from

Leo Tolstoy:
My Confession

the infuriated beast, and does not dare jump down to the bottom of the well, lest he be devoured by the dragon, and so clutches the twig of a wild bush growing in a cleft of the well and holds on to it. His hands grow weak and he feels that soon he shall have to surrender to the peril which awaits him at either side; but he still holds on and sees two mice, one white, the other black, in even measure making a circle around the main trunk of the bush to which he is clinging, and nibbling at it on all sides. Now, at any moment, the bush will break and tear off, and he will fall into the dragon's jaws. The traveller sees that and knows that he will inevitably perish; but while he is still clinging, he sees some drops of honey hanging on the leaves of the bush, and so reaches out for them with his tongue and licks the leaves. Just so I hold on to the branch of life, knowing that the dragon of death is waiting inevitably for me, ready to tear me to pieces, and I cannot understand why I have fallen on such suffering. And I try to lick that honey which used to give me pleasure; but now it no longer gives me joy, and the white and the black mouse day and night nibble at the branch to which I am holding on. I clearly see the dragon, and the honey is no longer sweet to me. I see only the inevitable dragon and the mice, and am unable to turn my glance away from them. That is not a fable, but a veritable, indisputable, comprehensible truth.

The former deception of the pleasures of life, which stifled the terror of the dragon, no longer deceives me. No matter how much one should say to me, "You cannot understand the meaning of life, do not think, live!" I am unable to do so, because I have been doing it too long before. Now I cannot help seeing day and night, which run and lead me up to death. I see that alone, because that alone is the truth. Everything else is a lie.

The two drops of honey that have longest turned my eyes away from the cruel truth, the love of family and of authorship, which I have called an art, are no longer sweet to me. . . .

I lived for a long time in this madness, which, not in words, but in deeds, is particularly characteristic of us, the most liberal and learned of men. But, thanks either to my strange, physical love for the real working class, which made me understand it and to see that it is not so stupid as we suppose, or to the sincerity of my conviction which was that I could know nothing and that the best that I could do was to hang myself,— I felt that if I wanted to live and understand the meaning of life, I ought naturally to look for it, not among those who had lost the meaning of life and wanted to kill themselves, but among those billions departed and living men who had been carrying their own lives and ours upon their shoulders. And I looked around at the enormous masses of deceased and living men,—not learned and wealthy, but simple men,—and I saw something quite different. I saw that all these billions of men that lived or had lived, all, with rare exceptions, did not fit into my subdivisions, and that I could not recognize them as not understanding the question, because they themselves put it and answered it with surprising clearness. Nor could I recognize them as Epicureans, because their lives were composed rather of privations and suffering than of enjoyment. Still less could I recognize them as senselessly living out their meaningless lives, because every act of theirs and death itself was explained by them. They regarded it as the greatest evil to kill themselves. It appeared, then, that all humanity was in possession of a knowledge of the meaning of life, which I did not recognize and which I condemned. It turned out that rational knowledge did not give any meaning to life, excluded life, while the meaning which by billions of people, by all humanity, was ascribed to life was based on some despised, false knowledge. . . .

Thus, outside the rational knowledge, which had to me appeared as the only one, I was inevitably led to recognize that all living humanity had a certain other irrational knowledge, faith, which made it possible to live. . . .

The rational knowledge brought me to the recognition that life was meaningless,— my life stopped, and I wanted to destroy myself. When I looked around at people, at all humanity, I saw that people lived and asserted that they knew the meaning of life. I looked back at myself: I lived so long as I knew the meaning of life. As to other people, so even to me, did faith give the meaning of life and the possibility of living. . . .

Then I began to cultivate the acquaintance of the believers from among the poor, the simple and unlettered folk, of pilgrims, monks, dissenters, peasants. The doctrine of these people from among the masses was also the Christian doctrine that the quasi-believers of our circle professed. With the Christian truths were also mixed in very many superstitions, but there was this difference: the superstitions of our circle were quite unnecessary to them, had no connection with their lives, were only a kind of an Epicurean amusement, while the superstitions of the believers from among the laboring classes were to such an extent blended with their life that it would have been impossible to imagine it without these superstitions,—it was a necessary condition of that life. I began to examine closely the lives and beliefs of these people, and the more I examined them, the more did I become convinced that they had the real faith, that their faith was necessary for them, and that it alone gave them a meaning and possibility of life. In contradistinction to what I saw in our circle, where life without faith was possible, and where hardly one in a thousand professed to be a believer, among them there was hardly one in a thousand who was not a believer. In contradistinction to what I saw in our circle, where all life passed in idleness, amusements, and tedium of life, I saw that the whole life of these people was passed in hard work, and that they were satisfied with life. In contradistinction to the people of our circle, who struggled and murmured against fate because of their privations and their suffering, these people accepted diseases and sorrows without any perplexity or opposition, but with the calm and firm conviction that it was all for good. In contradistinction to the fact that the more intelligent we are, the less do we understand the meaning of life and the more do we see a kind of a bad joke in our suffering and death, these people live, suffer, and approach death, and suffer in peace and more often in joy. . . . I cast a broader glance about me. I examined the life of past and present vast masses of men, and I saw people who in like manner had understood the meaning of life, who had known how to live and die, not two, not three, not ten, but hundreds, thousands, millions. All of them, infinitely diversified as to habits, intellect, culture, situation, all equally and quite contrary to my ignorance knew the meaning of life and of death, worked calmly, bore privations and suffering, lived and died, seeing in that not vanity, but good.

I began to love those people. The more I penetrated into their life, the life of the men now living, and the life of men departed, of whom I had read and heard, the more did I love them, and the easier it became for me to live. Thus I lived for about two years, and within me took place a transformation, which had long been working within me, and the germ of which had always been in me. What happened with me was that the life of our circle,—of the rich and the learned,—not only disgusted me, but even lost all its meaning. All our acts, reflections, sciences, arts,—all that appeared to me in a new light. I saw that all that was mere pampering of the appetites, and that no meaning could be found in it; but the life of all the working masses, of all humanity, which created life, presented itself to me in its real significance. I saw that that was life itself and that the meaning given to this life was truth, and I accepted it.[6]

Figure 18.6 Gandhi was not a Christian. Did he nevertheless lead a meaningful life? What about Socrates? Einstein?

So Tolstoy says he found the true meaning of life through a leap of faith, not through the rational knowledge of his circle of sophisticates. He chose the religious path trod by millions of the poor and unlearned.

Nonbelievers, however, would not be impressed by Tolstoy's appeal to faith. They would insist that his position be backed by reasons and arguments. But theistic belief is difficult to support this way. Moreover, some critiques of Tolstoy's view do not depend on a denial of God's existence. Several philosophers have argued that the notion of a God assigning a purpose to humans should be objectionable to believers and nonbelievers alike. This is how Baggini expresses the point:

Julian Baggini: *What's It All About?*

8. How do you think Tolstoy would respond to the claim that many people appear to have very meaningful lives? What would he say, for example, about meaning in the life of Mahatma Gandhi or Albert Einstein?

"Ever more people today have the means to live, but no meaning to live for."
—Viktor E. Frankl

[I]t is often said that we are here to do God's will. If this were true. . . [o]ur lives would have a purpose for the being that created us but not a purpose for us. We would each be like Sartre's being-in-itself—an object to be used for the ends of others and not a being-for-itself—a conscious being making choices meaningful for itself. If we found that our sole purpose was to serve God then we might think that was a worse fate than to have no predetermined purpose at all. Is it better to be slaves with a role in the universe or to be free people left to create a role for ourselves?

This view that we are created to serve God is not only objectionable on the grounds that it robs humanity of its dignity. It also has to be seen as extremely implausible within the world-view of the religions that sometimes propound it. After all, what could seem more unlikely than that the supreme being would feel the need to create human beings, with all their complexity, and with all the suffering and toil that human life entails, solely so that it can have creatures to serve it? This is an image of God as an egotistical tyrant, determined to use its power to surround itself with acolytes and have praise heaped upon it. This is not the God which most religious believers worship, and so the idea that we are here just to serve such a God is not one that should be seriously countenanced either. . . .

I think that most reflective religious believers would agree that saying God's purpose for us is to serve it or live full lives is not adequate. They might prefer to say that the existence of God shows that there must be a purpose, since God wouldn't have created us without one, but that we do not know what that purpose is. Faith requires us to trust God and its purposes for us. As Jesus is reported in John's Gospel to have said, 'Trust in God; trust also in me. In my Father's house are many rooms' (14:1-2). This is a perfectly coherent position and probably the one most sensible religious believers occupy. But doing so requires an honest acceptance that they have no more idea as to what the purpose of life is than the atheist has.

The leap of faith required to adopt such a position also needs to be clearly understood. This is faith that a God we cannot know to exist has a purpose we cannot discern for an afterlife we have no evidence is to come. Further, we would also be trusting that this purpose is one we would be pleased with. If it turned out that our purpose was to fight Satan's hordes for eternity or just to have lived as a beacon of fortitude under duress on earth before dying, we might not be too pleased that God had a purpose for us after all.

A belief that we were created by God for a purpose does not then provide us with the kind of adequate account of life's meaning we might expect. Religions are not clear about what this purpose is. The idea that it is to serve God seems deeply implausible and contrary to most conceptions of God's nature. The idea that it is to live life to the full is a platitude, only turned into something more by a belief in an afterlife. The idea that God's purpose is something we just have to trust is an admission that we have no answer to the question of why we are here and must leave everything to the unknown.[7]

9. According to Baggini, how is God's creating us for his purposes supposed to denigrate human life? Do you agree?

"Religion is the state of being grasped by an ultimate concern, a concern which qualifies all other concerns as preliminary and which itself contains the answer to the question of a meaning of our life."
—Paul Tillich

Meaning from Below

Internalists believe they can have meaningful lives without relying on the concepts of God or transcendent realms. They hold that they can confer meaning on their own lives. The proof of this, they might say, is all around us. There are many people who seem to lead meaningful lives, and we would judge this to be the case even if we thought no external being or force existed to confer meaning. Consider Socrates, Mahatma Gandhi, Martin Luther King, Jr., Rosa Parks, Elizabeth Cady Stanton, Marie Curie, George Washington, Confucius—these men and women, by all accounts, were driven by a sense of purpose and led lives full of meaning.

But exactly what property or state of affairs is the conveyor of meaning? Internalists differ on that score. Here is Paul Edwards's view:

Figure 18.7 Baggini asks, "Is it better to be slaves with a role in the universe or to be free people left to create a role for ourselves?"

Paul Edwards, *The Encyclopedia of Philosophy*

[W]hen we ask whether a *particular* person's life has or had any meaning, we are usually concerned not with cosmic issues but with the question of whether certain purposes are to be found *in* his life. Thus, most of us would say without hesitation that a person's life had meaning if we knew that he devoted himself to a cause (such as the spread of Christianity or communism or the reform of mental institutions), or we would at least be ready to say that it "acquired meaning" once he became sufficiently attached to his cause. Whether we approve of what they did or not, most of us would be ready to admit—to take some random examples—that Dorothea Dix, Pasteur, Lenin, Margaret Sanger, Anthony Comstock, and Winston Churchill led meaningful lives. We seem to mean two things in characterizing such lives as meaningful: we assert, first, that the life in question had some dominant, over-all goal or goals which gave direction to a great many of the individual's actions and, second, that these actions and possibly others not immediately related to the overriding goal were performed with a special zest that was not present before the person became attached to his goal or that would not have been present if there had been no such goal in his life. It is not necessary, however, that a person should be devoted to a cause, in the sense just indicated, before we call his life meaningful. It is sufficient that he should have some attachments that are not too shallow.[8]

A common reply to any internalist view is that the prospect of death and the eventual obliteration of all human creations rob our lives of meaning. How can our lives be meaningful, they ask, when life is so short and death is certain? What's the point of living if everything we are and do will soon sink into nothingness?

Many philosophers reject this dismal outlook, arguing that the fact of death and the ephemeral nature of human endeavors are irrelevant to the meaningfulness or meaninglessness of a person's existence. If life is meaningful, then it is meaningful no matter how long or short it is. Edwards is one of the philosophers who make this point:

Let us consider some everyday occurrences: A man with a toothache goes to a dentist, and the dentist helps him so that the toothache disappears. A man is falsely accused of a crime and is faced with the possibility of a severe sentence as well as with the loss of his reputation; with the help of a devoted attorney his innocence is established, and he is acquitted. It is true that a hundred years later all of the participants in these events will be dead and none of them will *then* be able to enjoy the fruits of any of the efforts involved. But this most emphatically does not imply that the dentist's efforts were not worthwhile or that the attorney's work was not worth doing. To bring in considerations of what will or will not happen in the remote future is, in [this and other] human situations, totally irrelevant. Not only is the finality of death irrelevant here; equally irrelevant are the facts, if they are facts, that life is an endless cycle of the same kind of activities and that the history of the universe is not a drama with a happy ending.[9]

Internalists can be divided into two camps: those who believe that meaning is something they create (*subjectivists*) and those who think meaning is something they discover (*objectivists*).

> I would rather live my life as if there is a God and die to find out there isn't, than live my life as if there isn't and die to find out there is.
> —Albert Camus

10. Do you agree with Edwards that the length of one's life does not by itself determine whether life is meaningful?

Among the subjectivists, we can count not only Baggini and Edwards, but also the philosophers R. M. Hare (1919–2002), Bertrand Russell (1872–1970), Richard Taylor (1919–2003), Kai Nielsen, Jean-Paul Sartre (1905–1980), Robert Solomon (1942–2007), E. D. Klemke (1926–2000), and Lucretius (c. 100–55 BCE).

For subjectivists, meaning is relative to each person and depends on his or her attitudes, desires, and goals. So subjectivists might say their lives are meaningful if they do what they deem most important or satisfy their strongest desires or act out of love or concern. A common criticism of subjectivist views is that it's intuitively obvious that sometimes objective standards apply. If satisfying our strongest desires leads to obviously immoral or trivial acts, subjectivism is implausible. Things aren't meaningful just because we say they are.

The classic example of a subjectivist is Sartre. As one of the modern founders of existentialism, he argues that humans are profoundly free to create their own lives and thus are entirely responsible for defining the meaning and moral relevance of their existence. There are no objective standards to define what is and is not meaningful for them. "Man," he says, "is nothing else but what he makes of himself."

Consider these two subjectivists who lived two millennia apart but came to much the same conclusion about meaning in life. E. D. Klemke, editor of the highly regarded anthology *The Meaning of Life*, was an astute subjectivist philosopher. In a well-known essay, "Living Without Appeal: An Affirmative Philosophy of Life," he responded to those who claim that (1) there exists a "transcendent ultimate" (a deity, for example) with which we can have a relationship through faith; (2) without such an entity and faith in it, life is meaningless; and (3) without such meaning, life is not worthwhile.

Regarding the first claim, he asks what evidence supports it. The assertions of some sacred text prove nothing, he says, since they prove only that "someone *believed* that a transcendent ultimate exists." Likewise the testimony of large numbers of believers proves nothing. The traditional arguments for the existence of a god all fail to provide reasons for believing, and arguments from religious experience can prove no more than that "someone has had an unusual experience." He concludes that there is zero evidence for the existence of a transcendent anything.

As to the second claim—that without faith in the transcendent, human existence is without meaning—Klemke answers by distinguishing between objective meaning and subjective meaning. An objective meaning is one that is either structurally part of the universe (apart from human evaluation) or dependent on some nonhuman external agency. If there is objective meaning, he says, there is no reason why it must be linked to a transcendent being. But even more important, "I find the notion of an objective meaning as difficult to accept as I do the notion of a transcendent being. It seems to me that there is no shred of evidence for the existence of an objective meaning in the universe. . . . From the standpoint of present evidence, evaluational components such as meaning or purpose are not to be found in the universe as objective aspects of it."[10] Klemke also rejects the related claims that subjective meaning is possible but only through the transcendent, or that even subjective meaning is impossible without faith in the transcendent. He says of the latter assertion, "I know of many humans who have found a meaningful existence without faith in the transcendent."[11]

In response to the third claim—that without meaning, life is not worthwhile—Klemke says that it confuses objective and subjective meaning. He says that indeed life has no objective meaning, "but from this it does not follow that life is not *worthwhile*, for it can still be subjectively meaningful. . . . I, for one, am *glad* that the universe has no meaning, for thereby is *man all the more glorious*. I willingly accept the fact that external meaning is non-existent (or if existent, certainly not apparent), for this leaves me free to *forge my own meaning*."[12] He declares that he has found subjective meaning through knowledge, art, love, and work, for with his consciousness, he can endow events, objects, and persons with value.

Lucretius, a Roman poet and philosopher, believes that life can be meaningful even in a completely materialistic universe bereft of the supernatural. He is best known for a seven-thousand-line poem on science and philosophy called *The Nature of Things*, or *De rerum natura*, a masterpiece that has influenced many thinkers throughout the centuries as well as in modern life.

Lucretius was an atomist. Two millennia ago some philosophers argued that the world consists entirely of atoms moving in space, just as modern science has shown us. He declares that everything—humans, animals, the earth, the stars, the sun—is made of atoms. The universe is infinite and entirely material. There is no designer who created everything. The universe is eternal; it has always been here. Things have come about through the laws of nature and chance. The soul is also material, which means that it dies just as the body does. There is no afterlife; the present world is all we have.

This view may seem dreary, but Lucretius thinks the opposite. Because death is final, we need not fear it, because we will not be present to confront it. As he says, "Death is nothing to us." There will be no pain, anguish, or torment after death.

Religion causes pain, Lucretius says, because it instills a fear of everlasting torment or some other uncertain fate after death. Religion causes anxiety because it teaches superstitions about mischief or terror caused by demons, angels, or ghosts. Religion discourages the pursuit of happiness and pleasure, when these things should be central to our lives. Religion causes ruin when it holds out the false hope of miraculously transcending our finite lives. The most famous line of Lucretius's poem refers to a particularly evil act performed in the name of religion. He says, "So potent was religion in persuading to do wrong."

Lucretius wasn't an atheist exactly, for he believed there were gods, but he thought the gods had no interest in, and nothing to do with, humans. To be truly happy, he says, we must dispel illusions about our ability to live forever, find perfect satisfaction, control events, and be the center of the universe's attention. By avoiding these delusions, we can attain a realistic measure of happiness, even joy.

Lucretius declares that we can experience a sense of awe, gratitude, and reverence when we see that the universe is beautiful and boundlessly complex. We are made of the same stuff as stars and seas and trees and clouds. We humans are all connected—to each other and to every part of the cosmos. We also experience awe when we contemplate the mysteries that science reveals, and we feel the delight of discovery when we solve those mysteries.

Lucretius believes that the meaning of life can be found in pleasure-seeking that is rational and realistic. One of his disciples said that it is not possible to live a life of

DETAILS

The Perfectionist Trap

For many people, the worst enemy of meaning in their lives is perfectionism. Iddo Landau, professor of philosophy and author of *Finding Meaning in an Imperfect World*, explains:

> Of all the presuppositions that bring people to believe that their lives are meaningless, the most common is probably the perfectionist presupposition. According to this presupposition, meaningful lives must include some perfection or excellence or some rare and difficult achievements, and lives that do not show this characteristic cannot be seen as meaningful. Meaningful lives, then, must transcend the common and the mundane.
>
> A surprisingly large number of philosophers who write on the topic of the meaning of life endorse the perfectionist presupposition. To the extent that Nietzsche should be interpreted as calling for meaningful lives, he too presents ideals that are difficult, or almost impossible, to achieve. . . . Camus takes our life to be absurd because we cannot attain perfect knowledge that would unify everything under one principle and recognize the eternal relations between things. According to Camus, anything less than that arouses a sense of absurdity. . . .
>
> It is not just philosophers who find the perfectionist supposition to be intuitive. Most people who have told me that they found their life meaningless held one version or another of the perfectionist supposition. Many of them mention, among other issues, that they are not absolutely authentic, absolutely immune to peer pressure, absolutely truthful, absolutely unaffected by egoistic motivations, or absolutely courageous. . . .
>
> What marks perfectionists is that they fail to see the worth that inheres also in the nonperfect; they despise and reject it. Both perfectionist and many nonperfectionist students think that receiving a grade of 100 percent on an exam is better than receiving any other grade, and both would be glad to receive it. But the perfectionists are those who, when they receive a 98, feel that they failed. For them, this 98 is like a zero. They do not want it; they fail to see the worth in receiving such a grade. Perfectionists believe that if our city is not the most beautiful in the world, it is disgustingly ugly, that if one is not Einstein one is a fool; and that if a person does not write as Shakespeare did, she had better just give up writing altogether. Noticing that our city is not the most beautiful in the world, criticizing what is wrong with it, wishing to improve it, and trying to do so does not make one a perfectionist. But we are perfectionists if, after noticing that our city is not the most beautiful in the world, we become blind to the beauty and value that it does have.
>
> Thus perfectionists are so busy with the search for the perfect that they neglect to see and find satisfaction in the good.

Landau argues that perfectionist views of the meaning of life are implausible, inconsistent, and even cruel. Perfectionist tendencies, he says, fly in the face of the obvious fact that "many nonperfect things or achievements, or things or achievements that are common and easy to attain, are good, important, and worthy."[13]

pleasure "without living prudently and honorably and justly, and also without living courageously and temperately and magnanimously, and without making friends, and without being philanthropic."

For objectivists, meaning is mind-independent. Objectively worthwhile activities or states convey objective meaning that everyone can recognize as such. If a life is meaningful, it is so because it has objective value, not because of someone's subjective preferences or desires. An objectivist might say that helping others and creating art are generally believed to give meaning to life, and the best explanation for such beliefs is objectivism—some things are inherently worthwhile.

Notable objectivists include James Rachels (1941–2003), Susan Wolf, Terry Eagleton, John G. Messerly, Christopher Belshaw, Thaddeus Metz, Victor Frankl (1905–1997), and Moritz Schlick (1882–1936).

Susan Wolf, philosopher and author of *Meaning in Life and Why It Matters*, argues that meaning in life must consist of both subjective and objective elements. As she says, "Meaningful lives are lives of active engagement in projects of worth."[14] Active engagement is involvement in something that grips or excites a person, something that arouses passion. But this subjective response alone is not enough to add significant meaning to someone's life. Mere passion about an activity is, in itself, insufficient to contribute meaningfulness to a life. The passion must be directed at projects that are in themselves worthwhile. "What is clear to me," she says, "is that there can be no sense to the idea of meaningfulness without a distinction between more and less worthwhile ways to spend one's time, where the test of worth is at least partly independent of a subject's ungrounded preferences or enjoyment."[15]

This view belies the often-expressed notion that what someone does doesn't matter as long as the person enjoys it or prefers it or gets satisfaction out of it. Counterexamples abound. People do wonder sometimes if an activity they enjoy is in fact worthwhile. Some people with satisfying lives do feel that their existence is meaningless.

Wolf lists some of the activities that seem objectively worthwhile: "Moral and intellectual accomplishments and the ongoing activities that lead to them. Relationships with friends and relatives are perhaps even more important for most of us. Aesthetic enterprises (both creative and appreciative), the cultivation of personal virtues, and religious practices frequently loom large."

She sums up her view in a slogan: "Meaning arises when subjective attraction meets objective attractiveness."[16]

The contemporary philosopher Christopher Belshaw, another objectivist, examines some of the reasons that lead people to think life may be meaningless. Perhaps life is meaningless because it is so brief, because we and our world are so minuscule compared to the inconceivably vast cosmos, because life for us is so filled with misery and loss, and because there is no god or creator to give us a purpose or plan for living. But, Belshaw says, none of these reasons shows that life is meaningless. Why should the brevity of life or our relative size matter? These facts seem irrelevant. Yes, life is fraught with suffering, but it also contains moments of joy and satisfaction. And as for being part of God's plan, Belshaw wonders if our worries about the meaninglessness or pointlessness of our lives are really going to be put to rest because God has a

DETAILS

What Can and Cannot Give Life Meaning

Here is a quiz to help you assess your views on life's meaning. For each statement below, indicate whether you agree or disagree with it (or have no opinion on it). This is the easy part. The more difficult task is to support your beliefs with good arguments or evidence. This exercise asks you to specify not what has *caused* your beliefs but what *justifies* them.

Figure 18.8 Determining whether your life has meaning usually requires a broad, encompassing view of things.

1. Unless there is an eternal afterlife, human life can have no meaning.

2. Life has meaning only if there is a God who has created us for a purpose.

3. Life has meaning if you are happy.

4. Life has no meaning and no purpose.

5. Having a meaningful or purposeful life does not matter; what matters is the next life of everlasting bliss.

6. People cannot give meaning to their own lives; life's meaning is derived from God or some other transcendental reality.

7. A study of people past and present would show that some of them live or have lived meaningful lives, and this sense of meaning does not depend on their belief in God.

8. Death has no bearing on whether we can live meaningful lives.

9. The eventual obliteration of everything we have created or strived for is irrelevant to whether our lives can be meaningful.

10. The notion that God has assigned to humans a purpose or plan to live by is an affront to human dignity.

11. Without a transcendental reality, and humanity's relationship to it through faith, human life is meaningless.

12. Some moral, aesthetic, or intellectual goals or endeavors are enough to confer meaning on one's life.

13. As Tolstoy says, a meaningful life requires a leap of faith.

14. People who trust that God has a plan for their lives have no understanding of what the purpose of their lives is.

15. Socrates, Mahatma Gandhi, Marie Curie, and Confucius led meaningful lives.

scheme into which we fit. "Are we really going to be satisfied by finding that we fit into someone else's grand scheme?" Belshaw asks. "There's some sort of meaning and purpose in this, but is it the sort we want?"[17]

He suggests that what we really want is our own meaning that we find for ourselves. But the meaning can't be completely subjective; meaning cannot be whatever we think it is. "Whether or not your life is successful depends on how it matches up against certain external criteria," Belshaw says. "It doesn't depend simply on how you feel about it. And I think it's the same for whether your life is meaningful. Here, too, thinking doesn't make it so."[18]

What are some of the things that objectively matter? "Relationships," he says, "pursuing some plan or project, living a good life."[19]

WRITING AND REASONING	CHAPTER 18

1. Devise an argument for the proposition that life is (or is not) meaningful.

2. Explain Tolstoy's case for believing that life can have meaning through a leap of faith—then show how skeptics have argued against Tolstoy's view. Conclude by stating which side in this controversy you think is stronger.

3. Some maintain that we are here to do God's will. Lay out an argument showing that such a purpose would or would not make life meaningful.

4. State whether you believe that Socrates and Marie Curie led meaningful lives. Give reasons for your assertion.

5. Does the prospect of death undermine life's meaningfulness? Give reasons for your answer.

REVIEW NOTES

18.1 THE SEARCH FOR MEANING

- Most who have thought about it believe that questions concerning the meaning of human existence are extremely important and relevant.

- The process of examining the question of life's meaning is personal—no one can do it for you.

- The main impediment to clear thinking about life's meaning is confusion about what *meaning* refers to. The word can refer to external meaning or internal meaning.

18.2 PESSIMISM: LIFE HAS NO MEANING

- Pessimists believe that life has no meaning; optimists believe that it does. Some optimists believe that life's meaning is external; other optimists think it's internal.

- Tolstoy (at one point in his life), Schopenhauer, and Darrow are pessimists. Baggini thinks they mix up the two senses of meaning; when they say "life is meaningless," they likely mean only that life has no meaning in the external sense.

18.3 OPTIMISM: LIFE CAN HAVE MEANING

- Most of those who take the externalist approach view the matter from a religious standpoint. Typically they believe that a human life has meaning only because it is part of God's plan. Tolstoy took this view and maintained that finding meaning in life requires a leap of faith.

- Unbelievers would insist the religious view of meaning be backed by reasons and arguments. Several philosophers have argued that the notion of a God assigning a purpose to humans should be objectionable to believers and nonbelievers alike. They maintain that this idea of God creating people for a purpose is an affront to human dignity.

- Internalists believe they can have meaningful lives without relying on the concepts of God or transcendent realms. They hold that they can confer meaning on their own lives.

- Many philosophers reject the notion that death robs people of meaning in life. They argue that the fact of death and the ephemeral nature of human endeavors are irrelevant to the meaningfulness or meaningless of a person's existence. If life is meaningful, then it is meaningful no matter how long or short it is.

Notes

1. Albert Camus, *The Myth of Sisyphus*, trans. J. O'Brien (New York: Alfred A. Knopf, 1955), i.
2. Leo Tolstoy, *My Confession*, trans. Leo Wierner (New York: J. M. Dent and Sons, 1905).
3. Arthur Schopenhauer, "On the Sufferings of the World," *Parerga and Paralipomena*, trans. T. Bailey Saunders (1851).
4. Clarence Darrow, "Is Life Worth Living?" (debate), March 28, 1920.
5. Julian Baggini, *What's It All About?*: *Philosophy and the Meaning of Life* (Oxford: Oxford University Press, 2005), 160–161.
6. Tolstoy, *My Confession*.
7. Baggini, *What's It All About?*, 17, 19–20.
8. Paul Edwards, *The Encyclopedia of Philosophy*, vol. 4, ed. Paul Edwards (New York: Macmillan, 1967).
9. Edwards, *The Encyclopedia of Philosophy*.
10. E. D. Klemke, "Living Without Appeal: An Affirmative Philosophy of Life," in *The Meaning of Life*: *A Reader*, ed. E. D. Klemke and Steven M. Cahn (New York: Oxford University Press, 2008), 190.
11. Klemke, "Living Without Appeal," 191.
12. Klemke, "Living Without Appeal," 193.
13. Iddo Landau, *Finding Meaning in an Imperfect World* (New York: Oxford University Press, 2017), 31–36, 48.
14. Susan Wolf, "Meaning in Life," in *The Meaning of Life*: *A Reader*, ed. E. D. Klemke and Steven M. Cahn (New York: Oxford University Press, 2008), 232.

15. Wolf, "Meaning in Life," 233.

16. Wolf, "Meaning in Life," 234.

17. Christopher Belshaw, *10 Good Questions about Life and Death* (Oxford: Blackwell, 2005), 113.

18. Belshaw, *10 Good Questions*, 115.

19. Belshaw, *10 Good Questions*, 116.

For Further Reading

Julian Baggini, *What's It All About?*: *Philosophy and the Meaning of Life* (Oxford: Oxford University Press, 2005). An excellent primer on meaning in life; argues that meaning can have an internal source.

Kurt Baier, "The Meaning of Life," 1957, reprinted in *The Meaning of Life*: *A Reader*, eds. E. D. Klemke and Steven M. Cahn (New York: Oxford University Press, 2008), 82–113. A classic essay on the basic issues.

Christopher Belshaw, *10 Good Questions about Life and Death* (Malden, MA: Blackwell, 2005).

E. D. Klemke and Steven M. Cahn, eds., *The Meaning of Life*: *A Reader* (New York: Oxford University Press, 2008). A good anthology featuring most of the must-read articles.

Iddo Landau, *Finding Meaning in an Imperfect World* (New York: Oxford University Press, 2017).

Bertrand Russell, "A Free Man's Worship," *Why I Am Not a Christian* (London: George Allen & Unwin, 1957). A much-anthologized essay by the famous twentieth-century philosopher; discusses how life can have meaning in a godless world.

Susan Wolf, *Meaning in Life and Why It Matters* (Princeton, NJ: Princeton University Press, 2010).

Online Resources

"The Meaning of Life," in The Stanford Encyclopedia of Philosophy, June 3, 2013, https://plato.stanford.edu/entries/life-meaning/

Seachris, J., 2011, "Meaning of Life: The Analytic Perspective," in Internet Encyclopedia of Philosophy, J. Fieser and B. Dowden (eds.)

Iddo Landau, "Mistakes about the Meaning of Life," The Philosophers' Magazine, May 14, 2018, https://www.philosophersmag.com/essays/185-mistake-about-the-meaning-of-life

John G. Messerly, "Meaning," in Reason and Meaning (blog), https://reasonand-meaning.com/ (July 13, 2020)

Julian Baggini, "Revealed—the Meaning of Life," The Guardian, September 20, 2004, https://www.theguardian.com/theguardian/2004/sep/20/features11.g2

How to Write a Philosophy Paper

In conversations, letters to the editor, or online discussions, have you ever taken a position on an issue and offered reasons why your view is correct? If so, then you have defended a thesis. You have presented an argument, giving reasons for accepting a particular thesis, or conclusion. If you elaborate on your argument in a written paper, you create something even more valuable—a *thesis defense* (or *argumentative*) *essay*. In a thesis defense essay, you try to show the reader that your view is worthy of acceptance by offering reasons that support it. Your thesis may assert your position on a philosophical, social, or political issue; on the arguments or claims of other writers (including some famous or not-so-famous philosophers); or on the interpretation of a single work or several works. In every case, you affirm a thesis and give reasons for your affirmation.

This type of essay is not merely an analysis of claims, a summary of points made by someone else, or a reiteration of what other people believe or say—though a good thesis defense essay may contain some of these elements. A thesis defense essay is supposed to be a demonstration of what you believe and why you believe it. What other people think is, ultimately, beside the point.

BASIC ESSAY STRUCTURE

Thesis defense essays usually contain the following elements, though not necessarily in this order:

I. Introduction (or opening)

    A. Thesis statement (the claim to be supported)

    B. Plan for the paper

    C. Background for the thesis

II. Argument supporting the thesis

III. Assessment of objections

IV. Conclusion

Introduction

The introduction often consists of the paper's first paragraph, sometimes just a sentence or two. Occasionally it is longer, perhaps several paragraphs. The length depends on how much ground you must cover to introduce the argument. Whatever the length, the introduction should be no longer than necessary. In most cases the best introductions are short.

If there is a rule of thumb for what the introduction must contain, it is this: *The introduction should set forth the thesis statement.* The thesis statement usually appears in the first paragraph. It is the claim that you hope to support or prove in your essay, the conclusion of the argument that you intend to present. You may want to pose the thesis statement as the answer to a question that you raise, or as the solution to a problem that you wish to discuss. However presented, your thesis statement is the assertion you must support with reasons. It is like a compass to your readers, guiding them from paragraph to paragraph, premise to premise, showing them a clear path from introduction to conclusion. It also helps you stay on course. It reminds you to relate every sentence and paragraph to your one controlling idea.

Your thesis statement should be restricted to a claim that you can defend in the space allowed. You want to state it in a single sentence and do so as early as possible. You may need to add a few words to explain or elaborate on the statement if you think its meaning or implications unclear.

The other two parts of an introduction—the plan for the paper (B) and background information for the thesis (C)—may or may not be necessary, depending on your thesis and your intent. In more formal essays, you will need not only to state your thesis, but also to spell out how you intend to argue for it. You will have to summarize your whole argument—each of your premises and conclusion—or, if your argument is long or complex, at least the most important points. Providing background information for your thesis is a matter of explaining what your thesis means (which includes defining terms and clarifying concepts), what its implications are, why the issue is so important or pressing, or why you have decided to address it. Sometimes the needed background information is so extensive that you must supply much of it after the introduction. At any rate, by adding the right kind of background information, you give your readers good reason to care about what you are saying and to continue reading.

In many philosophy papers, the background information includes a summary or sketch of the views of other philosophers—what they have said that is relevant to the issue or to your thesis. Providing this kind of material can help the reader understand why your topic is worth exploring and why your argument is relevant.

Argument Supporting the Thesis

Between your paper's introduction and conclusion is the *body* of the essay. The basic components of the body are (1) the premises of your argument plus the material that supports or explains them and (2) an evaluation of objections to your thesis. Each premise must be clearly stated, carefully explained and illustrated, and properly backed up by examples, statistics, expert opinion, argument, or other reasons or evidence. You may be able to adequately develop the essay by devoting a single paragraph to each premise, or you may have to use several paragraphs per premise.

Whatever tack you take, you must stick to the central rule of paragraph development: Develop just one main point in each paragraph, embodying that point in a topic sentence. Make sure that each paragraph in turn relates to your thesis statement.

If your essay is a critique of someone else's arguments, you should examine them in the body, explaining how they work and laying out the author's response to any major criticisms of them. Your account of the arguments should be accurate and complete, putting forth the author's best case and providing enough detail for your readers to understand the import of your own argument. After the presentation of the author's side of things, you can then bring in your critique, asserting and explaining each premise.

Some premises, of course, may be so obvious that they do not require support. The determining factor is whether your readers would be likely to question them. If your readers are likely to accept a premise as it is, no backup is required. If they are not, you need to support the premise. A common mistake is to assume that a premise would be accepted by everyone when in fact it is controversial.

Recall that in a good argument the conclusion logically follows from the premises, and the premises are true. Your task in the body of your essay is to put forth such an argument and to do so plainly—to demonstrate clearly to your readers that your premises are properly related to your conclusion and that they are true. You should leave no doubt about what you are trying to prove and how you are trying to prove it. In longer papers, you may want to back up your thesis with more than one argument. This is an acceptable way to proceed, providing you make the relationships between the separate arguments and your thesis clear.

Assessment of Objections

Very often an argumentative essay includes an *assessment of objections*—a sincere effort to take into account any objections or doubts that readers are likely to have about points in your essay. (In some cases, however, there may be no significant objections to assess.) You must show your readers that the objections are unfounded, that your argument is not fatally wounded by likely criticisms. Contrary to what some may think, when you deal effectively with objections in your essay, *you do not weaken it—you strengthen it*. You lend credibility to it by making an attempt to be fair and thorough. You make your position stronger by removing doubts from your readers' minds. If you don't confront likely objections, your readers may conclude that you are either ignorant of the objections or you don't have a good reply to them. An extra benefit is that in dealing with objections, you may see ways to make your argument stronger.

On the other hand, you may discover that you do not have an adequate answer to the objections. Then what? Then you look for ways to change your arguments or thesis to overcome the criticisms. You can weaken your thesis by making it less sweeping or less probable. Or you may need to abandon your thesis altogether in favor of one that is stronger. Discovering that your beloved thesis is full of holes is not necessarily a setback. You have increased your understanding by finding out which boats will float and which will not.

Conclusion

Unless your essay is very short, it should have a *conclusion*. The conclusion usually appears in the last paragraph. Many conclusions simply reiterate the thesis statement and then go on to emphasize how important it is. Others issue a call to action, present a compelling perspective on the issue, or discuss further implications of the thesis statement. Some conclusions contain a summary of the essay's argument. A summary is always a good idea if the argument is complex, long, or formal.

WRITING THE ESSAY: STEP BY STEP

Now we examine the steps involved in crafting a good thesis defense essay. You have the best chance of writing a good essay if you try to follow these steps. Just remember that the process is not linear. You may not be able to follow the steps in the sequence suggested. You may have to backtrack or rearrange the order of the steps. This kind of improvising on the fly is normal—and often necessary. At any stage in the process, you may discover that your argument is not as good as you thought, or that you did not take an important fact into account, or that there is a way that you can alter the essay to make it stronger. You may then want to go back and rework your outline or tinker with the draft you are working on—and your essay will be better for it. Rethinking and revising are normal procedures for even the best writers.

Here are the steps:

1. Select a topic and narrow it to a specific issue.
2. Research the issue.
3. Write a thesis statement.
4. Create an outline of the whole essay.
5. Write a first draft.
6. Study and revise your first draft.
7. Produce a final draft.

Step 1. Select a topic and narrow it to a specific issue.

This step is first for a reason. It is here to help inexperienced writers avoid a tempting but nasty trap: picking a thesis out of the air and writing their paper on it. Caution: *Any thesis that you dream up without knowing anything about it is likely to be unusable*—and a waste of time. It is better to begin by selecting a topic or issue and narrowing it through research and hard thinking to a manageable thesis.

A topic is simply a broad category of subject matter, such as *human cloning, the mind, capital punishment*, and *God*. Within topics there lurk an infinite number of issues—that is, questions that are in dispute. From the topic of capital punishment, for example, countless issues arise: whether executing criminals deters crime, whether executing a human being is ever morally permissible, whether it is ethical to execute people who are insane or mentally impaired, whether the system of capital punishment in the United States is unfair, whether the death penalty should be mandatory for serial killers, whether executing juveniles is immoral . . . the list could go on and on. The basic idea is to select from the roster of possibilities an issue that (1) you are interested in and (2) you can adequately address in the space allowed.

Step 2. Research the issue.

The main reason for researching an issue is to find out what viewpoints and arguments are involved. Often your instructor will suggest good sources to research for a particular writing assignment. Your assigned reading may be the only source you need to check. Otherwise, you can read articles and books, talk to people who have studied the issue or at least thought about it carefully, or go online to review topical or philosophical sites.

Step 3. Write a thesis statement.

The conclusion of your selected argument will serve as the basis for your thesis statement. Often the conclusion *is* your thesis statement. Writing a good thesis statement is an essential step, because the entire essay is built on it. An imprecise or clumsy thesis statement can lead to an imprecise or clumsy argument, which can wreck any argumentative essay.

At this stage, you should try to get the wording of your statement just right, even though you may revise it later on. Its scope should be restricted to what you can handle in the space you have. It should also be focused on just one idea, not several. A good thesis statement must be clear. No one should have to guess about the meaning of your thesis. The thesis "Same-sex marriages are intolerable," for example, is intolerably vague, since there are many ways that something can be intolerable. It gives us very little information about what will be discussed in the essay.

It is possible to devise a thesis statement that is restricted, focused, clear—and trivial. A trivial thesis statement is one that either concerns an insignificant issue or makes an insignificant claim. People generally don't care about insignificant issues, and few would bother to disagree with an insignificant claim. Who cares whether pens are better than pencils, or whether gambling is more fun than beachcombing? And who would care to contest the claim that pleasure is better than pain? An essay built on a trivial thesis statement wastes your readers' time (if they bother to read it at all), and you learn nothing and change nothing by writing it. Thesis statements should be worthy.

Here are some thesis statements that meet the preceding criteria:

- Jeremy Bentham's moral theory known as act-utilitarianism conflicts with our commonsense ideas about human rights.
- The U.S. government should be allowed to arrest and indefinitely imprison without trial any American citizen who is suspected of terrorism.
- Subjective relativism—the view that truth depends on what someone believes—is self-refuting.
- Racial profiling should not be used to do security screening of airline passengers.

Step 4. Create an outline of the whole essay.

If you can write out your thesis statement and outline the argument used to defend it, you have already come far. Your argument and thesis statement will constitute the skeleton of your essay. The next step is to flesh out the bones with introductory or explanatory material, responses to objections, and support for the premises (which may consist of subordinate arguments, examples, explanations, analogies, statistics, scientific research, expert opinion, or other evidence). Producing a detailed, coherent outline of the whole essay is the best way to manage this task, and if you already have an outline of your argument, creating an outline for the whole essay will be easy. An outline helps you fill out your argument in an orderly fashion, showing you how the pieces fit together, and whether any parts are missing or misaligned. This filling-out process will probably require you to research your thesis further—to check the truth of premises, examine alternative arguments, look for additional evidence, or assess the strength of objections to your argument.

Do not be afraid to alter your outline at any stage. As you write, you may realize that your thesis is weak, your argument flawed, or your premises vague. If so, you should go back and adjust the outline before writing any further. Writing is an act of exploration, and good writers are not afraid to revise when they find something amiss.

When you outline your essay, include your full thesis statement in the introduction. Then, as you work on the outline, you can refer to the statement for guidance. The major points of your outline will include the premises, conclusion, objections, and responses to objections.

You will find that as you tweak the outline, you may need to adjust the thesis statement. And as you perfect the thesis statement, you may need to adjust the outline. In the end, you want to satisfy yourself that the outline is complete, accurate, and structurally sound, tracing a clear and logical progression of points.

Step 5. Write a first draft.

Good writers revise . . . and revise and revise. They either write multiple drafts, revising in successive passes, or they revise continuously as they write. They know that their first tries will always be in need of improvement. Inexperienced writers, on the other hand, too often dash off a first draft without a second look—then turn it in! A much more reasonable approach (and the best one for most students) is to at least write a first draft and a final draft or—better—several drafts and a final one.

In argumentative essays, because of the importance of articulating an argument carefully, and the difficulty of writing later drafts of the essay unless the first one is in reasonable shape, the first draft should be fairly solid. That is, in your first draft, you should write a tentative version of each paragraph, and the wording of your thesis statement, and all premises should be at least close to final form.

Give your draft a good introduction that lays out your thesis statement, provides background information on the issue, and draws your readers into the essay. Make it interesting, informative, and pertinent to the question at hand. Do not assume that your readers will automatically see that your paper is worth reading.

Every paragraph in your paper should relate to the thesis; every sentence in each paragraph should relate to a topic sentence. Delete any sentence that does not serve the essay's purpose. Ensure that paragraphs appear in a logical sequence and are clearly linked by transitional words and phrases or references to material in preceding paragraphs. Your readers should never have to wonder what the connection is between parts of your paper.

Step 6. Study and revise your first draft.

Your first draft is likely to have problems, both big and small. At this stage, though, you should scrutinize mostly the big ones. This is no time for proofreading (correcting spelling, fixing punctuation, repairing typos, and the like). This is the time to make substantive changes.

Step 7. Produce a final draft.

After completing all substantive changes, you should generate a final draft, the one you will turn in. The final draft should reflect not only the big changes, but the corrections of all minor errors as well—misspellings, typos, grammatical errors, misplaced words, faulty punctuation, and documentation mistakes. This task should be primarily a proofreading job. At this stage, you should also format the manuscript according to your instructor's requirements.

The key to producing a clean final draft is *down time*—an interim in which you leave the last draft alone and focus on something else. Coming back to your paper after a day or so away from it can help you see errors that passed right by you before. You may be surprised how many mistakes this fresh look can reveal. If you cannot set the essay aside, ask a friend to read it and give you some constructive criticism.

FORMATTING YOUR PAPER

The formatting conventions discussed here are used in the humanities and are consistent with the general guidelines in *The Chicago Manual of Style*, 16th edition. The formatting preferences of your instructor, of course, trump anything in this appendix.

General Specifications

- Use good-quality paper (neither onion-skin thickness nor card stock), 8½ × 11, white.
- Use a 12-point standard font such as Times New Roman, a common word-processing font.
- Ensure that there are margins of at least one inch at the top, bottom, and sides of the page. Double-space the text.
- Assign consecutive numbers to all pages, starting with 1, and insert the numbers in the upper right corner of each page. The first page is the title page. Do not show the page number on the title page. The first visible page number should begin on the next page—page 2.
- On the title page, center (1) the full title of your essay, (2) your name, (3) the title of the course, (4) your instructor's name, and (5) the date.

Quotations and Citations

- Indent and double-space block quotations. Leave a blank line before and after the block quote and by indenting the left edge of the block quote four or five spaces.
- Start endnotes on their own page. Number the endnote pages along with the rest of the pages. Center *Notes* at the top of the page. Indent endnotes as shown in the sample paper.
- Single-space each endnote. Insert one line space between entries.
- Start a list of works cited on its own page. Number the pages with the rest of the paper. Center *Works Cited* at the top of the page. Indent entries as shown in the sample paper.
- Double-space each line of works cited notes.

A SAMPLE PHILOSOPHY PAPER

The Dilemma of the Divine Command Theory
by Jane Doe
Philosophy 101
March 10, 2017

What is the connection between God and morality? In the past, many people would take this question to be about whether someone can behave morally even if they are atheists. But nowadays most people in the West would probably answer yes to this question. If there are moral standards of behavior, then it seems that anyone can live by them. A more important question (for both the religious and nonreligious) is not whether someone can be moral without belief in God, but *whether morality itself is possible without God*. The answer that many give to this question is the divine command theory, the view that morality absolutely requires God.

Introduces topic.

It says that an action is right if God commands or wills it. In other words, certain actions are right or wrong only because God says they are, for he is the author of the moral law. God's commanding an action is what makes it right; God's forbidding it is what makes it forbidden.[1]

Defines key term.

Further explains the divine command theory.

Those who accept the divine command theory could consistently think that they should perform actions that promote the common good, as an act-utilitarian would. Or they could believe that they should always act to serve their own interests, as an ethical egoist does.[2] Or they could assume that their duty is to act according to a set of deontological principles. But no matter what approach they take, they would still maintain that ultimately an action is right because God commands it.

But is the divine command theory plausible? Does God make right? I intend to argue that the theory is untenable—and for reasons that both theists and nontheists can appreciate. I will show that there is a crucial difficulty for the theory that would come to fore even if God's existence and our knowledge of his will are assured. The source of the problem is that the divine command theory forces a dilemma on us that can be satisfactorily resolved only by abandoning the theory.[3]

Thesis statement.

Provides background for the issue.

Plato lays out the dilemma in his dialogue *Euthyphro*. In it Socrates asks, in effect, Are actions right because God commands them, or does God command them because they are right? The first option says that God creates morality, and the divine command theory is true. The second option says that the divine command theory is false: morality exists independently of God's will, and even he must obey it.

If one accepts the theory, unpalatable implications arise. If an action is morally right only because God says so, then any action at all could be morally right. If God so willed, the torture of children or the murder of innocents would be morally right. As the divine command theory would have it, there could be no reasons for God's willing one way or the other. He just commands, and that makes an action right (or wrong). But if God has no reasons for his commands, no standards other than his say-so, his commands are arbitrary. If the theory is correct, then God doesn't have reasons—and doesn't need reasons—to make the moral rules. But in that case, God's decisions would amount to no more than a throw of the dice. If rape and murder are morally wrong (or morally right), they are arbitrarily so. This result is implausible, and both theists and nontheists agree. In fact, most Christian philosophers reject the divine command theory.[4]

The main argument for the thesis.

To reject the theory is to give up the idea that God is the maker of the moral law and to acknowledge that morality is independent of God's will. Actions are right or wrong for reasons that do not depend on God. We try to do right because it's right, not because a divine power has made an arbitrary decision. Theists who reject the divine command theory believe that God commands humans to obey moral standards that exist regardless of what God commands. God is perfect. He obeys the moral law and expects his children to obey it also.

Writer explains and rebuts the chief argument against the thesis.

The chief argument against the charge of arbitrariness is this: God would never command the murder of one's neighbors, the torture of children, or any other evil acts because God is all-good. And because God is all-good, his commands would not be arbitrary—they would be good. But to say this is to argue in a circle and undermine—not strengthen—the divine command theory. The theory is supposed to tell us what morality is, or what makes something good. But if goodness is a defining property of God, then God cannot be used to define goodness. Such a tack would result in an empty definition of the divine command theory: Good actions are those commanded by an all-good God. When theists say that God is good, they surely mean more than this.[5]

In conclusion, the divine command theory is unfounded. To avoid the arbitrariness problem, and to preserve a credible idea of goodness, the theory must be rejected. The much more plausible view is located on the other side of Socrates' dilemma: The moral law is independent of God and applies to both God and man.

Conclusion and brief reiteration of the argument in its favor.

Notes

1. Alasdair MacIntyre, *A Short History of Ethics* (New York: Macmillan, 1966), 178–79.

2. Michael Beaty, *Christian Theism and the Problems of Philosophy* (Notre Dame: University of Notre Dame Press, 1990), 5.

3. Russ Shafer-Landau, *Whatever Happened to Good and Evil?* (New York: Oxford University Press, 2004), 81–82.

4. MacIntyre, *A Short History of Ethics*, 190.

5. John Chandler, "Divine Command Theories and the Appeal to Love," *American Philosophical Quarterly* 22 (1985): 231–239.

Works Cited

Audi, Robert, and William Wainwright, eds. *Rationality, Religious Belief, and Moral Commitment*. Ithaca, NY: Cornell University Press, 1986.

Beaty, Michael, ed. *Christian Theism and the Problems of Philosophy*. Notre Dame: University of Notre Dame Press, 1990.

Chandler, John. "Divine Command Theories and the Appeal to Love." *American Philosophical Quarterly* 22.1 (1985).

Darwall, Stephen L. *The Second-Person Standpoint: Morality, Respect, and Accountability*. Cambridge, MA: Harvard University Press, 2006.

MacIntyre, Alasdair. *A Short History of Ethics*. New York: Macmillan, 1966.

Shafer-Landau, Russ. *Whatever Happened to Good and Evil?* New York: Oxford University Press, 2004.

APPENDIX B
Deductive and Inductive Arguments

Checking the validity or strength of an argument is often a plain, commonsense undertaking. Using our natural reasoning ability, we can examine how the premises are linked to the conclusion and can see quickly whether the conclusion follows from the premises. We are most likely to make an easy job of it when the arguments are simple. Many times, however, we need some help, and help is available in the form of methods and guidelines for evaluating arguments.

Having a familiarity with common argument patterns, or forms, is especially useful when assessing the validity of deductive arguments. We are likely to encounter these forms again and again. Here is a prime example:

Argument 1

1. If the surgeon operates, then the patient will be cured.
2. The surgeon is operating.
3. Therefore, the patient will be cured.

This argument form contains a *conditional* premise—that is, a premise consisting of a conditional, or if-then, statement (actually a compound statement composed of two constituent statements). Premise 1 is a conditional statement. A conditional statement has two parts: the part beginning with *if* (called the *antecedent*), and the part beginning with *then* (known as the *consequent*). So the antecedent of Premise 1 is "If the surgeon operates," and the consequent is "then the patient will be cured."

The best way to appreciate the structure of such an argument (or any deductive argument, for that matter) is to translate it into traditional argument symbols in which each statement is symbolized by a letter. Here is the symbolization for Argument 5:

1. If *p*, then *q*.
2. *p*.
3. Therefore, *q*.

We can see that *p* represents "the surgeon operates," and *q* represents "the patient will be cured." But notice that we can use this same symbolized argument form to represent countless other arguments—arguments with different statements but having the same basic structure.

It just so happens that the underlying argument form for Argument 1 is extremely common—common enough to have a name, *modus ponens* (or affirming the antecedent). The truly useful fact about *modus ponens* is that any argument having this form is valid. We can plug any statements we want into the formula and the result will be a valid argument, a circumstance in which if the premises are true, the conclusion must be true.

An equally prevalent argument form is *modus tollens* (or denying the consequent). For example:

Argument 2

1. If the dose is low, then the healing is slow.
2. The healing is not slow.
3. Therefore, the dose is not low.

1. If *p*, then *q*.
2. Not *q*.
3. Therefore, not *p*.

Modus tollens is also a valid form, and any argument using this form must also be valid.

There are also common argument forms that are invalid. Here are two of them:

Affirming the Consequent

Argument 3

1. If the mind is an immaterial substance, then ESP is real.
2. ESP is real.
3. Therefore, the mind is an immaterial substance.

1. If *p*, then *q*.
2. *q*.
3. Therefore, *p*.

Denying the Antecedent

Argument 4

1. If morality is relative to persons (that is, if moral rightness or wrongness depends on what people believe), then moral disagreement between persons would be nearly impossible.
2. Morality is not relative to persons.
3. Therefore, moral disagreement between persons is not nearly impossible.

1. If *p*, then *q*.
2. Not *p*.
3. Therefore, not *q*.

The advantage of being able to recognize these and other common argument forms is that you can use that skill to readily determine the validity of many deductive arguments. You know, for example, that any argument having the same form as *modus ponens* or *modus tollens* must be valid, and any argument in one of the common invalid forms must be invalid.

Inductive arguments also have distinctive forms. In *enumerative induction*, for example, we arrive at a generalization about an entire group of things after observing just some members of the group. Consider these:

Argument 5

Every light fixture I have bought from the hardware store has been defective.

Therefore, all light fixtures sold at the hardware store are probably defective.

Argument 6

All the hawks that I have observed in this wildlife sanctuary have had red tails.

Therefore, all the hawks in this sanctuary probably have red tails.

Argument 7

Sixty percent of the Bostonians I have interviewed in various parts of the city are pro-choice.

Therefore, 60 percent of all Bostonians are probably pro-choice.

As you can see, enumerative induction has this form:

X percent of the observed members of group A have property P.

Therefore, X percent of all members of group A probably have property P.

The observed members of the group are simply a sample of the entire group. So based on what we know about this sample, we can generalize to all the members. But how do we know whether such an argument is strong? Everything depends on the sample. If the sample is large enough and representative enough, we can safely assume that our generalization drawn from the sample is probably an accurate reflection of the whole group of members. A sample is representative of an entire group only if each member of the group has an equal chance of being included in the sample. In general, the larger the sample, the greater the probability that it accurately reflects the nature of the group as a whole. Often common sense tells us when a sample is too small.

We do not know how many light fixtures from the hardware store are in the sample mentioned in Argument 5. But if the number is several dozen and the fixtures were bought over a period of weeks or months, the sample is probably sufficiently large and representative. If so, the argument is strong. Likewise, in Argument 6 we don't know the size of the sample or how it was obtained. But if the sample was taken from all the likely spots in the sanctuary where hawks live, and if several hawks were observed in each location, the sample is probably adequate—and the argument is strong. In Argument 7, if the sample consists of a handful of Bostonians interviewed on a few street corners, the sample is definitely inadequate and the argument is weak.

DETAILS

Valid and Invalid Argument Forms

Valid Argument Forms

Affirming the Antecedent
(*Modus Ponens*)
If *p*, then *q*.
p.
Therefore, *q*.

Example:
If Spot barks, a burglar is in the house.
Spot is barking.
Therefore, a burglar is in the house.

Denying the Consequent
(*Modus Tollens*)
If *p*, then *q*.
Not *q*.
Therefore, not *p*.

Example:
If it's raining, the park is closed.
The park is not closed.
Therefore, it's not raining.

Invalid Argument Forms

Affirming the Consequent
If *p*, then *q*.
q.
Therefore, *p*.

Example:
If Donald Trump owns Paris, then he's rich.
Donald Trump is rich.
Therefore, he own's Paris.

Denying the Antecedent
If *p*, then *q*.
Not *p*.
Therefore, not *q*.

Example:
If Joe Biden was born in California, then he's
an American.
Joe Biden was not born in California.
Therefore, he is not an American.

But if the sample consists of several hundred people, and if every member of the whole group has an equal chance of being included in the sample, then the sample would be good enough to allow us to accurately generalize about the whole population. Typically, selecting such a sample of a large population is done by professional polling organizations.

In the argument form known as *analogical induction* (or *argument by analogy*), we reason in this fashion: Two or more things are similar in several ways; therefore, they are probably similar in one further way.

Argument 8

Humans can walk upright, use simple tools, learn new skills, and devise deductive arguments.

Chimpanzees can walk upright, use simple tools, and learn new skills.

Therefore, chimpanzees can probably devise deductive arguments.

This argument says that because chimpanzees are similar to humans in several respects, they probably are similar to humans in one further respect.

Here's an argument by analogy that has become a classic in philosophy:

Argument 9

A watch is a complex mechanism with many parts that seem arranged to achieve a specific purpose—a purpose chosen by the watch's designer. In similar fashion, the universe is a complex mechanism with many parts that seem arranged to achieve a specific purpose. Therefore, the universe must also have a designer.

We can represent the form of an argument by analogy in this way:

X has properties P1, P2, P3 plus the property P4.

Y has properties P1, P2, and P3.

Therefore, Y probably has property P4.

The strength of an analogical induction depends on the relevant similarities between the two things compared. The more relevant similarities there are, the greater the probability that the conclusion is true. In argument 8, several similarities are noted. But there are some unmentioned dissimilarities. The brain of a chimpanzee is smaller and more primitive than that of a human, a difference that probably inhibits higher intellectual functions such as logical argument. Argument 8, then, is weak. A common response to argument 9 is that the argument is weak because, although the universe resembles a watch in some ways, in other ways it does not resemble a watch. Specifically, the universe also resembles a living thing.

A third type of inductive argument is known as *inference to the best explanation*, a kind of reasoning that we all use daily and that is at the heart of scientific investigations and many philosophical theories. Recall that an argument gives us reasons for believing *that* something is the case. An *explanation*, on the other hand, states *how* or *why* something is the case. It attempts to clarify or elucidate, not offer proof. For example:

1. Megan definitely understood the material, for she could answer every question on the test.

2. Megan understood the material because she has a good memory.

Sentence 1 is an argument. The conclusion is "Megan definitely understood the material," and the reason (premise) given for believing that the conclusion is true is "for she could answer every question on the test." Sentence 2, however, is an explanation. It does not try to present reasons for believing something; it has nothing to prove. Instead, it tries to show why something is the way it is (why Megan understood the material). Sentence 2 assumes that Megan understood the material and then tries to explain why. Such explanations play a crucial role in inference to the best explanation.

In this type of inductive argument, we begin with premises about a phenomenon or state of affairs to be explained. Then we reason from those premises to an explanation for that state of affairs. We try to produce not just any old explanation but the best explanation among several possibilities. The best explanation is the one most likely to be true. The conclusion of the argument is that the preferred explanation is indeed probably true. For example:

Argument 10

Tariq flunked his philosophy course. The best explanation for his failure is that he didn't read the material. Therefore, he probably didn't read the material.

Argument 11

Ladies and gentlemen of the jury, the defendant was found with the murder weapon in his hand, blood on his clothes, and the victim's wallet in his pocket. We have an eyewitness putting the defendant at the scene of the crime. The best explanation for all these facts is that the defendant committed the murder. There can be very little doubt—he's guilty.

Here's the form of inference to the best explanation:

Phenomenon Q.

E provides the best explanation for Q.

Therefore, it is probable that E is true.

In any argument of this pattern, if the explanation given is really the best, then the argument is inductively strong. If the explanation is not the best, the argument is inductively weak. If the premises of the strong argument are true, then the argument is cogent. If the argument is cogent, then we have good reason to believe that the conclusion is true.

The biggest challenge in using inference to the best explanation is determining which explanation is the best. Sometimes this feat is easy. If our car has a flat tire, we may quickly uncover the best explanation for such a state of affairs. If we see a nail sticking out of the flat, and there is no obvious evidence of tampering or of any other extraordinary cause (that is, there are no good alternative explanations), we may safely conclude that the best explanation is that a nail punctured the tire.

In more complicated situations, we may need to do what scientists do to evaluate explanations, or theories—use special criteria to sort through the possibilities. Scientists call these standards the criteria of adequacy. Despite this fancy name, these criteria are basically just common sense, standards that you have probably used yourself.

One of these criteria is called *conservatism*. This criterion says that, all things being equal, the best explanation or theory is the one that fits best with what is already known or established. For example, if a Facebook friend of yours says—in all seriousness—that she can fly to the moon without using any kind of rocket or spaceship, you probably wouldn't believe her (and might even think she needed psychiatric help). Your reasons for doubting her would probably rest on the criterion of conservatism—that what she says conflicts with everything science knows about space flight, human anatomy, aerodynamics, laws of nature, and much more. It is logically possible that she really can fly to the moon, but her claim's lack of conservatism (the fact that it conflicts with so much of what we already know about the world) casts serious doubt on it.

Here is another useful criterion for judging the worth of explanations: *simplicity*. Other things being equal, the best explanation is the one that is the simplest—that is, the one that rests on the fewest assumptions. The theory making the fewest assumptions is less likely to be false because there are fewer ways for it to go wrong. In the example about the flat tire, one possible (but strange) explanation is that space aliens punctured the tire. You probably wouldn't put much credence in this explanation because you would have to assume too many unknown entities and processes—namely, space aliens who have come from who knows where using who knows what methods to move about and puncture your tires. The nail-in-the-tire theory is much simpler (it assumes no unknown entities or processes) and therefore is much more likely to be true.

Glossary

a posteriori knowledge Knowledge that depends entirely on sense experience.

a priori knowledge Knowledge gained independently of or prior to sense experience.

absolute idealism The doctrine that the universe is an objective reality consisting of ideas in the universal mind.

absurdity In existentialism, a sense of meaninglessness and irrationality in the world arising from the conflict between our need for meaning in life and the meaningless, indifferent universe.

act-utilitarianism The idea that the rightness of actions depends solely on the overall well-being produced by *individual actions*.

ahimsa The principle of not harming living beings (often referred to as the "non-harm" or "nonviolence" principle).

Analects Confucian text containing the conversations of Confucius and his followers.

analytic statement A logical truth whose denial results in a contradiction.

anatta The impermanence of the self; or not-self, or no-soul.

ancient atomism The theory that reality consists of an infinite number of minute, indivisible bits called atoms moving randomly in an infinite void, or empty space.

anicca Impermanence; the ephemeral nature of everything.

appeal to ignorance. The fallacy of trying to prove something by appealing to what we don't know. It is arguing either that (1) a claim is true because it hasn't been proven false or (2) a claim is false because it hasn't been proven true.

appeal to popularity The fallacy of arguing that a claim must be true not because it is backed by good reasons but simply because many people believe it.

appeal to the person (ad hominem fallacy) The fallacy of rejecting a statement on the grounds that it comes from a particular person, not because the statement itself is false or dubious.

appearances The way things in the world appear to us.

argument A group of statements in which one of them (the conclusion) is supported by the others (the premises).

aristocracy A society ruled by a privileged class.

asceticism The denial of physical comfort or pleasures for religious ends.

atman One's soul or self.

axiology The study of value, including both aesthetic value and moral value.

begging the question The fallacy of trying to prove a conclusion by using that very same conclusion as support.

Bhagavad-Gita The most highly venerated and influential scriptures in Hinduism.

Brahman The impersonal, all-pervading spirit that is the universe yet transcends all space and time.

brahmin A priest or teacher; a man of the priestly caste.

465

capitalism A socioeconomic system in which wealth goes to anyone who can acquire it in a free marketplace.

categorical imperative Kant's fundamental moral principle, which he formulates as (1) "I am never to act otherwise than so *that I could also will that my maxim should become a universal law*," and (2) "So act as to treat humanity, whether in thine own person or in that of any other, in every case as an end withal, never as a means only."

communism A term broadly synonymous with socialism but associated with nominally Marxist countries such as the Soviet Union in the twentieth century.

composition The fallacy of arguing erroneously that what can be said of the parts can also be said of the whole.

conclusion In an argument, the statement being supported by premises.

consequentialist theory A moral theory in which the rightness of actions depends solely on their consequences or results.

cosmological arguments Arguments that reason from the existence of the universe, or cosmos (or some fundamental feature of it) to the conclusion that God exists.

cosmopolitanism The idea that we have moral duties to all persons, even those outside our family and community.

cultural relativism The view that the truth about something depends on what cultures believe.

Dao The "Way" in Daoism, the mysterious first principle of the universe; the eternal source of all that is real and the underpinning of the world.

deconstruction A way of unpacking a text (philosophical, literary, or other) to reveal hidden assumptions and contradictions that subvert the ostensible meaning.

deductive argument An argument intended to give logically conclusive support to its conclusion.

democracy Rule by the people as a whole.

deontological (or nonconsequentialist) **theory** A moral theory in which the rightness of actions is determined not solely by their consequences but partly or entirely by their intrinsic nature.

distributive justice (or social justice) The fair distribution of society's benefits and burdens—such things as jobs, income, property, liberties, rights, welfare aid, taxes, and public service.

division The fallacy of arguing erroneously that what can be said of the whole can be said of the parts.

doctrine of double effect The moral principle that performing a bad action to bring about a good effect is never morally acceptable but that performing a good action may sometimes be acceptable even if it produces a bad effect.

dualism The view that the mind (or soul) and matter (or body) are two disparate things.

dukkha The inevitable suffering and dissatisfaction inherent in existence.

efficient cause The main source or initiator of a change.

empiricism The view that our knowledge of the world comes solely from sense experience.

empiricists Those who believe that our knowledge of the world comes solely from sense experience.

Epicureanism The philosophy of Epicurus; the view that life's highest aim is happiness attained through moderate pleasures and the avoidance of mental disturbance.

epistemology The philosophical study of knowledge.

equivocation The fallacy of assigning two different meanings to the same significant word in an argument.

ethics (moral philosophy) The study of morality using the methods of philosophy.

ethics of care A moral perspective that emphasizes the unique demands of specific situations and the virtues and feelings that are central to close personal relationships.

evidentialism The view that we are justified in believing something only if it is supported by sufficient evidence.

existentialism A term applied to different philosophies that share themes about the uniqueness of each human being, the central importance of choice, and the individual's response to an indifferent, absurd universe.

fallacy A common but bad argument.

fallibilism The view that our claims to knowledge may turn out to be false.

false dilemma The fallacy of arguing erroneously that since there are only two alternatives to choose from, and one of them is unacceptable, the other one must be true.

feminist ethics An approach to morality aimed at advancing women's interests, underscoring their distinctive experiences and characteristics, and advancing the obvious truth that women and men are morally equal.

fideism The notion that religious belief is grounded in faith, not reason.

final cause What a thing is for or for what purpose it exists.

form The shape, pattern, or function of material stuff.

formal cause A thing's structure and properties that make it what it is.

Forms In Plato's philosophy, the objectively real, eternal abstract entities that serve as models or universals of higher knowledge.

genetic fallacy Arguing that a statement can be judged true or false based on its source.

hedonism The doctrine that pleasure is the supreme good.

Hellenistic era The period from the death of Alexander in 323 BCE to the end of the Roman Republic in 31 BCE in which Epicureanism, Stoicism, and skepticism flourished.

inductive argument An argument intended to give probable support to its conclusion.

instrumental good Something good because it helps us attain something else good; something good for the sake of something else.

intrinsic good Something good in itself; something good for its own sake.

invalid argument A deductive argument that fails to provide conclusive support for its conclusion.

justice The idea that people should get what is fair or what is their due.

karma The universal principle that governs the characteristics and quality of each rebirth, or future life.

language-game A pattern of social activity in which words play a crucial role and derive their meaning from how they are used in the activity.

li In early Confucianism, ritual, etiquette, principle, and propriety; conscientious behavior and right action.

logic The study of correct reasoning.

logos Heraclitus' central idea—the *principle*, *formula*, or *law* of the world order.

Lyceum Aristotle's school of philosophy and science, named after its location, a grove just outside Athens dedicated to the god Apollo Lyceus.

material cause A thing's material composition.

meritocracy A system of rule by those most qualified to govern.

metaphysics The study of reality.

monads Leibniz's term for the only true substances—immaterial, mental entities that constitute reality.

moral evil Evil that comes from human choices and actions.

moral theory A theory that explains why an action is right or wrong or why a person or a person's character is good or bad.

morality Beliefs about right and wrong actions and good and bad persons or character.

mysticism The belief in the alleged ability to access, through trances or visions, divine knowledge that is unattainable through sense experience or reason.

natural law theory The view that right actions are those that conform to moral standards discerned in nature through human reason.

necessary truth A truth that could not have been false.

Neoplatonism The philosophical view consisting of a blend of Plato's metaphysics (primarily concerning the theory of the Forms) and other nonmaterialist or religious ideas.

nirvana A state of bliss and well-being attained when one extinguishes the flames of desire and thus halts the repeating cycle of death and rebirth.

ontological arguments Arguments that reason from the concept of God to the existence of God.

panentheism The view that God is in every part of the universe but is also more than the universe.

pantheism The view that God is identical with everything.

phenomenology A way of painstakingly describing the data of consciousness without the distortions of preconceived ideas.

philosophical method The systematic use of critical reasoning to try to find answers to fundamental questions about reality, morality, and knowledge.

picture theory of meaning The view that the logical structures of language mirror the structures of the world.

pragmatism The doctrine that the meaning or truth of a belief is synonymous with the practical results of accepting it.

premise A statement that supports the conclusion of an argument.

pre-Socratics The first philosophers, most of whom flourished before Socrates (fifth century BCE).

principle of induction The presumption that events that followed one another in the past will do the same in the future, that the future will be like the past.

propositional knowledge Knowledge of a proposition.

rationalism The view that some or all of our knowledge about the world is gained independently of sense experience.

rationalists Those who believe that some or all of our knowledge about the world is gained independently of sense experience.

reductio ad absurdum An argument form in which a set of statements is assumed, and absurd or false statements are derived from the set, showing that at least one of the original statements must be rejected.

relativism The doctrine that the truth about something depends on what persons or cultures believe.

ren The essential Confucian virtues, including benevolence, sympathy, kindness, generosity, respect for others, and human-heartedness.

rhetoric The art of verbal persuasion.

rule-utilitarianism The doctrine that a right action is one that conforms to a rule that, if followed consistently, would create for everyone involved the most beneficial balance of well-being over suffering.

samsara One's cycle of repeated deaths and rebirths.

skepticism The view that we lack knowledge in some fundamental way.

slippery slope The fallacy of arguing erroneously that a particular action should not be taken because it will lead inevitably to other actions resulting in some dire outcome.

social contract theory The view that justice is secured, and the state is made legitimate, through an agreement among citizens of the state or between the citizens and the rulers of the state.

socialism The political and economic view that the means of production (property, factories, businesses) should be owned and controlled by the state for the general welfare.

Socratic method Question-and-answer dialogue in which propositions are methodically scrutinized to uncover the truth.

sophists Itinerant professors who, for a fee, would teach a range of subjects that could be of practical or intellectual benefit.

statement (or claim) An assertion that something is or is not the case and is therefore the kind of utterance that is either true or false.

Stoicism The view that we can attain happiness and peace of mind if we focus on controlling only what is up to us (attitudes, intentions, perceptions, and feelings) and ignoring what is not up to us (body, reputation, property, and political office), thereby restraining our desires, cultivating virtue, and conforming our lives to Nature (or God).

straw man The fallacy of misrepresenting a person's views so they can be more easily attacked or dismissed.

subjective relativism The notion that truth depends on what a person believes.

syllogism A deductive argument made up of three statements—two premises and a conclusion.

synthetic statement A statement that is not analytic.

teleological arguments Arguments that reason from apparent signs of design or purposeful creation in the world to the existence of a supreme designer.

teleology The existence of purpose or ends inherent in persons or things.

term A word that names a class, or category, of things in a deductive argument.

Upanishads Vedic literature concerning the self, Brahman, *samsara*, and liberation.

utilitarianism The view that right actions are those that result in the most beneficial balance of good over bad consequences for everyone involved.

valid argument A deductive argument that succeeds in providing conclusive support for its conclusion.

Vedas Early Hindu scriptures, developed between 1500 and 600 BCE.

virtue A disposition to behave in line with a standard of excellence.

will to power The fundamental nature of existence as a drive to control and dominate.

Credits

Chapter 1

1.1 Photoservice Electa/Universal Images Group/SuperStock

1.2 Universal Images Group/Universal Images Group/SuperStock

1.3 Vasiliki Varvaki/iStockphoto

1.4 Photo 12/Alamy Stock Photo

1.5 slobo/iStockphoto

1.6 Library of Congress Prints and Photographs Division Washington, D.C. 20540 USA

1.7 Bettmann/Getty Images

1.8 SuperStock/SuperStock

Chapter 2

2.1 Courtesy of the Yale University Art Gallery

2.2 OUP 9780195397703

2.3 Bettmann/Getty Images

2.4 Photo by Prisma/UIG/Getty Images

2.5 CTR design LLC/iStockphoto

2.6 Photo by DeAgostini/Getty Images

2.7 skullsinthestars.com

2.8 RedDaxLuma/Shutterstock

2.9 Georgios Kollidas/Shutterstock

2.10 Wikimedia Commons

2.11 © CORBIS/Corbis via Getty Images

2.12 Photo12/UIG via Getty Images

2.13 Photo by ANDREW HOLBROOKE/ Corbis via Getty Images

Chapter 3

3.1 Hans Laubel/iStockphoto

3.2 Brigida Soriano/Shutterstock

3.3 neftali/Shutterstock

3.4 Bettmann/Getty Images

3.5 Moshe Torgovitsky/Alamy Stock Photo

3.6 Photo by VCG Wilson/Corbis via Getty Images

3.7 Jessica Kuras/Shutterstock

Chapter 4

4.1 Bettmann/Getty Images

4.2 Anastasios71/Shutterstock

4.3 Cameraphoto Arte, Venice/Art Resource, NY © 2016 Artists Rights Society (ARS), New York/SIAE, Rome

4.4 fotoVoyager/iStockphoto

4.5 Muhla1/iStockphoto

4.6 Wikimedia Commons

4.7 Fine Art Images/Fine Art Images/ SuperStock

4.8 Pictorial Press Ltd/Alamy Stock Photo

Chapter 5

5.1 Photo By DEA PICTURE LIBRARY/ De Agostini/Getty Images

5.2 Brianna May/iStockphoto

5.3 Bettmann/Getty Images

5.4 SuperStock/SuperStock

5.5 Wikimedia Commons

5.6 ANA MPA

5.7 V&A Images, London/Art Resource, NY

5.8 damedeeso/iStockphoto

5.9 Zenphotography/Shutterstock

5.10 Purdue University

5.11 bikeriderlondon/Shutterstock

Chapter 6

6.1 saiko3p/Shutterstock

6.2 Mitchell Kanashkevich/Getty Images

6.3 robertharding/Alamy Stock Photo

6.4 Murali Nath/iStockphoto

6.5 STEVE RAYMER/National Geographic Creative

6.6 mura/iStockphoto

6.7 FredFroese/iStockphoto

6.8 Luciano Mortula/Shutterstock

6.9 AP Photo/Gemunu Amarasinghe

6.10 vipflash/Shutterstock

6.11 Photo by Ann Ronan Pictures/Print Collector/Getty Images

6.12 Hung Chung Chih/Shutterstock

6.13 Bettmann/Getty Images

Chapter 7

7.1 Photo By DEA/G. DAGLI ORTI/De Agostini/Getty Images

7.2 National Geographic Creative/Alamy Stock Photo

7.3 Photo by Fine Art Images/Heritage Images/Getty Images

7.4 Photo by Spencer Arnold/Getty Images

7.5 Chronicle/Alamy Stock Photo

7.6 AF archive/Alamy Stock Photo

7.7 U.S. Navy Photo

7.8 Wikipedia

7.9 Bplanet/Shutterstock

Chapter 8

8.1 Carlos Caetano/Shutterstock

8.2 National Gallery of Art

8.3 Alinari/Art Resource, NY

8.4 DEA/A. DAGLI ORTI/Getty Images

8.5 bilwissedition Ltd. & Co. KG/Alamy Stock Photo

8.6 tropicalpix/iStockphoto

8.7 Flickr

8.8 Gena96/Shutterstock

8.9 MARK GARLICK/Getty Images

8.10 Wolfgang_Steiner/iStockphoto

8.11 Elzbieta Sekowska/iStockphoto

8.12 Georgios Kollidas/iStockphoto

8.13 Luisma Tapia/Shutterstock

8.14 Zvonimir Atletic/Shutterstock

8.15 Photo by Hulton Archive/Getty Images

Chapter 9

9.1 Georgios Kollidas/Shutterstock

9.2 HIP/Art Resource, NY

9.3 nicolamargaret/iStockphoto

9.4 Oktay Ortakcioglu/iStockphoto

9.5 Pictorial Press Ltd/Alamy Stock Photo

9.6 Photo by Stefano Bianchetti/Corbis via Getty Images

Chapter 10

10.1 Georgios Kollidas/Shutterstock

10.2 Bettmann/Getty Images

10.3 Bettmann/Getty Images

10.4 pictore/iStockphoto

10.5 Photo by Culture Club/Getty Images

10.6 Photo by Culture Club/Getty Images

10.7 Duncan Walker/iStockphoto

10.8 jeremy sutton-hibbert/Alamy Stock Photo

10.9 Photo by Culture Club/Getty Images

10.10 Bettmann/Getty Images

10.11 GeorgiosArt/iStockphoto

Chapter 11

11.1 Nicku/Shutterstock

11.2 Kevin Fleming/Getty Images

11.3 Darko Veselinovic/iStockphoto

11.4 traveler1116/iStockphoto

11.5 Brainden.com

11.6 Brainden.com

11.7 123OpticalIllusions

11.8 Clark Brennan/Alamy Stock Photo

11.9 Flik47/Shutterstock

11.10 dpa picture alliance archive/Alamy Stock Photo

11.11 traveler1116/iStockphoto

Chapter 12

12.1 Photo by adoc-photos/Corbis via Getty Images

12.2 Jeffrey Blackler/Alamy Stock Photo

12.3 Subsociety/iStockphoto

12.4 Bettmann/Getty Images

12.5 Bettmann/Getty Images

Chapter 13

13.1 Grafissimo/iStockphoto

13.2 Nicku/Shutterstock

13.3 alexkuehni/iStockphoto

13.4 Michael Nicholson/Corbis via Getty Images

13.5 ojka/Shutterstock

13.6 L. Kragt Bakker/Shutterstock

Chapter 14

14.1 Bettmann/Getty Images

14.2 Geoffrey Taunton/Alamy Stock Photo

14.3 Nicku/Shutterstock

14.4 Nicku/Shutterstock

14.5 Sergey Goryachev/Shutterstock

14.6 Photo by adoc-photos/Corbis via Getty Images

14.7 Dave G. Houser/Getty Images

14.8 Photo by Jack Burlot/Apis/Sygma/Sygma via Getty Images

14.9 Bettmann/Getty Images

14.10 Bettmann/Getty Images

14.11 Olga Popova/Shutterstock

14.12 AF archive/Alamy Stock Photo

Chapter 15

15.1 Bettmann/Getty Images

15.2 epa european pressphoto agency b.v./Alamy Stock Photo

15.3 Bettmann/Getty Images

15.4 Bettmann/Getty Images

15.5 Roman Sigaev/Shutterstock

Chapter 16

16.1 IanDagnall Computing/Alamy Stock Photo

16.2 traveler1116/iStockphoto

16.3 Kathy deWitt/Alamy Stock Photo

16.4 Pictorial Press Ltd/Alamy Stock Photo

16.5 deadlyphoto.com/Alamy Stock Photo

Chapter 17

17.1 Photo by Frank Wojciechowski

17.2 epa european pressphoto agency b.v./Alamy Stock Photo

17.3 MediaPunch Inc/Alamy Stock Photo

17.4 Bettmann/Getty Images

17.5 Photo by © Flip Schulke/CORBIS/Corbis via Getty Images

17.6 Courtesy of David Chalmers

17.7 © Richard Melloul/Sygma/CORBIS/Sygma via Getty Images

17.8 Photo by Sophie Bassouls/Sygma/Sygma via Getty Images

Chapter 18

18.1 Marek Uliasz/iStockphoto

18.2 Peter Barritt/Alamy Stock Photo

18.3 Pantheon/Pantheon/SuperStock

18.4 ImagineGolf/iStockphoto

18.5 Georgios Kollidas/Alamy Stock Photo

18.6 Silvio Fiore/Silvio Fiore/SuperStock

18.7 Alex Motrenko/iStockphoto

18.8 Ascent/PKS Media Inc./Getty Images

Text Credits

Page 168, Epicurus, *Letter to Menoeceus*: Epicurus, *The Extant Remains*, translated by Cyril Bailey (Oxford: Clarendon Press, 1926). By permission of Oxford University Press. www.oup.com

Page 178, "Five Reasons Why Stoicism Matters Today": Rob Goodman and Jimmy Soni, "Five Reasons Why Stoicism Matters Today." From *Forbes*, September 28, 2012. © 2012 Forbes. All rights reserved. Used by permission and protected by the Copyright Laws of the United States. The printing, copying, redistribution, or retransmission of this Content without express written permission is prohibited. www.forbes.com

Page 196, Immanuel Kant, *Critique of Pure Reason*: Immanuel Kant, *Critique of Pure Reason*, translated by Norman Kemp Smith (London: Macmillan & Co., 1929). Reproduced with permission of Palgrave Macmillan.

Page 318, Albert Einstein, "Why Socialism?": Albert Einstein, "Why Socialism?" *Monthly Review* (May 1949). Reproduced by permission of Monthly Review Foundation via Copyright Clearance Center.

Page 340, Fredrich Nietzsche, *The Gay Science*: Friedrich Nietzsche, "The Madman," from *The Portable Nietzsche* by Friedrich Nietzsche, translated and edited by Walter Kaufmann, copyright © 1954, 1968. Copyright renewed 1982 by Penguin Random House LLC. Used by permission of Viking Books, an imprint of Penguin Publishing Group, a division of Penguin Random House LLC. All rights reserved.

Page 345, Jean-Paul Sartre, *Existentialism*: Jean-Paul Sartre, "Existentialism Is a Humanism." Originally a 1946 lecture in French entitled "L'Existentialisme est un Humanisme." Copyright © 1996 by Editions Gallimard. Reprinted by permission of Georges Borchardt, Inc., for Editions Gallimard.

Page 350, Albert Camus, *The Myth of Sisyphus*: Albert Camus, "The Myth of Sisyphus" from *The Myth of Sisyphus and Other Essays* by Albert Camus, translated by Justin O'Brien, translation copyright © 1955, copyright renewed 1983 by Alfred A. Knopf, a division of Penguin Random House LLC. Used by permission of Alfred A. Knopf, an imprint of the Knopf Doubleday Publishing Group, a division of Penguin Random House LLC. All rights reserved.

Page 352, "The Top 10 Existential Movies of All Time": George Dvorsky, "The Top 10 Existential Movies of All Time," June 7, 2009, http://www .sentientdevelopments.com/2009/06/top-10-existential-movies-of-all-time.html (3 November 2013).

Page 382, Simone de Beauvoir, *The Second Sex*: Simone de Beauvoir, excerpts from *The Second Sex* by Simone de Beauvoir and translated by Constance Borde and Sheila Malovany-Chevallier, translation copyright © 2009 by Constance Borde and Sheila Malovany-Chevallier. Used by permission of Alfred A. Knopf, an imprint of the Knopf Doubleday Publishing Group, a division of Penguin Random House LLC. All rights reserved.

Page 388, Virginia Held, *The Ethics of Care*: Virginia Held, *The Ethics of Care: Personal, Political, and Global*. Copyright © 2005 by Oxford University Press, Inc. By permission of Oxford University Press USA

Page 392, Eva Browning Cole, *Philosophy and Feminist Criticism*: Eve Browning Cole, *Philosophy and Feminist Criticism*. Copyright © 1993 by Paragon House. Reprinted by permission of the publisher.

Page 404, Martha Nussbaum, *The New Religious Intolerance*: Martha C. Nussbaum, *The New Religious Intolerance: Overcoming the Politics of Fear in an Anxious Age*. Cambridge, MA: The Belknap Press

Index of Marginal Quotations

General Index

Page numbers in **bold** indicate figures or tables.